T0332155

Modeling in Event-B

A practical text suitable for an introductory or advanced course in formal methods, this book presents a mathematical approach to modeling and designing systems using an extension of the B formalism: Event-B.

Based on the idea of refinement, the author's systematic approach allows the user to construct models gradually and to facilitate a systematic reasoning method by means of proofs. Readers will learn how to build models of programs and, more generally, discrete systems, but this is all done with practice in mind. The numerous examples provided arise from various sources of computer system developments, including sequential programs, concurrent programs, and electronic circuits.

The book also contains a large number of exercises and projects ranging in difficulty. Each of the examples included in the book has been proved using the Rodin Platform tool set, which is available free for download at www.event-b.org.

JEAN-RAYMOND ABRIAL was a guest professor and researcher in the Department of Computer Science at ETH Zurich.

Modeling in Event-B
System and Software Engineering

Jean-Raymond Abrial

CAMBRIDGE
UNIVERSITY PRESS

CAMBRIDGE
UNIVERSITY PRESS

Shaftesbury Road, Cambridge CB2 8EA, United Kingdom

One Liberty Plaza, 20th Floor, New York, NY 10006, USA

477 Williamstown Road, Port Melbourne, VIC 3207, Australia

314–321, 3rd Floor, Plot 3, Splendor Forum, Jasola District Centre, New Delhi – 110025, India

103 Penang Road, #05–06/07, Visioncrest Commercial, Singapore 238467

Cambridge University Press is part of Cambridge University Press & Assessment, a department of the University of Cambridge.

We share the University's mission to contribute to society through the pursuit of education, learning and research at the highest international levels of excellence.

www.cambridge.org
Information on this title: www.cambridge.org/9780521895569

First published 2010

A catalogue record for this publication is available from the British Library

Library of Congress Cataloging-in-Publication data
Abrial, Jean-Raymond.
Modeling in event-b : system and software engineering / Jean-Raymond Abrial.
p.   cm.
Includes bibliographical references and index.
ISBN 978-0-521-89556-9 (hardback)
1. Formal methods (Computer science)   2. Computer science – Mathematical models.
3. Computer systems – Verification.   I. Title.
QA76.9.F67A27   2010
004.01′51 – dc22   2010001382

ISBN   978-0-521-89556-9   Hardback

Additional resources for this publication at www.event-b.org

Contents

Prologue: Faultless systems – yes we can!   *page* xi
Acknowledgments   xxv

1   **Introduction**   1
     1.1   Motivation   1
     1.2   Overview of the chapters   2
     1.3   How to use this book   8
     1.4   Formal methods   10
     1.5   A little detour: blueprints   12
     1.6   The requirements document   13
     1.7   Definition of the term "formal method" as used in this book   16
     1.8   Informal overview of discrete models   18
     1.9   References   22

2   **Controlling cars on a bridge**   24
     2.1   Introduction   24
     2.2   Requirements document   25
     2.3   Refinement strategy   27
     2.4   Initial model: limiting the number of cars   27
     2.5   First refinement: introducing the one-way bridge   50
     2.6   Second refinement: introducing the traffic lights   70
     2.7   Third refinement: introducing car sensors   88

3   **A mechanical press controller**   100
     3.1   Informal description   100
     3.2   Design patterns   103
     3.3   Requirements of the mechanical press   114
     3.4   Refinement strategy   116
     3.5   Initial model: connecting the controller to the motor   117
     3.6   First refinement: connecting the motor buttons to the controller   119

3.7   Second refinement: connecting the controller to the clutch   127
3.8   Another design pattern: weak synchronization of two strong reactions   127
3.9   Third refinement: constraining the clutch and the motor   135
3.10   Fourth refinement: connecting the controller to the door   137
3.11   Fifth refinement: constraining the clutch and the door   138
3.12   Another design pattern: strong synchronization of two strong reactions   139
3.13   Sixth refinement: more constraints between clutch and door   146
3.14   Seventh refinement: connecting the controller to the clutch buttons   147

4   **A simple file transfer protocol**   149
4.1   Requirements   149
4.2   Refinement strategy   150
4.3   Protocol initial model   151
4.4   Protocol first refinement   158
4.5   Protocol second refinement   167
4.6   Protocol third refinement   169
4.7   Development revisited   172
4.8   Reference   175

5   **The Event-B modeling notation and proof obligation rules**   176
5.1   The Event-B notation   176
5.2   Proof obligation rules   188

6   **Bounded re-transmission protocol**   204
6.1   Informal presentation of the bounded re-transmission protocol   204
6.2   Requirements document   210
6.3   Refinement strategy   211
6.4   Initial model   212
6.5   First and second refinements   213
6.6   Third refinement   215
6.7   Fourth refinement   216
6.8   Fifth refinement   221
6.9   Sixth refinement   225
6.10   Reference   226

7   **Development of a concurrent program**   227
7.1   Comparing distributed and concurrent programs   227
7.2   The proposed example   228
7.3   Interleaving   233
7.4   Specifying the concurrent program   237
7.5   Refinement strategy   242
7.6   First refinement   245
7.7   Second refinement   250

	7.8	Third refinement	253
	7.9	Fourth refinement	255
	7.10	Reference	257
8		**Development of electronic circuits**	**258**
	8.1	Introduction	258
	8.2	A first example	267
	8.3	Second example: the arbiter	280
	8.4	Third example: a special road traffic light	291
	8.5	The Light circuit	299
	8.6	Reference	305
9		**Mathematical language**	**306**
	9.1	Sequent calculus	306
	9.2	The propositional language	310
	9.3	The predicate language	316
	9.4	Introducing equality	319
	9.5	The set-theoretic language	321
	9.6	Boolean and arithmetic language	331
	9.7	Advanced data structures	334
10		**Leader election on a ring-shaped network**	**353**
	10.1	Requirement document	353
	10.2	Initial model	355
	10.3	Discussion	356
	10.4	First refinement	359
	10.5	Proofs	361
	10.6	Reference	366
11		**Synchronizing a tree-shaped network**	**367**
	11.1	Introduction	367
	11.2	Initial model	369
	11.3	First refinement	371
	11.4	Second refinement	375
	11.5	Third refinement	377
	11.6	Fourth refinements	384
	11.7	References	386
12		**Routing algorithm for a mobile agent**	**387**
	12.1	Informal description of the problem	387
	12.2	Initial model	392
	12.3	First refinement	396
	12.4	Second refinement	399

12.5	Third refinement: data refinement	403
12.6	Fourth refinement	405
12.7	References	405

13 Leader election on a connected graph network — 406
13.1	Initial model	407
13.2	First refinement	407
13.3	Second refinement	410
13.4	Third refinement: the problem of contention	412
13.5	Fourth refinement: simplification	414
13.6	Fifth refinement: introducing cardinality	415

14 Mathematical models for proof obligations — 417
14.1	Introduction	417
14.2	Proof obligation rules for invariant preservation	418
14.3	Observing the evolution of discrete transition systems: traces	420
14.4	Presentation of simple refinement by means of traces	424
14.5	General refinement set-theoretic representation	431
14.6	Breaking the one-to-one relationship between abstract and concrete events	441

15 Development of sequential programs — 446
15.1	A systematic approach to sequential program development	446
15.2	A very simple example	450
15.3	Merging rules	453
15.4	Example: binary search in a sorted array	454
15.5	Example: minimum of an array of natural numbers	458
15.6	Example: array partitioning	460
15.7	Example: simple sorting	463
15.8	Example: array reversing	466
15.9	Example: reversing a linked list	469
15.10	Example: simple numerical program computing the square root	473
15.11	Example: the inverse of an injective numerical function	476

16 A location access controller — 481
16.1	Requirement document	481
16.2	Discussion	484
16.3	Initial model of the system	486
16.4	First refinement	488
16.5	Second refinement	492
16.6	Third refinement	497
16.7	Fourth refinement	501

17 Train system 508

17.1 Informal introduction 508

17.2 Refinement strategy 527

17.3 Initial model 528

17.4 First refinement 536

17.5 Second refinement 543

17.6 Third refinement 544

17.7 Fourth refinement 546

17.8 Conclusion 548

17.9 References 549

18 Problems 550

18.1 Exercises 551

18.2 Projects 557

18.3 Mathematical developments 572

18.4 References 582

Index 584

Prologue: Faultless systems – yes we can!

This title is certainly provocative. We all know that this claim corresponds to something that is impossible. No! We cannot construct faultless systems; just have a look around. If it were possible, it would have been already done a long time ago. And anyway, to begin with, what is a "fault"?

So, how can we imagine the contrary? We might think: yet another guru trying to sell us his latest universal panacea. Dear reader, be reassured, this Prologue does not contain any new bright solutions and, moreover, it is not technical; you'll have no complicated concepts to swallow. The intention is just to remind you of a few simple facts and ideas that you might use if you wish to do so.

The idea is to play the role of someone who is faced with a terrible situation (yes, the situation of computerized system development is not far from being terrible – as a measure, just consider the money thrown out of the window when systems fail). Faced with a terrible situation, we might decide to change things in a brutal way; it never works. Another approach is to gradually introduce some simple features that *together* will eventually result in a global improvement of the situation. The latter is the philosophy we will use here.

Definitions and requirements document

Since it is our intention to build correct systems, we need first to carefully define the way we can judge what it is we are doing. This is the purpose of a "definitions and requirements" document, which has to be carefully written before embarking on any computerized system development.

But, you say, lots of industries have such documents; they already exist, so why bother? Well, it is my experience that most of the time, requirements documents that are used in industry are *very poor*; it is often very hard just to understand what the

Jean-Raymond Abrial. Faultless Systems: Yes We Can! *Computer*, **42**(9): 30–36, September 2009, doi:10.1109/MC.2009.283. ©IEEE 2009. Reproduced with permission.

requirements are and thus to extract them from these documents. People too often justify the appropriateness of their requirements document by the fact that they use some (expensive) tools!

I strongly recommend that a requirements document is rewritten along the simple lines presented in this section.

Such a document should be made up of two kinds of texts embedded in each other: the *explanatory* text and the *reference* text. The former contains explanations needed to understand the problem at hand. Such explanations are supposed to help a reader who encounters a problem for the first time and who needs some elementary account. The latter contains definitions and requirements mainly in the form of short natural language statements that are labeled and numbered. Such definitions and requirements are more formal than the accompanying explanations. However, they must be self-contained and thus constitute a unique reference for correctness.

The definitions and requirements document bears an analogy with a book of mathematics where fragments of the *explanatory* text (where the author explains informally his approach and sometimes gives some historical background) are intermixed with fragments of more formal items – definitions, lemmas, and theorems – all of which form the *reference* text and can easily be separated from the rest of the book.

In the case of system engineering, we label our reference definitions and requirements along two axes. The first one contains the purpose (functions, equipment, safety, physical units, degraded modes, errors . . .) while the second one contains the abstraction level (high, intermediate, low . . .).

The first axis must be defined carefully before embarking on the writing of the definitions and requirements document since it might be different from one project to the next. Note that the "functional" label corresponds to requirements dealing with the specific task of the intended software, whereas the "equipment" label deals with *assumptions* (which we also call requirements) that have to be guaranteed concerning the environment situated around our intended software. Such an environment is made of some pieces of equipment, some physical varying phenomena, other pieces of software, as well as system users. The second axis places the reference items within a hierarchy, going from very general (abstract) definitions or requirements down to more and more specific ones imposed by system promoters.

It is very important that this stage of the definitions and requirements document be agreed upon and signed by the stakeholders.

At the end of this phase however, we have *no guarantee* that the desired properties of our system we have written down can indeed be fulfilled. It is not by writing that an intended airplane must fly that it indeed will. However, quite often after the writing of such a document, people rush into the programming phase and we know very well what the outcome is. What is needed is an intermediate phase to be undertaken *before programming*; this is the purpose of what is explained in the next section.

Modeling vs. programming

Programming is the activity of constructing a piece of formal text that is supposed to instruct a computer how to fulfil certain tasks. *Our intention is not to do that.* What we intend to build is a system within which there is a certain piece of software (the one we shall construct), which is a component among many others. This is the reason why our task is not limited to the software part only.

In doing this as engineers, we are not supposed to instruct a computer; rather, we are supposed to instruct ourselves. To do this in a rigorous way, we have no choice but to build a complete *model* of our future system, including the software that will eventually be constructed, as well as its environment, which, again, is made of equipment, varying physical phenomena, other software, and even users. Programming languages are of no help in doing this. All this has to be carefully modeled so that the exact assumptions within which our software is going to behave are known.

Modeling is the main task of system engineers. Programming then becomes a subtask which might very well be performed automatically.

Computerized system modeling has been done in the past (and still is) with the help of simulation languages such as SIMULA-67 (the ancestor of object-oriented programming languages). What we propose here is also to perform a simulation, but rather than doing it with the help of a simulation language, the outcome of which can be inspected and analyzed, we propose to do it by constructing *mathematical models* which will be analyzed by doing *proofs*. Physicists or operational researchers proceed in this way. We will do the same.

Since we are not instructing a computer, we do not have to say what is to be done, we have rather to explain and formalize what we can *observe*. But immediately comes the question: how can we observe something that does not yet exist? The answer to this question is simple: it certainly does not exist yet in the physical world, but, for sure, it exists in our minds. Engineers or architects always proceed in this way: they construct artefacts according to the pre-defined representation they have of them in their minds.

Discrete transition systems and proofs

As said in the previous section, modeling is not just formalizing our mental representation of the future system, it also consists in *proving* that this representation fulfils certain desired properties, namely those stated informally in the definitions and requirements document briefly described above.

In order to perform this joint task of simulation and proofs, we use a simple formalism, that of *discrete transition systems*. In other words, whatever the modeling task we have to perform, we always represent the components of our future systems by means of a succession of *states* intermixed with sudden transitions, also called *events*.

From the point of view of modeling, it is important to understand that there are *no fundamental differences* between a human being pressing a button, a motor starting or stopping, or a piece of software executing certain tasks – all of them being situated within the same global system. Each of these activities is a discrete transition system, working on its own and communicating with others. They are together embarked on the distributed activities of the system as a whole. This is the way we would like to do our modeling task.

It happens that this very simple paradigm is extremely convenient. In particular, the proving task is partially performed by demonstrating that the transitions of each component preserve a number of desired global properties which must be permanently obeyed by the states of our components. These properties are the so-called invariants. Most of the time, these invariants are transversal properties involving the states of multiple components in our system. The corresponding proofs are called the *invariant preservation proofs*.

States and events

As seen in previous section, a discrete transition component is made of a state and some transitions. Let us describe this here in simple terms.

Roughly speaking, a *state* is defined (as in an imperative program) by means of a number of variables. However, the difference with a program is that these variables might be any integer, pairs, sets, relations, functions, etc. (i.e. any mathematical object representable within set theory), not just computer objects (i.e. limited integer and floating point numbers, arrays, files, and the like). Besides the variables' definitions, we might have invariant statements, which can be any predicate expressed within the notation of first-order logic and set theory. By putting all this together, a state can be simply abstracted to a set.

Exercises: What is the state of the discrete system of a human being able to press a button? What is the state of the discrete system of a motor being able to start and stop?

Taking this into account, an *event* can be abstracted to a simple binary relation built on the state set. This relation represents the connection existing between two successive states considered just before and just after the event "execution." However, defining an event directly as a binary relation would not be very convenient. A better notation consists in splitting an event into two parts: the *guards* and the *actions*.

A guard is a predicate and all the guards conjoined together in an event form the domain of the corresponding relation. An action is a simple assignment to a state variable. The actions of an event are supposed to be "executed" simultaneously on different variables. Variables that are not assigned are unchanged.

This is all the notation we are using for defining our transition systems.

Exercises: What are the events of the discrete system of a human being able to press a button? What are the events of the discrete system of a motor being able to start and stop? What is the possible relationship between both these systems?

At this stage, we might be slightly embarrassed and discover that it is not so easy to answer the last question. In fact, to begin with, we have not followed our own prescriptions! Perhaps it would have been better to first write down a definitions and requirements document concerned with the user/button/motor system. In doing this, we might have discovered that this relationship between the motor and the button is not that simple after all. Here are some questions that might come up: do we need a single button or several of them (i.e. a start button and a stop button)? Is the latter a good idea? In the case of several buttons, what can we observe if the start button is pressed while the motor is already started? In this case, do we have to release the button to re-start the motor later? And so on. We could also have figured out that, rather than considering separately a button system and a motor system and then *composing* them, it might have been better to consider first a single problem which might later be *decomposed* into several. Now, how about putting a piece of software between the two? And so on.

Horizontal refinement and proofs

The modeling of a large system containing many discrete transition components is not a task that can be done in one shot. It has to be done in successive steps. Each of these steps make the model richer by first creating and then enriching the states and transitions of its various components, first in a very abstract way and later by introducing more concrete elements. This activity is called *horizontal refinement* (or superposition).

In doing this, the system engineer explores the definitions and requirements document and gradually extracts from it some elements to be formalized; he thus starts the *traceability* of the definitions and requirements within the model. Notice that quite often it is discovered by modeling that the definitions and requirements document is incomplete or inconsistent; it then has to be edited accordingly.

By applying this horizontal refinement approach, we have to perform some proofs, namely that a more concrete refinement step does not invalidate what has been done in a more abstract step: these are the *refinement proofs*.

Note, finally, that the horizontal refinement steps are complete when there do not remain any definitions or any requirements that have not been taken into account in the model.

In making an horizontal refinement, we do not care about implementability. Our mathematical model is done using the set-theoretic notation to write down the state invariants and the transitions.

When making an horizontal refinement, we extend the state of a model by adding new variables. We can strengthen the guards of an event or add new guards. We also add new actions in an event. Finally, it is possible to add new events.

Vertical refinement and proofs

There exists a second kind of refinement that takes place when all horizontal refinement steps have been performed. As a result, we do not enter any more new details of the problem in the model, we rather transform some state and transitions of our discrete system so that it can easily be implemented on a computer. This is called *vertical refinement* (or data refinement). It can often be performed by a semi-automatic tool. *Refinement proofs* have also to be performed in order to be sure that our implementation choice is coherent with the more abstract view.

A typical example of vertical refinement is the transformation of finite sets into boolean arrays together with the corresponding transformations of set-theoretic operations (union, intersection, inclusion, etc.) into program loops.

When making a vertical refinement, we can remove some variables and add new ones. An important aspect of vertical refinement is the so-called gluing invariant linking the concrete and abstract states.

Communication and proofs

A very important aspect of the modeling task is concerned with the *communication* between the various components of the future system. We have to be very careful here to proceed by successive refinements. It is a mistake to model immediately the communication between components as they will be in the final system. A good approach to this is to consider that each component has the "right" to *access directly* the state of other components (which are still very abstract too). In doing that we "cheat", as it is clearly not the way it works in reality. But it is a very convenient way to approach the initial horizontal refinement steps as our components are gradually refined with their communication becoming gradually richer as one moves along the refinement steps. It is *only at the end* of the horizontal refinement steps that it is appropriate to introduce various channels corresponding to the real communication schemes at work between components and to possibly decompose our global system into several communicating sub-systems.

We can then figure out that each component reacts to the transitions of others with a fuzzy picture of their states. This is because the messages between the components do take some time to travel. We then have to prove that, in spite of this time shift, things remain "as if" such a shift did not exist. This is yet another *refinement proof* that we have to perform.

Being faultless: what does it mean?

We are now ready to make precise what we mean by a "faultless" system, which represents our ultimate goal as the title of this prologue indicates.

If a program controlling a train network is not developed to be correct by construction, then, after writing it, we can certainly never prove that this program will guarantee that two trains will never collide. It is too late. The only thing we might sometimes (not always unfortunately) be able to test or prove is that such a program has not got array accesses that are out of bounds, or dangerous null pointers that might be accessed, or that it does not contain the risk of some arithmetic overflow (although, remember, this was precisely the undetected problem that caused the Ariane 5 crash on its maiden voyage).

There is an important difference between a solution validation versus a problem validation. It seems that there is considerable confusion here as people do not make any clear distinction between the two.

A solution validation is concerned solely with the constructed software and it validates this piece of code against a number of *software properties* as mentioned above (out-of-bound array access, null pointers, overflows). On the contrary, a problem validation is concerned with the *overall purpose* of our system (i.e. to ensure that trains travel safely within a given network). To do this, we have to prove that all components of the system (not only the software) harmoniously participate in the global goal.

To prove that our program will guarantee that two trains will never collide, we have to construct the program by modeling the problem. And, of course, a significant part of this is that the property in question must be *part of the model* to begin with.

We should notice, however, that people sometimes succeed in doing some sort of problem proofs directly as part of the solution (the program). This is done by incorporating some so-called ghost variables dealing with the problem inside the program. Such variables are then removed from the final code. We consider that this approach is a rather artificial afterthought. The disadvantage of this approach is that it focuses attention on the software rather than on the wider problem. In fact, this use of ghost variables just highlights the need for abstraction when reasoning at the problem level. The approach advocated here is precisely to start with the abstractions, reason about these, and introduce the programs later.

During the horizontal refinement phase of our model development, we shall take account of many properties. At the end of the horizontal refinement phase, we shall then know exactly what we mean by this non-collision property. In doing so, we shall make precise all *assumptions* (in particular, environment assumptions) by which our model will guarantee that two trains will never collide.

As can be seen, the property alone is not sufficient. By exhibiting all these assumptions, we are doing a problem validation that is completely different in nature from the one we can perform on the software only.

Using this kind of approach for all properties of our system will allow us to claim that, at the end of our development, our system is faultless by construction. For this, we have made very precise what we call the "faults" under consideration (and, in particular, their relevant assumptions).

However, we should note a delicate point here. We pretended that this approach allows us to produce the final software that is correct by construction relative to its surrounding environment. In other words, the global system is faultless. This has been done by means of proofs performed during the modeling phase where we constructed a model of the environment. Now we said earlier that this environment was made up of equipment, physical phenomena, pieces of software, and also users. It is quite clear that these elements cannot be formalized completely. Rather than say that our software is correct relative to its environment, it would be more appropriate to be more modest by saying that our software is correct relative to the model of the environment we have constructed. This model is certainly only an approximation of the physical environment. Should this approximation be too far from the real environment, then it would be possible that our software would fail under unforeseen external circumstances.

In conclusion, we can only pretend that we have a relative faultless construction, not an absolute one, which is clearly impossible. A problem where the solution is still in its infancy is that of finding the right methodology to perform an environment modeling that is a "good" approximation of the real environment. It is clear that a probabilistic approach would certainly be very useful when doing this.

About proofs

In previous sections, we mentioned several times that we have to perform proofs during the modeling process. First of all, it must be clear that we need a tool for generating automatically what we have to prove. It would be foolish (and error prone) to let a human being write down explicitly the formal statements that must be proved, for the simple reason that it is common to have thousands of such proofs. Second, we also need a tool to perform the proofs automatically: a typical desirable figure here is to have 90% of the proofs being discharged automatically.

An interesting question is then to study what happens when an automatic proof fails. It might be because: (1) the automatic prover is not smart enough, or (2) the statement to prove is false, or else (3) the statement to prove cannot be proved. In case (1), we have to perform an interactive proof (see the "Tool" section below). In case (2), the model has to be significantly modified. In case (3), the model has to be enriched. Cases (2) and (3) are very interesting; they show that the proof activity plays the same role for models as the one played by testing for programs.

Also notice that the final percentage of automatic proofs is a good indication of the quality of the model. If there are too many interactive proofs, it might signify that the model is too complicated. By simplifying the model, we often also significantly augment the percentage of automatically discharged proofs.

Design pattern

Design patterns were made very popular some years ago by a book written on them for object-oriented software development [3]. But the idea is more general than that: it can be fruitfully extended to any particular engineering discipline and in particular to system engineering as envisaged here.

The idea is to write down some predefined small engineering recipes that can be reused in many different situations, provided these recipes are instantiated accordingly. In our case, it takes the form of some proved parameterized models, which can be incorporated in a large project. The nice effect is that it saves redoing proofs that have been done once and for all in the pattern development. Tools can be developed to easily instantiate and incorporate patterns in a systematic fashion.

Animation

Here is a strange thing: in previous sections, we heavily proposed to base our correctness assurance on modeling and *proving*. And, in this section, we are going to say that, well, it might also be good to "animate" (that is "execute") our models!

But, we thought that mathematics was sufficient and that there was no need to execute. Is there any contradiction here? Are we in fact not so sure after all that our mathematical treatment is sufficient, that mathematics are always "true"? No, after the proof of the Pythagorean Theorem, no mathematician would think of measuring the hypotenuse and the two sides of a right triangle to check the validity of the theorem! So why execute our models?

We have certainly proved something and we have no doubts about our proofs, but more simply are we sure that what we proved was indeed the right thing to prove? Things might be difficult to swallow here: we wrote (painfully) the definitions and requirements document precisely for that reason, to know exactly what we have to prove. And now we claim that perhaps what the requirements document said was not what is wanted. Yes, that is the way it is: things are not working in a linear fashion.

Animating directly the model (we are not speaking here of doing a special simulation, we are using the very model which we proved) and showing this animation of the entire system (not only the software part) on a screen is very useful to check in another way (besides the requirements document) that what we want is indeed what we wrote. Quite often, by doing this, we discover that our requirements document was not accurate enough or that it required properties that are not indispensable or even different from what we want.

Animation complements modeling. It allows us to discover that we might have to change our minds very early on. The interesting thing is that it does not cost that much money, far less indeed than doing a real execution on the final system and discovering (but far too late) that the system we built is not the system we want.

It seems that animation has to be performed after proving, as an additional phase before the programming phase. No, the idea is to use animation as early as possible during the horizontal refinement phase, even on very abstract steps. The reason is that if we have to change our requirements (and thus redo some proofs), it is very important to know exactly what we can save in our model and where we have to modify our model construction.

There is another positive outcome in animating and proving simultaneously. Remember, we said that proving was a way to debug our model: a proof that cannot be done is an indication that we have a "bug" in our model or that our model is too poor. The fact that an invariant preservation proof cannot be done can be pointed out and explained by an animation even before doing the proof. Deadlock freedom counter-examples are quite often discovered very easily by animation. Notice that animation does not mean that we can suspend our proof activity, we just wanted to say that it is a very useful complement to it.

Tools

Tools are important to develop correct systems. Here we propose to depart from the usual approach where there exists a (formal) text file containing models and their successive refinement. It is far more appropriate to have a *database* at our disposal. This database handles modeling objects such as models, variables, invariant, events, guards, actions, and their relationships, as we have presented them in previous sections.

Usual *static analyzers* can be used on these components for lexical analysis, name clash detection, mathematical text syntactic analysis, refinement rules verification, and so on.

As said above, an important tool is the one called the *proof obligation generator*, that analyzes the models (invariants, events) and their refinements in order to produce corresponding statements to prove.

Finally, some *proving tools* (automatic and interactive) are needed to discharge the proof obligations provided by the previous tool. An important thing to understand here is that the proofs to be performed are not the kind of proofs a professional mathematician would tackle (and be interested in). Our proving tool has to take this into account.

In a mathematical project, the mathematician is interested in proving one theorem (say, the four-color theorem) together with some lemmas (say, 20 of them). The mathematician does not use mathematics to accompany the construction of an artefact. During the mathematical project, the problem does not change (this is still the four-color problem).

In an engineering project, thousands of predicates have to be proved. Moreover, what we have to prove is not known right from the beginning. Note that again we do not prove that trains do not collide; we prove that the system we are constructing ensures that, under certain hypotheses about the environment, trains do not collide. What we have to prove evolves with our understanding of the problem and our (non-linear) progress in the construction process.

As a consequence, an engineering prover needs to have some functionalities which are not needed in provers dedicated to perform proofs for mathematicians. To cite two of these functionalities: differential proving (how to figure out which proofs have to be redone when a slight modification to the model occurs) and proving in the presence of useless hypotheses.

Around the tools we have presented in this section, it is very useful to add a number of other tools using the same core database: animating tools, model-checking tools, UML transformation tools, design pattern tools, composition tools, decomposition tools, and so on. It means that our tooling system must be built in such a way that this extension approach is facilitated. A tool developed according to this philosophy is the Rodin platform which can be freely downloaded from [4].

The problem of legacy code

The legacy code question has a dual aspect: either (1) we want to develop a new piece of software which is connected to some legacy code, or (2) we want to renovate a certain legacy code.

Problem (1) is the most common one; it is almost always found in the development of a new piece of software. In this case, the legacy code is just an element of the environment of our new product. The challenge is to be able to model the behavior we can observe of the legacy code so that we can enter it in the model as we do it with any other element of the environment. To do this, the requirements document of our new product must contain some elements concerned with the legacy code. Such requirements (assumptions) have to be defined informally as we explained above.

The goal is to develop in our model the minimal interface which is compatible with the legacy code. As usual, the key is abstraction and refinement: how can we gradually introduce the legacy code in our model in such a way that we take full account of the concrete interface it offers.

Problem (2) is far more difficult than the previous one. In fact, such renovations often give very disappointing results. People tend to consider that the legacy code "is" the requirements document of the renovation. This is an error.

The first step is to write a brand new requirements document, not hesitating to depart from the legacy code by defining abstract requirements that are independent from the precise implementation seen in the legacy code.

The second step is to renovate the legacy code by developing and proving a model of it. The danger here is to try to mimic too closely the legacy code because it might contain aspects that are not comprehensible (except for the absent legacy code programmer(s)) and that are certainly not the result of a formal modeling approach.

Our advice here is to think twice before embarking on such a renovation. A better approach is to develop a new product. People think it might be more time consuming than a simple renovation; experience shows that this is rarely the case.

The use of set-theoretic notation

Physicists or operational researchers, who also proceed by constructing models, never invent specific languages to do so; they all use classical set-theoretic notations.

Computer scientists, because they have been educated to program only, believe that it is necessary to invent specific languages to do the modeling. This is an error. Set-theoretic notations are well suited to perform our system modeling, and, moreover, we can understand what it means when we write a formal statement!

We also hear very frequently that we must hide the use of mathematical notation, because engineers will not understand it and be afraid of it. This is nonsense. Can we imagine that it is necessary to hide the mathematical notation used in the design of an electrical network because electrical engineers will be frightened by it?

Other validation approaches

For decades, there have been various approaches dedicated to the validation of software. Among them are tests, abstract interpretation, and model checking.

These approaches validate the solution, the software, not the problem, the global system. In each case, we construct a piece of software and then (and only then) try to validate it (although it is not entirely the case with model checking, which is also used for problem validation). To do so, we think of a certain desired property and check that the software is indeed consistent with it. If it is not, then we have to modify the software and thus, quite often, introduce more problems. It is also well known that such approaches are very expensive, far more than the pure development cost.

We do not think that these approaches alone are appropriate. However, we are not saying of course that we should reject them; we are just saying they might complement the modeling and proving approach.

Innovation

Big industrial corporations are often unable to innovate. They sometimes do so however, provided a very large amount of money is given to them precisely for this. Needless to say, it is very rare. It is well known that many, so-called, research and development (R&D) divisions of big companies are not providing any significant technologies for their business units.

Nevertheless, financing agencies still insist on having practical research proposals connected with such large companies. This is an error. They would do a better job by accepting connections with far smaller more innovative entities.

It is my belief that the introduction into industry of the approach advocated here should be done through small innovative companies rather than big corporations

Education

Most of the people presently involved in large software engineering projects are not correctly educated. Companies think that programming jobs can be done by junior people with little or no mathematical background and interest (quite often programmers do not like mathematics; this is why they choose computing in the first place). All this is bad. The basic background of a system engineer must be a *mathematical education* at a good (even high) level.

Computing should come second, after the necessary mathematical background has been well understood. As long as this is not the case, progress will not be made. Of course, it is clear that many academics will disagree with this; it is not the smallest problem we have to face. Many academics still confuse computation and mathematics.

It is far less expensive to have a few well-educated people than an army of people who are not educated at the right level. This is not an elitist attitude: who would think that a doctor or an architect can perform well without the right education in his discipline? Again, the fundamental basic discipline of system and software engineers is (discrete) mathematics.

Two specific topics to be taught to future software engineers are: (1) the writing of requirements documents (this is barely present in the practical software engineering curriculum), and (2) the construction of mathematical models. Here the basic approach is a practical one; it has to be taught by means of many examples and projects to be undertaken by the students. Experience shows that the mastering of the mathematical approach (including the proofs) is not a problem for students with a good *previous* mathematical background.

Technology transfer

Technology transfer of this kind in industry is a serious problem. It is due to the extreme reluctance of managers to modify their development process. Usually such processes are difficult to define and more difficult to be put into practice. This is the reason why managers do not like to modify them.

The incorporation in the development process of the important initial phase of requirements document writing, followed by another important phase of modeling, is usually regarded as dangerous, as these additional phases impose some significant expenses at the beginning of a project. Again, managers do not believe that spending more initially will mean spending less at the end. However, experience shows that the overall expenditure is drastically reduced, since the very costly testing phase at the end can be significantly less, as is the considerable effort needed to patch design errors.

Above all, the overall initial action needed in order to transfer a technology to industry is to perform a very significant preliminary education effort. Without that initial effort, any technology transfer attempt is due to fail.

It should be noted that there exist also some fake technology transfers where people pretend to use a formal approach (although they did not) just to get the "formal" stamp given to them by some authority.

References

The ideas presented in this short prologue are not new. Most of them come from the seminal ideas of Action Systems developed in the eighties and nineties. Important papers on Action Systems (among many others) are [1] and [2].

More recently, some of the ideas presented here have been put into practice. You can consult the web site [4] and, of course, read this book for more information, examples, and tool description.

[1]   R. Back and R. Kurki-Suonio. Decentralization of process nets with centralized control. *2nd ACM SIGACT-SIGOPS Symposium on Principles of Distributing Computing* (1983)

[2]   M. Butler. Stepwise refinement of communicating systems. *Science of Computer Programming* **27**, 139–173 (1996)

[3]   E. Gamma *et al. Design Patterns: Elements of Reusable Object Oriented Software.* Addison-Wesley (1995).

[4]   http://www.event-b.org

Acknowledgments

The development of this book on Event-B was a long process, taking me more than ten years.

A book of this importance in size and content cannot be produced by one person alone. During my years at ETH Zurich (one of the two Swiss Federal Institutes of Technology), I gradually elaborated the many examples which are presented here. This was done with the help of many people and also the insightful feedback of my students.

I am extremely grateful for the permanent help given to me by Dominique Cansell. Without him, this book would have been very different! In many cases, I was completely blocked and could only proceed thanks to Dominique's advice. He has continually read the versions of the book as it has developed, always giving very important suggestions for improvements. Dominique, many thanks to you.

Another significant source of help came from the Rodin and Deploy teams in Zurich (Rodin and Deploy are the names of European Projects which participated in the financing of this effort). Members of the teams were Laurent Voisin, Stefan Hallerstede, Thai Son Hoang, Farhad Mehta, François Terrier, and Matthias Schmalz. Numerous discussions were necessary to gradually develop a fruitful cooperation between the Event-B corpus and the Rodin Platform, which is now available as an open source tool set. Among these people, Laurent Voisin played an outstanding role. Laurent is the architect of the tool; his immense competence in tool development allowed us to have now a tool which is the indispensable support of Event-B. Laurent was also at the origin of some key concepts in Event-B. Laurent, many thanks to you.

Members of the teams mentioned above also assisted me with numerous courses (both introductory and advanced) I gave on this topic at ETH Zurich. They invented many exercises and projects that were proposed to students. Adam Darvas, as well as the aforementioned team members, was also an assistant for my lectures. I was surprised by his ability to quickly master these subjects and to give interesting feedback. Gabriel Katz, a student at ETH, also joined the team of assistants and later became a temporary member of the development team.

Other people at ETH were involved in one way or another in the Event-B development: David Basin, Peter Müller, and Christoph Sprenger. More generally, members of the ETH Formal Methods Club, which met once a week, were very active in bringing comments and feedback on the ongoing development of Event-B: among them were Joseph Ruskiewicz, Stephanie Balzer, Bernd Schöller, Vijay D'silva, Burkhart Wolf, and Achim Brucker.

Outside Zurich, a number of people were also active participants in this effort. Among them, I am very happy to mention Christophe Métayer. He plays an outstanding part in the usage of Event-B in industry and also in the development of some additional tools. More generally, Systerel, the company led by François Bustany, where Laurent Voisin and Christophe Métayer are now working, is playing a key role in the development of Event-B in industry.

As members of the Rodin and Deploy European Projects, Michael Butler and Michael Leuschel were very helpful with their competence in formal methods during the many years of the lives of these Projects. Both Michael Butler in Southampton and Michael Leuschel in Düsseldorf built, together with their teams, very interesting tools enlarging those developed in Zurich.

Other people, such as Dominique Méry, Michel Sintzoff, Egon Börger, Ken Robinson, Richard Banach, Marc Frappier, Henri Habrias, Richard Bornat, Guy Vidal-Naquet, Carroll Morgan, Leslie Lamport, and Stephan Merz, helped in one way or another during the many scientific meetings that happened over the years.

Finally, I would like to thank particularly Tony Hoare and Ralph Back. Their influence on this work was extremely important. The seminal ideas of Edsger Dijkstra were also permanently applied in Event-B.

1

Introduction

1.1 Motivation

The intent of this book is to give some insights on *modeling* and *formal reasoning*. These activities are supposed to be performed *before* undertaking the effective coding of a computer system, so that the system in question will be *correct by construction*.

In this book, we will thus learn how to build models of programs and, more generally, discrete systems. But this will be done with *practice in mind*. For this we shall study a large number of examples coming from various sources of computer system development: sequential programs, concurrent programs, distributed programs, electronic circuits, reactive systems, etc.

We will understand that the model of a program is quite different from the program itself. And we will learn that it is far easier to *reason* about the model than about the program. We will be made aware of the very important notions of *abstraction* and *refinement*; the idea being that an executable program is only obtained at the final stage of a sometimes long sequence consisting of gradually building more and more accurate models of the future program (think of the various blueprints made by an architect).

We shall make it very clear what we mean by *reasoning* about a model. This will be done by using some simple mathematical methods, which will be presented first by means of some examples then by reviewing classical logic (propositional and predicate calculus) and set theory. We will understand the necessity of performing proofs in a very rigorous fashion.

We will also understand how it is possible to detect the presence of inconsistencies in our models just by the fact that some proofs cannot be done. The failure of the proof will provide us with some helpful clues about what is wrong or insufficiently defined in our model. We will use such tools and see how easy it is to perform proofs with a computer.

The formalism we use throughout the book is called Event-B. It is a simplification as well as an extension of the B formalism [1] which was developed ten years ago and which has been used in a number of large industrial projects [4], [3]. The formal concepts used in Event-B are by no means new. They were proposed a long time ago in a number of parent formalisms, such as Action Systems [6], TLA$^+$ [2], and UNITY [5].

The book is organized around examples. Each chapter contains a new example (sometimes several) together with the necessary formalism allowing the mathematical concepts being used to be understood. Of course, such concepts are not repeated from one chapter to the other, although they are sometimes made more precise. As a matter of fact, each chapter is an almost independent essay. The proofs done in each chapter have all been performed using the tools of the open source Rodin Platform [7] (see also the website "event-b.org").

The book can be used as a textbook by presenting each chapter in one or more lectures. After giving a small summary of the various chapters in the next section, a possible use for the book in an introductory as well as an advanced course will be proposed.

1.2 Overview of the chapters

Let us now list the various chapters of the book and give a brief outline of each of them.

Chapter 1: Introduction

The intent of this first (non-technical) chapter is to introduce you to the notion of a *formal method*. It also intends to make clear what we mean by *modeling*. We shall see what kind of systematic *conventions* we shall use for modeling. But we shall also notice that there is no point in embarking on the modeling of a system without knowing what the requirements of this system are. For this, we are going to study how a *requirements document* has to be written.

Chapter 2: Controlling cars on a bridge

The intent of this chapter is to introduce a complete example of a small system development. We develop the model of a system controlling cars on a one-way bridge between an island and the mainland. As an additional constraint, the number of cars on the island is limited. The physical equipment is made of traffic lights and car sensors

During this development, we will be made aware of the systematic approach we are using: it consists in developing a series of more and more accurate models of the system we want to construct. Note that each model does not represent the programming of our system using a high-level programming language, it rather formalizes what an *external observer* of this system could perceive of it.

Each model will be analyzed and proved, thus enabling us to establish that it is *correct* relative to a number of criteria. As a result, when the last model is finished, we shall be able to say that this model is *correct by construction*. Moreover, this model will be so close to a final implementation that it will be very easy to transform it into a genuine program.

The correctness criteria alluded to above will be made completely clear and systematic by giving a number of *proof obligation rules*, which will be applied to our models. After applying such rules, we shall have to prove formally a number of statements. To this end, we shall also give a reminder of the classical *rules of inference of the sequent calculus*. Such rules concern propositional logic, equality, and basic arithmetic. The idea here is to give the reader the opportunity to manually prove the statements as given by the proof obligation rules. Clearly, such proofs could easily be discharged by theorem provers (as the ones used in the Rodin Platform), but we feel it important at this stage that the reader takles these proofs before using an automatic theorem prover. Notice that we do not claim that a theorem prover would perform these proofs the way it is proposed here; quite often, a tool does not work like a human being does.

Chapter 3: A mechanical press controller

In this chapter, we develop again the controller of a complete system: a mechanical press. The intention is to show how this can be done in a systematic fashion in order to obtain the correct final code. We first present, as usual, the requirement document of this system. Then we develop two general *design patterns* which we shall subsequently use. The development of these patterns will be made by using the proofs as a means of discovering the invariants and the guards of the events. Finally, the main development of the mechanical press will take place.

In this chapter, we illustrate how the usage of formal design patterns can help tackling systematic correct developments.

Chapter 4: A simple file transfer protocol

The example introduced in this chapter is quite different from the previous ones, where the program was supposed to control an external situation (cars on a bridge or a mechanical press). Here we present a, so-called, protocol to be used on a computer network by two agents. This is the very classical two-phase handshake protocol. A very nice presentation of this example can be found in the book by L. Lamport [2].

This example will allow us to extend our usage of the mathematical language with such constructs as partial and total functions, domain and range of functions, and function restrictions. We shall also extend our logical language by introducing *universally quantified formulas* and corresponding inference rules.

Chapter 5: The Event-B Modeling notation and proof obligation rules

In the previous chapters, we used the Event-B notation and the various corresponding proof obligation rules without introducing them in a systematic fashion. We presented them instead in the examples when they were needed. This was sufficient for the simple examples studied so far because we used part of the notation and part of the proof obligation rules only. But it might not be adequate to continue like this when presenting more complicated examples in subsequent chapters.

The purpose of this chapter is thus to correct this. First, we present the Event-B notation as a whole, in particular the parts we have not used so far, then we present all the proof obligation rules. This will be illustrated with a simple running example. Note that the mathematical justifications of the proof obligation rules will be covered in Chapter 14.

Chapter 6: Bounded re-transmission protocol

In this chapter, we extend the file transfer protocol example of Chapter 4. The added constraint with regard to the previous simple example is that we now suppose that the channels situated between the two sites are *unreliable*. As a consequence, the effect of the execution of the bounded re-transmission protocol is to only *partially* copy a sequential file from one site to another. The purpose of this example is precisely to study how we can cope with this kind of problem, i.e. dealing with fault tolerances and how we can formally reason about them. This example has been studied in many papers among which is [8].

Notice that, in this chapter, we do not develop proofs to the extent we did in the previous chapters, we only give some hints and let the reader develop the formal proof.

Chapter 7: Development of a concurrent program

In previous chapters, we saw examples of *sequential* program developments (note that we shall come back to sequential program developments in Chapter 15) and *distributed* program developments. Here we show how we can develop *concurrent* program developments. Such concurrent programs are different from distributed programs where various processes are executed on different computers in such a way that they *cooperate* (by exchanging messages in a well-defined manner) in order to achieve a well-specified goal. This was typically the case in the examples presented in Chapters 4 and 6. It will also be the case in Chapters 10, 11, 12, and 13.

In the case of concurrent programs, we also have different processes, but this time they are usually situated on the same computer and they *compete* rather than co-operate in order to gain access to some shared resources. The concurrent programs do not communicate by exchanging messages (they ignore each other), but they can interrupt each other in a rather random way. We illustrate this approach by developing the concurrent program known to be "Simpson's 4-slot Fully Asynchronous Mechanism" [14].

Chapter 8: Development of electronic circuits

In this chapter, we present a methodology to develop electronic circuits in a systematic fashion. In doing so, we can see that the Event-B approach is general enough to be adapted to different execution paradigms. The approach used here is similar to the one we shall use for developing sequential programs in Chapter 15: the circuit is first defined by means of a single event doing the job "in one shot", then the initial very abstract transition is refined into several transitions until it becomes possible to apply some syntactic rules able to merge the various transitions into a single circuit.

Chapter 9: Mathematical language

This chapter does not contain any examples as in previous chapters (except Chapter 5). It rather contains the formal definition of the mathematical language we use in this book. It is made up of four sections introducing successively the propositional language, the predicate language, the set-theoretic language, and the arithmetic language. Each of these languages will be introduced as an extension of the previous one.

Before introducing these languages, however, we shall also give a brief summary of the sequent calculus. Here we shall insist on the concept of proof.

At the end of the chapter, we present the way various classical but "advanced" concepts are formalized: transitive closure, various graph properties (in particular strong connectivity), lists, trees, and well-founded relations. Such concepts will be used in subsequent chapters.

Chapter 10: Leader election on a ring-shaped network

In this chapter, we study another interesting problem in distributed computation. We have a possibly large (but finite) number of agents, not just two as in the examples of Chapters 4 and 6 (file transmission protocols). These agents are disposed on different sites that are connected by means of unidirectional channels forming a ring. Each agent is executing the same piece of coding. The distributed execution of all these identical programs should result in a *unique agent* being "elected the leader". This example comes from a paper written by G. Le Lann in the 1970s [9].

The purpose of this chapter is to learn more about modeling, in particular in the area of non-determinism. We shall also use more mathematical conventions, such as the image of a set under a relation, the relational overriding operator, and the relational composition operator, conventions which have all been introduced in the previous chapter. Finally, we are going to study some interesting data structures: ring and linear list, also introduced in the previous chapter.

Chapter 11: Synchronizing a tree-shaped network

In the example presented in this chapter, we have a network of nodes, which is slightly more complicated than in the previous case where we were dealing with a ring. Here we have a tree. At each node of the tree, we have a process performing a certain task, which is the same for all processes (the exact nature of this task is not important). The constraint we want these processes to observe is that they remain *synchronized*. An additional constraint of our distributed algorithm states that each process can only communicate with its immediate neighbors in the tree. This example has been treated by many researchers [10], [11].

In this chapter, we shall encounter another interesting mathematical object: a tree. We shall thus learn how to formalize such a data structure and see how we can fruitfully reason about it using an induction rule. We remind the reader that this data structure has already been introduced in Chapter 9.

Chapter 12: Routing algorithm for a mobile agent

The purpose of the example developed in this chapter is to present an interesting routing algorithm for sending messages to a mobile phone. In this example, we shall again encounter a tree structure as in the previous chapter, but this time the tree structure will be dynamically modified. We shall also see another example (besides the "bounded re-transmission protocol" of Chapter 6) where the usage of clocks will play a fundamental role. This example is taken from [12].

Chapter 13: Leader election on a connected graph network

The example presented in this chapter resembles the one presented in Chapter 10; it is again a leader election protocol, but here the network is more complicated than a simple ring. More precisely, the goal of the IEEE-1394 protocol, [13], is to elect in a finite time a specific node, called the leader, in a network made of a finite number of nodes linked by some communication channels. This election is done in a distributed and non-deterministic way.

The network has got some specific properties. As a mathematical structure, it is called a *free tree*; it is a finite graph, which is symmetric, irreflexive, connected, and acyclic. In this chapter, we shall thus learn how to deal and reason with such a complex data structure, which was already presented in Chapter 9.

Chapter 14: Mathematical models for proof obligations

In this chapter, some mathematical justifications are presented to the proof obligation rules introduced in Chapter 5. This is done by constructing some set-theoretic mathematical models based on the trace semantics of Event-B developments. We show that the proof obligation rules used in this book are equivalent to those dictated by the mathematical models of Event-B developed in this chapter.

Chapter 15: Development of sequential programs

This chapter is devoted entirely to the development of sequential programs. We shall first study the structure of such programs. They are made up of a number of assignment statements, glued together by means of a number of operators: sequential composition, conditional, and loop. We shall see how this can be modeled by means of simple transitions, which are the essence of the Event-B formalism. Once such transitions are developed gradually by means of a number of refinement steps, we shall see how they can be put together using a number of merging rules, the nature of which is completely syntactic.

All this will be illustrated with many examples, ranging from simple array and numerical programs to more complex pointer programs.

Chapter 16: A location access controller

The purpose of this chapter is to study another example dealing with a complete system such as the one we studied in Chapters 2 and 3, where we controlled cars on a bridge and a mechanical press. We shall construct a system which will be able to control the access of certain people to different locations of a "workplace", for example: a university campus, an industrial site, a military compound, a shopping mall, etc.

The system we now study is a little more complicated than the previous ones. In particular, the mathematical data structure we are going to use is more advanced. Our intention is also to show that during the reasoning of the model, we shall discover a number of important missing points in the requirements document.

Chapter 17: Train system

The purpose of this chapter is to show the specification and construction of a complete computerized system. The example we are interested in is called a *train system*. By this, we mean a system that is practically managed by a *train agent*, whose role is to control the various trains crossing part of a certain *track network* situated under his supervision. The computerized system we want to construct is supposed to help the train agent in doing this task.

This example presents an interesting case of quite complex data structures (the track network) where mathematical properties have to be defined with great care – we want to show that this is possible.

This example also shows a very interesting case where the reliability of the final product is absolutely fundamental: several trains have to be able to safely cross the network under the complete automatic guidance of the software product we want to construct. For this reason, it will be important to study the bad incidents that could happen and which we want to either completely avoid or safely manage.

The software must take account of the external environment which is to be carefully controlled. As a consequence, the formal modeling we propose here will contain not only a model of the future software we want to construct, but also a detailed model of its environment. Our ultimate goal is to have the software working in perfect synchronization with the external equipment, namely the track circuits, the points (or "switch"), the signals, and also the train drivers. We want to *prove* that trains obeying the signals, set by the software controller, and then (blindly) circulating on the tracks where the points (switches) have been positioned, again by the software controller, will do so in a completely safe manner.

Chapter 18: Problems

This last chapter contains only problems which readers might try to tackle. Rather than spreading exercises and projects through each chapter of the book, we preferred to put them all in a single chapter.

All problems have to be performed with the Rodin Platform, which, again, can be downloaded from the web site "event-b.org".

Besides exercises (supposed to be rather easy) and projects (supposed to be larger and more difficult than exercises), we propose some mathematical developments which can also be proved with the Rodin Platform.

1.3 How to use this book

The material presented in this book has been used to teach various courses, essentially either introductory courses or advanced courses. Here is what can be proposed for these two categories of courses.

Introductory course The danger with such an introductory course is to present too much material. The risk is to have the attendees being completely overwhelmed. What can be presented then is the following:

- Chapter 1 (introduction),
- Chapter 2 (cars on a bridge),
- Chapter 3 (mechanical press),
- Chapter 4 (simple file transfer),
- some parts of Chapter 5 (Event-B notation),
- some parts of Chapter 9 (mathematical language),
- some parts of Chapter 15 (sequential program development).

The idea is to avoid encountering complex concepts, only simple mathematical constructs: propositional calculus, arithmetic, and simple set-theoretic constructs.

Chapter 2 (cars on a bridge) is important because the example is extremely easy to understand and the basic notions of Event-B and of classical logic are introduced by means of that simple example. However, we have to be careful to present this chapter very slowly, doing carefully the proofs with the students because they are usually very confused when they encounter this kind of material for the first time. In this example, the data structures are very simple: numbers and booleans.

Chapter 3 (mechanical press) shows again a complete development. It is simple and the usage of formal design patterns is helpful to construct the controller in a systematic fashion.

Chapter 4 (simple file transfer) allows us to present a very simple distributed program. Students will learn how this can be specified and later refined in order to obtain a very well-known distributed protocol. They have to understand that such a protocol can be constructed by starting from a very abstract (non-distributed) specification, which is gradually distributed among various (here two) processes. This example contains some more elaborated data structures than those used in the previous chapter: intervals, functions, restrictions.

Chapter 5 (Event-B notation) contains a summary of the Event-B notation and of the proof obligation rules. It is important that the students see that they use a well-defined, although simple, notation, which is given a mathematical interpretation through, the proof obligation rules. It is not necessary however to go too deeply into fine details in such an introductory course

Chapter 9 (mathematical language) allows us to depart a bit from the examples. It is a refresher of the mathematical concepts in the middle of the course. The important aspect here is to have the students becoming more familiar with proofs undertaken in set-theoretic concepts. Students have to be given a number of exercises for translating set-theoretic constructs into predicate calculus. It is not necessary to cover this chapter from beginning to end.

Chapter 15 (sequential program development) is partly an introductory course because students are used to writing programs. It is important to understand that programs can be constructed in a systematic fashion; to understand eventually the distinction between formal program construction (which we do here) versus program verification (where the program is "proved" once developed). Some of the examples must be avoided in an introductory course, namely those dealing with pointers that are too difficult.

At the end of the course, students should be comfortable with the notions of abstraction and refinement. They should also be less afraid of tackling formal proofs of simple mathematical statements. Finally, they should be convinced that it is possible to develop programs that work first time!

Students could be made aware of the Rodin Platform tool [7], which is devoted to Event-B. But we think that they must first do some proofs by hand in order to understand what the tool is doing.

Advanced course Here we suppose that the students have already attended the introductory course. In this case, it is not necessary to repeat the presentations of Chapters 2 and 3. However, students will be encouraged to read them again. The course then consists in presenting all the other chapters.

It is important for the students to understand that the same Event-B approach can be used to model systems with very different execution paradigms: sequential, distributed, concurrent, and parallel.

Students should be comfortable reasoning with complex data structures: list, trees, DAGs, arbitrary graphs. They must understand that set theory allows us to build very complex data structures. For these reasons, the examples presented in Chapters 11 (synchronizing processes in a tree), 12 (mobile agent), 13 (IEEE protocol), and 17 (train system) are all important.

In this course, students should not do manual proofs any more as was the case in the previous introductory course. They must use a tool such as the Rodin Platform, which is specially devoted to Event-B and associated plugins [7].

1.4 Formal methods

The term "formal method" leads nowadays to *great confusion* because its usage has been enlarged to cover many different activities. Some typical questions we can ask about such methods are the following: Why use formal methods? What are they used for? When do we need to use such methods? Is UML a formal method? Are they needed in object-oriented programming? How can we define formal methods?

We will look at these questions gradually. Formal methods have to be used by people who have recognized that the (internal) *program development process* they use is inadequate. There may be several reasons for such inadequacies, e.g. failure, cost, risk.

The choice of a formal method is not an easy one. Partly because there are many formal method vendors. More precisely, the adjective "formal" does not mean anything. Here are some questions you may ask a formal method vendor. Is there any theory behind your formal method? What kind of language is your formal method using? Does there exist any kind of refinement mechanism associated with your formal method? What is your way of reasoning with your formal method? Do you prove anything when using your formal method?

People might claim that using formal methods is impossible because there are some intrinsic difficulties in doing so. Here are a few of these claimed difficulties: You have to be a mathematician. The proposed formalism is hard to master. It is not visual enough (boxes, arrows are missing). People will not be able to perform proofs.

I mostly disagree with the above points of view, but I recognize that there are some real difficulties, which, in my mind, are the following:

(i) When using formal methods, you have to think a lot before coding, which is not, as we know, the current practice.

(ii) The use of formal methods has to be incorporated within a certain development process, and this incorporation is not easy. In industry, people develop their products under very precise guidelines, which they have to follow very carefully. Usually, the introduction of such guidelines in an industry takes a significant time before being accepted and fully observed by engineers. Now, changing such guidelines to incorporate the use of formal methods is something that managers are very reluctant to do because they are afraid of the time and cost this process modification will take.

(iii) Model building is not a simple activity; remember that this is what we will be learning in this book. We have to be careful not to confuse modeling and programming. Sometimes people do some kind of pseudo-programming instead of modeling. More precisely, the initial model of a program describes the properties that the program must fulfil. It does not describe the algorithm contained in the program, but rather the way by which we can eventually judge that the final program is correct. For example, the initial model of a file-sorting program does not explain how to sort. It rather explains what the properties of a sorted file are and which relationship exists between the initial non-sorted file we want to sort and the final sorted one.

(iv) Modeling has to be accompanied by reasoning. In other words, the model of a program is not just a piece of text, whatever the formalism being used. It also contains proofs that are related to this text. For many years, formal methods have just been used as a means of obtaining abstract descriptions of the program we wanted to construct. Again, descriptions are not enough. We must justify what we write by proving some consistency properties. Now the problem is that software practitioners are not used to constructing such proofs, whereas people in other engineering disciplines are far more familiar with doing so. And one of the difficulties in making this part of the daily practice of software engineers is the lack of good proving tool support for proofs, which could be used on a large scale.

(v) Finally, one important difficulty encountered in modeling is the very frequent lack of good requirement documents associated with the programming task we have to perform. Most of the time, the requirement document, which can be found in industry, is either almost non-existent or far too verbose. In my opinion, it is vital, most of the time, to completely rewrite such documents before starting any modeling. We shall come back to this point in what follows.

1.5 A little detour: blueprints

It is my belief that the people in charge of the development of large and complex computer systems should adopt a point of view shared by all mature engineering disciplines, namely that of *using an artifact to reason about their future system during its construction*. In these disciplines, people use *blueprints* in the wider sense of the term, which allows them to reason formally during the very construction process. Here are a number of mature engineering disciplines: avionics, civil engineering, mechanical engineering, train control systems, ship building, etc. In these disciplines, people use blueprints and they consider these as very important parts of their engineering activity.

Let us analyze for a while what a blueprint is. A blueprint is a certain representation of the future system. It is not a mock-up however because the basis is lacking – you cannot drive the blueprint of a car! The blueprint allows you to reason about the future system you want to construct during its very construction process.

Reasoning about a future system means defining and calculating its behavior and its constraints. It also allows you to construct an architecture gradually. It is based on some dedicated underlying theories: strength of material, fluid mechanics, gravitation, etc.

It is possible to use a number of "blueprinting" techniques, which we are going to review now. While blueprinting, we are using a number of pre-defined conventions, which help reasoning but also allow the blueprints to be shared among large communities. Blueprints are usually organized as sequences of more and more accurate versions (again think of the blueprints made by architects), where each more recent version is adding details which could not be visible in previous ones. Likewise, blueprints can be decomposed into smaller ones in order to enhance readability. It is also possible for some early blueprints to be not completely determined, thus leaving open options which will be later refined (in further blueprints). Finally, it is very interesting to have libraries of old blueprints, where the engineer can browse in order to re-use some work that has already been done. All this (refinement, decomposition, re-use) clearly requires that blueprints are used with care so that the entire blueprint development of a system is coherent. For example, we have to be sure that a more accurate blueprint does not contradict a previous less precise one.

Most of the time, in our engineering discipline of software construction, people do not use such blueprinting artifacts. This results in a very heavy testing phase on the final product, which, as is well known, quite often happens too late. The blueprint drawing of our discipline consists of *building models* of our future systems. In no way is the model of a program, the program itself. But the model of a program and more generally of a complex computer system, although not executable, allows us to clearly identify the properties of the future system and to prove that they will be present in it.

1.6 The requirements document

The blueprint we quickly described in the previous section is not however the initial phase of the development process. It is preceded by a very important one which consists of writing a so-called *requirement document*. Most of the time such a document is either missing or very badly written. This is the reason why we are going to dwell for a while on this question and try to give an adequate answer to it.

1.6.1 Life cycle

First, we are going to recall what is the right time for this activity, namely that of the requirements document writing, within the life cycle of a program development. Here is a rough list of the various phases of the life cycle: system analysis, *requirements document*, technical specification, design, implementation, tests, maintenance.

Let us briefly summarize what the contents of these phases are. The system analysis phase contains the preliminary feasibility studies of the system we want to construct. The requirements document phase clearly states what the functions and constraints of the system are. It is mostly written in natural language. The technical specification contains the structured formalization of the previous document using some modeling techniques. The design phase develops the previous one by taking and justifying the decisions which implement the previous specification and also defines the architecture of the future system. The implementation phase contains the translation of the outcome of the previous phase into hardware and software components. The test phase consists of the experimental verifications of the final system. The maintenance phase contains the system upgrading.

As noticed above, the requirements document phase is quite often a *very weak point* in this life cycle. This results in lots of difficulties in subsequent phases. In particular, the famous syndrome of the inescapable specification changes occurring during the design phases originates in the weakness of the requirements document. When such a document is well written, these kinds of difficulties tend to disappear. This is the reason why it is so important to see how this phase can be improved.

1.6.2 Difficulties with the requirements document

Writing a good requirements document is a difficult task. We have to remember that the readers of such a document are the people who are conducting the next phases, namely technical specification and design. It is usually very difficult for them to exploit the requirements document because they cannot clearly identify what they have to take into account and in which order.

Quite often too, some important points are missing in the requirements document. I have seen a huge requirements document for the alarm system of an aircraft where the simple fact that this system should not deliver false alarms was simply missing. When the authors of this document were interrogated on this missing point, the answer they gave was rather surprising: it was not necessary to put such a detail in the requirements document because "of course everybody knows that the system should not deliver any false alarms." Sometimes, on the contrary, the requirements document is over-specified with a number of irrelevant details.

What is difficult for the reader of the requirements document is to make a clear distinction between which part of the text is devoted to *explanations* and which part is devoted to genuine *requirements*. Explanations are needed initially for the reader to understand the future system. But when the reader is more acquainted with the purpose of the system, explanations are less important. At that time, what counts is to remember what the real requirements are in order to know exactly what has to be taken into account in the system to be constructed.

1.6.3 A useful comparison

There exist other documents (rather books) which also contain explanations and, in a sense, requirements. These are books of mathematics. The "requirements" are definitions and theorems. Such items are usually easily recognizable because they are labeled by their function (definition, lemma, theorem), numbered in a systematic fashion, and usually written with a font which differs from that used elsewhere in the book. Here is an example:

2.8 The Cantor–Bernstein theorem *If $a \preceq b$ and $b \preceq a$, then a and b are equinumerous.*

This theorem was first conjectured by Cantor in 1895, and proved by Bernstein in 1898.

Proof. Since $b \preceq a$, then a has a subset c such that $b \approx c$ ...

$\square$

In this quotation extracted from a book of mathematics, we can clearly see the "requirement" as indicated on the first line: the theorem number, the theorem name, and the theorem statement (written in italic). Next are the associated "explanations": historical comments and proof.

This distinction is extremely interesting and useful for the reader. If it is our first contact with this material, then the explanation is fundamental. Later, we might only be interested in having just a look at the precise statement of the theorem; we are not interested any more in the historical comments or even in the proof. There are some books of mathematics where the "requirements" – that is, the definitions and the theorems – are summarized at the end of the book in an appendix that can be conveniently consulted.

Structuring the requirements document

Following this analogy of a book of mathematics, the idea is to have our requirements document organized around two texts embedded in each other: the *explanatory text* and the *reference text*. These two texts should be immediately separable, so that it is possible to summarize the reference text independently.

Usually, the reference text takes the form of *labeled and numbered short statements* written using natural language, which must be very easy to read independently from the explanatory text. For this, we shall use a special font for the reference text. These fragments must be self contained without the explanations. They together form the requirements. The explanations are just there to give some comments which could help a first reader. But after an initial period, the reference text is the only one that counts.

The labels of the requirement fragments are very important. They may vary from one system to the other. Common labels are the following:

FUN: for functional requirements,
ENV: for environment requirements,
SAF: for safety properties,
DEG: for degraded mode requirements,
DEL: for requirements concerned with delays, etc.

An important activity to be undertaken before writing the requirements document is that of defining with care the various labels we are going to use. Numbering these requirements is also very important as they will be referenced in later stages of the development. This is called *traceability*. The idea is to have these labeled numbers appearing in later stages (technical specification, design, even implementation) so that it will be easy to recognize how each requirement has indeed been taken into account during the construction of our system and in its final operational version.

Most of the time, the requirement fragments are made of short statements. But we might also have other styles: date description tables, transition diagrams, mathematical formulae, physical unit tables, figures, etc.

The order and more generally the structure of the entire requirements document is not so important at this stage. This will be taken care of in later development phases.

1.7 Definition of the term "formal method" as used in this book

Formal methods are techniques used to build blueprints adapted to our discipline. Such blueprints are called *formal models*.

As for real blueprints, we shall use some *pre-defined conventions* to write our models. There is no point in inventing a new language; we are going to use the language of *classical logic* and *set theory*. These conventions will allow us to easily communicate our models to others, as these languages are known by everyone having some mathematical backgrounds. The use of such a mathematical language will allow us to do some reasoning in the form of mathematical proofs, which we shall conduct as usual.

Note again that, as with blueprints, the basis is lacking; *our model will thus not in general be executable*.

The kind of systems we are interested in developing are *complex* and *discrete*. Let us develop these two ideas for a while.

1.7.1 Complex systems

Here is the kind of questions we might ask to begin with. What is common among, say, an electronic circuit, a file transfer protocol, an airline seat booking system, a sorting program, a PC operating system, a network routing program, a nuclear plant control system, a SmartCard electronic purse, a launch vehicle flight controller, etc.? Does there exist any kind of unified approach to in-depth study and formally prove the requirements, the specification, the design, and the implementation of *systems* that are so different in size and purpose?

We shall only give for the moment a very general answer. Almost all such systems are *complex* in that they are made of many parts interacting with a highly evolving and sometimes hostile environment. They also quite often involve several concurrent executing agents. They require a high degree of correctness. Finally, most of them are the result of a construction process which is spread over several years and which requires a large and talented team of engineers and technicians.

1.7.2 Discrete systems

Although their behavior is certainly ultimately continuous, the systems listed in the previous section operate most of the time in a *discrete fashion*. This means that their behavior can be faithfully *abstracted* by a succession of steady states intermixed with jumps that cause sudden state changes. Of course, the number of such possible changes is enormous, and they are occurring in a concurrent fashion at an unthinkable frequency. But this number and this high frequency do not change the very nature of the problem: such systems are intrinsically discrete. They fall under the generic name of *transition systems*. Having said this does not give us a method, but it gives us at least *a common point of departure*.

Some of the examples envisaged above are pure programs. In other words, their transitions are essentially concentrated in *one medium* only. The electronic circuit and the sorting program clearly fall into this category. Most of the other examples however are far more complex than just pure programs because they involve many different executing agents and also a heavy interaction with their environment. This means that the transitions are executed by different kinds of entities acting concurrently. But, again, this does not change the very discrete nature of the problem, it only complicates matters.

1.7.3 Test reasoning versus model (blueprint) reasoning

A very important activity, at least in terms of time and money, concerned with the construction of such complex discrete systems is certainly that of verifying that the final implementations are operating in a, so-called, *correct* fashion. Most of the time nowadays, this activity is realized during a very heavy testing phase, which we shall call a "laboratory execution".

The validation of a discrete system by means of such "laboratory executions" is certainly far more complicated, if not impossible in practice, to realize in the multiple medium case than in the single medium one. And we already know that program testing used as a validation process in almost all programming projects is far from being a complete process. Not so much, in fact, because of the impossibility of achieving a total cover of all executing cases. The incompleteness is rather, for us, the consequence of the very often *lack of oracles* which would give, *beforehand* and independently of the tested objects, the expected results of a future testing session.

It is nevertheless the case that today complex system constructions is still dependent on a very small design team of smart people, managing an army of implementers, eventually concluding the construction process with a long and heavy testing phase. And it is a well-known fact that the testing cost is at least twice that of the pure development effort. Is this a reasonable approach nowadays? Our opinion is that a technology using such an approach is still in its infancy. This was the case at the beginning of last century for some technologies, which have now reached a more mature status (e.g. avionics).

The technology we consider in this short presentation is concerned with the construction of *complex discrete systems*. As long as the main validation method used is testing, we consider that this technology will remain in an underdeveloped state. Testing does not involve any kind of sophisticated reasoning. It rather consists of *always postponing any serious thinking* during the specification and design phase. The construction of the system will always be re-adapted and re-shaped according to the testing results (trial and error). But, as we know, it is quite often too late.

In conclusion, testing always gives a shortsighted operational view of the system under construction: that of execution. In other technologies, say again avionics, it is certainly the case that people eventually do test what they are constructing, but the testing is just the *routine confirmation* of a sophisticated design process rather than a fundamental phase in it. As a matter of fact, most of the reasoning is done *before* the very construction of the final object. It is performed on various blueprints, in the broad sense of the term, by applying to them some well-defined practical theories.

The purpose of this book is to incorporate such a "blueprint" approach in the design of complex discrete systems. It also aims at presenting a theory that is able to facilitate the elaboration of some *proved reasoning* on such blueprints. Such reasoning will thus take place far before the final construction. In the present context, the "blueprints" are called *discrete models*. We shall now give a brief informal overview of the notion of discrete models.

1.8 Informal overview of discrete models

In this section, we give an informal description of discrete models. A discrete model is made of a state and a number of transitions. For the sake of understanding, we then give an operational interpretation of discrete models. We then present the kind of formal reasoning we want to express. Finally, we address the problem of mastering the complexity of models by means of three concepts: refinement, decomposition, and generic development.

1.8.1 State and transitions

Roughly speaking, a discrete model is made of a *state* represented by some constants and variables at a certain level of abstraction with regard to the real system under study. Such variables are very much the same as those used in applied sciences (physics, biology, operational research) for studying natural systems. In such sciences, people also build models. It helps them to infer some laws about the real world by means of reasoning about these models.

Besides the state, the model also contains a number of *transitions* that can occur under certain circumstances. Such transitions are called here "events." Each event is first made of a *guard*, which is a predicate built on the state constants and variables. It represents the *necessary* conditions for the event to occur. Each event is also made up of an *action*, which describes the way certain state variables are modified as a consequence of the event occurrence.

1.8.2 Operational interpretation

As can be seen, a discrete dynamical model thus indeed constitutes a kind of state transition machine. We can give such a machine an extremely simple *operational interpretation*. Notice that such an interpretation should not be considered as providing any operational semantics in our models (this will be given later by means of a proof system), it is just given here to support their *informal understanding*.

First of all, the execution of an event, which describes a certain observable transition of the state variables, is considered to take *no time*. Moreover, no two events can occur simultaneously. The execution is then the following:

- When no event guards are true, then the model execution stops; *it is said to have deadlocked*.
- When some event guards are true, then one of the corresponding events necessarily occurs and the state is modified accordingly; subsequently, the guards are checked again, and so on.

This behavior clearly shows some possible non-determinism (called external non-determinism) as several guards may be true simultaneously. We make *no assumption* concerning the specific event which is indeed executed among those whose guards are true. When only one guard is true at all times, the model is said to be deterministic.

Notice that the fact that a model eventually finishes is *not at all mandatory*. As a matter of fact, most of the systems we study never deadlock; they run for ever.

1.8.3 Formal reasoning

The very elementary transition machine we have described in the previous section, although primitive is nevertheless sufficiently elaborate to allow us to undertake some interesting formal reasoning. In the following, we envisage two kinds of discrete model properties.

The first kind of properties that we want to prove about our models, and hence ultimately about our real systems, are so-called *invariant properties*. An invariant is a condition on the state variables that must hold permanently. In order to achieve this, it is just required to *prove* that, under the invariant in question and under the guard of each event, the invariant still holds after being modified according to the action associated with that event.

We might also consider more complicated forms of reasoning, involving conditions which, in contrast to the invariants, do not hold permanently. The corresponding statements are called *modalities*. In our approach, we only consider a very special form of modality, called *reachability*. What we would like to prove is that an event whose guard is not necessarily true now will nevertheless certainly occur within a certain finite time.

1.8.4 Managing the complexity of closed models

Note that the models we are going to construct will not just describe the control part of our intended system, they will also contain a certain representation of the environment within which the system we build is supposed to behave. In fact, we shall quite often essentially construct *closed models,* which are able to exhibit the actions and reactions taking place between a certain environment and a corresponding, possibly distributed, controller.

In doing so, we shall be able to insert the model of the controller within an abstraction of its environment, which is formalized as yet another model. The state of such a closed system thus contains physical variables, describing the environment state, as well as logical variables, describing the controller state. And, in the same way, the transitions will fall into two groups: those concerned with the environment and those concerned with the controller. We shall also have to put into the model the way these two entities communicate.

But, as we mentioned earlier, the number of transitions in the real systems under study is certainly enormous. And, needless to say, the number of variables describing the state of such systems is also extremely large. How are we going to practically manage such complexity? The answer to this question lies in three concepts: *refinement* (Section 1.8.5), *decomposition* (Section 1.8.6), and *generic instantiation* (Section 1.8.7). It is important to notice here that these concepts are linked together. As a matter of fact, we refine a model to later decompose it, and, more importantly, we decompose it to further refine it more freely. And, finally, a generic model development can be later instantiated, thus saving the user from redoing similar proofs.

1.8.5 Refinement

Refinement allows us to build a model *gradually* by making it more and more precise, so that it is closer to the reality. In other words, we are not going to build a single model representing once and for all our reality; this is clearly impossible due to the size of the state and the number of its transitions. It would also make the resulting model very difficult to master. We are rather going to construct an ordered sequence of embedded models, where each of them is supposed to be a refinement of the one preceding it in a sequence. This means that a refined, more concrete, model will have more variables than its abstraction; such new variables are a visible consequence of a view of our system from closer range.

A useful analogy here is that of the scientist looking through a microscope. In doing so, the reality is the same, the microscope does not change it, but *our view of it is more accurate*: some previously invisible parts of the reality are now revealed by the microscope. An even more powerful microscope will reveal more parts, etc. A refined model is thus one which is spatially larger than its previous abstractions.

Analogously to this *spatial extension*, there is a corresponding *temporal extension*. This is because the new variables are now able to be modified by some transitions, which could not have been present in the previous abstractions, simply because the concerned variables did not exist in them. Practically, this is realized by means of *new events,* involving the new variables only. Such new events refine some implicit events doing nothing to the abstraction. Refinement will thus result in a discrete observation of our reality, which is now performed using a *finer time granularity*.

Refinement is also used in order to modify the state so that it can be implemented on a computer by means of some programming language. This second usage of refinement is called *data refinement*. It is used as a second technique, once all the important properties have been modeled.

1.8.6 Decomposition

Refinement does not solve completely the problem of the complexity. As a model is more and more refined, the number of its state variables and that of its transitions may augment in such a way that it becomes impossible to manage them as a whole. At this point, it is necessary to cut our single refined model into several almost independent pieces.

Decomposition is precisely the process by which a single model can be split into various component models in a systematic fashion. In doing so, we reduce the complexity of the whole by studying, and thus refining, each component model independently of the others. The very definition of such a decomposition implies that independent refinements of the component models could always be put together again to form a single model that is guaranteed to be a refinement of the original one. This decomposition process can be further applied to the components, and so on. Note that the component model could already exist and be developed, thus allowing to mix a top-down and a bottom-up approach.

1.8.7 Generic development

Any model development done by applying refinement and decomposition is parameterized by some carrier sets and constants defined by means of a number of properties.

Such a generic model may be instantiated within another development in the same way as a mathematical theory, e.g. group theory, can be instantiated in a more specific mathematical theory. This can be done providing that we have been able to prove that the axioms of the abstract theory are mere theorems in the second one.

The interest of this approach of generic instantiation is that it saves us redoing the proofs already done in the abstract development.

1.9 References

[1]   J. R. Abrial. *The B-book: Assigning Programs to Meanings.* Cambridge University Press, 1996

[2]   L. Lamport. *Specifying Systems: The TLA+ Language and Tools for Hardware and Software Engineers.* Addison-Wesley, 1999.

[3]   F. Badeau. Using B as a high level programming language in an industrial project: Roissy val. In *Proceedings of ZB'05*, 2005.

[4]   P. Behm. Meteor: A successful application of B in a large project. In *Proceedings of FM'99*, 1999.

[5]   K. M. Chandy and J. Misra. *Parallel Program Design: A Foundation.* Addison-Wesley, 1988.

[6]   R. J. Back and R. Kurki-Suonio. Distributed cooperation with action systems. *ACM Transactions on Programming Languages and Systems.* **10**(4): 513–554, 1988.

[7]   Rodin. *European Project Rodin.* http://rodin.cs.ncl.ac.uk.

[8]   J. F. Groote and J.C. Van de Pol. A bounded retransmission protocol for large data packets – a case study in computer checked algebraic verification. *Algebraic Methodology and Software Technology: 5th International Conference AMAST '96, Munich.* Lecture Notes in Computer Science 1101.

[9]   G. Le Lann. Distributed systems – towards a formal approach. In B. Gilchrist, editor, *Information Processing 77* North-Holland, 1977.

[10] N. Lynch. *Distributed Algorithms.* Morgan Kaufmann Publishers, 1996.

[11] W. H. J. Feijen and A. J. M. van Gasteren. *On a Method of Multi-programming.*, Springer. 1999.

[12] L. Moreau. Distributed Directory Service and Message Routers for Mobile Agent. *Science of Computer Programming* **39**(2–3): 249–272, 2001.

[13] IEEE Standard for a High Performance Serial Bus. *Std 1394–1995*, August 1995.

[14] H. R. Simpson. Four-slot fully asynchronous communication mechanism. *Computer and Digital Techniques*. IEE Proceedings. **137** (1) (Jan 1990).

2

Controlling cars on a bridge

2.1 Introduction

The intent of this chapter is to introduce a complete example of a small system development. During this development, we will become aware of the systematic approach we are using: it consists in developing a series of more and more accurate models of the system we want to construct. This technique is called *refinement*. The reason for building consecutive models is that a unique one would be far too complicated to reason about. Note that each model does not represent the programming of our system using a high-level programming language, it rather formalizes what an *external observer* of this system could perceive of it.

Each model will be analyzed and proved, thus enabling us to establish that it is *correct* relative to a number of criteria. As a result, when the last model is finished, we will be able to say that this model is *correct by construction*. Moreover, this model will be so close to a final implementation that it will be very easy to transform it into a genuine program.

The correctness criteria alluded to above will be made completely clear and systematic by giving a number of *proof obligation rules* which will be applied on our models. After applying such rules, we shall have to prove formally a number of statements. To this end, we shall also give a reminder of the classical *rules of inference of the sequent calculus*. Such rules concern propositional logic, equality, and basic arithmetic. The idea here is to give the reader the possibility to manually prove the statements as given by the proof obligation rules. Clearly, such proofs could easily be discharged by a theorem prover, but we feel that it is important at this stage for the reader to tackle the exercise before using an automatic theorem prover. Notice that we do not claim that a theorem prover would perform these proofs the way it is proposed here; quite often, a tool does not work like a human being does.

This chapter is organized as follows. Section 2.2 contains the requirement document of the system we would like to develop. For this, we shall use the principles explained in the previous chapter. Section 2.3 explains our refinement strategy; it essentially assigns the various requirements to the various development steps. The four remaining sections are devoted to the development of the initial models and those of the three subsequent refinements.

2.2 Requirements document

The system we are going to build is a piece of software, called the *controller*, connected to some equipment, called the *environment*. There are thus two kinds of requirements: those concerned with the functionalities of the controller labeled FUN, and those concerned with the environment labeled ENV.

Note that the model we are going to build is a *closed model*, comprising the controller *as well as its environment*. The reason is that we want to define with great care the assumptions we are making concerning the environment. In other words, the controller we shall build eventually will be *correct* as long as these assumptions are fulfilled by the environment: outside these assumptions, the controller is not guaranteed to perform correctly. We shall come back to this in Section 2.7.

Let us now turn our attention to the requirements of this system. The main function of this system is to control cars on a narrow bridge. This bridge is supposed to link the mainland to a small island:

The system is controlling cars on a bridge connecting the mainland to an island	FUN-1

This system is equipped with two traffic lights:

The system is equipped with two traffic lights with two colors: green and red	ENV-1

One of the traffic lights is situated on the mainland and the other one on the island. Both are close to the bridge:

The traffic lights control the entrance to the bridge at both ends of it	ENV-2

Drivers are supposed to obey the traffic lights by not passing when a traffic light is red:

Cars are not supposed to pass on a red traffic light, only on a green one	ENV-3

There are also some car sensors situated at both ends of the bridge:

The system is equipped with four sensors with two states: on or off	ENV-4

These sensors are supposed to detect the presence of cars intending to enter or leave the bridge. There are four such sensors. Two of them are situated on the bridge and the other two are situated on the mainland and on the island respectively:

The sensors are used to detect the presence of a car entering or leaving the bridge: "on" means that a car is willing to enter the bridge or to leave it	ENV-5

The pieces of equipment which have been described are illustrated Fig. 2.1. The system has two main additional constraints: the number of cars on the bridge and island is limited:

The number of cars on bridge and island is limited	FUN-2

and the bridge is one-way:

The bridge is one-way or the other, not both at the same time	FUN-3

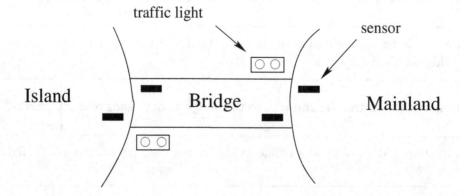

Fig. 2.1. The bridge control equipment

2.3 Refinement strategy

Before engaging in the development of such a system, it is profitable to clearly identify what our design strategy will be. This is done by listing the order in which we are going to take account of the various requirements we proposed in the requirement document of the previous section. Here is our strategy:

- We start with a very simple model allowing us to take account of requirement FUN-2 concerned with the maximum number of cars on the island and the bridge (Section 2.4)
- Then the bridge is introduced into the picture, and we thus take account of requirement FUN-3 telling us that the bridge is one way or the other (Section 2.5).
- In the next refinement, we introduce the traffic lights. This corresponds to requirements ENV-1, ENV-2, and ENV-3 (Section 2.6).
- In the last refinement, we introduce the various sensors corresponding to requirements ENV-4 and ENV-5 (Section 2.7). In this refinement, we shall also introduce eventually the *architecture* of our closed model made up of the controller, the environment, and the communication channels between the two.

You may have noticed that we have not mentioned requirement FUN-1 telling us what the main function of this system is. This is simply because it is fairly general. It is in fact taken care of at each development step.

2.4 Initial model: limiting the number of cars

2.4.1 Introduction

The first model we are going to construct is very simple. We do not consider at all the various pieces of equipment, namely the traffic lights and sensors; they will be introduced in subsequent refinements. Likewise, we do not even consider the bridge, only a *compound* made of the bridge and the island together.

This is an approach taken frequently. We start by building a model that is *far more abstract* than the final system we want to construct. The idea is to take account initially of only a very few constraints. This is because we want to be able to reason about this system in a simple way, considering in turn each requirement.

As a useful analogy, we will observe the situation from high in the sky. Although we cannot see the bridge, we suppose however that we can "see" the cars on the island–bridge compound and observe the two transitions, ML_out and ML_in, corresponding to cars entering and leaving the island–bridge compound. All this is illustrated in Fig. 2.2.

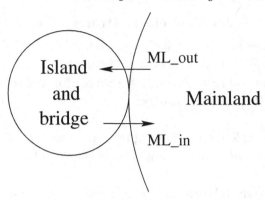

Fig. 2.2. The mainland and the island–bridge

Our first task is to formalize the *state* of this simple version of our system (Section 2.4.2). We shall then formalize the two *events* we can observe (Section 2.4.3).

2.4.2 *Formalizing the state*

The state of our model is made up of two parts: the *static part* and the *dynamic part*. The static part contains the definition and axioms associated with some *constants*, whereas the dynamic part contains the *variables* which are modified as the system evolves. The static part is also called the *context* of our model.

The context of our first model is very simple. It contains a single constant d, which is a natural number denoting the maximum number of cars allowed to be on the island–bridge compound at the same time. The constant d has a simple axiom: it is a natural number. As can be seen below, we have given this axiom the name **axm0_1**:

constant: d	**axm0_1:** $d \in \mathbb{N}$

The dynamic part is made up of a single variable n, which denotes the actual number of cars in the island–bridge compound at a given moment. This is simply written as shown in the following boxes:

variable: n	**inv0_1:** $n \in \mathbb{N}$ **inv0_2:** $n \le d$

The variable n is defined by means of two conditions which are called the *invariants*. They are named **inv0_1** and **inv0_2**. The reason for calling them invariants is straightforward: despite the changes over time in the value of n, these conditions always remain true. Invariant **inv0_1** says that n is a natural number. And the *first basic requirement* of our system, namely FUN-2, is taken into account at this stage by stating in **inv0_2** that the number n of cars in the compound is always smaller than or equal to the maximum number d.

The labels **axm0_1**, **inv0_1**, and **inv0_2** we have used above are chosen in a systematic fashion. The prefix **axm** stands for the *axiom* of the constant d, whereas the prefix **inv** stands for the *invariant* of the variable n. The **0**, as in **axm0_1** or **inv0_2**, stands for the fact that these conditions are introduced in the initial model. Subsequent models will be the first refinement, the second refinement, and so on. They will be numbered **1**, **2**, etc. Finally, the second number, as **2** in **inv0_2**, is a simple serial number. In what follows, we shall use such a systematic labeling scheme for naming our state conditions. Sometimes, but rarely, we shall change the prefixes **axm** and **inv** for others. We found this naming scheme convenient, but, of course, any other naming scheme can be used provided it is systematic.

2.4.3 Formalizing the events

At this stage, we can observe two transitions, which we shall henceforth call *events*. They correspond to cars entering the island–bridge compound or leaving it. In Fig. 2.3 there is an illustration of the situation just before and just after an occurrence of the first event, ML_out (the name ML_out stands for "going out of mainland"). As can be seen, the number of cars in the compound is incremented as a result of this event.

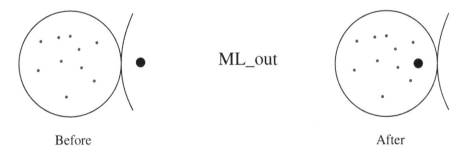

Before   After

Fig. 2.3. Event ML_out

Likewise, Fig. 2.4 shows the situation just before and just after an occurrence of the second event, ML_in (the name ML_in stands for "getting on to the mainland"). As can be seen, the number of cars in the compound is decremented as a result of this event.

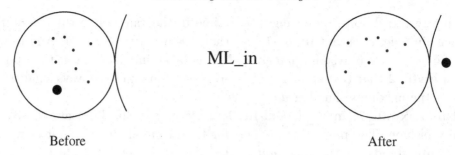

Before   After

Fig. 2.4. Event ML_in

In a *first approximation*, we define the events of the initial model in a simple way as follows:

ML_out	ML_in
$n := n + 1$	$n := n - 1$

An event has a *name*: here ML_out and ML_in. It contains an *action*: here $n := n+1$ and $n := n - 1$. These statements can be read as follows: "*n* becomes equal to $n + 1$" and "*n* becomes equal to $n - 1$". Such statements are called *actions*. It is important to notice that, in writing these actions, *we are not programming*. We are just formally representing what can be observed in discrete evolutions of our system. We are giving a formal representation to our observation.

You might have noticed that we have said above that the two events are proposed "in a first approximation." There are two reasons for writing this:

(i) Our model observation is done in an *incremental fashion*. In other words, we are not defining immediately the final state and events of our system. Remember, *we are not programming*, we are defining models of the system we want to construct, and these models cannot be defined at once in full generality; this requires some gradual introduction of state components and transitions.

(ii) We propose here a state and various events, but we are not yet sure that these elements are consistent. This will have to be proved formally, and in doing this we might discover that what we have proposed is not correct.

2.4.4 Before–after predicates

In this section, we present the concept of *before–after predicates*. This concept will be helpful to define the proof obligation rules in subsequent sections.

To each event defined as an action there corresponds a so-called before–after predicate. The before–after predicate associated with an action denotes the relationship that exists between the value of the concerned variable *just before* and *just after* the transition. This is indicated as shown below:

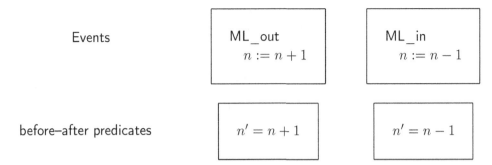

As can be seen, the before–after predicate is easily obtained from the action: the variable on the left-hand side of the action symbol ":=" is primed, the action symbol ":=" is changed to an equality symbol "=", and, finally, the expression on the right-hand side of the action symbol is taken as is.

In a before–after predicate, a primed variable such as n' denotes, *by convention*, the value of the variable n *just after* the transition has occurred, whereas n represents its value *just before*. For instance, just after an occurrence of the event ML_out, the value of the variable n is equal to the value it had just before plus one, that is $n' = n + 1$.

The before–after predicates we present here have got very simple shapes, where the primed value is equal to some expression depending on the non-primed value. Of course, more complicated shapes can be encountered, but in this example, which is *deterministic*, we shall not encounter more complicated cases.

2.4.5 Proving invariant preservation

When writing the actions corresponding to the events ML_in and ML_out, we did not necessarily take into account invariants **inv0_1** and **inv0_2**, because we only concentrated on the way the variable n was modified. As a consequence, there is no reason *a priori* for these invariants to be preserved by these events. In fact, *it has to be proved in a rigorous fashion*. The purpose of this section is thus to define precisely what we have to prove in order to ensure that the invariants are indeed invariant!

The statement to be proved is generated in a systematic fashion by means of a rule, called INV, which is defined once and for all. Such a rule is called a *proof obligation* rule or a *verification condition* rule.

Generally speaking, suppose that our constants are collectively called c. And let $A(c)$ denote the axioms associated with these constants c. More precisely, $A(c)$ stands for the list: $A_1(c), A_2(c), \ldots$ of axioms associated with the constants. In our example model, $A(c)$ is reduced to a list consisting of the single element **axm0_1**. Likewise, let v denote the variables and let $I(c, v)$ denote the invariants of these variables. As for the axioms of the constants, $I(c, v)$ stands for the list $I_1(c, v), I_2(c, v), \ldots$ of invariants. In our example, $I(c, v)$ is reduced to a list consisting of the two elements **inv0_1** and **inv0_2**. Finally, let $v' = E(c, v)$ be the before–after predicate associated with an event. The invariant preservation statement which we have to prove for this event and for a specific invariant $I_i(c, v)$, taken from the set of invariants $I(c, v)$, is then the following:

$$\boxed{A(c), \ I(c, v) \ \vdash \ I_i(c, E(c, v)) \quad \Big| \quad \text{INV}}$$

This statement, which is called a *sequent* (wait till the next section for a precise definition of sequents), can be read as follows: "hypotheses $A(c)$ and hypotheses $I(c, v)$ *entail* predicate $I_i(c, E(c, v))$". This is what we have to prove for each event and for each invariant $I_i(c, v)$. It is easy to understand. Just before the transition, we can assume clearly that each axiom of the set $A(c)$ holds. We can also assume that each invariant of the set $I(c, v)$ holds. As a consequence, we can assume $A(c)$ and $I(c, v)$. Now, just after the transition, where the value of v has been changed to $E(c, v)$, then the invariant statement $I_i(c, v)$ becomes $I_i(c, E(c, v))$, and it must hold too since it is claimed to be an *invariant*.

To simplify writing and ease reading, we shall write sequents vertically when there are several hypotheses. In the case of our rule INV, this yields the following:

$$\boxed{\begin{array}{l} A(c) \\ I(c, v) \\ \vdash \\ \quad I_i(c, E(c, v)) \end{array} \quad \Bigg| \quad \text{INV}}$$

As this formulation of proof obligation rule INV might seem a bit difficult to remember, let us rewrite it in another way, which is less formal:

$$\boxed{\begin{array}{l} \text{Axioms} \\ \text{Invariants} \\ \vdash \\ \quad \text{Modified invariant} \end{array} \quad \Bigg| \quad \text{INV}}$$

The proof obligation rule INV states *what we have to formally prove* in order to be certain that the various events maintain the invariants. But we have not yet defined what we mean by "formally prove": this will be explained in Sections 2.4.8 to 2.4.11. We shall also explain how we can construct formal proofs in a systematic fashion. Finally, note that such sequents which correspond to applying rule INV are generated easily by a tool, which is called a *proof obligation generator*.

2.4.6 Sequent

In the previous section, we introduced the concept of sequent in order to express our proof obligation rule. In this section, we give more information about such a construct.†
As explained above, a statement of the following form is called a *sequent*:

$$\mathbf{H} \vdash \mathbf{G}$$

The symbol ⊢ is named the *turnstile*. The part situated on the left-hand side of the turnstile, here **H**, denotes a finite set of predicates called the *hypotheses* (or *assumptions*). Notice that the set **H** can be empty. The part situated on the right-hand side of the turnstile, here **G**, denotes a predicate called the *goal* (or *conclusion*).

The intuitive meaning of such a statement is that the goal **G** is provable *under* the set of assumptions **H**. In other words, the turnstile can be read as the verb "entail," or "yield"; the assumptions **H** yield the conclusion **G**.

In what follows, we shall always generate such sequents (and try to prove them) in order to analyze our models. We shall also give rules to prove sequents in a formal way.

2.4.7 Applying the invariant preservation rule

Coming back to our example, we are now in a position to clearly state what we have to prove; this is what we are going to do in this section. The proof obligation rule INV given in Section 2.4.5 yields several sequents to prove. We have one application of this proof obligation rule per event and per invariant: in our case, we have two events, namely ML_out and ML_in, and we have two invariants, namely **inv0_1** and **inv0_2**. This makes four sequents to prove: two sequents for each of the two events.

In order to remember easily what proof obligations we are speaking about, we are going to give *compound names* to them. Such a proof obligation name first mentions the event we are concerned with, then the invariant, and we finally include the label INV in order to remember that it is an invariant preservation proof obligation (as there will be some other kinds of proof obligations‡). In our case, the four proof obligations are named as follows:

---

† Sequents and the sequent calculus are reviewed in a more formal way in Section 1 of Chapter 9.
‡ All proof obligations are reviewed in Section 2 of Chapter 5.

ML_out / **inv0_1** / INV   ML_out / **inv0_2** / INV
ML_in / **inv0_1** / INV   ML_in / **inv0_2** / INV

Let us now apply proof obligation rule INV to the two events and the two invariants. Here is what we have to prove concerning event ML_out and invariant **inv_01**:

Axiom **axm0_1**
Invariant **inv0_1**
Invariant **inv0_2**
⊢
Modified invariant **inv0_1**

$$d \in \mathbb{N}$$
$$n \in \mathbb{N}$$
$$n \le d$$
⊢
$$n + 1 \in \mathbb{N}$$

ML_out / **inv0_1** / INV

Remember that event ML_out has the before–after predicate $n' = n + 1$. This is why predicate $n \in \mathbb{N}$ corresponding to invariant **inv0_1** in the assumptions has been replaced by predicate $n + 1 \in \mathbb{N}$ in the goal. Here is what we have to prove concerning event ML_out and invariant **inv0_2**:

Axiom **axm0_1**
Invariant **inv0_1**
Invariant **inv0_2**
⊢
Modified invariant **inv0_2**

$$d \in \mathbb{N}$$
$$n \in \mathbb{N}$$
$$n \le d$$
⊢
$$n + 1 \le d$$

ML_out / **inv0_2** / INV

Here is what we have to prove concerning event ML_in and invariant **inv0_1** (remember that the before–after predicate of event ML_in is $n' = n - 1$):

Axiom **axm0_1**
Invariant **inv0_1**
Invariant **inv0_2**
⊢
Modified invariant **inv0_1**

$$d \in \mathbb{N}$$
$$n \in \mathbb{N}$$
$$n \le d$$
⊢
$$n - 1 \in \mathbb{N}$$

ML_in / **inv0_1** / INV

Here is what we have to prove concerning event ML_in and invariant **inv0_2**:

Axiom **axm0_1**
Invariant **inv0_1**
Invariant **inv0_2**
⊢
Modified invariant **inv0_2**

$d \in \mathbb{N}$
$n \in \mathbb{N}$
$n \leq d$
⊢
$n - 1 \leq d$

ML_in / **inv0_2** / INV

2.4.8 Proving the proof obligations

We know exactly which sequents we have to prove. Our next task is now to prove them: this is the purpose of the present section. The formal proofs of the previous sequents are done by applying some *transformations* on sequents, yielding one or several other sequents to prove, until we reach sequents that are considered proved without any further justification. The transformation of one sequent into new ones corresponds to the idea that proofs of the latter are sufficient to prove the former. For example, our first sequent, namely:

$$
\begin{array}{l}
d \in \mathbb{N} \\
n \in \mathbb{N} \\
n \leq d \\
\vdash \\
n + 1 \in \mathbb{N}
\end{array}
\tag{2.1}
$$

can be simplified by removing some *irrelevant hypotheses* (clearly hypotheses $d \in \mathbb{N}$ and $n \leq d$ are useless for proving our goal $n + 1 \in \mathbb{N}$), yielding the following simpler sequent:

$$
n \in \mathbb{N} \vdash n + 1 \in \mathbb{N}
\tag{2.2}
$$

What we have admitted here as a step in the proof is the fact that a proof of sequent (2.2) is *sufficient* to prove sequent (2.1). In other words, if we succeed now in proving sequent (2.2), then we have also a proof of sequent (2.1). The proof of the sequent (2.2) is reduced to nothing. In other words, it is accepted as being proved without further justification. It says that, under the assumption that n is a natural number, then $n + 1$ is also a natural number.

2.4.9 Rules of inference

In the previous section, we applied informally some rules either to transform a sequent into another one or to accept a sequent without further justification. Such rules can be rigorously formalized, they are called *rules of inference*. This is what we do now. The first rule of inference we have used can be stated as follows:

$$
\frac{\mathbf{H1} \vdash \mathbf{G}}{\mathbf{H1, H2} \vdash \mathbf{G}} \quad \text{MON}
$$

Here is the structure of such a rule. On top of the horizontal line, we have a set of sequents (here just one). These sequents are called the *antecedents* of the rule. Below the horizontal line, we always have a single sequent called the *consequent* of the rule. On the right of the rule, we have a name, here MON; this is the name of the inference rule. In this case, this name stands for *monotonicity* of hypotheses.

The rule is to be read as follows: in order to prove the consequent, it is sufficient to have proofs of each sequent in the antecedents. In the present case, it says that in order to have a proof of goal **G** under the two sets of assumptions **H1** and **H2**, it is sufficient to have a proof of **G** under **H1** only. We have indeed obtained the effect we wanted: the removing of possibly irrelevant hypotheses **H2**.

Note that in applying this rule we do not require that the subset of assumptions **H2** is entirely situated after the subset **H1** as is strictly indicated in the rule. In fact, the subset **H2** is to be understood as *any* subset of the hypotheses. For example, in applying this rule to our proof obligation (2.1) in the previous section, we removed the assumption $d \in \mathbb{N}$ situated before assumption $n \in \mathbb{N}$ and after assumption $n \leq d$.

The second rule of inference can be stated as follows:

$$
\frac{}{\mathbf{H}, \mathbf{n} \in \mathbb{N} \vdash \mathbf{n+1} \in \mathbb{N}} \quad \text{P2}
$$

Here we have a rule of inference with no antecedent. For this reason, it is called an *axiom*. This is the second Peano Axiom for natural numbers; hence the name P2. It says that, in order to have a proof of the consequent, it is not necessary to prove anything. Under the hypothesis that **n** is a natural number, **n**+1 is also a natural number. Notice that the presence of the additional hypotheses **H** is optional here. This is so because it is always possible to remove the additional hypotheses using rule MON. Thus the rule could have been stated more simply as follows (this is the convention we shall follow from now on):

$$
\overline{\rule{4cm}{0pt}} \quad \text{P2}
$$
$$
\mathbf{n} \in \mathbb{N} \;\vdash\; \mathbf{n}+1 \in \mathbb{N}
$$

A similar but more constraining rule will be used in what follows. It concerns decrementing a natural number:

$$
\overline{\rule{4cm}{0pt}} \quad \text{P2}'
$$
$$
0 < \mathbf{n} \;\vdash\; \mathbf{n}-1 \in \mathbb{N}
$$

This rule says that $\mathbf{n}-1$ is a natural number under the assumption that $\mathbf{n}$ is *positive*. We shall also use two other rules of inference called INC and DEC:

$$
\overline{\rule{4cm}{0pt}} \quad \text{INC}
$$
$$
\mathbf{n} < \mathbf{m} \;\vdash\; \mathbf{n}+1 \le \mathbf{m}
$$

Rule of inference INC says that $\mathbf{n}+1$ is smaller than or equal to $\mathbf{m}$ under the assumption that $\mathbf{n}$ is strictly smaller than $\mathbf{m}$:

$$
\overline{\rule{4cm}{0pt}} \quad \text{DEC}
$$
$$
\mathbf{n} \le \mathbf{m} \;\vdash\; \mathbf{n}-1 < \mathbf{m}
$$

Rule of inference DEC says that $\mathbf{n}-1$ is smaller than $\mathbf{m}$ under the assumption that $\mathbf{n}$ is already smaller than or equal to $\mathbf{m}$. We shall clearly need more rules of inference dealing with elementary logic and also with natural numbers. But, for the moment, we only need those we have just presented in this section.

Notice that it is well known that inference rules P2', INC, and DEC are *derived* inference rules; it simply means that such inference rules can be deduced from more basic inference rules such as P2 above and others. But, in this presentation, we are not so much interested in this, we want just to construct a *library* of useful inference rules.

2.4.10 Meta-variables

You might have noticed that the various identifiers, namely **H1**,**H2**, **G**, **n**, **m** we have used in the rules of inferences proposed in the previous section, were emphasized; we have not used the standard mathematical font for them, namely $H1$, $H2$, G, n, m. This is because such variables are not part of the mathematical language we are using. They are called *meta-variables*.

More precisely, each proposed rule of inference stands for a schema of rules corresponding to all the possible *matches* we could ever perform. For example rule P2:

$$\frac{\phantom{\mathbf{n} \in \mathbb{N} \vdash \mathbf{n}+1 \in \mathbb{N}}}{\mathbf{n} \in \mathbb{N} \;\vdash\; \mathbf{n}+1 \in \mathbb{N}} \quad \text{P2}$$

describes the second Peano axiom in very general terms; it can be applied to the sequent:

$$a+b \in \mathbb{N} \;\vdash\; a+b+1 \in \mathbb{N}$$

by *matching* meta-variable **n** to the mathematical language expression $a + b$.

2.4.11 Proofs

Equipped with a number of rules of inference, we are now ready to perform some elementary formal proofs. This is the purpose of this section. A proof is just a sequence of sequents connected by the name of the rule of inference, which allows us to go from one sequent to the next in the sequence. The sequence of sequents ends with the name of a rule of inference with no antecedent. We shall see in Section 2.4.24 that proofs have a more general shape, but one is sufficient for the moment.

For example, the proof of our first proof obligation ML_out / **inv0_1** / INV is the following. It corresponds exactly to what has been said informally in Section 2.4.8, namely removing some useless hypotheses and then accepting the second sequent without any further proof:

$$
\boxed{\begin{array}{l} d \in \mathbb{N} \\ n \in \mathbb{N} \\ n \leq d \\ \vdash \\ n+1 \in \mathbb{N} \end{array}} \quad \text{MON} \quad
\boxed{\begin{array}{l} n \in \mathbb{N} \\ \vdash \\ n+1 \in \mathbb{N} \end{array}} \quad \text{P2}
$$

The next proof, corresponding to proof obligation ML_out / **inv0_2** / INV, fails because we cannot apply rule INC on the final sequent as we do not have an assumption telling us that $n < d$ holds as required by rule INC; we only have the weaker assumption $n \leq d$. For this reason, we have put a "?" at the end of the sequence of sequents:

$$
\boxed{\begin{array}{l} d \in \mathbb{N} \\ n \in \mathbb{N} \\ n \leq d \\ \vdash \\ n + 1 \leq d \end{array}} \quad \text{MON} \quad \boxed{\begin{array}{l} n \leq d \\ \vdash \\ n + 1 \leq d \end{array}} \quad ?
$$

Likewise, the proof of ML_in / **inv0_1** / INV fails. Here we cannot apply inference rule P2' on the last sequent because we do not have the required assumption $0 < n$, only the weaker one $n \in \mathbb{N}$:

$$
\boxed{\begin{array}{l} d \in \mathbb{N} \\ n \in \mathbb{N} \\ n \leq d \\ \vdash \\ n - 1 \in \mathbb{N} \end{array}} \quad \text{MON} \quad \boxed{\begin{array}{l} n \in \mathbb{N} \\ \vdash \\ n - 1 \in \mathbb{N} \end{array}} \quad ?
$$

The last proof, that of ML_in / **inv0_2** / INV, succeeds:

$$
\boxed{\begin{array}{l} d \in \mathbb{N} \\ n \in \mathbb{N} \\ n \leq d \\ \vdash \\ n - 1 \leq d \end{array}} \quad \text{MON} \quad \boxed{\begin{array}{l} n \leq d \\ \vdash \\ n - 1 < d \ \vee \ n - 1 = d \end{array}} \quad \text{OR\_R1} \quad \boxed{\begin{array}{l} n \leq d \\ \vdash \\ n - 1 < d \end{array}} \quad \text{DEC}
$$

Notice that in the second step we felt free to replace $n - 1 \leq d$, that is $n - 1$ is smaller than *or* equal to d, by the equivalent formal statement $n - 1 < d \ \vee \ n - 1 = d$, where $\vee$ is the disjunctive operator "or." Then, we apply inference rule OR_R1 (see next section) in order to obtain the goal $n - 1 < d$, which is easily proved using rule DEC.

2.4.12 More rules of inference

At the end of previous section, we applied our first logical rule of inference named OR_R1.† Later on, there will be further logical rules of inference, but this is the first one we need. We present it together with the companion rule OR_R2:

$$
\frac{H \vdash P}{H \vdash P \lor Q} \quad \text{OR\_R1}
\qquad\qquad
\frac{H \vdash Q}{H \vdash P \lor Q} \quad \text{OR\_R2}
$$

Both rules state obvious facts about proving a disjunctive goal $P \lor Q$ involving two predicates P and Q. To prove their disjunction, it is sufficient to prove one of them: P in the case of rule OR_R1 and Q in the case of rule OR_R2.

Notice that in the _R1 or _R2 suffixes of these rule names, the R stands for "right": it means that this rule transforms a goal, that is a statement situated on the *right*-hand side of the turnstile. Other logical inference rules presented below will be named using the suffix L when the transformed predicate is an hypothesis, that is a predicate situated on the *left*-hand side of the turnstile.

2.4.13 Improving the two events: introducing guards

Coming back to our example, we have now to make some modifications to our model due to the fact that some proofs have failed. We figure out that proving has the same effect as debugging. In other words, *a failed proof reveals a bug*.

In order to correct the deficiencies we have discovered while carrying out the proof, we have to add *guards* to our events. Taken together, these guards denote the *necessary conditions* for an event to be enabled. More precisely, when an event is enabled, it means that the transition corresponding to the event can take place. On the contrary, when an event is not enabled (that is when at least one of its guards does not hold), it means that the corresponding transition cannot occur.

For event ML_out to be enabled, we shall require that n be strictly smaller than d, that is $n < d$. And for event ML_in to be enabled, we shall require that n be strictly positive, that is $0 < n$. Notice that such guarding conditions are exactly the conditions that were missing in the sequents we had to prove in the previous section; we have been guided by the failure of the proofs. Adding guards to events is done

---

† All rules of inference are reviewed in Chapter 9.

as follows:

As can be seen, we have a simple piece of syntax here: the guard is situated between the keywords **when** and **then**, whereas the action is situated between the keywords **then** and **end**. Note that we may have several guards in an event, although it is not the case here.

2.4.14 Improving the invariant preservation rule

When dealing with a guarded event with the set of guards denoted by $G(c, v)$ and before–after predicate of the form $v' = E(c, v)$ (where c denotes the constants and v the variables as introduced in Section 2.4.5), our previous proof obligation rule INV has to be modified by adding the set of guards $G(c, v)$ to the hypotheses of the sequent. This yields the following more general proof obligation for events that have guards:

2.4.15 Reproving invariant preservation

The statements to prove by applying the amended proof obligation rule INV are modified accordingly and are now easily provable. Here is the sequent to prove to ensure that event ML_out preserves invariant **inv0_2**:

Axiom **axm0_1**
Invariant **inv0_1**
Invariant **inv0_2**
Guard of ML_out
$\vdash$
  Modified invariant **inv0_2**

$d \in \mathbb{N}$
$n \in \mathbb{N}$
$n \leq d$
$n < d$
$\vdash$
$n + 1 \leq d$

ML_out / **inv0_2** / INV

Here is what we have to prove concerning event ML_in and invariant **inv0_1**:

Axiom **axm0_1**
Invariant **inv0_1**
Invariant **inv0_2**
Guard of ML_in
$\vdash$
  Modified invariant **inv0_1**

$d \in \mathbb{N}$
$n \in \mathbb{N}$
$n \leq d$
$0 < n$
$\vdash$
$n - 1 \in \mathbb{N}$

ML_in / **inv0_1** / INV.

The two missing proofs can now be performed easily:

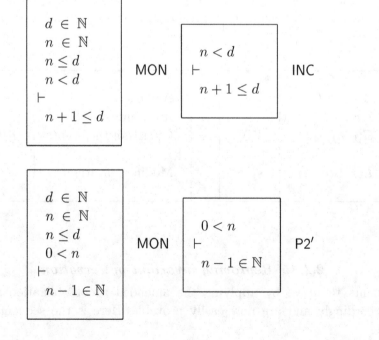

Notice that the proofs we have already done for proof obligations ML_out / **inv0_1** / INV and ML_in / **inv0_2** / INV in Section 2.4.11 need not to be redone. This is because we are just adding a new hypothesis to these proof obligations: remember inference rule MON (Section 2.4.9), which says that for proving a goal under certain hypotheses **H**, it is sufficient to perform the proof of the same goal under *less* hypotheses. So, conversely adding an hypothesis to a proof which is already done does not invalidate that proof.

2.4.16 Initialization

In the previous sections, we defined the two events ML_in and ML_out and the invariants of the model, namely **inv0_1** and **inv0_2**. We also proved that these invariants were preserved by the transition defined by the events. But we have not defined what happens at the beginning. For this, it is necessary to define a special initial event that is systematically named init. In our case, this event is the following:

$$\boxed{\begin{array}{l} \text{init} \\ \quad n := 0 \end{array}}$$

As can be seen, the initializing event corresponds to the observation that initially there are no cars in the compound. Notice that this event has no guard; this must always be the case with the initializing event init. In other words, initialization must always be possible!

Also note that the expression situated on the right-hand sign of := in the action of the event init cannot refer to any variable of the model. This is because we are *initializing*. In our case, the variable n cannot be assigned an expression depending on n. The corresponding before–after predicate of init is thus always rather an "after predicate" only. In our case, it is the following (as can be seen, this predicate does not mention n, only n'):

$$\boxed{n' = 0}$$

2.4.17 Invariant establishment rule for the initializing event init

Event init cannot preserve the invariants because before init the system state "does not exist." Event init must just *establish the invariant* for the first time. In this way, other events, which by definition are only observable after initialization has taken place, can be enabled in a situation where the invariants hold.

We have thus to define a proof obligation rule for this invariant establishment. It is almost identical to the proof obligation rule INV we have already presented in Section 2.4.5. The difference is that in the proof obligation rule presented now the invariants are not mentioned in the hypotheses of the sequent. More precisely, given a system with constants c, with a set of axioms $A(c)$, with variables v and an invariant $I_i(c, v)$, and an initializing event with after predicate $v' = K(c)$, then the proof obligation rule INV for invariant establishment is the following:

$$
\boxed{\begin{array}{c} A(c) \\ \vdash \\ I_i(c, K(c)) \end{array}} \quad \text{INV}
\qquad
\boxed{\begin{array}{c} \text{Axioms} \\ \vdash \\ \text{Modified invariant} \end{array}} \quad \text{INV}
$$

2.4.18 Applying the invariant establishment rule

The application of the previous rule to our initializing event init yields the following to prove:

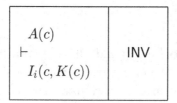

Axiom **axm0_1**
$\vdash$
Modified invariant **inv0_1**

$$\boxed{d \in \mathbb{N} \ \vdash \ 0 \in \mathbb{N}}$$ **inv0_1** / INV

Axiom **axm0_1**
$\vdash$
Modified invariant **inv0_2**

$$\boxed{d \in \mathbb{N} \ \vdash \ 0 \le d}$$ **inv0_2** / INV

2.4.19 Proving the initialization proof obligations: more inference rules

The proof obligations of the previous section cannot be formally proved without other inference rules. The first one is named P1: it is the first Peano axiom which says that 0 is a natural number. Notice that the sequent that defines the consequent of this inference rule has no assumption:

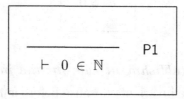

$$\boxed{\dfrac{\phantom{\vdash 0 \in \mathbb{N}}}{\vdash \ 0 \in \mathbb{N}}} \quad \text{P1}$$

The second rule of inference we need is a consequence of the third Peano axiom, which says that 0 is not the successor of any natural number. We can prove that this can be rephrased as follows: 0 is the smallest natural number. In other words, under the assumption that **n** is a natural number, then 0 is smaller than or equal to **n**. For convenience, we shall name it P3:

$$
\frac{}{\mathbf{n} \in \mathbb{N} \ \vdash \ 0 \le \mathbf{n}} \quad \text{P3}
$$

We leave it as an exercise to the reader to now prove the two previous initialization proof obligations.

2.4.20 Deadlock freedom

Since our two main events ML_in and ML_out are now guarded, it means that our model might *deadlock* when both guards are false: none of the events would be enabled; the system would be blocked. Sometimes this is what we want, but certainly not here, where this is to be avoided. As a matter of fact, we discover that this non-blocking property was *missing* in our requirement document of Section 2.2. So we edit this document by adding this new requirement:

Once started, the system should work for ever	FUN-4

2.4.21 Deadlock freedom rule

Given a model with constants c, set of axioms $A(c)$, variables v, and set of invariants $I(c, v)$, we have thus to prove a proof obligation rule called DLF (for deadlock freedom) stating that one of the guards $G_1(c, v)$, ..., $G_m(c, v)$ of the various events is always true. In other words, in our case, cars can always either enter the compound or leave it. This is to be proved under the set of axioms $A(c)$ of the constants c and under the set of invariants $I(c, v)$. The proof obligation rule can be stated as follows in general terms:

$$
\begin{array}{l}
A(c) \\
I(c, v) \\
\vdash \\
G_1(c, v) \ \lor \ \dots \ \lor \ G_m(c, v)
\end{array} \quad \text{DLF}
\qquad
\begin{array}{l}
\text{Axioms} \\
\text{Invariants} \\
\vdash \\
\text{Disjunction of the guards}
\end{array} \quad \text{DLF}
$$

Note that the application of this rule is *not mandatory*; not all systems need to be deadlock free.

2.4.22 Applying the deadlock freedom proof obligation rule

Here is what we have to prove according to rule DLF:

$$
\begin{array}{ll}
\text{Axiom } \mathbf{axm0\_1} & \quad d \in \mathbb{N} \\
\text{Invariant } \mathbf{inv0\_1} & \quad n \in \mathbb{N} \\
\text{Invariant } \mathbf{inv0\_2} & \quad n \leq d \qquad\qquad \text{DLF} \\
\vdash & \quad \vdash \\
\text{Disjunction of the guards} & \quad n < d \ \vee \ 0 < n
\end{array}
$$

2.4.23 More inference rules

The previous deadlock freedom proof obligation cannot be proved without more rules of inference. The first one is a logical rule, which corresponds to the classical technique of a *proof by cases*. It is named OR_L as it has to do with the "or" symbol $\vee$ situated in the "left-hand" assumption part of a sequent. Notice that the antecedent of this rule has two sequents. More precisely, in order to prove a goal under a disjunctive assumption $\mathbf{P} \vee \mathbf{Q}$, it is sufficient to *prove independently* the same goal under assumption $\mathbf{P}$ and also under assumption $\mathbf{Q}$:

$$
\frac{\mathbf{H}, \mathbf{P} \ \vdash\ \mathbf{R} \qquad\qquad \mathbf{H}, \mathbf{Q} \ \vdash\ \mathbf{R}}{\mathbf{H}, \ \mathbf{P} \vee \mathbf{Q} \ \vdash\ \mathbf{R}} \quad \text{OR\_L}
$$

For the sake of completeness, we provide again the two logical inference rules we have already presented in Section 2.4.12:

$$
\frac{\mathbf{H} \ \vdash\ \mathbf{P}}{\mathbf{H} \ \vdash\ \mathbf{P} \vee \mathbf{Q}} \quad \text{OR\_R1}
\qquad\qquad
\frac{\mathbf{H} \ \vdash\ \mathbf{Q}}{\mathbf{H} \ \vdash\ \mathbf{P} \vee \mathbf{Q}} \quad \text{OR\_R2}
$$

Our final logical rules have to do with the essence of a sequent. The first rule, HYP says that when the goal of a sequent is present as an assumption of that sequent, then the sequent is proved. The second rule, FALSE_L, says that a sequent with a false assumption is proved. We denote false with the symbol ⊥:

$$\frac{}{\mathbf{P} \vdash \mathbf{P}} \text{ HYP} \qquad \frac{}{\bot \vdash \mathbf{P}} \text{ FALSE\_L}$$

Our next two rules of inference are dealing with equality. They explain how we can exploit an assumption which is an equality.

$$\frac{\mathbf{H(F)}, \mathbf{E} = \mathbf{F} \vdash \mathbf{P(F)}}{\mathbf{H(E)}, \mathbf{E} = \mathbf{F} \vdash \mathbf{P(E)}} \text{ EQ\_LR} \qquad \frac{\mathbf{H(E)}, \mathbf{E} = \mathbf{F} \vdash \mathbf{P(E)}}{\mathbf{H(F)}, \mathbf{E} = \mathbf{F} \vdash \mathbf{P(F)}} \text{ EQ\_RL}$$

In rule EQ_LR, we have a sequent with a goal $\mathbf{P(E)}$, which is a predicate *depending* on the expression $\mathbf{E}$. We also have a set of hypotheses $\mathbf{H(E)}$ depending of $\mathbf{E}$. Finally, we have the equality hypothesis $\mathbf{E} = \mathbf{F}$. The rule says that we can then replace this sequent by another one where all occurrences of $\mathbf{E}$ in $\mathbf{P(E)}$ and in $\mathbf{H(E)}$ have been replaced by $\mathbf{F}$. The label LR is to remind us that we apply the equality from "Left" to "Right". Rule EQ_RL exploits the same equality by applying it now from right to left, that is replacing $\mathbf{F}$ by $\mathbf{E}$ in $\mathbf{P(F)}$ and $\mathbf{H(F)}$ yielding $\mathbf{P(E)}$ and $\mathbf{H(E)}$. Note that we have not formally explained exactly what we mean when we say that a predicate "depends" on an expression $\mathbf{E}$. This will be made more precise later.

Our final rule, dealing with equality, says that any expression $\mathbf{E}$ is equal to itself. This rule in not used immediately in the next proof, but it is quite natural to introduce it now:

$$\frac{}{\vdash \mathbf{E} = \mathbf{E}} \text{ EQL}$$

2.4.24 *Proving the deadlock freedom proof obligation*

Coming back to our example, we are going to give a tentative proof of our deadlock freedom proof obligation DLF, which we repeat now:

$$
\begin{array}{l}
d \in \mathbb{N} \\
n \in \mathbb{N} \\
n \leq d \\
\vdash \\
n < d \ \lor \ 0 < n
\end{array}
\qquad \text{DLF}
$$

Here, we are going to apply inference rule OR_L, because the assumption $n \leq d$ is in fact equivalent to the disjunctive predicate $n < d \ \lor \ n = d$. As can be seen, the usage of inference rule OR_L induces a tree shape to the proof. This is because we have two antecedents in this rule. This tree shape is the normal shape of a proof:

$$
\begin{array}{l}
d \in \mathbb{N} \\
n \in \mathbb{N} \\
n < d \ \lor \ n = d \\
\vdash \\
n < d \ \lor \ 0 < n
\end{array}
\quad \text{MON}
\qquad
\begin{array}{l}
n < d \ \lor \ n = d \\
\vdash \\
n < d \ \lor \ 0 < n
\end{array}
\quad \text{OR\_L} \ \ldots
$$

$$
\ldots \left\{
\begin{array}{l}
\begin{array}{l}
n < d \\
\vdash \\
n < d \lor 0 < n
\end{array}
\quad \text{OR\_R1}
\quad
\boxed{n < d \vdash n < d}
\quad \text{HYP} \\[2em]
\begin{array}{l}
n = d \\
\vdash \\
n < d \lor 0 < n
\end{array}
\quad \text{EQ\_LR}
\quad
\boxed{\vdash d < d \ \lor \ 0 < d}
\quad \text{OR\_R2}
\quad
\boxed{\vdash 0 < d}
\quad ?
\end{array}
\right.
$$

We now discover that the last sequent cannot be proved. We have thus to add the following axiom, named **axm0_2**, which was obviously forgotten:

$$\textbf{axm0\_2:} \quad 0 < d$$

We notice that this additional axiom allows us to have a more precise requirement FUN-2:

The number of cars on bridge and island is limited but positive	FUN-2

Adding this axiom to avoid deadlock is very intuitive because, when $d = 0$, the system is deadlocked right from the beginning since no car can ever enter the compound. Again, note that adding this new axiom for the constant d does not invalidate the proofs we have already made so far; this is a consequence of the monotonicity rule MON introduced in Section 2.4.9.

2.4.25 Conclusion and summary of the initial model

As we have seen, the proofs (or rather the failed proof attempts) allowed us to discover that our events were too naive (we had to add guards in Section 2.4.13) and also that one axiom was missing for constant d. This is quite frequently the case: proofs help us to discover inconsistencies in a model. In fact, this is the heart of the modeling method! Here is the final version of the state for our initial model:

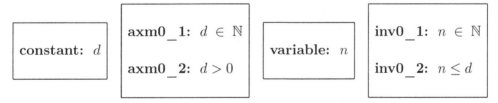

And here is the final version of the events of our initial model:

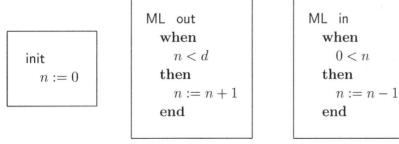

2.5 First refinement: introducing the one-way bridge

2.5.1 Introduction

We are now going to proceed with a *refinement* of our initial model. A refinement is a more precise model than the initial one. It is more precise, but it should not contradict the initial model. Therefore, we shall certainly have to *prove* that the refinement is consistent with the initial model. This will be made clear in this section.

In this first refinement, we introduce the bridge. This means that we are able to observe more accurately our system. Together with this more accurate observation, we can also see more events, namely cars entering and leaving the island. These events are called IL_in and IL_out. Note that events ML_out and ML_in, which were present in the initial model, still exist in this refinement: they now correspond to cars leaving the mainland and entering the bridge or leaving the bridge and entering the mainland. All this is illustrated in Fig. 2.5.

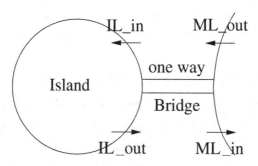

Fig. 2.5. Island and bridge

2.5.2 Refining the state

The state, which was defined by the constant d and variable n in the initial model, now becomes more accurate. The constant d remains, but the variable n is now *replaced by three variables*. This is because now we can see cars on the bridge and on the island, something which we could not distinguish in the previous abstraction. Moreover, we can see where cars on the bridge are going: either towards the island or towards the mainland.

For these reasons, the state is now represented by means of three variables a, b, and c. Variable a denotes the number of cars on the bridge and going to the island, variable b denotes the number of cars on the island, and variable c denotes the number of cars on the bridge and going to the mainland. This is illustrated in Fig. 2.6.

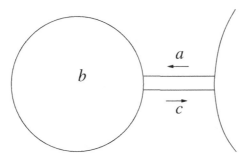

Fig. 2.6. The concrete state

The state of the initial model is called the *abstract state* and the state of the refined model is called the *concrete state*. Likewise, variable n of the abstract state is called an *abstract variable*, whereas variables a, b, and c of the concrete state are called *concrete variables*.

The concrete state is represented by a number of invariants, which we call the *concrete invariants*. First, variables a, b, and c are all natural numbers. This is stated in invariants **inv1_1**, **inv1_2**, and **inv1_3** below:

variables: a, b, c	

inv1_1:	$a \in \mathbb{N}$
inv1_2:	$b \in \mathbb{N}$
inv1_3:	$c \in \mathbb{N}$

inv1_4:	$a + b + c = n$
inv1_5:	$a = 0 \ \lor \ c = 0$

Then we express that the sum of these variables is equal to the previous abstract variable n, which has disappeared. This is expressed in invariant **inv1_4**, which relates the concrete state represented by the three variables a, b, and c to the abstract state represented by the variable n. And, finally, we state that the bridge is one-way; this is our basic requirement FUN-3. This is expressed by saying that a or c is equal to zero. Clearly, they cannot both be positive since the bridge is one-way, but they can both be equal to zero if the bridge is empty. This one-way property is expressed in invariant **inv1_5**.

Notice that among the concrete invariants, some are dealing with the concrete variables only. These are **inv1_1**, **inv1_2**, **inv1_3**, and **inv1_5**, and one is dealing with concrete and abstract variables; this is **inv1_4**.

2.5.3 Refining the abstract events

The two abstract events ML_out and ML_in now have to be *refined* as they are no longer dealing with the abstract variable n, but with the concrete variables a, b, and c. Here is the proposed *concrete versions* (sometimes also called refined versions) of events ML_in and ML_out:

$$
\boxed{
\begin{aligned}
&\textsf{ML\_in} \\
&\quad \textbf{when} \\
&\qquad 0 < c \\
&\quad \textbf{then} \\
&\qquad c := c - 1 \\
&\quad \textbf{end}
\end{aligned}
}
\qquad
\boxed{
\begin{aligned}
&\textsf{ML\_out} \\
&\quad \textbf{when} \\
&\qquad a + b < d \\
&\qquad c = 0 \\
&\quad \textbf{then} \\
&\qquad a := a + 1 \\
&\quad \textbf{end}
\end{aligned}
}
$$

Notice that event ML_out has two guards, namely $a + b < d$ and $c = 0$. Also notice that although our refined model now has three variables a, b, and c, only one of them is mentioned in each event: c in event ML_in and a in event ML_out. In fact, the other two are, in each case, implicitly mentioned as being *left unchanged*.

It is easy to understand what these events are doing. In event ML_in, the action decrements variable c as there will be one car less on the bridge, and this can be done if there are some cars on the bridge going to the mainland, that is when $0 < c$ holds (notice that we are sure that there are no cars on the bridge going to the island as a must be equal to 0 since c is positive).

In event ML_out, the action increments variable a as there will be one more car on the bridge. But this is possible only if c is equal to 0, because of the one-way constraint of the bridge. Moreover, this will also be possible only if the new car entering the bridge does not break the constraint that there are a maximum number of d cars in the compound, that is when $a + b + c < d$ holds, which reduces to $a + b < d$ since c is equal to 0.

2.5.4 Revisiting the before–after predicates

The observation concerning the actions of the concrete events in the previous section forces us to be more precise now concerning the construction of the before–after predicate. The before–after predicate of the action corresponding to an event situated in a model containing *several variables* must mention explicitly that the missing variables in the action are not modified; this is done by stating that their primed after-values are equal to their non-primed before-values. In the case of our example, the following before–after predicates are associated with the corresponding event actions as follows:

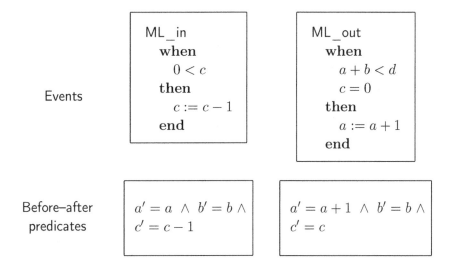

As can be seen, the before–after predicate of the action $c := c - 1$ contains $c' = c - 1$ as expected, but also $a' = a$ and $b' = b$. We have similar equalities corresponding to the action $a := a + 1$.

2.5.5 Informal proofs of refinement

In the next section, we shall clearly define what is required for the concrete version of an event *to refine its abstraction*. For now, we just present some informal arguments. For this, we are going to compare the abstract and concrete versions of our two events respectively. Here are the two versions of the event ML_out:

(abstract_)ML_out
  when
    $n < d$
  then
    $n := n + 1$
  end

(concrete_)ML_out
  when
    $a + b < d$
    $c = 0$
  then
    $a := a + 1$
  end

As can be seen, the concrete version of this event has guards which are completely different from that of the abstraction. We can already "feel" that the concrete version is *not contradictory* with the abstract one. When the concrete version is enabled, that is when its guards hold, then certainly the abstract one is enabled too. This is so because the two concrete guards $a + b < d$ and $c = 0$ together imply $a + b + c < d$, that is $n < d$, which is the abstract guard, according to invariant **inv1_4**, which states that $a + b + c$ is equal to n. Moreover, when a is incremented and the other variables left unchanged as stated in the action $a := a + 1$ in the concrete version, this clearly corresponds to the fact that n is incremented in the abstract one, according again to the invariant **inv1_4**. Likewise, here are the two versions of the event ML_in:

(abstract_)ML_in **when** $\quad 0 < n$ **then** $\quad n := n - 1$ **end**

(concrete_)ML_in **when** $\quad 0 < c$ **then** $\quad c := c - 1$ **end**

A similar informal "proof" can be conducted on these two versions of event ML_in, showing that the concrete one does not contradict the abstract one.

2.5.6 *Proving the correct refinements of abstract events*

We are now going to give systematic rules defining exactly what we have to prove in order to ensure that a concrete event indeed refines its abstraction. In fact, we have to prove two different things. First a statement concerning the guards, and second a statement concerning the actions.

Guard strengthening We first have to prove that the concrete guard is *stronger* than the abstract one. The term "stronger" means that the concrete guard *implies* the abstract guard. In other words, it is not possible to have the concrete version enabled when the abstract one is not. Otherwise, it would be possible to have a concrete transition with no counterpart in the abstraction. This has to be proved under the abstract axioms of the constants, the abstract invariants and the concrete invariants. We shall see in Section 2.5.16 that we cannot strengthen the refined guards too much because it might result in unwanted deadlocks.

In more general terms, let c denote the constants, $A(c)$ the set of constant axioms, v the abstract variables, $I(c, v)$ the set of abstract invariants, w the concrete variables, $J(c, v, w)$ the set of concrete invariants. Let an abstract event have the set of guards $G(c, v)$. In other words, $G(c, v)$ stands for the list $G_1(c, v), G_2(c, v), \dots$. Let the corresponding concrete event have the set of guards $H(c, w)$. We have then to prove the following for each concrete guard $G_i(c, v)$:

$\begin{array}{l} A(c) \\ I(c,v) \\ J(c,v,w) \\ H(c,w) \\ \vdash \\ G_i(c,v) \end{array}$	GRD

$\begin{array}{l} \text{Axioms} \\ \text{Abstract invariants} \\ \text{Concrete invariants} \\ \text{Concrete guards} \\ \vdash \\ \text{Abstract guard} \end{array}$	GRD

Notice again that the set of concrete invariants denoted by $J(c, v, w)$ contains some elementary invariants dealing with concrete variables w only, while others are dealing with both abstract and concrete variables v and w. This is the reason why we collectively denote this set of concrete invariants by $J(c, v, w)$.

Also note that it is possible to introduce new constants in a refinement. But we have not stated this in the concrete invariants $J(c, v, w)$ in order to keep the formulae small.

Correct refinement We have to prove that the concrete event transforms the concrete variables w into w', in a way which does not contradict the abstract event. While this transition happens, the abstract event changes the abstract variables v, which are related to w by the concrete invariant $J(c, v, w)$, into v', which must be related to w' by the modified concrete invariant $J(c, v', w')$. This is illustrated in the following diagram:

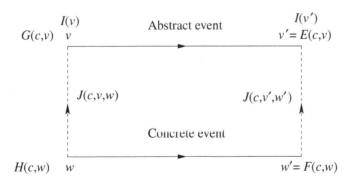

With our usual conventions, this leads to the following proof obligation rule named INV, where $J_j(c, v, w)$ denotes a single invariant of the set of concrete invariants

$J(c, v, w)$:

$A(c)$ $I(c, v)$ $J(c, v, w)$ $H(c, w)$ $\vdash$ $J_j(c, E(c, v), F(c, w))$	INV

Axioms Abstract invariant Concrete invariant Concrete guard $\vdash$ Modified concrete invariant	INV

2.5.7 Applying the refinement rules

Coming back to our example, we apply rule GRD to both refined events ML_out and ML_in. This leads to some sequents, which look complicated but are easy to prove.

Applying guard strengthening to event ML_out Here is what we have to prove for event ML_out:

axm0_1	$d \in \mathbb{N}$	
axm0_2	$0 < d$	
inv0_1	$n \in \mathbb{N}$	
inv0_2	$n \leq d$	
inv1_1	$a \in \mathbb{N}$	
inv1_2	$b \in \mathbb{N}$	
inv1_3	$c \in \mathbb{N}$	ML_out / GRD.
inv1_4	$a + b + c = n$	
inv1_5	$a = 0 \ \lor \ c = 0$	
Concrete guards of ML_out	$a + b < d$	
	$c = 0$	
$\vdash$	$\vdash$	
Abstract guards of ML_out	$n < d$	

This huge, impressive sequent can be dramatically simplified. First, we can remove useless hypotheses by applying MON. Then we can apply the equality present in the hypothesis – that is $c = 0$ – thus transforming hypothesis $a + b + c = n$ first into $a + b + 0 = n$ and then into $a + b = n$. Then, we can apply this equality, thus replacing hypothesis $a + b < d$ by the simpler one $n < d$. And now we discover that this is exactly the goal we wanted to prove; we can apply HYP. More formally, this leads to the following successive transformations of our original sequent (obtained after applying rule MON):

$$
\boxed{\begin{array}{l} a + b + c = n \\ a + b < d \\ c = 0 \\ \vdash \\ n < d \end{array}} \ \text{EQ\_LR} \ \boxed{\begin{array}{l} \underline{a + b + 0 = n} \\ a + b < d \\ \vdash \\ n < d \end{array}} \ \text{ARI} \ \boxed{\begin{array}{l} a + b = n \\ a + b < d \\ \vdash \\ n < d \end{array}} \ \text{EQ\_LR} \ \boxed{\begin{array}{l} n < d \\ \vdash \\ n < d \end{array}} \ \text{HYP}
$$

As can be seen, we have introduced a generic rule of inference named ARI. This is to say in a less formal way that the justification is based on simple arithmetic properties. We could have defined corresponding specific rules of inference, but there is no point in doing this here for the moment. In order to make clear which arithmetic properties we are thinking of, the relevant assumptions or goals are underlined in the sequent situated to the left of this ARI justification.

Applying guard strengthening to event ML_in After applying MON, we obtain the following sequent:

$$
\boxed{\begin{array}{l} b \in \mathbb{N} \\ a + b + c = n \\ a = 0 \ \lor \ c = 0 \\ 0 < c \\ \vdash \\ 0 < n \end{array}}
$$

The disjunctive assumption suggests doing a proof by cases. Then we may apply the equalities, thus simplifying the sequents to be proved. The proof is finished by applying a number of simple arithmetic transformations. Here is the proof of this sequent:

$$
\begin{array}{l}
b \in \mathbb{N} \\
a + b + c = n \\
a = 0 \ \lor \ c = 0 \\
0 < c \\
\vdash \\
0 < n
\end{array}
\quad \text{OR\_L}
\left\{
\begin{array}{l}
\begin{array}{l}
b \in \mathbb{N} \\
a + b + c = n \\
a = 0 \\
0 < c \\
\vdash \\
0 < n
\end{array}
\quad \text{EQ\_LR}
\quad
\begin{array}{l}
b \in \mathbb{N} \\
\dfrac{0 + b + c = n}{0 < c} \\
\vdash \\
0 < n
\end{array}
\quad \text{ARI} \ldots \\[3em]
\begin{array}{l}
b \in \mathbb{N} \\
a + b + c = n \\
c = 0 \\
0 < c \\
\vdash \\
0 < n
\end{array}
\quad \text{EQ\_LR}
\quad
\begin{array}{l}
b \in \mathbb{N} \\
a + b + 0 = n \\
0 < 0 \\
\vdash \\
0 < n
\end{array}
\quad \text{MON} \ldots
\end{array}
\right.
$$

$$
\ldots
\begin{array}{l}
b \in \mathbb{N} \\
\dfrac{b + c = n}{0 < c} \\
\vdash \\
0 < n
\end{array}
\quad \text{ARI}
\quad
\begin{array}{l}
\dfrac{c \leq n}{0 < c} \\
\vdash \\
0 < n
\end{array}
\quad \text{ARI}
\quad
\begin{array}{l}
0 < n \\
\vdash \\
0 < n
\end{array}
\quad \text{HYP}
$$

$$
\ldots
\begin{array}{l}
\dfrac{0 < 0}{} \\
\vdash \\
0 < n
\end{array}
\quad \text{ARI}
\quad
\begin{array}{l}
\bot \\
\vdash \\
0 < n
\end{array}
\quad \text{FALSE\_L}
$$

Applying proof obligation rule INV leads to ten predicates to prove since we have two events and five concrete invariants. We shall only present some of them, the others being left as exercises for the reader.

Invariant inv1_4 preservation with event ML_out After applying MON, here is the proof we obtain:

$$\boxed{\begin{array}{l} a+b+c=n \\ \vdash \\ \underline{a+1+b+c=n+1} \end{array}} \;\text{ARI}\; \boxed{\begin{array}{l} a+b+c=n \\ \vdash \\ a+b+c+1=n+1 \end{array}} \;\text{EQ\_LR}\; \boxed{\; \vdash\; n+1=n+1\;} \;\text{EQL.}$$

Invariant inv1_5 preservation with event ML_in After applying MON, here is the proof we obtain:

$$\boxed{\begin{array}{l} a=0 \vee c=0 \\ 0<c \\ \vdash \\ a=0 \vee c-1=0 \end{array}} \;\text{OR\_L}\; \left\{ \begin{array}{l} \boxed{\begin{array}{l} a=0 \\ 0<c \\ \vdash \\ a=0 \vee c-1=0 \end{array}} \;\text{OR\_R1}\; \boxed{\begin{array}{l} a=0 \\ 0<c \\ \vdash \\ a=0 \end{array}} \;\text{MON}\; \boxed{\begin{array}{l} a=0 \\ \vdash \\ a=0 \end{array}} \;\text{HYP} \\[2em] \boxed{\begin{array}{l} c=0 \\ 0<c \\ \vdash \\ a=0 \vee c-1=0 \end{array}} \;\text{EQ\_LR} \cdots \end{array} \right.$$

$$\cdots \quad \boxed{\; \underline{0<0}\; \vdash\; a=0 \vee -1=0 \;} \;\text{ARI}\; \boxed{\; \bot\; \vdash\; a=0 \vee -1=0 \;} \;\text{FALSE\_L}$$

2.5.8 Refining the initialization event Init

We also have to define the refinement of the special event init. This event can be stated obviously as follows:

$$\boxed{\begin{array}{l} \text{init} \\ \quad a := 0 \\ \quad b := 0 \\ \quad c := 0 \end{array}}$$

Here we see for the first time a *multiple action*. The corresponding before–after predicate is what we expect:

$$\boxed{\; a'=0 \;\wedge\; b'=0 \;\wedge\; c'=0 \;}$$

2.5.9 Correct proof obligation refinement rule for the initialization event init

The proof obligation rule we have to apply in the case of the init event is a special case of the proof obligation rule INV. It is also called INV. If the abstract initialization has an after predicate of the form $v' = K(c)$ and the concrete initialization has an after predicate of the form $w' = L(c)$, then the proof obligation rule is the following:

$$\begin{array}{|c|c|} \hline \begin{array}{l} A(c) \\ \vdash \\ \quad J_j(c, K(c), L(c)) \end{array} & \text{INV} \\ \hline \end{array} \qquad \begin{array}{|c|c|} \hline \begin{array}{l} \text{Axioms} \\ \vdash \\ \quad \text{Modified concrete invariant} \end{array} & \text{INV} \\ \hline \end{array}$$

Notice that we have no proof obligation rule for guard strengthening since, by definition, the initialization event is not guarded.

2.5.10 Applying the initialization proof obligation refinement rule

The application of the proof obligation rule introduced in the previous section is straightforward in our example. Out of the five predicates, we give only the most important ones. Here is what we have to prove concerning invariant **inv1_4**:

$$\begin{array}{|l|} \hline \begin{array}{l} \textbf{axm0\_1} \\ \textbf{axm0\_2} \\ \vdash \\ \text{Modified concrete invariant } \textbf{inv1\_4} \end{array} \\ \hline \end{array} \qquad \begin{array}{|l|} \hline \begin{array}{l} d \in \mathbb{N} \\ d > 0 \\ \vdash \\ 0 + 0 + 0 = 0 \end{array} \\ \hline \end{array} \quad \textbf{inv1\_4} \: / \: \text{INV}$$

Here is what we have to prove concerning invariant **inv1_5**:

$$\begin{array}{|l|} \hline \begin{array}{l} \textbf{axm0\_1} \\ \textbf{axm0\_1} \\ \vdash \\ \text{Modified concrete invariant } \textbf{inv1\_5} \end{array} \\ \hline \end{array} \qquad \begin{array}{|l|} \hline \begin{array}{l} d \in \mathbb{N} \\ d > 0 \\ \vdash \\ 0 = 0 \: \lor \: 0 = 0 \end{array} \\ \hline \end{array} \quad \textbf{inv1\_5} \: / \: \text{INV}$$

The proofs of these sequents are left to the reader.

2.5.11 Introducing new events

We now have to introduce some new events corresponding to cars entering and leaving the island. Next are the proposed new events:

```
IL_in
    when
        0 < a
    then
        a := a - 1
        b := b + 1
    end
```

```
IL_out
    when
        0 < b
        a = 0
    then
        b := b - 1
        c := c + 1
    end
```

We have here again some *multiple actions*. These actions are incomplete however, since in the first one variable c is missing, whereas variable a is missing in the second one. Such multiple actions are associated with the following before–after predicates:

$$a' = a - 1 \ \wedge \ b' = b + 1 \ \wedge \ c' = c$$

$$a' = a \ \wedge \ b' = b - 1 \ \wedge \ c' = c + 1$$

It is also easy to understand what these events are doing. Event IL_in corresponds to a car leaving the bridge and entering the island. The action thus decrements the number a of cars on the bridge and simultaneously increments the number b of cars on the island. But this can only be done when there are cars on the bridge, that is when the condition $0 < a$ holds.

Event IL_out corresponds to a car leaving the island and entering the bridge. The action clearly decreases b and simultaneously increases c. But this can be done only if there are cars on the island, that is if the condition $0 < b$ holds. A second condition for event IL_out to be enabled is that there are no cars on the bridge going to the island (remember, the bridge is one-way), that is if the condition $a = 0$ holds.

2.5.12 The empty action skip

As we shall explain in the next section, the new events have to be proved to refine a "dummy event" that is non-guarded and *does nothing* in the abstraction. Such a void action is denoted by means of the empty action skip.

It is very important to note that the before–after predicate of skip depends on the state of the model in which it is located. In the present case, we shall speak first of such an empty action in the initial model, which has the single variable n. Its before–after predicate is thus the following:

$$n' = n$$

But a **skip** action residing in the concrete state, where we have the three variables a, b, and c, would be associated with the following different before–after predicate:

$$a' = a \ \land \ b' = b \ \land \ c' = c$$

2.5.13 Proving that the new events are correct

The new events that we have introduced in Section 2.5.11 were not visible in the abstraction. Although not visible, it does not mean that they did not exist and occur. When you are looking through a microscope, you can see things that were not visible without the microscope. By analogy, refinement is the same thing as looking at a system through a microscope. The transitions corresponding to the new events IL_in and IL_out were not visible in the abstraction but, again, they existed. Formalizing this idea consists in saying that the new events refine a non-guarded event with the empty action **skip**. As a consequence, we can use proof obligation rule INV to prove that our new events are correct. Here is what we have to prove for event IL_in and concrete invariant **inv1_4**:

axm0_1	$d \in \mathbb{N}$	
axm0_2	$0 < d$	
inv0_1	$n \in \mathbb{N}$	
inv0_2	$n \leq d$	
inv1_1	$a \in \mathbb{N}$	
inv1_2	$b \in \mathbb{N}$	
inv1_3	$c \in \mathbb{N}$	IL_IN / inv1_4 / INV.
inv1_4	$a + b + c = n$	
inv1_5	$a = 0 \ \lor \ c = 0$	
Concrete guards of IL_in	$0 < a$	
$\vdash$	$\vdash$	
Modified invariant **inv1_4**	$a - 1 + b + 1 + c = n$	

Notice that n is not modified as the event refines a non-guarded event with a **skip** action in the abstraction. After applying MON, we obtain the following proof:

$$
\begin{array}{l}
a + b + c = n \\
\vdash \\
\overline{a - 1 + b + 1 + c = n}
\end{array}
\qquad \text{ARI}
\qquad
\begin{array}{l}
a + b + c = n \\
\vdash \\
a + b + c = n
\end{array}
\qquad \text{HYP}
$$

Here is what we have to prove for event IL_in and concrete invariant **inv1_5**:

$$
\begin{array}{l}
\ldots \\
\textbf{inv1\_1} \\
\textbf{inv1\_2} \\
\textbf{inv1\_3} \\
\textbf{inv1\_4} \\
\textbf{inv1\_5} \\
\text{Concrete guards of IL\_in} \\
\vdash \\
\text{Modified invariant } \textbf{inv1\_5}
\end{array}
\qquad
\begin{array}{l}
\ldots \\
a \in \mathbb{N} \\
b \in \mathbb{N} \\
c \in \mathbb{N} \\
a + b + c = n \\
a = 0 \;\vee\; c = 0 \\
0 < a \\
\vdash \\
a - 1 = 0 \;\vee\; c = 0
\end{array}
\qquad \text{IL\_IN / inv1\_5 / INV}
$$

After applying MON, we obtain the following proof:

$$
\begin{array}{l}
a = 0 \vee c = 0 \\
0 < a \\
\vdash \\
a - 1 = 0 \vee \\
c = 0
\end{array}
\;\text{OR\_L}\;
\left\{
\begin{array}{l}
\begin{array}{l}
a = 0 \\
0 < a \\
\vdash \\
a - 1 = 0 \vee \\
c = 0
\end{array}
\;\text{EQ\_LR}\;
\begin{array}{l}
0 < 0 \\
\vdash \\
-1 = 0 \vee \\
c = 0
\end{array}
\;\text{ARI}\;
\begin{array}{l}
\bot \\
\vdash \\
-1 = 0 \vee \\
c = 0
\end{array}
\;\text{FALSE\_L} \\[2em]
\begin{array}{l}
c = 0 \\
0 < a \\
\vdash \\
a - 1 = 0 \vee c = 0
\end{array}
\;\text{OR\_R2}\;
\begin{array}{l}
c = 0 \\
0 < a \\
\vdash \\
c = 0
\end{array}
\;\text{MON}\;
\begin{array}{l}
c = 0 \\
\vdash \\
c = 0
\end{array}
\;\text{HYP}
\end{array}
\right.
$$

We leave it as an exercise to the reader to state and prove the remaining sequents corresponding to the other predicates and the other new event IL_out.

2.5.14 *Proving the convergence of the new events*

In the case where we introduce some new events, we have to prove something else, namely that they *do not diverge*. In other words, the new events must not be indefinitely enabled. Should it be the case, then the concrete versions of the existing events, here ML_out and ML_in, could be postponed indefinitely, which is certainly something we want to avoid since such events could possibly occur in the abstraction. For proving this, we have to exhibit a natural number expression called a *variant* and prove that it is *decreased by all new events*. This leads to two proof obligation rules: one states that the proposed variant is a natural number and the other states that the variant is decreased by the new events.

In the first proof obligation rule, called NAT, we prove that the exhibited variant $V(c, w)$ is a natural number. This is to be done assuming the axioms $A(c)$ of the constants c, the abstract invariants $I(c, v)$, the concrete invariants $J(c, v, w)$, and the guards of each new event $H(c, w)$. The guard $H(c, w)$ is put in the antecedent as we are not interested in proving that the exhibited variant is a natural number when the guard of a new event does not hold (it could be negative in this case):

$A(c)$ $I(c, v)$ $J(c, v, w)$ $H(c, w)$ $\vdash$ $V(c, w) \in \mathbb{N}$	NAT	Axioms Abstract invariants Concrete invariants Concrete guards of a new event $\vdash$ Variant $\in \mathbb{N}$	NAT	

The second proof obligation rule states that the variant $V(c, w)$ is decreased. This has to be proved for each new event with guards $H(c, w)$ and before–after predicate $w' = F(c, w)$:

$A(c)$ $I(c, v)$ $J(c, v, w)$ $H(c, w)$ $\vdash$ $V(c, F(c, w)) < V(c, w)$	VAR	Axioms Abstract invariants Concrete invariants Concrete guards of a new event $\vdash$ Modified variant $<$ variant	VAR	

Note that the variant is unique. In other words, the *same variant* has to be decreased by each new event. Sometimes the variant might be a little more complicated than a simple natural number expression, but in this example we only need a natural number variant.

2.5.15 Applying the non-divergence proof obligation rules

In our case, the proposed variant is the following:

$$\textbf{variant\_1}: \quad 2 * a + b$$

Applying proof obligation rule VAR on event IL_in leads to the following large but obvious sequent to prove:

axm0_1	$d \in \mathbb{N}$	
axm0_2	$0 < d$	
inv0_1	$n \in \mathbb{N}$	
inv0_2	$n \le d$	
inv1_1	$a \in \mathbb{N}$	
inv1_2	$b \in \mathbb{N}$	
inv1_3	$c \in \mathbb{N}$	IL_in / VAR.
inv1_4	$a + b + c = n$	
inv1_5	$a = 0 \ \lor \ c = 0$	
Concrete guards of IL_in	$0 < a$	
$\vdash$	$\vdash$	
Modified variant $<$ variant	$2 * (a - 1) + b + 1 < 2 * a + b$	

Next is the application of proof obligation rule VAR to event IL_out:

axm0_1	$d \in \mathbb{N}$	
axm0_2	$0 < d$	
inv0_1	$n \in \mathbb{N}$	
inv0_2	$n \le d$	
inv1_1	$a \in \mathbb{N}$	
inv1_2	$b \in \mathbb{N}$	
inv1_3	$c \in \mathbb{N}$	IL_out / VAR.
inv1_4	$a + b + c = n$	
inv1_5	$a = 0 \ \lor \ c = 0$	
Concrete guards of IL_out	$0 < b$	
	$a = 0$	
$\vdash$	$\vdash$	
Modified variant $<$ variant	$2 * a + b - 1 < 2 * a + b$	

Both these sequents are proved by simple arithmetic calculations. Proofs are omitted.

2.5.16 Relative deadlock freedom

Finally, we have to prove that all concrete events (old and new together) do not deadlock more often than the abstract events. We have thus to prove that the disjunction of the abstract guards $G_1(c,v), \ldots, G_m(c,v)$ imply the disjunction of the concrete guards $H_1(c,w), \ldots, H_n(c,w)$. This proof obligation rule is called DLF:

$A(c)$ $I(c,v)$ $J(c,v,w)$ $G_1(c,v) \lor \ldots \lor G_m(c,v)$ $\vdash$ $H_1(c,w) \lor \ldots \lor H_n(c,w)$	DLF

Axioms Abstract invariants Concrete invariants Disjunction of abstract guards $\vdash$ Disjunction of concrete guards	DLF

2.5.17 Applying relative deadlock freedom proof obligation

The application of proof obligation rule DLF leads to the following to prove. Notice that we have removed the disjunction of the abstract guards in the antecedent of the implication because we have already proved them in the initial model:

axm0_1 **axm0_2** **inv0_1** **inv0_2** **inv1_1** **inv1_2** **inv1_3** **inv1_4** **inv1_5** $\vdash$ Disjunction of concrete guards	$d \in \mathbb{N}$ $0 < d$ $n \in \mathbb{N}$ $n \leq d$ $a \in \mathbb{N}$ $b \in \mathbb{N}$ $c \in \mathbb{N}$ $a + b + c = n$ $a = 0 \lor c = 0$ $\vdash$ $(a + b < d \land c = 0) \lor$ $c > 0 \lor$ $a > 0 \lor$ $(b > 0 \land a = 0)$	DLF.

2.5.18 More inference rules

In the previous sequent, we had to prove the *disjunction* of various predicates. A convenient way to do this (using commutativity and associativity of disjunction) is to apply the following rule that moves the negation of one of the disjuncts of the goal into the assumptions of the sequent. Here is the corresponding rule:

$$\frac{\mathbf{H}, \neg \mathbf{P} \;\vdash\; \mathbf{Q}}{\mathbf{H} \;\vdash\; \mathbf{P} \vee \mathbf{Q}} \quad \text{OR\_R}$$

The next two rules allow us to simplify conjunctive predicates appearing either in the assumptions or in the goal of a sequent:

$$\frac{\mathbf{H}, \mathbf{P}, \mathbf{Q} \;\vdash\; \mathbf{R}}{\mathbf{H}, \mathbf{P} \wedge \mathbf{Q} \;\vdash\; \mathbf{R}} \quad \text{AND\_L}$$

$$\frac{\mathbf{H} \;\vdash\; \mathbf{P} \qquad \mathbf{H} \;\vdash\; \mathbf{Q}}{\mathbf{H} \;\vdash\; \mathbf{P} \wedge \mathbf{Q}} \quad \text{AND\_R}$$

Proving the deadlock freedom proof obligation Equipped with these new inference rules, we may now prove the deadlock freedom proof obligation (after applying MON):

$$
\begin{array}{l}
0 < d \\
a \in \mathbb{N} \\
b \in \mathbb{N} \\
c \in \mathbb{N} \\
\vdash \\
(a + b < d \wedge \\
\quad c = 0) \vee \\
c > 0 \vee \\
a > 0 \vee \\
(b > 0 \wedge a - 0)
\end{array}
\;\;\text{OR\_R}\;\;
\begin{array}{l}
0 < d \\
a \in \mathbb{N} \\
b \in \mathbb{N} \\
\underline{c \in \mathbb{N}} \\
\neg (c > 0) \\
\vdash \\
(a + b < d \wedge \\
\quad c = 0) \vee \\
a > 0 \vee \\
(b > 0 \wedge a = 0)
\end{array}
\;\;\text{ARI}\;\;
\begin{array}{l}
0 < d \\
a \in \mathbb{N} \\
b \in \mathbb{N} \\
c = 0 \\
\vdash \\
(a + b < d \wedge \\
\quad c = 0) \vee \\
a > 0 \vee \\
(b > 0 \wedge a = 0)
\end{array}
\;\;\text{EQ\_LR} \ldots
$$

$$
\cdots
\boxed{
\begin{array}{l}
0 < d \\
a \in \mathbb{N} \\
b \in \mathbb{N} \\
\vdash \\
(a + b < d \wedge \\
0 = 0) \vee \\
a > 0 \vee \\
(b > 0 \wedge a = 0)
\end{array}
}
\;\text{OR\_R}\;
\boxed{
\begin{array}{l}
0 < d \\
\underline{a \in \mathbb{N}} \\
b \in \mathbb{N} \\
\neg\,(a > 0) \\
\vdash \\
(a + b < d \wedge \\
0 = 0) \vee \\
(b > 0 \wedge a = 0)
\end{array}
}
\;\text{ARI}\;
\boxed{
\begin{array}{l}
0 < d \\
a = 0 \\
b \in \mathbb{N} \\
\vdash \\
(a + b < d \wedge \\
0 = 0) \vee \\
(b > 0 \wedge a = 0)
\end{array}
}
\;\text{EQ\_LR}\;\cdots
$$

$$
\cdots
\boxed{
\begin{array}{l}
0 < d \\
\underline{b \in \mathbb{N}} \\
\vdash \\
(0 + b < d \;\wedge \\
\quad\;\; 0 = 0) \;\vee \\
(b > 0 \;\wedge\; 0 = 0)
\end{array}
}
\;\text{ARI}\;\cdots
$$

$$
\cdots
\boxed{
\begin{array}{l}
0 < d \\
b = 0 \;\vee\; b > 0 \\
\vdash \\
(b < d \;\wedge\; 0 = 0) \;\vee \\
(b > 0 \;\wedge\; 0 = 0)
\end{array}
}
\;\text{OR\_L}\;
\left\{
\begin{array}{l}
\boxed{
\begin{array}{l}
0 < d \\
b = 0 \\
\vdash \\
(b < d \;\wedge\; 0 = 0) \;\vee \\
(b > 0 \;\wedge\; 0 = 0)
\end{array}
}
\;\text{OR\_R1}\;\cdots \\
\\
\boxed{
\begin{array}{l}
0 < d \\
b > 0 \\
\vdash \\
(b < d \;\wedge\; 0 = 0) \;\vee \\
(b > 0 \;\wedge\; 0 = 0)
\end{array}
}
\;\text{OR\_R2}\;\cdots
\end{array}
\right.
$$

$\cdots$ $\boxed{\begin{array}{l} 0 < d \\ b = 0 \\ \vdash \\ b < d \wedge 0 = 0 \end{array}}$ EQ_LR $\boxed{\begin{array}{l} 0 < d \\ \vdash \\ 0 < d \wedge 0 = 0 \end{array}}$ AND_R $\left\{ \begin{array}{l} \boxed{0 < d \vdash 0 < d} \quad \text{HYP} \\[2em] \boxed{0 < d \vdash 0 = 0} \quad \text{EQL} \end{array} \right.$

$\cdots$ $\boxed{0 < d,\ b > 0 \vdash b > 0 \wedge 0 = 0}$ AND_R $\left\{ \begin{array}{l} \boxed{0 < d,\ b > 0 \vdash b > 0} \quad \text{HYP} \\[2em] \boxed{0 < d,\ b > 0 \vdash 0 = 0} \quad \text{EQL} \end{array} \right.$

2.5.19 Summary of the first Refinement

Here is a summary of the state of the first refinement:

$\boxed{\begin{array}{l} \textbf{constants: } d \\[1em] \textbf{variables: } a, b, c \end{array}}$
$\boxed{\begin{array}{l} \textbf{inv1\_1: } a \in \mathbb{N} \\[1em] \textbf{inv1\_2: } b \in \mathbb{N} \\[1em] \textbf{inv1\_3: } c \in \mathbb{N} \end{array}}$
$\boxed{\begin{array}{l} \textbf{inv1\_4: } a + b + c = n \\[1em] \textbf{inv1\_5: } a = 0 \ \vee \ c = 0 \\[1em] \textbf{variant1: } 2 * a + b \end{array}}$

Here is a summary of the events of the first refinement:

$\boxed{\begin{array}{l} \text{ML\_in} \\ \quad \textbf{when} \\ \qquad 0 < c \\ \quad \textbf{then} \\ \qquad c := c - 1 \\ \quad \textbf{end} \end{array}}$
$\boxed{\begin{array}{l} \text{ML\_out} \\ \quad \textbf{when} \\ \qquad a + b < d \\ \qquad c = 0 \\ \quad \textbf{then} \\ \qquad a := a + 1 \\ \quad \textbf{end} \end{array}}$
$\boxed{\begin{array}{l} \text{IL\_in} \\ \quad \textbf{when} \\ \qquad 0 < a \\ \quad \textbf{then} \\ \qquad a := a - 1 \\ \qquad b := b + 1 \\ \quad \textbf{end} \end{array}}$
$\boxed{\begin{array}{l} \text{IL\_out} \\ \quad \textbf{when} \\ \qquad 0 < b \\ \qquad a = 0 \\ \quad \textbf{then} \\ \qquad b := b - 1 \\ \qquad c := c + 1 \\ \quad \textbf{end} \end{array}}$

$$\boxed{\begin{array}{l} \text{init} \\ \quad a := 0 \\ \quad b := 0 \\ \quad c := 0 \end{array}}$$

2.6 Second refinement: introducing the traffic lights

In its present form, the model of the bridge appears to be a bit magical. It seems, from our observation, that car drivers can count cars and thus decide to enter into the bridge from the mainland (event ML_out) or from the island (event IL_out). This means they can observe the state of the system. Clearly, this is not realistic. In reality, as we know, drivers follow the indication of some traffic lights; they clearly do not count cars!

This refinement then consists in introducing first the two traffic lights, named ml_tl and il_tl, then the corresponding invariants, and, finally, some new events that can change the colors of the traffic lights. Fig. 2.7 illustrates the new physical situation, which can be observed in this refinement.

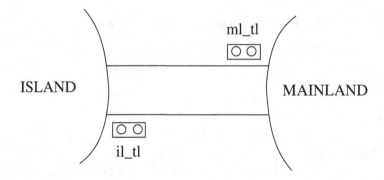

Fig. 2.7. The traffic lights

2.6.1 Refining the state

At this stage, we must extend our set of constants by first introducing the set $COLOR$ and its two distinct values *red* and *green*. It is done as follows:

set:	$COLOR$
constants:	$red, green$

axm2_1:	$COLOR = \{green, red\}$
axm2_2:	$green \neq red$

Two new variables are then introduced, namely ml_tl (for mainland traffic light) and il_tl (for island traffic light). These variables are defined as colors: this is formalized in invariants named **inv2_1** and **inv2_2** below. Since drivers are allowed to pass only when traffic lights are green, we better ensure, by two *conditional invariants* named **inv2_3** and **inv2_4**, that when ml_tl is green then the abstract guard of event ML_out holds, and that when il_tl is green then the abstract guard of event IL_out holds. Notice that we are here taking account of requirements ENV-1, ENV-2, and ENV-3. Here are the refined variables:

variables: . . . ml_tl il_tl	**inv2_1:** $ml\_tl \in COLOR$ **inv2_2:** $il\_tl \in COLOR$ **inv2_3:** $ml\_tl = green \ \Rightarrow \ a + b < d \ \wedge \ c = 0$ **inv2_4:** $il\_tl = green \ \Rightarrow \ 0 < b \ \wedge \ a = 0$

Note again that invariants **inv2_3** and **inv2_4** are *conditional invariants*. Such invariants are introduced by means of the logical implication operator "$\Rightarrow$". Clearly, we shall need inference rules dealing with this logical operator. We shall introduce such inference rules in Section 2.6.6.

At this point, it seems that we are in a situation which is a bit different from the one we had in the previous refinement, where concrete variables a, b, and c were replacing the more abstract variable n. Here we are just adding two new variables ml_tl and il_tl and we are keeping the abstract variables a, b, and c. Such a special refinement scheme is called a *superposition*. We shall see in Section 2.6.4 that superposition refinement requires an additional proof obligation rule.

2.6.2 Refining abstract events

Events ML_out and IL_out are now refined by changing their guards to the test of the green value of the corresponding traffic lights. This is where we implicitly assume that drivers obey the traffic lights, as indicated by requirements ENV-3. Note that events IL_in (entering the island from the bridge) and ML_in (entering the mainland from the bridge) are not modified in this refinement. Here is the new version of event ML_out presented together with its abstraction:

```
(abstract_)ML_out
  when
    c = 0
    a + b < d
  then
    a := a + 1
  end
```

```
(concrete_)ML_out
  when
    ml_tl = green
  then
    a := a + 1
  end
```

Here is the new version of event IL_out presented together with its abstraction:

```
(abstract_)IL_out
  when
    a = 0
    0 < b
  then
    b, c := b − 1, c + 1
  end
```

```
(concrete_)IL_out
  when
    il_tl = green
  then
    b, c := b − 1, c + 1
  end
```

2.6.3 Introducing new events

We have to introduce two new events to turn the value of the traffic lights color to green when they are red and the conditions are appropriate. The appropriate conditions are exactly the guards of the abstract events ML_out and IL_out. Here are the proposed new events:

```
ML_tl_green
  when
    ml_tl = red
    a + b < d
    c = 0
  then
    ml_tl := green
  end
```

```
IL_tl_green
  when
    il_tl = red
    0 < b
    a = 0
  then
    il_tl := green
  end
```

2.6.4 Superposition: adapting the refinement rule

In this section, we depart again from our example and explain the superposition with some general terms. When we have a case of superposition where some abstract variables are kept in the concrete state we have to adapt the refinement proof obligation rule INV. The other refinement rules need not be adapted.

Suppose we have variables u and v in the abstract state and variables v and w in the concrete state. Variables v are thus common to the abstract and concrete states. Let $I(c, u, v)$ denote the abstract invariants and $J(c, u, v, w)$ denote the concrete invariants. In order to be able to apply the proof obligation rule INV, the abstract and concrete states must be *completely disjoint*, and this is clearly not the situation we have in the present case of superposition.

In order to get back to a disjoint situation, we can rename the variables in the concrete state, changing v to, say, $v1$ and *adding the additional concrete invariant* $v1 = v$. Suppose now that the before–after predicates of an event in the abstract state are $u' = E(c, u, v)$ and $v' = M(c, u, v)$. Suppose that the before–after predicates of the corresponding concrete event are $v' = N(c, v, w)$ and $w' = F(c, v, w)$ in the concrete state. Suppose the guards of this concrete event are denoted by $H(c, v, w)$. Applying the proof obligation refinement rule INV yields two kinds of sequent to prove:

Axioms of constants	$A(c)$	$A(c)$
Abstract invariants	$I(c, u, v)$	$I(c, u, v)$
Concrete invariants	$J(c, u, v1, w)$	$J(c, u, v1, w)$
	$v1 = v$	$v1 = v$
Concrete guards	$H(c, v1, w)$	$H(c, v1, w)$
$\vdash$	$\vdash$	$\vdash$
Modified invariants	$J_j(c, E(c, u, v), M(c, u, v), F(c, v1, w))$	$M(c, u, v) = N(c, v1, w)$

Applying now the equality $v1 = v$, that is replacing every occurrence of $v1$ by v in the previous sequents, leads to the following where $v1$ has disappeared. This is the adaptation we wanted to perform on the proof obligation refinement rule INV. We can interpret this adaptation as adding to the basic proof obligation rule INV another proof obligation rule which says that the abstract and concrete expressions assigned to the common variables in the abstract and concrete states are equal under the assumption of the concrete invariants $J(c, u, v, w)$:

$$A(c)$$
$$I(c, u, v)$$
$$J(c, u, v, w)$$
$$H(c, v, w)$$
$$\vdash$$
$$J(c, E(c, u, v), M(c, u, v), F(c, v, w))$$

$$A(c)$$
$$I(c, u, v)$$
$$J(c, u, v, w)$$
$$H(c, v, w)$$
$$\vdash$$
$$M(c, u, v) = N(c, v, w)$$

The first sequent corresponds to proof obligation rule INV as before and the second, and new one named SIM, simply states the equality of the abstract and concrete expressions assigned to the common variables:

$A(c)$ $I(c,u,v)$ $J(c,u,v,w)$ $H(c,v,w)$ $\vdash$ $M(c,u,v) = N(c,v,w)$	SIM

Axioms of constants Abstract invariants Concrete invariants Concrete guards $\vdash$ Equality of the expressions assigned to the common variables

2.6.5 Proving that the events are correct

In order to prove that the concrete old events refine their abstractions, we now have to apply three proof obligations: GRD, SIM, and INV.

Events IL_in and ML_in are identical to their abstraction, so proof obligations GRD and SIM applied to them do not imply anything to prove. It is easy to prove that proof obligation rule INV applied to them leads to statements that are trivial: we have to prove that the concrete invariants **inv2_3** and **inv2_4** are preserved.

Proof obligation SIM applied to events events IL_out and ML_out is also trivial because the abstract and concrete actions of these events are exactly the same. Applying proof obligation rule GRD to these events leads to simple proofs: we have to use invariants **inv2_3** and **inv2_4** to prove that the guards are strengthened. This is what we did informally in Section 2.6.2.

What remains to be done therefore are the proofs obtained by applying proof obligation rule INV to events IL_out and ML_out. We shall see below that this raises some difficulties.

2.6.6 More logical inference rules

We now add some new logical rules of inference that will be needed in order to perform our proofs. The next two rules allow us to simplify implicative predicates appearing either in the assumptions or in the goal of a sequent. We also present a rule dealing with a negative assumption:†

$$
\frac{\textbf{H}, \textbf{P}, \textbf{Q} \vdash \textbf{R}}{\textbf{H}, \textbf{P}, \textbf{P} \Rightarrow \textbf{Q} \vdash \textbf{R}} \text{ IMP\_L}
\qquad
\frac{\textbf{H}, \textbf{P} \vdash \textbf{Q}}{\textbf{H} \vdash \textbf{P} \Rightarrow \textbf{Q}} \text{ IMP\_R}
\qquad
\frac{\textbf{H}, \textbf{P} \vdash \neg \textbf{Q}}{\textbf{H}, \neg \textbf{P} \vdash \textbf{Q}} \text{ NOT\_L}
$$

2.6.7 Tentative proofs and solutions

Proving that event ML_out preserves invariant inv2_4 Here is the sequent to prove:

axm0_1	$d \in \mathbb{N}$	
axm0_2	$0 < d$	
axm2_1	$COLOR = \{green, red\}$	
axm2_2	$green \neq red$	
inv0_1	$n \in \mathbb{N}$	
inv0_2	$n \leq d$	
inv1_1	$a \in \mathbb{N}$	
inv1_2	$b \in \mathbb{N}$	
inv1_3	$c \in \mathbb{N}$	ML_out / **inv2_4** / INV.
inv1_4	$a + b + c = n$	
inv1_5	$a = 0 \vee c = 0$	
inv2_1	$ml\_tl \in \{red, green\}$	
inv2_2	$il\_tl \in \{red, green\}$	
inv2_3	$ml\_tl = green \Rightarrow a + b < d \wedge c = 0$	
inv2_4	$il\_tl = green \Rightarrow 0 < b \wedge a = 0$	
Guard of ML_out	$ml\_tl = green$	
$\vdash$	$\vdash$	
Modified **inv2_4**	$il\_tl = green \Rightarrow 0 < b \wedge a + 1 = 0$	

† We remind the reader that all rules of inference are reviewed in Chapter 9.

Here is a tentative proof of this sequent (after applying MON):

$$
\begin{array}{l}
green \neq red \\
il\_tl = green \Rightarrow 0 < b \wedge a = 0 \\
ml\_tl = green \\
\vdash \\
il\_tl = green \Rightarrow 0 < b \wedge a + 1 = 0
\end{array}
\quad \text{IMP\_R}
$$

$$
\begin{array}{l}
green \neq red \\
il\_tl = green \Rightarrow 0 < b \wedge a = 0 \\
ml\_tl = green \\
il\_tl = green \\
\vdash \\
0 < b \wedge a + 1 = 0
\end{array}
\quad \text{IMP\_L}\ldots
$$

$$
\ldots \quad
\begin{array}{l}
green \neq red \\
0 < b \wedge a = 0 \\
ml\_tl = green \\
il\_tl = green \\
\vdash \\
0 < b \wedge a + 1 = 0
\end{array}
\quad \text{AND\_L}
$$

$$
\begin{array}{l}
green \neq red \\
0 < b \\
a = 0 \\
ml\_tl = green \\
il\_tl = green \\
\vdash \\
0 < b \wedge a + 1 = 0
\end{array}
\quad \text{AND\_R} \quad \ldots
$$

$$
\ldots \left\{
\begin{array}{l}
green \neq red \\
0 < b \\
a = 0 \\
ml\_tl = green \\
il\_tl = green \\
\vdash \\
0 < b
\end{array}
\quad \text{MON} \quad
\begin{array}{l}
0 < b \\
\vdash \\
0 < b
\end{array}
\quad \text{HYP}
\right.
$$

$$
\begin{array}{l}
green \neq red \\
0 < b \\
a = 0 \\
ml\_tl = green \\
il\_tl = green \\
\vdash \\
a + 1 = 0
\end{array}
\quad \text{EQ\_LR}
\begin{array}{l}
green \neq red \\
ml\_tl = green \\
il\_tl = green \\
\vdash \\
\underline{0 + 1 = 0}
\end{array}
\quad \text{ARI}
\begin{array}{l}
green \neq red \\
ml\_tl = green \\
il\_tl = green \\
\vdash \\
1 = 0
\end{array}
\quad \text{?}
$$

Clearly, the last sequent cannot be proved.

Proving that event IL_out preserves invariant inv2_3 Here is what we have to prove for the preservation of invariant **inv2_3** by event IL_out:

$$
\begin{array}{l|l}
\ldots & \ldots \\
\textbf{axm2\_1} & COLOR = \{green, red\} \\
\textbf{axm2\_2} & green \neq red \\
\textbf{inv2\_1} & ml\_tl \in \{red, green\} \\
\textbf{inv2\_2} & il\_tl \in \{red, green\} \\
\textbf{inv2\_3} & ml\_tl = green \;\Rightarrow\; a + b < d \;\wedge\; c = 0 \\
\textbf{inv2\_4} & il\_tl = green \;\Rightarrow\; 0 < b \;\wedge\; a = 0 \\
\text{Guard of IL\_out} & il\_tl = green \\
\vdash & \vdash \\
\text{Modified } \textbf{inv2\_3} & ml\_tl = green \;\Rightarrow\; a + b - 1 < d \;\wedge\; c + 1 = 0
\end{array}
\qquad \text{IL\_out} / \textbf{inv2\_3} / \text{INV}
$$

Here is the tentative proof (after applying MON):

$$
\begin{array}{l}
green \neq red \\
ml\_tl = green \Rightarrow \\
\quad a + b < d \;\wedge\; c = 0 \\
il\_tl = green \\
\vdash \\
ml\_tl = green \;\Rightarrow \\
\quad a + b - 1 < d \;\wedge\; c + 1 = 0
\end{array}
\quad \text{IMP\_R}
\qquad
\begin{array}{l}
green \neq red \\
ml\_tl = green \Rightarrow \\
\quad a + b < d \;\wedge\; c = 0 \\
il\_tl = green \\
ml\_tl = green \\
\vdash \\
a + b - 1 < d \;\wedge\; c + 1 = 0
\end{array}
\quad \text{IMP\_L} \ldots
$$

$$
\ldots
\begin{array}{l}
green \neq red \\
a + b < d \;\wedge\; c = 0 \\
il\_tl = green \\
ml\_tl = green \\
\vdash \\
a + b - 1 < d \;\wedge \\
c + 1 = 0
\end{array}
\quad \text{AND\_L}
\qquad
\begin{array}{l}
green \neq red \\
a + b < d \\
c = 0 \\
il\_tl = green \\
ml\_tl = green \\
\vdash \\
a + b - 1 < d \;\wedge \\
c + 1 = 0
\end{array}
\quad \text{AND\_R} \ldots
$$

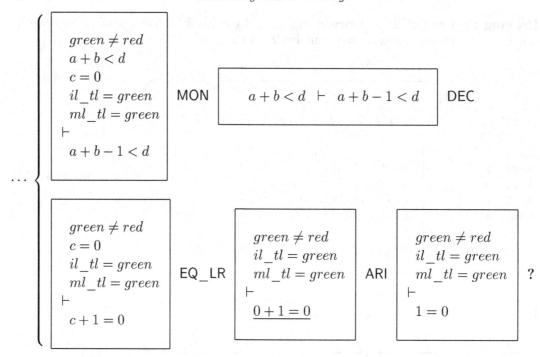

Clearly the last sequent cannot be proved either.

The solution The two previous proofs failed because we had to prove the following sequent:

$$
\begin{array}{l}
green \neq red \\
il\_tl = green \\
ml\_tl = green \\
\vdash \\
1 = 0
\end{array}
$$

What this shows is that both lights cannot be green at the same time. This is an *obvious fact*, which we have nevertheless completely forgotten to express. We thus now introduce it as an additional invariant:

inv2_5: $ml\_tl = red \ \lor \ il\_tl = red$

We note that this invariant could have been a requirement, although it could have been deduced from requirement, ENV-3, which says that "cars are not supposed to pass on a red traffic light, only a green one", and requirement FUN-3, which says that "the bridge

is one way or the other, *not both at the same time*". Adding this invariant will solve
the problem, since then we have the following extension to our proofs:

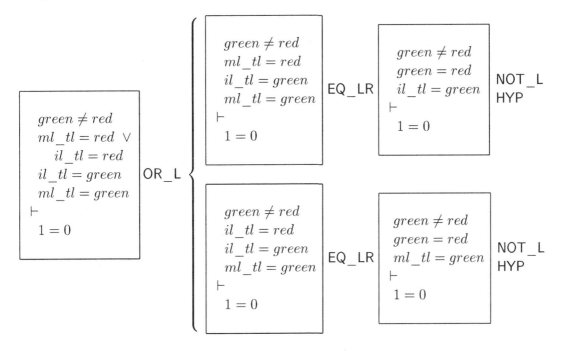

Modifying events ML_tl_green and IL_tl_green This new invariant **inv2_5** has
to be preserved and this is clearly not the case with the new events ML_tl_green and
IL_tl_green we proposed earlier in Section 2.6.3, unless we correct them by turning to
red the other traffic light, yielding:

```
ML_tl_green
    when
        ml_tl = red
        a + b < d
        c = 0
    then
        ml_tl := green
        il_tl := red
    end
```

```
IL_tl_green
    when
        il_tl = red
        0 < b
        a = 0
    then
        il_tl := green
        ml_tl := red
    end
```

Proving that event ML_out preserves invariant inv2_3 When trying to prove
the preservation of invariant **inv2_3** by event ML_out, we are again in trouble. Next

is what we have to prove:

$$
\begin{array}{l|l}
\ldots & \ldots \\
\mathbf{inv2\_3} & ml\_tl = green \Rightarrow a + b < d \ \wedge \ c = 0 \\
\mathbf{inv2\_4} & il\_tl = green \Rightarrow 0 < b \ \wedge \ a = 0 \\
\text{Guard of ML\_out} & ml\_tl = green \\
\vdash & \vdash \\
\text{Modified } \mathbf{inv2\_3} & ml\_tl = green \Rightarrow a + 1 + b < d \ \wedge \ c = 0
\end{array}
\qquad \text{ML\_out / } \mathbf{inv2\_3} \text{ / INV}
$$

Here is the tentative proof (after applying MON):

$$
\begin{array}{l}
ml\_tl = green \Rightarrow a + b < d \ \wedge \ c = 0 \\
\vdash \\
ml\_tl = green \Rightarrow a + 1 + b < d \ \wedge \ c = 0
\end{array}
\quad \text{IMP\_R}
\qquad
\begin{array}{l}
ml\_tl = green \Rightarrow \\
\quad a + b < d \ \wedge \ c = 0 \\
ml\_tl = green \\
\vdash \\
a + 1 + b < d \ \wedge \ c = 0
\end{array}
\quad \text{IMP\_L} \ldots
$$

$$
\ldots \quad
\begin{array}{l}
a + b < d \ \wedge \ c = 0 \\
ml\_tl = green \\
\vdash \\
a + 1 + b < d \ \wedge \ c = 0
\end{array}
\quad \text{AND\_L}
\qquad
\begin{array}{l}
a + b < d \\
c = 0 \\
ml\_tl = green \\
\vdash \\
a + 1 + b < d \ \wedge \ c = 0
\end{array}
\quad \text{AND\_R} \ldots
$$

$$
\ldots \left\{
\begin{array}{l}
\begin{array}{l}
a + b < d \\
c = 0 \\
ml\_tl = green \\
\vdash \\
a + 1 + b < d
\end{array}
\quad ? \\[2em]
\begin{array}{l}
a + b < d \\
c = 0 \\
ml\_tl = green \\
\vdash \\
c = 0
\end{array}
\quad \text{MON}
\qquad
\begin{array}{l}
c = 0 \\
\vdash \\
c = 0
\end{array}
\quad \text{HYP}
\end{array}
\right.
$$

As can be seen, the first of the last two sequents cannot be proved when $a + 1 + b = d$ unless ml_tl is set to red. In fact, when $a + 1 + b = d$, then the entering car is the last one allowed to enter at this stage because more cars would violate requirement FUN-3, which says that there are no more than d cars on the island and on the bridge. This indicates that event ML_out has to be split into two events (both refining their abstraction however) as follows:

ML_out_1
when
  $ml\_tl = green$
  $\underline{a + b + 1 \neq d}$
then
  $a := a + 1$
end

ML_out_2
when
  $ml\_tl = green$
  $\underline{a + b + 1 = d}$
then
  $a := a + 1$
  $\underline{ml\_tl := red}$
end

Proving that event IL_out preserves invariant inv2_4 For similar reasons, invariant **inv2_4** cannot be maintained by event IL_out when b is equal to 1. In this case, the last car is leaving the island. As a consequence, the island traffic light has to turn red. As for event ML_out in the previous section, we have to split event IL_out as follows:

IL_out_1
when
  $il\_tl = green$
  $\underline{b \neq 1}$
then
  $b, c := b - 1, c + 1$
end

IL_out_2
when
  $il\_tl = green$
  $\underline{b = 1}$
then
  $b, c := b - 1, c + 1$
  $\underline{il\_tl := red}$
end

2.6.8 Convergence of new events

We have now to prove that the new events cannot diverge. For this, we must exhibit a certain variant that must be decreased by the new events. In fact, it turns out to be impossible. For instance, when a and c are both equal to 0, meaning that there is no car on the bridge in either direction, then the traffic lights could freely change color for ever as we can figure out by looking at the new events ML_tl_green and IL_tl_green:

```
ML_tl_green
  when
    ml_tl = red
    a + b < d
    c = 0
  then
    ml_tl := green
    il_tl := red
  end
```

```
IL_tl_green
  when
    il_tl = red
    0 < b
    a = 0
  then
    il_tl := green
    ml_tl := red
  end
```

What could then happen is that the light colors are changing so rapidly that the drivers can never pass. We have to make the colors change in a more disciplined way, that is only when a car has passed in the other direction. For this, we introduce two more variables ml_pass and il_pass. Each of them can take two values TRUE or FALSE; they are members of the pre-defined set BOOL made of the two distinct values TRUE and FALSE. When ml_pass is equal to TRUE, it means that one car at least has passed on the bridge going to the island since the mainland traffic light last turned green. And similarly when il_pass is equal to TRUE. These variables are formalized in the following invariants:

```
variables:      ...
                ml_pass,
                il_pass
```

```
inv2_6:    ml_pass ∈ BOOL

inv2_7:    il_pass ∈ BOOL
```

We must now modify events ML_out_1, ML_out_2, IL_out_1, and IL_out_2 to set ml_pass or il_pass to TRUE since a car has passed in the proper direction:

```
ML_out_1
  when
    ml_tl = green
    a + b + 1 ≠ d
  then
    a := a + 1
    ml_pass := TRUE
  end
```

```
ML_out_2
  when
    ml_tl = green
    a + b + 1 = d
  then
    a := a + 1
    ml_tl := red
    ml_pass := TRUE
  end
```

```
IL_out_1
   when
      il_tl = green
      b ≠ 1
   then
      b := b − 1
      c := c + 1
      il_pass := TRUE
   end
```

```
IL_out_2
   when
      il_tl = green
      b = 1
   then
      b := b − 1
      c := c + 1
      il_tl := red
      il_pass := TRUE
   end
```

But we must also modify event ML_tl_green and IL_tl_green to reset ml_pass and il_pass to FALSE and also add in their guards the conditions $il\_pass = \text{TRUE}$ and $ml\_pass = \text{TRUE}$ respectively in order to be sure that indeed a car has passed in the other direction. This yields:

```
ML_tl_green
   when
      ml_tl = red
      a + b < d
      c = 0
      il_pass = TRUE
   then
      ml_tl := green
      il_tl := red
      ml_pass := FALSE
   end
```

```
IL_tl_green
   when
      il_tl = red
      0 < b
      a = 0
      ml_pass = TRUE
   then
      il_tl := green
      ml_tl := red
      il_pass := FALSE
   end
```

Having done all that, we can now state what is to be proved in order to guarantee that there is no divergence of the new events. The variant we can exhibit is:

$$\textbf{variant\_2:} \quad ml\_pass + il\_pass$$

However, this variant is not correct as variables ml_pass and $ilpass$ are not natural number variables but boolean variables. To correct this, we have to transform boolean expressions into numeric expressions. This can be done in a straightforward way by defining the following constants b_2_n, which is a function from the set $BOOL$ to the set $\{0, 1\}$:

constants: ...
                b_2_n

axm2_3: $b\_2\_n \in \text{BOOL} \rightarrow \{0, 1\}$

axm2_4: $b\_2\_n(\text{TRUE}) = 1$

axm2_4: $b\_2\_n(\text{FALSE}) = 0$

The variant can be now properly defined as follows:

variant_2: $b\_2\_n(ml\_pass) + b\_2\_n(il\_pass)$

The sequents to be proved by applying proof obligation rule VAR on events ML_tl_green and IL_tl_green are:

$$ml\_tl = red$$
$$a + b < d$$
$$c = 0$$
$$il\_pass = \text{TRUE}$$
$$\vdash$$
$$b\_2\_n(il\_pass) < b\_2\_n(ml\_pass) + b\_2\_n(il\_pass)$$

$$il\_tl = red$$
$$b > 0$$
$$a = 0$$
$$ml\_pass = \text{TRUE}$$
$$\vdash$$
$$b\_2\_n(ml\_pass) < b\_2\_n(ml\_pass) + b\_2\_n(il\_pass)$$

At this point, we figure out that it cannot be proved unless $ml\_pass = \text{TRUE}$ in the first case (so that $b\_2\_n(ml\_pass)$ is equal to 1) and $il\_pass = \text{TRUE}$ in the second case for a similar reason. This suggests adding the following invariants:

$$\textbf{inv2\_8:} \quad ml\_tl = red \;\Rightarrow\; ml\_pass = \text{TRUE}$$

$$\textbf{inv2\_9:} \quad il\_tl = red \;\Rightarrow\; il\_pass = \text{TRUE}$$

It remains now for us to prove that the two new invariants **inv2_8** and **inv2_9** are indeed preserved by all events. We leave this as an exercise to the reader.

2.6.9 Relative deadlock freedom

It remains now to prove that the relative deadlock freedom proof obligation rule DLF holds. Note that the "relative" deadlock freedom becomes in our example an "absolute" deadlock freedom since we have already proved that the previous abstractions are deadlock-free. The statement to prove is then the disjunction of the various guards with some simplified assumptions (we do not need all invariants):

$$
\begin{array}{l}
d \in \mathbb{N} \\
0 < d \\
ml\_tl \in COLOR \\
il\_tl \in COLOR \\
ml\_pass \in \text{BOOL} \\
il\_pass \in \text{BOOL} \\
a \in \mathbb{N} \\
b \in \mathbb{N} \\
c \in \mathbb{N} \\
ml\_tl = red \Rightarrow ml\_pass = \text{TRUE} \\
il\_tl = red \Rightarrow il\_pass = \text{TRUE} \\
\vdash \\
(ml\_tl = red \,\wedge\, a + b < d \,\wedge\, c = 0 \,\wedge\, ml\_pass = \text{TRUE} \,\wedge\, il\_pass = \text{TRUE}) \;\vee \\
(il\_tl = red \,\wedge\, a = 0 \,\wedge\, b > 0 \,\wedge\, ml\_pass = \text{TRUE} \,\wedge\, il\_pass = \text{TRUE}) \;\vee \\
ml\_tl = green \;\vee \\
il\_tl = green \;\vee \\
a > 0 \;\vee \\
c > 0
\end{array}
$$

DLF

Here is a sketch of the corresponding proof. In this sketch, many intermediate steps have been omitted, this is indicated by the symbol $\rightsquigarrow$, which stands for the missing intermediate steps:

$$
\begin{array}{l}
d \in \mathbb{N} \\
0 < d \\
b \in \mathbb{N} \\
ml\_tl = red \\
il\_tl = red \\
ml\_tl = red \Rightarrow ml\_pass = \text{TRUE} \\
il\_tl = red \Rightarrow il\_pass = \text{TRUE} \\
\vdash \\
(b < d \wedge ml\_pass = \text{TRUE} \wedge \\
\quad il\_pass = 1) \vee \\
(b > 0 \wedge ml\_pass = \text{TRUE} \wedge \\
\quad il\_pass = 1)
\end{array}
\quad \leadsto \quad
\begin{array}{l}
d \in \mathbb{N} \\
0 < d \\
b \in \mathbb{N} \\
ml\_tl = red \\
il\_tl = red \\
ml\_pass = \text{TRUE} \\
il\_pass = \text{TRUE} \\
\vdash \\
(b < d \wedge ml\_pass = \text{TRUE} \wedge \\
\quad il\_pass = \text{TRUE}) \vee \\
(b > 0 \wedge ml\_pass = \text{TRUE} \wedge \\
\quad il\_pass = \text{TRUE})
\end{array}
\quad \leadsto \cdots
$$

$$
\cdots
\begin{array}{l}
0 < d \\
b \in \mathbb{N} \\
\vdash \\
b < d \vee b > 0
\end{array}
\quad \text{OR\_R1} \quad
\begin{array}{l}
0 < d \\
b = 0 \\
\vdash \\
b < d
\end{array}
\quad \text{EQ\_LR} \quad
\boxed{0 < d \vdash 0 < d}
\quad \text{HYP}
$$

2.6.10 Conclusion and summary of the second refinement

During this refinement, we have seen again how the proofs (or rather the failed proof attempts) have helped us correct our mistakes or improve our model. In fact, we discovered four errors, we introduced several additional invariants, we corrected four events, and we introduced two more variables. Here is the final version of this second refinement:

$$
\begin{array}{ll}
\textbf{variables:} & \ldots \\
& ml\_tl \\
& il\_tl \\
& ml\_pass \\
& il\_pass
\end{array}
$$

$$
\begin{array}{ll}
\textbf{inv2\_1:} & ml\_tl \in COLOR \\[6pt]
\textbf{inv2\_2:} & il\_tl \in COLOR \\[6pt]
\textbf{inv2\_3:} & ml\_tl = green \Rightarrow a + b < d \wedge c = 0 \\[6pt]
\textbf{inv2\_4:} & il\_tl = green \Rightarrow 0 < b \wedge a = 0
\end{array}
$$

inv2_5: $ml\_tl = red \lor il\_tl = red$

inv2_6: $ml\_pass \in BOOL$

inv2_7: $il\_pass \in BOOL$

inv2_8: $ml\_tl = red \Rightarrow ml\_pass = TRUE$

inv2_9: $il\_tl = red \Rightarrow il\_pass = TRUE$

variant_2: $b\_2\_n(ml\_pass) + b\_2\_n(il\_pass)$

And here are the events of the second refinement:

```
ML_out_1
   when
      ml_tl = green
      a + b + 1 ≠ d
   then
      a := a + 1
      ml_pass := TRUE
   end
```

```
ML_out_2
   when
      ml_tl = green
      a + b + 1 = d
   then
      a := a + 1
      ml_tl := red
      ml_pass := TRUE
   end
```

```
IL_out_1
   when
      il_tl = green
      b ≠ 1
   then
      b := b − 1
      c := c + 1
      il_pass := TRUE
   end
```

```
IL_out_2
   when
      il_tl = green
      b = 1
   then
      b := b − 1
      c := c + 1
      il_tl := red
      il_pass := TRUE
   end
```

```
ML_in
   when
      0 < c
   then
      c := c − 1
   end
```

```
IL_in
   when
      0 < a
   then
      a := a − 1
      b := b + 1
   end
```

```
ML_tl_green
   when
      ml_tl = red
      a + b < d
      c = 0
      il_pass = TRUE
   then
      ml_tl := green
      il_tl := red
      ml_pass := FALSE
   end
```

```
IL_tl_green
   when
      il_tl = red
      0 < b
      a = 0
      ml_pass = TRUE
   then
      il_tl := green
      ml_tl := red
      il_pass := FALSE
   end
```

2.7 Third refinement: introducing car sensors

2.7.1 Introduction

The sensors In this refinement, we introduce the sensors, which are devices capable of detecting the physical presence of cars entering or leaving the bridge. We remind the reader that such sensors are situated on each side of the road and at both extremities of the bridge. This is indicated in Fig. 2.8.

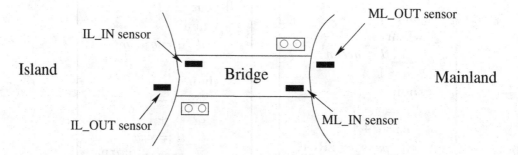

Fig. 2.8. The bridge control equipment

Closed model of the controller and its environment The presence of the sensor must now make clearer the separation between our future *software controller* and its *physical environment*, which was mentioned at the beginning of Section 2.2. This can be sketched as indicated in Fig. 2.9

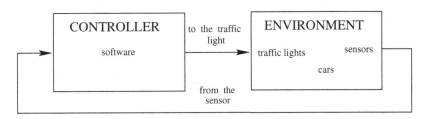

Fig. 2.9. Controller and environment

As can be seen, the software controller is equipped with two sets of *channels*: output channels connecting the controller to the traffic lights and input channels connecting the sensors to the software controller. Our intention is to build now a *closed model* corresponding to a complete mathematical simulation of the pair formed by the software controller and its environment. The reason for building such a model is that we want to be sure that the controller works in perfect harmony with the environment, provided, of course, the latter obeys a number of assumptions which have to be made completely clear (this will be made precise in Section 2.7.2). We would like to review now the variables that help us construct the models of the various constituents of our closed model.

Controller variables The model of the software controller has a number of variables which we have already encountered: variables a, b, and c denoting the number of cars on the bridge (a and c) and on the island (b) and two boolean variables *il_pass* and *ml_pass* which were introduced in the previous section. What is important to understand here is that variables a, b, and c do not correspond exactly to the physical numbers of cars on the bridge and on the island, which we shall introduce in the next sub-section. In fact, the controller is always working with an approximate picture of the environment, but we want to *prove* that, despite this, it is able to control the environment in a correct fashion; this is the heart of the modeling process.

Environment variables The environment is formalized by means of four variables corresponding to the state of the sensors. More precisely, a sensor can be in one of two states: either "on" or "off". It is "on" when a car is on it; "off" otherwise. As a consequence, we shall enlarge our state with four variables corresponding to each sensor state: ML_OUT_SR, ML_IN_SR, IL_OUT_SR, and IL_IN_SR. Notice that we use upper-case letters to name these variables, this is to remind us that they are *physical variables* denoting objects of the real world. We shall also introduce three variables A, B, and C denoting the *physical* number of cars on the bridge going to the island (A), on the island (B), and on the bridge going to the mainland (C).

Output channels Now we have to explain how the controller and the environment communicate. We have already introduced variables ml_tl and il_tl; they correspond to the output channels from the controller to the environment. To simplify matters and as an abstraction, we suppose that the physical traffic lights are also directly represented by these variables. It is an abstraction as we can imagine that there is a (very) slight delay between the controller changing one of these channels color and the real change occurring on the physical traffic light, but we consider the corresponding delay so small that we can take it to be equal to zero.

Input channels It remains now for us to explain how the sensors communicate with the controller. We are not interested in the precise technology used in the sensors, only in their external behavior. As said above, a sensor can be in two different states: either "on" or "off." When the state of a sensor moves from "off" to "on," this means that a car has just been detected as arriving on it: nothing has to be sent to the controller in this case. Note that the state of a sensor can remain "on" for a certain time when the car has to wait because the associated traffic light is red. When the state of a sensor moves from "on" to "off," this means that a car that was on it has just left. In that case, a message has to be sent to the controller. All this is illustrated in Fig. 2.10

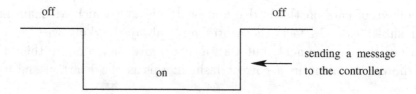

Fig. 2.10. Controller and environment

We thus introduce four input channel variables corresponding to the different sensors: ml_out_10, ml_in_10, il_in_10, and il_out_10.

Summary Here is a summary of the different kinds of variables we have just presented:

Input channels	$ml\_out\_10, ml\_in\_10, il\_in\_10, il\_out\_10$
Controller	$a, b, c, ml\_pass, il\_pass$
Output channels	ml_tl, il_tl
Environment	$A, B, C, ML\_OUT\_SR,$ $ML\_IN\_SR, IL\_OUT\_SR, IL\_IN\_SR$

Fig. 2.11 shows the various categories of variables of our closed system. In principle, the input channel variables are set by the environment and tested by the controller. Likewise, the output channel variables are set by the controller and tested by the environment. But, as we shall explain at the end of Section 2.7.3, in this example there will be an exception to these rules. On the other hand, the controller variables are set and tested by the controller only while the environment variables are set and tested solely by the environment. There is no exception to these rules.

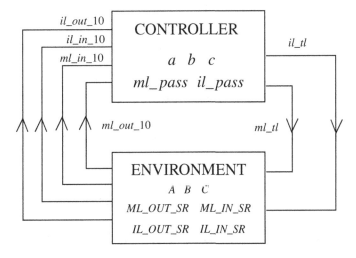

Fig. 2.11. Controller, environment, and their variables

2.7.2 Refining the state

We first introduce an additional carrier set defining the various states ("on" and "off") of a sensor. This is done as follows:

sets: $\quad \ldots, SENSOR$	**axm3_1:** $\quad SENSOR = \{on, off\}$
constants: $\quad \ldots, on, off$	**axm3_2:** $\quad on \neq off$

Here are the new variables together with their basic typing invariants **inv3_1** to **inv3_11**:

inv3_1: $\quad ML\_OUT\_SR \in SENSOR$	**inv3_5:** $\quad A \in \mathbb{N}$
inv3_2: $\quad ML\_IN\_SR \in SENSOR$	**inv3_6:** $\quad B \in \mathbb{N}$
inv3_3: $\quad IL\_OUT\_SR \in SENSOR$	**inv3_7:** $\quad C \in \mathbb{N}$
inv3_4: $\quad IL\_IN\_SR \in SENSOR$	**inv3_8:** $\quad ml\_out\_10 \in BOOL$
	inv3_9: $\quad ml\_in\_10 \in BOOL$
	inv3_10: $\quad il\_out\_10 \in BOOL$
	inv3_11: $\quad il\_in\_10 \in BOOL$

We are now going to state the more interesting invariants concerned with these variables. First, we have an invariant stating that when the sensor IL_IN_SR is *on*, then A is positive. In other words, there is at least one physical car on the bridge, namely the one that sits on the sensor IL_IN_SR. We have similar invariants for IL_OUT_SR and ML_IN_SR, yielding:

inv3_12: $\quad IL\_IN\_SR = on \;\Rightarrow\; A > 0$
inv3_13: $\quad IL\_OUT\_SR = on \;\Rightarrow\; B > 0$
inv3_14: $\quad ML\_IN\_SR = on \;\Rightarrow\; C > 0$

Second, when input channel ml_out_10 is TRUE, it means that a car has just left the sensor ML_OUT_SR. For this to be possible, the mainland traffic light must be green. This invariant formalizes the fact that car drivers obey the traffic light indications. We have a similar case with input channel il_out_10. This is formalized by means of the following two invariants:

> **inv3_15 :** $\quad ml\_out\_10 = \text{TRUE} \;\Rightarrow\; ml\_tl = green$
>
> **inv3_16 :** $\quad il\_out\_10 = \text{TRUE} \;\Rightarrow\; il\_tl = green$

Our next group of invariants is dealing with the relationship between the sensor status and the messages sent to the controller. They say that no message is on an input channel when a car is on the corresponding sensor. Here are these invariants:

> **inv3_17 :** $\quad IL\_IN\_SR = on \;\Rightarrow\; il\_in\_10 = \text{FALSE}$
>
> **inv3_18 :** $\quad IL\_OUT\_SR = on \;\Rightarrow\; il\_out\_10 = \text{FALSE}$
>
> **inv3_19 :** $\quad ML\_IN\_SR = on \;\Rightarrow\; ml\_in\_10 = \text{FALSE}$
>
> **inv3_20 :** $\quad ML\_OUT\_SR = on \;\Rightarrow\; ml\_out\_10 = \text{FALSE}$

These invariants state that when a car is on a sensor, then the previous message coming from that sensor has been treated by the controller. There are two possible interpretations for these invariants:

(A) cars must wait before touching a sensor until the controller is ready;
(B) the controller is fast enough so as to be always ready for the next car.

Obviously, (A) is not acceptable. So, we postulate choice (B). Were this not to hold, then the controller could miss some cars entering or leaving the system. In other words, *this assumption has to be checked when installing the system*. In fact, it corresponds to a requirement which is obviously missing in our requirement document:

The controller must be fast enough so as to be able to treat all the information coming from the environment	FUN-5

Our next series of invariants deals with the relationship that exists between the physical number of cars (A, B, and C) and the corresponding numbers dealt with by the controller (a, b, and c):

$$\textbf{inv3\_21}: \quad il\_in\_10 = \text{TRUE} \land ml\_out\_10 = \text{TRUE} \;\Rightarrow\; A = a$$

$$\textbf{inv3\_22}: \quad il\_in\_10 = \text{FALSE} \land ml\_out\_10 = \text{TRUE} \;\Rightarrow\; A = a + 1$$

$$\textbf{inv3\_23}: \quad il\_in\_10 = \text{TRUE} \land ml\_out\_10 = \text{FALSE} \;\Rightarrow\; A = a - 1$$

$$\textbf{inv3\_24}: \quad il\_in\_10 = \text{FALSE} \land ml\_out\_10 = \text{FALSE} \;\Rightarrow\; A = a$$

These invariants are easy to understand. When, say, $il\_in\_10 = \text{TRUE}$, this means that a car has left the bridge to enter the island, but the controller does not know it yet: thus A is incremented and B in decremented, while a and b are left unchanged. Likewise, when $ml\_out\_10 = \text{TRUE}$, this means that a new car has entered the bridge coming from the mainland, but the controller does not know it yet; thus A is incremented, while a is left unchanged. We have similar invariants dealing with B and b and with C and c as shown below:

$$\textbf{inv3\_25}: \quad il\_in\_10 = \text{TRUE} \land il\_out\_10 = \text{TRUE} \;\Rightarrow\; B = b$$

$$\textbf{inv3\_26}: \quad il\_in\_10 = \text{TRUE} \land il\_out\_10 = \text{FALSE} \;\Rightarrow\; B = b + 1$$

$$\textbf{inv3\_27}: \quad il\_in\_10 = \text{FALSE} \land il\_out\_10 = \text{TRUE} \;\Rightarrow\; B = b - 1$$

$$\textbf{inv3\_28}: \quad il\_in\_10 = \text{FALSE} \land il\_out\_10 = \text{FALSE} \;\Rightarrow\; B = b$$

$$\textbf{inv3\_29}: \quad il\_out\_10 = \text{TRUE} \land ml\_in\_10 = \text{TRUE} \;\Rightarrow\; C = c$$

$$\textbf{inv3\_30}: \quad il\_out\_10 = \text{TRUE} \land ml\_in\_10 = \text{FALSE} \;\Rightarrow\; C = c + 1$$

$$\textbf{inv3\_31}: \quad il\_out\_10 = \text{FALSE} \land ml\_in\_10 = \text{TRUE} \;\Rightarrow\; C = c - 1$$

$$\textbf{inv3\_32}: \quad il\_out\_10 = \text{FALSE} \land ml\_in\_10 = \text{FALSE} \;\Rightarrow\; C = c$$

The last two, and probably most important, invariants in this refinement are the ones which say that the two main properties (one-way bridge and limited number of cars) *hold for the physical number of cars:*

$$\mathbf{inv3\_33}: \quad A = 0 \ \lor \ C = 0$$

$$\mathbf{inv3\_34}: \quad A + B + C \le d$$

In other words, the controller, although working with slightly time-shifted information concerning A, B, and C (the controller bases its decision on a, b, and c), nevertheless maintains the basic properties on the physical numbers of cars A, B, and C.

2.7.3 Refining abstract events in the controller

It is now easy to proceed with the refinement of abstract events. This is done in a straightforward fashion as follows:

ML_out_1
  when
    $ml\_out\_10 = \text{TRUE}$
    $\overline{a + b + 1 \ne d}$
  then
    $a := a + 1$
    $ml\_pass := \text{TRUE}$
    $\overline{ml\_out\_10 := \text{FALSE}}$
  end

ML_out_2
  when
    $ml\_out\_10 = \text{TRUE}$
    $\overline{a + b + 1 = d}$
  then
    $a := a + 1$
    $ml\_tl := red$
    $ml\_pass := \text{TRUE}$
    $\overline{ml\_out\_10 := \text{FALSE}}$
  end

IL_out_1
  when
    $il\_out\_10 = \text{TRUE}$
    $\overline{b \ne 1}$
  then
    $b := b - 1$
    $c := c + 1$
    $il\_pass := \text{TRUE}$
    $\overline{il\_out\_10 :- \text{FALSE}}$
  end

IL_out_2
  when
    $il\_out\_10 = \text{TRUE}$
    $\overline{b = 1}$
  then
    $b := b - 1$
    $c := c + 1$
    $il\_tl := red$
    $il\_pass := \text{TRUE}$
    $\overline{il\_out\_10 := \text{FALSE}}$
  end

Notice that in their abstract versions these events were testing the green status of the corresponding traffic lights. In these refined versions, it is not necessary any more since these events are now triggered by the input channels ml_out_10 or il_out_10, which ensure through invariants **inv3_15** and **inv3_16** that the corresponding lights are green.

ML_in
 when
  $ml\_in\_10 = \text{TRUE}$
  $c > 0$
 then
  $c := c - 1$
  $ml\_in\_10 := \text{FALSE}$
 end

IL_in
 when
  $il\_in\_10 = \text{TRUE}$
  $a > 0$
 then
  $a := a - 1$
  $b := b + 1$
  $il\_in\_10 := \text{FALSE}$
 end

In the six above events, which are triggered by the input channels, we can see that the channels in question are all reset by the events. This is to indicate that the corresponding controller operation has finished. Events xxx_arr in the next section will test such resetting in their guards so as to "allow" another car to occupy the relevant sensor. This interplay is a formal way to express the rapid reaction of the controller, running faster than cars may arrive!

ML_tl_green
 when
  $ml\_tl = red$
  $a + b < d$
  $c = 0$
  $il\_pass = \text{TRUE}$
  $il\_out\_10 = \text{FALSE}$
 then
  $ml\_tl := green$
  $il\_tl := red$
  $ml\_pass := \text{FALSE}$
 end

IL_tl_green
 when
  $il\_tl = red$
  $0 < b$
  $a = 0$
  $ml\_pass = \text{TRUE}$
  $ml\_out\_10 = \text{FALSE}$
 then
  $il\_tl := green$
  $ml\_tl := red$
  $il\_pass := \text{FALSE}$
 end

The new guard $il\_out\_10 = \text{FALSE}$ in event ML_tl_green is indispensable to maintain invariant **inv3_16**: that is:

---

inv3_16 : $il\_out\_10 = \text{TRUE} \;\Rightarrow\; il\_tl = green$

This is so because il_tl is set to *red* in event ML_tl_green. We have a similar guard ($ml\_out\_10 = \text{FALSE}$) in event IL_tl_green; it is necessary in order to maintain invariant **inv3_15**.

It would be possible to add other guards in the two previous events. The idea would be to turn a light to green only if there is a car willing to pass. In order to do so, we would have to make the two sensors, which are situated close to the traffic lights, send additional information when a car is coming on to them. We leave it to the reader to make this extension.

2.7.4 Adding new events in the environment

We now add four new events corresponding to cars arriving on the various sensors:

ML_out_arr
  when
    $ML\_OUT\_SR = off$
    $ml\_out\_10 = \text{FALSE}$
  then
    $ML\_OUT\_SR := on$
  end

ML_in_arr
  when
    $ML\_IN\_SR = off$
    $ml\_in\_10 = \text{FALSE}$
    $C > 0$
  then
    $ML\_IN\_SR := on$
  end

IL_in_arr
  when
    $IL\_IN\_SR = off$
    $il\_in\_10 = \text{FALSE}$
    $A > 0$
  then
    $IL\_IN\_SR := on$
  end

IL_out_arr
  when
    $IL\_OUT\_SR = off$
    $il\_out\_10 = \text{FALSE}$
    $B > 0$
  then
    $IL\_OUT\_SR := on$
  end

In each case, we suppose that the previous message has been treated; the input channels are all tested for FALSE. Moreover, the physical number of cars is tested as expected.

It expresses the fact that the setting to "on" of a sensor is due to the presence of cars. This is compatible with our requirement ENV-5 saying that the sensors are used to detect the presence of a car entering or leaving the bridge. We finally have four events corresponding to a car leaving a sensor:

ML_out_dep
  when
    $ML\_OUT\_SR = on$
    $ml\_tl = green$
  then
    $ML\_OUT\_SR := off$
    $ml\_out\_10 := TRUE$
    $A := A + 1$
  end

ML_in_dep
  when
    $ML\_IN\_SR = on$
  then
    $ML\_IN\_SR := off$
    $ml\_in\_10 := TRUE$
    $C = C - 1$
  end

IL_in_dep
  when
    $IL\_IN\_SR = on$
  then
    $IL\_IN\_SR := off$
    $il\_in\_10 := TRUE$
    $A = A - 1$
    $B = B + 1$
  end

IL_out_dep
  when
    $IL\_OUT\_SR = on$
    $il\_tl = green$
  then
    $IL\_OUT\_SR := off$
    $il\_out\_10 := TRUE$
    $B = B - 1$
    $C = C + 1$
  end

It is important to notice that a car leaving the mainland out-sensor can do so provided the corresponding traffic light is green. Likewise, a car leaving the island out-sensor can do so provided the corresponding traffic light is green. Here we take into account requirement ENV-3 saying that "cars are not supposed to pass on a red traffic light, only on a green one." It is also possible to see that in each case a message is sent to the controller. Finally, the physical number of cars are modified as expected; we simulate what happens in the environment.

2.7.5 Convergence of the new events

We have to exhibit a variant which is decreased by all new events. Here it is:

variant_3: $12 - (ML\_OUT\_SR + ML\_IN\_SR + IL\_OUT\_SR$
$+ IL\_IN\_SR +$
$2 * (ml\_out\_10 + ml\_in\_10 + il\_out\_10 + il\_in\_10))$

Notice that, as for **variant_2**, the previous variant is not correct. we have to convert the boolean or sensor expressions to numerical expressions. We leave this to the reader.

2.7.6 No deadlock

We leave it to the reader to prove that this third refinement does not deadlock.

3

A mechanical press controller

In this chapter, we develop the controller of another complete example: a mechanical press. The intention is to show how this can be done in a systematic fashion in order to obtain the correct final code. In Section 1, we present an informal description of this system. In Section 2, we develop two general patterns that we shall subsequently use. The development of these patterns will be made by using the proofs as a mean of discovering the invariants and the guards of the events. In Section 3, we define the requirement document in a more precise fashion by using the terminology developed in the definition of the patterns. The main development of the mechanical press will take place in further sections where more design patterns will be presented.

3.1 Informal description

3.1.1 Basic equipment

A mechanical press is essentially made of the following pieces of equipment:

- a *vertical slide*, which is either stopped or moving up and down very rapidly;
- an *electrical rotating motor*, which can be stopped or working;
- a *connecting rod*, which transmits the movement of the electrical motor to that of the slide;
- a *clutch*, which allows to engage or disengage the motor on the connecting rod.

This is illustrated in Fig. 3.1.

3.1.2 Basic commands and buttons

The following *commands* can be performed by means of buttons named respectively B1, B2, B3, and B4.

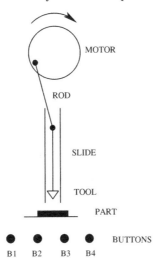

Fig. 3.1. Schematic view of the press

Command 1 Start motor (this is performed by depressing button B1).
Command 2 Stop motor (this is performed by depressing button B2).
Command 3 Engage clutch (this is performed by depressing button B3).
Command 4 Disengage clutch (this is performed by depressing button B4).

3.1.3 Basic user action

The following *actions* can be performed by the user (it is clearly better to do so when the vertical slide has stopped!).

Action 1 Change the tool at the lower extremity of the vertical slide.
Action 2 Put a part to be treated by the press at a specific place under the slide.
Action 3 Remove the part that has been treated by the press.

The very first schematic structure of the system could be thought of as being the one shown in Fig. 3.2.

Fig. 3.2. First schematic view of the system

3.1.4 *User session*

A typical *user session* is the following (we suppose that, *initially*, the motor is stopped and the clutch is disengaged):

1. Start motor (*Command* 1).
2. Change tool (*Action* 1).
3. Put a part (*Action* 2).
4. Engage the clutch (*Command* 3); the press now works.
5. Disengage the clutch (*Command* 4); the press is stopped.
6. Remove the part (*Action* 3).
7. Repeat zero or more times items 3 to 6.
8. Repeat zero or more times items 2 to 7.
9. Stop motor (*Command* 2).

As can be seen, the philosophy of this mechanical press is that it can work without stopping the motor.

3.1.5 *Danger: necessity of a controller*

Clearly, Action 1 (change the tool), Action 2 (put a part), and Action 3 (remove a part) are dangerous because the user has to manipulate objects (tools, parts) in places which are just situated below the vertical slide. *Normally*, this slide should not move while doing such actions because the clutch must have been disengaged. However, the user could have forgotten to do so or a malfunction could have caused it not to happen. As a consequence, a *controller* is placed between the commands and the equipment in order to make sure that things are working properly. In order to prevent malfunctions, the equipment is also reporting its own status to the controller. All this results in the second, more precise, system structure shown in Fig. 3.3.

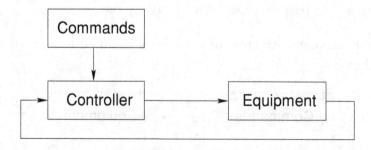

Fig. 3.3. Second schematic view of the system

3.1.6 The door

Placing a controller between the commands and the equipment is certainly not sufficient: we have also to make these commands more sophisticated *in order to protect the user*. In fact, the key is clearly the two commands for engaging and disengaging the clutch. For this, a *door* is put in front of the press. This is illustrated in Fig. 3.4.

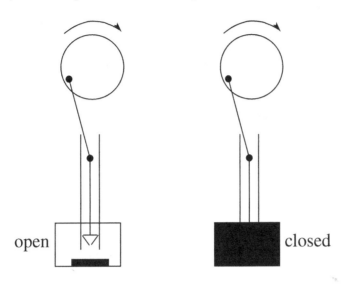

Fig. 3.4. The door

Initially, the door is open. When the user depresses button B3 to engage the clutch, then the door is first closed *before* engaging the clutch, and when the user depresses button B4 to disengage the clutch, then the door is opened *after* disengaging the clutch.

3.2 Design patterns

In this example, there are many cases where a user can depress a button, which is eventually followed by a certain reaction of the system. For example buttons B1 and B2 have an eventual action on the motor. This is not a direct action however. In other words, there is no direct connection between these buttons and the motor. Direct actions on the motor are initiated by the controller, which sends commands after receiving some information coming from buttons B1 or B2.

For example, when the motor does not work, the effect of depressing button B1 is to eventually have the motor working. Likewise, when the motor is working, the effect of depressing button B2 is that the motor will eventually stop. Note that when the user depresses such a button, say button B1, and releases it very quickly, it might be the case that nothing happen simply because the controller has not got enough time to figure out that this button was depressed.

Another interesting case is the one where the user depresses button B1 and keeps on depressing it by not removing his finger. Once the motor starts working, the user depresses button B2 with another finger. This results in the motor eventually stopping. But the fact that now button B1 is still depressed must not have any effect, the motor must not restart. This is due to the fact that any button must be first released in order to be taken into account once again.

A more complicated case corresponds to the following sequence of actions as indicated in Fig. 3.5:

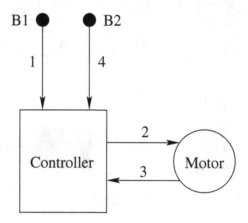

Fig. 3.5. Race conditions between 3 and 4

(1) the user depresses button B1 (starting motor) and, not too quickly, releases it;
(2) the controller responds to this depressing of button B1 by sending the start command to the motor;
(3) the motor sends back to the controller information informing that it has started working;
(4) the user depresses button B2 (stopping motor) and, not too quickly, releases it.

The difficulty is that actions (3) and (4) are done in parallel by the motor and by the user. Both these actions have to be taken into account by the controller. If action (3) (feedback from the motor) wins, then action (4) (depressing the stop button) is followed by a controller reaction, whose purpose is to send to the motor the stop command. But if action (4) wins, then the reaction of the controller cannot be performed as the controller does not know yet whether the motor is working since it has not received the corresponding information from the motor. In that case, depressing button B2 is not taken into account.

What we would like to do in this section is to have a *formal general study* of such cases. This will allow us to have a very systematic approach to the construction of our mechanical press reactive system in further sections.

3.2.1 Action and reaction

The general paradigm in what we mentioned in the previous section is that of *actions* and *reactions*. Actions and reactions can be illustrated as shown in Fig. 3.6. We have an action, named a and represented by the plain line, followed by a reaction, named r and represented by the dashed line. Action and reaction can take two values: 0 or 1. We note that r, the reaction, always takes place *after a*, the action. In other words, r goes up (1) after a has gone up (1). Likewise, r goes down (0) after a has gone down (0).

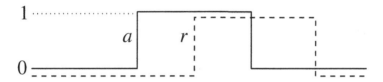

Fig. 3.6. Action and reaction

3.2.2 First case: a simple action and reaction pattern without retro-action

Introduction This first case corresponds to two possible scenarios. In the first one, it is possible that a goes up and down several times, while r is not able to react so quickly; it stays down all the time. This is indicated in Fig. 3.7.

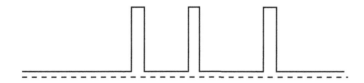

Fig. 3.7. Action and weak reaction (case 1)

As a second similar scenario, it is possible that once r has gone up, then a goes down and then up again very quickly, so that r comes down only after a has gone down several times. This is indicated in Fig. 3.8.

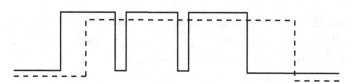

Fig. 3.8. Action and weak reaction (case 2)

When the behavior of an action–reaction system corresponds to what we have just described, it is said that we have a *weak synchronization* between the action and the reaction.

Modeling These two cases will be handled by the same model. Besides variables a and r denoting the state of the action and reaction (invariant **pat0_1** and **pat0_2** below), we introduce two counters: the first one is named ca and is associated with a and the second one is named cr and is associated with r (invariant **pat0_3** and **pat0_4** below). These counters denote the number of times each action and reaction respectively have gone up. The role of these counters is precisely to formalize the concept of a weak reaction. This is done in the main invariant, **pat0_5**, which says that cr is never greater than ca.

Note that these counters will not be present in our final definition of the patterns; they are there just *to make precise the constraint of the pattern*. For that reason, variables ca and cr will not be allowed in the guards of events; they will be present in event actions only:

variables:	a
	r
	ca
	cr

pat0_1:	$a \in \{0,1\}$
pat0_2:	$r \in \{0,1\}$
pat0_3:	$ca \in \mathbb{N}$
pat0_4:	$cr \in \mathbb{N}$
pat0_5:	$cr \leq ca$

Initially, no action and reaction have taken place (event init below). Events a_on and a_off correspond to the action a. As can be seen, these events are not constrained by the reaction:

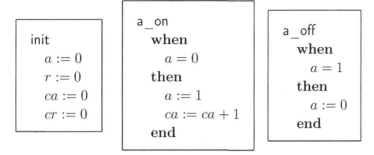

This is not the case for r_on and r_off corresponding to the reaction r. These events are synchronized with some occurrences of events a_on and a_off. This is due to the presence of the guards $a = 1$ and $a = 0$ in the guards of events r_on and r_off.

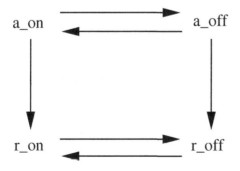

The weak synchronization of action and reaction is illustrated in Fig. 3.9. In this figure, the arrows simply express that the occurrence of an event relies on the previous occurrences of some others. For example, the occurrence of event r_on depends on that of event a_on and on that of event r_off. Note that these arrows have to be understood informally only.

Fig. 3.9. Weak synschronization of the events

Proofs The proofs of invariant preservation are straightforward. Unfortunately, one of them fails. This is the proof of the preservation of invariant **pat0_5** by event r_on: that is, r_on/**pat0_5**/INV.

$$
\begin{array}{l}
\text{r\_on} \\
\quad \textbf{when} \\
\qquad r = 0 \\
\qquad a = 1 \\
\quad \textbf{then} \\
\qquad r := 1 \\
\qquad cr := cr + 1 \\
\quad \textbf{end}
\end{array}
$$

We have to prove the following (after some simplifications):

Invariant **pat0_5**	$cr \leq ca$
Guards of	$r = 0$
event r_on	$a = 1$
$\vdash$	$\vdash$
Modified invariant **pat0_5**	$cr + 1 \leq ca$

We could solve the difficulty by adding the predicate $cr < ca$ in the guard of event r_on. This is certainly the most economical solution, as it does not affect the rest of the model. But, as was pointed out earlier, we do not want to incorporate counter variables in event guards. This suggests the following implicative invariant:

$$a = 1 \;\Rightarrow\; cr < ca,$$

which is clearly preserved by event a_on, which simultaneously sets a to 1 and increments ca, also trivially by events a_off (setting a to 0 and keeping cr and ca untouched) and r_off (keeping a, cr, and ca untouched). But, unfortunately, this invariant is not preserved, again by event r_on. In this case, we have to prove:

New proposed invariant	$a = 1 \;\Rightarrow\; cr < ca$
Guards of	$r = 0$
event r_on	$a = 1$
$\vdash$	$\vdash$
Modified proposed invariant	$a = 1 \;\Rightarrow\; cr + 1 < ca$

This can be simplified to:

$$cr < ca$$
$$r = 0$$
$$a = 1$$
$$\vdash$$
$$cr + 1 < ca.$$

This shows that our first proposed invariant, $a = 1 \Rightarrow cr < ca$ was not strong enough. The reader could also convince himself that the invariant $r = 0 \Rightarrow cr < ca$, would not be sufficient either. Thus, we have to also suppose that $r = 0$ holds. This leads to the following new invariant:

$$\boxed{\quad \textbf{pat0\_6:} \qquad a = 1 \;\wedge\; r = 0 \;\Rightarrow\; cr < ca \quad}$$

Invariant **pat0_6**	$a = 1 \wedge r = 0 \Rightarrow cr < ca$
Guards of	$r = 0$
event r_on	$a = 1$
$\vdash$	$\vdash$
Modified invariant **pat0_6**	$a = 1 \wedge 1 = 0 \Rightarrow cr + 1 < ca.$

This simplifies to the following, which holds trivially since there is a false assumption, namely $1 = 0$:

$$cr < ca$$
$$r = 0$$
$$a = 1$$
$$1 = 0$$
$$\vdash$$
$$cr + 1 < ca$$

3.2.3 Second case: a simple action pattern with a retro-acting reaction

Introduction In this section, we refine the previous model by imposing now that the situations illustrated in Figs. 3.8 and 3.7 are not possible. We now have a *strong synchronization* between the action and the reaction. The only well-synchronized possibilities are those indicated in Fig. 3.10.

Modeling We have exactly the same variables as in the previous case, with an additional invariant stipulating that ca cannot exceed cr by more than one. In other words,

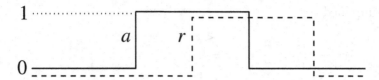

Fig. 3.10. Action and strong reaction

either ca and cr are equal or ca is equal to $cr + 1$. This yields:

$$\boxed{\textbf{pat1\_1:} \qquad ca \leq cr + 1}$$

Proofs To begin with, since we do not know how to modify the events, we do not modify them at all. The idea again is that the failure of some proofs will give us some clues on how to improve the situation. In fact, all proofs succeed except one. Event a_on cannot maintain the new invariant **pat1_1**:

$$
\begin{array}{l}
\text{a\_on} \\
\quad \textbf{when} \\
\qquad a = 0 \\
\quad \textbf{then} \\
\qquad a := 1 \\
\qquad ca := ca + 1 \\
\quad \textbf{end}
\end{array}
$$

After some simplifications, we have to prove:

$$
\begin{array}{ll}
\text{Invariant } \textbf{pat0\_5} & cr \leq ca \\
\text{Invariant } \textbf{pat1\_1} & ca \leq cr + 1 \\
\text{Guard of a\_on} & a = 0 \\
\vdash & \vdash \\
\text{Modified invariant } \textbf{pat1\_1} & ca + 1 \leq cr + 1:
\end{array}
$$

that is:

$$
\begin{array}{l}
cr \leq ca \\
ca \leq cr + 1 \\
a = 0 \\
\vdash \\
ca \leq cr.
\end{array}
$$

The impossibility of proving this statement suggests the following invariant since ca cannot be strictly smaller than cr because of invariant **pat0_5** ($cr \leq ca$):

$$\boxed{\textbf{pat1\_2:} \qquad a = 0 \;\Rightarrow\; ca = cr}$$

Unfortunately, this time event a_off cannot preserve this invariant.

$$\boxed{\begin{array}{l} \textsf{a\_off} \\ \quad \textbf{when} \\ \qquad a = 1 \\ \quad \textbf{then} \\ \qquad a := 0 \\ \quad \textbf{end} \end{array}}$$

After some simplification, we are left to prove:

$$\begin{array}{ll} \text{Guards of a\_off} & a = 1 \\ \vdash & \vdash \\ \text{Modified invariant } \textbf{pat1\_2} & 0 = 0 \;\Rightarrow\; ca = cr. \end{array}$$

Note that we already have the following (this is **pat0_6**):

$$a = 1 \;\wedge\; r = 0 \;\Rightarrow\; cr < ca.$$

This suggests trying the following invariant:

$$\boxed{\textbf{pat1\_3:} \qquad a = 1 \;\wedge\; r = 1 \;\Rightarrow\; ca = cr}$$

But, unfortunately, we have no guarantee that $r = 1$ when we are using event a_off, *unless*, of course, we add $r = 1$ as a new guard for event a_off. We thus try to refine a_off by strengthening its guard as follows:

$$
\boxed{\begin{array}{l}
\textsf{a\_off} \\
\quad \textbf{when} \\
\qquad a = 1 \\
\qquad r = 1 \\
\quad \textbf{then} \\
\qquad a := 0 \\
\quad \textbf{end}
\end{array}}
$$

Unfortunately, this time we have a problem with a_on:

$$
\boxed{\begin{array}{l}
\textsf{a\_on} \\
\quad \textbf{when} \\
\qquad a = 0 \\
\quad \textbf{then} \\
\qquad a := 1 \\
\qquad ca := ca + 1 \\
\quad \textbf{end}
\end{array}}
$$

The preservation of the proposed invariant **pat1_3** leads to the following to prove:

Invariant **pat1_2**	$a = 0 \;\Rightarrow\; ca = cr$
Guards of a_on	$a = 0$
$\vdash$	$\vdash$
Modified invariant **pat1_3**	$1 = 1 \;\wedge\; r = 1 \;\Rightarrow\; ca + 1 = cr$

This can be simplified to:

$$
\begin{array}{l}
ca = cr \\
a = 0 \\
r = 1 \\
\vdash \\
ca + 1 = cr
\end{array}
$$

The only possibility of proving this is to have an additional guard in a_on in order to obtain a contradiction. The natural one is thus $r = 0$ (it will contradict $r = 1$). We thus refine a_on by strengthening its guard as follows:

```
a_on
    when
        a = 0
        r = 0
    then
        a := 1
        ca := ca + 1
    end
```

And now we discover that *all invariant preservation proofs succeed*. Notice that we can put the two invariants **pat1_2** and **pat1_3** together:

$$\textbf{pat1\_2:} \quad a = 0 \ \Rightarrow \ ca = cr$$

$$\textbf{pat1\_3:} \quad a = 1 \ \wedge \ r = 1 \ \Rightarrow \ ca = cr$$

This leads to the following invariant, which can replace the two previous ones:

$$\textbf{pat1\_4:} \quad a = 0 \ \vee \ r = 1 \ \Rightarrow \ ca = cr$$

It is very instructive to put invariant **pat0_6** next to this one:

$$\textbf{pat0\_6:} \quad a = 1 \ \wedge \ r = 0 \ \Rightarrow \ cr < ca$$

As can be seen, the antecedent of **pat0_6** is the negation of that of **pat1_4**. And now we can see from Fig. 3.11 the places where these invariants hold.

To summarize, here are the events for this strong synchronization case. We have removed the counters which were present just to formalize the relationship between

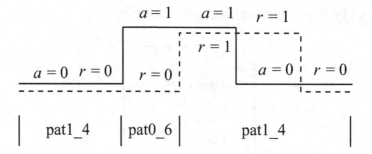

Fig. 3.11. Showing where the invariants hold

the events:

a_on	a_off	r_on	r_off
when	**when**	**when**	**when**
$a = 0$	$a = 1$	$r = 0$	$r = 1$
$r = 0$	$r = 1$	$a = 1$	$a = 0$
then	**then**	**then**	**then**
$a := 1$	$a := 0$	$r := 1$	$r := 0$
end	**end**	**end**	**end**

The strong synchronization is illustrated in Fig. 3.12.

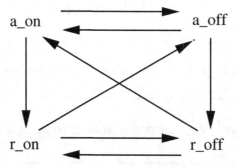

Fig. 3.12. Strong synchronization

3.3 Requirements of the mechanical press

In view of what we have seen above, we now can clearly present the requirements of our mechanical press. We first have three requirements defining the equipment

The system has got the following pieces of equipment: a motor, a clutch, and a door	EQP_1

Four buttons are used to start and stop the motor, and engage and disengage the clutch	EQP_2

A controller is supposed to manage these equipment	EQP_3

Then we present the ways the equipment is connected to the controller:

Buttons and controller are weakly synchronized	FUN_1

Controller and equipment are strongly synchronized	FUN_2

Next are the two main safety requirements of the system:

When the clutch is engaged, the motor must work	SAF_1

When the clutch is engaged, the door must be closed	SAF_2

Finally, more constraints are put in place between the clutch and the door:

When the clutch is disengaged, the door cannot be closed several times, ONLY ONCE	FUN_3

When the door is closed, the clutch cannot be disengaged several times, ONLY ONCE	FUN_4

Opening and closing the door is not independent. It must be synchronized with disengaging and engaging the clutch	FUN_5

The overall structure of the system is presented in Fig. 3.13.

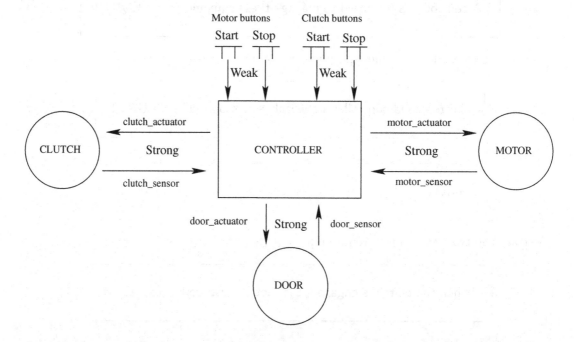

Fig. 3.13. The press controller

3.4 Refinement strategy

In the following sections, we are going to develop the design of the mechanical press according to the following strategy:

- Initial model: connecting the controller to the motor.
- 1st refinement: connecting the motor button to the controller.

- 2nd refinement: connecting the controller to the clutch.
- 3rd refinement: constraining the clutch and the motor.
- 4th refinement: connecting the controller to the door.
- 5th refinement: constraining the clutch and the door.
- 6th refinement: more constraints between the clutch and the door.
- 7th refinement: connecting the clutch button to the controller.

In each case, we are going to do so by instantiating some design patterns.

3.5 Initial model: connecting the controller to the motor

3.5.1 Introduction

This initial model formalizes the connection of the controller to the motor as illustrated in Fig. 3.14

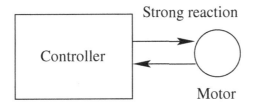

Fig. 3.14. Connecting the controller to the motor

We take partially into account requirement FUN_2:

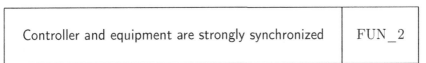

3.5.2 Modeling

We first define a context with the set $STATUS$ defining the two different statuses of the motor: *stopped* or *working*:

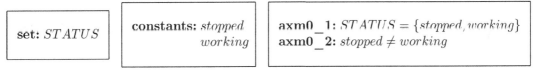

Then we define two variables corresponding to the connection of the motor to the controller: *motor_actuator* and *motor_sensor*. Variable *motor actuator* formalizes the connection of the controller to the motor. It corresponds to the command sent by the controller, either to start or to stop the motor. The variable *motor_sensor*

formalizes the connection of the motor to the controller. It corresponds to the feedback sent by the motor concerning its *physical status*:

variables: $motor\_actuator$	**inv0_1:** $motor\_sensor \in STATUS$
$motor\_sensor$	**inv0_2:** $motor\_actuator \in STATUS$

In this connection, the controller acts as an *action*, whereas the motor acts as a *reaction*. As we know, the reaction of the motor is strongly synchronized to the action of the controller. The idea then is to use the corresponding pattern (Section 3.2.3) by *instantiating* it to the problem at hand. More precisely, we are going to instantiate the strong pattern as follows:

$$
\begin{array}{lll}
a & \rightsquigarrow & motor\_actuator \\
r & \rightsquigarrow & motor\_sensor \\
0 & \rightsquigarrow & stopped \\
1 & \rightsquigarrow & working \\
a\_on & \rightsquigarrow & treat\_start\_motor \\
a\_off & \rightsquigarrow & treat\_stop\_motor \\
r\_on & \rightsquigarrow & Motor\_start \\
r\_off & \rightsquigarrow & Motor\_stop
\end{array}
$$

This leads first to the following events, which are supposed to represent the action of the controller:

```
a_on
  when
    a = 0
    r = 0
  then
    a := 1
  end
```

```
treat_start_motor
  when
    motor_actuator = stopped
    motor_sensor = stopped
  then
    motor_actuator := working
  end
```

```
a_off
  when
    a = 1
    r = 1
  then
    a := 0
  end
```

```
treat_stop_motor
  when
    motor_actuator = working
    motor_sensor = working
  then
    motor_actuator := stopped
  end
```

In this section and in the rest of this chapter, we shall follow the convention that the names of the events pertaining to the controller all start with the prefix "**treat-**". On the other hand, events the names of which do not start with the prefix "**treat-**" are physical events occurring in the environment.

The following events are supposed to represent the physical reaction of the motor:

```
r_on
   when
      r = 0
      a = 1
   then
      r := 1
   end
```

```
Motor_start
   when
      motor_sensor = stopped
      motor_actuator = working
   then
      motor_sensor := working
   end
```

```
r_off
   when
      r = 1
      a = 0
   then
      r := 0
   end
```

```
Motor_stop
   when
      motor_sensor = working
      motor_actuator = stopped
   then
      motor_sensor := stopped
   end
```

3.5.3 Summary of the events

- Environment

    motor_start
    motor_stop

- Controller

    treat_start_motor
    treat_stop_motor

3.6 First refinement: connecting the motor buttons to the controller

3.6.1 Introduction

We now extend the connection introduced in the previous section by connecting the motor buttons B1 (start motor) and B2 (stop motor) to the controller. This corresponds to Fig. 3.15

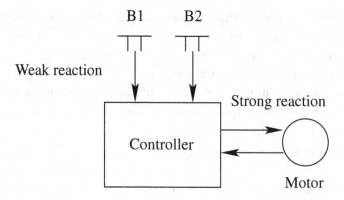

Fig. 3.15. Connecting the motor buttons to the controller

We take partially into account requirement FUN_1:

Buttons and controller are weakly synchronized	FUN_1

3.6.2 Modeling

We define two boolean variables corresponding to the connection of the motor buttons B1 and B2 to the controller: *start_motor_button* and *stop_motor_button*. These physical variables denote the status of buttons B1 and B2 respectively: when equal to TRUE, it means that the corresponding button is physically depressed; when equal to FALSE, it means that it is physically released.

We define two more boolean variables: this the time controller variables: *start_motor_impulse* and *stop_motor_impulse*. These variables denote the *knowledge* by the controller of the physical status of the buttons. They are clearly distinct from the two previous variables, as the change of the physical status of a button occurs *before* the controller can be aware of it:

variables: ... *start_motor_button* *stop_motor_button* *start_motor_impulse* *stop_motor_impulse*	**inv1_1:** *stop_motor_button* ∈ BOOL **inv1_2:** *start_motor_button* ∈ BOOL **inv1_3:** *stop_motor_impulse* ∈ BOOL **inv1_4:** *start_motor_impulse* ∈ BOOL

As we know, the controller weakly reacts to the buttons: it means that the buttons can be sometimes quickly depressed and released without the controller reacting to it: the behavior is clearly an instantiation of the weak reaction pattern we studied in Section 3.2.2. Thus, we are going to instantiate the weak pattern as follows:

a_on	⤳	push_start_motor_button
a_off	⤳	release_start_motor_button
r_on	⤳	treat_start_motor
r_off	⤳	treat_release_start_motor_button
a	⤳	*start_motor_button*
r	⤳	*start_motor_impulse*
0	⤳	FALSE
1	⤳	TRUE

Here are the first two events:

<table>
<tr><td>

a_on
  when
    $a = 0$
  then
    $a := 1$
  end

</td><td>

push_start_motor_button
  when
    start_motor_button = FALSE
  then
    start_motor_button := TRUE
  end

</td></tr>
</table>

<table>
<tr><td>

a_off
  when
    $a = 1$
  then
    $a := 0$
  end

</td><td>

release_start_motor_button
  when
    start_motor_button = TRUE
  then
    start_motor_button := FALSE
  end

</td></tr>
</table>

Here are the two other events. As can be seen, the event **treat_start_motor**, which used to be the instantiation of an *action* in the initial model, is now the instantiation of a *reaction.* It is renamed below treat_push_start_motor_button:

<table>
<tr>
<td>

r_on

when
  $r = 0$
  $a = 1$

then
  $r := 1$

end

</td>
<td>

treat_push_start_motor_button
  refines
    treat_start_motor
  when
    $start\_motor\_impulse = \text{FALSE}$
    $start\_motor\_button = \text{TRUE}$
    $motor\_actuator = stopped$
    $motor\_sensor = stopped$
  then
    $start\_motor\_impulse := \text{TRUE}$
    $motor\_actuator := working$
  end

</td>
</tr>
</table>

<table>
<tr>
<td>

r_off
  when
    $r = 1$
    $a = 0$
  then
    $r := 0$
  end

</td>
<td>

treat_release_start_motor_button
  when
    $start\_motor\_impulse = \text{TRUE}$
    $start\_motor\_button = \text{FALSE}$
  then
    $start\_motor\_impulse := \text{FALSE}$
  end

</td>
</tr>
</table>

In order to understand what is happening here, let us show again the abstract event treat_start_motor:

<table>
<tr>
<td>

treat_start_motor
  when
    $motor\_actuator = stopped$
    $motor\_sensor = stopped$
  then
    $motor\_actuator := working$
  end

</td>
</tr>
</table>

We can see how the new pattern is *superposed* on the previous one:

> treat_push_start_motor_button
> > **refines**
> > > treat_start_motor
> >
> > **when**
> > > $\underline{start\_motor\_impulse = \text{FALSE}}$
> > > $\underline{start\_motor\_button = \text{TRUE}}$
> > > $motor\_actuator = stopped$
> > > $motor\_sensor = stopped$
> >
> > **then**
> > > $\underline{start\_motor\_impulse := \text{TRUE}}$
> > > $motor\_actuator := working$
> >
> > **end**

The guard of the concrete version of event treat_push_start_motor_button is made stronger and the action is enlarged: the new version of this event is indeed a refinement of the previous one. But, at the same time, the new version of this event is also *a refinement of the pattern* (up to renaming).

We now instantiate the weak pattern as follows:

a_on	$\rightsquigarrow$	push_stop_motor_button
a_off	$\rightsquigarrow$	release_stop_motor_button
r_on	$\rightsquigarrow$	treat_stop_motor
r_off	$\rightsquigarrow$	treat_release_stop_motor_button
a	$\rightsquigarrow$	$stop\_motor\_button$
r	$\rightsquigarrow$	$stop\_motor\_impulse$
0	$\rightsquigarrow$	FALSE
1	$\rightsquigarrow$	TRUE

Once again, we can see that the event treat_stop_motor, which used to be the instantiation of an action in the initial model, is now the instantiation of a reaction. It is renamed treat_push_stop_motor_button:

> a_on
> > **when**
> > > $a = 0$
> >
> > **then**
> > > $a := 1$
> >
> > **end**

> push_stop_motor_button
> > **when**
> > > $stop\_motor\_button = \text{FALSE}$
> >
> > **then**
> > > $stop\_motor\_button := \text{TRUE}$
> >
> > **end**

```
a_off
   when
      a = 1
   then
      a := 0
   end
```

```
release_stop_motor_button
   when
      stop_motor_button = TRUE
   then
      stop_motor_button := FALSE
   end
```

```
r_on



   when
      r = 0
      a = 1



   then
      r := 1

   end
```

```
treat_push_stop_motor_button
   refines
      treat_stop_motor
   when
      stop_motor_impulse = FALSE
      stop_motor_button = TRUE
      motor_sensor = working
      motor_actuator = working
   then
      stop_motor_impulse := TRUE
      motor_actuator := stopped
   end
```

```
r_off
   when
      r = 1
      a = 0
   then
      r := 0
   end
```

```
treat_release_stop_motor_button
   when
      stop_motor_impulse = TRUE
      stop_motor_button = FALSE
   then
      stop_motor_impulse := FALSE
   end
```

In Fig. 3.16, you can see a combined synchronization of the various events.

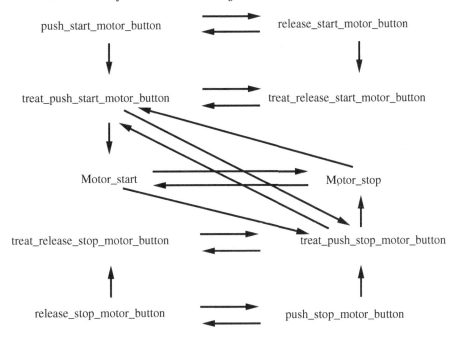

Fig. 3.16. Combined synchronizations

3.6.3 Adding "false" events

The problem we tackle now has to do with the superposition of a pattern on an existing event. A typical example is the following event:

```
treat_push_start_motor_button
  refines
    treat_start_motor
  when
    start_motor_impulse = FALSE
    start_motor_button = TRUE
    motor_actuator = stopped
    motor_sensor = stopped
  then
    start_motor_impulse := TRUE
    motor_actuator := working
  end
```

In case the following condition is false:

$$motor\_actuator = stopped \land motor\_sensor = stopped$$

while the following condition is true:

$$start\_motor\_impulse = \text{FALSE} \land start\_motor\_button = \text{TRUE};$$

then the event cannot be "executed", but nevertheless the button has been depressed so that the assignment:

$$start\_motor\_impulse := \text{TRUE}$$

must be "executed". As a consequence, it is necessary to define the following additional event:

```
treat_push_start_motor_button_false
  when
    start_motor_impulse = FALSE
    start_motor_button = TRUE
    ¬ (motor_actuator = stopped ∧
        motor_sensor = stopped)
  then
    start_motor_impulse := TRUE
  end
```

In what follows, we shall encounter similar cases for all buttons.

3.6.4 Summary of the events

- Environment

    motor_start
    motor_stop
    push_start_motor_button
    release_start_motor_button
    push_stop_motor_button
    release_stop_motor_button

- Controller

    treat_push_start_motor_button
    treat_push_start_motor_button_false
    treat_push_stop_motor_button
    treat_push_stop_motor_button_false
    treat_release_start_motor_button
    treat_release_stop_motor_button

3.7 Second refinement: connecting the controller to the clutch

We now connect the controller to the clutch. As it follows exactly the same approach as the one we have already used for the connection of the controller to the motor in Section 3.6, we simply copy (after renaming "motor" to "clutch") what has been done in the initial model.

3.7.1 Summary of the events

- Environment

  motor_start
  motor_stop
  clutch_start
  clutch_stop
  push_start_motor_button
  release_start_motor_button
  push_stop_motor_button
  release_stop_motor_button

- Controller

  treat_push_start_motor_button
  treat_push_start_motor_button_false
  treat_push_stop_motor_button
  treat_push_stop_motor_button_false
  treat_release_start_motor_button
  treat_release_stop_motor_button
  treat_start_clutch
  treat_stop_clutch

3.8 Another design pattern: weak synchronization of two strong reactions

Our next step in designing the mechanical press is to take account of the following additional safety constraint:

When the clutch is engaged, the motor must work	SAF_1

It means that engaging the clutch is not independent of the starting of the motor as was the case in the previous refinement, where we had two completely independent strongly synchronized connections: that of the motor and that of the clutch. To study this in general, we now consider another design pattern.

3.8.1 Introduction

In this design pattern, we have two strongly synchronized patterns as indicated in Fig. 3.17, where in each case the arrows indicate the strong synchronization at work. Note that the first action and reaction are called a and r as before, whereas the second ones are called b and s.

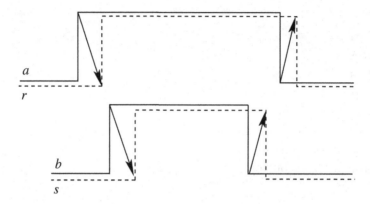

Fig. 3.17. Two strongly synchronized action-reactions

We would like now to synchronize these actions and reactions so that the second reaction, s, only occurs when the first one, r, is enabled. In other words, we would like to ensure the following: $s = 1 \Rightarrow r = 1$.

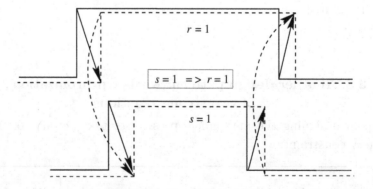

Fig. 3.18. Synchronizing two strongly synchronized action–reactions

This is illustrated in Fig. 3.18, where the dashed arrows indicate this new synchronization. But this synchronization between the two is supposed to be weak only. For

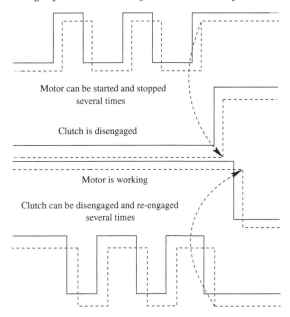

Fig. 3.19. Weak synchronization of the motor and the clutch

example, in our case, it is possible that the motor is started and stopped several times before the clutch is indeed engaged. Likewise, it is possible that the clutch is disengaged and re-engaged several times before the motor is stopped. All that is illustrated in Fig. 3.19.

In Fig. 3.19, the new relationship between the various events is illustrated by the dashed arrows. The reason why these arrows are dashed is that we have an additional constraint stating that *we do not want to modify the reacting events* s_on *and* r_off. This is illustrated in Fig. 3.20. More precisely, we want to act at the level of the actions which have enabled these events. This is what we shall formalize in the next section.

3.8.2 Modeling

Next is a blind copy of the two strongly synchronized patterns:

dbl0_1: $a \in \{0,1\}$	**dbl0_7:** $b \in \{0,1\}$
dbl0_2: $r \in \{0,1\}$	**dbl0_8:** $s \in \{0,1\}$
dbl0_3: $ca \in \mathbb{N}$	**dbl0_9:** $cb \in \mathbb{N}$
dbl0_4: $cr \in \mathbb{N}$	**dbl0_10:** $cs \in \mathbb{N}$
dbl0_5: $a = 1 \wedge r = 0 \Rightarrow ca = cr + 1$	**dbl0_11:** $b = 1 \wedge s = 0 \Rightarrow cb = cs + 1$
dbl0_6: $a = 0 \vee r = 1 \Rightarrow ca = cr$	**dbl0_12:** $b = 0 \vee s = 1 \Rightarrow cb = cs$

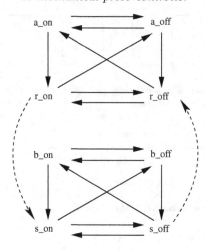

Fig. 3.20. Weak synchronization of two strongly synchronized action–reactions

a_on **when** $a = 0$ $r = 0$ **then** $a, ca := 1, ca + 1$ **end**	a_off **when** $a = 1$ $r = 1$ **then** $a := 0$ **end**	r_on **when** $r = 0$ $a = 1$ **then** $r, cr := 1, cr + 1$ **end**	r_off **when** $r = 1$ $a = 0$ **then** $r := 0$ **end**
b_on **when** $b = 0$ $s = 0$ **then** $b, cb := 1, cb + 1$ **end**	b_off **when** $b = 1$ $s = 1$ **then** $b := 0$ **end**	s_on **when** $s = 0$ $b = 1$ **then** $s, cs := 1, cs + 1$ **end**	s_off **when** $s = 1$ $b = 0$ **then** $s := 0$ **end**

We now refine these patterns by introducing our new requirement:

dbl1_1: $s = 1 \Rightarrow r = 1$

The only events that might cause a problem in proving this invariant are s_on (setting s to 1) and r_off (setting r to 0). In order to solve this problem, it seems sufficient to add the guards $r = 1$ and $s = 0$ to events s_on and r_off respectively:

```
s_on
   when
      s = 0
      b = 1
      r = 1
   then
      s, cs := 1, cs + 1
   end
```

```
r_off
   when
      r = 1
      a = 0
      s = 0
   then
      r := 0
   end
```

But, as indicated above, *we do not want to touch these reacting events.* In order to obtain the same effect, it is sufficient to add the following invariants:

$$\textbf{dbl1\_2:} \quad b = 1 \;\Rightarrow\; r = 1$$

$$\textbf{dbl1\_3:} \quad a = 0 \;\Rightarrow\; s = 0$$

In order to maintain invariant **dbl1_2**, we have to modify event b_on by adding the guard $r = 1$ to it since it sets b to 1:

```
b_on
   when
      b = 0
      s = 0
   then
      b := 1
      cb := cb + 1
   end
```

$\rightsquigarrow$

```
b_on
   when
      b = 0
      s = 0
      r = 1
   then
      b := 1
      cb := cb + 1
   end
```

To maintain invariant **dbl1_2**, we have also to add the guard $b = 0$ to event r_off since it sets r to 0:

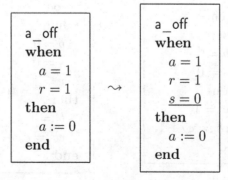

But, again, *we do not want to touch this reacting event*, so we introduce the following invariant:

$$\textbf{dbl1\_4:} \quad a = 0 \;\Rightarrow\; b = 0$$

In order to maintain invariant **dbl1_3**: that is:

$$\textbf{dbl1\_3:} \quad a = 0 \;\Rightarrow\; s = 0 \quad,$$

we have to refine event a_off as follows (guard strengthening):

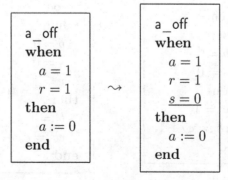

We have also to refine event s_on as follows (guard strengthening):

s_on
when
$s = 0$
$b = 1$
then
$s := 1$
$cs := cs + 1$
end

$\rightsquigarrow$

s_on
when
$s = 0$
$b = 1$
$\underline{a = 1}$
then
$s := 1$
$cs := cs + 1$
end

But, again, we do not want to touch this event, so that we have to introduce the following invariant:

$$b = 1 \;\Rightarrow\; a = 1$$

Fortunately, this is exactly **dbl1_4** contraposed:

$$\textbf{dbl1\_4:} \quad a = 0 \;\Rightarrow\; b = 0$$

In order to maintain invariant **dbl1_4**, we have to refine a_off again:

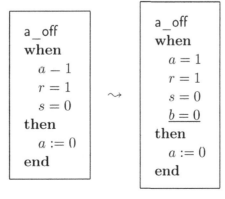

And also event b_on again:

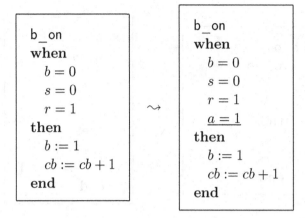

Now we have obtained the desired effect, namely that of weakly synchronizing the reactions r and s by acting on their respective actions a and b. This is indicated in Fig. 3.21.

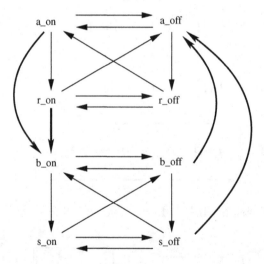

Fig. 3.21. Weak synchronizing two strongly synchronized action–reactions

Here is a summary of the introduced invariants:

dbl1_1:	$s = 1 \Rightarrow r = 1$		**dbl1_3:**	$a = 0 \Rightarrow s = 0$
dbl1_2:	$b = 1 \Rightarrow r = 1$		**dbl1_4:**	$a = 0 \Rightarrow b = 0$

Here is also a summary of the modified events a_off and b_on (where we have removed the incrementation of counter cb):

a_off	b_on
when	**when**
$a = 1$	$b = 0$
$r = 1$	$s = 0$
$\underline{s = 0}$	$\underline{r = 1}$
$\underline{b = 0}$	$\underline{a = 1}$
then	**then**
$a := 0$	$b := 1$
end	**end**

Note that the four previous invariants can be equivalently reduced to the following unique one, which can be "read" now from Fig. 3.22:

$$\textbf{dbl1\_5:} \quad b = 1 \ \lor \ s = 1 \ \Rightarrow \ a = 1 \ \land \ r = 1$$

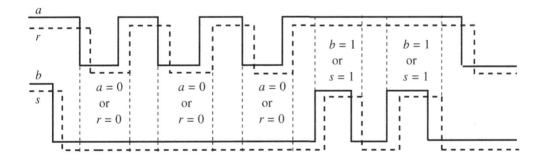

Fig. 3.22. $b = 1 \ \lor \ s = 1 \ \Rightarrow \ a = 1 \ \land \ r = 1$

3.9 Third refinement: constraining the clutch and the motor

Coming back to our development, we now incorporate the following requirement:

When the clutch is engaged, the motor must work	SAF_1

This can be formalized by means of the following new invariant:

> **inv3_1:** $clutch\_sensor = engaged \Rightarrow motor\_sensor = working$

This is an instance of the design pattern developed in Section 3.8, which we instantiate as follows:

a	$\rightsquigarrow$	$motor\_actuator$	a_on	$\rightsquigarrow$	treat_push_start_motor_button
r	$\rightsquigarrow$	$motor\_sensor$	a_off	$\rightsquigarrow$	treat_push_stop_motor_button
0	$\rightsquigarrow$	$stopped$	r_on	$\rightsquigarrow$	Motor_start
1	$\rightsquigarrow$	$working$	r_off	$\rightsquigarrow$	Motor_stop
b	$\rightsquigarrow$	$clutch\_actuator$	b_on	$\rightsquigarrow$	treat_start_clutch
s	$\rightsquigarrow$	$clutch\_sensor$	b_off	$\rightsquigarrow$	treat_stop_clutch
0	$\rightsquigarrow$	$disengaged$	s_on	$\rightsquigarrow$	Clutch_start
1	$\rightsquigarrow$	$engaged$	s_off	$\rightsquigarrow$	Clutch_stop

The invariant are as follows:

dbl1_1: $\quad s = 1 \Rightarrow r = 1$	**inv3_1:** $\quad clutch\_sensor = engaged \Rightarrow motor\_sensor = working$
dbl1_2: $\quad b = 1 \Rightarrow r = 1$	**inv3_2:** $\quad clutch\_actuator = engaged \Rightarrow motor\_sensor = working$
dbl1_3: $\quad a = 0 \Rightarrow s = 0$	**inv3_3:** $\quad motor\_actuator = stopped \Rightarrow clutch\_sensor = disengaged$
dbl1_4: $\quad a = 0 \Rightarrow b = 0$	**inv3_4:** $\quad motor\_actuator = stopped \Rightarrow clutch\_actuator = disengaged$

The two modified events are as follows:

b_on	treat_start_clutch
when	**when**
$b = 0$	$clutch\_actuator = disengaged$
$s = 0$	$clutch\_sensor = disengaged$
$r = 1$	$motor\_sensor = working$
$a = 1$	$motor\_actuator = working$
then	**then**
$b := 1$	$clutch\_actuator := engaged$
end	**end**

a_off	treat_stop_motor
when	**when**
	$stop\_motor\_impulse = \text{FALSE}$
	$stop\_motor\_button = \text{TRUE}$
$a = 1$	$motor\_actuator = working$
$r = 1$	$motor\_sensor = working$
$s = 0$	$clutch\_sensor = disengaged$
$b = 0$	$clutch\_actuator = disengaged$
then	**then**
$a := 0$	$motor\_actuator := stopped$
	$stop\_motor\_impulse := \text{TRUE}$
end	**end**

3.10 Fourth refinement: connecting the controller to the door

3.10.1 Copying

We copy (after renaming "motor" to "door") what has been done in the initial model (Section 3.6)

3.10.2 Summary of the events

- Environment

  motor_start
  motor_stop
  clutch_start
  clutch_stop

     door_close
     door_open
     push_start_motor_button
     release_start_motor_button
     push_stop_motor_button
     release_stop_motor_button

- Controller

     treat_push_start_motor_button
     treat_push_start_motor_button_false
     treat_push_stop_motor_button
     treat_push_stop_motor_button_false
     treat_release_start_motor_button
     treat_release_stop_motor_button
     treat_start_clutch
     treat_stop_clutch
     treat_close_door
     treat_open_door

3.11 Fifth refinement: constraining the clutch and the door

We now incorporate the following additional safety constraint:

When the clutch is engaged, the door must be closed	SAF_2

This is done by copying (after renaming "motor" to "door") what has been done in the third model (Section 3.9). At this point, we figure out that we have forgotten something concerning the door: clearly it must be open when the motor is stopped so that the user can replace the part or change the tool. This can be stated by adding the following requirement:

When the motor is stopped, the door must be open	SAF_3

It is interesting to present this requirement under its equivalent contraposed form SAF_3':

When the door is closed, the motor must work	SAF_3'

We can take care of this requirement by copying (after renaming "clutch" to "door") what has been done in the third model (Section 3.9). It is interesting now to put the two previous requirements SAF_1 and SAF_2 next to SAF_3':

When the clutch is engaged, the motor must work	SAF_1

When the clutch is engaged, the door must be closed	SAF_2

This shows that SAF_1 *is redundant* as it can be obtained by combining SAF_2 and SAF_3'! The moral of the story is that the third refinement (Section 3.9) can be removed completely, and thus our refinement strategy (Section 3.4) could have been simplified as follows:

- Initial model: connecting the controller to the motor.
- 1st refinement: connecting the motor button to the controller.
- 2nd refinement: connecting the controller to the clutch.
- 3rd (4th) refinement: connecting the controller to the door.
- 4th (5th) refinement: constraining the clutch and the door and the motor and the door.
- 5th (6th) refinement: more constraints between the clutch and the door.
- 6th (7th) refinement: connecting the clutch button to the controller.

3.12 Another design pattern: strong synchronization of two strong reactions

3.12.1 Introduction

We consider now the following requirements FUN_3 and FUN_4 concerning the relationship between the clutch and the door:

When the clutch is disengaged, the door cannot be closed several times

When the door is closed, the clutch cannot be disengaged several times

This is also a case of synchronization between two strong reactions. This time however the weak synchronization is not sufficient any more: we need a strong synchronization. This is indicated in Fig. 3.23. The full picture is indicated in Fig. 3.24.

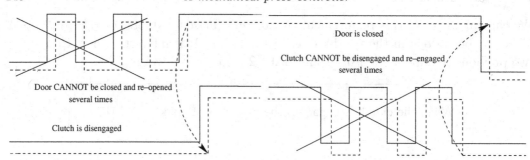

Fig. 3.23. Strong synchronization between the clutch and the door

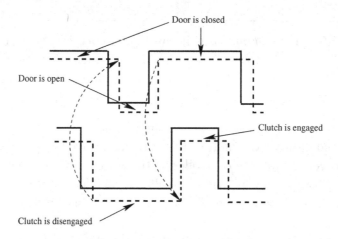

Fig. 3.24. The full picture of strong synchronization

3.12.2 Modeling

The modeling of this new constraints will be presented as a refinement of the "weak–strong" model of Section 3.8. In order to formalize this new kind of synchronization, we have to consider again the counters ca, cr, cb, and cs as indicated in Fig. 3.25.

What we want to achieve is expressed in the following properties:

$$ca = cb \ \lor \ ca = cb + 1$$

$$cr = cs \ \lor \ cr = cs + 1$$

Let us first treat the case of counters ca and cb as illustrated in Fig. 3.26. It seems that the condition $ca = cb + 1$ is implied by the condition $a = 1 \land b = 0$ as indicated

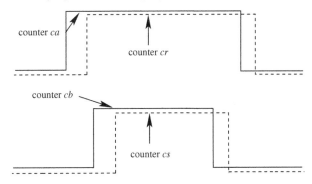

Fig. 3.25. The counters

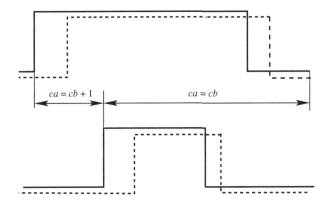

Fig. 3.26. Counters ca and cb

in Fig. 3.27. However, this guess is wrong as can be seen from Fig. 3.28. The solution consists in introducing a new variable m as in Fig. 3.29.

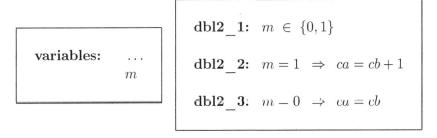

Let us now treat the case of counters cr and cs as indicated in Fig. 3.30. It seems that the condition $cr = cs + 1$ is implied by the condition $r = 1 \wedge s = 0$ as indicated in Fig 3.31. But again this guess is wrong as illustrated in Fig 3.32. The solution is shown in Fig. 3.33. This led to the following additional invariants **dbl2_4** and **dbl2_5**:

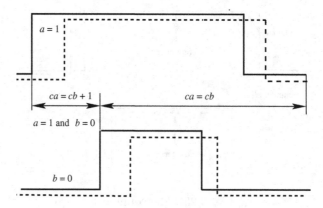

Fig. 3.27. A guess

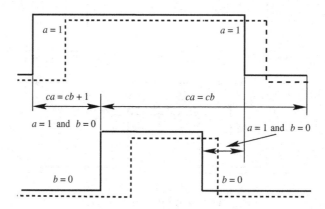

Fig. 3.28. The guess is wrong

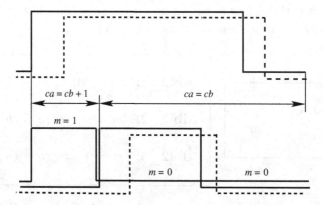

Fig. 3.29. Introducing a new variable m

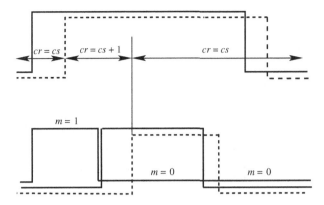

Fig. 3.30. Counters cr and cs

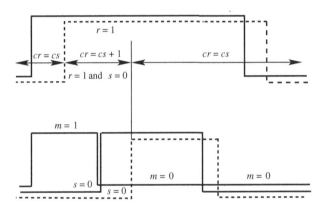

Fig. 3.31. A guess

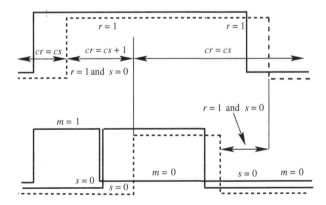

Fig. 3.32. The guess is wrong

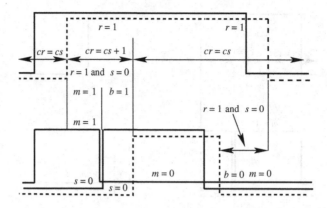

Fig. 3.33. The solution

dbl2_1: $m \in \{0,1\}$

dbl2_2: $m = 1 \;\Rightarrow\; ca = cb + 1$

dbl2_3: $m = 0 \;\Rightarrow\; ca = cb$

dbl2_4: $r = 1 \;\wedge\; s = 0 \;\wedge\; (m = 1 \;\vee\; b = 1) \;\Rightarrow\; cr = cs + 1$

dbl2_5: $r = 0 \;\vee\; s = 1 \;\vee\; (m = 0 \;\wedge\; b = 0) \;\Rightarrow\; cr = cs$

Let us now turn our attention to the modified events. This is indicated in Fig. 3.34. As can be seen, the events of concern are a_on, b_on, and a_off. Here are the proposals for these events:

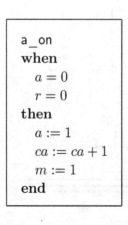

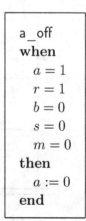

a_on
when
  $a = 0$
  $r = 0$
then
  $a := 1$
  $ca := ca + 1$
  $m := 1$
end

b_on
when
  $r = 1$
  $a = 1$
  $b = 0$
  $s = 0$
  $m = 1$
then
  $b := 1$
  $cb := cb + 1$
  $m := 0$
end

a_off
when
  $a = 1$
  $r = 1$
  $b = 0$
  $s = 0$
  $m = 0$
then
  $a := 0$
end

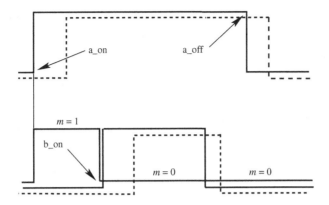

Fig. 3.34. The events

It remains now for us to do the proofs. Similar techniques as the ones used in Sections 3.2 and 3.8 lead us to define the following additional invariants **dbl2_6** and **dbl2_7**:

dbl2_1: $m \in \{0, 1\}$

dbl2_2: $m = 1 \Rightarrow ca = cb + 1$

dbl2_3: $m = 0 \Rightarrow ca = cb$

dbl2_4: $r = 1 \wedge s = 0 \wedge (m = 1 \vee b = 1) \Rightarrow cr = cs + 1$

dbl2_5: $r = 0 \vee s = 1 \vee (m = 0 \wedge b = 0) \Rightarrow cr = cs$

dbl2_6: $m = 0 \Rightarrow a = 0 \vee r = 1$

dbl2_7: $m = 1 \Rightarrow b = 0 \wedge s = 0 \wedge a = 1$

After this last invariant extension, the proofs are done easily.

3.13 Sixth refinement: more constraints between clutch and door

It remains now for us to instantiate the "strong–strong" pattern of the previous section. We do this as follows:

$$
\begin{array}{llll}
a & \rightsquigarrow & door\_actuator & \quad b \rightsquigarrow clutch\_actuator \\
r & \rightsquigarrow & door\_sensor & \quad s \rightsquigarrow clutch\_sensor \\
0 & \rightsquigarrow & open & \quad 0 \rightsquigarrow disengaged \\
1 & \rightsquigarrow & closed & \quad 1 \rightsquigarrow engaged \\
\end{array}
$$

$$
\begin{array}{lll}
a\_on & \rightsquigarrow & treat\_close\_door \\
a\_off & \rightsquigarrow & treat\_open\_door \\
b\_on & \rightsquigarrow & treat\_start\_clutch \\
\end{array}
$$

This leads to the following event instantiations:

```
a_on                    treat_close_door
when                        when
    a = 0                       door_actuator = open
    r = 0                       door_sensor = open
                                motor_actuator = working
                                motor_sensor = working
then                        then
    a := 1                      door_actuator := closed
    m := 1                      m := 1
end                         end
```

```
b_on                    treat_start_clutch
when                        when
                                motor_actuator = working
                                motor_sensor = working
    b = 0                       clutch_actuator = disengaged
    s = 0                       clutch_sensor = disengaged
    r = 1                       door_sensor = closed
    a = 1                       door_actuator = closed
    m = 1                       m = 1
then                        then
    b := 1                      clutch_actuator := engaged
    m := 0                      m := 0
end                         end
```

a_off	treat_open_door
when	**when**
$a = 1$	$door\_actuator = closed$
$r = 1$	$door\_sensor = closed$
$s = 0$	$clutch\_sensor = disengaged$
$b = 0$	$clutch\_actuator = disengaged$
$m = 0$	$m = 0$
then	**then**
$a := 0$	$door\_actuator := open$
end	**end**

The final synchronization of the door and the clutch is shown in Fig. 3.35, where the underlined events are environment events.

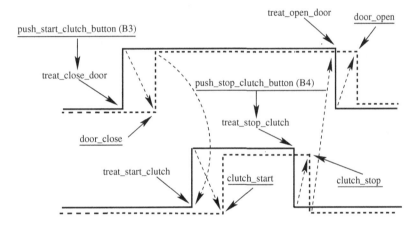

Fig. 3.35. The final synchronization of the door and the clutch

3.14 Seventh refinement: connecting the controller to the clutch buttons

3.14.1 Copying

We simply connect button B3 to the event treat_close_door and button B4 to the events treat_stop_clutch.

3.14.2 Summary of events

- Environment

  motor_start
  motor_stop

clutch_start

clutch_stop

door_close

door_open

push_start_motor_button

release_start_motor_button

push_stop_motor_button

release_stop_motor_button

push_start_clutch_button

release_start_clutch_button

push_stop_clutch_button

release_stop_clutch_button

- Controller

treat_push_start_motor_button

treat_push_start_motor_button_false

treat_push_stop_motor_button

treat_push_stop_motor_button_false

treat_release_start_motor_button

treat_release_stop_motor_button

treat_start_clutch

treat_stop_clutch

treat_close_door

treat_open_door

treat_close_door_false

4

A simple file transfer protocol

The example introduced in this chapter is quite different from the previous one, where the program was supposed to control an external situation (cars on a bridge or a mechanical press). Here we present a so-called protocol to be used on a computer network by two agents. This is the very classical two-phase handshake protocol. This example has been presented in many places. A very nice presentation is the one given in the book by L. Lamport [1].

This example will allow us to extend our usage of the mathematical language with such constructs as partial and total functions, domain and range of functions, and function restrictions. We shall also extend our logical language by introducing universally quantified formulas and corresponding inference rules.

4.1 Requirements

The purpose of the protocol is to transfer a sequential file from one agent, the sender, to another one, the receiver. The transmitted file should be equal to the original file:

The protocol ensures the copy of a file from one site to another one	FUN-1

The sequential file, as its name indicates, is made of a number of items disposed in an ordered fashion:

The file is supposed to be made of a sequence of items	FUN-2

These agents are supposed to reside on *different sites*, so that the transfer is not made by a simple copy of the file, it is rather realized gradually by two distinct programs exchanging various kinds of messages on the network:

The file is sent piece by piece between the two sites	FUN-3

Such programs are working on different machines: the overall protocol is indeed a *distributed program*.

4.2 Refinement strategy

We are not going to model the final protocol right away; this would be too complicated and error prone. The refinement strategy we are going to adopt is explained now.

In the initial model (Section 4.3), the idea is to present the final result of the protocol which we can observe when the protocol is finished. At this initial stage, the two participants in the protocol – the sender and the receiver – are not supposed to reside on different sites. This is a technique we shall always use when modeling protocols. This initial model is important because it tells us exactly *what the protocol is supposed to achieve without telling us how.*

In the first refinement (Section 4.4), we shall separate the sender and the receiver. Moreover, the file will be transmitted piece by piece between them, not in one shot as in the initial model. However, this separation of the sender and the receiver will not be complete; we suppose that the receiver can "see" what remains to be transmitted in the sender's site and is able to take "directly" the next item from the sender and add it to its own file. At this stage, we explain the essence of the algorithm, but we do not see the details yet of the distributed behavior as performed on each site. This kind of refinement is very important in the modeling of a protocol: we simplify our task by allowing separate participants to "cheat" by looking directly into other participants private memories.

In the next refinement (Section 4.5), the receiver is not cheating any more: it is not able to access directly the sender's site. In fact, the sender will *send messages* that the receiver will read. The receiver then responds to these messages by returning some *acknowledgment messages* to the sender. The fine details of the distributed algorithm are revealed in full. What is important here is that the messages between the participants can be seen as a means of implementing the previous abstraction where the receiver could have direct access to the contents of the sender's memory. Again, this is a technique we shall frequently use in protocol modeling.

In the final refinement (Section 4.6), we shall optimize what is sent between the two participants. The protocol is not modified any more; it is made just more efficient.

4.3 Protocol initial model

What we are going to develop here is *not* directly the distributed program in question. We are rather going to construct a *model of its distributed execution.* In the context of this model, the file to transfer is formalized by means of a finite sequence f. The file f is supposed to "reside" at the sender's site. At the end of this protocol execution, we want the file f to be copied without loss or duplication at the receiver's site on a file named g supposed to be empty initially. This is illustrated on Figure 4.1.

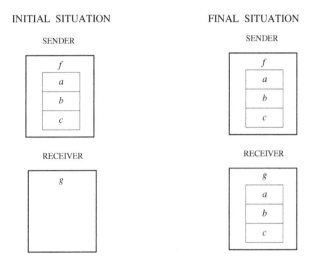

Fig. 4.1. Initial and final situations

4.3.1 The state

The context is made of a set D, which is called a *carrier set.* This set represents the data that are stored in the file. The only implicit property that we assume concerning carrier sets is that they are not empty. The presence of this set makes our development *generic.* It means that the set D could be instantiated later to a particular set. Furthermore, we have two constants. First the constant n, which is a positive natural number, and second the constant f, which is a *total function* from the interval $1 \ldots n$ to the set D. This is the way we formalize finite sequences. These properties are written below as **axm0_1** and **axm0_2**:

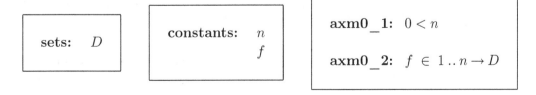

We have a variable, g, which is a *partial function* from the interval $1..n$ to the set D. It is written below in invariant **inv0_1**. We have also a boolean variable b stating when the protocol is finished ($b = \text{TRUE}$). As we shall see later in Section 4.3.3, variable g is empty when the protocol is not finished, whereas it is equal to f when the protocol is finished. This is formalized in invariants **inv0_2** and **inv0_3**:

variables:	g
	b

inv0_1: $\quad g \in 1..n \rightarrowtail D$

inv0_2: $\quad b = \text{FALSE} \Rightarrow g = \varnothing$

inv0_3: $\quad b = \text{TRUE} \Rightarrow g = f$

4.3.2 Reminder of mathematical notations

In the previous sections, we have used some mathematical concepts such as intervals, partial functions, and total functions. We recall here a few notations and definitions concerning such concepts and similar ones.

Given two natural numbers a and b, the interval between a and b is the set of natural numbers x where $a \leq x$ and $x \leq b$. It is denoted by the construct $a..b$. Note that when b is smaller than a, the interval $a..b$ is empty:

$x \in S$	set membership operator
$\mathbb{N}$	set of natural numbers: $\{0, 1, 2, 3, \ldots\}$
$a..b$	interval from a to b: $\{a, a+1, \ldots, b\}$ (empty when $b < a$)

Given two sets S and T, and two elements a and b belonging to S and T respectively, the *ordered pair* made of a and b in that order is denoted by the construct $a \mapsto b$. The set of all such ordered pairs made out of S and T is called the *Cartesian product* of S and T. It is denoted by the construct $S \times T$.

Given a set T, the fact that a set S is a *subset* of T is denoted by the predicate $S \subseteq T$. The set of all subsets of a set S is called the *power set* of S. It is denoted by the construct $\mathbb{P}(S)$:

$a \mapsto b$	pair constructing operator
$S \times T$	Cartesian product operator: the set of all pairs from S to T
$S \subseteq T$	set inclusion operator
$\mathbb{P}(S)$	power set operator: set of all subsets of a given set S

Given two sets S and T, the power set of their Cartesian product is called the set of *binary relations* built on S and T. It is denoted by $\mathbb{P}(S \times T)$, usually abbreviated by the construct $S \leftrightarrow T$. A binary relation is thus a set of pairs. It can be empty. In this case, it is denoted by the empty set $\varnothing$.

Given a binary relation r built on two sets S and T (thus r belongs to the set $S \leftrightarrow T$), the *domain* of r is the subset of S whose elements x are such that there exists an element y belonging to T such that the pair $x \mapsto y$ belongs to r. It is denoted by the construct $\text{dom}(r)$.

Symmetrically, the *range* of r is the subset of T whose elements y are such that there exists an element x of S such that the pair $x \mapsto y$ belongs to r. It is denoted by the construct $\text{ran}(r)$:

$S \leftrightarrow T$	set of binary relations from S to T
$\text{dom}(r)$	domain of a relation r
$\text{ran}(r)$	range of a relation r

Next is an illustration of a binary relation r between sets S and T:

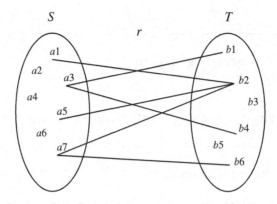

Given two sets S and T, a *partial function* f from S to T is a binary relation from S to T, where any two pairs $x \mapsto y$ and $x \mapsto z$ belonging to f are such that y is equal to z. The set of all partial functions from S to T is denoted by the construct $S \nrightarrow T$.

Given two sets S and T, a *total function* f from S to T is a partial function from S to T whose domain is exactly S. The set of all total functions from S to T is denoted by the construct $S \rightarrow T$:

$S \nrightarrow T$	set of partial functions from S to T
$S \rightarrow T$	set of total functions from S to T

Next is an illustration of a partial function f from set S to set T, where the domain of f is the set $\{a1, a3, a5, a7\}$ and its range is the the set $\{b2, b4, b6\}$:

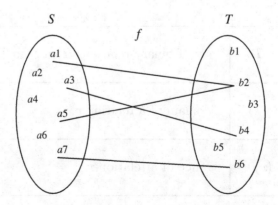

Now comes an illustration of a total function f from set S to set T. As can be seen, the domain of f is now exactly S:

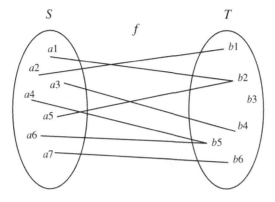

4.3.3 The events

Coming back to our example, let us now define the events of our first model. Initially, g is empty. This is indicated in the special event init below. The very global transfer action of the protocol can be abstracted by means of a *single* event called final:

init

$g := \varnothing$
$b := \text{FALSE}$

final
  when
    $b = \text{FALSE}$
  then
    $g := f$
    $b := \text{TRUE}$
  end

Event final does not exist by itself. In other words, it is not part of the protocol; it is just a *temporal snapshot* that we would like hopefully to *observe*. In reality, the transfer of the file f is not done in one shot; it is made gradually. But, at this very initial stage of our approach, we are not interested in this. In other words, *as an abstraction*, and regardless of what will happen in the details of the distributed execution of the protocol, its final action must result in the possibility to observe that the file f has indeed been copied into the file g.

At this point, it should be noted that we are not committed to any particular protocol; this model is thus, in a sense, the most general one corresponding to a given class of protocols, namely that of file transfers. Some more sophisticated specifications could have been proposed, in which the file might have only been partially transfered (this case will be studied in Chapter 6), but such an extension is not studied in the present example.

4.3.4 Proofs

Let us now turn our attention to the proofs. At this stage, the only proofs to be considered are invariant proofs and the deadlock freeness proof. Here are the proof obligations concerning the establishment of invariants **inv0_1** and **inv0_2** by the initialization event init. Here is the first proof obligation concerning the establishment of invariant **inv0_1** by event init:

$$
\begin{array}{l}
\textbf{axm0\_1} \\
\textbf{axm0\_2} \\
\vdash \\
\quad \text{modified } \textbf{inv0\_1}
\end{array}
\qquad
\left|
\begin{array}{l}
0 < n \\
f \in 1\,..\,n \to D \\
\vdash \\
\varnothing \in 1\,..\,n \nrightarrow D
\end{array}
\right.
\qquad \text{init} \;/\; \textbf{inv0\_1} \;/\; \text{INV}
$$

The corresponding proof will be done by using informal arguments only: clearly the empty function is a partial function from $1\,..\,n$ to D. For proofs involving set-theoretic constructs, we shall not provide specific inference rules as we have done in Chapter 2 for propositional logic and equality, we shall instead use a "generic" inference rule named SET, which we shall justify informally each time. Here are the proof obligations concerning the establishment of invariant **inv0_2** and **inv0_3** by event init:

$$
\begin{array}{l}
\textbf{axm0\_1} \\
\textbf{axm0\_2} \\
\vdash \\
\quad \text{modified } \textbf{inv0\_2}
\end{array}
\qquad
\left|
\begin{array}{l}
0 < n \\
f \in 1\,..\,n \to D \\
\vdash \\
\text{FALSE} = \text{FALSE} \;\Rightarrow\; \varnothing = \varnothing
\end{array}
\right.
\qquad \text{init} \;/\; \textbf{inv0\_2} \;/\; \text{INV}
$$

$$
\begin{array}{l}
\textbf{axm0\_1} \\
\textbf{axm0\_2} \\
\vdash \\
\quad \text{modified } \textbf{inv0\_3}
\end{array}
\qquad
\left|
\begin{array}{l}
0 < n \\
f \in 1\,..\,n \to D \\
\vdash \\
\text{FALSE} = \text{TRUE} \;\Rightarrow\; \varnothing = f
\end{array}
\right.
\qquad \text{init} \;/\; \textbf{inv0\_3} \;/\; \text{INV}
$$

The corresponding proofs can be done easily. Here is the proof obligation concerning the preservation of invariant **inv0_1** by event final:

$$
\begin{array}{ll}
\begin{array}{l}
\textbf{axm0\_1} \\
\textbf{axm0\_2} \\
\textbf{inv0\_1} \\
\textbf{inv0\_2} \\
\textbf{inv0\_3} \\
\text{guard} \\
\vdash \\
\text{modified } \textbf{inv0\_1}
\end{array}
&
\boxed{
\begin{array}{l}
0 < n \\
f \in 1..n \rightarrow D \\
g \in 1..n \nrightarrow D \\
b = \text{FALSE} \Rightarrow g = \varnothing \\
b = \text{TRUE} \Rightarrow g = f \\
b = \text{FALSE} \\
\vdash \\
f \in 1..n \nrightarrow D
\end{array}
}
\quad \text{final / } \textbf{inv0\_1} \text{ / INV}
\end{array}
$$

After applying MON, the proof goes as indicated below. A total function from one set to another is indeed a partial function built on the same sets:

$$
\boxed{
\begin{array}{l}
f \in 1..n \rightarrow D \\
\vdash \\
f \in 1..n \nrightarrow D
\end{array}
}
\quad \text{SET}
$$

Here are the proof obligations concerning the preservation of invariant **inv0_2** and **inv0_3** by event final:

$$
\begin{array}{ll}
\begin{array}{l}
\textbf{axm0\_2} \\
\textbf{axm0\_3} \\
\textbf{inv0\_1} \\
\textbf{inv0\_2} \\
\textbf{inv0\_3} \\
\text{guard} \\
\vdash \\
\text{modified } \textbf{inv0\_2}
\end{array}
&
\boxed{
\begin{array}{l}
0 < n \\
f \in 1..n \rightarrow D \\
g \in 1..n \nrightarrow D \\
b = \text{FALSE} \Rightarrow g = \varnothing \\
b = \text{TRUE} \Rightarrow g = f \\
b = \text{FALSE} \\
\vdash \\
\text{TRUE} = \text{FALSE} \Rightarrow g = \varnothing
\end{array}
}
\quad \text{final / } \textbf{inv0\_2} \text{ / INV}
\end{array}
$$

axm0_2	$0 < n$
axm0_3	$f \in 1\mathbin{..}n \to D$
inv0_1	$g \in 1\mathbin{..}n \nrightarrow D$
inv0_2	$b = \text{FALSE} \Rightarrow g = \varnothing$
inv0_3	$b = \text{TRUE} \Rightarrow g = f$
guard	$b = \text{FALSE}$
$\vdash$	$\vdash$
modified **inv0_3**	$\text{TRUE} = \text{TRUE} \Rightarrow f = f$

final / **inv0_3** / INV

The corresponding proofs can be done easily using inference rules introduced in Chapter 2.

4.4 Protocol first refinement

4.4.1 Informal presentation

We are now going to *refine* the file transfer done in one shot by the previous *abstract* event final acting "magically" on the receiver's side. For this, we have an additional *concrete* event named receive corresponding to an intermediate phase of the protocol. It aims at transferring the file *piece by piece*. Of course, the abstract event final should not disappear; it will have a concrete counterpart in which the same observation as in the abstraction can be done.

In Fig. 4.2, we can see on the top what could have been observed in the abstraction, namely the init event followed by the final event. On the bottom, we can see what we can observe during this refinement. We can say that the eyes of the observer are now open more often than in the abstraction. It is possible to observe a number of occurrences of event receive in between that of event init and that of event final.

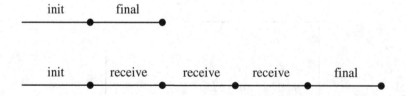

Fig. 4.2. Initial abstraction and first refinement observations

We change the variable g to another one, h, which is modified by event receive. In fact, this event will gradually copy the file f from the sender's side to the receiver's side. For this it will use an index r, which is progressing as indicated in Fig. 4.3 below.

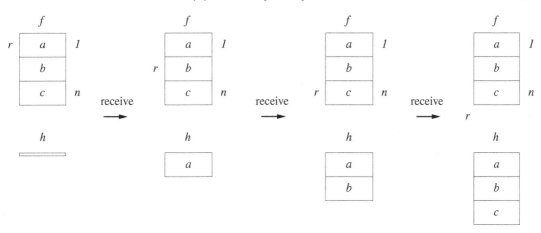

Fig. 4.3. A trace of the first refinement behaviour

As can be seen, event receive is adding an element to file h by copying the rth element of file f to file h. It will be interesting to see what event final does now (wait until Section 4.4.4).

4.4.2 The state

We enlarge our state by adding to it a variable r which is a natural number. This variable is initialized to 1. It will serve as an index on the file f; it is thus within the interval $1 .. n + 1$ as indicated in invariant **inv1_1** below. We also replace the variable g by another one named h. Variable h is exactly equal to the constant f with domain *restricted* to the interval $1 .. r - 1$ (see the next section). This is written by means of the following construct: $(1 .. r - 1) \lhd f$. In other words, in $(1 .. r - 1) \lhd f$, we are considering only those pairs $x \mapsto y$ of f where x is in the set $1 .. r - 1$. This is recorded in invariant **inv1_2**. Finally, we have to establish the connection between the concrete variable h and the abstract variable g; at the end of the protocol (when b is TRUE), r must be equal to $n + 1$. This is stated in invariant **inv1_3**. It is then easy to prove Theorem **thm1_1**, stating that g is equal to h when b is equal to TRUE.

variables: b h r	**inv1_1:** $r \in 1 .. n + 1$ **inv1_2:** $h = (1 .. r - 1) \lhd f$ **inv1_3:** $b = \text{TRUE} \Rightarrow r = n + 1$	**thm1_1:** $b = \text{TRUE} \Rightarrow g = h$

4.4.3 More mathematical symbols

In the previous section, we have introduced the operator $\lhd$ for restricting the domain of a relation. In this section, we introduce more restriction operators.

Given a relation r form S to T and a subset s of S, expression $s \lhd r$ denotes the relation r with only those pairs whose first element is in s. It is called a domain restriction.

Given a relation r form S to T and a subset s of S, expression $s \ensuremath{\mathbin{\vartriangleleft\!\!\!\!-}} r$ denotes the relation r with only those pairs whose first element is not in s. It is called domain subtraction.

Given a relation r form S to T and a subset t of T, expression $r \rhd t$ denotes the relation r with only those pairs whose second element is in t. It is called a range restriction.

Given a relation r form S to T and a subset s of S, expression $r \ensuremath{\mathbin{-\!\!\!\!\vartriangleright}} t$ denotes the relation r with only those pairs whose second element is not in t. It is called range subtraction:

$s \lhd r$	domain restriction operator
$s \mathbin{\vartriangleleft\!\!\!-} r$	domain subtraction operator
$r \rhd t$	range restriction operator
$r \mathbin{-\!\!\!\vartriangleright} t$	range subtraction operator

Next is an illustration where the dotted lines correspond to $\{a3,\ a7\} \lhd f$.

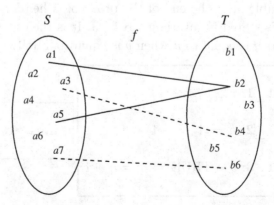

Now comes an illustration where the dotted lines correspond to $\{a3, a7\} \lhd f$.

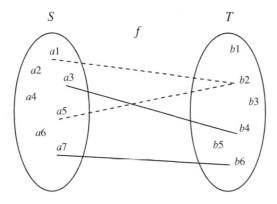

And now an illustration where the dotted lines correspond to $f \rhd \{b2, b4\}$.

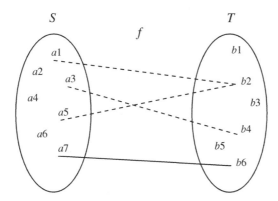

Finally, an illustration where the dotted lines correspond to $f \rhd\!\!\!\!- \{b2, b4\}$.

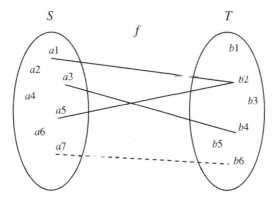

4.4.4 *The events*

Coming back to our example, let us now define the events of this refinement. The initializing event init set b to FALSE as in the abstraction, h to the empty set and r to 1. Event receive is adding an element to file h by copying the rth element of file f into h, it also increments r, and event final does nothing (just sets b to TRUE as in the abstraction)! This seems strange, but we shall prove that it refines its abstraction. In fact, it just acts now as a witness; when its guard is true, that is when condition $r = n + 1$ holds and b is FALSE, then file g must be equal to file f as stipulated in its abstraction:

init
$b := $ FALSE
$h := \varnothing$
$r := 1$

receive
  status
    convergent
  when
    $r \leq n$
  then
    $h := h \cup \{r \mapsto f(r)\}$
    $r := r + 1$
  end

final
  when
    $r = n + 1$
    $b = $ FALSE
  then
    $b := $ TRUE
  end

Notice the **status** of event receive; it is convergent, meaning that we have to prove that it cannot "keep control" for ever. To prove this, we have to exhibit a numerical **variant** and prove that event receive decreases it. This will be done in Section 4.4.6.

4.4.5 *Refinement proofs*

The proof for the initializing event init is simple. Here is the proof obligation for the establishment of invariant **inv1_1**:

$$
\begin{array}{ll}
\textbf{axm0\_1} \\
\textbf{axm0\_2} \\
\vdash \\
\text{modified } \textbf{inv1\_1}
\end{array}
\qquad
\begin{array}{l}
0 < n \\
f \in 1 .. n \to D \\
\vdash \\
1 \in 1 .. n + 1
\end{array}
\qquad
\text{init / } \textbf{inv1\_1} \text{ / INV}
$$

The proof is done easily by transforming the goal $1 \in 1 .. n + 1$ into $1 \leq 1 \wedge 1 \leq n + 1$. Then we apply inference rule AND_R followed by simple arithmetic calculations.

Here is now the proof obligation for the establishment of invariant **inv1_2**:

$$
\begin{array}{c|c}
\textbf{axm0\_1} & 0 < n \\
\textbf{axm0\_2} & f \in 1 \mathinner{\ldotp\ldotp} n \to D \\
\vdash & \vdash \\
\text{modified } \textbf{inv1\_2} & \varnothing = (1 \mathinner{\ldotp\ldotp} 1 - 1) \lhd f
\end{array}
\qquad \text{init} \,/\, \textbf{inv1\_2} \,/\, \mathsf{INV}
$$

To prove this, we first transform the interval $1 \mathinner{\ldotp\ldotp} 1 - 1$ into $1 \mathinner{\ldotp\ldotp} 0$, which is empty. Then we notice that the expression $\varnothing \lhd f$ denotes the empty set. We finally apply inference rule EQL. Finally, proving **inv1_3** is trivial.

More interesting are the refinement proofs for event **final**. First, we have to apply the proof obligation rule GRD, which is obvious since the guard of the concrete version, namely $r = n + 1$, is clearly stronger than that of the abstraction, which is missing (thus always true). Applying now rule INV to invariant **inv1_1** leads to the proof of the following sequent, whose proof is obvious according to inference rules MON and then HYP (since the goal $r \in 1 \mathinner{\ldotp\ldotp} n + 1$ is also an hypothesis):

$$
\begin{array}{c|c}
\ldots & \ldots \\
\textbf{inv1\_1} & r \in 1 \mathinner{\ldotp\ldotp} n + 1 \\
\ldots & \ldots \\
\text{guard of final} & r = n + 1 \\
\ldots & \ldots \\
\vdash & \vdash \\
\text{modified } \textbf{inv1\_1} & r \in 1 \mathinner{\ldotp\ldotp} n + 1
\end{array}
\qquad \text{final} \,/\, \textbf{inv1\_1} \,/\, \mathsf{INV}
$$

Likewise, invariant **inv1_2** is trivially proved using inference rules MON and HYP:

$$
\begin{array}{c|c}
\ldots & \ldots \\
\textbf{inv1\_2} & h = (1 \mathinner{\ldotp\ldotp} r - 1) \lhd f \\
\ldots & \ldots \\
\text{guard of final} & r = n + 1 \\
\ldots & \ldots \\
\vdash & \vdash \\
\text{modified } \textbf{inv1\_2} & h = (1 \mathinner{\ldotp\ldotp} r - 1) \lhd f
\end{array}
\qquad \text{final} \,/\, \textbf{inv1\_2} \,/\, \mathsf{INV}
$$

The preservation of invariant **inv1_3** by event final requires proving the following, which is obvious:

$$
\begin{array}{l|l}
\ldots & \ldots \\
\text{guard of final} & r = n+1 \\
\ldots & \ldots \\
\vdash & \vdash \\
\text{modified } \mathbf{inv1\_3} & \text{TRUE} = \text{TRUE} \Rightarrow r = n+1
\end{array}
\qquad \text{final} \ / \ \mathbf{inv1\_3} \ / \ \text{INV}
$$

The preservation of invariant **inv1_1** by event receive requires proving:

$$
\begin{array}{l|l}
\ldots & \ldots \\
\mathbf{inv1\_1} & r \in 1\,..\,n+1 \\
\ldots & \ldots \\
\text{guard of receive} & r \le n \\
\vdash & \vdash \\
\text{modified } \mathbf{inv1\_1} & r+1 \in 1\,..\,n+1
\end{array}
\qquad \text{receive} \ / \ \mathbf{inv1\_1} \ / \ \text{INV}
$$

Here is the proof after applying MON:

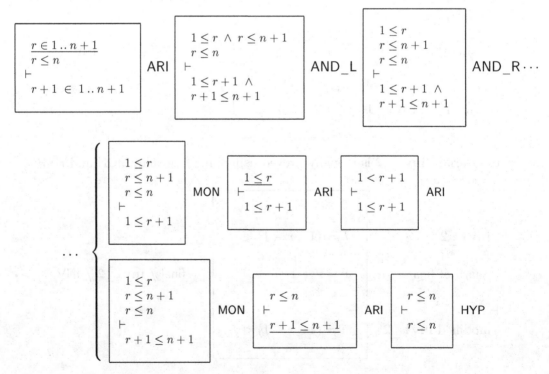

The preservation of invariant **inv1_2** by event receive requires proving:

$$
\begin{array}{l|l}
\cdots & \cdots \\
\textbf{inv1\_1} & r \in 1 \mathinner{..} n+1 \\
\textbf{inv1\_2} & h = (1 \mathinner{..} r - 1) \lhd f \\
\cdots & \cdots \\
\text{guard of receive} & r \leq n \\
\vdash & \vdash \\
\text{mod. } \textbf{inv1\_2} & h \cup \{r \mapsto f(r)\} = (1 \mathinner{..} r + 1 - 1) \lhd f
\end{array}
\qquad \text{receive/}\textbf{inv1\_2}\text{/INV\_REF}
$$

Here is the proof after applying MON:

$$
\begin{array}{l}
f \in 1 \mathinner{..} n \to D \\
\underline{r \in 1 \mathinner{..} n+1} \\
h = (1 \mathinner{..} r - 1) \lhd f \\
r \leq n \\
\vdash \\
h \cup \{r \mapsto f(r)\} = (1 \mathinner{..} r + 1 - 1) \lhd f
\end{array}
\quad \text{ARI}
\quad
\begin{array}{l}
f \in 1 \mathinner{..} n \to D \\
1 \leq r \\
h = (1 \mathinner{..} r - 1) \lhd f \\
r \leq n \\
\vdash \\
h \cup \{r \mapsto f(r)\} = (1 \mathinner{..} r) \lhd f
\end{array}
\quad \text{EQ\_LR} \ldots
$$

$$
\ldots
\begin{array}{l}
f \in 1 \mathinner{..} n \to D \\
1 \leq r \\
r \leq n \\
\vdash \\
(1 \mathinner{..} r - 1) \lhd f \ \cup\ \{r \mapsto f(r)\} \ = \ (1 \mathinner{..} r) \lhd f
\end{array}
\quad \text{SET}
$$

The last sequent is discharged by noticing that adding the mini-function $\{r \mapsto f(r)\}$ (where r is in the domain of f) to the function f restricted to the interval $1 \mathinner{..} r - 1$ yields exactly f restricted to the interval $1 \mathinner{..} r$. The preservation of invariant **inv1_3** by event receive requires proving:

$$
\begin{array}{l|l}
\cdots & \cdots \\
\textbf{inv1\_3} & b = \text{TRUE} \ \Rightarrow\ r = n + 1 \\
\text{guard of receive} & r \leq n \\
\vdash & \vdash \\
\text{modified } \textbf{inv1\_3} & b = \text{TRUE} \ \Rightarrow\ r + 1 = n + 1
\end{array}
\qquad \text{receive / }\textbf{inv1\_3}\text{ / INV\_REF}
$$

The proof goes as follows after applying MON:

$$
\boxed{
\begin{array}{l}
b = \text{TRUE} \;\Rightarrow\; r = n + 1 \\
r \le n \\
\vdash \\
b = \text{TRUE} \;\Rightarrow\; r + 1 = n + 1
\end{array}
}
\quad \text{IMP\_R}
\qquad
\boxed{
\begin{array}{l}
b = \text{TRUE} \;\Rightarrow\; r = n + 1 \\
r \le n \\
b = \text{TRUE} \\
\vdash \\
r + 1 = n + 1
\end{array}
}
\quad \text{IMP\_L} \;\ldots
$$

$$
\ldots
\boxed{
\begin{array}{l}
r = n + 1 \\
r \le n \\
b = \text{TRUE} \\
\vdash \\
r + 1 = n + 1
\end{array}
}
\quad \text{EQL\_LR}
\qquad
\boxed{
\begin{array}{l}
\dfrac{n + 1 \le n}{b = \text{TRUE}} \\
\vdash \\
r + 1 = n + 1
\end{array}
}
\quad \text{ARI}
\qquad
\boxed{
\begin{array}{l}
\bot \\
b = \text{TRUE} \\
\vdash \\
r + 1 = n + 1
\end{array}
}
\quad \text{FALSE\_L}
$$

4.4.6 Convergence proof of event receive

We have to prove that the new event **receive** converges. For this, we have to exhibit a variant, that is a non-negative expression which is decreased by event **receive**. The most obvious variant is the following:

$$
\boxed{\quad \textbf{variant1:}\quad n + 1 - r \quad}
$$

Proving that this variant is decreased is easy. We have to apply proof obligation rules NAT (the variant denotes a natural number) and VAR (the variant is decreased by event **receive**). The proof of the decreasing of this variant is extremely important because it shows that the concrete "execution" of event **final** might be *eventually reachable*. In other words, it shows that our initial goal stated in the abstract version of **final** might be reachable in the concrete version, despite the new event **receive**. We have written "might be" on purpose, because what we have proved is that event **receive** cannot be executed for ever. But it might stop in a position where event **final** cannot be enabled because its guard would not be true. It is precisely the purpose of the next section to prove that this cannot happen.

4.4.7 Proving relative deadlock freeness

We are now going to prove that this system never deadlocks (as was the case for the abstraction). Applying rule DLF, it is easy to prove that the disjunction of the guards of events receive and final is always true. Applying the rule leads to the following, after some simplifications:

$$
\begin{array}{l}
r \ \in \ 1 \,..\, n+1 \\
\vdash \\
r \le n \ \lor \ r = n+1
\end{array}
$$

As can be seen, the "execution" is the following: init, followed by one or more "executions" of event receive, followed by a single "execution" of event final.

4.5 Protocol second refinement

The previous refinement is not satisfactory, as the event receive, supposedly "executed" by the receiver, has a direct access to the file f, which is supposed to be situated at the sender site. We want to have a more distributed execution of this protocol. Our observer's eyes are now open more frequently and he can see that another event, send, occurs before each occurrence of event receive. In Fig. 4.4, we can see first what the observer could see at earlier stages and, in the bottom, what he can see now.

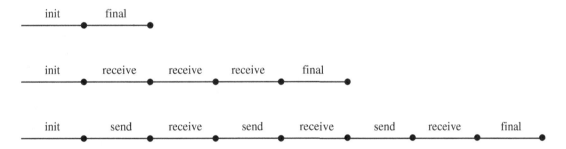

Fig. 4.4. A trace of the second refinement behavior

4.5.1 The state and the events

The sender has a local counter, s, which records the index of the next item to be sent to the receiver (initially, s is set to 1). When a transmission does occur, the data item d, which is equal to $f(s)$, is sent to the receiver, the counter s is incremented, and the new value of s is also sent together with d to the receiver (event send). Notice that the sender does not immediately send the next item. It waits until it receives an *acknowledgement* from the receiver. This acknowledgement, as we shall see, is the counter r.

When the receiver receives a pair "index-item", it compares the received counter with r and accepts the item if the counter it receives is different from r (event **receive**). In this case, r is incremented and then sent as an acknowledgment. When the sender receives a number r which is equal to its own counter s, it considers this to be an acknowledgement and proceeds with the next item, and so on.

The sender and the receiver are thus connected by means of two channels as indicated in Fig. 4.5: the data channel and the acknowledgement channel.

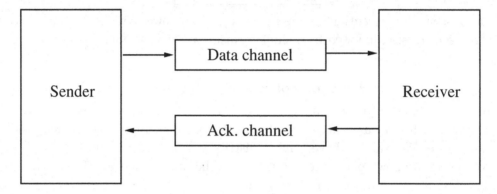

Fig. 4.5. The channels

Invariant **inv2_1** and **inv2_2** below correspond to the main properties of s. It states that the value of the counter s is at most one more than that of the counter r. It remains now for us to formalize the channels. For the moment (in this refinement), the data channel contains the counter s of the sender and also the data item d. As the counter s has already been formalized, we only have to define the invariants corresponding to d. This is done in invariants **inv2_3**, which states that the transmitted data item d is exactly the rth element of the input file f when s is different from r (that is when s is equal to $r+1$ according to invariant **inv2_2**). The Acknowledgment channel just contains the counter r of the receiver:

variables: b	**inv2_1:** $s \le n+1$
h	
s	**inv2_2:** $s \in r..r+1$
r	
d	**inv2_3:** $s = r+1 \;\Rightarrow\; d = f(r)$

Next are the various events. They encode the informal behavior of the protocol as described above:

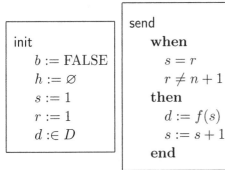

Notice our usage of the non-deterministic assignment $d :\in D$ in event init. Non-deterministic assignment will be explained in greater detail in Section 5.1.8 of Chapter 5. We have just to understand for now that d is assigned *any value* pertaining to the set D.

4.5.2 Proofs

All proofs are left as exercises to the reader. We encourage the reader to only take weaker invariants than those proposed in the previous section. More precisely, first drop invariant **inv2_2** and replace invariant **inv2_1** by a weaker one such as $s \in \mathbb{N}$, so that it is possible to see exactly where they are needed. Remember that it will be necessary to prove in turn that:

- event init establishes the invariants;
- event receive and final correctly refine their more abstract versions;
- event send refines the implicit event skip;
- event send converges; for this, a variant expression will need to be exhibited;
- taken together, events never deadlock.

Also do not forget that for variables that are the same as those in the abstraction, here b, h, and r, it will be necessary to prove that the actions done on them by old events receive and final are identical.

4.6 Protocol third refinement

In this refinement, we shall give the final implementation of the two-phase handshake protocol. The idea is to observe that it is not necessary to transmit the entire counters s and r on the data and acknowledgment channels. This is so for three reasons: (1) the only tests made on both sites are equality tests ($s = r$ or $s \neq r$, as can be seen in the events defined at the end of Section 4.5.1); (2) the only modifications of the counters are simple incrementations (again, this can be seen in the events defined in the Section 4.5.1); and (3) the difference between s and r is at most 1 (look at invariant **inv2_2**). As a consequence, these equality tests can be performed on the *parities* of these pointers only. These are thus the quantities we are going to transfer between the sites.

4.6.1 The state

Here are a few obvious definitions concerning the parities of natural numbers. The parity of 0 is 0 and the parity of $x + 1$ is $1 - parity(x)$:

constants: ... parity

axm3_1: $parity \in \mathbb{N} \rightarrow \{0, 1\}$
axm3_2: $parity(0) = 0$
axm3_3: $\forall x \cdot x \in \mathbb{N} \Rightarrow parity(x + 1) = 1 - parity(x)$

Notice that in **axm3_3**, we see for the first time a predicate logic formula, which is introduced by the quantifier $\forall$ (to be read "forall").

It is then easy to prove the following result (in Section 4.6.3), which we are going to exploit. It says that the comparison of two natural numbers is identical to the comparison of their parities when the difference between these two numbers is at most 1:

thm3_1: $\quad \forall x, y \cdot \begin{aligned} & x \in \mathbb{N} \\ & y \in \mathbb{N} \\ & x \in y .. y + 1 \\ & parity(x) = parity(y) \\ & \Rightarrow \\ & x = y \end{aligned}$

This is a theorem, i.e. a *consequence* to be proved, of what has been said elsewhere, namely properties of constants and invariants. We now refine the state and introduce two new variables p and q defined to be the parities of s and r respectively:

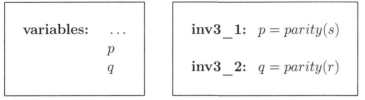

4.6.2 The events

The refined events are as follows:

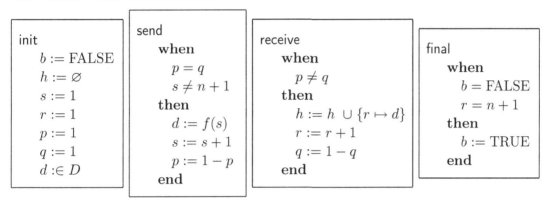

It can be seen that each counter s and r is now modified on one site only. So the only data transmitted from one site to the other are d and p from the sender to the receiver and q from the receiver to the sender. Again, all proofs are left as exercises to the reader.

4.6.3 Inference rules for universally quantified predicates

Before proving Theorem **thm3_1**, we need clearly some inference rules dealing with universally quantified formulas. As for elementary logic, we need two rules: one for universally quantified assumptions (left rule) and one for a universally quantified goal (right rule). Here are these rules:

$$\frac{\mathbf{H}, \; \forall \mathbf{x} \cdot \mathbf{P(x)}, \; \mathbf{P(E)} \vdash \mathbf{Q}}{\mathbf{H}, \; \forall \mathbf{x} \cdot \mathbf{P(x)} \vdash \mathbf{Q}} \; \mathsf{ALL\_L}$$

$$\frac{\mathbf{H} \vdash \mathbf{P(x)}}{\mathbf{H} \vdash \forall \mathbf{x} \cdot \mathbf{P(x)}} \; \mathsf{ALL\_R} \quad (\mathbf{x} \text{ not free in } \mathbf{H})$$

The first rule ($\mathsf{ALL\_L}$) allows us to add another assumption when we have a universally quantified one. This new assumption is obtained by instantiating the quantified variable $\mathbf{x}$ by any expression $\mathbf{E}$ in the predicate $\mathbf{P(x)}$. The second rule (ALL_R) allows us to remove the "$\forall$" quantifier appearing in the goal. This can be done however only if the quantified variable (here $\mathbf{x}$) *does not appear free* in the the set of assumptions $\mathbf{H}$: this requirement is called a side condition.

Equipped with the rule introduced in this section, we can now prove Theorem **thm3_1**. The proof obligation for this theorem consists in building a sequent with **thm3_1** as a goal and all relevant axioms as assumptions, yielding the following:

$$
\begin{aligned}
&\ldots \\
&parity \ \in \ \mathbb{N} \rightarrow \{0,1\} \\
&parity(0) = 0 \\
&\forall\, x \cdot x \in \mathbb{N} \ \Rightarrow \ parity(x+1) = 1 - parity(x) \\
&\vdash \\
&\quad \forall\, x, y \cdot \ \ x \in \mathbb{N} \\
&\qquad\qquad\quad y \in \mathbb{N} \\
&\qquad\qquad\quad x \in y \mathbin{..} y + 1 \\
&\qquad\qquad\quad parity(x) = parity(y) \\
&\qquad\qquad \Rightarrow \\
&\qquad\qquad\quad x = y
\end{aligned}
$$

This proof is left to the reader.

4.7 Development revisited

4.7.1 Motivation and the introduction of anticipated events

In the development undertaken so far, we were changing the file variable g of the initial model to another file variable h in the first refinement. Moreover, in order to establish the relationship between both variables (gluing invariants **inv0_2** and **inv0_3**), we had to introduce the boolean variable b, which is not really a variable of the protocol. All this seems a bit artificial.

In fact, the reason why we had to change from variable g in the initial model to variable h in the first refinement is purely technical. This is because the new event receive introduced in the first refinement must refine skip (as each new event does). But this new event modifies h: it adds to h an item taken in f. As a consequence, it cannot do that on g: h must be distinct from g.

In order to circumvent this difficulty, we introduce the concept of an *anticipated* event.† In the initial model, we introduce the event receive as "anticipated". Its only action is to possibly modify the variable g in a non-deterministic way. More generally, if a new anticipated event is introduced in a refinement (which is not the case here), it

---

† This concept was developed together with D. Cansell and D. Méry.

does not need to decrease a variant; it will do that only when it becomes convergent in a further refinement. However, an anticipated event must not increment the current variant (if any).

In this new development, event **receive** becomes **convergent** in the first refinement. It is exactly as event **receive** in the previous development, except that it works now with variable g. By this, we avoid introducing the artificial file variable h and the boolean variable b.

In the following section, we quickly present this technique applied to our current development. As you will see, it is simpler than the previous one, thanks to the introduction of an anticipated event in the initial model.

4.7.2 Initial model

$$\boxed{\textbf{variables:} \quad g} \qquad \boxed{\textbf{inv0\_1:} \quad g \in \mathbb{N} \leftrightarrow D}$$

$$\boxed{\begin{array}{l} \text{init} \\ \quad g :\in \mathbb{N} \leftrightarrow D \end{array}}$$

$$\boxed{\begin{array}{l} \text{final} \\ \quad \textbf{when} \\ \qquad g = f \\ \quad \textbf{then} \\ \qquad \text{skip} \\ \quad \textbf{end} \end{array}}$$

$$\boxed{\begin{array}{l} \text{receive} \\ \quad \textbf{status} \\ \qquad \text{anticipated} \\ \quad \textbf{when} \\ \qquad g \neq f \\ \quad \textbf{then} \\ \qquad g :\in \mathbb{N} \leftrightarrow D \\ \quad \textbf{end} \end{array}}$$

4.7.3 First refinement

$$\boxed{\begin{array}{ll} \textbf{variables:} & g \\ & r \end{array}} \qquad \boxed{\begin{array}{l} \textbf{inv1\_1:} \quad r \in 1\,..\,n+1 \\[2mm] \textbf{inv1\_2:} \quad g = (1\,..\,r-1) \lhd f \\[2mm] \textbf{variant1:} \quad n+1-r \end{array}}$$

```
                  receive
                    status
                      convergent
                    when
                      r ≤ n
                    then
                      g := g ∪ {r ↦ f(r)}
                      r := r + 1
                    end
```

```
  init
    g := ∅
    r := 1
```

```
  final
    when
      r = n + 1
    then
      skip
    end
```

4.7.4 Second refinement

```
  variables:    g
                s
                r
                d
```

```
  inv2_1:   s ≤ n + 1

  inv2_2:   s ∈ r .. r + 1

  inv2_3:   s = r + 1  ⇒  d = f(r)

  variant2:  r + 1 − s
```

```
  init
    g := ∅
    s := 1
    r := 1
    d :∈ D
```

```
  send
    status
      convergent
    when
      s = r
      r ≠ n + 1
    then
      d := f(s)
      s := s + 1
    end
```

```
  receive
    when
      s = r + 1
    then
      g := g ∪ {r ↦ d}
      r := r + 1
    end
```

```
  final
    when
      r = n + 1
    then
      skip
    end
```

4.7.5 Third refinement

variables: ...
p
q

inv3_1: $p = parity(s)$

inv3_2: $q = parity(r)$

init
$g := \varnothing$
$s := 1$
$r := 1$
$p := 1$
$q := 1$
$d :\in D$

send
when
$p = q$
$s \neq n + 1$
then
$d := f(s)$
$s := s + 1$
$p := 1 - p$
end

receive
when
$p \neq q$
then
$g := g \cup \{r \mapsto d\}$
$r := r + 1$
$q := 1 - q$
end

final
when
$r = n + 1$
then
skip
end

4.8 Reference

[1] L. Lamport. *Specifying Systems: The TLA+ Language and Tools for Hardware and Software Engineers.* Addison-Wesley, 1999.

5

The Event-B modeling notation and proof obligation rules

In previous chapters, we used the Event-B notation and the various corresponding proof obligation rules without introducing them initially in a systematic fashion. We presented them instead in the examples when they were needed. This was sufficient for the simple examples we studied because we used part of the notation and part of the proof obligation rules only. But it might not be adequate to continue in this way when presenting more elaborate examples in subsequent chapters. The purpose of this chapter is thus to correct this. First, we present the Event-B notation as a whole, in particular the bits not used so far, and then we present all the proof obligation rules. This will be illustrated with a simple running example.

5.1 The Event-B notation

5.1.1 Introduction: machines and contexts

The primary concept in doing formal developments in Event-B is that of a *model*. A model contains the complete mathematical development of a *Discrete Transition System*. It is made of several *components* of two kinds: *machines* and *contexts*. Machines contain the dynamic parts of a model, namely variables, invariants, theorems, variants, and events, whereas contexts contain the static parts of a model, namely carrier sets, constants, axioms, and theorems. This is illustrated in Fig. 5.1. Items belonging to machines or contexts (variables, invariants, etc.) are called *modeling elements*.

A model can contain contexts only, or machines only, or both. In the first case, the model represents a pure mathematical structure with sets, constants, axioms, and theorems. In the third case, the model is parameterized by the contexts. Finally, the second case represents a model which is not parameterized.

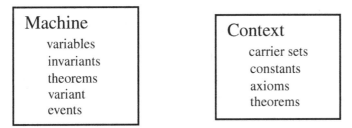

Fig. 5.1. Machine and context

5.1.2 Machine and context relationships

Machines and contexts have various relationships: a machine can be "refined" by another one, and a context can be "extended" by another one. Moreover, a machine can "see" one or several contexts. Machine and context relationships are illustrated in Fig. 5.2. Here are some visibility rules which must be followed by machines and contexts:

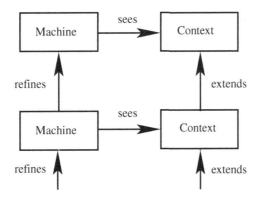

Fig. 5.2. Machine and context relationships

- A machine can see explicitly several contexts (or no context at all).
- A context can extend explicitly several contexts (or no context at all).
- The notion of context extension is transitive: a context C1 explicitly extending a context C2, implicitly extends all contexts extended by C1.
- When a context C1 extends a context C2, then the sets and constants of C2 can be used in C1.
- A machine implicitly sees all contexts extended by an explicitly seen context.
- When a machine M sees a context C, it means that the sets and constants of C can be used in M.
- The "refines" and "extends" relationships put together must not lead to any cycle.
- A machine only refines at most one other machine.

- The set of explicitly or implicitly seen contexts of a machine must be as large as the one of the abstraction of this machine.

All this is illustrated in Fig. 5.3, where it can be seen that machine M0 sees both context C01 and C02 explicitly, whereas machine M1 sees context C1 explicitly and contexts C01 and C02 implicitly. Note that the "sees" link between M2 and C1 is indispensable.

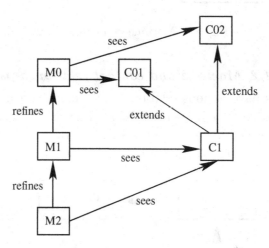

Fig. 5.3. Examples of correct visibilities

5.1.3 Context structure

The most general context structure is the one shown in Fig. 5.4. As can be seen, a context is made of various clauses introduced by specific keywords. Figure 5.4 presents the way these clauses are shown within the Rodin Platform, where they are *prede-fined*. This means that it is not necessary to enter the various keywords explicitly, they are there permanently. Clauses are not mandatory; some (or all) of them can be empty.

As can be seen, some clauses contain modeling elements introduced together with labels: axioms and theorems. These labels must be clearly all distinct; in the Rodin Platform, they are generated automatically (although users can change them). Let us now describe the contents of each clause:

- Each context has a name, which must be distinct from all other component (machine or context) names within the same model.
- Clause "extends" lists the contexts, which this context extends explicitly. This means that the present context can reference sets and constants of the explicitly extended contexts and of their extended contexts.

- Clause "sets" lists the newly introduced carrier sets which define pairwise disjoint types. The only property we can implicitly assume about such carrier sets is that they are not empty.
- Clause "constants" list the various constants introduced in this context. The constant identifiers must be all distinct and also distinct from the identifiers of the constants and sets situated in the extended contexts.
- Clause "axioms" lists the various predicates which the constants obey. Such predicates will be present as hypotheses in all proof obligations (Section 5.2).
- Clause "theorems" lists the various theorems which have to be proved within the context. In order to prove a theorem, we assume the axioms and theorems which are present in the extended context, the local axioms, but also the local theorems which are written before the theorem to be proved.

```
< context_identifier >
   extends
     < context_identifier_list >
   sets
     < set_identifier_list >
   constants
     < constant_identifier_list >
   axioms
     < label >:  < predicate >
        . . .
   theorems
     < label >:  < predicate >
        . . .
   end
```

Fig. 5.4. Context structure

5.1.4 Context example

An example of context is presented in Fig. 5.5. A set D is defined in context ctx_0. Moreover, three constants, n, f, and v, are defined in this context: n is a natural number (axm1), f is a total function from the interval $1..n$ to the set D (axm2), and v is supposed to belong to the range of f (axm3). A theorem is proposed: n is a positive number (thm1).

Notice that in this book we shall never write a context as it is shown in Fig. 5.5 because it might be difficult to read when getting bigger. As we have already done in previous chapters, we shall always present a context with separate boxes (one per

```
ctx_0
   sets
      D
   constants
      n
      f
      v
   axioms
      axm1 :   n ∈ ℕ
      axm2 :   f ∈ 1..n → D
      axm3 :   v ∈ ran(f)
   theorems
      thm1 :   n > 0
   end
```

Fig. 5.5. Context example

clause) as indicated in Fig. 5.6. Moreover, the "extends" clause will be obvious from the text.

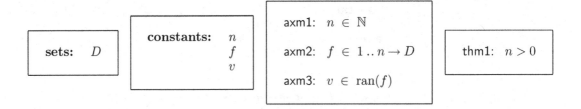

Fig. 5.6. Context example as presented in this book

5.1.5 Machine structure

The most general machine structure is shown in Fig. 5.7. As can be seen, a machine, like a context, is made of various clauses introduced by specific keywords. Figure 5.7 presents the way these clauses are shown within the Rodin Platform, where they are *predefined*. Clauses are not all mandatory, some (or all) of them can be empty.

As can be seen, some clauses contain modeling elements introduced together with labels: invariants and theorems. These labels must be clearly all distinct; in the Rodin Platform, they are generated automatically (although users can change them). Let us now describe the contents of each clause:

```
< machine_identifier >
    refines
        < machine_identifier >
    sees
        < context_identifier_list >
    variables
        < variable_identifier_list >
    invariants
        < label >:  < predicate >
        ...
    theorems
        < label >:  < predicate >
        ...
    variant
        < variant >
    events
        < event_list >
    end
```

Fig. 5.7. Machine structure

- A machine has a name, which must be distinct from all other component (machine or context) names within the same model.
- Clause "refines" contains (if any) the machine which this machine refines.
- Clause "sees" lists the contexts explicitly referenced by the machine. The machine can use the sets and constants defined in the explicitly or implicitly seen contexts.
- Clause "variables" list the various variables introduced in this machine. The variable identifiers must all be distinct, but, unlike the contexts, some variables can be the same as some variables in the abstract machine (if any).
- Clause "invariants" lists the various predicates which the variables must obey. Variables of the refined machine (if any) can occur in an invariant. When it is the case, this invariant is said to be a *gluing invariant*; as this indicates, it "glues" the space of the present machine to that of the refined machine.
- Clause "theorems" lists the various theorems which have to be proved within the machine. In order to prove a theorem, we assume the axioms and theorems of the seen contexts, the invariants and theorems of the abstract machines, the local invariants, and also the theorems which are written before the present one.
- The "variant" clause appears in a machine containing some **convergent** events (see Section 5.1.7). The variant behavior is explained in Section 5.2.9 describing the corresponding proof obligation rule.

- Clause "events" lists the various events of the machine. Events are described in Section 5.1.7.

5.1.6 Machine example

An example of machine is presented in Fig. 5.8. Machine m_0a sees context ctx_0. A variable i is defined which belongs to the interval $1..n$ (n is defined in context ctx_0). The events of this machine are defined in Section 5.1.9. Just as for contexts, in this book machines are never shown; this is illustrated in Fig. 5.8. Each clause is defined in a separate box as shown in Fig 5.9. Seen contexts as well as the abstract machines are obvious from the text.

```
m_0a
   sees
      ctx_0
   variables
      i
   invariants
      inv1 :  i ∈ 1..n
   events
      ...
   end
```

Fig. 5.8. Machine example

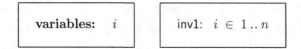

Fig. 5.9. Machine example as presented in this book

5.1.7 Events

The most general event structure is shown in Fig. 5.10. An event contains several clauses introduced by specific keywords. Figure 5.10 presents the way these clauses are shown on the Rodin Platform, where they are also *predefined*. Clauses can be missing except the clause "status".

```
< event_identifier >
  status
    {ordinary, convergent, anticipated}
  refines
    < event_identifier_list >
  any
    < parameter_identifier_list >
  where
    < label >: < predicate >
    ...
  with
    < label >: < witness >
    ...
  then
    < label >: < action >
    ...
  end
```

Fig. 5.10. Event structure

Let us now describe the contents of each clause.

- Clause "status" can be one of ordinary, convergent (the event has to decrease the variant), or anticipated (the event must not increase the variant).
- Clause "refines" lists the abstract events (if any) this event refines.
- Clause "any" lists the parameters (if any) of the event.
- Clause "where" contains the various guards of the event. Guards are the necessary conditions for the event to be enabled. Notice that when the "any" clause is missing, then keyword **where** is replaced by keyword **when** in the pretty print of the Rodin Platform.
- Clause "with" in an event contains the *witnesses* of the corresponding abstract event. A witness has to be provided in a refining event *for each disappearing parameter* of the abstract event and *for each disappearing abstract variable* assigned in a "non-deterministic way" in the abstract event (see Section 5.1.8). The witness for parameter or variable a is defined as follows: $a : P(a)$, where $P(a)$ is a predicate involving a. A witness predicate can be either *deterministic* or *non-deterministic*. A deterministic witness $P(a)$ is of the form $a = E$ (with E free of a).
- Clause "then" contains the list of actions of the event. Actions are explained in Section 5.1.8.

Each machine must contain a special initialization event.

5.1.8 Actions

An event action can be either *deterministic* or *non-deterministic*. In the first case, it is made of a variable identifier, followed by :=, followed by an expression. This is illustrated as follows:

$$< variable\_identifier > \ := \ < expression >$$

Here is an example of a list of deterministic actions in an event situated in a machine with variables x. y, and z:

$$
\begin{aligned}
\mathsf{act1}: \quad & x \ := \ x + z \\
\mathsf{act2}: \quad & y \ := \ y - x
\end{aligned}
$$

Variables x and y are modified as indicated, whereas variable z is not modified. It is important to notice that such actions are "performed" *simultaneously*. In other words, the order of actions in such a list is meaningless. In action act2, the value of x which is referred to in the right-hand side is the value of x *before* the action act1 modifying x takes place.

A special case of deterministic assignment is the following:

$$< identifier > (< expression\_1 >) \ := \ < expression\_2 >$$

where $< identifier >$ denotes a function variable. This form is a shorthand for:

$$< identifier > \ := \ < identifier > \ \mathbin{⩤} \ \{< expression\_1 > \mapsto < expression\_2 >\}$$

where $\mathbin{⩤}$ is the relation overriding operator.

Alternatively, an action can be non-deterministic, in which case it is made of a list of distinct variable identifiers, followed by :|, followed by a before–after predicate. This is illustrated below:

$$< variable\_identifier\_list > \ :| \ < before\_after\_predicate >$$

The *before–after predicate* may contain all the variables of the machine: they denote the corresponding values *just before* the action takes place. It can also contain some of the variable identifiers of the list. Such identifiers are primed; they denote the corresponding values *just after* the action has taken place. As an example, suppose we have three variables x, y, and z; here is a non-deterministic action:

$$\mathsf{act1}: \quad x, y \ :| \ x' > y \ \wedge \ y' > x' + z.$$

Variable x becomes greater than y and variable y becomes greater than x' (the new value for x) added to z (a variable which is not modified).

A final option is to define a non-deterministic action as a variable identifier, followed by :∈, followed by a set expression. This is illustrated below:

$$< variable\_identifier > \ :\in \ < set\_expression >$$

This form is just a special case of the previous one. It can always be translated to a non-deterministic case as shown in the following example. Suppose a machine with variables A, x, and y, here is an action:

$$\text{act1}: \quad x \quad :\in \quad A \cup \{y\}$$

It is the same as:

$$\text{act1}: \quad x \quad :| \quad x' \in A \cup \{y\}.$$

Variable x becomes a member of the set $A \cup \{y\}$, whereas variables A and y are not modified.

Note that the most general form for all actions in an event is in fact the non-deterministic form. As an example, our initial deterministic case:

$$\begin{aligned} x &:= x + z \\ y &:= y - x \end{aligned}$$

can be equivalently "translated" as follows:

$$x, y \quad :| \quad x' = x + z \ \wedge \ y' = y - z.$$

This is the form which is used systematically in the tool. It unifies the three forms of actions presented in this section.

Note, finally, that actions in the same list have to deal with *distinct variables*. For example, the following is not allowed since variable x is modified in both act1 and act2:

$$\begin{aligned} \text{act1}: \quad & x \quad := \quad x + z \\ \text{act2}: \quad & x, y \quad :| \quad x' > y \ \wedge \ y' \leq x' + z, \end{aligned}$$

whereas the following is:

$$\begin{aligned} \text{act1}: \quad & x \quad := \quad x + z \\ \text{act2}: \quad & y, z \quad :| \quad z' > y \ \wedge \ y' \leq z' + x. \end{aligned}$$

5.1.9 Examples of events

Events associated with machine m_0a are presented in Fig. 5.11: initialization and search. This is the way events are shown in this book, where things are simplified. In ordinary events, the status is missing; moreover, when an event is made of a single "then" clause, the **then** keyword is omitted as in event initialization. On the Rodin

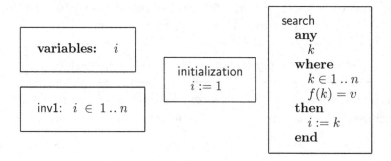

Fig. 5.11. Events associated with machine m_0a

Platform, the presentation is slightly different: a label is defined with each guard and each action.

The **search** event describes the purpose of machine m_0a, namely to find an index i in array f such that $f(i)$ is equal to the constant v. On Fig. 5.12, another machine, m_0b, is presented with a different **search** event containing a non-deterministic action.

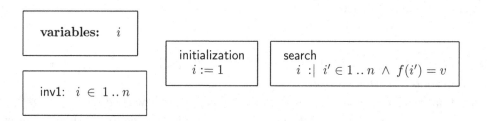

Fig. 5.12. Another machine m_0b

A refinement of machine m_0a by machine m_1a is shown in Fig. 5.13. A new variable j is introduced. Notice the "with" clause in event **search**: it provide a witness for the parameter k of the abstract event **search** in machine m_0a, which has disappeared in the concrete event **search** of machine m_1a. A new **convergent** event **progress** is introduced. Notice the "variant" clause in machine m_1a with numeric variant $n - j$: this variant is decreased by event **progress**.

A refinement of machine m_0b by machine m_1b is shown in Fig. 5.14. The "with" clause in event **search** is not needed because variable i is kept in the concrete version of event **search**. Notice the "variant" clause defining the finite set variant $j \mathbin{..} n$. These are the *only differences* with refining machine m_1a.

variables: i
j

search
  when
    $f(j+1) = v$
  with
    $k: \quad j+1 = k$
  then
    $i := j+1$
  end

inv1: $j \in 0 .. n$

inv2: $v \notin f[i .. j]$

thm1: $v \in f[j+1 .. n]$

variant: $n - j$

initialization
$i := 1$
$j := 0$

progress
  status
    convergent
  when
    $f(j+1) \neq v$
  then
    $j := j+1$
  end

Fig. 5.13. Machine m_1a refines machine m_0a

variables: i
j

initialization
$i := 1$
$j := 0$

inv1: $j \in 0 .. n$

inv2: $v \notin f[i .. j]$

search
  when
    $f(j+1) = v$
  then
    $i := j+1$
  end

thm1: $v \in f[j+1 .. n]$

variant: $j .. n$

progress
  status
    convergent
  when
    $f(j+1) \neq v$
  then
    $j := j+1$
  end

Fig. 5.14. Machine m_1b refines machine m_0b

5.2 Proof obligation rules

5.2.1 Introduction

The proof obligations define what is to be proved for an Event-B model. They are automatically generated by a Rodin Platform tool called the *proof obligation generator*. This tool static-checks context or machine texts. It decides then what is to be proved in these texts. The outcome is various sequents, which are transmitted to the provers performing automatic or interactive proofs. Here is summary of the main Rodin Platform kernel tools: the static checkers (comprising the lexical analyzer, the syntactic analyzer, and the type checker), the proof obligation generator, and the provers.

In what follows, we describe the different kinds of proof obligation rules. This is done by defining for each kind of proof obligation rule the specific form of the corresponding sequent generated by the tool. In what follows, we shall always denote the action of an event by means of a non-deterministic action (see Section 5.1.8), since, as we know, an action can always be put under this normalized form.

In order to define rules dealing with an event (this is the case for most rules), we shall use systematically a schematic event defined as follows:

```
evt
    any  x  where
        G(s, c, v, x)
    then
        v :| BA(s, c, v, x, v')
    end
```

where s denotes the seen sets, c the seen constants, and v the variables of the machine. Seen axioms and theorems are collectively denoted by $A(s, c)$, whereas invariants and local theorems are denoted by $I(s, c, v)$. In a refining machines, the concrete variables will be denoted by w and the local invariants and theorems by $J(s, c, v, w)$. In order to simplify matters, we shall suppose that no additional contexts are seen in an refined machine (we shall thus still use s for the sets and c for the constants).

5.2.2 Invariant preservation proof obligation rule: INV

This proof obligation rule ensures that each invariant in a machine is preserved by each event. For an event evt and an invariant inv(s, c, v), the PO is named: "evt / inv / INV."

Let evt be the following event:

$$
\boxed{
\begin{array}{l}
\text{evt} \\
\quad \textbf{any} \quad x \quad \textbf{where} \\
\qquad G(s, c, v, x) \\
\quad \textbf{then} \\
\qquad v :\mid BA(s, c, v, x, v') \\
\quad \textbf{end}
\end{array}
}
$$

The rule is then the following:

Axioms and theorems Invariants and theorems Guards of the event Before–after predicate of the event $\vdash$ Modified specific invariant	evt/inv/INV

$$
\begin{array}{l}
A(s, c) \\
I(s, c, v) \\
G(s, c, v, x) \\
BA(s, c, v, x, v') \\
\vdash \\
\text{inv}(s, c, v')
\end{array}
$$

For the machine m_0a shown in Fig. 5.11 the tool generates the following proof obligations: "initialization / inv1 / INV" and "search / inv1 / INV". Here is proof obligation "initialization / inv1 / INV":

axm1 axm2 axm3 thm1 BA predicate $\vdash$ modified inv1	$n \in \mathbb{N}$ $f \in 1 .. n \rightarrow D$ $v \in \mathrm{ran}(f)$ $n > 0$ $\underline{i' = 1}$ $\vdash$ $i' \in 1 .. n$	$n \in \mathbb{N}$ $f \in 1 .. n \rightarrow D$ $v \in \mathrm{ran}(f)$ $n > 0$ $\vdash$ $1 \in 1 .. n$

Simplification performed
by the PO Generator

Here is proof obligation "**search** / **inv1** / **INV**":

axm1	$n \in \mathbb{N}$	$n \in \mathbb{N}$
axm2	$f \in 1 .. n \to D$	$f \in 1 .. n \to D$
axm3	$v \in \mathrm{ran}(f)$	$v \in \mathrm{ran}(f)$
thm1	$n > 0$	$n > 0$
inv1	$i \in 1 .. n$	$i \in 1 .. n$
grd1	$k \in 1 .. n$	$k \in 1 .. n$
grd2	$f(k) = v$	$f(k) = v$
BA predicate	$i' = k$	
$\vdash$	$\vdash$	$\vdash$
modified inv1	$i' \in 1 .. n$	$k \in 1 .. n$

Simplification performed
by the PO Generator

As can be seen, the tool has performed some trivial simplifications before sending the proof obligation to the prover. From now on, in further examples we shall show the simplified form only.

The **INV** proof obligation rule is also used in the invariant of a refinement. Let **evt0** be an event and **evt** be one of its refinements:

```
evt0
    any
        ...
    where
        ...
    then
        v :| ...
    end
```

```
evt
    refines
        evt0
    any
        y
    where
        H(y, s, c, w)
    with
        ...
        v' : W2(v', s, c, w, y, w')
    then
        w :| BA2(s, c, w, y, w')
    end
```

Let $inv(s, c, v, w)$ be a specific invariant in this refinement, then the proof obligation rule is the following:

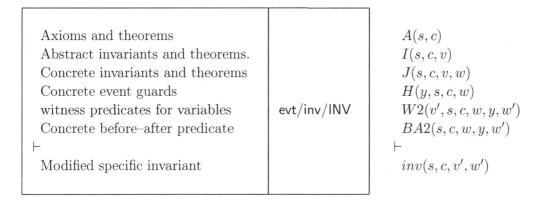

5.2.3 Feasibility proof obligation rule: FIS

The purpose of this proof obligation is to ensure that a non-deterministic action is feasible. For an event **evt** and a non-deterministic action **act** in it, the name of this proof obligation is "evt/act/FIS." Let **evt** be the following event:

evt
   any x **where**
     $G(s, c, v, x)$
   then
     act : $v :| BA(s, c, v, x, v')$
   end

The rule is then the following:

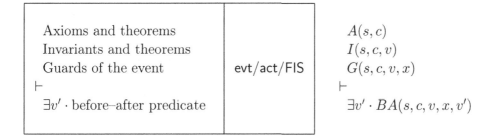

For the machine m_0b shown in Fig. 5.12, the tool generates the following proof obligation:

<table>
<tr><td>

axm1
axm2
axm3
thm1
inv1
grd
⊢

$\exists i' \cdot$ before-after predicate

</td><td>

$n \in \mathbb{N}$
$f \in 1\mathbin{..}n \to D$
$v \in \mathrm{ran}(f)$
$n > 0$
$i \in 1\mathbin{..}n$
no guard in event **search**
⊢
$\exists i' \cdot i' \in 1\mathbin{..}n \ \wedge \ f(i') = v$

</td></tr>
</table>

5.2.4 Guard strengthening proof obligation rule: GRD

The purpose of this proof obligation is to make sure that the concrete guards in a concrete event are stronger than the abstract ones in the abstract event. This ensures that when a concrete event is enabled, so is the corresponding abstract one. For a concrete event **evt** and an abstract guard **grd** in the corresponding abstract event, the name of this proof obligation is: "evt/grd/GRD". Let **evt0** be an event and **evt** be its refinement:

<table>
<tr><td>

evt0
  any
    x
  where
    grd : $g(s, c, v, x)$
    . . .
  then
    . . .
  end

</td><td>

evt
  refines
    evt0
  any
    y
  where
    $H(y, s, c, w)$
  with
    $x : W(x, s, c, w, y)$
  then
    . . .
  end

</td></tr>
</table>

Notice the witness predicate $W(x, y, s, c, w)$, which is due to the fact that the abstract parameters x are *different* from the concrete parameters y. Then the proof obligation rule is the following:

Axioms and theorems		$A(s, c)$
Abstract invariants and theorems		$I(s, c, v)$
Concrete invariants and theorems		$J(s, c, v, w)$
Concrete event guards	evt/grd/GRD	$H(y, s, c, w)$
Witness predicates for parameters		$W(x, s, c, w, y)$
$\vdash$		$\vdash$
Abstract event specific guard		$g(s, c, v, x)$

From the machine m_1a shown in Fig. 5.13, the tool generates the following proof obligation:

axm1	$n \in \mathbb{N}$
axm2	$f \in 1 .. n \to D$
axm3	$v \in \operatorname{ran}(f)$
thm1 of ctx_0	$n > 0$
inv1 (abstract)	$i \in 1 .. n$
inv1 (concrete)	$j \in 0 .. n$
inv2 (concrete)	$v \notin f[1 .. j]$
thm1 of m_1a	$v \in f[j + 1 .. n]$
grd1 (concrete)	$f(j + 1) = v$
witness predicate for k	$j + 1 = k$
$\vdash$	$\vdash$
grd2 (abstract)	$f(k) = v$

5.2.5 The guard merging proof obligation rule: MRG

This proof obligation rule ensures that the guard of a concrete event merging two abstract events is stronger than the disjunction of the guards of the abstract events. For a merging event evt, the name of the rule is "evt / MRG". Let evt01 and evt02 be two abstract events with the same parameters and the same action, and let **evt** be the concrete merging event:

```
evt01
    any
        x
    where
        G1(s, c, v, x)
    then
        S
    end
```

```
evt02
    any
        x
    where
        G2(s, c, v, x)
    then
        S
    end
```

```
evt
    refines
        evt01
        evt02
    any
        x
    where
        H(s, c, v, x)
    then
        S
    end
```

The rule is as follows:

Axioms and theorems		$A(s, c)$
Abstract invariants and theorems		$I(s, c, v)$
Concrete event guards	evt/MRG	$H(s, c, v, x)$
$\vdash$		$\vdash$
Disjunction of abstract guards		$G1(s, c, v, x) \lor G2(s, c, v, x)$

5.2.6 Simulation proof obligation rule: SIM

The purpose of this proof obligation is to make sure that each action in an abstract event is correctly simulated in the corresponding refinement. This ensures that when a *concrete event is "executed"* what it does is *not contradictory* with what the corresponding *abstract event does*. For a concrete event **evt** and an abstract action **act**, the name of this proof obligation is "evt/act/SIM". Let **evt0** be an event and **evt** be its refinement:

```
evt0
   any
      x
   where
      . . .
   then
      v :| BA1(s, c, v, x, v')
   end
```

```
evt
   refines
      evt0
   any
      y
   where
      H(y, s, c, w)
   with
      x :  W1(x, s, c, w, y, w')
      v' : W2(v', s, c, w, y, w')
   then
      w :| BA2(s, c, w, y, w')
   end
```

The case presented in these events is the *most general one* that can be encountered. Both events have parameters (introduced by keyword **any**) and also some non-deterministic actions. We suppose that the abstract and concrete parameters x and y are pairwise disjoint. Likewise, we suppose that the abstract and concrete variables v and w are pairwise disjoint. As a result, we have two witness predicates: $W1(x, s, c, w, y, w')$ for the abstract parameters x and $W2(v', s, c, w, y, w')$ for the abstract variable after-value v'. The proof obligation rule is as follows:

Axioms and theorems		$A(s, c)$
Abstract invariants and theorems		$I(s, c, v)$
Concrete invariants and theorems		$J(s, c, v, w)$
Concrete event guards		$H(y, s, c, w)$
witness predicates for parameters	evt/act/SIM	$W1(x, s, c, w, y, w')$
witness predicates for variables		$W2(v', s, c, w, y, w')$
Concrete before–after predicate		$BA2(s, c, w, y, w')$
$\vdash$		$\vdash$
Abstract before–after predicate		$BA1(s, c, v, x, v')$

In order to illustrate this proof obligation rule, we use a specific example. Here is machine with variable v and event inc:

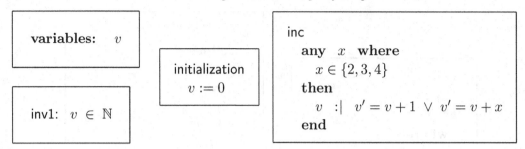

Here is now a refinement of this machine:

variables: w		inc

```
variables:   w

initialization
   w := 0

inv1:  w = 2 * v

inc
   any  y  where
      y ∈ {6, 8}
   with
      x :    y = 2 * x
      v' :   w' = 2 * v'
   then
      w  :|  w' = w + 2  ∨  w' = w + y
   end
```

Suppose the abstract action in event inc is labeled act, then the generated proof obligation is the following:

Abstract invariant		$v \in \mathbb{N}$
Concrete invariant		$w = 2 * v$
Concrete event guard		$y \in \{6, 8\}$
witness predicate for parameter	inc/act/SIM	$y = 2 * x$
witness predicate for variable		$w' = 2 * v'$
Concrete before–after predicate		$w' = w + 2 \ \lor \ w' = w + y$
$\vdash$		$\vdash$
Abstract before–after predicate		$v' = v + 1 \ \lor \ v' = v + x$

Another usage of the **SIM** proof obligation rule is when (part of) the abstract variables are kept in the concrete machine. To simplify matters, we give here the rule when all abstract variables are kept in the concrete machine without even adding new variables there. The generalization is simple.

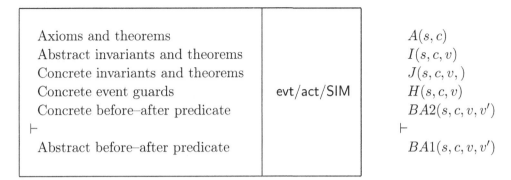

We can illustrate this case with the following machine:

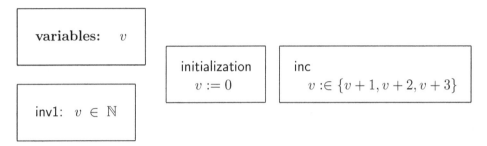

This machine is refined as follows:

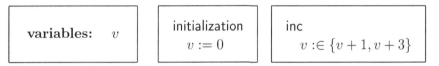

The generated **SIM** proof obligation is then the following (**act** is supposed to be the label associated with the abstract action):

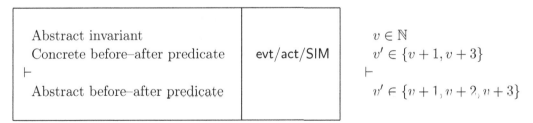

5.2.7 The numeric variant proof obligation rule: NAT

This rule ensures that under the guards of each convergent or anticipated event, a proposed numeric variant is indeed a natural number. For a convergent (or anticipated) event **evt**, the name of this rule is **evt** / **NAT**. Given a machine and a convergent event defined as follows:

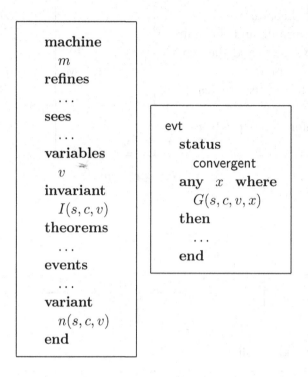

Then the **NAT** proof obligation rule is the following:

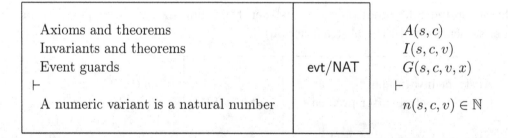

5.2.8 *The finite set variant proof obligation rule:* FIN

This rule ensures that under the guards of each convergent or anticipated event, a proposed set variant is indeed a *finite* set. For a convergent (or anticipated) event **evt**, the name of this rule is evt / FIN. Given a machine and a convergent event defined as follows:

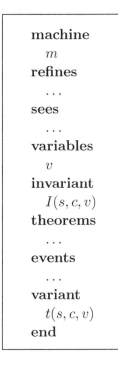

Then the FIN proof obligation rule is the following:

Axioms and theorems		$A(s,c)$
Invariants and theorems		$I(s,c,v)$
Event guards	evt/FIN	$G(s,c,v,x)$
$\vdash$		$\vdash$
Finiteness of set variant		$\mathrm{finite}(t(s,c,v))$

5.2.9 The variant proof obligation rule: VAR

This proof obligation rule ensures that each convergent event decreases the proposed numeric variant or proposed finite set variant. It also ensures that each anticipated event does not increase the proposed numeric variant or proposed finite set variant.

For a convergent or anticipated event **evt**, the name of this rule is "**evt** / **VAR**". Given a convergent event defined as follows:

$$
\begin{array}{l}
\textbf{evt} \\
\quad \textbf{status} \\
\quad\quad \text{convergent} \\
\quad \textbf{any} \;\; x \;\; \textbf{where} \\
\quad\quad G(x, s, c, v) \\
\quad \textbf{then} \\
\quad\quad v :\mid BA(s, c, v, x, v') \\
\quad \textbf{end}
\end{array}
$$

The proof obligation rule is the following if the variant $n(s, c, v)$ is numeric:

	evt/VAR	
Axioms and theorems		$A(s, c)$
Invariants and theorems		$I(s, c, v)$
Guards of the event		$G(s, c, v, x)$
Before–after predicate of the event		$BA(s, c, v, x, v')$
$\vdash$		$\vdash$
Modified variant smaller than variant		$n(s, c, v') < n(s, c, v)$

The proof obligation rule is the following if the variant $t(s, c, v)$ is a finite set:

	evt/VAR	
Axioms and theorems		$A(s, c)$
Invariants and theorems		$I(s, c, v)$
Guards of the event		$G(s, c, v, x)$
Before–after predicate of the event		$BA(s, c, v, x, v')$
$\vdash$		$\vdash$
Modified variant strictly included in variant		$t(s, c, v') \subset t(s, c, v)$

Given an anticipated event defined as follows:

```
evt
    status
        anticipated
    any  x  where
        G(s, c, v, x)
    then
        v :| BA(s, c, v, x, v')
    end
```

The proof obligation rule is the following if the variant $n(s, c, v)$ is numeric:

Axioms and theorems		$A(s, c)$
Invariants and theorems		$I(s, c, v)$
Guards of the event	evt/VAR	$G(s, c, v, x)$
Before–after predicate of the event		$BA(s, c, v, x, v')$
$\vdash$		$\vdash$
Modified variant not greater than variant		$n(s, c, v') \leq n(s, c, v)$

The proof obligation rule is the following if the variant $t(s, c, v)$ is a finite set:

Axioms and theorems		$A(s, c)$
Invariants and theorems		$I(s, c, v)$
Guards of the event	evt/VAR	$G(s, c, v, x)$
Before–after predicate of the event		$BA(s, c, v, x, v')$
$\vdash$		$\vdash$
Modified variant included in or equal to variant		$t(s, c, v') \subseteq t(s, c, v)$

5.2.10 The non-deterministic witness proof obligation rule: WFIS

This proof obligation rule ensures that each witness proposed in the witness predicate of a concrete event indeed exists. For a concrete event **evt**, and an abstract parameter x, the name of this rule is: evt/x/WFIS. Let the following be a concrete event where a witness predicate $W(x, s, c, w, y)$ is defined for the abstract parameter x (a similar case can be handled for a witness corresponding to an abstract after-value):

```
evt
    refines
        evt0
    any
        y
    where
        H(y, s, c, w)
    with
        x : W(x, s, c, w, y, w')
    then
        BA2(s, c, w, y, w')
    end
```

The proof obligation rule is defined as follows:

Axioms and theorems		$A(s, c)$
Abstract invariants and theorems		$I(s, c, v)$
Concrete invariants and theorems		$J(s, c, v, w)$
Concrete event guards	evt/x/WFIS	$H(y, s, c, w)$
Concrete before–after predicate		$BA2(s, c, w, y, w')$
$\vdash$		$\vdash$
$\exists x \cdot$ witness		$\exists x \cdot W(x, s, c, w, y, w')$

5.2.11 *The theorem proof obligation rule:* THM

This rule ensures that a proposed context or machine theorem is indeed provable. Theorems are important in that they might simplify some proofs. For a theorem thm in a context or machine, the name of this rule is thm/ THM.

5.2.12 *The well-definedness proof obligation rule:* WD

This proof obligation rule ensures that a potentially ill-defined axiom, theorem, invariant, guard, action, variant, or witness is indeed well defined. For a given modeling element (axm, thm, inv, grd, act or a variant, or a witness x in an event evt), the names are: axm / WD, thm / WD, inv / WD, grd / WD, act / WD, VWD , evt /x/ WWD. The specific form of this proof obligation rule depends on the potentially ill-defined expression. This is indicated in the following table:

Mathematical expression	Well-definedness condition
$\text{inter}(S)$	$S \neq \varnothing$
$\bigcap x \cdot P \mid T$	$\exists x \cdot P$
$f(E)$	f is a partial function $E \in \text{dom}(f)$
E/F	$F \neq 0$
$E \bmod F$	$0 \leq E \wedge 0 < F$
$\text{card}(S)$	$\text{finite}(S)$
$\min(S)$	$S \neq \varnothing \wedge \exists x \cdot (\forall n \cdot n \in S \Rightarrow x \leq n)$
$\max(S)$	$S \neq \varnothing \wedge \exists x \cdot (\forall n \cdot n \in S \Rightarrow x \geq n)$

6

Bounded re-transmission protocol

In this chapter, we extend the *file transfer protocol* example of Chapter 4. The added constraint with regard to the previous simple example is that we suppose now that the data and acknowledgment channels situated between the two sites are *unreliable*. As a consequence, the effect of the execution of the bounded re-transmission protocol (for short BRP) is to only *partially* copy (but sometimes totally also) a sequential file from one site to another. The purpose of this example is precisely to study how we can cope with this kind of problem of dealing with *fault tolerance* and how we can formally reason about them. Notice that, in this chapter, we do not develop proofs as much as in the previous chapters; we only give some hints and let the reader develop the formal proof. This example has been studied in many papers among which is the one by J.F. Groote and J.C. Van de Pool [1].

6.1 Informal presentation of the bounded re-transmission protocol
6.1.1 Normal behavior

The sequential file to be transmitted is supposed to be transported piece by piece from one site, the sender site, to another one, the receiver site. For that purpose, the sender sends a certain data item on the so-called data channel connecting the sender to the receiver. As soon as the receiver receives this data item, it stores it in its own file and sends back an acknowledgment to the sender on the so-called acknowledgment channel connecting the receiver to the sender. As soon as the sender receives this acknowledgment, it sends the next data item, and so on. We suppose that the *final* data item sent by the sender contains a special item of information so that the receiver is able to know when the file transmission is completed. Notice that it has nevertheless to send a final acknowledgment.

All this can be represented in Fig. 6.1 where the events (SND_snd, RCV_rcv, RCV_snd, and SND_rcv) are supposed to represent the various phases we have just described, together with their synchronization as indicated by the arrows.

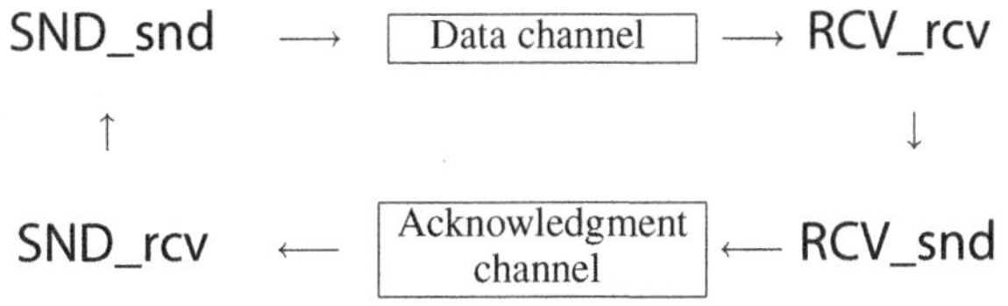

SND_snd $\longrightarrow$ [Data channel] $\longrightarrow$ RCV_rcv

$\uparrow$ $\downarrow$

SND_rcv $\longleftarrow$ [Acknowledgment channel] $\longleftarrow$ RCV_snd

Fig. 6.1. Schematic view of the transmission protocol

What we have just described is the normal behavior of the protocol, where an entire file is transmitted from the sender to the receiver. We shall also describe below a degraded behavior, where the sender's file is transmitted only partially to the receiver due to some problems on the transmission channels.

6.1.2 Unreliability of the communications

The transmission channels (data and acknowledgement) situated between the sender and the receiver might be faulty; that is, some data items sent by the sender or some acknowledgments sent by the receiver might be lost. In order to cope with the unreliability of these channels, the sender starts a timer when it sends a data item. This device is adjusted so that it wakes up the sender (provided, of course, it has not received an acknowledgment in the meantime) after a certain delay. This delay is *guaranteed* to be greater than the *maximum* delay, dl, which is required to first send a data item and subsequently receive back the corresponding acknowledgment. In other words, the sender can conclude that a message has necessarily been lost when the time is over, that is if a delay, dl, has passed since the last data item has been sent to the receiver without receiving a corresponding acknowledgment.

But, of course, when the timer wakes it up, the sender does not know whether the lost message corresponds to the data item that it has been sent or to the corresponding acknowledgment supposed to have been sent back by the receiver. In any case, the sender re-transmits the previous data item and waits for the corresponding acknowledgment. This is the reason why the protocol is called a *re-transmission* protocol.

6.1.3 Protocol abortion

In case of successive losses of messages, the process of data re-transmission can be repeated a number of times; this is recorded at the sender site in the, so-called, *re-try counter*. When this counter reaches a certain pre-defined limit M, the sender decides that the transmission is definitely broken and aborts the protocol (from its own point of view). This is the reason why the protocol is called the *bounded* re-transmission protocol.

The question that arises immediately is then, of course, that of the synchronization with the receiver. In other words, how does the receiver know that the protocol has aborted? Clearly, the sender cannot communicate any longer with the receiver in order to send it this abortion information because the communication is now broken.

This problem is solved by means of a second timer situated in the receiver's site. This timer is activated by the receiver when it receives a new data item (that is, not a re-transmitted one). This timer is adjusted so that it wakes up the receiver (provided, of course, it has not received a new data item in the meantime) after a certain delay that is *guaranteed* to be such that the receiver can be certain that the sender has already aborted the protocol. Clearly, this delay has to be greater than or equal to the quantity $(M + 1) \times dl$, since after that delay the sender must have given up as we have seen above. When the second timer wakes it up, the receiver aborts the protocol (from its own point of view). As can be seen, in case of problems, the two participants are indirectly synchronized by means of these timers.

6.1.4 Alternating bit

As we have seen above, the sender may re-transmit the same data item several times. But, it may also transmit two (or more) successive data items, which might happen to have the *same value*. Of course, this is annoying, since the receiver may confuse a re-transmitted data item with a new one that is identical to its predecessor. In order to solve this problem, each data item is accompanied by a bit whose value is alternating from one item to the next. When the receiver receives two successive items accompanied by the same bit, it can thus be certain (is it?) that the latter is a re-transmission of the former.

6.1.5 Final situation of the protocol

At the end of the protocol execution, we might be in one of the following three situations:

(i) The protocol has successfully been able to transfer the entire file from the sender to the receiver and the sender has indeed received the last acknowledgment from the receiver. In that case, both the sender and the receiver know that the protocol has ended successfully; the file has been entirely copied and both sites know it.

(ii) The protocol has successfully been able to transfer the entire file from the sender to the receiver, but the sender has never received the last acknowledgment (in spite of successive re-transmissions, this message is definitely lost in the acknowledgment channel) so that the sender aborts the protocol, whereas the receiver does not.

(iii) The protocol has been aborted on both sites.

Notice that the fourth possibility – where the receiver would have aborted the protocol, whereas the sender would not – is not possible (is it true?).

6.1.6 A pseudo-code description of the BRP

In this section, we present a pseudo-code version of our protocol. The rôle of this description is to make a little more precise the completely informal presentation of the previous section. Each event of the protocol (that is, SND_snd, RCV_rcv, RCV_snd, and SND_rcv) and the two additional events corresponding to the timers (which we call, SND_timer and RCV_timer) are described in terms of an *enabling condition*, introduced as we have done in previous chapters by the keyword **when**, followed by an *action part*, introduced by the keyword **then**. The former contains the condition under which the event *may* be enabled, whereas the latter contains a description of what the event is supposed to do once it is enabled.

Event SND_snd Our first event, SND_snd, is enabled by a condition expressing that this event is indeed woken up (we shall see below that this is done either by the event SND_rcv or by the event SND_timer). The action of SND_snd consists in acquiring the next data item from the sender's file, storing it on the data channel together with the corresponding alternating bit, starting the sender's timer, and finally activating the data channel (effectively sending the data and the bit). Below, on the left, is the pseudo-code of this event:

```
SND_snd
    when
        SND_snd is woken up
    then
        acquire data from sender's file;
        store acquired data on data channel;
        store sender's bit on data channel;
        start sender's timer;
        activate data channel;
    end
```

```
RCV_rcv
    when
        data channel interrupt occurs
    then
        acquire sender's bit from data channel;
        if sender's bit = receiver's bit then
            acquire data from data channel;
            store data on receiver's file;
            modify receiver's bit;
            if data item is not the last one then
                start receiver's timer;
            end
        end
        reset data channel interrupt;
        wake up event RCV_snd;
    end
```

Event RCV_rcv The next event, RCV_rcv, proposed above on the right, is enabled by the interruption of the data channel on the receiver's site. The action consists first in testing whether the alternating bit sent by the sender is identical to the alternating bit previously stored by the receiver. If this is the case, then this means, by convention, that we have a new data item. This item is extracted from the data channel, it is subsequently stored on the receiver's file, the receiver's alternating bit is modified, and, finally, the receiver's timer is started if the received item is not the final one. In any case, the interrupt of the data channel is de-activated, whereas event RCV_snd is woken up.

Event RCV_snd The next event, RCV_snd, is enabled by event RCV_rcv as we have seen in the previous section. Its action simply consists in activating the acknowledgment channel. This event is shown below on the left.

```
RCV_snd
  when
    RCV_snd is woken up
  then
    activate acknowledgment channel;
  end
```

```
SND_rcv
  when
    acknowledgment channel interrupt occurs;
  then
    remove data from sender's file;
    reset retry counter;
    modify sender's bit;
    reset acknowledgment channel interrupt;
    if  sender's file is not empty  then
        wake up event SND_snd;
    end
  end
```

Event SND_rcv The next event, SND_rcv, is enabled by the interruption of the acknowledgment channel on the sender's site. The action consists in removing the previously sent item from the sender's file (although that data item has already been sent, it was nevertheless kept in the file in case of a re-transmission; now it can be definitely removed since we have just received the acknowledgment telling us that the receiver has indeed received it). The sender's alternating bit can now be modified for the next data item, the event SND_snd is woken up, and, finally, the acknowledgment channel is de-activated.

Event SND_timer The event, SND_timer, is enabled when the sender's timer reaches its specified delay. The action consists in testing whether the re-try counter has reached its maximum value, in which case the protocol is aborted (from the point of view of the sender). When this is not the case, then the re-try counter is incremented and, of course, the event SND_snd is woken up for a re-transmission:

```
SND_timer
   when
      sender's timer interrupt occurs
   then
      if  retry counter is equal to M+1   then
         abort protocol on sender's site
      else
         increment retry counter;
         wake up event SND_snd;
      end
   end
```

```
RCV_timer
   when
      receiver's timer interrupt occurs
   then
      abort protocol on receiver's site
   end
```

Event RCV_timer The event RCV_timer is enabled when the receiver's timer reaches its specified delay. The action consists in aborting the protocol (from the point of view of the receiver).

Note: The sender knows that the file has been successfully sent and received when event SND_rcv observes that the file is empty (we suppose that the file is not empty at the beginning). It seems (but are we sure?) that event SND_timer cannot wake up event SND_snd while the file is empty.

Likewise, the sender knows that the file has been entirely sent, but that the last data has not been necessarily received. This happens when event SND_timer aborts the protocol, while the sender's file has just got one piece of data left.

The receiver knows that the protocol ends successfully when it receives the last data; this is supposed to be indicated by a special information put on the last data itself.

6.1.7 About the pseudo-code

The definition of our protocol by means of this pseudo-code (or by means of any other similar descriptive notation) raises a number of questions. Are we sure that such a description is correct in the sense that it effectively corresponds to a *file transfer* protocol? Are we sure that the described protocol does terminate (no infinite loop, no deadlock)? What kind of properties should this protocol maintain?

It is our opinion that these questions cannot be answered on the basis of such an informal description only. Nevertheless, we believe that it is quite useful to have such a description at our disposal, since it may act as a *goal* to our future protocol construction. In the sequel, and as said above, we shall formally construct our protocol starting from a mathematical specification of its main properties, and ending up with a formal description of its components, which we might then fruitfully *compare* to their informal pseudo-code counterparts.

The main drawback of such descriptions, which are often said to constitute the *specification* of these protocols, is that they describe a rather informal *implementation*. This is the reason why it is so important to rewrite clearly our informal specification as a proper *requirements document*. This is what we intend to do in the next section.

6.2 Requirements document

The requirements document which we propose now is *far less precise* than the previous informal explanations we have given. It is far less precise in that *it does not propose an implementation*. It essentially consists in explaining what kind of *belief* each site may have at the end of the protocol. We also make precise when such beliefs are indeed true. Here are our requirements for the bounded retransmission protocol. We first make precise the overall purpose of the protocol:

The bounded retransmission protocol is a file transfer protocol. Its goal is to totally or partially transfer a certain non-empty original sequential file from one site, the sender, to another, the receiver.	FUN-1

Then we explain what a "total transfer" means:

A "total transfer" means that the transmitted file is an exact copy of the original one.	FUN-2

We also explain what a "partial transfer" means:

A "partial transfer" means that the transmitted file is a prefix of the original one.	FUN-3

We describe now what both sites may *believe* at the end of the protocol:

Each site may end up in any of the two situations: either it believes that the protocol has terminated successfully, or it believes that the protocol has aborted before being successfully terminated.	FUN-4

We relate the beliefs of both the sender and the receiver:

When the sender believes that the protocol has terminated successfully, then the receiver believes so too. Conversely, when the receiver believes that the protocol has aborted, then the sender believes so too.	FUN-5

We explain that it is possible that these beliefs are not shared by both participants:

However, it is possible for the sender to believe that the protocol has aborted, while the receiver believes that it has terminated successfully.	FUN-6

We explain finally that the belief of the receiver is always true:

When the receiver believes that the protocol has terminated successfully, this is because the original file has been entirely copied on the receiver's site. In other words, the receiver's belief is true.	FUN-7

When the receiver believes that the protocol has aborted, this is because the original file has not been copied entirely on the receiver's site. Again, the receiver's belief is true.	FUN-8

6.3 Refinement strategy

In this short section, we present our strategy for constructing the bounded re-transmission protocol. This will be done by means of an initial model followed by six refinements.

- The initial model set up the scene by taking account of requirements **FUN-4** stating the final situation of both participants of the protocol.
- In the first and second refinement, we take care of the requirements **FUN-5** and **FUN-6**, stating some relationship between the status of the two participants.
- In the third refinement, we introduce the transmitted file. It takes account of requirement **FUN-1** to **FUN-3**. In this refinement, the receiver only enters into the scene.

- In the fourth refinement, we introduce the sender, which sends messages to the receiver and vice-versa.
- In the fifth refinement, we introduce the unreliability of the channels.
- In the last refinement, we optimize the information transmitted between the sender and the receiver.

6.4 Initial model

Our initial model contains a very partial specification of the bounded re-transmission protocol. It deals with requirements FUN-4:

Each site may end up in any of the two situations: either it believes that the protocol has terminated successfully, or it believes that the protocol has aborted before being successfully terminated.	FUN-4

6.4.1 The state

In this initial very abstract model, we introduce the concept of status. For this, we define a carrier set named $STATUS$. It is made of three distinct elements: $working$, $success$, and $failure$ as shown below:

sets: $STATUS$	**axm1_1:** $STATUS = \{working, success, failure\}$
	axm0_2: $working \neq success$
constants: $working$	**axm0_3:** $working \neq failure$
$success$	
$failure$	**axm0_4:** $success \neq failure$

There are two variables s_st and r_st defining the status of the two participants:

variables: s_st	**inv0_1:** $s\_st \in STATUS$
r_st	**inv0_2:** $r\_st \in STATUS$

6.4.2 The events

Initially, the participants are *working*. We have then an *observer* event named brp, which is fired when both participants are not working any more.

```
init
    s_st := working
    r_st := working
```

```
brp
    when
        s_st ≠ working
        r_st ≠ working
    then
        skip
    end
```

In what follows, we use the technique of *anticipated* events, which was introduced and motivated in Section 7 of Chapter 4. We have thus two *anticipated* events claiming to have both participants being eventually in either status *success* or status *failure*:

```
SND_progress
    status
        anticipated
    when
        s_st = working
    then
        s_st :∈ {success, failure}
    end
```

```
RCV_progress
    status
        anticipated
    when
        r_st = working
    then
        r_st :∈ {success, failure}
    end
```

6.5 First and second refinements

These refinements take account of requirement FUN-5:

When the sender believes that the protocol has terminated successfully, then the receiver believes so too. Conversely, when the receiver believes that the protocol has aborted, then the sender believes so too.	FUN-5

,

and of requirement FUN-6:

However, it is possible for the sender to believe that the protocol has aborted, while the receiver believes that it has terminated successfully.	FUN-6

.

Finally, it makes more precise what is meant by the previous *anticipated* event.

6.5.1 The state

Invariant **inv1_1** below formalizes requirement FUN-4. As it is not an equivalence, it take accounts indirectly of requirement FUN-6:

$$\textbf{inv1\_1: } s\_st = success \Rightarrow r\_st = success$$

6.5.2 Events of first refinement

We now split events progress into success and failure. Notice that events SND_success (in this section) and RCV_failure (in the next section) are both "cheating" as they contain the status of the other participant in their guards. We prove that these events are indeed convergent; it is done in two separate refinements:

SND_success
refines
 SND_progress
status
 convergent
when
 $s\_st = working$
 $r\_st = success$
then
 $s\_st := success$
end

SND_failure
refines
 SND_progress
status
 convergent
when
 $s\_st = working$
then
 $s\_st := failure$
end

$$\textbf{variant1: } \{success, failure\} \setminus \{s\_st\}$$

6.5.3 Events of second refinement

RCV_success
refines
  RCV_progress
status
  convergent
when
  $r\_st = working$
then
  $r\_st := success$
end

RCV_failure
refines
  RCV_progress
status
  convergent
when
  $r\_st = working$
  $s\_st = failure$
then
  $r\_st := failure$
end

variant2: $\{success, failure\} \setminus \{r\_st\}$

6.6 Third refinement

In this refinement, we consider requirements FUN-1 to FUN-3 concerned with the transfer of the file. We also take account of requirement FUN-7 and FUN-8, expressing that the receiver belief is true.

6.6.1 The state

First, we extend our context by defining the sequential file f to be transmitted from the sender to the receiver:

sets: D

constants: n
f

axm0_1: $0 < n$

axm0_2: $f \in 1..n \rightarrow D$

The transmitted file is denoted by a variable q of length r. Invariant **inv3_2** formalizes that the transmitted file is always a prefix of the original file. Invariant **inv3_3** formalizes that the receiver succeeds exactly when the file has been transmitted entirely:

$$
\begin{array}{ll}
\textbf{inv3\_1:} & r \in 0..n \\[1em]
\textbf{inv3\_2:} & g = 1..r \lhd f \\[1em]
\textbf{inv3\_3:} & r\_st = success \Leftrightarrow r = n
\end{array}
$$

6.6.2 The events

New Event RCV_rcv_current_data and refined event RCV_success both cheat as they contain direct references to information belonging to the sender, namely $f(r+1)$ and n. Event init is not shown here: it sets r to 0:

RCV_rcv_current_data
   status
      convergent
   when
      $r\_st = working$
      $r + 1 < n$
   then
      $r := r + 1$
      $g := g \cup \{r + 1 \mapsto f(r+1)\}$
   end

RCV_success
   when
      $r\_st = working$
      $r + 1 = n$
   then
      $r\_st := success$
      $r := r + 1$
      $g := g \cup \{r + 1 \mapsto f(n)\}$
   end

variant3: $n - r$

6.6.3 Synchronization of the events

In this refinement, the events are synchronized according to Fig. 6.2. In this figure, the new events are written in *italic* and the dashed line corresponds to the only synchronization we had in the abstraction.

6.7 Fourth refinement

In this refinement, the sender will enter into the scene by cooperating with the receiver in order to transmit the file. In fact, the receiver will no longer directly access the

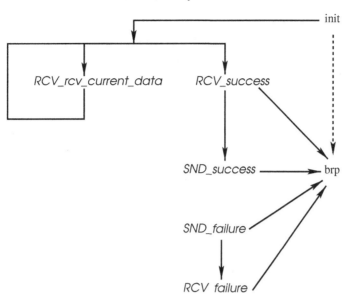

Fig. 6.2. Synchronization of the events

original file f as was the case in the previous refinement; this will be done by the sender who then sends the corresponding data to the receiver through the, so-called, *data channel*. We then introduce this data channel and also the symmetric *acknowledgment channel*. Such channels are situated between the two sites. Notice that we do not introduce yet the fact that these channels are unreliable; this will be done in the next refinement only.

6.7.1 The state

The state is first enlarged with an activation bit, w, to be used by the sender. This variable is boolean as indicated implicitly in invariants **inv2_3**. When w is equal to TRUE, it means that the sender event sending information to the receiver can be activated:

variables: ...
w
s
d

inv4_1: $s \in 0..n-1$

inv4_2: $r \in s..s+1$

inv4_3: $w = \text{FALSE} \Rightarrow d = f(s+1)$

The state is also enlarged with a sender pointer s, which is such that $s+1$ points to the next item, $f(s+1)$, of the original file f to be transmitted to the receiver. It is defined by invariant **inv4_1**. Also notice the very important property relating pointer s to the size r of the transmitted file: r is either equal to s or to $s+1$ as indicated by invariant **inv4_2**.

The state is further enlarged with the data container d, which is part of the data channel and which contains the next item to be transmitted. Its main property is defined in invariant **inv4_3**, which states that d is equal to $f(s+1)$ when the data channel is active, that is when $w = \text{FALSE}$.

6.7.2 The events

Events brp, SND_failure, and RCV_failure are not modified in this refinement. The initialization event is extended in a straightforward fashion as indicated below. The activation bit w is set to TRUE at the beginning so that the only two events which can be fired are the ones described now:

$$
\begin{array}{|l|}
\hline
\text{init} \\
\quad r := 0 \\
\quad g := \varnothing \\
\quad r\_st := working \\
\quad s\_st := working \\
\quad w := \text{TRUE} \\
\quad s := 0 \\
\quad d :\in D \\
\hline
\end{array}
$$

The next event SND_snd_data is new. It corresponds to the main action of the sender, namely to prepare the information to be sent through the data channel. What are sent through this channel are the data d and the sender pointer s:

$$
\begin{array}{|l|}
\hline
\text{SND\_snd\_data} \\
\quad \textbf{when} \\
\qquad s\_st = working \\
\qquad w = \text{TRUE} \\
\quad \textbf{then} \\
\qquad d := f(s+1) \\
\qquad w := \text{FALSE} \\
\quad \textbf{end} \\
\hline
\end{array}
$$

The next two events correspond to the receiver receiving information on the data channel. As can be seen, the receiver checks that the received pointer s from the sender is equal to its own pointer r. The first event, RCV_rcv_current_data, corresponds to the receiver receiving an information which is not the last one ($r + 1 < n$). The second one corresponds to the receiver receiving the last item ($r + 1 = n$). In this case, the receiver succeeds:

$$
\boxed{
\begin{array}{l}
\text{RCV\_rcv\_current\_data} \\
\quad \textbf{when} \\
\qquad r\_st = working \\
\qquad w = \text{FALSE} \\
\qquad r = s \\
\qquad r + 1 < n \\
\quad \textbf{then} \\
\qquad r := r + 1 \\
\qquad g := g \cup \{r + 1 \mapsto d\} \\
\quad \textbf{end}
\end{array}
}
\qquad
\boxed{
\begin{array}{l}
\text{RCV\_success} \\
\quad \textbf{when} \\
\qquad r\_st = working \\
\qquad w = \text{FALSE} \\
\qquad r = s \\
\qquad r + 1 = n \\
\quad \textbf{then} \\
\qquad r\_st := success \\
\qquad r := r + 1 \\
\qquad g := g \cup \{r + 1 \mapsto d\} \\
\quad \textbf{end}
\end{array}
}
$$

Notice that the receiver is still "cheating" as it is able (in the guards above) to check the value of its pointer r against the constant size n of the original file, which is in the sender's site. This anomaly will be corrected in the next refinement.

The next two events correspond to the sender receiving the acknowledgment from the receiver. The first one, SND_rcv_current_ack, is a new event. When the sender receives the last acknowledgment (when $s + 1 = n$ in event SND_success), the sender succeeds, otherwise (when $s + 1 < n$ in event SND_rcv_current_ack) it increments its pointer s and activates the events SND_snd_data by setting the activation bit w to TRUE:

$$
\boxed{
\begin{array}{l}
\text{SND\_rcv\_current\_ack} \\
\quad \textbf{when} \\
\qquad s\_st = working \\
\qquad w = \text{FALSE} \\
\qquad s + 1 < n \\
\qquad r = s + 1 \\
\quad \textbf{then} \\
\qquad w := \text{TRUE} \\
\qquad s := s + 1 \\
\quad \textbf{end}
\end{array}
}
\qquad
\boxed{
\begin{array}{l}
\text{SND\_success} \\
\quad \textbf{when} \\
\qquad s\_st = working \\
\qquad w = \text{FALSE} \\
\qquad s + 1 = n \\
\qquad r = s + 1 \\
\quad \textbf{then} \\
\qquad s\_st := success \\
\quad \textbf{end}
\end{array}
}
$$

We finally introduce an event that modifies the activation pointer w. This event will receive a full explanation in the next refinement:

> SND_time_out_current
> > **when**
> > > $s\_st = working$
> > > $w = \text{FALSE}$
> > **then**
> > > $w := \text{TRUE}$
> > **end**

6.7.3 Synchronization of the events

In this refinement, the events are synchronized according to Fig. 6.3, where the new events are written in *italic*. These new events are inserted in the previous synchronization diagram, Fig. 6.2. Events SND_failure, RCV_failure, and SND_time_out_current are presently "spontaneous". They will receive more explanations in the next refinement.

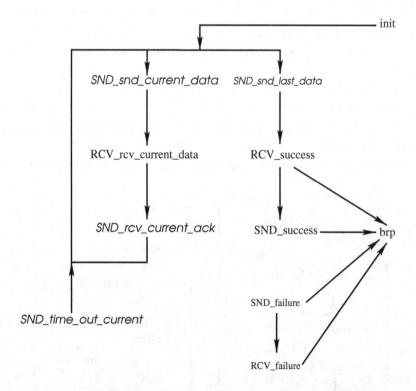

Fig. 6.3. Synchronization of the events in the fourth refinement

6.8 Fifth refinement

6.8.1 The state

In this refinement, we introduce the unreliability of the channels. This is done by first adding three activation bits: db, ab, and v. At most one of these bits, together with w already introduced in previous refinements, is equal to TRUE; this is expressed in invariants **inv5_1** to **inv5_6**. The use of the activation bits is illustrated in Fig. 6.4:

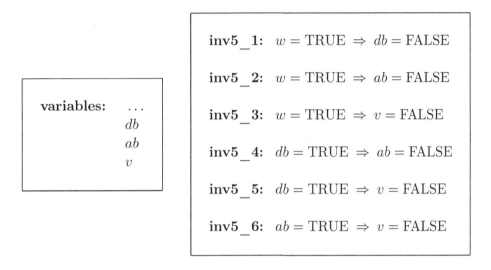

variables: ...
db
ab
v

inv5_1: $w = \text{TRUE} \Rightarrow db = \text{FALSE}$

inv5_2: $w = \text{TRUE} \Rightarrow ab = \text{FALSE}$

inv5_3: $w = \text{TRUE} \Rightarrow v = \text{FALSE}$

inv5_4: $db = \text{TRUE} \Rightarrow ab = \text{FALSE}$

inv5_5: $db = \text{TRUE} \Rightarrow v = \text{FALSE}$

inv5_6: $ab = \text{TRUE} \Rightarrow v = \text{FALSE}$

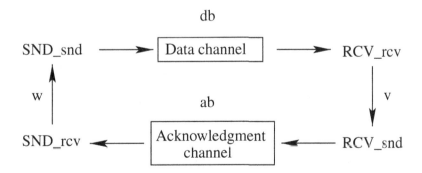

Fig. 6.4. The activation bits

We introduce an additional boolean variable, l, which denotes the last item indicator. It is sent by the sender to the receiver (together with d and s). When equal to TRUE, this bit indicates that the sent item is the last one (invariants **inv5_7** and **inv5_8**):

variables: ... l	**inv5_7:** $db = \text{TRUE} \wedge r = s \wedge l = \text{FALSE} \Rightarrow r + 1 < n$ **inv5_8:** $db = \text{TRUE} \wedge r = s \wedge l = \text{TRUE} \Rightarrow r + 1 = n$

Finally, we introduce a constant MAX and a variable c. Constant MAX denotes the maximum number of re-tries and variable c denotes the current number of re-tries. In invariant **inv3_10**, it is explained that when c exceeds MAX, then the sender fails:

constants: ... MAX	**axm3_1:** $MAX \in \mathbb{N}$

variables: ... c	**inv3_9:** $\quad c \in 0 \mathbin{..} MAX + 1$ **inv3_10:** $\quad c = MAX + 1 \Leftrightarrow s\_st = failure$

6.8.2 The events

The initial event is extended in a straightforward fashion. Event brp is not modified in this refinement:

```
init
    r := 0
    g := ∅
    r_st := working
    s_st := working
    s := 0
    d :∈ D
    w := TRUE
    db := FALSE
    ab := FALSE
    v := FALSE
    l := FALSE
    c := 0
```

```
brp
    when
        r ≠ working
        s ≠ working
    then
        skip
    end
```

The following events are modified as indicated by the underlined actions. We split now abstract event SND_snd_data into two events according to the sending of the last data or not. The activation bit, *db*, of the data channel is set to TRUE:

SND_snd_current_data
  refines
    SND_snd_data
  when
    $s\_st = working$
    $w = \text{TRUE}$
    $\underline{s + 1 < n}$
  then
    $d := f(s + 1)$
    $w := \text{FALSE}$
    $\underline{db := \text{TRUE}}$
    $\underline{l := \text{FALSE}}$
  end
	SND_snd_last_data
	  refines
	    SND_snd_data
	  when
	    $s\_st = working$
	    $w = \text{TRUE}$
	    $\underline{s + 1 = n}$
	  then
	    $d := f(s + 1)$
	    $w := \text{FALSE}$
	    $\underline{db := \text{TRUE}}$
	    $\underline{l := \text{TRUE}}$
	  end

In the next two receiver events, the abstract "cheating" guards $r + 1 < n$ and $r + 1 = n$ have disappeared. They have been replaced by guards $l = \text{FALSE}$ and $l = \text{TRUE}$, respectively. Invariants **inv3_11** and **inv3_12** defined below ensure guard strengthening. The receiver activation bit v is set to TRUE:

RCV_rcv_current_data
  when
    $r\_st = working$
    $\underline{db = \text{TRUE}}$
    $r = s$
    $\underline{l = \text{FALSE}}$
  then
    $r := r + 1$
    $h := h \cup \{r + 1 \mapsto d\}$
    $\underline{db := \text{FALSE}}$
    $\underline{v := \text{TRUE}}$
  end
	RCV_success
	  when
	    $r\_st = working$
	    $\underline{db = \text{TRUE}}$
	    $r = s$
	    $\underline{l = \text{TRUE}}$
	  then
	    $r\_st := success$
	    $r := r + 1$
	    $h := h \cup \{r + 1 \mapsto d\}$
	    $\underline{db := \text{FALSE}}$
	    $\underline{v := \text{TRUE}}$
	  end

The next two events are new. Event RCV_rcv_retry corresponds to the receiver receiving a re-try. The receiver detects this by the fact that its own pointer r is different from the one, s, it receives from the sender. The activation bit v is set to TRUE. The second event, RCV_snd_ack, is activated when v is equal to TRUE. It sends the acknowledgment to the sender by setting the activation bit ab of the acknowledgment channel to TRUE. Notice that that no information is sent:

```
RCV_rcv_retry
  when
    db = TRUE
    r ≠ s
  then
    db := FALSE
    v := TRUE
  end
```

```
RCV_snd_ack
  when
    v = TRUE
  then
    v := FALSE
    ab := TRUE
  end
```

In the next two sender events, the abstract guard $r = s + 1$ has disappeared. It has been replaced by the guard $ab = \text{TRUE}$. In order to ensure guard strengthening, we have to add the following invariants:

inv3_11: $ab = \text{TRUE} \;\Rightarrow\; r = s + 1$

inv3_12: $v = \text{TRUE} \;\Rightarrow\; r = s + 1$

The second invariant helps prove the first one in event RCV_snd_ack:

```
SND_rcv_current_ack
  when
    s_st = working
    ab = TRUE
    s + 1 < n
  then
    w := TRUE
    s := s + 1
    c := 0
    ab := FALSE
  end
```

```
SND_success
  when
    s_st = working
    ab = TRUE
    s + 1 = n
  then
    s_st := success
    c := 0
    ab := FALSE
  end
```

The next two new events correspond to the daemons breaking the channels. They result in activation bits w, db, v, and ab being all equal to FALSE. Notice that these events can occur asynchronously when the corresponding channels are active:

DMN_data_channel
when
  $db = TRUE$
then
  $db = FALSE$
end

DMN_ack_channel
when
  $ab = TRUE$
then
  $ab = FALSE$
end

The next three events correspond to the timers. The first two are the sender timer. The first one occurs when the retransmission has not yet reach the maximum MAX, whereas the second one corresponds to this maximum: in this case, the sender fails. The last one corresponds to the receiver failure. This occurs when the sender has already failed according to invariant **inv3_10**. As can be seen, the time slot given to the receiver timer implicitly assumes that this event can only occur when the sender has failed:

SND_time_out_current
when
  $s\_st = working$
  $w = FALSE$
  $\underline{ab = FALSE}$
  $\underline{db = FALSE}$
  $\underline{v = FALSE}$
  $\underline{c < MAX}$
then
  $\underline{w := TRUE}$
  $\underline{c := c + 1}$
end

SND_failure
when
  $s\_st = working$
  $w = FALSE$
  $\underline{ab = FALSE}$
  $\underline{db = FALSE}$
  $\underline{v = FALSE}$
  $\underline{c = MAX}$
then
  $s\_st := failure$
  $c := c + 1$
end

RCV_failure
when
  $r\_st = working$
  $c = MAX + 1$
then
  $r\_st := failure$
end

6.8.3 Synchronization of the events

The last synchronization of the events is shown in Fig. 6.5.

6.9 Sixth refinement

The sixth refinement consists in sending the parity of pointer s from the sender to the receiver, and the parity of pointer r in the other direction. The definition of this

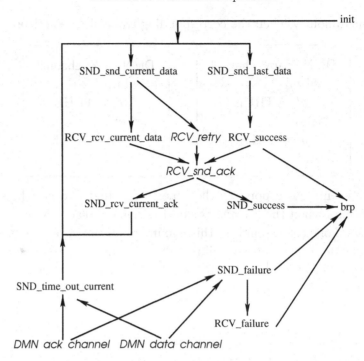

Fig. 6.5. Synchronization of the events in the third refinement

refinement is left to the reader. The technique to be used is the one used in Section 6 of this chapter.

6.10 Reference

[1]   J. F. Groote and J. C. Van de Pol. A bounded retransmission protocol for large data packets – a case study in computer checked algebraic verification. *Lecture Notes in Computer Science* 1101. Algebraic Methodology and Software Technology, 5th International Conference AMAST '96, Munich.

7

Development of a concurrent program[†]

In this book, we are studying the correct development of *distributed programs* by means of various examples. So far we have done this in Chapter 4 (file transfer protocol) and in Chapter 6 (bounded retransmission protocol). In later chapters, we shall also study some distributed program developments: leader election on a ring-shaped network in Chapter 10, synchronizing processes on a tree in Chapter 11, routing algorithm in Chapter 12, leader election on a connected network in Chapter 13. We shall also study the correct development of *sequential programs* in Chapter 15. In this chapter, we shall study another kind of execution paradigm, namely that of *concurrent programs*.

7.1 Comparing distributed and concurrent programs

The distinction between sequential and distributed programs must be clear. But the one between distributed and concurrent ones might be less obvious. Here are the main differences which we consider between the two.

7.1.1 Distributed programs

In the case of distributed programs, the entire algorithm is performed by various agents executing some sequential programs (sometimes the same one) on *different computers*. But, at the same time, these agents are supposed to *cooperate* in order to achieve together a well-defined goal, which is the purpose of the algorithm.

This cooperation could be made easy by having a centralized agency, the role of which would be to schedule the various participating agents. But we suppose that such an agency does not exist. In other words, the various agents cooperate only by communicating with each other in some well-defined ways, which have to be clearly defined before embarking in a distributed development. This is typically the case in the leader election algorithms developed in Chapters 10 and 13, where each agent executes

[†] This chapter was written in close cooperation with Dominique Cansell

227

the *same* short sequential program in order to achieve a single goal, that of electing a node to be the leader. In these examples, the geometry of the network dictates the way the agents can communicate.

7.1.2 Concurrent programs

In the case of concurrent programs, we still have different agents working concurrently by executing some sequential programs. But, this time, the various executions, which may correspond to different programs, are performed on the *same computer*. Moreover, the agents do not cooperate as was the case in a distributed program, they rather *compete* in order to use a common shared resource, which must be handled according to certain rules preserving its integrity.

Here too, an obvious way to do this would be to have a centralized agency protecting the resource in question so that its integrity is preserved. To this end, each agent would ask the centralized agency permission to use for a while the shared resource. But we want to avoid the usage of such a centralized agency. In other words, we would like each agent to consider that it can use the resource by executing its own program as if the other agents did not exist. But, of course, we have a final constraint which is the following: the sequential program executed by an agent can be interrupted by any other program executed by another agent in an almost totally random way. Of course, the places where the program of each agent can be interrupted are well defined: they correspond to what is called the *atomicity* of the various "instructions" of such programs. Such atomicity constraints are dictated by the hardware of the computer where the concurrent programs are supposed to be executed. This has to be clearly defined before embarking on such a concurrent development.

7.2 The proposed example

7.2.1 Informal presentation

The technique we are using for developing such concurrent programs will be completely systematic. In this chapter, we describe and illustrate it on a famous example introduced by H.R. Simpson in [1]: the "Four-slot Fully Asynchronous Mechanism."

Here is a first simplified explanation of this mechanism. We have two participants: a writer and a reader. The writer writes some information (which he gets somehow) on a shared memory. The reader must be able to read the information stored in that memory. As a very first approximation, we consider that the shared memory is made of a pair of slots where the writer writes alternatively. This is illustrated in Fig. 7.1 where the two slots are named "0" and "1".

Still as an approximation, we need a second pair of slots where the writer and the reader are writing and reading alternatively (again, it is an approximation for the moment). This is illustrated in Fig. 7.2 where the two pairs are named "0" and "1":

Fig. 7.1. The two slots

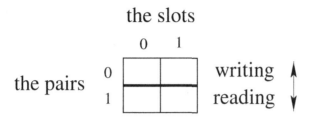

Fig. 7.2. The two pairs of two slots

We are now ready to present the sequential programs of the writer and the reader. But before doing that, we need to define the global variables, which are shared between the two participants:

$$data \in \{0,1\} \rightarrow (\{0,1\} \rightarrow D)$$

$$reading \in \{0,1\}$$

$$latest \in \{0,1\}$$

$$slot \in \{0,1\} \rightarrow \{0,1\}$$

The set D is a generic; it represents the data which are written and read. The variable *data* defines the two pairs of two slots. The first dimension defines the pair and the second dimension defines the slot. For example, $data(1)(0)$ is indicated by "X" in Fig. 7.3.

The variable *reading* denotes the pair used by the reader. The pair used by the writer is therefore $1 - reading$. The variable *latest* denotes the last pair used by the writer, which the reader may now use if it is willing to read. Finally, the variable *slot* indicates the slot in which the writer or the reader are currently writing or reading. More precisely, $slot(reading)$ indicates the slot where the reader is currently reading

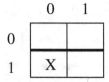

Fig. 7.3. Using the slots

and $slot(1 - reading)$ indicates the slot where the writer is currently writing. The sequential program of the writer uses two local variables:

$$pair\_w \in \{0, 1\}$$

$$indx\_w \in \{0, 1\}$$

The local variable $pair\_w$ denotes the pair used by the writer. The local variable $indx\_w$ denotes the current slot used by the writer. Now, the pidgin program of the writer (with parameter x) is the following:

Writer(x)	
$pair\_w := 1 - reading;$	Choosing a pair different from that used by the reader
$indx\_w := 1 - slot(pair\_w);$	Choosing a slot different from that used in the previous writing
$data(pair\_w)(indx\_w) := x;$	Writing
$slot(pair\_w) := indx\_w;$	Storing the last written slot
$latest := pair\_w$	Storing the last written pair

The sequential program of the reader uses one local variable:

$$indx\_r \in \{0, 1\}$$

The local variable $indx\_r$ denotes the current slot used by the reader. Now, the pidgin program of the reader (with returned value y) is the following:

Reader	
$reading := latest;$	Choosing the last written pair
$indx\_r := slot(reading);$	Choosing the last written slot
$y := data(reading)(indx\_r)$	Reading

The usage of "last" in the previous comments, "Choosing the *last* written pair" and "Choosing the *last* written slot", is not correct as we shall see later. More precisely, it is correct provided the **Reader** program is executed in a non-concurrent fashion with the **Writer** program: in other words, when they never interrupt each other. But it is not correct when the **Reader** program accesses the first instruction, $reading := latest$, while the **Writer** program has already written another piece of data by executing the instruction $data(pair\_w)(indx\_w) := x$.

7.2.2 Non-concurrent animations

In order to understand more accurately the behaviors of both the writer and the reader, let us define some short animations where the reader and the writer are, for the moment, working independently of each other. We suppose the following initial condition:

$$reading = 1 \qquad\qquad slot = \{0 \mapsto 1, 1 \mapsto 1\}$$

Writing successively the three values a, b, and c yields the following successive values of the state after the execution of the **Writer** pidgin program:

Writer(a)

	0	1
0	a	–
1	–	–

Writer(b)

	0	1
0	a	b
1	–	–

Writer(c)

	0	1
0	c	b
1	–	–

$$pair\_w = 0 \qquad pair\_w = 0 \qquad pair\_w = 0$$
$$indx\_w = 0 \qquad indx\_w = 1 \qquad indx\_w = 0$$
$$reading = 1 \qquad reading = 1 \qquad reading = 1$$
$$slot(pair\_w) = 0 \qquad slot(pair\_w) = 1 \qquad slot(pair\_w) = 0$$
$$latest = 0 \qquad latest = 0 \qquad latest = 0$$

Now, we read twice and then write d. This results in the following succession of states:

	Reader			**Reader**			**Writer(d)**	
	0	1		0	1		0	1
0	c	b	0	c	b	0	c	b
1	–	–	1	–	–	1	d	–
	0	1		0	1		0	1

$$indx\_r = 0 \qquad\quad indx\_r = 0 \qquad\quad pair\_w = 1$$
$$reading = 0 \qquad\quad reading = 0 \qquad\quad indx\_w = 0$$
$$slot(reading) = 0 \quad slot(reading) = 0 \quad reading = 0$$
$$data(0)(0) = c \qquad data(0)(0) = c \qquad slot(pair\_w) = 0$$
$$latest = 1$$

Finally, we write e and f and we read once. This results in the following succession of states:

	Writer(e)			**Writer(f)**			**Reader**	
	0	1		0	1		0	1
0	c	b	0	c	b	0	c	b
1	d	e	1	f	e	1	f	e

$$pair\_w = 1 \qquad\quad pair\_w = 1 \qquad\quad indx\_r = 0$$
$$indx\_w = 1 \qquad\quad indx\_w = 0 \qquad\quad reading = 1$$
$$reading = 0 \qquad\quad reading = 0 \qquad\quad slot(reading) = 0$$
$$slot(pair\_w) = 1 \quad slot(pair\_w) = 0 \quad data(1)(0) = f$$
$$latest = 1 \qquad\qquad latest = 1$$

According to this short animation, we can observe the following facts concerning the **Reader** program:

– it always reads the last written data: c and f;
– it can read several times the same data: c;
– it can miss some written data: a, b, d, and e.

7.2.3 Defining atomicity

We suppose that each instruction of the **Writer** and **Reader** programs are atomic. But we require that the reading and writing operations never occur "simultaneously" on the same slot. In other words, if the **Writer** program is about to write a piece of data in $data(pair\_w)(indx\_w)$ and simultaneously the **Reader** program is about to read some data in $data(reading)(indx\_r)$, then we require that either $pair\_w$ and $reading$ are distinct, or, if they are identical, then $indx\_w$ and $indx\_r$ are distinct. More formally:

$$pair\_w = reading \;\Rightarrow\; indx\_w \neq indx\_r$$

This definition of atomicity is highly subjective. It could be argued that a finer atomicity is needed because the hardware might not be able to achieve this one. We agree with that remark, but shall not enter into this discussion here as it is not our present problem.

Our present problem at the moment is to perform this concurrent development. But we face immediately a difficult question. In fact, what is not clear at all at this point is *what the specification of this problem is*. As a result, we do not know what kind of proof we have to perform in order to guarantee that our concurrent development is correct. In other words, we do not know what to do!

7.3 Interleaving

Before clearly defining what the specification of our problem is (this will be done in Section 7.4), we shall stop for a while on the question of *interleaving*.

7.3.1 The problem

The animation we have been able to observe in the previous section was very simple because there was no interruptions between the executions of the **Writer** and **Reader** programs. But a real concurrent execution of both programs is far more complicated than this as it is possible to have interleaving of both programs' instructions. For example, here is one interleaving we can observe among many others:

Writer	**Reader**
...	...
1. $pair\_w := 1 - reading$	
	1. $reading := latest$
2. $indx\_w := 1 - slot(pair\_w)$	
	2. $indx\_r := slot(reading)$
	3. $y := data(reading)(indx\_r)$
3. $data(pair\_w)(indx\_w) := x$	
	1. $reading := latest$
4. $slot(pair\_w) := indx\_w$	
5. $latest := pair\_w$	
	2. $indx\_r := slot(reading)$
1. $pair\_w := 1 - reading$	
	3. $y := data(reading)(indx\_r)$
2. $indx\_w := 1 - slot(writing)$	
3. $data(pair\_w)(indx\_w) := x$	
	1. $reading := latest$
...	...

As can be seen, each program remains sequential but it can be interrupted by the other between two successive instructions and vice-versa. A possible reasoning about such interleaved programs is to envisage studying all possible interleaving corresponding to a significant number of executions of the **Writer** and **Reader** programs, thus making a complete checking of all these situations. Before doing that however, it might be interesting to formally compute the number of interleavings we have, just to know whether such a complete checking is indeed feasible.

7.3.2 Computing the number of different interleavings

We are given two sequential programs with respectively m and n instructions, where m and n are natural numbers. Notice that we might have m or n equal to 0; this corresponds to empty programs. Let $U(m, n)$ be the number of interleavings of these two programs. First of all, we certainly have:

$$\boxed{\begin{array}{l} U(m, 0) = 1 \\ \\ U(0, n) = 1 \end{array}},$$

since interleaving the instructions of a program with another empty one results in one interleaving! Now supposing m and n are both different from 0, then we have:

$$U(m, n) = U(m - 1, n) + U(m, n - 1)$$

This can be explained easily. If the last instruction of the first program is situated after the last instruction of the second one, then the number of interleavings is $U(m - 1, n)$. And if the last instruction of the first program is not situated after the last instruction of the second one, then the number of interleavings is $U(m, n - 1)$.

We can calculate $U(m, n)$ by means of a recursive program, but it would be rather inefficient because we shall calculate identical quantities many times. A far better technique is that of *dynamic programming*, where a matrix M of size $m + 1$ and $n + 1$ is calculated step by step after filling its first line $M(i, 0)$ (for i in $0 \mathinner{.\,.} m$) and its first column $M(0, j)$ (for j in $0 \mathinner{.\,.} n$) with ones. The result is given by $M(m, n)$. Here is the C program calculating $U(m, n)$:

```
int U(int m, int n)
  {int M[m+1][n+1],i,j;
   for (i=0; i<=m; ++i) M[i][0]=1;
   for (j=0; j<=n; ++j) M[0][j]=1;
   for (i=1; i<=m; ++i)
      for (j=1; j<=n; ++j)
         M[i][j]=M[i-1][j]+M[i][j-1];
   return M[m][n];
  }
```

This program has to be modified however as the calculation might result in an overflow. This is the case when a certain calculation leads to a number which would be greater than INT_MAX (the greatest integer of the "C machine"). In order to take care of this, we define a new version returning 0 (an impossible normal result) when there is a possible overflow:

```
int U(int m, int n)
  {int M[m+1][n+1],i,j,a,b;
   for (i=0; i<=m; ++i) M[i][0]=1;
   for (j=0; j<=n; ++j) M[0][j]=1;
   for (i=1; i<=m; ++i)
      for (j=1; j<=n; ++j)
         {a=M[i-1][j];
          b=M[i][j-1];
```

```
        if (a>INT_MAX-b) return 0;
        M[i][j]=a+b;
      }
  return M[m][n];
  }
```

7.3.3 The results

The results are quite interesting. Our **Writer** program has five instructions and our **Reader** program has three instructions. Let us calculate the number of interleavings for zero **Writer** working with zero **Reader**, that is $U(0,0)$, one **Writer** working with one **Reader**, that is $U(5,3)$, then two **Writer** with two **Reader**, that is $U(10,6)$, and so on. Here is the main program calculating these values:

```
main(void)
   {int i,a,b,r,ok=1;
    for (i=0; ok; ++i)
      {a=5*i;
       b=3*i;
       r=U(a,b);
       if (r==0)
         {printf("   U(%d,%d)   = OVERFLOW\n",a,b);
          ok=0;
          }
       else
          printf("   U(%d,%d)   = %d\n",a,b,r);
       }
    }
```

Here are the results:

```
U(0,0)    = 1
U(5,3)    = 56
U(10,6)   = 8008
U(15,9)   = 1307504
U(20,12)  = 225792840
U(25,15)  = OVERFLOW
```

What is shown by this result is that the number of interleavings becomes quickly extremely large. With only five writings and five readings (that is, $U(25,15)$) the number is already greater than INT_MAX, that is 2,147,483,647. The moral of the story is that it is clearly out of the question to reason on concurrent programs by checking all possible cases on a significant number of successive executions!

7.4 Specifying the concurrent program

Coming back to our example, we define in this section how our concurrent program can be specified.

7.4.1 Writing and reading traces

The idea is to consider that the **Writer** and **Reader** programs are not entirely seen in the specification. We suppose that we only see what happens at the very moment where they are supposed to have finished writing or reading. Taking account of these moments in the reasoning can be done by storing the complete history of what has been written and read so far; this gives rise to a *writing trace* and to a *reading trace*. The specification of our concurrent programs is then the definition of the *relationship between these traces*. The formal definition of the writing and reading traces, wt and rd respectively, are straightforward. The variables w and r denote the lengths of these traces:

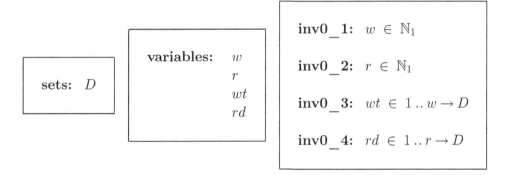

$$
\begin{array}{ll}
\textbf{sets:} \quad D \\[4pt]
\textbf{variables:} \quad w & \textbf{inv0\_1:} \quad w \in \mathbb{N}_1 \\
\qquad\qquad\;\; r & \textbf{inv0\_2:} \quad r \in \mathbb{N}_1 \\
\qquad\qquad\;\; wt & \textbf{inv0\_3:} \quad wt \in 1\,..\,w \to D \\
\qquad\qquad\;\; rd & \textbf{inv0\_4:} \quad rd \in 1\,..\,r \to D
\end{array}
$$

7.4.2 Relationship between the traces

We have now to express various properties of the reading trace with regard to the writing traces:

(i) what is read has been written before;
(ii) what is read follows the order of what is written;
(iii) some writing might be missing in the reading trace;
(iv) some reading might be repeated in the reading trace.

This can be formulated partially by means of a function f relating the reading and the writing traces:

variables: f	**inv0_5:** $f \in 1..r \rightarrow 1..w$ **inv0_6:** $rd = (f\,;wt)$

The variable f is a total function mapping the domain of the reading trace to that of the writing trace (**inv0_5**). The reading trace is exactly the forward composition of f with wt (**inv0_6**). In Fig. 7.4, we show an example of traces together with their basic relationship. As can be seen, the function f relating both traces of this example is:

$$f = \{1 \mapsto 1,\ 2 \mapsto 1,\ 3 \mapsto 5,\ 4 \mapsto 8,\ 5 \mapsto 8,\ 6 \mapsto 11,\ ...\}$$

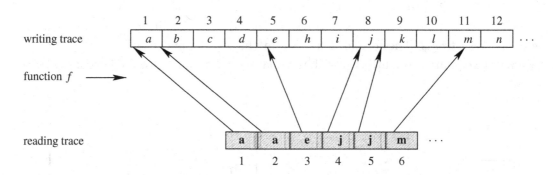

Fig. 7.4. The writing and reading traces and their basic relationship

The specification we have defined so far in the invariants does not take into account our intuition about the reading trace. In fact, a **Reader** program always reading the first element of the writing trace would be a perfect implementation of the present specification. In order to make impossible such an implementation, we have to say that the reading trace *makes necessary some progress.*

To begin with, what is missing in our specification is the exact situation of the writing trace when a value is entered in the reading trace. To do that, we introduce a second function g also connecting like f the domain of the reading trace to that of the writing trace (**inv0_7**):

variables: g	**inv0_7:** $g \in 1..r \rightarrow 1..w$

Given a point i in the domain of the reading trace (thus $i \in 1 .. r$), then $g(i)$ denotes the last point in the writing trace that has occurred just before the end of the reading trace. This is illustrated in Fig. 7.5.

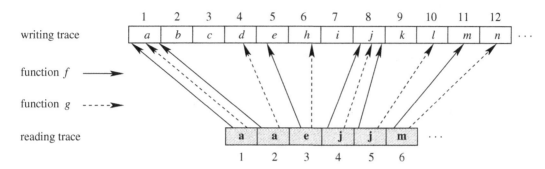

Fig. 7.5. The writing and reading traces and their relationship

The functions f and g allow us (in principle) to put together both traces as indicated in Fig. 7.6. As can be seen, the second reading, **a**, is done on the first writing, although the writing that just precedes that second reading is the fourth writing, **d**. This is due to the interleaving of the **Reader** and **Writer** programs. If the reader executes its first instruction, it assigns a new value to the variable *reading* (it performs *reading* := *latest*). If the **reader** stops now, then any new execution of the writer will write on the slot different from *reading*, and it can do so many times. As a consequence, when the reader starts again, it can read a very old value.

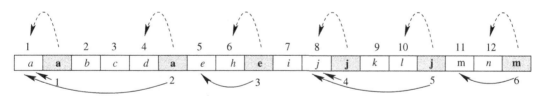

Fig. 7.6. The writing and reading traces together

We now express very simply that what is read corresponds to something that has been written already, namely $f(i) \leq g(i)$ for all i in $1 .. r$ (**inv0_8**). Again, the reason for not having an equality here is that the **Writer** program might have moved forward (sometimes a lot) while the **Reader** program has already decided what it is going to read but has not done it yet:

$$\boxed{\textbf{inv0\_8:} \quad \forall i \cdot i \in 1 .. r \;\Rightarrow\; f(i) \leq g(i)}$$

What remains to be expressed now is the fact that the writing index of what is read at some point $i + 1$ (for some i in $1 .. r - 1$), that is at the index $f(i + 1)$ of the writing trace, is greater than or equal to the index of what has be written at index $g(i)$ just before the previous reading i. This is invariant **inv0_9** which follows:

$$\textbf{inv0\_9:} \quad \forall i \cdot i \in 1 .. r - 1 \Rightarrow g(i) \leq f(i + 1)$$

Putting together **inv0_8** and **inv0_9**, we obtain the following for all i in $1 .. r - 1$:

$$f(i + 1) \in g(i) .. g(i + 1).$$

This is illustrated in Fig. 7.7 where the domain of the writing trace is shown at the top, whereas that of the reading trace is shown at the bottom.

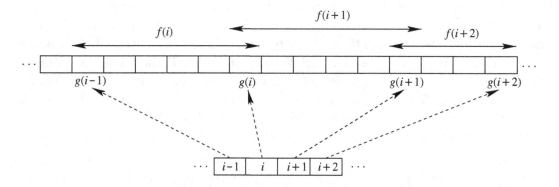

Fig. 7.7. The relationship between functions f and g

As can be seen, the reader certainly makes some progress if there is *at least one writing between two successive readings*. More precisely, if $g(i + 1) = g(i) + 1$, then the minimal value of $f(i + 2)$, which is equal to $g(i + 1)$, is thus equal to $g(i) + 1$, whereas the maximal value of $f(i)$ is $g(i)$. In this case, the reader makes progress between i and $i + 2$. This is illustrated in Fig. 7.8, where we have indicated that the ith reading can be **a**, **b**, or **c**, the $(i + 1)$th reading can be **c**, or **d**, and the $(i + 2)$th reading can be **d**, **e**, or **h**.

This example can be made clearer by putting together the two traces as shown in Fig. 7.9. As can be seen, there is writing (**d**) between the ith and $(i + 1)$th readings. As a consequence, there is progress in reading between the ith reading, where **a**, **b**, or **c** can be read, and the $(i + 2)$th reading where **d**, **e**, or **h** can be read (not any of **a**, **b**, or **c**).

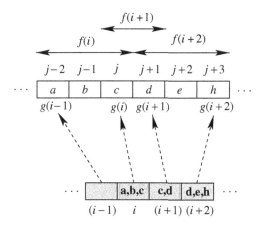

Fig. 7.8. The reader is making progress

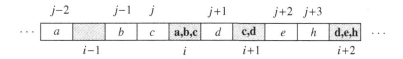

Fig. 7.9. The reader is making progress

7.4.3 Summary of the invariants

Next is a summary of the invariants of the initial step:

inv0_1: $w \in \mathbb{N}_1$

inv0_2: $r \in \mathbb{N}_1$

inv0_3: $wt \in 1 .. w \to D$

inv0_4: $rd \in 1 .. r \to D$

inv0_5: $f \in 1 .. r \to 1 .. w$

inv0_6: $rd = (f \, ; wt)$

inv0_7: $g \in 1 .. r \to 1 .. w$

inv0_8: $\forall i \cdot i \in 1 .. r \Rightarrow f(i) \leq g(i)$

inv0_9: $\forall i \cdot i \in 1 .. r - 1 \Rightarrow g(i) \leq f(i+1)$

7.4.4 The events

In order to simplify matters, we suppose that a certain value $d0$ has been written and then read initially:

constants: $d0$	**axm0_1:** $d0 \in D$

With this in mind, the initial events are straightforward:

```
init
    w := 1
    r := 1
    wt := {1 ↦ d0}
    rd := {1 ↦ d0}
    f := {1 ↦ 1}
    g := {1 ↦ 1}
```

```
write
    any d where
        d ∈ D
    then
        w := w + 1
        wt(w + 1) := d
    end
```

```
read
    any v where
        v ∈ g(r)..w
    then
        r := r + 1
        f(r + 1) := v
        g(r + 1) := w
        rd(r + 1) := wt(v)
    end
```

In event **read**, the guard, $v \in g(r)..w$, and the two actions, $f(r+1) := v$ and $g(r+1) := w$, ensure the preservation of the invariants:

– for invariant **inv0_8**: $f(r+1) \le g(r+1)$ since $f(r+1) = v \le w = g(r+1)$;
– for invariant **inv0_9**: $g(r) \le f(r+1)$ since $g(r) \le v = f(r+1)$.

7.5 Refinement strategy

The technique we use for developing our concurrent program consists in *cutting* events **write** and **read** proposed in the previous section into smaller pieces. This technique is very general; it can be applied to many concurrent algorithms.

7.5.1 Sketch of the final refinement

At the end of the development, the formalization of each instruction of both programs must correspond to a specific event so that the interleaving will be obtained by the non-determinacy between the writing and reading events. More precisely, we shall have two variables denoting the address counters of the **Writer** and **Reader** programs, namely

adr_w and adr_r:

$$adr\_w \in 1..5$$

$$adr\_r \in 1..3$$

Besides the initialization event (setting both address counters to 1), the various events corresponding to the **Writer** and **Reader** programs will then have the following forms:

```
init
adr_w := 1
adr_r := 1
...
```

```
Writer_1
any d where
  d ∈ D
  adr_w = 1
then
  x := D
  pair_w := 1 − reading
  adr_w := 2
end
```

```
Writer_2
when
  adr_w = 2
then
  indx_w := 1 − slot(pair_w)
  adr_w := 3
end
```

```
Writer_3
when
  adr_w = 3
then
  data(pair_w)(index_w) := x
  adr_w := 4
end
```

```
Writer_4
when
  adr_w = 4
then
  slot(pair_w) := indx_w
  adr_w := 5
end
```

```
Writer_5
when
  adr_w = 5
then
  latest := pair_w
  adr_w := 1
end
```

```
Reader_1
when
  adr_r = 1
then
  reading := latest
  adr_r := 2
end
```

```
Reader_2
when
  adr_r = 2
then
  indx_r := slot(reading)
  adr_r := 3
end
```

```
Reader_3
when
  adr_r = 3
then
  y := data(reading)(indx_r)
  adr_r := 1
end
```

It is worth comparing these events with the two concurrent programs, which were presented in Section 7.2.1:

Writer(x)

$pair\_w := 1 - reading;$

$indx\_w := 1 - slot(pair\_w);$

$data(pair\_w)(indx\_w) := x$

$slot(pair\_w) := indx\_w;$

$latest := pair\_w$

Reader

$reading := latest;$

$indx\_r := slot(reading);$

$y := data(reading)(indx\_r)$

As can be seen, each individual instruction corresponds to an independent event. Note however that event Writer_1 also stores the input parameter in a variable x. It could have been done in an additional initial event Writer_0.

7.5.2 Purpose of refinements

Our goal is now clarified. We have to refine the initial model presented in Section 7.4 in order to obtain the final model presented in Section 7.5.1. This will be done by:

- gradually splitting the writing and reading actions done in one shot in the abstraction;
- gradually removing the reading and writing traces;
- gradually introducing the data structure of the final concurrent programs.

The more precise refinement strategy is the following:

  (i) Splitting the writer and reader into two parts; removing the reading trace.
  (ii) Introducing Simpson's algorithm data structure; splitting the reader into one more part.
 (iii) Removing the writing trace.
 (iv) Splitting the writer into three parts.

7.6 First refinement

In this refinement, we introduce the address counters of both the writer and the reader, we remove the reading trace, and we also cut the writing in the writing trace into various places.

7.6.1 The reader state

The address counters are named adr_w, ranging from 1 to 5, and adr_r, ranging from 1 to 3. They are defined in invariants **inv1_1** and **inv1_2** below:

variables: ...
adr_r
adr_w

inv1_1: $adr\_r \in \{1, 2, 3\}$

inv1_2: $adr\_w \in \{1, 2, 3, 4, 5\}$

Let us recall below the **read** event of the initial model:

read
  any v **where**
    $v \in g(r) .. w$
  then
    $r := r + 1$
    $f(r + 1) := v$
    $g(r + 1) := w$
    $rd(r + 1) := wt(v)$
  end

We can see that we only use and modify f and g at index r and new index $r + 1$. As a consequence, we can forget about the entire reading trace and only use two variables u and m denoting respectively $g(r)$ and $f(r)$. This is done in invariants **inv1_3** and **inv1_4** below. The variable y denotes the result of the reading operation. Therefore, it is a member of the set D (**inv1_5**). We must also express that this variable corresponds to the *last* value of the reading trace rd, that is $rd(r)$. We do this in invariant **inv1_6** below:

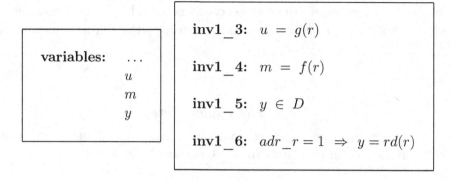

$$\mathbf{inv1\_3:} \quad u = g(r)$$

$$\mathbf{inv1\_4:} \quad m = f(r)$$

$$\mathbf{inv1\_5:} \quad y \in D$$

$$\mathbf{inv1\_6:} \quad adr\_r = 1 \Rightarrow y = rd(r)$$

7.6.2 The reading events

The reader events are now defined below. We have two new events (refining skip): Reader_1 and Reader_3. For the moment, event Reader_1 is just a dummy. Abstract event read is renamed Reader_2. This is illustrated in Fig. 7.10.

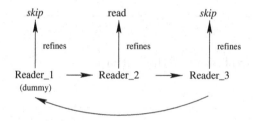

Fig. 7.10. Refinement of the reader

Among the three events, Reader_2 is the one that refines the abstract event read. The reason for this choice is explained informally by looking at the Reader program:

Reader

$reading := latest;$

$indx\_r := slot(reading);$

$y := data(reading)(indx\_r)$

In fact, it happens that after the second instruction of this program, the data which are read, namely $data(reading)(indx\_r)$, do not change whatever the behavior of the writing programs. This will be proved formally in the fourth refinement. So we choose to state that what is read is defined after the second instruction, hence our choice of refining event read with event Reader_2.

In event Reader_2, the non-deterministic choice for v, which was in $g(r) .. w$ in the abstraction, is now in $u .. w$ (remember invariant **inv1_3**, which says that u is equal to $g(r)$). The result of the reading in variable y is done in event Reader_3. Remember that invariant **inv1_6** says that just after an occurrence of event Reader_3 (when adr_r is equal to 1), y is equal to the last item of the reading trace, $rd(r)$, which is $wtp(f(r))$ – that is $wtp(m)$ since $m = f(r)$ – (this is invariant **inv1_4**):

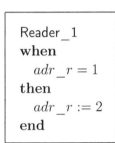

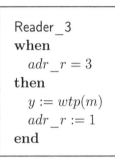

7.6.3 The writer state

We define now the concrete writing trace wtp, which is slightly different from the abstract writing trace wt. It is different because, in this refinement, the writing trace wtp is modified in an event (Writer_1), while the writing index w is incremented in two different events: Writer_42 or Writer_51. All this is expressed in the following invariants:

variables: ...
wtp

inv1_7: $wtp \in \mathbb{N}_1 \rightarrowtail D$

inv1_8: $wt \subseteq wtp$

inv1_9: $adr\_w = 1 \Rightarrow \mathrm{dom}(wtp) = 1 .. w$

inv1_10: $adr\_w \in \{2, 3, 4\} \Rightarrow \mathrm{dom}(wtp) = 1 .. w + 1$

inv1_11: $adr\_w = 5 \Rightarrow \mathrm{dom}(wtp) \in \{1 .. w,\ 1 .. w + 1\}$

7.6.4 The writing events

Now come the writing events. We have five new events (refining **skip**): Writer_1, Writer_2, Writer_3, Writer_41, and Writer_52. For the moment, events Writer_2, Writer_3, Writer_41, and Writer_52 are simple dummies. Events Writer_42 and Writer_51 are *both* refining abstract event **write**. All this is illustrated in Fig. 7.11.

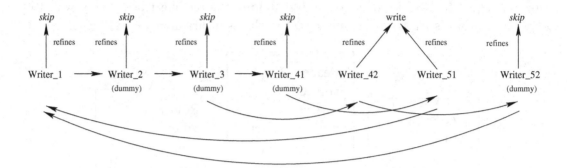

Fig. 7.11. Refinement of the writer

The choice of the event refining abstract event **write** is more delicate than that for the reading case. To explain it informally, let us study the **Writer** program:

$$\textbf{Writer}(x)$$

$$pair\_w := 1 - reading;$$

$$indx\_w := 1 - slot(pair\_w);$$

$$data(pair\_w)(indx\_w) := x$$

$$slot(pair\_w) := indx\_w;$$

$$latest := pair\_w$$

The instruction that must correspond to what we can observe in the abstraction is not the third one where the writing is done. The reason for not choosing that instruction is that the last two instructions modify some data (*slot* and *latest*) which are *shared* by the **Reader** program. So, we have to choose the last instruction. But, in fact, this last instruction is sometimes doing nothing; this is when *latest* is already equal to *pair_w*. It can happen when the **Reader** program has been quiet for a while and has not modified the variable *reading*. In that case, *pair_w* is not modified in the first instruction; hence *latest* is not modified. As a consequence, the abstract end of the writing is either on the fourth or on the fifth instruction. Therefore, we define two events for the fourth instruction, Writer_41 and Writer_42, and two events for the fifth instruction, Writer_51 and Writer_52.

The writing in *wtp* occurs in event Writer_1, while the incrementation of the index *w* is only done in event Writer_42 or Writer_51. Note the guards in events Writer_51 and Writer_52. They ensure that *w* is always incremented, but only once either in event Writer_42 or in event Writer_51:

```
Writer_1
any d where
    d ∈ D
    adr_w = 1
then
    wtp(w + 1) := d
    adr_w := 2
end
```

```
Writer_2
when
    adr_w = 2
then
    adr_w := 3
end
```

```
Writer_3
when
    adr_w = 3
then
    adr_w := 4
end
```

```
Writer_41
when
    adr_w = 4
then
    adr_w := 5
end
```

```
Writer_42
refines
    write
when
    adr_w = 4
with
    d = wtp(w + 1)
then
    w := w + 1
    adr_w := 5
end
```

```
Writer_51
refines
    write
when
    adr_w = 5
    dom(wtp) = 1 .. w + 1
with
    d = wtp(w + 1)
then
    w := w + 1
    adr_w := 1
end
```

```
Writer_52
when
    adr_w = 5
    dom(wtp) = 1 .. w
then
    adr_w := 1
end
```

7.7 Second refinement

In this refinement, we introduce the data structure of Simpson's algorithm

7.7.1 The state

The data structures of the algorithm, which we already presented in Section 7.2.1, are formally defined below. Note that there are two exceptions: (1) variable *idata* does not contain a data value but rather an index to the writing trace – it will be refined to the final variable *data* in the third and fourth refinements – and (2) variable *indx_wp* is slightly different from the final variable *indx_w*, which will be introduced in the fourth refinement. Note that we remove variables u and m, which are no longer useful:

variables: ...
       reading
       pair_w
       latest
       indx_r
       indx_wp
       slot
       idata

inv2_1: $reading \in \{0,1\}$

inv2_2: $pair\_w \in \{0,1\}$

inv2_3: $latest \in \{0,1\}$

inv2_4: $indx\_r \in \{0,1\}$

inv2_5: $indx\_wp \in \{0,1\}$

inv2_6: $slot \in \{0,1\} \rightarrow \{0,1\}$

inv2_7: $idata \in \{0,1\} \rightarrow (\{0,1\} \rightarrow \mathrm{dom}(wtp))$

7.7.2 The events and some additional invariants

Here are the refined reader events:

Reader_1
when
  $adr\_r = 1$
then
  $reading := latest$
  $adr\_r := 2$
end

Reader_2
when
  $adr\_r = 2$
with
  $v = idata(reading)(slot(reading))$
then
  $indx\_r := slot(reading)$
  $adr\_r := 3$
end

Reader_3
when
  $adr\_r = 3$
then
  $y := wtp(idata(reading)(indx\_r))$
  $adr\_r := 1$
end

Next are the abstract versions of event Reader_2 and Reader_3:

```
(abstract-)Reader_2
refines
    read
any  v  where
    adr_r = 2
    v ∈ u .. w
then
    m := v
    u := w
    adr_r := 3
end
```

```
(abstract-)Reader_3
when
    adr_r = 3
then
    y := wtp(m)
    adr_r := 1
end
```

This will allow us to understand the necessity of the next invariants, which were discovered while doing the proofs. In fact, **inv2_8** helps prove Reader_2, **inv2_9** helps prove Reader_3, and **inv2_9** helps prove the preservation of **inv2_8** by Reader_1:

inv2_8: $adr\_r = 2 \Rightarrow idata(reading)(slot(reading)) \in u .. w$

inv2_9: $adr\_r = 3 \Rightarrow m = idata(reading)(indx\_r)$

inv2_10: $idata(latest)(slot(latest)) = w$

Here are the writer events. As events Writer_2 and Writer_3 are not modified from the previous refinement, they are not shown now:

```
Writer_1
any  d  where
    d ∈ D
    adr_w = 1
then
    pair_w := 1 − reading
    indx_wp := 1 − slot(1 − reading)
    idata(1 − reading)(1 − slot(1 − reading)) := w + 1
    wtp(w + 1) := d
    adr_w := 2
end
```

```
Writer_41
when
    adr_w = 4
    pair_w ≠ latest
then
    slot(pair_w) := indx_wp
    adr_w := 5
end
```

```
Writer_42
when
    adr_w = 4
    pair_w = latest
then
    slot(pair_w) := indx_wp
    w := w + 1
    adr_w := 5
end
```

```
Writer_51
when
    adr_w = 5
    pair_w ≠ latest
then
    latest := pair_w
    w := w + 1
    adr_w := 1
end
```

```
Writer_52
when
    adr_w = 5
    pair_w = latest
then
    latest := pair_w
    adr_w := 1
end
```

The preservation of the previous invariants requires introducing the next series of invariants; they are all proved very easily:

inv2_11: $\quad adr\_w = 1 \Rightarrow pair\_w = latest$

inv2_12: $\quad reading = pair\_w \Rightarrow latest = reading$

inv2_13: $\quad adr\_w \in \{1, 5\} \Rightarrow indx\_wp = slot(pair\_w)$

inv2_14: $\quad adr\_w \in \{2, 3, 4\} \Rightarrow indx\_wp = 1 - slot(pair\_w)$

inv2_15: $\quad adr\_w = 5 \Rightarrow (latest = pair\_w \Leftrightarrow \mathrm{dom}(wtp) = 1\,..\,w)$

inv2_16: $\quad idata(pair\_w)(indx\_w) = \max(\mathrm{dom}(wtp))$

Notice that max(dom(*wtp*)) is well defined since dom(*wtp*) is not empty and finite (dom(*wtp*) ⊆ 1..*w* + 1 as stipulated in invariants **inv1_9** to **inv1_11** and also *w* ≥ 1 as stipulated by invariant **inv0_1**). Here is finally the initialization event:

init
    $adr\_w := 1$
    $adr\_r := 1$
    $w := 1$
    $wtp := \{1 \mapsto d0\}$
    $y := d0$
    $pair\_w := 0$
    $reading := 0$
    $latest := 0$
    $slot := \{0 \mapsto 0, 1 \mapsto 0\}$
    $idata := \{0 \mapsto \{0 \mapsto 1, 1 \mapsto 1\},$
                     $1 \mapsto \{0 \mapsto 1, 1 \mapsto 1\}\}$
    $indx\_wp := 0$
    $indx\_r := 0$

7.8 Third refinement

In this refinement, we remove the writing trace *wtp*. We can thus remove variable *w*. As a consequence, the action of events Write_41 and Write_42 are becoming identical; these events will be merged in the next refinement. The same thing happens to events Write_51 and Write_52; these events will also be merged in the next refinement.

7.8.1 The state

The variables *idata* and *wtp* are replaced by variable *Data*, which contains data values (this is indicated in the gluing invariant **inv3_2**):

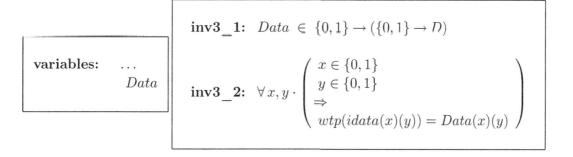

variables: ...
    Data

inv3_1: $Data \in \{0,1\} \rightarrow (\{0,1\} \rightarrow D)$

inv3_2: $\forall x, y \cdot \left(\begin{array}{l} x \in \{0,1\} \\ y \in \{0,1\} \\ \Rightarrow \\ wtp(idata(x)(y)) = Data(x)(y) \end{array} \right)$

7.8.2 *The events*

Here are the events. Notice that the first writing event still concentrates three actions. It will be split in the next refinement in events write_2 and write_3:

```
init
adr_w := 1
adr_r := 1
y := d0
pair_w := 0
reading := 0
latest := 0
slot := {0 ↦ 0, 1 ↦ 0}
Data := {0 ↦ {0 ↦ d0, 1 ↦ d0},
          1 ↦ {0 ↦ d0, 1 ↦ d0}}
indx_wp := 0
indx_r := 0
```

```
Writer_1
any d where
    d ∈ D
    adr_w = 1
then
    pair_w := 1 − reading
    indx_wp := 1 − slot(1 − reading)
    Data(1 − reading)(1 − slot(1 − reading)) := d
    adr_w := 2
end
```

```
Writer_41
when
    adr_w = 4
    pair_w ≠ latest
then
    slot(pair_w) := indx_wp
    adr_w := 5
end
```

```
Writer_42
when
    adr_w = 4
    pair_w = latest
then
    slot(pair_w) := indx_wp
    adr_w := 5
end
```

```
Writer_51
when
    adr_w = 5
    pair_w ≠ latest
then
    latest := pair_w
    adr_w := 1
end
```

```
Writer_52
when
    adr_w = 5
    pair_w = latest
then
    latest := pair_w
    adr_w := 1
end
```

```
Reader_1
when
    adr_r = 1
then
    reading := latest
    adr_r := 2
end
```

```
Reader_2
when
    adr_r = 2
then
    indx_r := slot(reading)
    adr_r := 3
end
```

```
Reader_3
when
    adr_r = 3
then
    y := Data(reading)(indx_r)
    adr_r := 1
end
```

7.9 Fourth refinement

7.9.1 The state

This is the final touch: event Writer_1 is split. We obtain exactly the sketch we proposed in Section 7.5.1. The variable *data* replaces *Data*, and the variable *indx_w* replaces *indx_wp*:

```
variables:    ...
              data
              indx_w
              x
```

inv4_1: $data \in \{0,1\} \to (\{0,1\} \to D)$

inv4_2: $indx\_w \in \{0,1\}$

inv4_3: $x \in D$

inv4_4: $adr\_w \in \{1,4,5\} \Rightarrow Data = data$

inv4_5: $adr\_w \in \{2,3\}$
$\Rightarrow$
$Data = data \mathbin{\lhd\mkern-9mu-} \{pair\_w \mapsto (data(pair\_w) \mathbin{\lhd\mkern-9mu-} \{indx\_wp \mapsto x\})\}$

inv4_6: $adr\_w \in \{1,3,4,5\} \Rightarrow indx\_w = indx\_wp$

inv4_7:
$$\begin{array}{l} adr\_w = 3 \\ adr\_r = 3 \\ pair\_w = reading \\ \Rightarrow \\ indx\_r \neq indx\_wp \end{array}$$

inv4_8:
$$\begin{array}{l} adr\_w = 2 \\ adr\_r = 3 \\ pair\_w = reading \\ \Rightarrow \\ indx\_r \neq indx\_wp \end{array}$$

Notice **inv4_7**, which was required in Section 7.2.3. It says that we are never writing and reading at the same place concurrently.

7.9.2 The events

```
init
adr_w := 1
adr_r := 1
. . .
```

```
Writer_1
when
    adr_w = 1
then
    x :∈ D
    pair_w := 1 − reading
    adr_w := 2
end
```

```
Writer_2
when
    adr_w = 2
then
    indx_w := 1 − slot(pair_w)
    adr_w := 3
end
```

```
Writer_3
when
    adr_w = 3
then
    data(pair_w)(index_w) := x
    adr_w := 4
end
```

```
Writer_4
refines
    Writer_41
    Writer_42
when
    adr_w = 4
then
    slot(pair_w) := indx_w
    adr_w := 5
end
```

```
Writer_5
refines
    Writer_51
    Writer_52
when
    adr_w = 5
then
    latest := pair_w
    adr_w := 1
end
```

| Reader_1
when
$adr\_r = 1$
then
$reading := latest$
$adr\_r := 2$
end | Reader_2
when
$adr\_r = 2$
then
$indx\_r := slot(reading)$
$adr\_r := 3$
end | Reader_3
when
$adr\_r = 3$
then
$y := data(reading)(indx\_r)$
$adr\_r := 1$
end |

In the following diagram, we represent the various transformations of the **write** event:

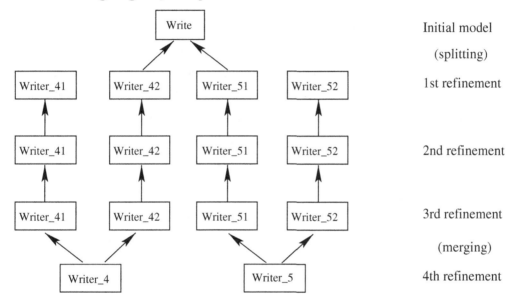

7.10 Reference

[1] H. R. Simpson. Four-slot fully asynchronous communication mechanism. Computer and Digital Techniques. *IEE Proceedings*. Vol. 137 (1) (January 1990).

8

Development of electronic circuits

8.1 Introduction

In this chapter, a simple methodology supporting the *progressive proved development* of synchronous electronic circuits is presented. A typical circuit is shown in Fig. 8.1

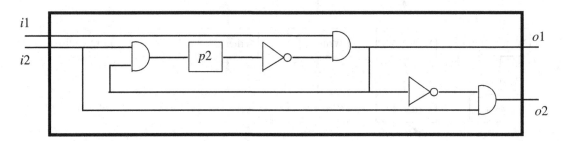

Fig. 8.1. A typical circuit

This circuit is made of the following components: two input wires $i1$ and $i2$ carrying boolean values, two output wires $o1$ and $o2$ carrying boolean values, various *gates* (here three and-gates and two not-gates), and a *register* $p2$ containing a boolean value. We would like to develop such circuits in a systematic fashion.

8.1.1 Synchronous circuits

A synchronous circuit is viewed as a box which has a certain *state*; let us call this state *cir_state*. Some *input* lines are entering into the box, and some *output* lines are emerging out of it. Input and output lines are supposed to carry boolean values. All this is indicated in Fig. 8.2.

As a sufficient abstraction, we can say that the circuit is *synchronized* by a clock, which pulses regularly between two alternative positions, *low* and *high*, as indicated in Fig. 8.3.

258

Fig. 8.2. A circuit as a box with some input and output wires

Fig. 8.3. A clock

This abstraction of the clock is interpreted as follows: (1) when the clock is *low*, *cir_state* and the *output* lines are supposed to be idle, only the *input* lines may change; conversely, (2) when the clock is *high*, the *input* lines are supposed to stay idle, whereas *cir_state* may be modified as well as the *output* line. From now on, we consider that the circuit state *cir_state* and the output wire *output* together form the *circuit*, whereas the input line constitutes its *environment*. Note that the environment may also comprise a state, which we call *env_state*.

8.1.2 Coupling the circuit with its environment

With this view of circuit and environment in mind, the notion of clock can be made more abstract by simply saying that it gives us two alternative ways of *observing the closed system* made of the circuit and its environment.

We can thus consider that we have two *modes* of observation: one, *env*, corresponds to observing the environment independently of the circuit, and another one, *cir*, corresponds to observing the circuit independently of the environment. Such modes alternate for ever. From now on, we shall follow that view and forget about the clock. This has the consequence that we shall never develop a circuit in isolation, but always *together with its environment*. Such a *coupling* is shown in Fig. 8.4.

8.1.3 Dynamic view of the coupling

Suppose *cir_state* is formalized by means of a number of boolean variables c. The various dynamic evolutions of the circuit can be formalized by means of a number of

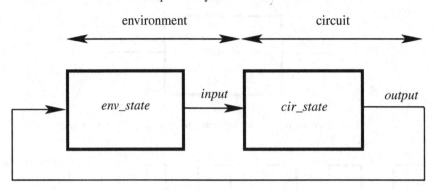

Fig. 8.4. A circuit and its environment

events defined as follows:

```
cir_event_i
  when
    mode = cir
    GC_i(input, c)
  then
    mode := env
    c, output :| PC_i(input, c, c′, output′)
  end
```

Likewise, the environment is formalized by means of a number of variables e. The various dynamic evolutions of the environment can be formalized by means of a number of events defined as follows:

```
env_event_j
  when
    mode = env
    GE_j(output, e)
  then
    mode := cir
    e, input :| PE_j(output, e, e′, input′)
  end
```

As can be seen, there is an important distinction to be made between the way the *input* line and environment variables e are modified when the *mode* is *env*, and the *output* line and circuit variables c are modified when the *mode* is *cir*. The modification of the environment may follow some specific rules but in no case is it influenced by the circuit variables (it may be influenced by the *output* however). Conversely, the modification in the circuit may depend on the *input* line and on the circuit variables c, but not on the environment variables e however.

Also notice that, in an abstract view of our circuit and environment, the status of the *input* and *output* lines and of c and e are not necessarily represented by boolean values (which will probably be the case in a refined implementation). For instance, in an abstract specification, variables e and c can very well carry the entire history of what has happened since the interaction between the circuit and its environment has started.

8.1.4 Static view of the coupling

So far we have only envisaged a very *operational* (although abstract) view of our circuit and environment; we have just described how these entities behave dynamically while time is passing, but we have not at all explained *why* they should behave like this. Another completely *independent* approach is one by which a *static view* is presented by means of some conditions C and D describing the way these entities are *permanently* related to each other. These conditions express the way the circuit is *coupled* with its environment:

$$mode = env \quad \Rightarrow \quad C(e, input, c, output)$$

$$mode = cir \quad \Rightarrow \quad D(e, input, c, output)$$

Condition C states what the circuit should establish (for the environment) provided it behaves in a situation where D holds. Conversely, condition D states what the environment should establish (for the circuit) provided it behaves in a situation where C holds.

8.1.5 Consistency conditions

Nothing guarantees however that the dynamics envisaged above and the statics we have just described are coherent; this is something that has to be proved rigorously. It can be stated as follows:

$$
\begin{array}{l}
C(e, input, c, output) \\
GE\_j(output, e) \\
PE\_j(output, e, e', input') \\
\Rightarrow \\
D(e', input', c, output))
\end{array}
$$

$$
\begin{array}{l}
D(e, input, c, output) \\
GC\_i(input, c) \\
PC\_i(input, c, c', output') \\
\Rightarrow \\
C(e, input, c', output')
\end{array}
$$

Informally, this means that when *mode* is *env* and the static condition C holds, then D must hold after any accepted modifications e' and *input'* made by the environment. Likewise, when *mode* is *cir* and the static condition D holds, then C must hold after any accepted modifications c' and *output'* made by the circuit.

8.1.6 A warning

Note that this formulation corresponds to what we must obtain towards the *end of a formal development* where there should exist a very clear distinction between the circuit and the environment. During the development however, such a distinction is not necessarily as strict. For instance, we might allow for the possibility of the environment accessing the previous *input* and even accessing the state of the circuit. Likewise, we have to accept the circuit accessing its previous *output* and even the entire state of the environment. What must still be clearly followed however, even in an abstraction, is the limitation of modification: the environment modifies the *input* and its state only, whereas the circuit modifies its state and the *output* only.

One of the objectives of the design of a circuit is precisely that of making the circuit and environment communicate eventually through the input and output lines only. For this, we have to *localize* their respective states.

8.1.7 Final construction of the circuit

A final refinement situation is obtained when the following conditions hold:

  (i) the circuit variables must all be boolean;
  (ii) the inputs must be boolean;
  (iii) the outputs must be boolean;
  (iv) the circuit must be deadlock free;

(v) the circuit must be internally deterministic – this concerns circuit variables and outputs;

(vi) the circuit must be externally deterministic – circuit guards are mutually exclusive;

(vii) the environment does not access the circuit variables except the output;

(viii) the circuit does not access the environment variables except the input.

Note that the environment might still be externally as well as internally non-deterministic. As a result, a circuit event has the following shape:

$$
\begin{aligned}
&\text{cir\_event\_i} \\
&\quad \textbf{when} \\
&\qquad mode = cir \\
&\qquad GC\_i(input, c) \\
&\quad \textbf{then} \\
&\qquad mode := env \\
&\qquad c := C\_i(input, c) \\
&\qquad output := O\_i(input, c) \\
&\quad \textbf{end}
\end{aligned}
$$

We are going to prove now that each circuit event can be refined in such a way that all have the *same action* on the circuit state and output. Here is one such refinement:

$$
\begin{aligned}
&\text{cir\_event\_i} \\
&\quad \textbf{when} \\
&\qquad mode = cir \\
&\qquad GC\_i(input, c) \\
&\quad \textbf{then} \\
&\qquad mode := env \\
&\qquad c := \text{bool} \left(\begin{array}{l} \ldots \ \vee \\ (GC\_i(input, c) \ \wedge \ C\_i(input, c) = \text{TRUE}) \ \vee \\ \ldots \end{array} \right) \\
&\qquad output := \text{bool} \left(\begin{array}{l} \ldots \ \vee \\ (GC\_i(input, c) \ \wedge \ O\_i(input, c) = \text{TRUE}) \ \vee \\ \ldots \end{array} \right) \\
&\quad \textbf{end}
\end{aligned}
$$

Notice our usage of the operator "bool" transforming a predicate into a boolean expression. It is defined by means of the following equivalence:

$$E = \text{bool}(P) \quad \Leftrightarrow \quad \left(\begin{array}{l} P \Rightarrow E = \text{TRUE} \\ \neg P \Rightarrow E = \text{FALSE} \end{array} \right)$$

The refinement proof is now straightforward. It amounts to proving the following concerning variable c (the proof to be done concerning *output* is similar and thus not shown):

$GC\_i(input, c)$
$\vdash$

$$C\_i(input, c) = \text{bool} \left(\begin{array}{l} \dots \quad \vee \\ (\, GC\_i(input, c) \wedge C\_i(input, c) = \text{TRUE}\,) \quad \vee \\ \dots \end{array} \right)$$

According to the definition of the operator bool, this reduces to proving two statements. Here is the first:

$GC\_i(input, c)$
$$\left(\begin{array}{l} \dots \quad \vee \\ (\, GC\_i(input, c) \wedge C\_i(input, c) = \text{TRUE}\,) \quad \vee \\ \dots \end{array} \right)$$
$\vdash$
$C\_i(input, c) = \text{TRUE}$

Thanks to the mutual exclusion of the guards (that is $GC\_i(input, c) \Rightarrow \neg GC\_j$ $(input, c)$ when $i \neq j$), this first statement reduces to the following which holds trivially:

$GC\_i(input, c)$
$C\_i(input, c) = \text{TRUE}$
$\vdash$
$C\_i(input, c) = \text{TRUE}$

Here is now the second statement:

$GC\_i(input, c)$
$$\neg \left(\begin{array}{l} \dots \quad \vee \\ (\, GC\_i(input, c) \wedge C\_i(input, c) = \text{TRUE}\,) \quad \vee \\ \dots \end{array} \right)$$
$\vdash$
$C\_i(input, c) = \text{FALSE}$

By applying de Morgan's law to remove the external negation, this second statement is equivalent to:

$$GC\_i(input, c)$$
$$\dots$$
$$\neg\, GC\_i(input, c)\ \vee\ C\_i(input, c) = \text{FALSE}$$
$$\dots$$
$$\vdash$$
$$C\_i(input, c) = \text{FALSE}$$

that is, the following, which holds trivially:

$$GC\_i(input, c)$$
$$\dots$$
$$C\_i(input, c) = \text{FALSE}$$
$$\dots$$
$$\vdash$$
$$C\_i(input, c) = \text{FALSE}$$

Since the circuit events are deadlock free (disjunction of guards holds under condition $mode = cir$) and have identical actions, they can all be merged into a single event as follows:

```
cir_event
  when
     mode = cir
  then
     mode := env
                   / ... ∨                                          \
     c := bool    |  GC_i(input, c)  ∧  C_i(input, c) = TRUE  ∨     |
                   \ ...                                            /
                        / ... ∨                                      \
     output := bool |  GC_i(input, c)  ∧  O_i(input, c) = TRUE  ∨   |
                        \ ...                                        /
  end
```

Notice that when $C_i(input, c)$ is syntactically equal to TRUE, then $C_i(input, c) = $ TRUE can be removed, and when $C_i(input, c)$ is syntactically equal to FALSE, then $GC_i(input, c) \wedge C_i(input, c) = $ TRUE can be removed. We have similar simplifications for $O\_i(input, c)$. This last event *is* our circuit. From this, the circuit can be drawn in a systematic fashion.

8.1.8 A very small illustrative example

Suppose we end up with a development with the following circuit events:

```
env1
   when
      mode = env
      input_1 = TRUE
      input_2 = TRUE
   then
      mode := cir
      output := TRUE
   end
```

```
env2
   when
      mode = env
      input_1 = TRUE
      input_2 = FALSE
   then
      mode := cir
      output := TRUE
   end
```

```
env3
   when
      mode = env
      input_1 = FALSE
      input_2 = TRUE
   then
      mode := cir
      output := TRUE
   end
```

```
env4
   when
      mode = env
      input_1 = FALSE
      input_2 = FALSE
   then
      mode := cir
      output := FALSE
   end
```

Clearly, these events are internally as well as externally deterministic and also deadlock-free. By applying the merging rule presented in the previous section, we obtain the following for the assignment of the variable *output*:

$$
\text{bool} \begin{pmatrix}
(input\_1 = \text{TRUE} \ \wedge \ input\_2 = \text{TRUE} \ \wedge \ \text{TRUE} = \text{TRUE}) & \vee \\
(input\_1 = \text{TRUE} \ \wedge \ input\_2 = \text{FALSE} \ \wedge \ \text{TRUE} = \text{TRUE}) & \vee \\
(input\_1 = \text{FALSE} \ \wedge \ input\_2 = \text{TRUE} \ \wedge \ \text{TRUE} = \text{TRUE}) & \vee \\
(input\_1 = \text{FALSE} \ \wedge \ input\_2 = \text{FALSE} \ \wedge \ \text{FALSE} = \text{TRUE})
\end{pmatrix} ,
$$

reducing as expected to:

$$
\text{bool}(input\_1 = \text{TRUE} \ \vee \ input\_2 = \text{TRUE}).
$$

As a result, these events can be merged into the following unique event:

```
or_gate
  when
    mode = env
  then
    mode := cir
    output := bool ( input_1 = TRUE ∨ input_2 = TRUE )
  end
```

8.2 A first example

As the previous discussion may appear to be rather dry, we shall now illustrate our approach by describing a little example of circuit specification and design.

8.2.1 Informal specification

The circuit we propose to study is a well-known benchmark that has been analyzed in different contexts: it is called the *Single Pulser* (Pulser for short). Here is a first informal specification taken from [1]:

> We have a debounced push-button, on (true) in the down position, off (false) in the up position. Devise a circuit to sense the depression of the button and assert an output signal for one clock pulse. The system should not allow additional assertions of the output until after the operator has released the button.

Here is another related specification [1], which is given under the form of three properties concerning the input I and the output O of the circuit:

1. Whenever there is a rising edge at I, O becomes true some time later.
2. Whenever O is true, it becomes false in the next time distance and it remains false at least until the next rising edge on I.
3. Whenever there is a rising edge, and assuming that the output pulse does not happen immediately, there are no more rising edges until that pulse happens (There cannot be two rising edges on I without a pulse on O between them).

A subjective impression after reading these specifications is that they are rather difficult to understand. We would prefer to plunge the circuit to specify within a possible environment as follows:

1. We have a button that can be depressed and released by an operator. The button is connected to the input of the circuit.

2. We have a lamp that is able to be lit and subsequently turned down. The lamp is connected to the output of the circuit.

3. The circuit, situated between the button and the lamp, must always make the lamp flash as many times as the button is depressed and subsequently released.

A schematic representation of this closed system is shown in Fig. 8.5.

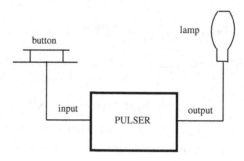

Fig. 8.5. A pulser and its environment

Note that the scenario we have described can be *observed* by an external witness. We can count the number of times the button is depressed by the operator and also the number of times the lamp flashes and we can *compare* these numbers. For example, Fig. 8.6 shows two wave diagrams: the first one represents a succession of depressions of the button followed by subsequent releases, while the second shows various corresponding flashes of the lamp.

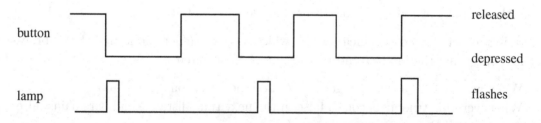

Fig. 8.6. Relationship between the button depression and the lamp flash

As can be seen, the flash can be situated just after a button depression, or in between a depression and a subsequent release, or else just after a release.

8.2.2 Initial model

The State Before defining the state, we must formalize the set $MODE$ and its two values *env* and *cir*:

sets: $MODE$

constants: env, cir

axm0_1: $MODE = \{env, cir\}$

axm0_2: $env \neq cir$

Rather than directly representing the environment by the concrete input line and the circuit by the concrete output line (and probably some concrete internal state), we consider an *abstraction* where the environment is represented by two natural variables, *push* and *pop*, denoting respectively the number of times the button is depressed and the number of times it is released (since the system has started). This yields the following invariants, stating quite naturally that *push* is at least as *pop* and at most one more than *pop*:

variables: $mode$
     $push$
     pop

inv0_1: $mode \in MODE$

inv0_2: $push \in \mathbb{N}$

inv0_3: $pop \in \mathbb{N}$

inv0_4: $pop \leq push$

inv0_5: $push \leq pop + 1$

The abstract circuit is represented by a single variable, *flash*, denoting the number of times the lamp flashes. We then have the following properties showing the *coupling* between the abstract environment and the abstract circuit: *push* is at least as *flash* and at most one more than *flash*. In other words, you push the button then the lamp later flashes (the lamp being turned down when the circuit is started):

variables: $\ldots, flash$

inv0_6: $flash \in \mathbb{N}$

inv0_7: $flash \leq push$

inv0_8: $push \leq flash + 1$

The events Besides the initialization event, the dynamics of the environment are straightforward: we have three events corresponding respectively to pushing the button (event **env1**), releasing it (event **env2**), and, finally, doing nothing (event **env3**). Clearly, we can depress the button only when *pop* is equal to *push*, and we can release it when *push* is different from *pop* (it is then one more than *pop* according to invariants **inv0_4** and **inv0_5**); finally, we can do nothing in all circumstances:

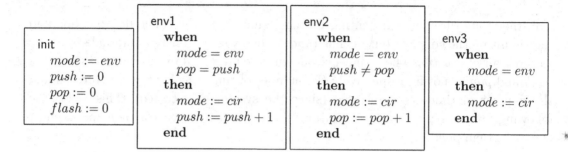

The dynamics of the abstract circuit is a little more complicated. There are two events corresponding to flashing the lamp (event **cir1**) or doing nothing (event **cir2**). We can flash the lamp when *push* is different from *flash*:

$$
\boxed{
\begin{array}{l}
\text{cir1}\\
\quad\textbf{when}\\
\qquad mode = cir\\
\qquad push \neq flash\\
\quad\textbf{then}\\
\qquad mode := env\\
\qquad flash := flash + 1\\
\quad\textbf{end}
\end{array}
}
$$

The circumstances in which the circuit does nothing need to be studied carefully. When the button is depressed, the flash of the lamp can be done either immediately (Case 1) or later as indicated in Fig. 8.7 (Case 2 and 3). The latest time for the

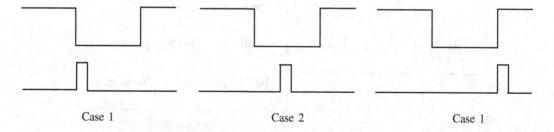

Case 1   Case 2   Case 1

Fig. 8.7. The various cases where the circuit does nothing

flash occurrence is just after the user releases the button (Case 3). As a consequence, the circuit can do nothing in three different circumstances denoted A, B, and C in Fig. 8.8.

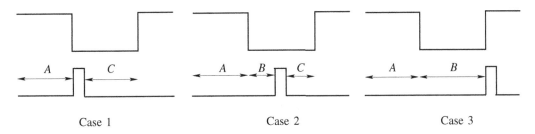

Case 1   Case 2   Case 3

Fig. 8.8. The various conditions where the circuit does nothing

Conditions A, B, and C can be formalized more rigorously as follows:

$$\text{Condition } A: \quad push = pop \;\wedge\; push = flash$$

$$\text{Condition } B: \quad push \neq pop \;\wedge\; push \neq flash$$

$$\text{Condition } C: \quad push \neq pop \;\wedge\; push = flash$$

The guard of the "do-nothing" event of the circuit corresponds to the disjunction of these conditions, namely:

$$A \vee B \vee C \;\Leftrightarrow\; push \neq pop \vee push = flash$$

```
cir2
  when
    mode = cir
    push ≠ pop ∨ push = flash
  then
    mode := env
  end
```

Proofs The proof of consistency between the static properties and the events requires introducing the following additional invariant:

$$\textbf{inv0\_9:} \quad mode = env \;\Rightarrow\; flash = push \vee flash = pop$$

It may seem at first glance that the disjunction $flash = push \vee flash = pop$ is always true (even when $mode = cir$). In fact, this is almost always the case, except when the flash occurs at the latest as indicated in Fig. 8.9.

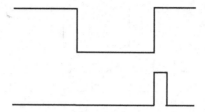

Fig. 8.9. The special case where $flash = push \vee flash = pop$ does not hold

Then just after the occurrence of event env2 (releasing the button), we have $mode = cir$ and $push = pop = flash + 1$, thus clearly $flash = push \vee flash = pop$ does not hold.

8.2.3 Refining the circuit by diminishing its non-determinacy

In this section, we shall present a first way of refining our circuit. This corresponds to removing some of its possible non-deterministic behaviors. Let us reconsider the two events of our circuit:

```
cir1
   when
      mode = cir
      push ≠ flash
   then
      mode := env
      flash := flash + 1
   end
```

```
cir2
   when
      mode = cir
      push ≠ pop ∨ push = flash
   then
      mode := env
   end
```

The guards, clearly, may overlap when $push \neq flash$ and $push \neq pop$ hold simultaneously. This occurs when we are in between a depression and a release ($push \neq pop$) and when the flash has not yet occurred ($push \neq flash$). In this situation, it is possible for the circuit to either flash the lamp or do nothing.

We can see that there are two different ways of making this system of events deterministic: (1) by replacing the guard of cir2 by $push = flash$, or (2) by adding the guard $push = pop$ to that of the event cir1. In both cases, we are strengthening the guards. The net effect, in both cases, is to make each guard the negation of the other: the circuit has become deterministic indeed. The first solution, which we call PULSER1, corresponds to flashing the lamp as early as possible. It is illustrated in Fig. 8.10.

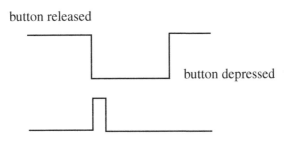

button released

button depressed

Fig. 8.10. The flash occurs as early as possible

```
cir1_PULSER1
    when
        mode = cir
        push ≠ flash
    then
        mode := env
        flash := flash + 1
    end
```

```
cir2_PULSER1
    when
        mode = cir
        push = flash
    then
        mode := env
    end
```

In this case, the following invariant can be proved:

inv1_pulser1: $pop \neq push \ \wedge \ mode = env \ \Rightarrow \ flash \neq pop$

When the button is depressed ($pop \neq push$) and the mode is environment ($mode = env$), then the flash has occurred; thus, the number of flashes is one more than the number of pops, or alternatively the flash number is equal to the push number ($flash = push$).

The second solution, which we call PULSER2, corresponds to flashing the lamp as late as possible. It is illustrated in Fig. 8.11.

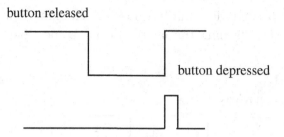

button released

button depressed

Fig. 8.11. The flash occurs as late as possible

cir1_PULSER2
  when
    $mode = cir$
    $push = pop \ \wedge \ push \neq flash$
  then
    $mode := env$
    $flash := flash + 1$
  end

cir2_PULSER2
  when
    $mode = cir$
    $push \neq pop \ \vee \ push = flash$
  then
    $mode := env$
  end

In this case, the following invariant can be proved:

inv1_pulser2: $pop \neq push \ \Rightarrow \ flash \neq push$

When the button is depressed ($pop \neq push$), then the number of flashes is one less than the number of pushes ($flash \neq push$) or alternatively the flash number is equal to the pop number ($flash = pop$).

8.2.4 Refining the circuits by changing the data space

The two circuits PULSER1 and PULSER2 we have obtained, although now completely deterministic, are still rather abstract. We would like to converge now towards some "real" circuits. In particular, the input and output wires should be defined, and the abstract variables *push*, *pop*, and *flash* should be abandoned. The purpose of this section is to show how refinement allow us to change our data space.

We have two new variables *input* and *output*, which correspond to the input and output lines respectively. These variables are boolean:

variables:	*mode*		**inv2_1:**	*input* $\in$ BOOL
	input			
	output		**inv2_2:**	*output* $\in$ BOOL

The variable *input* is an environment variable: it is modified by both events **env1** and **env2**. The abstract variable *push* is supposed to denote the number of times the variable *input* moves from FALSE to TRUE. Likewise, the abstract variable *pop* is supposed to denote the number of times the variable *input* moves from TRUE to FALSE. This leads to the following new events **env1** and **env2**:

```
env1
   when
      mode = env
      input = FALSE
   then
      mode := cir
      input := TRUE
   end
```

```
env2
   when
      mode = env
      input = TRUE
   then
      mode := cir
      input := FALSE
   end
```

```
env3
   when
      mode = env
   then
      mode := cir
   end
```

For these events to be correct refinements of their abstract counterparts, each concrete guard must imply the corresponding abstract guard. Here is a copy of the abstractions:

```
(abstract-)env1
   when
      mode = env
      pop = push
   then
      mode := cir
      push := push + 1
   end
```

```
(abstract-)env2
   when
      mode = env
      pop ≠ push
   then
      mode := cir
      pop := pop + 1
   end
```

```
(abstract-)env3
   when
      mode = env
   then
      mode := cir
   end
```

The correct refinement thus clearly involves proving the following relationship between the concrete environment space and the abstract one:

| **inv2_3:** | $input = \text{TRUE} \iff pop \neq push$ |

Let us now turn to the implementation of the abstract circuit PULSER1. We have the following abstract circuit events:

```
(abstract-)cir1_PULSER1
  when
    mode = cir
    push ≠ flash
  then
    mode := env
    flash := flash + 1
  end
```

```
(abstract-)cir2_PULSER1
  when
    mode = cir
    push = flash
  then
    mode := env
  end
```

The abstract circuit variable *flash* has to disappear. It counts the number of times the concrete variable *output* moves from FALSE to TRUE. For this, the guard of the concrete event cir1 must check that the abstract variable *push* has just been modified by the environment. As we know, this is when the input line *input* moves from FALSE to TRUE. Clearly, we can access the actual value of *input*, but certainly *not its previous value*. We have no choice then but to introduce a register, *reg*, internal to our circuit, and whose role is to store the previous value of *input*. We also have an equality between *reg* and *input* when *mode = env* holds (**invi2_5**):

```
variables: mode, input, output, reg
```

```
inv2_4:  reg ∈ BOOL

invi2_5:  mode = env ⇒ reg = input
```

This leads to the following implementation of the events cir1 and cir2 for PULSER1:

```
cir1_PULSER1
  when
    mode = cir
    input = TRUE ∧ reg = FALSE
  then
    mode := env
    output := TRUE
    reg := input
  end
```

```
cir2_PULSER1
  when
    mode = cir
    input = FALSE ∨ reg = TRUE
  then
    mode := env
    output := FALSE
    reg := input
  end
```

The concrete guards must imply the abstract ones. All this leads to the following properties to be maintained:

$$
\textbf{inv2\_PULSER1\_6:} \quad mode = cir \;\Rightarrow\; \left(\begin{array}{c} input = \text{TRUE} \;\wedge\; reg = \text{FALSE} \\ \Leftrightarrow \\ push \neq flash \end{array} \right)
$$

We have a similar implementation of the events cir1 and cir2 for PULSER2:

```
cir1_PULSER2
  when
    mode = cir
    input = FALSE ∧ reg = TRUE
  then
    mode := env
    output := TRUE
    reg := input
  end
```

```
cir2_PULSER2
  when
    mode = cir
    input = TRUE ∨ reg = FALSE
  then
    mode := env
    output := FALSE
    reg := input
  end
```

And we have to ensure the following additional invariant:

$$
\textbf{inv2\_PULSER2\_6:} \quad mode = cir \;\Rightarrow\; \left(\begin{array}{c} input = \text{FALSE} \;\wedge\; reg = \text{TRUE} \\ \Leftrightarrow \\ push \neq flash \;\wedge\; push = pop \end{array} \right)
$$

8.2.5 Building the final circuits

Our next design step is to depart from the closed system and consider the circuit PULSER1 and PULSER2 in isolation. Here is a copy of the PULSER1 events:

```
cir1_PULSER1
  when
    mode = cir
    input = TRUE ∧ reg = FALSE
  then
    mode := env
    output := TRUE
    reg := input
  end
```

```
cir2_PULSER1
  when
    mode = cir
    input = FALSE ∨ reg = TRUE
  then
    mode := env
    output := FALSE
    reg := input
  end
```

Applying the technique developed in Section 8.1.7, we obtain:

> PULSER1
>   **when**
> $mode = cir$
>   **then**
> $mode := env$
> $output := \text{bool}((input = \text{TRUE} \wedge reg = \text{FALSE} \wedge \text{TRUE} = \text{TRUE}) \vee$
> $(\ldots \wedge \text{FALSE} = \text{TRUE}))$
> $reg \quad := \text{bool}(input = \text{TRUE} \wedge (input = \text{TRUE} \wedge reg = \text{FALSE}) \vee$
> $input = \text{TRUE} \wedge (input = \text{FALSE} \vee reg = \text{TRUE}))$
>   **end**

which reduces to:

> PULSER1
>   **when**
> $mode = cir$
>   **then**
> $mode := env$
> $output := \text{bool}(input = \text{TRUE} \wedge reg = \text{FALSE})$
> $reg \quad := \text{bool}(input = \text{TRUE})$
>   **end**

We have eventually constructed our little circuit **PULSER1** as shown on Fig. 8.12.

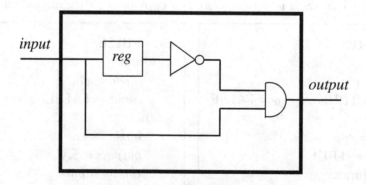

Fig. 8.12. The circuit **PULSER1**

We can construct the following circuit PULSER2 similarly:

```
cir1_PULSER2
    when
        mode = cir
        input = FALSE ∧ reg = TRUE
    then
        mode := env
        output := TRUE
        reg := input
    end
```

```
cir2_PULSER2
    when
        mode = cir
        input = TRUE ∨ reg = FALSE
    then
        mode := env
        output := FALSE
        reg := input
    end
```

Applying the technique developed in Section 8.1.7, we obtain:

```
PULSER2
    when
        mode = cir
    then
        mode := env
        output := bool((input = FALSE ∧ reg = TRUE ∧ TRUE = TRUE) ∨
                    (... ∧ FALSE = TRUE))
        reg    := bool(input = TRUE ∧ (input = FALSE ∧ reg = TRUE) ∨
                    input = TRUE ∧ (input = TRUE ∨ reg = FALSE))
    end
```

which reduces to:

```
PULSER2
    when
        mode = cir
    then
        mode := env
        output := bool(input = FALSE ∧ reg = TRUE)
        reg    := bool(input = TRUE)
    end
```

This leads to the circuit of Fig. 8.13.

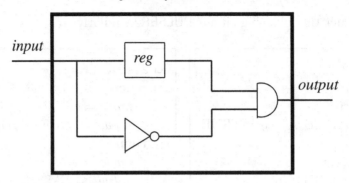

Fig. 8.13. The circuit PULSER2

8.3 Second example: the arbiter

8.3.1 Informal specification

This simple circuit is called the (binary) *Arbiter*. It has two boolean input lines called i_1 and i_2 and two boolean output lines called o_1 and o_2. This is indicated in Fig. 8.14.

The circuit has two boolean inputs i_1 and i_2 and two boolean outputs o_1 and o_2	FUN-1

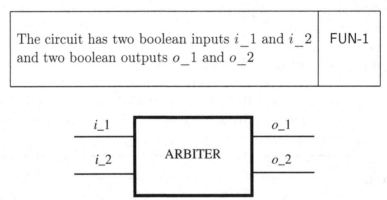

Fig. 8.14. The arbiter

When input i_i is valued to TRUE, this means that a certain *user_i*, associated by construction with the line i_i, has required (asked for) the usage of a certain shared resource (the specific resource in question as well as the nature of the users do not play any rôle in this system):

A TRUE input means a user (associated with that input) is asking for a certain resource	FUN-2

When the circuit, used with input i_i valued to TRUE, reacts with the output o_i valued to TRUE, this means that the circuit has indeed granted the resource to *user_i*. Of course, an output o_i can only be valued to TRUE when the corresponding input i_i is TRUE:

The circuit reacts positively to a request by setting the corresponding output to TRUE	FUN-3

Conversely, the circuit should react as soon as it can. But this reaction is constrained by the fact that the circuit can only grant the resource to *at most one user* at a time:

The circuit can react positively to only one request at a time (mutual exclusion)	FUN-4

Notice that each winning user is supposed to immediately release the resource so that it can ask for it again immediately after getting it.

Each user frees the resource immediately	FUN-5

We have a number of additional constraints:

- No requiring user can be indefinitely denied the right to obtain the resource (this could be the case, should the other user always require the resource again immediately after getting it). Notice that, in this example, we shall make this constraint more precise by asking that a requiring user should not wait for more than one clock pulse before being served. In other words, a new requesting user, if not served at the next circuit reaction, must necessarily be served at the one that follows the next:

A requesting user cannot be postponed indefinitely	FUN-6

- We suppose that a requiring user shall not give up requiring the resource without being served (this is just a simplification that could have been relaxed):

A user asking for a resource continues to ask for it as long as it is not served	FUN-7

- Finally, we require that the circuit correctly reacts to the void case where no user is asking for the resource. In that case, the resource must not then be granted to any user:

The resource cannot be granted without a user asking for it	FUN-8

We do not know whether it is possible to build such a circuit. Also, we do not know either whether such a circuit, supposedly constructed, is free from any deadlock in some situations.

8.3.2 Initial model

The state In the formal specification, we shall abstract from the boolean input and output lines as described in the previous section. We consider that in the environment, we can count the numbers $r1$ and $r2$ of requests made by each user and the corresponding numbers $a1$ and $a2$ of acknowledgements made by the circuit. The constraint of the informal specification imposes the following straightforward permanent invariant where it is stated that the number of requests is at most one more than the number of acknowledgements (**inv0_5** to **inv0_8**):

variables: $r1$ $r2$ $a1$ $a2$	**inv0_1:** $r1 \in \mathbb{N}$ **inv0_2:** $r2 \in \mathbb{N}$ **inv0_3:** $a1 \in \mathbb{N}$ **inv0_4:** $a2 \in \mathbb{N}$	**inv0_5:** $a1 \leq r1$ **inv0_6:** $r1 \leq a1 + 1$ **inv0_7:** $a2 \leq r2$ **inv0_8:** $r2 \leq a2 + 1$

We have not yet stated however that no user must wait indefinitely. For this, we introduce two boolean variables in the circuit: $p1$ and $p2$. When, say, pi is TRUE, it means that *user_i* now waits for the resource. Clearly, $p1$ and $p2$ cannot be both equal to TRUE simultaneously (**inv011**) because that would mean that the circuit has not reacted immediately. In fact, when *mode* is *env*, $pi = \text{FALSE}$ is equivalent to $ri = ai$; no request is pending for *user_i* (**inv0_12** and **inv0_13**):

| variables: | $p1$ |
| | $p2$ |

inv0_9: $p1 \in \text{BOOL}$

inv0_10: $p2 \in \text{BOOL}$

inv0_11: $p1 = \text{FALSE} \lor p2 = \text{FALSE}$

inv0_12: $mode = env \Rightarrow (r1 = a1 \Leftrightarrow p1 = \text{FALSE})$

inv0_13: $mode = env \Rightarrow (r2 = a2 \Leftrightarrow p2 = \text{FALSE})$

Events The various environment events correspond to new requests being posted either individually (env1 and env2) or simultaneously (env3), or to the environment doing nothing (env0):

env1
  when
    $mode = env$
    $r1 = a1$
  then
    $mode := cir$
    $r1 := r1 + 1$
  end

env2
  when
    $mode = env$
    $r2 = a2$
  then
    $mode := cir$
    $r2 := r2 + 1$
  end

env3
  when
    $mode = env$
    $r1 = a1$
    $r2 = a2$
  then
    $mode := cir$
    $r1 := r1 + 1$
    $r2 := r2 + 1$
  end

env0
  when
    $mode = env$
  then
    $mode := cir$
  end

The events of the circuit are very simple. In case a request is pending (in events cir1 and cir2), the event increments the acknowledgement counter and sets the corresponding variables, say $p1$ for event cir1, to FALSE. Notice that it can be the case already. It does so, however, provided the other user has not itself required the resource for more than one clock pulse; hence the guard $p2 = $ FALSE. When no request is made (in event cir0), the event does nothing except set $p1$ and $p2$ to FALSE:

```
cir1
  when
    mode = cir
    r1 ≠ a1
    p2 = FALSE
  then
    mode := env
    a1 := a1 + 1
    p1 := FALSE
    p2 := bool(r2 ≠ a2)
  end
```

```
cir2
  when
    mode = cir
    r2 ≠ a2
    p1 = FALSE
  then
    mode := env
    a2 := a2 + 1
    p2 := FALSE
    p1 := bool(r1 ≠ a1)
  end
```

```
cir0
  when
    mode = cir
    r1 = a1
    r2 = a2
  then
    mode := env
    p1 := FALSE
    p2 := FALSE
  end
```

Proving deadlock freedom Nothing guarantees, of course, that the circuit events are not stuck because their guards do not hold. We have thus to prove the following, stating that while in the *cir* mode, the disjunction of the guards of the circuit always holds:

$$\textbf{thm0\_1:} \quad mode = cir \Rightarrow \left(\begin{array}{l} r1 \neq a1 \ \wedge \ p2 = \text{FALSE} \ \vee \\ r2 \neq a2 \ \wedge \ p1 = \text{FALSE} \ \vee \\ r1 = a1 \ \wedge \ r2 = a2 \end{array} \right)$$

To prove this, it is necessary to add the following invariants:

$$\textbf{inv0\_14:} \quad mode = cir \Rightarrow (r1 = a1 \Rightarrow p1 = \text{FALSE})$$

$$\textbf{inv0\_15:} \quad mode = cir \Rightarrow (r2 = a2 \Rightarrow p2 = \text{FALSE})$$

Note that the circuit is still non-deterministic; this is the case when both users are just require the resource simultaneously (thus $p1 = \text{FALSE}$ and $p2 = \text{FALSE}$ hold simultaneously). In this case, both circuit events, cir1 and cir2, can be fired.

8.3.3 First refinement: generating binary outputs from the circuit

The state In the previous section, the circuit events, cir1 and cir2, incremented directly the acknowledgement counters, $a1$ and $a2$. These counters both formed the abstract outputs of our circuit. We shall now postpone this incrementation and have the circuit only generating an offset (that is, a 0 or a 1), the proper incrementation itself being done by the environment on two slightly time-shifted counters, say $b1$ and $b2$. But we want the circuit to produce boolean values only. For this, we introduce a constant function b_2_01, transforming a boolean value into a numeric value.

$$\textbf{constants:} \quad b\_2\_01$$

$$\textbf{axm1\_1:} \quad b\_2\_01 \in \text{BOOL} \rightarrow \{0, 1\}$$

$$\textbf{axm1\_2:} \quad b\_2\_01(\text{TRUE}) = 1$$

$$\textbf{axm1\_3:} \quad b\_2\_01(\text{FALSE}) = 0$$

This refinement introduces thus four variables typed as follows:

variables:	$b1, o1, b2, o2$

inv1_1: $b1 \in \mathbb{N}$

inv1_2: $o1 \in \text{BOOL}$

inv1_3: $b2 \in \mathbb{N}$

inv1_4: $o2 \in \text{BOOL}$

The "gluing" invariant that holds between the abstract counters $a1$ and $a2$ and the new concrete variables we have just introduced is the following:

inv1_5: $mode = cir \Rightarrow a1 = b1$

inv1_6: $mode = cir \Rightarrow a2 = b2$

inv1_7: $mode = env \Rightarrow a1 = b1 + b\_2\_01(o1)$

inv1_8: $mode = env \Rightarrow a2 = b2 + b\_2\_01(o2)$

The last two statements indicate that, while we are observing the environment (just after the reaction of the circuit), the abstract counters ai are already incremented (by the abstract circuit), while the concrete counters bi are not. In fact, they will be incremented in the environment, thanks to the contents of the output oi. On the other hand, the first two statements indicate that, while observing the circuit, the abstract and concrete counters are now "in phase".

The events The environment events are all modified in a straightforward way:

```
env1
  when
    mode = env
    r1 = b1 + b_2_01(o1)
  then
    mode := cir
    r1 := r1 + 1
    b1 := b1 + b_2_01(o1)
    b2 := b2 + b_2_01(o2)
  end
```

```
env2
  when
    mode = env
    r2 = b2 + b_2_01(o2)
  then
    mode := cir
    r2 := r2 + 1
    b1 := b1 + b_2_01(o1)
    b2 := b2 + b_2_01(o2)
  end
```

```
env3
  when
    mode = env
    r1 = b1 + b_2_01(o1)
    r2 = b2 + b_2_01(o2)
  then
    mode := cir
    r1 := r1 + 1
    r2 := r2 + 1
    b1 := b1 + b_2_01(o1)
    b2 := b2 + b_2_01(o2)
  end
```

The circuit events are modified accordingly:

```
cir1
  when
    mode = cir
    r1 ≠ b1
    p2 = FALSE
  then
    mode := env
    o1 := TRUE
    o2 := FALSE
    p1 := FALSE
    p2 := bool(r2 ≠ b2)
  end
```

```
cir2
  when
    mode = cir
    r2 ≠ b2
    p1 = FALSE
  then
    mode := env
    o1 := FALSE
    o2 := TRUE
    p1 := bool(r1 ≠ b1)
    p2 := FALSE
  end
```

```
cir0
  when
    mode = cir
    r1 = b1
    r2 = b2
  then
    mode := env
    o1 := FALSE
    o2 := FALSE
    p1 := FALSE
    p2 := FALSE
  end
```

8.3.4 Second refinement

The state The environment events are now accessing environment variables only ($r1$, $r2$, $b1$, and $b2$) together with the outputs of the circuit ($o1$ and $o2$). But, the circuit events still access the environment variables ($r1$, $r2$, $b1$, and $b2$). In this refinement, we introduce proper inputs $i1$ and $i2$ to the circuit.

The inputs to the circuit, rather than being the number r_i of requests and the number b_i of acknowledgements could very well be only their *difference*, which is at most 1, as we know from invariants **inv0_5** to **inv0_8**. For this, we introduce two new binary variables i_1 and i_2:

$$\boxed{\textbf{variables:}\quad i1, i2}$$

$$\boxed{\begin{array}{l} \textbf{inv2\_1:}\quad i1 \in \text{BOOL} \\[2ex] \textbf{inv2\_2:}\quad i2 \in \text{BOOL} \end{array}}$$

The invariants relating $i1$ and $i2$ to $r1$, $r2$, $b1$, and $b2$ are straightforward:

$$\boxed{\begin{array}{l} \textbf{inv2\_2:}\quad mode = cir \;\Rightarrow\; (i1 = \text{FALSE} \Leftrightarrow r1 = b1) \\[2ex] \textbf{inv2\_3:}\quad mode = cir \;\Rightarrow\; (i2 = \text{FALSE} \Leftrightarrow r2 = b2) \end{array}}$$

The modification of the environment events are very simple:

env1	env2
when	**when**
$mode = env$	$mode = env$
$r1 = b1 + b\_2\_01(o1)$	$r2 = b2 + b\_2\_01(o2)$
then	**then**
$mode := cir$	$mode := cir$
$r1 := r1 + 1$	$r2 := r2 + 1$
$b1 := b1 + b\_2\_01(o1)$	$b1 := b1 + b\_2\_01(o1)$
$b2 := b2 + b\_2\_01(o2)$	$b2 := b2 + b\_2\_01(o2)$
$i1 := \text{TRUE}$	$i1 := \text{bool}(r1 \neq b1 + b\_1\_01(o1))$
$i2 := \text{bool}(r2 \neq b2 + b\_2\_01(o2))$	$i2 := \text{TRUE}$
end	**end**

```
env3
  when
    mode = env
    r1 = b1 + b_2_01(o1)
    r2 = b2 + b_2_01(o2)
  then
    mode := cir
    r1 := r1 + 1
    r2 := r2 + 1
    b1 := b1 + b_2_01(o1)
    b2 := b2 + b_2_01(o2)
    i1 := TRUE
    i2 := TRUE
  end
```

```
env0
  when
    mode = env
  then
    mode := cir
    b1 := b1 + b_2_01(o1)
    b2 := b2 + b_2_01(o2)
    i1 := bool(r1 ≠ b1 + b_1_01(o1))
    i2 := bool(r1 ≠ b2 + b_1_01(o2))
  end
```

Here are the new circuit events:

```
cir1
  when
    mode = cir
    i1 = TRUE
    p2 = FALSE
  then
    mode := env
    o1 := TRUE
    o2 := FALSE
    p1 := FALSE
    p2 := i2
  end
```

```
cir2
  when
    mode = cir
    i2 = TRUE
    p1 = FALSE
  then
    mode := env
    o1 := FALSE
    o2 := TRUE
    p1 := i1
    p2 := FALSE
  end
```

```
cir0
  when
    mode = cir
    i1 = FALSE
    i2 = FALSE
  then
    mode := env
    o1 := FALSE
    o2 := FALSE
    p1 := FALSE
    p2 := FALSE
  end
```

8.3.5 Third refinement: reducing non-determinacy of the circuit

The state The circuit we have obtained in the previous section is now complete and simple, but *still non-deterministic*: when $i1$ and $i2$ are both equal to TRUE with $p1$ and $p2$ both equal to FALSE, the circuit can choose to set $o1$ or $o2$ to TRUE. In other words, both events cir1 and cir2 are enabled. In order to make the circuit completely deterministic, we decide that, in this case, $o1$ say, will be the winner. In fact, we remove variables $p1$.

The events The environment events remain the same, whereas the circuit events are modified as follows:

```
cir1
   when
      mode = cir
      i1 = TRUE
      p2 = FALSE
   then
      mode := env
      o1 := TRUE
      o2 := FALSE
      p2 := i2
   end
```

```
cir2
   when
      mode = cir
      i2 = TRUE
      ¬ (i1 = TRUE ∧ p2 = FALSE)
   then
      mode := env
      o1 := FALSE
      o2 := TRUE
      p2 := FALSE
   end
```

```
cir0
   when
      mode = cir
      i1 = FALSE
      i2 = FALSE
   then
      mode := env
      o1 := FALSE
      o2 := FALSE
      p2 := FALSE
   end
```

The circuit events are now clearly internally as well as externally deterministic.

Revisiting deadlock freedom The interesting and fundamental last statement to prove is that the events of the circuit are deadlock free. For this, we have to prove that, under the hypothesis $mode = cir$, the disjunction of the guards of the circuit events are true (the interactive proof of this statement is easy), namely:

$$\mathbf{thm3\_1:} \; mode = cir \Rightarrow \left(\begin{array}{l} i1 = \text{TRUE} \; \wedge \; p2 = \text{FALSE}) \vee \\ i2 = \text{TRUE} \; \wedge \; \neg \, (i1 = \text{TRUE} \; \wedge \; p2 = \text{FALSE}) \vee \\ i1 = \text{FALSE} \; \wedge \; i2 = \text{FALSE} \end{array} \right)$$

8.3.6 Fourth refinement: building the final circuit

The circuit and environment now fulfill all the final conditions stated in Section 8.1.7. As a result, we can construct our final circuit in a systematic fashion:

---

arbiter
  when
    $mode = cir$
  then
    $mode := env$
    $o1 := \text{bool}\,((i1 = \text{TRUE} \wedge p2 = \text{FALSE} \wedge \text{TRUE} = \text{TRUE}) \vee$
               $(\ldots \wedge \text{FALSE} = \text{TRUE}) \vee$
               $(\ldots \wedge \text{FALSE} = \text{TRUE}))$
    $o2 := \text{bool}\,((\ldots \wedge \text{FALSE} = \text{TRUE}) \vee$
               $(i2 = \text{TRUE} \wedge \neg\,(i1 = \text{TRUE} \wedge p2 = \text{FALSE}) \wedge \text{TRUE} = \text{TRUE}) \vee$
               $(\ldots \wedge \text{FALSE} = \text{TRUE}))$
    $p2 := \text{bool}\,((i1 = \text{TRUE} \wedge p2 = \text{FALSE} \wedge i2 = \text{TRUE}) \vee$
               $(\ldots \wedge \text{FALSE} = \text{TRUE}) \vee$
               $(\ldots \wedge \text{FALSE} = \text{TRUE}))$
  end

This can be simplified as follows:

---

arbiter
  when
    $mode = cir$
  then
    $mode := env$
    $o1 := \text{bool}\,(i1 = \text{TRUE} \wedge p2 = \text{FALSE})$
    $o2 := \text{bool}\,(i2 = \text{TRUE} \wedge \neg\,(i1 = \text{TRUE} \wedge p2 = \text{FALSE}))$
    $p2 := \text{bool}\,(i1 = \text{TRUE} \wedge p2 = \text{FALSE} \wedge i2 = \text{TRUE})$
  end

This leads to the circuit of Fig. 8.15.

8.4 Third example: a special road traffic light

The example we develop in this section is one where a complete (but still simple) system is considered with a circuit aimed at controlling a physical environment by

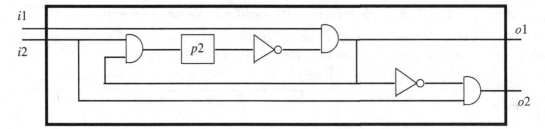

Fig. 8.15. The arbiter

reacting appropriately. In this example, we also experiment with the idea of *connecting* various circuits together.

8.4.1 Informal specification

We intend to install a traffic light at the crossing between a main road and a small road. The idea is to have these lights behaving in such a way that the traffic on the main road is somehow given a certain advantage over that on the small road. The corresponding policy is explained (and commented) in the following informally stated rules:

Rule 1 When the light controlling the main road is green, it only turns orange (and subsequently red) when some cars are present on the small road (the presence of such cars is detected by appropriate sensors). As a consequence, when no cars are present on the small road, the traffic on the main road is not disturbed.

Rule 2 This potential loss of priority on the main road is however only possible provided that road has already kept the priority for at least a certain (long) fixed delay. In other words, within that delay, the main road keeps the priority even if there are cars waiting on the small road. As a consequence, when there are cars frequently coming on the small road, the traffic on the main road is still flowing smoothly.

Rule 3 On the other hand, the small road, when given priority, keeps it is as long as there are cars willing to cross the main road.

Rule 4 This keeping of the priority by the small road is however only possible provided a (long) delay (the same delay as for the main road) has not passed. When the delay is over, the priority systematically returns to the main road, even if there are still some cars present on the small road. As a consequence, when there are many cars on the small road, these cars cannot block the main road for too long a period of time.

Rule 5 As already alluded to above, a green light does not turn red immediately. An orange color appears as usual for a (small) amount of time before the light definitely turns red. This sequential behavior is the same on the lights of both roads.

Rule 6 As usual, the safety of the drivers is ensured by the fact that the light, when green or orange on one road, is always red on the other one, and vice-versa. Safety is also ensured, of course, provided the drivers obey the law of not trespassing a red light (but this is another matter, not under the responsibility of the circuit!).

8.4.2 A separation of concern approach

By reading the previous informal requirements, it appears that there are apparently *two separate questions* in this problem: (1) one is dealing with the modification of the priority from the main to the small road and vice-versa (this corresponds to **Rule 1** and to **Rule 4** above), and (2) another is dealing with the realization of that change of priority in a way that is meaningful to drivers (this corresponds to **Rule 5** and **Rule 6**): this concerns the modification of the colours of each light (from successively, say, green to orange, then to red, and then to green again, etc), and the obvious non-contradiction between the lights governing each road (no two green lights at the same time, etc).

It seems that these two questions are rather "orthogonal" in that a modification in the road priority policy should not affect the proper behaviors of the lights, and vice-versa. Clearly, a modification in classical behavior of the lights is not something that we would reasonably envisage, as it is rather universal. On the other hand, a modification in the priority policy is a possibility that could not be rejected a priori. In that case, we would like to have the circuit built in such a way that this modification could be done in an easy way (sub-circuit replacement).

We should also notice that the first of these two questions deals with the essential *function* of this system, namely to alternate the priority between two roads in an unbalanced way. On the other hand, the second question rather deals with the *safety* and possible *progress* of the users. In other words, we must ensure that drivers: (i) are always in a safe situation provided they obey the usual conventions indicated by the colours of the lights, and (ii) are also not blocked indefinitely (everybody has experienced at least once a situation where, for instance, both lights are red!).

Our initial idea is thus to make the design of *two distinct circuits*, which will be eventually connected. One is the Priority circuit, and the other is the Light circuit. The

Priority circuit delivers a signal to the Light circuit stating that the priority has to be changed from one road to the other. In this way, the latter can translate this "priority" information in terms of a corresponding "traffic light" information.

8.4.3 The priority circuit: initial model

The state The simplest Priority circuit we can think of is one with two boolean inputs, *car* and *clk*: *car* corresponds to the information elaborated by the car sensors disposed on the small road and *clk* is an alarm coming from an external "timer" saying that the long delay is over. The priority circuit has two boolean outputs, *chg* and *prt*. *chg* yields the information concerning a *change* in the priority, whereas *prt* yields the priority in use. All this is indicated on Fig. 8.16.

This timer sends an alarm on the boolean entry *clk* when (and as long as) the long delay described above is over. The circuit "decides" to possibly change the priority depending on three factors: (1) the actual priority (main road or small road) stored in the circuit, (2) the presence of cars on the small road, and (3) the state of the alarm coming from the timer. The Priority circuit has an internal register, *prt*, holding the actual priority. The output *chg* is used externally to reset the external timer. The overall picture is indicated on Fig. 8.17.

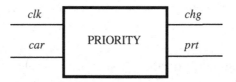

Fig. 8.16. The priority circuit

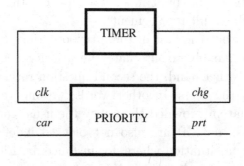

Fig. 8.17. Connection of the priority circuit with the Timer Circuit

The variables of the priority circuit are declared as follows:

<table>
<tr><td>

variables: car, clk, chg, prt

</td><td>

inv0_1: $car \in \text{BOOL}$

inv0_2: $clk \in \text{BOOL}$

inv0_3: $chg \in \text{BOOL}$

inv0_4: $prt \in \text{BOOL}$

</td></tr>
</table>

We have the following conventions: (1) car valued to TRUE means that some cars are waiting on the small road; (2) clk valued to TRUE means that the long delay is over; and (3) chg valued to TRUE means that the priority has to change. The variable prt is valued FALSE (priority on main road) or TRUE (priority on small road).

The events The events of the Priority circuit elaborate priority changes. We have two such events, called main_to_small and small_to_main. Their guards formally state under which circumstances the priority can change. This is explained in what follows:

(i) Event main_to_small can be fired when the priority is on main road ($prt = $ FALSE), when some car are present on the small road ($car = $ TRUE), and when the long delay has passed ($clk = $ TRUE): this corresponds to **Rule 1** and **Rule 2** above.

(ii) Event small_to_main_ can be fired when the priority is on small road ($prt = $ TRUE) and when no cars are present on the small road ($car = $ FALSE) or when the long delay has passed ($clk = $ TRUE): this corresponds to **Rule 3** and **Rule 4**.

In both cases, the priority changes ($chg := $ TRUE) and variable prt is modified accordingly. Here are the events:

<table>
<tr><td>

main_to_small
  when
    $mode = cir$
    $prt = \text{FALSE}$
    $car = \text{TRUE}$
    $clk = \text{TRUE}$
  then
    $mode := env$
    $prt := \text{TRUE}$
    $chg := \text{TRUE}$
  end

</td><td>

small_to_main
  when
    $mode = cir$
    $prt = \text{TRUE}$
    $car = \text{FALSE} \vee clk = \text{TRUE}$
  then
    $mode := env$
    $prt := \text{FALSE}$
    $chg := \text{TRUE}$
  end

</td></tr>
</table>

Another series of events corresponds to the circuit doing nothing except resetting the *chg* output to FALSE (no change). This occurs in two circumstances:

(i) Event do_nothing_1 can be fired when the priority is on main road ($prt = $ FALSE) and when there are no cars on the small road ($car = $ FALSE) or the delay has not passed yet ($clk = $ FALSE). This corresponds to **Rule 1** and **Rule 2** above.

(ii) Event do_nothing_2 can be fired when the priority is on small road ($prt = $ TRUE), when there are cars present on the small road ($car = $ TRUE), and when the delay has not passed yet ($clk = $ FALSE). This corresponds to **Rule 3** and **Rule 4**.

Here are these events:

```
do_nothing_1
  when
    mode = cir
    prt = FALSE
    car = FALSE ∨ clk = FALSE
  then
    mode := env
    chg := FALSE
  end
```

```
do_nothing_2
  when
    mode = cir
    prt = TRUE
    car = TRUE
    clk = FALSE
  then
    mode := env
    chg := FALSE
  end
```

The unique environment event is the following:

```
env1
  when
    mode = env
  then
    mode := cir
    car :∈ BOOL
    clk :∈ BOOL
  end
```

Notice that this event is not very realistic as cars may come and then disappear in a rather random way. In Section 8.4.4, we shall make this event more realistic by splitting it.

Deadlock freedom The Priority circuit is deadlock free as stated in this theorem:

$$
\textbf{thm0\_1: } mode = cir \Rightarrow \left(\begin{array}{l} prt = \text{FALSE} \wedge car = \text{TRUE} \wedge clk = \text{TRUE} \\ prt = \text{TRUE} \wedge (car = \text{FALSE} \vee clk = \text{TRUE}) \\ prt = \text{FALSE} \wedge (car = \text{FALSE} \vee clk = \text{FALSE}) \\ prt = \text{TRUE} \wedge car = \text{TRUE} \wedge clk = \text{FALSE} \end{array} \right)
$$

8.4.4 The final Priority circuit

The priority circuit fulfills the condition of Section 8.1.7. Notice that events do_nothing_1 and do_nothing_2 do not mention variable prt; in fact, we could consider that they both have the action $prt := prt$. With this in mind, the circuit generation goes as follows:

```
priority
  when
    mode = cir
  then
    mode := env
```

$$
prt := \text{bool} \left(\begin{array}{l} (prt = \text{FALSE} \wedge car = \text{TRUE} \wedge clk = \\ \qquad\qquad \text{TRUE} \wedge \text{TRUE} = \text{TRUE}) \vee \\ (prt = \text{FALSE} \wedge (car = \text{FALSE} \vee clk = \text{FALSE}) \wedge prt = \\ \qquad\qquad \text{TRUE}) \vee \\ (prt = \text{TRUE} \wedge car = \text{TRUE} \wedge clk = \text{FALSE} \wedge prt = \\ \qquad\qquad \text{TRUE}) \end{array} \right)
$$

$$
chg := \text{bool} \left(\begin{array}{l} (prt = \text{FALSE} \wedge car = \text{TRUE} \wedge clk = \text{TRUE} \wedge \text{TRUE} \\ \qquad\qquad = \text{TRUE}) \vee \\ (prt = \text{TRUE} \wedge (car = \text{FALSE} \vee clk = \text{TRUE}) \wedge \text{TRUE} \\ \qquad\qquad = \text{TRUE}) \vee \\ (\ldots \wedge \text{FALSE} = \text{TRUE}) \vee \\ (\ldots \wedge \text{FALSE} = \text{TRUE})) \end{array} \right)
$$

```
  end
```

This reduces trivially to the following:

$$
\begin{array}{l}
\textsf{priority} \\
\quad \textbf{when} \\
\qquad mode = cir \\
\quad \textbf{then} \\
\qquad mode := env \\
\qquad prt := \text{bool} \left(\begin{array}{l} (prt = \text{FALSE} \ \wedge \ car = \text{TRUE} \ \wedge \ clk = \text{TRUE}) \ \vee \\ (prt = \text{TRUE} \ \wedge \ car = \text{TRUE} \ \wedge \ clk = \text{FALSE}) \end{array} \right) \\
\\
\qquad chg := \text{bool} \left(\begin{array}{l} (prt = \text{FALSE} \ \wedge \ car = \text{TRUE} \ \wedge \ clk = \text{TRUE}) \ \vee \\ (prt = \text{TRUE} \ \wedge \ (car = \text{FALSE} \ \vee \ clk = \text{TRUE})) \end{array} \right) \\
\quad \textbf{end}
\end{array}
$$

This circuit can be further transformed in the following equivalent fashion:

$$
\begin{array}{l}
\textsf{priority} \\
\quad \textbf{when} \\
\qquad mode = cir \\
\quad \textbf{then} \\
\qquad mode := env \\
\qquad prt := \text{bool} \left(\begin{array}{l} (prt = \text{TRUE} \ \wedge \ \neg \left(\begin{array}{l} (car = \text{TRUE} \ \wedge \ clk = \text{TRUE}) \ \vee \\ (car = \text{FALSE} \ \wedge \ prt = \text{TRUE}) \end{array} \right) \ \vee \\[18pt] (prt = \text{FALSE} \ \wedge \ \left(\begin{array}{l} (car = \text{TRUE} \ \wedge \ clk = \text{TRUE}) \ \vee \\ (car = \text{FALSE} \ \wedge \ prt = \text{TRUE}) \end{array} \right) \end{array} \right) \\
\\
\qquad chg := \text{bool} \left(\begin{array}{l} (car = \text{TRUE} \ \wedge \ clk = \text{TRUE}) \ \vee \\ (car = \text{FALSE} \ \wedge \ prt = \text{TRUE}) \end{array} \right) \\
\quad \textbf{end}
\end{array}
$$

It is easy to figure out that these two events are equivalent. Hint: (1) do a proof by cases ($prt = \text{TRUE}$, then $prt = \text{FALSE}$) to prove the equivalence concerning the assignment to prt, and (2) do a proof by cases ($car = \text{TRUE}$, then $car = \text{FALSE}$) to prove the equivalence concerning the assignment to chg. The last event is interesting because it contains three times the following fragment, which can thus be computed only once:

$$
\begin{array}{l}
car = \text{TRUE} \ \wedge \ clk = \text{TRUE} \ \vee \\
car = \text{FALSE} \ \wedge \ prt = \text{TRUE}.
\end{array}
$$

In this last version, we notice also several occurrences of predicates of the form:

$$
(P \wedge Q) \ \vee \ (\neg P \wedge R).
$$

This will be economically represented by an IF gate, considered to be an atomic one. Such a gate is pictorially represented in Fig. 8.18.

Equipped with such an IF gate, we can draw our Priority circuit as indicated in Fig. 8.19.

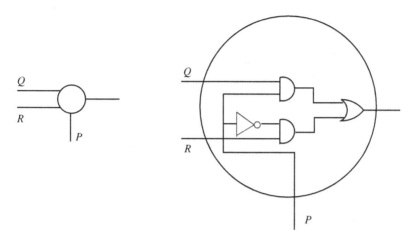

Fig. 8.18. An IF gate

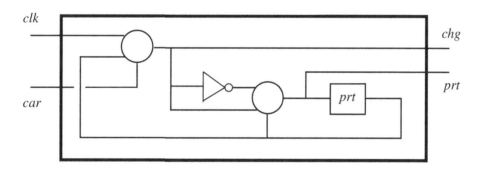

Fig. 8.19. The priority circuit

8.5 The Light circuit

We now connect our Priority circuit to the Light circuit. The Light circuit delivers the various colours of both traffic lights. This is indicated in Fig. 8.20.

8.5.1 An abstraction: the Upper circuit

We start with a simplified circuit whose rôle is to ensure the sequencing of a single traffic light, that of the *main road*. This is shown in Fig. 8.21.

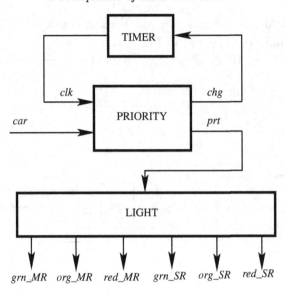

Fig. 8.20. The priority circuit connected to the light circuit

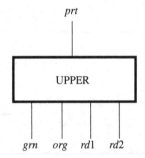

Fig. 8.21. The upper light circuit

We shall later extend that circuit to handle two synchronous traffic lights. The circuit has a single boolean entry *prt*, which, when valued to TRUE, indicates that a light appearance should give priority to the small road. It has four boolean outputs called *grn*, *org*, *rd*1, and *rd*2. The reason for decomposing the red colour into two colours is one of symmetry. Exactly one of them at a time is valued to TRUE. This can be formalized as follows:

variables: $prt, grn, org, rd1, rd2$

inv0_1:	$prt \in \text{BOOL}$
inv0_2:	$grn = \text{TRUE} \ \vee \ org = \text{TRUE} \ \vee \ rd1 = \text{TRUE} \ \vee \ rd2 = \text{TRUE}$
inv0_3:	$grn = \text{TRUE} \Rightarrow org = \text{FALSE} \ \wedge \ rd1 = \text{FALSE} \ \wedge \ rd2 = \text{FALSE}$
inv0_4:	$org = \text{TRUE} \Rightarrow rd1 = \text{FALSE} \ \wedge \ rd2 = \text{FALSE}$
inv0_5:	$rd1 = \text{TRUE} \Rightarrow rd2 = \text{FALSE}$
inv0_6:	$mode \in MODE$

The events of the circuit are straightforward:

```
grn_to_org
    when
        mode = cir
        prt = TRUE
        grn = TRUE
    then
        mode := env
        grn := FALSE
        org := TRUE
    end
```

```
org_to_rd1
    when
        mode = cir
        org = TRUE
    then
        mode := env
        org := FALSE
        rd1 := TRUE
    end
```

```
rd1_to_rd2
    when
        mode = cir
        prt = FALSE
        rd1 = TRUE
    then
        mode := env
        rd1 := FALSE
        rd2 := TRUE
    end
```

```
rd2_to_grn
    when
        mode = cir
        rd2 = TRUE
    then
        mode := env
        grn := TRUE
        rd2 := FALSE
    end
```

We have two "do-nothing" events in the circuit and also an environment event assigning *prt* in a non-deterministic way. These are as follows:

```
grn_to_nth
  when
    mode = cir
    grn = TRUE
    prt = FALSE
  then
    mode := env
  end
```

```
rd1_to_nth
  when
    mode = cir
    rd1 = TRUE
    prt = TRUE
  then
    mode := env
  end
```

```
env_evt
  when
    mode = env
  then
    mode := cir
    prt :∈ BOOL
  end
```

8.5.2 A refinement: adding the Lower circuit

We refine the circuit by having now six outputs corresponding the the light appearance of both traffic lights. First those of the main road: grn_MR, org_MR, and red_MR. Then those of the small road: grn_SR, org_SR, and red_SR:

variables: $prt, grn, org, rd1, rd2$

grn_MR, org_MR, red_MR

grn_SR, org_SR, red_SR

The final colours are related to the variables of the initial model in a straightforward way:

inv1_1: $grn\_MR = grn$

inv1_2: $org\_MR = org$

inv1_3: $red\_MR = \text{TRUE} \Leftrightarrow (rd1 = \text{TRUE} \lor rd2 = \text{TRUE})$

inv1_4: $grn\_SR = rd1$

inv1_5: $org\_SR = rd2$

inv1_6: $red\_SR = \text{TRUE} \Leftrightarrow (grn = \text{TRUE} \lor org = \text{TRUE})$

We can prove the following safety theorems:

$$\textbf{thm1\_1:} \quad red\_MR = \text{TRUE} \Leftrightarrow (grn\_SR = TRUE \lor org\_SR = \text{TRUE})$$

$$\textbf{thm1\_2:} \quad red\_SR = \text{TRUE} \Leftrightarrow (grn\_MR = TRUE \lor org\_MR = \text{TRUE})$$

Next are the refinements of the events:

```
grn_to_org
  when
    mode = cir
    prt = TRUE
    grn = TRUE
  then
    mode := env
    grn := FALSE
    org := TRUE
    grn_MR := FALSE
    org_MR := TRUE
  end
```

```
org_to_rd1
  when
    mode = cir
    org = TRUE
  then
    mode := env
    org := FALSE
    rd1 := TRUE
    org_MR := FALSE
    red_MR := TRUE
    grn_SR := TRUE
    red_SR := FALSE
  end
```

```
rd1_to_rd2
  when
    mode = cir
    prt = FALSE
    rd1 = TRUE
  then
    mode := env
    rd1 := FALSE
    rd2 := TRUE
    org_SR := TRUE
    grn_SR := FALSE
  end
```

```
rd2_to_grn
  when
    mode = cir
    rd2 = TRUE
  then
    mode := env
    grn := TRUE
    rd2 := FALSE
    grn_MR := TRUE
    red_MR := FALSE
    org_SR := FALSE
    red_SR := TRUE
  end
```

The various circuit events can be unified as usual:

---

light
  when
    $mode = cir$
  then
    $mode := env$
    $grn := \text{bool}(\, rd2 = \text{TRUE} \ \lor\ (prt = \text{FALSE} \ \land\ grn = \text{TRUE})\,)$
    $org := \text{bool}(\, prt = \text{TRUE} \ \land\ grn = \text{TRUE}\,)$
    $rd1 := \text{bool}(\, org = \text{TRUE} \ \lor\ (prt = \text{TRUE} \ \land\ rd1 = \text{TRUE})\,)$
    $rd2 := \text{bool}(\, prt = \text{FALSE} \ \land\ rd1 = \text{TRUE}\,)$
    $grn\_MR := \text{bool}(\, rd2 = \text{TRUE} \ \lor\ (prt = \text{FALSE} \ \land\ grn = \text{TRUE})\,)$
    $org\_MR := \text{bool}(\, prt = \text{TRUE} \ \land\ grn = \text{TRUE}\,)$
    $red\_MR := \text{bool}(\, org = \text{TRUE} \ \lor\ (prt = \text{TRUE} \ \land\ rd1 = \text{TRUE}) \ \lor$
                 $(prt = \text{FALSE} \ \land\ rd1 = \text{TRUE})\,)$
    $grn\_SR := \text{bool}(\, org = \text{TRUE} \ \lor\ (prt = \text{TRUE} \ \land\ rd1 = \text{TRUE})\,)$
    $org\_SR := \text{bool}(\, prt = \text{FALSE} \ \land\ rd1 = \text{TRUE}\,)$
    $red\_SR := \text{bool}(\, rd2 = \text{TRUE} \ \lor\ (prt = \text{FALSE} \ \land\ grn = \text{TRUE}) \ \lor$
                 $(prt = \text{TRUE} \ \land\ grn = \text{TRUE})\,)$
  end

The final Light circuit is shown in Fig. 8.22.

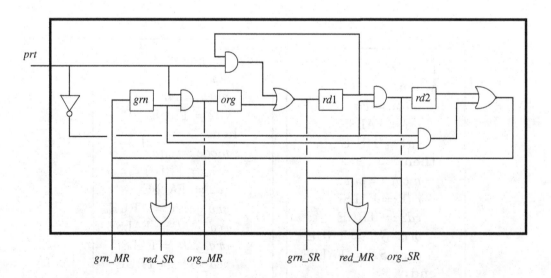

Fig. 8.22. The light circuit

8.6 Reference

[1] T. Kropf. *Formal Hardware Verification: Methods and Systems in Comparison.* LNCS State-of-the-art Survey. Springer, 1991

9

Mathematical language

This chapter contains the definition of the *mathematical language* we use in this book. It is made of seven sections. The first one contains a preliminary definition of sequents, inference rules, and proofs. Then we have the presentation of our mathematical language. It is defined as follows: the propositional language (Section 9.2), the predicate language (Section 9.3), the equality language (Section 9.4), the set-theoretic language (Section 9.5), and the boolean and arithmetic language (Section 9.6). Each of these languages will be presented as an extension of the previous one. A final section contains a definition of the various data structures we are going to use in subsequent chapters, among which are lists, rings, and trees.

9.1 Sequent calculus

9.1.1 Definitions

In this section, we give some definitions which will be helpful to present the sequent calculus.

(1) A *sequent* is a generic name for "something we want to prove". For the moment, this is just an informally defined notion, which we shall refine later in Section 9.1.2. The important thing to note at this point is that we can associate a *proof* with a sequent. For the moment, we do not know what a proof is however. It will only be defined at the end of this section.

(2) An *inference rule* is a device used to construct proofs of sequents. It is made of two parts: the *antecedent* part and the *consequent* part. The antecedent denotes a finite set of sequents, while the consequent denotes a single sequent. An inference rule, named say **R1**, with antecedent A and consequent C is usually written as follows:

$$\frac{A}{C} \quad \textbf{R1}$$

It is to be read:

> Inference rule **R1** yields a proof of sequent C
> as soon as we have proofs of each sequent of A.

The antecedent A might be empty. In this case, the inference rule, named say **R2**, is written as follows:

$$\frac{}{C} \quad \textbf{R2}$$

It is to be read:

> Inference rule **R2** yields a proof of sequent C.

(3) A *theory* is a set of inference rules.

(4) The *proof of a sequent* within a theory is simply a finite tree with certain constraints. The nodes of such a tree have two components: a sequent s and a rule r of the theory. Here are the constraints for each node of the form (s, r): the consequent of the rule r is s, and the offspring of this node are nodes whose sequents are exactly all the sequents of the antecedent of rule r. As a consequence, the leaves of the tree contain rules with no antecedent. Moreover, the root node of the tree contains the sequent to be proved. As an example, we give the following theory involving sequents $S1$ to $S7$ and rules **R1** to **R7**:

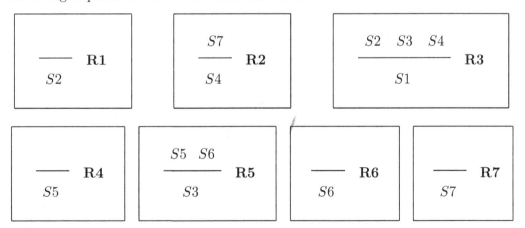

In Fig. 9.1 you can see a proof of sequent $S1$:

As can be seen, the root of the tree contains sequent $S1$, which is the one we want to prove. And it is easy to check that each node, say node $(S3, \textbf{R5})$, is indeed such that the consequent of its rule is the sequent of the node. More precisely,

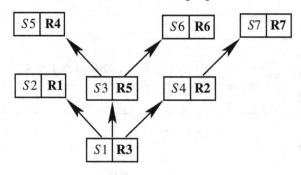

Fig. 9.1. A proof

$S3$ in this case, is the consequent of rule **R5**. Moreover, we can check that the sequents of the offspring nodes of node $(S3, \mathbf{R5})$, namely, $S5$ and $S6$, are exactly the sequents forming the antecedents of rule **R5**.

This tree can be interpreted as follows: In order to prove $S1$, we prove $S2$, $S3$, and $S4$, according to rule **R3**. In order to prove $S2$, we prove nothing more, according to rule **R1**. In order to prove $S3$, we prove $S5$ and $S6$, according to **R5**. And so on.

This tree can be represented as we have done in Chapter 2; this is indicated on Fig. 9.2. In this chapter, we shall adopt this representation as well.

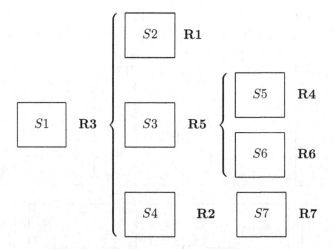

Fig. 9.2. Another representation of the proof tree

9.1.2 Sequents for a mathematical language

We now refine our notion of sequent in order to define the way we shall make proofs with our mathematical language. Such a language contains constructs called *predicates*.

For the moment, this is all that we know about our mathematical language. Within this framework, a sequent S, as defined in the previous section, now becomes a more complex object. It is made of two parts: the *hypotheses* part and the *goal* part. The hypothesis part denotes a finite set of predicates, while the goal part denotes a single predicate. A sequent with hypotheses H and goal G is written as follows:

$$\mathsf{H} \vdash G$$

This sequent is to be read as follows:

Goal G holds under the set of hypotheses H

This is the sort of sequents we want to prove. It is also the sort of sequents we shall have in the theories associated with our mathematical language. Note that the set of hypotheses of a sequent might be empty and that the order and repetition of hypotheses in the set H is meaningless.

9.1.3 Initial theory

We now have enough elements at our disposal to define the first rules of our proving theory. Note again that we still do not know what a predicate is. We just know that predicates are constructs we shall be able to define within our future mathematical language. We start with three basic rules which we first state informally and then define more rigorously. They are called **HYP**, **MON**, and **CUT**. Here are their definitions:

- **HYP**: If the goal P of a sequent belongs to the set of hypotheses of this sequent, then it is proved.

$$\frac{}{\mathsf{H},\, P \,\vdash\, P} \quad \textbf{HYP}$$

- **MON**: In order to prove a sequent, it is sufficient to prove another sequent with the same goal but with fewer hypotheses:

$$\frac{\mathsf{H} \,\vdash\, Q}{\mathsf{H},\, P \,\vdash\, Q} \quad \textbf{MON}$$

- **CUT**: If you succeed in proving a predicate P under a set of hypotheses H, then P can be added to the set of hypotheses H for proving a goal Q:

$$\frac{\mathsf{H} \vdash P \qquad \mathsf{H}, P \vdash Q}{\mathsf{H} \vdash Q} \quad \text{CUT}$$

Note that in the previous rules, the letters H, P, and Q are, so-called, *meta-variables*. The letter H is a meta-variable standing for a finite set of predicates, whereas the letters P and Q are meta-variables standing for predicates. Clearly, then, each of the previous "rules" stands for more than just one rule; it is better to call it a *rule schema*. This will always be the case in what follows.

9.2 The propositional language

In this section, we present a first simple version of our mathematical language, it is called the propositional language. It will be later refined to more complete versions: predicate language (Section 9.3), equality language (Section 9.4), set-theoretic language (Section 9.5), and arithmetic language (Section 9.6).

9.2.1 Syntax

Our first version is built around five constructs called *falsity, negation, conjunction, disjunction,* and *implication*. Given two predicates P and Q, we can construct their conjunction $P \wedge Q$, their disjunction $P \vee Q$, and their implication $P \Rightarrow Q$. And given a predicate P, we can construct its negation $\neg P$. This can be formalized by means of the following syntax:

$$
\begin{aligned}
predicate \quad ::= \quad & \bot \\
& \neg\, predicate \\
& predicate \, \wedge \, predicate \\
& predicate \, \vee \, predicate \\
& predicate \, \Rightarrow \, predicate
\end{aligned}
$$

This syntax is clearly ambiguous, but we do not care about it at this stage. Only note that conjunction and disjunction operators have stronger syntactic priorities than the implication operator. Moreover, conjunction and disjunction have the same syntactic priorities, so that parentheses will always be necessary when several such distinct operators are following each other. Also note that this syntax does not contain any "base" predicate (except $\perp$); such predicates will come later in Sections 9.4 and 9.5.

9.2.2 *Enlarging the initial theory*

The initial theory of Section 9.1.3 is enlarged with the following inference rules:

$$\frac{}{H, \perp \vdash P} \quad \textbf{FALSE\_L}$$

$$\frac{H \vdash P \quad H \vdash \neg P}{H \vdash \perp} \quad \textbf{FALSE\_R}$$

$$\frac{H, \neg Q \vdash P}{H, \neg P \vdash Q} \quad \textbf{NOT\_L}$$

$$\frac{H, P \vdash \perp}{H \vdash \neg P} \quad \textbf{NOT\_R}$$

$$\frac{H, P, Q \vdash R}{H, P \wedge Q \vdash R} \quad \textbf{AND\_L}$$

$$\frac{H \vdash P \quad H \vdash Q}{H \vdash P \wedge Q} \quad \textbf{AND\_R}$$

$$\frac{H, P \vdash R \quad H, Q \vdash R}{H, P \vee Q \vdash R} \quad \textbf{OR\_L}$$

$$\frac{H, \neg P \vdash Q}{H \vdash P \vee Q} \quad \textbf{OR\_R}$$

$$\frac{\text{H}, P, Q \vdash R}{\text{H}, P, P \Rightarrow Q \vdash R} \quad \textbf{IMP\_L} \qquad \frac{\text{H}, P \vdash Q}{\text{H} \vdash P \Rightarrow Q} \quad \textbf{IMP\_R}$$

As can be seen, each kind of predicates, namely falsity, negation, conjunction, disjunction, and implication, is given two rules: a left rule, labeled with **_L**, and a right rule, labeled with **_R**. This corresponds to the predicate appearing either in the hypothesis part (left) or in the goal part (right) of the consequent of the rule.

9.2.3 Derived rules

Besides the previous rules, the following *derived* rule (among many others) is quite useful. It says that, for proving a goal P, it is sufficient to prove it first under hypothesis Q and then under hypothesis $\neg Q$:

$$\frac{\text{H}, Q \vdash P \qquad \text{H}, \neg Q \vdash P}{\text{H} \vdash P} \quad \textbf{CASE}$$

For proving a derived rule, we assume its antecedents (if any) and prove its consequent. With this in mind, here is the proof of derived rule **CASE**:

With the help of this new (derived) rule **CASE**, we can now generalize rule **NOT_L** by rule **CT_L**:

$$\frac{\mathsf{H}.\,\neg Q \;\vdash\; \neg P}{\mathsf{H},\,P \;\vdash\; Q} \quad \textbf{CT\_L}$$

Proof of rule **CT_L**:

$$\boxed{\mathsf{H},P\vdash Q}\;\textbf{CASE}\begin{cases}\boxed{\mathsf{H},P,Q\vdash Q}\;\textbf{HYP}\\[2em]\boxed{\mathsf{H},P,\neg Q\vdash Q}\;\textbf{CUT}\begin{cases}\boxed{\mathsf{H},P,\neg Q\vdash \neg P}\;\textbf{MON}\ldots\\[1.5em]\boxed{\mathsf{H},P,\neg Q,\neg P\vdash Q}\;\textbf{NOT\_L}\ldots\end{cases}\end{cases}$$

$$\ldots\quad\boxed{\mathsf{H},\neg Q \;\vdash\; \neg P}\quad\textbf{assumed antecedent}$$

$$\ldots\quad\boxed{\mathsf{H},P,\neg Q,\neg Q \;\vdash\; P}\quad\textbf{HYP}$$

We can also generalize rule **NOT_R** by rule **CT_R**:

$$\frac{\mathsf{H},\neg P \;\vdash\; \bot}{\mathsf{H} \;\vdash\; P} \quad \textbf{CT\_R}$$

Proof of rule **CT_R**:

$$
H \vdash P \quad \boxed{\textbf{CASE}} \left\{
\begin{array}{l}
\boxed{H, P \vdash P} \quad \textbf{HYP} \\[2em]
\boxed{H, \neg P \vdash P} \quad \textbf{CUT} \left\{
\begin{array}{l}
\boxed{H, \neg P \vdash \bot} \quad \text{assumed antecedent} \\[1.5em]
\boxed{H, \neg P, \bot \vdash P} \quad \textbf{FALSE\_L}
\end{array}
\right.
\end{array}
\right.
$$

In a similar way, we can prove the following derived rules, which we used in Chapter 2:

$$
\frac{H \vdash P}{H \vdash P \vee Q} \quad \textbf{OR\_R1}
\qquad\qquad
\frac{H \vdash Q}{H \vdash P \vee Q} \quad \textbf{OR\_R2}
$$

9.2.4 Methodology

The method we are going to use to build our mathematical language must start to be clearer: it will be very systematic. It is made of two steps: first we augment our syntax. Then either the extension corresponds to a simple facility. In that case, we give simply the definition of the new construct in terms of previous ones. Or the new construct is not related to any previous constructs. In that case, we augment our current theory.

9.2.5 Extending the proposition language

The proposition language is now extended by adding one more construct called *equivalence*. Given two predicates P and Q, we can construct their equivalence $P \Leftrightarrow Q$. We also add one predicate: $\top$. As a consequence, our syntax is now the following:

$$
\begin{array}{lll}
predicate & ::= & \bot \\
& & \top \\
& & \neg\, predicate \\
& & predicate \,\wedge\, predicate \\
& & predicate \,\vee\, predicate \\
& & predicate \,\Rightarrow\, predicate \\
& & predicate \,\Leftrightarrow\, predicate
\end{array}
$$

Note that implication and equivalence operators have the same syntactic priorities so that parentheses will be necessary when several such distinct operators are following each other. Such extensions are defined in terms of previous ones by mere rewriting rules:

Predicate	Rewritten
$\top$	$\neg\,\bot$
$P \Leftrightarrow Q$	$(P \Rightarrow Q) \wedge (Q \Rightarrow P)$

The following derived rules can be proved easily:

$$
\frac{H \,\vdash\, P}{H, \top \,\vdash\, P}\ \textbf{TRUE\_L}
\qquad\qquad
\frac{}{H \,\vdash\, \top}\ \textbf{TRUE\_R}
$$

Note that rule **TRUE_L** can be proved using rule **MON**, but the reverse rule (exchanging antecedent and consequent), which holds as well, cannot. We leave it as an exercise to the reader to prove these rules.

9.3 The predicate language

9.3.1 Syntax

In this section, we introduce the predicate language. The syntax is extended with a number of new kinds of predicates and also with the introduction of two new syntactic categories called *expression* and *variable*. A *variable* is a simple identifier. Given a non-empty list of variables x made of pairwise distinct identifiers and a predicate P, the construct $\forall x \cdot P$ is called a *universally quantified predicate*. Likewise, given a non-empty list of variables x made of pairwise distinct identifiers and a predicate P, the construct $\exists x \cdot P$ is called an *existentially quantified predicate*. An *expression* is either a variable or else a *paired expression* $E \mapsto F$, where E and F are two expressions. Here is this new syntax:

$$
\begin{aligned}
predicate \quad &::= \quad \bot \\
&\qquad \top \\
&\qquad \neg\, predicate \\
&\qquad predicate \wedge predicate \\
&\qquad predicate \vee predicate \\
&\qquad predicate \Rightarrow predicate \\
&\qquad predicate \Leftrightarrow predicate \\
&\qquad \forall var\_list \cdot predicate \\
&\qquad \exists var\_list \cdot predicate \\[1em]
expression \quad &::= \quad variable \\
&\qquad expression \mapsto expression \\[1em]
var\_list \quad &::= \quad variable \\
&\qquad variable,\ var\_list
\end{aligned}
$$

This syntax is also ambiguous. Note however that the scope of the universal or existential quantifiers extends to the right as much as they can, the limitation being expressed either by the end of the formula or by means of enclosing parentheses.

9.3.2 Predicates and expressions

It might be useful at this point to clarify the difference between a predicate and an expression. A predicate P is a piece of formal text which can be *proved* when embedded within a sequent as in:

$$H \vdash P.$$

A predicate does not denote anything. This is not the case of an expression which always denotes an *object*. An expression cannot be "proved". Hence predicates and expressions are incompatible. Note that for the moment the possible expressions we can define are quite limited. This will be considerably extended in the set-theoretic language defined in Section 9.5.

9.3.3 Inference rules for universally quantified predicates

The universally and existentially quantified predicates require introducing corresponding rules of inference. As for propositional calculus, in both cases we need two rules: one for quantified assumptions (left rule) and one for a quantified goal (right rule). Here are these rules for universally quantified predicates:

$$\frac{\text{H}, \forall x \cdot P, [x := E]P \;\vdash\; Q}{\text{H}, \forall x \cdot P \;\vdash\; Q} \quad \textbf{ALL\_L}$$

$$\frac{\text{H} \;\vdash\; P}{\text{H} \;\vdash\; \forall x \cdot P} \quad \textbf{ALL\_R} \quad (x \text{ not free in H})$$

The first rule (ALL_L) allows us to add another assumption when we have a universally quantified one. This new assumption is obtained by instantiating the quantified variable x by any expression E in the predicate P: this is denoted by $[x := E]P$. The second rule (ALL_R) allows us to remove the "$\forall$" quantifier appearing in the goal. This can be done however only if the quantified variable (here x) *does not appear free* in the the set of assumptions H: this requirement is called a *side condition*. In the sequel we shall write x <u>nfin</u> P to mean that variable x is not free in predicate P. The same notation is used with an expression E. We omit in this presentation to develop the syntactic rules allowing us to compute non-freeness as well as substitutions. We have similar rules for existentially quantified predicates:

$$\frac{\text{H}, P \;\vdash\; Q}{\text{H}, \exists x \cdot P \;\vdash\; Q} \quad \textbf{XST\_L} \quad (x \text{ not free in H and } Q)$$

$$\frac{\text{H} \;\vdash\; [x := E]P}{\text{H} \;\vdash\; \exists x \cdot P} \quad \textbf{XST\_R}$$

As an example, we prove now the following sequent:

$$\forall x \cdot (\exists y \cdot P_{x,y}) \Rightarrow Q_x \quad \vdash \quad \forall x \cdot (\forall y \cdot P_{x,y} \Rightarrow Q_x) \quad ,$$

where $P_{x,y}$ stands for a predicate containing variables x and y only as free variables, and Q_x stands for a predicate containing variable x only as a free variable.

$$
\begin{array}{ll}
\begin{array}{l}
\forall x \cdot (\exists y \cdot P_{x,y}) \Rightarrow Q_x \\
\vdash \\
\forall x \cdot (\forall y \cdot P_{x,y} \Rightarrow Q_x)
\end{array}
&
\begin{array}{l}
\text{ALL\_R} \\
\text{ALL\_R} \\
\text{IMP\_R}
\end{array}
\end{array}
\qquad
\begin{array}{ll}
\begin{array}{l}
\forall x \cdot (\exists y \cdot P_{x,y}) \Rightarrow Q_x \\
P_{x,y} \\
\vdash \\
Q_x
\end{array}
&
\text{CUT} \ldots
\end{array}
$$

$$
\ldots \left\{
\begin{array}{ll}
\begin{array}{l}
\forall x \cdot (\exists y \cdot P_{x,y}) \Rightarrow Q_x \\
P_{x,y} \\
\vdash \\
\exists y \cdot P_{x,y}
\end{array}
& \text{XST\_R}
\qquad
\begin{array}{l}
\forall x \cdot (\exists y \cdot P_{x,y}) \Rightarrow Q_x \\
P_{x,y} \\
\vdash \\
P_{x,y}
\end{array}
\quad \text{HYP}
\\[2em]
\begin{array}{l}
\forall x \cdot (\exists y \cdot P_{x,y}) \Rightarrow Q_x \\
P_{x,y} \\
\exists y \cdot P_{x,y} \\
\vdash \\
Q_x
\end{array}
&
\begin{array}{l}
\text{ALL\_L} \\
\text{IMP\_L}
\end{array}
\qquad
\begin{array}{l}
\forall x \cdot (\exists y \cdot P_{x,y}) \Rightarrow Q_x \\
Q_x \\
P_{x,y} \\
\exists y \cdot P_{x,y} \\
\vdash \\
Q_x
\end{array}
\quad \text{HYP}
\end{array}
\right.
$$

The proof of the following sequent is left to the reader:

$$\forall x \cdot (\forall y \cdot P_{x,y} \Rightarrow Q_x) \quad \vdash \quad \forall x \cdot (\exists y \cdot P_{x,y}) \Rightarrow Q_x$$

An interesting derived rule is the following, which allows us to simplify an existential goal by replacing it with another one, hopefully simpler:

$$\frac{\mathsf{H} \;\vdash\; \exists x \cdot Q \qquad \mathsf{H},\, Q \;\vdash\; P}{\mathsf{H} \;\vdash\; \exists x \cdot P} \quad \begin{array}{l} \mathbf{CUT\_XST} \\ (\text{x } \underline{\text{nfin}} \text{ H}) \end{array}$$

Proof of **CUT_XST**

$$\mathsf{H} \vdash \exists x \cdot P \quad \mathbf{CUT} \left\{ \begin{array}{l} \boxed{\mathsf{H} \vdash \exists x \cdot Q} \quad \textbf{assumed antecedent} \\[2em] \boxed{\mathsf{H}, \exists x \cdot Q \vdash \exists x \cdot P} \quad \begin{array}{l}\mathbf{XST\_L}\\\mathbf{XST\_R}\end{array} \quad \boxed{\mathsf{H}, Q \vdash P} \quad \begin{array}{l}\textbf{assumed}\\\textbf{antecedent}\end{array} \end{array} \right.$$

9.4 Introducing equality

The predicate language is once again extended by adding a new predicate, the *equality predicate*. Given two expressions E and F, we define their equality by means of the construct $E = F$. Here is the extension of our syntax:

$$
\begin{array}{lll}
predicate & ::= & \bot \\
 & & \top \\
 & & \neg\, predicate \\
 & & predicate \,\wedge\, predicate \\
 & & predicate \,\vee\, predicate \\
 & & predicate \,\Rightarrow\, predicate \\
 & & predicate \,\Leftrightarrow\, predicate \\
 & & \forall var\_list \cdot predicate \\
 & & \exists var\_list \cdot predicate \\
 & & expression = expression \\
 & & \\
expression & ::= & variable \\
 & & expression \mapsto expression \\
\end{array}
$$

Note that we shall henceforth use the operator $\neq$ to mean, as is usual, the negation of equality. The inference rules for equality are the following:

$$\frac{[x := F]\mathrm{H},\ E = F\ \vdash\ [x := F]P}{[x := E]\mathrm{H},\ E = F\ \vdash\ [x := E]P} \qquad \textbf{EQ\_LR}$$

$$\frac{[x := E]\mathrm{H},\ E = F\ \vdash\ [x := E]P}{[x := F]\mathrm{H},\ E = F\ \vdash\ [x := F]P} \qquad \textbf{EQ\_RL}$$

This allows us to *apply* an equality assumption in the remaining assumptions and in the goal. This can be made by using the equality from left to right or from right to left. Subsequent rules correspond to the reflexivity of equality and to the equality of pairs. They are both defined by rewriting some rules as follows:

Operator	Predicate	Rewritten
Equality	$E = E$	$\top$
Equality of pairs	$E \mapsto F = G \mapsto H$	$E = G \land F = H$

The following rewriting rules, within which x is supposed to be not free in E, are easy to prove. They are called the *one point rules*:

Predicate	Rewritten
$\forall x \cdot x = E \Rightarrow P$	$[x := E]P$
$\exists x \cdot x = E \land P$	$[x := E]P$

9.5 The set-theoretic language

Our next language, the set-theoretic language, is now presented as an extension to the previous predicate language.

9.5.1 Syntax

In this extension, we introduce some special kinds of expressions called *sets*. Note that not all expressions are sets: for instance a pair is not a set. However, in the coming syntax, we shall not make any distinction between expressions which are sets and expressions which are not.

We introduce another predicate the *membership predicate*. Given an expression E and a set S, the construct $E \in S$ is a membership predicate which says that expression E is a *member* of set S.

We also introduce the basic set constructs. Given two sets S and T, the construct $S \times T$ is a set called the *Cartesian product* of S and T. Given a set S, the construct $\mathbb{P}(S)$ is a set called the *power set of S*. Finally, given a list of variables x with pairwise distinct identifiers, a predicate P, and an expression E, the construct $\{x \cdot P \,|\, E\}$ is called a *set defined in comprehension*. Here is our new syntax:

$$
\begin{array}{lll}
predicate & ::= & \ldots \\
& & expression \in expression \\
\\
expression & ::= & variable \\
& & expression \mapsto expression \\
& & expression \times expression \\
& & \mathbb{P}(expression) \\
& & \{\, var\_list \cdot predicate \,|\, expression \,\}
\end{array}
$$

Note that we shall use the operator $\notin$ in the sequel to mean, as is usual, the negation of set membership.

9.5.2 Axioms of set theory

The axioms of the set-theoretic language are given under the form of equivalences to various set memberships. They are all defined in terms of rewriting rules. Note that the last of these rules defines equality for sets. It is called the *extensionality axiom*.

Operator	Predicate	Rewritten	Side cond.
Cartesian product	$E \mapsto F \in S \times T$	$E \in S \wedge F \in T$	
Power set	$E \in \mathbb{P}(S)$	$\forall x \cdot x \in E \Rightarrow x \in S$	$x \, \underline{\text{nfin}} \, E$ $x \, \underline{\text{nfin}} \, S$
Set comprehension	$E \in \{ x \cdot P \mid F \}$	$\exists x \cdot P \wedge E = F$	$x \, \underline{\text{nfin}} \, E$
Set equality	$S = T$	$S \in \mathbb{P}(T) \wedge T \in \mathbb{P}(S)$	

As a special case, set comprehension can sometimes be written $\{ F \mid P \}$, which can be read as follows: "the set of objects has shape F when P holds". However, as we can see, the list of variables x has now disappeared. In fact, these variables are then *implicitly determined* as being all the free variables in F. When we want that x represent only *some*, but not all, of these free variables, we cannot use this shorthand.

A more special case is one where the expression F is exactly a single variable x, that is $\{ x \cdot P \mid x \}$. As a shorthand, this can be written $\{ x \mid P \}$, which is very common in informally written mathematics. And then $E \in \{ x \mid P \}$ becomes $[x := E]P$ according to the second "one point rule" of Section 9.4.

9.5.3 Elementary set operators

In this section, we introduce the classical set operators: inclusion, union, intersection, difference, extension, and the empty set:

```
predicate        ::=   ...
                       expression ⊆ expression

expression       ::=   ...
                       expression ∪ expression
                       expression ∩ expression
                       expression \ expression
                       {expression_list}
                       ∅

expression_list  ::=   expression
                       expression, expression_list
```

Notice that the expressions in an *expression_list* are not necessarily distinct.

Operator	Predicate	Rewritten
Inclusion	$S \subseteq T$	$S \in \mathbb{P}(T)$
Union	$E \in S \cup T$	$E \in S \ \lor \ E \in T$
Intersection	$E \in S \cap T$	$E \in S \ \land \ E \in T$
Difference	$E \in S \setminus T$	$E \in S \ \land \ \neg(E \in T)$
Set extension	$E \in \{a, \ldots, b\}$	$E = a \ \lor \ \ldots \ \lor \ E = b$
Empty set	$E \in \varnothing$	$\bot$

9.5.4 Generalization of elementary set operators

The next series of operators consists in generalizing union and intersection to sets of sets. This takes the forms either of an operator acting on a set or of a quantifier:

$$
\begin{aligned}
&\ldots \\[4pt]
expression \quad ::= \quad &\ldots \\
&\mathrm{union}(expression) \\
&\bigcup var\_list \cdot predicate \,|\, expression \\
&\mathrm{inter}(expression) \\
&\bigcap var\_list \cdot predicate \,|\, expression
\end{aligned}
$$

Operator	Predicate	Rewritten	Side cond.
Generalized intersection	$E \in \text{union}(S)$	$\exists s \cdot s \in S \wedge E \in s$	$s \underline{\text{nfin}} S$ $s \underline{\text{nfin}} E$
Quantified union	$E \in \bigcup x \cdot P \mid T$	$\exists x \cdot P \wedge E \in T$	$x \underline{\text{nfin}} E$
Generalized intersection	$E \in \text{inter}(S)$	$\forall s \cdot s \in S \Rightarrow E \in s$	$s \underline{\text{nfin}} S$ $s \underline{\text{nfin}} E$
Quantified intersection	$E \in \bigcap x \cdot P \mid T$	$\forall x \cdot P \Rightarrow E \in T$	$x \underline{\text{nfin}} E$

The last two rewriting rules require that the set $\text{inter}(S)$ and $\bigcap x \cdot P \mid T$ be *well defined*. This is presented in the following table:

Set construction	Well-definedness condition
$\text{inter}(S)$	$S \neq \varnothing$
$\bigcap x \cdot P \mid T$	$\exists x \cdot P$

Well-definedness conditions are taken care of in proof obligations as explained in Section 5.2.12 of Chapter 5.

9.5.5 Binary relation operators

We now define a first series of binary relation operators: the set of binary relations built on two sets, the domain and range of a binary relation, and then various sets of binary relations.

$$
\begin{array}{lll}
\dots & & \\
expression & ::= & \dots \\
& & expression \leftrightarrow expression \\
& & \mathrm{dom}(expression) \\
& & \mathrm{ran}(expression) \\
& & expression \leftrightarrow\!\!\!\to expression \\
& & expression \leftarrow\!\!\!\to\!\!\!\to expression \\
& & expression \leftrightarrow\!\!\!\to\!\!\!\to expression
\end{array}
$$

Operator	Predicate	Rewritten	Side cond.
Set of all binary relations	$r \in S \leftrightarrow T$	$r \subseteq S \times T$	
Domain	$E \in \mathrm{dom}\,(r)$	$\exists y \cdot E \mapsto y \,\in\, r$	$y \ \underline{\mathsf{nfin}}\ E$ $y \ \underline{\mathsf{nfin}}\ r$
Range	$F \in \mathrm{ran}\,(r)$	$\exists x \cdot x \mapsto F \,\in\, r$	$x \ \underline{\mathsf{nfin}}\ F$ $x \ \underline{\mathsf{nfin}}\ r$
Set of all total relations	$r \in S \leftrightarrow\!\!\!\to T$	$r \in S \leftrightarrow T \,\wedge\, \mathrm{dom}\,(r) = S$	
Set of all surjective relations	$r \in S \leftrightarrow\!\!\!\to\!\!\!\to T$	$r \in S \leftrightarrow T \,\wedge\, \mathrm{ran}\,(r) = T$	
Set of all total and surjective relations	$r \in S \leftrightarrow\!\!\!\to\!\!\!\to T$	$r \in S \leftrightarrow\!\!\!\to T \,\wedge\, r \in S \leftrightarrow\!\!\!\to\!\!\!\to T$	

The next series of binary relation operators define the converse of a relation, various relation restrictions, and the image of a set under a relation.

$$
\begin{aligned}
expression \quad ::= \quad & \ldots \\
& expression^{-1} \\
& expression \lhd expression \\
& expression \rhd expression \\
& expression \lhd\!\!\!- expression \\
& expression -\!\!\!\rhd expression \\
& expression[expression]
\end{aligned}
$$

Operator	Predicate	Rewritten	Side cond.
Converse	$E \mapsto F \in r^{-1}$	$F \mapsto E \in r$	
Domain restriction	$E \mapsto F \in S \lhd r$	$E \in S \ \wedge \ E \mapsto F \in r$	
Range restriction	$E \mapsto F \in r \rhd T$	$E \mapsto F \in r \ \wedge \ F \in T$	
Domain subtraction	$E \mapsto F \in S \lhd\!\!\!- r$	$\neg E \in S \ \wedge \ E \mapsto F \in r$	
Range subtraction	$E \mapsto F \in r -\!\!\!\rhd T$	$E \mapsto F \in r \ \wedge \ \neg F \in T$	
Relational image	$F \in r[U]$	$\exists x \cdot x \in U \ \wedge \ x \mapsto F \in r$	$x \ \underline{\text{nfin}} \ F$ $x \ \underline{\text{nfin}} \ r$ $x \ \underline{\text{nfin}} \ U$

Let us illustrate the relational image. Given a binary relation r from a set S to a set T, the image of a subset U of S under the relation r is a subset of T. The image of U under r is denoted by $r[U]$. Here is its definition:

$$
r[U] \ = \ \{\, y \,|\, \exists x \cdot x \in U \ \wedge \ x \mapsto y \in r \,\}.
$$

This is illustrated in Fig. 9.3. As can be seen on this figure, the image of the set $\{a, b\}$ under relation r is the set $\{m, n, p\}$.

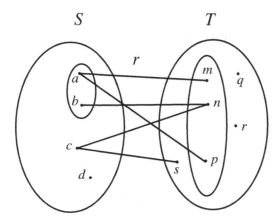

$$S \qquad\qquad T$$

Fig. 9.3. Image of a set under a relation

Our next series of operators defines the composition of two binary relations, the overriding of a relation by another one, and the direct and parallel products of two relations:

$$
\begin{aligned}
expression \quad ::= \quad & \ldots \\
& expression \; ; \; expression \\
& expression \circ expression \\
& expression \mathbin{\vartriangleleft} expression \\
& expression \otimes expression \\
& expression \parallel expression
\end{aligned}
$$

Operator	Predicate	Rewritten	Side cond.
Forward composition	$F \mapsto F \in f \; ; \; g$	$\exists x \cdot E \mapsto x \subset f \;\wedge\; x \mapsto \Gamma \in g$	$x\ \underline{\text{nfin}}\ E$ $x\ \underline{\text{nfin}}\ F$ $x\ \underline{\text{nfin}}\ f$ $x\ \underline{\text{nfin}}\ g$
Backward composition	$E \mapsto \Gamma \in g \circ f$	$E \mapsto F \in f \; ; \; g$	

Given a relation f from S to T and a relation g from T to U, the forward relational composition of f and g is a relation from S to U. It is denoted by the construct $f \,;g$. Sometimes it is denoted the other way around as $g \circ f$, in which case is is said to be the backward composition. Figure 9.4 illustrates forward composition.

Operator	Predicate	Rewritten
Overriding	$E \mapsto F \in f \lhdplus g$	$E \mapsto F \in (\mathrm{dom}\,(g) \lhd f) \,\cup\, g$
Direct product	$E \mapsto (F \mapsto G) \in f \otimes g$	$E \mapsto F \in f \,\wedge\, E \mapsto G \in g$
Parallel product	$(E \mapsto F) \mapsto (G \mapsto H) \in f \parallel g$	$E \mapsto G \in f \,\wedge\, F \mapsto H \in g$

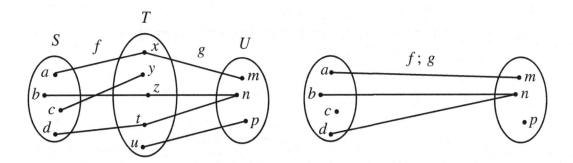

Fig. 9.4. Forward composition

The overriding operator is applicable in general to a relation f from, say, a set S to a set T, and a relation g also from S to T. Figure 9.5 illustrates overriding.

When f is a function and g is the singleton function $\{x \mapsto E\}$, then $f \lhdplus \{x \mapsto E\}$ replaces in f the pair $x \mapsto f(x)$ by the pair $x \mapsto E$. Notice that in the case where x is not in the domain of f, then $f \lhdplus \{x \mapsto E\}$ simply adds the pair $x \mapsto E$ to the function f. In this case, it is thus equal to $f \cup \{x \mapsto E\}$.

9.5.6 Function operators

In this section, we define various function operators: the sets of all partial and total functions, partial and total injections, partial and total surjections, and bijections. We also introduce the two projection functions as well as the identity function:

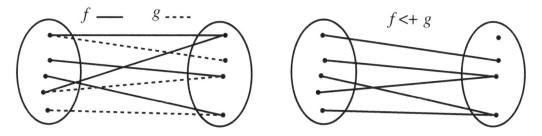

Fig. 9.5. Relation overriding

$$
\begin{array}{lll}
expression & ::= & \dots \\
& & \mathrm{id} \\
& & expression \nrightarrow expression \\
& & expression \rightarrow expression \\
& & expression \rightarrowtail\!\!\!\!\!\to expression \\
& & expression \rightarrowtail expression \\
& & expression \twoheadrightarrow expression \\
& & expression \rightarrow\!\!\!\!\to expression \\
& & expression \rightarrowtail\!\!\!\!\twoheadrightarrow expression \\
& & \mathrm{prj}_1 \\
& & \mathrm{prj}_2
\end{array}
$$

Operator	Predicate	Rewritten
Identity	$E \mapsto F \in \mathrm{id}$	$E = F$
Set of all partial functions	$f \in S \nrightarrow T$	$f \in S \leftrightarrow T \ \wedge \ (f^{-1}\,;f) \subseteq \mathrm{id}$
Set of all total functions	$f \in S \rightarrow T$	$f \in S \nrightarrow T \ \wedge \ S = \mathrm{dom}\,(f)$
Set of all partial injections	$f \in S \rightarrowtail\!\!\!\!\!\to T$	$f \in S \nrightarrow T \ \wedge \ f^{-1} \in T \nrightarrow S$
Set of all total injections	$f \in S \rightarrowtail T$	$f \in S \rightarrow T \ \wedge \ f^{-1} \in T \nrightarrow S$
Set of all partial surjections	$f \in S \twoheadrightarrow T$	$f \in S \nrightarrow T \ \wedge \ T = \mathrm{ran}\,(f)$
Set of all total surjections	$f \in S \rightarrow\!\!\!\!\to T$	$f \in S \rightarrow T \ \wedge \ T = \mathrm{ran}\,(f)$
Set of all bijections	$f \in S \rightarrowtail\!\!\!\!\twoheadrightarrow T$	$f \in S \rightarrowtail T \ \wedge \ f \in S \rightarrow\!\!\!\!\to T$

Operator	Predicate	Rewritten
First projection	$(E \mapsto F) \mapsto G \in \mathrm{prj}_1$	$G = E$
Second projection	$(E \mapsto F) \mapsto G \in \mathrm{prj}_2$	$G = F$

9.5.7 Summary of the arrows

Operator	Arrow
Binary relations	$S \leftrightarrow T$
Total relations	$S \leftarrow\!\!\leftrightarrow T$
Surjective relations	$S \leftrightarrow\!\!\rightarrow T$
Total surjective relations	$S \leftarrow\!\!\leftrightarrow\!\!\rightarrow T$
Partial functions	$S \nrightarrow T$
Total functions	$S \rightarrow T$

Operator	Arrow
Partial injections	$S \rightarrowtail\!\!\!\!\!\cdot\, T$
Total injections	$S \rightarrowtail T$
Partial surjections	$S \twoheadrightarrow\!\!\!\!\!\cdot\, T$
Total surjections	$S \twoheadrightarrow T$
Bijections	$S \rightarrowtail\!\!\!\!\!\twoheadrightarrow T$

9.5.8 Lambda abstraction and function invocation

We now define *lambda abstraction*, which is a way to construct functions, and also function invocation, which is a way to call functions. But first we have to define the notion of *pattern of variables*. A pattern of variables is either an identifier or a pair made of two patterns of variables. Moreover, all variables composing the pattern must be distinct. For example, here are three patterns of variables:

$$abc$$
$$abc \mapsto def$$
$$abc \mapsto (def \mapsto ghi)$$

Given a pattern of variables x, a predicate P, and an expression E, the construct $\lambda x \cdot P \mid E$ is a lambda abstraction, which is a function. Given a function f and an expression E, the construct $f(E)$ is an expression denoting a function invocation. Here is our new syntax:

$$
\begin{array}{lll}
expression & ::= & \ldots \\
& & expression(expression) \\
& & \lambda\, pattern \cdot predicate \mid expression \\
pattern & ::= & variable \\
& & pattern \mapsto pattern
\end{array}
$$

In the following table, l stands for the list of variables in the pattern L.

Operator	Predicate	Rewritten
Lambda abstraction	$F \in \lambda L \cdot P \mid E$	$F \in \{l \cdot P \mid L \mapsto E\}$
Function invocation	$F = f(E)$	$E \mapsto F \in f$

The function invocation construct $f(E)$ requires a well-definedness condition, which is the following:

Expression	Well-definedness condition
$f(E)$	$f^{-1} \,;\, f \subseteq \mathrm{id} \quad \wedge \quad E \in \mathrm{dom}(f)$

Some of the axioms of integers are presented in this section.

9.6 Boolean and arithmetic language

9.6.1 Syntax

In this section, we extend the expressions once more. An expression might be a boolean or a number. Booleans are either TRUE or FALSE (do not confuse them with $\top$ and $\perp$). Numbers are either 0, 1, ..., the sum, product, or power of two numbers. We also add the sets BOOL, $\mathbb{Z}$, $\mathbb{N}$, N1 and the functions succ and pred:

$$
\begin{array}{ll}
expression \quad ::= & \ldots \\
& \text{BOOL} \\
& \text{TRUE} \\
& \text{FALSE} \\
& \mathbb{Z} \\
& \mathbb{N} \\
& \mathbb{N}_1 \\
& \text{succ} \\
& \text{pred} \\
& 0 \\
& 1 \\
& \ldots \\
& expression + expression \\
& expression * expression \\
& expression \,\widehat{}\, expression
\end{array}
$$

9.6.2 Peano axioms and recursive definitions

The following predicates yield definition of the boolean and arithmetic expressions:

$$
\begin{array}{l}
\text{BOOL} \;=\; \{\text{TRUE}, \text{FALSE}\} \\[4pt]
\text{TRUE} \neq \text{FALSE} \\[4pt]
0 \in \mathbb{N} \\[4pt]
\text{succ} \in \mathbb{Z} \rightarrowtail\!\!\!\rightarrow \mathbb{Z} \\[4pt]
\text{pred} \;=\; \text{succ}^{-1} \\[4pt]
\forall S \cdot 0 \in S \;\wedge\; (\forall n \cdot n \in S \Rightarrow \text{succ}(n) \in S) \;\Rightarrow\; \mathbb{N} \subseteq S \\[4pt]
\forall a \cdot a + 0 \;=\; a \\[4pt]
\forall a \cdot a * 0 \;=\; 0 \\[4pt]
\forall a \cdot a \,\widehat{}\, 0 \;=\; \text{succ}(0) \\[4pt]
\forall a, b \cdot a + \text{succ}(b) = \text{succ}(a + b) \\[4pt]
\forall a, b \cdot a * \text{succ}(b) = (a * b) + a \\[4pt]
\forall a, b \cdot a \,\widehat{}\, \text{succ}(b) = (a \,\widehat{}\, b) * a
\end{array}
$$

9.6.3 Extension of the arithmetic language

We introduce the classical binary relations on numbers, the finiteness predicate, the interval between two numbers, the subtraction, division, modulo, cardinal, maximum, and minimum constructs:

```
        . . .

predicate    ::=    . . .
                    expression ≤ expression
                    expression < expression
                    expression ≥ expression
                    expression > expression
                    finite(expression)

expression   ::=    . . .
                    expression .. expression
                    expression − expression
                    expression / expression
                    expression mod expression
                    card(expression)
                    max(expression)
                    min(expression)
```

Operator	Predicate	Rewritten
smaller than or equal	$a \leq b$	$\exists c \cdot c \in \mathbb{N} \ \wedge \ b = a + c$
smaller than	$a < b$	$a \leq b \ \wedge \ a \neq b$
greater than or equal	$a \geq b$	$\neg \, (a < b)$
greater than	$a > b$	$\neg \, (a \leq b)$
interval	$c \in a .. b$	$a \leq c \ \wedge \ c \leq b$
subtraction	$c = a - b$	$a = b + c$
division	$c = a/b$	$\exists r \cdot (\, r \in \mathbb{N} \ \wedge \ r < b \ \wedge \\ \qquad a = c * b + r \,)$
modulo	$r = a \bmod b$	$a = (a/b) * b + r$
finiteness	finite(s)	$\exists n, f \cdot n \in \mathbb{N} \ \wedge \ f \in 1 .. n \rightarrowtail\!\!\!\!\rightarrow s$
cardinality	$n = \mathrm{card}(s)$	$\exists f \cdot f \in 1 .. n \rightarrowtail\!\!\!\!\rightarrow s$

Operator	Predicate	Rewritten
maximum	$n = \max(s)$	$n \in s \ \wedge \ (\forall x \cdot x \in s \ \Rightarrow x \leq n)$
minimum	$n = \min(s)$	$n \in s \ \wedge \ (\forall x \cdot x \in s \ \Rightarrow x \geq n)$

Division, modulo, cardinal, minimum, and maximum are subjected to some well-definedness conditions, which are the following:

Numeric expression	Well-definedness condition
a/b	$b \neq 0$
$a \bmod b$	$0 \leq a \ \wedge \ b > 0$
$\mathrm{card}(s)$	$\mathrm{finite}(s)$
$\max(s)$	$s \neq \varnothing \ \wedge \ \exists x \cdot (\forall n \cdot n \in s \ \Rightarrow \ x \geq n)$
$\min(s)$	$s \neq \varnothing \ \wedge \ \exists x \cdot (\forall n \cdot n \in s \ \Rightarrow \ x \leq n)$

9.7 Advanced data structures

In this section, we show how our basic mathematical language can still be extended to cope with some classical (advanced) data structures we shall use in subsequent chapters of the book, essentially strongly connected graphs, lists, rings, and trees. We present the axiomatic definitions of these data structures together with some theorems. We do not present proofs. In fact all such proofs have been done with the Rodin Platform.

9.7.1 Irreflexive transitive closure

We start with the definition of the irreflexive transitive closure of a relation, which is a very useful concept to be used in what follows. Given a relation r from a set S to itself, the irreflexive transitive closure of r, denoted by $cl(r)$, is also a relation from S to S. The characteristic properties of $cl(r)$ are:

(i) Relation r is included in $cl(r)$.
(ii) The forward composition of $cl(r)$ with r is included in $cl(r)$.
(iii) Relation $cl(r)$ is the smallest relation dealing with (i) and (ii).

This is illustrated in Fig. 9.6. It can be formalized as follows:

$$
\begin{aligned}
&\textbf{axm\_1}: \quad r \in S \leftrightarrow S \\[1ex]
&\textbf{axm\_2}: \quad cl(r) \in S \leftrightarrow S \\[1ex]
&\textbf{axm\_3}: \quad r \subseteq cl(r) \\[1ex]
&\textbf{axm\_4}: \quad cl(r)\,;r \subseteq cl(r) \\[1ex]
&\textbf{axm\_5}: \quad \forall p \cdot r \subseteq p \;\wedge\; p\,;r \subseteq p \;\Rightarrow\; cl(r) \subseteq p
\end{aligned}
$$

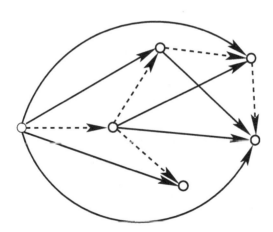

Fig. 9.6. A relation (dashed) and its irreflexive transitive closure (dashed and plain)

The following theorems can be proved:

$$
\begin{array}{ll}
\textbf{thm\_1}: & \mathrm{cl}(r)\,;\mathrm{cl}(r) \subseteq \mathrm{cl}(r) \\[2mm]
\textbf{thm\_2}: & \mathrm{cl}(r) = r \cup r\,;\mathrm{cl}(r) \\[2mm]
\textbf{thm\_3}: & \mathrm{cl}(r) = r \cup \mathrm{cl}(r)\,;r \\[2mm]
\textbf{thm\_4}: & \forall s \cdot r[s] \subseteq s \;\Rightarrow\; \mathrm{cl}(r)[s] \subseteq s \\[2mm]
\textbf{thm\_5}: & \mathrm{cl}(r^{-1}) = \mathrm{cl}(r)^{-1}
\end{array}
$$

These theorems are proved by finding some instantiations for the local variable p in the universally quantified axiom **axm_5**. In particular, the proof of **thm_1** is handled by instantiating p with†:

$$
\{\, x \mapsto y \mid cl(r)\,;\{x \mapsto y\} \subseteq cl(r)\,\}.
$$

9.7.2 Strongly connected graphs

Given a set V and a binary relation r from V to itself, the graph representing this relation is said to be *strongly connected* if any two distinct points m and n in V are possibly connected by a path built on r. This is illustrated in Fig. 9.7. This can be

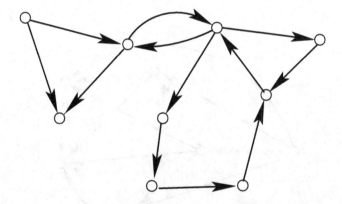

Fig. 9.7. A strongly connected graph

---

† This was suggested by D. Cansell

formalized as follows:

$$\mathbf{axm\_1}: \quad r \in V \leftrightarrow V$$

$$\mathbf{axm\_2}: \quad (V \times V) \setminus \mathrm{id} \subseteq \mathrm{cl}(r)$$

This definition is easy to understand: it simply says that every two distinct points of V are related through the irreflexive transitive closure $\mathrm{cl}(r)$ of r. But this definition is not very convenient to use in proof. Here is an *equivalent one*, which is more convenient:

$$\mathbf{thm\_1}: \quad \forall S \cdot S \neq \varnothing \wedge r[S] \subseteq S \Rightarrow V \subseteq S$$

The intuition behind this definition is the following: it says that the only set S (except the empty set), which is such that $r[S] \subseteq S$, is the entire set V. For example, suppose we have:

$$V = \{a, b\}$$

$$r = \{a \mapsto b\}$$

$$r[\{a\}] = \{b\}$$

$$r[\{b\}] = \varnothing$$

$$r[\{a, b\}] = \{b\}.$$

The graph r is not connected because the non-empty set $\{b\}$, which is different from V, is such that $r[\{b\}] \subseteq \{b\}$. Now suppose:

$$V = \{a, b\}$$

$$r = \{a \mapsto b, b \mapsto a\}$$

$$r[\{a\}] = \{b\}$$

$$r[\{b\}] = \{a\}$$

$$r[\{a, b\}] = \{a, b\}$$

The graph r is strongly connected since the only non-empty set S where $r[S] \subseteq S$ is $\{a, b\}$, that is indeed V.

Also note the following result which is very intuitive: if r is strongly connected then so is r^{-1}.

9.7.3 Infinite lists

An infinite list built on a set V is defined by means of a point f of V (the beginning of the list) and a bijective function n from V to $V \setminus \{f\}$. It is illustrated in Fig. 9.8.

This can be formalized as follows:

$$\textbf{axm\_1}: \quad f \in V$$

$$\textbf{axm\_2}: \quad n \in V \rightarrowtail\!\!\!\rightarrow V \setminus \{f\}$$

Fig. 9.8. An infinite list

But these two properties are not enough. We need a final property, which says that there are no cycles or backward infinite chains, which are not precluded by axioms **axm_1** and **axm_2**. We want to eliminate the backward infinite chain and the cycle which are shown in Fig. 9.9.

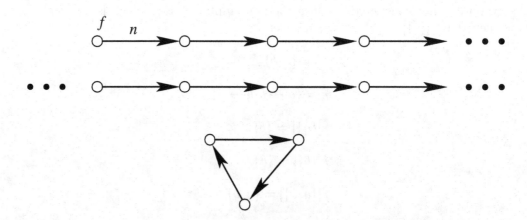

Fig. 9.9. Avoiding infinite backward chains and cycles

A set S containing a cycle or an infinite backward chain is one such that each point x in S is related to a point y in S by the relation n^{-1}. This can be formalized as follows:

$$\forall x \cdot x \in S \;\Rightarrow\; (\,\exists y \cdot y \in S \;\wedge\; y \mapsto x \in n\,) :$$

that is

$$S \;\subseteq\; n[S].$$

But as the empty set enjoys this property, we state in the following axiom that the only set with that property is precisely the empty set:

$$\textbf{axm\_3}: \quad \forall S \cdot S \subseteq n[S] \;\Rightarrow\; S = \varnothing$$

A classical example of an infinite list is one where V is the set of natural numbers $\mathbb{N}$, f is 0, and n is the successor function succ restricted to $\mathbb{N}$. This is illustrated in Fig. 9.10.

Fig. 9.10. The natural numbers

It clearly obeys **axm_1** and **axm_2**. It also obeys **axm_3**: let S be a non-empty subset of $\mathbb{N}$, then succ$[S]$ does not contain $\min(S)$; thus S is not included in succ$[S]$. In fact, **axm_1** and **axm_2** are exactly the first four Peano axioms. But clearly **axm_3** does not correspond to the last Peano axiom (recurrence). However, the following theorem shows that the last Peano axiom can be proved from **axm_3** (and vice-versa). This can be done easily by instantiating S in **axm_3** with $V \setminus T$:

$$\textbf{thm\_1}: \quad \forall T \cdot f \in T \;\wedge\; n[T] \subseteq T \;\Rightarrow\; V \subseteq T$$

By unfolding $n[T] \subseteq T$, we obtain:

$$\textbf{thm\_2}: \quad \forall T \cdot f \in T \;\wedge\; (\forall x \cdot x \in T \Rightarrow n(x) \in T) \;\Rightarrow\; V \subseteq T$$

Translating this to the natural numbers, we obtain the last Peano axiom:

$$\forall T \cdot 0 \in T \;\wedge\; (\forall x \cdot x \in T \Rightarrow x + 1 \in T) \;\Rightarrow\; \mathbb{N} \subseteq T$$

Next are three more theorems which might be useful. Observe **thm_4**, which says that backward chaining is finite. Theorem **thm_5** represents another way to state that there are no cycles. It does not say however that there is no backward infinite chains, so it is not equivalent to **axm_3**; it is only implied by **axm_3**.

$$\textbf{thm\_3}: \quad cl(n)[\{f\}] \cup \{f\} = V$$

$$\textbf{thm\_4}: \quad \forall x \cdot \text{finite}(cl(n^{-1})[\{x\}])$$

$$\textbf{thm\_5}: \quad cl(n) \cap \text{id} = \varnothing$$

Note that in the case of the natural numbers, $a \mapsto b \in cl(\text{succ})$ is the same as $a < b$, and $cl(\text{succ}^{-1})[\{a\}] \cup \{a\}$ (for any natural number a) is the same as the interval $0 \mathinner{.\,.} a$.

The list induction rule Theorem **thm_2** can be used to prove a property $P(x)$ for all nodes of a list. It is done in the following fashion. The property $P(x)$ is transformed into the following set:

$$\{\, x \mid x \in V \wedge P(x) \,\}.$$

And now proving that $P(x)$ holds for each node x of V is exactly the same as proving that V is included into that set, that is:

$$V \subseteq \{\, x \mid x \in V \wedge P(x) \,\}.$$

To do so, it suffices to instantiate T in **thm_2** with the set $\{\, x \mid x \in V \wedge P(x) \,\}$. This yields:

$$
\begin{array}{l}
f \in \{\, x \mid x \in V \wedge P(x) \,\} \\
\forall x \cdot x \in \{\, x \mid x \in V \wedge P(x) \,\} \;\Rightarrow\; n(x) \in \{\, x \mid x \in V \wedge P(x) \,\} \\
\Rightarrow \\
V \subseteq \{\, x \mid x \in V \wedge P(x) \,\}
\end{array}
$$

The first antecedent of this implication reduces to:

$$P(f)$$

The second antecedent can be rewritten:

$$\forall x \cdot x \in V \wedge P(x) \;\Rightarrow\; P(n(x))$$

And now, once we have proved the previous statements, then we can deduce the following, which was our initial goal:

$$V \subseteq \{\, x \mid x \in V \,\wedge\, \mathsf{P}(x)\,\},$$

that is:

$$\forall x \cdot x \in V \;\Rightarrow\; \mathsf{P}(x).$$

To summarize, when we have to prove a property $\mathsf{P}(x)$ for all elements x of a list, a possibility is to do the following:

- prove that $\mathsf{P}(f)$ holds for the first element f of the list;
- prove that $\mathsf{P}(n(x))$ holds for any x in V, under the assumption that $\mathsf{P}(x)$ holds.

In doing so, the property $\mathsf{P}(x)$ is said to be proved *by list induction*. All this can now be transformed in an inference rule as follows:

$$
\dfrac{\mathsf{H} \vdash \mathsf{P}(f) \qquad \mathsf{H},\, x \in V,\, \mathsf{P}(x) \vdash \mathsf{P}(n(x))}{\mathsf{H},\, x \in V \vdash \mathsf{P}(x)}
\qquad
\begin{array}{l} \mathsf{IND\_LIST} \\ (x \;\underline{\mathsf{nfin}}\; \mathsf{H}) \end{array}
$$

By translating this rule to the natural numbers, this yields:

$$
\dfrac{\mathsf{H} \vdash \mathsf{P}(0) \qquad \mathsf{H},\, x \in \mathbb{N},\, \mathsf{P}(x) \vdash \mathsf{P}(x+1)}{\mathsf{H},\, x \in \mathbb{N} \vdash \mathsf{P}(x)}
\qquad
\begin{array}{l} \mathsf{IND\_\mathbb{N}} \\ (x \;\underline{\mathsf{nfin}}\; \mathsf{H}) \end{array}
$$

9.7.4 Finite lists

A finite list constructed on the set V is defined by means of two points f (denoting the first element in the list) and l (denoting the last element in the list). The list itself is a bijection. It is illustrated in Fig. 9.11. Finally, an axiom similar to axiom **axm_3**

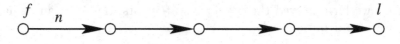

Fig. 9.11. A Finite list

of the infinite lists says that there is no backward chain or cycles:

$$
\begin{array}{ll}
\mathbf{axm\_1}: & f \in V \\[2mm]
\mathbf{axm\_2}: & l \in V \\[2mm]
\mathbf{axm\_3}: & n \in V \setminus \{l\} \rightarrowtail V \setminus \{f\} \\[2mm]
\mathbf{axm\_4}: & \forall S \cdot S \subseteq n[S] \;\Rightarrow\; S = \varnothing
\end{array}
$$

Notice that axiom **axm_4** is not symmetric with regard to both directions on the list. But this can be proved in a systematic manner. This is what is shown in the following theorems:

$$
\begin{array}{ll}
\mathbf{thm\_1}: & \forall T \cdot f \in T \,\wedge\, n[T] \subseteq T \;\Rightarrow\; V \subseteq T \\[2mm]
\mathbf{thm\_2}: & \mathrm{cl}(n)[\{f\}] \cup \{f\} = V \\[2mm]
\mathbf{thm\_3}: & \mathrm{cl}(n^{-1})[\{l\}] \cup \{l\} = V \\[2mm]
\mathbf{thm\_4}: & \forall T \cdot l \in T \,\wedge\, n^{-1}[T] \subseteq T \;\Rightarrow\; V \subseteq T \\[2mm]
\mathbf{thm\_5}: & \forall S \cdot S \subseteq n^{-1}[S] \;\Rightarrow\; S = \varnothing \\[2mm]
\mathbf{thm\_6}: & \mathrm{finite}(V) \\[2mm]
\mathbf{thm\_7}: & cl(n) \cap \mathrm{id} = \varnothing
\end{array}
$$

A classical example of finite lists are numerical intervals $a \mathbin{..} b$ (with $a \leq b$). This is illustrated in Fig. 9.12.

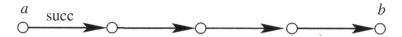

Fig. 9.12. A numerical interval

It is easy to prove the following:

$$a \in a \mathbin{..} b$$

$$b \in a \mathbin{..} b$$

$$(a \mathbin{..} b - 1) \lhd \mathrm{succ} \;\in\; (a \mathbin{..} b) \setminus \{b\} \rightarrowtail (a \mathbin{..} b) \setminus \{a\}$$

Coming back to our general finite lists, let us now define the set of elements $\mathrm{itvl}(x)$ belonging to a sublist from f to x in a finite list from f to l:

axm_5 : $\mathrm{itvl} \in V \to \mathbb{P}(V)$

axm_6 : $\forall x \cdot x \in V \;\Rightarrow\; \mathrm{itvl}(x) = cl(n^{-1})[\{x\}] \cup \{x\}$

The following theorems state some useful properties of these sets. Observe the recursive property stated in **thm_9**:

thm_8 : $\forall x \cdot x \in V \;\Rightarrow\; \{f, x\} \subseteq \mathrm{itvl}(x)$

thm_9 : $\forall x \cdot x \in V \setminus \{f\} \;\Rightarrow\; \mathrm{itvl}(x) = \mathrm{itvl}(n^{-1}(x)) \cup \{x\}$

thm_10 : $\mathrm{itvl}(l) = V$

The last theorem is just a rewording of **thm_3**.

9.7.5 Rings

A ring is defined by a bijection which is strongly connected. It is illustrated in Fig. 9.13. Thus we copy in **axm_2** part of the statement of **thm_2** of Section 9.7.2 showing the equivalence to strong connectivity.

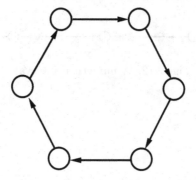

Fig. 9.13. A ring

$$\textbf{axm\_1}: \quad n \in V \rightarrowtail\mkern-14mu\rightarrow V$$

$$\textbf{axm\_2}: \quad \forall S \cdot S \neq \varnothing \,\wedge n^{-1}[S] \subseteq S \Rightarrow V \subseteq S$$

Since n is injective (bijective, in fact), we have the following:

$$\textbf{thm\_1}: \quad \forall S \cdot n^{-1}[S] \subseteq S \Leftrightarrow S \subseteq n[S]$$

This allows us to transform as follows the connectivity relationship of the ring:

$$\textbf{thm\_2}: \quad \forall S \cdot S \neq \varnothing \,\wedge\, S \subseteq n[S] \Rightarrow V \subseteq S$$

By cutting a ring between $n^{-1}(x)$ and x, we obtain a finite list from x to $n^{-1}(x)$. This is illustrated in Fig. 9.14. This finite list starts at x and ends at $n^{-1}(x)$. This is stated in the following theorems:

$$\textbf{thm\_1}: \quad \forall x \cdot x \in V \Rightarrow p \in V \setminus \{n^{-1}(x)\} \rightarrowtail\mkern-14mu\rightarrow V \setminus \{x\}$$

$$\textbf{thm\_2}: \quad \forall x \cdot x \in V \Rightarrow (\forall S \cdot S \subseteq p[S] \Rightarrow S = \varnothing)$$

where $\quad p$ is $\quad n \mathbin{\rhd\mkern-10mu\relax} \{x\}$

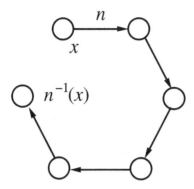

Fig. 9.14. A cut ring

Let us now define the sets of elements itvr$(x)(y)$ belonging to an interval on a ring from x to y.

---

axm_3 :   itvr $\in V \to (V \to \mathbb{P}(V))$

axm_4 : $\forall x, y \cdot x \in V \land y \in V \Rightarrow$ itvr$(x)(y) = cl(\{x\} \vartriangleleft n^{-1})[\{y\}] \cup \{y\}$

The following theorems state some useful properties of the intervals:

---

thm_3 : $\forall x \cdot x \in V \land y \in V \Rightarrow \{x, y\} \subseteq$ itvr$(x)(y)$

thm_4 : $\forall x \cdot x \in V \land y \in V \setminus \{x\} \Rightarrow$ itvr$(x)(y) =$ itvr$(x)(n^{-1}(y)) \cup \{y\}$

thm_5 : $\forall x \cdot x \in V \Rightarrow$ itvr$(x)(n^{-1}(x)) = V$

The last theorem is an adaptation of theorem **thm_10** of finite lists. A classical example of a ring is given by "addition-modulo" as illustrated in Fig. 9.15.

Notice that sometimes it is more convenient to use a ring than "addition-modulo": proofs are getting simpler.

9.7.6 Infinite trees

Infinite trees generalize infinite lists. The beginning f of the list is replaced by the top t of the tree. The function p replaces n^{-1} of the infinite list. This is illustrated in Fig. 9.16. This is expressed by axioms **axm_1** and **axm_2** below. Axiom **axm_3** has

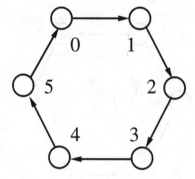

Fig. 9.15. A ring modulo 6

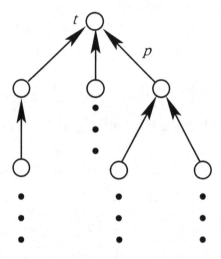

Fig. 9.16. An infinite tree

the same function as **axm_3** on infinite lists: it removes cycles and infinite backward chains:

$$
\begin{array}{ll}
\textbf{axm\_1}: & t \in V \\[2mm]
\textbf{axm\_2}: & p \in V \setminus \{t\} \twoheadrightarrow V \\[2mm]
\textbf{axm\_3}: & \forall S \cdot S \subseteq p^{-1}[S] \;\Rightarrow\; S = \varnothing
\end{array}
$$

The next theorem defines induction rules which generalize that of infinite lists:

$$\mathbf{thm\_1}: \quad \forall T \cdot t \in T \,\wedge\, p^{-1}[T] \subseteq T \,\Rightarrow\, V \subseteq T$$

$$\mathbf{thm\_2}: \quad \mathrm{cl}(p^{-1})[\{t\}] \cup \{t\} = V$$

The following theorem states that backwards chains are finite:

$$\mathbf{thm\_3}: \quad \forall x \cdot \mathrm{finite}(\mathrm{cl}(p)[\{x\}])$$

The list induction rule It is easy to prove that **thm_1** is equivalent to the following theorem **thm_4** (hint: instantiate T in **thm_1** with $\overline{N} \setminus T$):

$$
\mathbf{thm\_4}: \quad \forall T \cdot \quad
\begin{aligned}
& T \subseteq V \\
& t \in T \\
& p^{-1}[T] \subseteq T \\
& \Rightarrow \\
& V \subseteq T
\end{aligned}
$$

This theorem can be further unfolded to the following equivalent one:

$$
\mathbf{thm\_5}: \quad \forall T \cdot \quad
\begin{aligned}
& T \subseteq V \\
& t \in T \\
& \forall x \cdot x \in V \setminus \{t\} \,\wedge\, p(x) \in T \Rightarrow x \in T \\
& \Rightarrow \\
& V \subseteq T
\end{aligned}
$$

This is so because we have:

$$p^{-1}[T] \subseteq T$$
$$\Leftrightarrow$$
$$\forall x \cdot x \in p^{-1}[T] \Rightarrow x \in T$$
$$\Leftrightarrow$$
$$\forall x \cdot (\exists y \cdot y \in T \wedge x \mapsto y \in p) \Rightarrow x \in T$$
$$\Leftrightarrow$$
$$\forall x \cdot (\exists y \cdot y \in T \wedge x \in \mathrm{dom}(p) \wedge y = p(x)) \Rightarrow x \in T$$
$$\Leftrightarrow$$
$$\forall x \cdot x \in V \setminus \{t\} \wedge p(x) \in T \Rightarrow x \in T$$

Theorem **thm_5** can be used to prove a property $\mathsf{P}(x)$ for all nodes of a tree. It is done in the following fashion. The property $\mathsf{P}(x)$ is transformed into the following set:

$$\{ x \mid x \in V \wedge \mathsf{P}(x) \}.$$

And now proving that $\mathsf{P}(x)$ holds for each node x of V is exactly the same as proving that V is included into that set, that is:

$$V \subseteq \{ x \mid x \in V \wedge \mathsf{P}(x) \}$$

To do so, it suffices to instantiate T in **thm_5** with the set $\{ x \mid x \in V \wedge \mathsf{P}(x) \}$. This yields:

$$\{ x \mid x \in V \wedge \mathsf{P}(x) \} \subseteq V$$

$$t \in \{ x \mid x \in V \wedge \mathsf{P}(x) \}$$

$$\forall x \cdot \begin{pmatrix} x \in V \setminus \{t\} \\ p(x) \in \{ x \mid x \in V \wedge \mathsf{P}(x) \} \\ \Rightarrow \\ x \in \{ x \mid x \in V \wedge \mathsf{P}(x) \} \end{pmatrix}$$
$$\Rightarrow$$
$$V \subseteq \{ x \mid x \in V \wedge \mathsf{P}(x) \}$$

The first antecedent of this implication is obvious because the set $\{ x \mid x \in V \wedge \mathsf{P}(x) \}$ is indeed included in the set V, and the second antecedent reduces to:

$$\boxed{\mathsf{P}(t)}$$

The third antecedent can be rewritten:

$$\forall x \cdot x \in V \setminus \{t\} \; \wedge \; \mathsf{P}(p(x)) \; \Rightarrow \; \mathsf{P}(x)$$

And now, once we have proved the previous statements, then we can deduce the following which was our initial goal:

$$V \subseteq \{\, x \mid x \in V \wedge \mathsf{P}(x)\,\},$$

that is:

$$\forall x \cdot (\, x \in V \; \Rightarrow \; \mathsf{P}(x)\,)$$

To summarize, when we have to prove a property $\mathsf{P}(x)$ for all elements x of a tree, a possibility is to do the following:

- prove that $\mathsf{P}(t)$ holds for the top t of the tree;
- prove that $\mathsf{P}(x)$ holds for any x in $V \setminus \{t\}$, under the assumption that $\mathsf{P}(p(x))$ holds for the parent $p(x)$ of x in the tree.

In doing so, the property $\mathsf{P}(x)$ is said to be proved *by tree induction*. All this can now be transformed in an inference rule as follows:

$$
\frac{\mathsf{H} \vdash \mathsf{P}(t) \qquad \mathsf{H},\, x \in V \setminus \{t\},\, \mathsf{P}(p(x)) \vdash \mathsf{P}(x)}{\mathsf{H},\, x \in V \vdash \mathsf{P}(x)} \quad
\begin{array}{l}\text{IND\_TREE}\\[2pt](\mathbf{x}\ \underline{\mathsf{nfin}}\ \mathsf{H})\end{array}
$$

9.7.7 Finite depth trees

Finite depth trees generalize finite lists. We still have a top point t, which was f in the lists. But the last element l of the list is now replaced by a set L: these are the so-called leafs of the tree. All this is illustrated in Fig. 9.17. The axioms are as usual the following:

$$
\begin{aligned}
&\textbf{axm\_1}: && t \in V\\[6pt]
&\textbf{axm\_2}: && L \subseteq V\\[6pt]
&\textbf{axm\_3}: && p \in V \setminus \{t\} \twoheadrightarrow V \setminus L\\[6pt]
&\textbf{axm\_4}: && \forall S \cdot S \subseteq p^{-1}[S] \; \Rightarrow \; S = \varnothing
\end{aligned}
$$

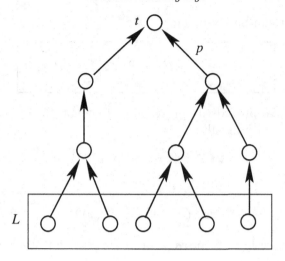

Fig. 9.17. A finite tree

The seven theorems of finite lists can be adapted to finite trees as follows:

$$\textbf{thm\_1}: \quad \forall T \cdot t \in T \ \wedge \ p^{-1}[T] \subseteq T \ \Rightarrow \ V \subseteq T$$

$$\textbf{thm\_2}: \quad \mathrm{cl}(p^{-1})[\{f\}] \cup \{f\} = V$$

$$\textbf{thm\_3}: \quad \mathrm{cl}(p)[L] \cup L = V$$

$$\textbf{thm\_4}: \quad \forall T \cdot L \subseteq T \ \wedge \ p[T] \subseteq T \ \Rightarrow \ V \subseteq T$$

$$\textbf{thm\_5}: \quad \forall S \cdot S \subseteq p[S] \ \Rightarrow \ S = \varnothing$$

$$\textbf{thm\_6}: \quad \mathrm{finite}(V)$$

$$\textbf{thm\_7}: \quad cl(p) \cap \mathrm{id} = \varnothing$$

9.7.8 Free trees

A free tree is a data structure that is often encountered in network modeling. Figure 9.18 shows a free tree. Given a finite set V (**axm_1**), a free tree is graph g with the following properties: it is a relation from V to V (**axm_2**), it is symmetric (**axm_3**), irreflexive (**axm_4**), connected (**axm_5**), and acyclic (**axm_6**) in spite of the symmetry.

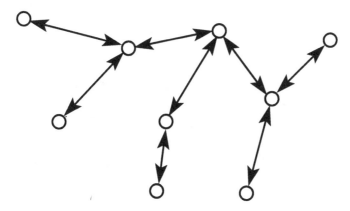

Fig. 9.18. A free tree

Axiom **axm_5** is a copy of Theorem **thm_2** of Section 9.7.2 dealing with strong connectivity. Note that axiom **axm_6** is not a copy of axiom **axm_4** of Section 9.7.7; we added the quantified variable h and two properties, namely $h \subseteq g$ and $h \cap h^{-1} = \varnothing$. This is due to the symmetry property of the graph, which we have somehow to "eliminate". The presence of h in **axm_6** has the effect of transforming the free tree into a finite tree. This is illustrated in Fig. 9.19.

$$
\begin{array}{ll}
\textbf{axm\_1}: & \text{finite}(V) \\[1.2ex]
\textbf{axm\_2}: & g \in V \leftrightarrow V \\[1.2ex]
\textbf{axm\_3}: & g \subseteq g^{-1} \\[1.2ex]
\textbf{axm\_4}: & g \cap \text{id} = \varnothing \\[1.2ex]
\textbf{axm\_5}: & \forall S \cdot S \neq \varnothing \,\wedge\, g[S] \subseteq S \,\Rightarrow\, V \subseteq S \\[1.2ex]
\textbf{axm\_6}: & \forall h, S \cdot \begin{array}[t]{l} h \subseteq g \\ h \cap h^{-1} = \varnothing \\ S \subseteq h[S] \\ \Rightarrow \\ S = \varnothing \end{array}
\end{array}
$$

Outer and inner nodes of a free tree The outer nodes of a free tree are those members x of the set V, which are connected to a single node y in the free tree:

$$\{\, x \mid x \in V \,\wedge\, \exists y \cdot g[\{x\}] = \{y\} \,\}.$$

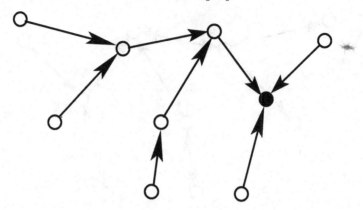

Fig. 9.19. A free tree transformed into a finite tree

The inner nodes are the other nodes. This is illustrated in Fig. 9.20, where the outer nodes are the black nodes, while the inner nodes are the white ones. The following theorem states that when a free tree is not empty, then its set of outer nodes is not empty either:

$$\mathbf{thm\_1}: \quad (\exists x \cdot V = \{x\}) \ \lor \ \exists x, y \cdot g[\{x\}] = \{y\}$$

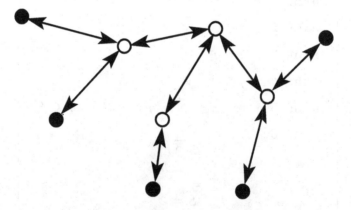

Fig. 9.20. The outer and inner nodes of the free tree

9.7.9 Well-founded relations and directed acyclic graphs

We leave it to the reader to generalize infinite trees to well-founded graphs and finite trees to directed acyclic graphs.

10

Leader election on a ring-shaped network

The purpose of this chapter is to learn more about modeling, in particular in the area of non-determinism. We are going to apply an interesting data structure: that of a ring. For this, we are going to use the general approach on advanced data structures introduced at the end of Chapter 9 (Section 9.7).

All this will be made through the study of another interesting problem in distributed computation. This example comes from a paper by Le Lann in the seventies [1].

10.1 Requirement document

We have a possibly large (but finite) number of agents, just not two as in the examples of Chapters 4 and 6 on file transfer. These agents are disposed on different sites that are connected by means of unidirectional channels forming a ring as indicated in Fig. 10.1.

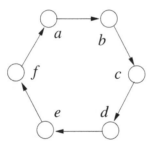

Fig. 10.1. The Ring

We have a finite set of nodes forming an oriented ring	ENV-1

Each agent is able to send messages to its right neighbor and receive ones form its left neighbor.

Each node can send a message to the next one in the ring	ENV-2

Such messages are not supposed to be transmitted immediately from one node to the next. In fact, we suppose that they can be buffered between the two and even freely reordered in these buffers:

Messages can be buffered in each node	ENV-3

This is illustrated in Fig. 10.2. As can be seen, a buffer is associated with each node.

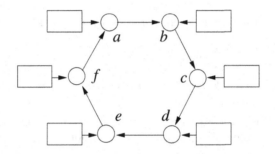

Fig. 10.2. The buffers

Messages can be re-ordered in their buffer	ENV-4

Moreover, each agent is supposed to execute the *same* piece of code.

The distributed program is made by the same piece of code executed by each node	ENV-5

The distributed execution of all these identical programs should result in a *unique agent* being "elected the leader":

The purpose of the distributed program is to have a unique node being elected the leader	FUN-1

This decision, based on certain local criteria, should be made by the winning agent itself. Of course, it must be proved that no other agent can reach the same conclusion. The determination of such a privileged agent might be useful when the ring is started or re-initiated.

Since every agent executes the same code, the problem seems to be unsolvable: what kind of distinction between them could indeed introduce a certain difference in their, otherwise homogeneous, behavior? Their position in the ring is certainly not such a distinction, since the very shape of the ring does not give the position of an agent any special distinction; no first, no last, only medium position. In fact, the only attribute that makes one agent different from the others is its name: the agents are indeed supposedly named and named differently. But by itself, this difference in names still is an homogeneous property: there is, a priori, no "more" distinction than the distinction itself.

In order to possibly introduce a supplementary distinction in these distinct names, we must have a certain structure in the name set. The simplest one we can think of is that of the natural numbers. In other words, we shall suppose that the names of the agents form a finite set of natural numbers.

Each node has a unique name which is a natural number	ENV-6

Clearly then, there exists a possible identifying distinction between these names: the largest one (or the smallest one as well). Now the problem can be restated as follows. How can one agent figure out that it bears a name that happens to be the largest number of the collection of names of all agents in the ring?

The leader must be the node with the largest name	FUN-2

10.2 Initial model

At this point, we have enough elements to start our formalization. We first define the constant set of agent names N, it is supposed to be a finite and non-empty subset of natural numbers. This is formalized in properties **axm0_1** to **axm0_3** below:

constants: N	**axm0_1:** $N \subseteq \mathbb{N}$
	axm0_2: finite(N)
	axm0_3: $N \neq \varnothing$

We have a variable w which is a node as indicated by invariant **inv0_1**. It will denote the winner of the election. Initially, w is set to any node:

variables: w	**inv0_1:** $w \in N$

As in other examples, we define a single event, here called elect, which solves the problem in one shot by assigning the maximum of N to the variable w as required by requirement FUN-2:

init	elect
$w :\in N$	$w := \max(N)$

Notice that the expression $\max(N)$ in event elect is *well defined* since the set N is finite and non-empty according to axioms **axm0_2** and **axm0_3**.

10.3 Discussion

In this section, we shall discuss various possibilities for determining the elected node as the one that bears the largest name.

10.3.1 First attempt

Here is a first simple procedure. To begin with, each agent has no choice but to send its own name to its right neighbor. An agent receiving a name from its left neighbor collects it in its private memory and sends it further to its right neighbor. When an agent receives its own name, it obviously means that it has collected all the names (since its own name must have made a complete turn of the ring) and can then decide whether its name is indeed the largest one by looking in its private collection.

However, this very primitive procedure does not work because messages can be re-ordered in the buffers as explained by requirement **ENV-4**. So that when one agent receives its own name, it does not mean that it has received all names.

10.3.2 Second attempt

The drawback of the first attempt can be circumvented by having each agent knowing the number, n, of distinct agents in the ring so that it can start the decision procedure not, as before, when receiving its own name from its left neighbor, but only after receiving n distinct agent names.

That would certainly work (although in a very tedious way), but we want to avoid agents having to know the number n in question for obvious practical reasons: the ring could be quite often dynamically extended or shrunk.

10.3.3 Third attempt

The other procedure that has been proposed resembles the first we mentioned above. But rather than transmitting systematically a name N from one agent named A to the one situated on its right, the idea is only to transmit N, provided it is strictly greater than A. Initially, each agent transmits its own name.

As a matter of fact, in the case where N is strictly smaller than A, then the potentially transmitted name cannot be the maximum we are looking for; consequently, there is no point in transmitting it since in no case could it be elected.

Finally, in the case where N is the same as A, then A is elected: its name is indeed the maximum of the agents names. We have the impression that it works, but *it certainly remains to be proved* in full generality (and in the presence of asynchronous channels, which may reorder messages in the buffers).

10.3.4 Informal presentation of the solution

The model we propose now is *not* one where we explicitly represent the channels between the nodes, or the corresponding "read" and "write" operations. We shall rather represent the actual state of the evolving situation by means of a partial function a linking some agent names x with the agent $a(x)$ which has to transmit it. We would say that x is in the buffer of $a(x)$. Notice that a is indeed a function, since no name can be in different buffers at the same time. And it is a partial function because some names are not in any buffer since they might have been eliminated. This is illustrated in Fig. 10.3. As can be seen, the function a is the following:

$$a = \{\, 1 \mapsto 6,\, 3 \mapsto 5,\, 4 \mapsto 6,\, 5 \mapsto 2,\, 6 \mapsto 4 \,\}.$$

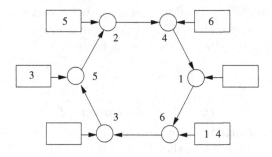

Fig. 10.3. The names in the buffers

From this state, the situation can evolve in many different ways. For example, 6 can move to node 1 since 6 is greater than 4, or 3 can be eliminated since 3 is smaller than 5, or 5 can move to node 4 since 5 is greater than 2, and so on. What appears here is a *huge non-determinism* in the way the situation is able to evolve. Initially, the agent has to transmit its name x to its neighbor in the ring. This is shown in Fig. 10.4

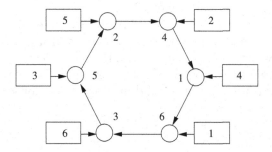

Fig. 10.4. Initial situation

Now suppose that a certain name, say 6, has moved successively to nodes 3, 5, 2, and 4 as indicated in Fig. 10.3. Name 6 is now waiting to be transmitted to node 1. Clearly, name 6 must be already greater than 3, 5, and 2 since otherwise it would not have been allowed to move to node 4. Therefore, the maximum of the set $\{6, 3, 5, 2\}$ is clearly 6. More generally, for all agent names x in the domain of a, x is the maximum of the *interval* between x and $n^{-1}(a(x))$ in the ring. And when x is the same as the node $a(x)$, then x is the maximum of the interval between this node x and node $n^{-1}(x)$, which is exactly the set N. This corresponds to the situation depicted in Fig. 10.5, where we have:

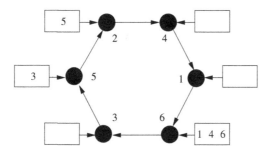

Fig. 10.5. The final situation

$$6 = \max(\{6, 3, 5, 2, 4, 1\}) = \max(N).$$

Notice that such a simple informal proof has been possible because we departed in our model from a close copy of the real environment of the future distributed program: no channels, no buffers, etc. It is important to make a clear distinction between the activity of building models and that of building programs. In the former, we are aiming at proving, hence it is convenient to use abstractions. In the latter, we are aiming at executing. Such a difference in goals induces a difference in forms.

10.4 First refinement

What we would like to do now is to completely formalize the informal proof we have presented in the previous section.

10.4.1 The state: formalizing a ring

Preliminary approach The first thing we define is the concept of a *ring*. A ring is defined on a set N by means of a function n (for next) representing the connection between each node and its, say, right neighbor. Clearly, n is a bijection from the set N to itself. We remind the reader that a bijection from a set S to a set T is a total function whose inverse is also a total function from set T to set S: it is denoted by $S \rightarrowtail\!\!\!\rightarrow T$.

constants: N, n, itvr

The next series of axioms is just a copy of some of the axioms and theorems for rings developed in Section 7.5 of Chapter 9.

---

axm1_1: $n \in N \rightarrowtail N$

axm1_2: $\forall S \cdot n^{-1}[S] \subseteq S \wedge S \neq \varnothing \Rightarrow N \subseteq S$

axm1_3: $\mathrm{itvr} \in N \rightarrow (N \rightarrow \mathbb{P}(N))$

axm1_4: $\forall x \cdot x \in N \wedge y \in N \setminus \{x\} \Rightarrow \mathrm{itvr}(x)(y) = \mathrm{itvr}(x)(n^{-1}(y)) \cup \{y\}$

axm1_5: $\forall x \cdot x \in N \Rightarrow \mathrm{itvr}(x)(n^{-1}(x)) = N$

10.4.2 The State: variables

Let us now come back to our original problem, namely electing a leader on a ring. We define the variable function a mentioned in Section 10.3.4. It is a partial function from N to itself as defined in **inv1_1**. Its main property is in **inv1_2**. It was informally stated in the Section 10.3.4. For each node x in the domain of a (remember a is only a partial function), x is the maximum of the interval starting in x and ending in $n^{-1}(a(x))$:

---

constants: w, a

inv1_1: $a \in N \nrightarrow N$

inv1_2: $\forall f \cdot f \in \mathrm{dom}\,(a) \Rightarrow f = \max(\mathrm{itvr}(f)(n^{-1}(a(f))))$

10.4.3 Events

Next are the events: **elect** that was already present in the abstraction and the new events **accept** and **reject**.

---

init
$w :\in N$
$a := n$

---

elect
  any x **where**
    $x \in \mathrm{dom}\,(a)$
    $x = a(x)$
  then
    $w := x$
  end

---

accept
  any x **where**
    $x \in \mathrm{dom}\,(a)$
    $a(x) < x$
  then
    $a(x) := n(a(x))$
  end

---

reject
  any x **where**
    $x \in \mathrm{dom}\,(a)$
    $x < a(x)$
  then
    $a := \{x\} \lhd a$
  end

Notice that the event **elect** in the abstraction has now become a parameterized event and the two new events **accept** and **reject** are also parameterized events. In all cases, the quantified variable x denotes a node that is in the domain of the function a.

10.5 Proofs

In this section, we give semi-formal proofs for the refinement of event **elect** and new events **accept** and **reject**. We also give an informal proof for the convergence of the new events. We close this section with an informal proof of deadlock freeness.

Notice that when using the proof obligation rules in each case, we shall only give parts of the elements required by each of them. In other words, we shall only give the properties and invariants that are needed in the proof, otherwise the complete transcription of the rules would be completely unreadable.

10.5.1 Proof for event elect

The refinement proof of event **elect**, which we show below together with its abstraction, does not require us to use the proof obligation rule GRD since the abstraction has no guard; it does not require the use of the proof obligation rule INV on the two invariants **inv1_1** and **inv1_2** since these invariants do not contain any references to variable w, which is the only variable modified by concrete event **elect**:

(abstract-)elect
$w := \max(N)$

(concrete-)elect
   any x **where**
     $x \in \mathrm{dom}\,(a)$
     $x = a(x)$
   then
     $w := x$
   end

The only proof obligation rule that remains to be used is then rule SIM, since the variable w is common to the two spaces and is modified by both events.

Axiom **axm1_5**	$\forall x \cdot (\, x \in N \;\Rightarrow\; \mathrm{itvr}(x)(n^{-1}(x)) = N \,)$
Invariant **inv1_1**	$a \in N \nrightarrow N$
Invariant **inv1_2**	$\forall f \cdot f \in \mathrm{dom}\,(a) \;\Rightarrow\; f = \max(\mathrm{itvr}(f)(n^{-1}(a(f))))$
Concrete guard	$x \in \mathrm{dom}\,(a)$
of event **elect**	$x = a(x)$
$\vdash$	$\vdash$
Equality of actions on	$x = \max(N).$
common variable w	

The proof is easy. We instantiate in both universal quantifications the quantified variable with x, yielding the following after some simplifications:

$$\text{itvr}(x)(n^{-1}(x)) = N$$
$$x = \max\left(\text{itvr}(x)(n^{-1}(a(x)))\right)$$
$$x = a(x)$$
$$\vdash$$
$$x = \max(N).$$

Then we replace $a(x)$ by x, yielding the following, which is obvious:

$$\text{itvr}(x)(n^{-1}(x)) = N$$
$$x = \max(\text{itvr}(x)(n^{-1}(x)))$$
$$\vdash$$
$$x = \max(N).$$

10.5.2 *Proof for event* accept

The new event accept is shown below:

```
accept
    any x where
        x ∈ dom (a)
        a(x) < x
    then
        a(x) := n(a(x))
    end
```

It must refine skip, which is obvious, since it does not touch the abstract variable w. We have first to prove that it preserves invariants **inv1_1**. This is stated as follows by using proof obligation rule INV:

inv1_1	$a \in N \nrightarrow N$
guards of event	$x \in \text{dom}(a)$
accept	$a(x) < x$
$\vdash$	$\vdash$
Modifed invariant **inv1_1**	$(\{x\} \ntriangleleft a) \cup \{x \mapsto n(a(x))\} \in N \nrightarrow N$

This is obvious since the left-hand side of the goal of this sequent is made of the union of two partial functions from N to N with non-intersecting domains. Then we have to prove that event **accept** preserves invariant **inv1_2**. The statement to prove is as follows by using proof obligation rule INV and after some simplifications:

Axiom **axm1_4**

$$\forall x, y \cdot \begin{pmatrix} x \in N \\ y \in N \setminus \{x\} \\ \Rightarrow \\ \text{itvr}(x)(y) = \text{itvr}(x)(n^{-1}(y)) \cup \{y\} \end{pmatrix}$$

Invariant **inv1_1** $ra \in N \nrightarrow N$
Invariant **inv1_2** $\forall f \cdot f \in \text{dom}(a) \Rightarrow f = \max(\text{itvr}(f)(n^{-1}(a(f))))$
Guards of event $x \in \text{dom}(a)$
accept $a(x) < x$
$\vdash$ $\vdash$
Modified invariant **inv1_2** $\forall f \cdot \begin{pmatrix} f \in \text{dom}(a \lhdominus \{x \mapsto n(a(x))\}) \\ \Rightarrow \\ x = \max(\text{itvr}(x)(n^{-1}((a \lhdominus \{x \mapsto n(a(x))\})(f)))) \end{pmatrix}.$

The universal quantification of the consequent can be decomposed (using rules ALL_R and IMP_R), yielding:

$$\forall x, y \cdot \begin{pmatrix} x \in N \\ y \in N \setminus \{x\} \\ \Rightarrow \\ \text{itvr}(x)(y) = \text{itvr}(x)(n^{-1}(y)) \cup \{y\} \end{pmatrix}$$
$a \in N \nrightarrow N$
$\forall f \cdot f \in \text{dom}(a) \Rightarrow f = \max(\text{itvr}(f)(n^{-1}(a(f))))$
$x \in \text{dom}(a)$
$a(x) < x$
$f \in \text{dom}(a \lhdominus \{x \mapsto n(a(x))\})$
$\vdash$
$f = \max(\text{itvr}(f)(n^{-1}((a \lhdominus \{x \mapsto n(a(x))\})(f)))).$

We now proceed with a *proof by cases*. We consider in turn the case where f is equal to x and then where it is different from x. Note that this is very frequently the case with proofs dealing with expressions containing the overriding operator $\lhdominus$.

First case: $f = x$ Notice that:

$$n^{-1}((a \lhdominus \{x \mapsto n(a(x))\})(x))$$

reduces to:

$$n^{-1}(n(a(x))),$$

that is, to $a(x)$ since n is a bijection. This yields:

$$\forall x,y \cdot \left(\begin{array}{l} x \in N \\ y \in N \setminus \{x\} \\ \Rightarrow \\ \mathrm{itvr}(x)(y) = \mathrm{itvr}(x)(n^{-1}(y)) \cup \{y\} \end{array} \right)$$
$$a \in N \twoheadrightarrow N$$
$$\forall f \cdot f \in \mathrm{dom}\,(a) \Rightarrow f = \max(\mathrm{itvr}(f)(n^{-1}(a(f))))$$
$$x \in \mathrm{dom}\,(a)$$
$$a(x) < x$$
$$\vdash$$
$$x = \max(\mathrm{itvr}(x)(a(x))).$$

In the first universal quantification, we instantiate x with x and y with $a(x)$. Notice that we have indeed $x \neq a(x)$ since $a(x) < x$. This yields:

$$\mathrm{itvr}(x)(a(x)) = \mathrm{itvr}(x)(n^{-1}(a(x))) \cup \{a(x)\}.$$

We can thus replace $\mathrm{itvr}(x)(a(x))$ by $\mathrm{itvr}(x)(n^{-1}(a(x)))\cup\{a(x)\}$ in $\max(\mathrm{itvr}(x)(a(x)))$. We also instantiate f with x in the second universal quantification. We thus obtain eventually the following:

$$x = \max(\mathrm{itvr}(x)(n^{-1}(a(x))))$$
$$a(x) < x$$
$$\vdash$$
$$x = \max(\mathrm{itvr}(x)(n^{-1}(a(x))) \cup \{a(x)\}).$$

This can be discharged easily by noticing that for two finite and non-empty sets of numbers s and t we have $\max(s \cup t) = \max(\{\max(s), \max(t)\})$. Finally, we also have for any number a: $\max(\{a\}) = a$. This yields the following, which is obvious:

$$a(x) < x$$
$$\vdash$$
$$x = \max(\{x, a(x)\}).$$

Second case: $f \neq x$ This yields:

$$a \in N \twoheadrightarrow N$$
$$\forall f \cdot f \in \mathrm{dom}\,(a) \Rightarrow f = \max(\mathrm{itvr}(f)(n^{-1}(a(f))))$$
$$f \in \mathrm{dom}\,(a)$$
$$\vdash$$
$$f = \max(\mathrm{itvr}(f)(n^{-1}(a(f)))).$$

By instantiating f in the universal quantification with f, we obtain the following, which is discharged by rule HYP:

$$f = \max(\mathrm{itvr}(f)(n^{-1}(a(f))))$$
$$\vdash$$
$$f = \max(\mathrm{itvr}(f)(n^{-1}(a(f)))).$$

10.5.3 Proofs for event reject

We leave it as an exercise for the reader to generate the proof statements for event reject and give them some informal proofs similar to the one we have just given for event accept.

10.5.4 Proof of non-divergence of the new events

We have to exhibit a variant quantity that will be decreased by both the new events accept and reject. Clearly event reject decreases the number of elements in the set $\mathrm{dom}(a)$ since it transforms a into $\{x\} \lhd a$, whereas the guards contain the condition $x \in \mathrm{dom}(a)$. But unfortunately, it is not the case for event accept, which only moves forward x from $a(x)$ to $n(a(x))$. But, in doing so, it certainly decreases the number of elements in the interval from $a(x)$ to x: $\mathrm{itvr}(a(x))(x)$.

The previous remark gives us a clue. We can take as a variant the sum of the cardinals of the various sets $\mathrm{itvr}(a(x))(x)$ for all x in the domain of a. This quantity is also decreased by the event reject, since it removes completely one of these intervals from the sum in question.

$$\textbf{variant1:} \quad \sum_{x \in \mathrm{dom}(a)} \textbf{card}\,(\mathrm{itvr}(a(x))(x))$$

Notice that the decrease in this variant can be proved by showing that the finite set:

$$\{\, x \mapsto y \mid x \in \mathrm{dom}(a) \ \wedge \ y \in \mathrm{itvr}(a(x))(x) \,\}$$

is made strictly smaller by the new event. Replacing the decrease in a variant of the sum of the cardinals of a finite set by the equivalent decrease in this set is generally a better technique than performing the proof directly on the cardinals.

10.5.5 Proof of deadlock freeness

The proof of deadlock freeness is easy when considering the various guards as shown below. Their disjunction is obviously true provided we are sure that $\mathrm{dom}(a)$ is never empty; a new invariant that we have to add and thus prove:

Event	Guard
elect	$\exists x \cdot (x \in \mathrm{dom}(a) \ \wedge \ x = a(x))$
accept	$\exists x \cdot (x \in \mathrm{dom}(a) \ \wedge \ a(x) < x)$
reject	$\exists x \cdot (x \in \mathrm{dom}(a) \ \wedge \ x < a(x))$

inv1_3: $\mathrm{dom}(a) \neq \varnothing$

10.6 Reference

[1] G. Le Lann. Distributed systems – towards a formal approach. In B. Gilchrist, editor, *Information Processing* **77**. North-Holland, 1977.

11

Synchronizing a tree-shaped network

In this chapter, we develop another distributed program example, where we shall encounter another interesting mathematical object: a tree. We shall thus learn how to formalize such a data structure and see how we can fruitfully reason about it using an induction rule. This example has been treated by many researchers; we have taken it from the following books [1], [2].

11.1 Introduction

In this example, we have a network of nodes, which is slightly more complicated than in the previous chapter, where we were dealing with a ring. Here we have a finite tree as indicated in Fig. 11.1.

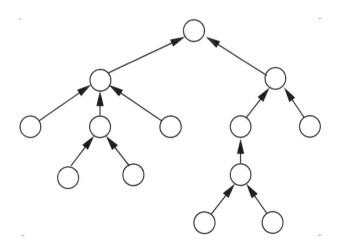

Fig. 11.1. A tree-shaped network

We have a set of nodes forming a finite tree	ENV-1

At each node of the tree, we have a process performing a certain task, which is the same for all processes (the exact nature of this task is not important). The constraint we want these processes to observe is that they remain *synchronized*. In other words, not one of them should be able to progress too much with regard to the others. In order to formalize this synchronization constraint, we assign a counter to each node of the tree. Intuitively, each counter represents the phase within which each process is currently running:

Each node has a counter, which is a natural number	FUN-1

In order to express that each process is at most one phase ahead of the others, we simply state that the difference between any two of these counters is at most equal to 1. This is illustrated in Fig. 11.2.

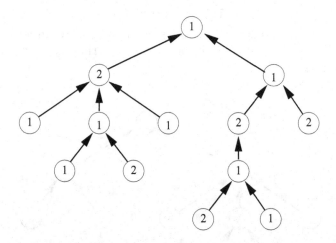

Fig. 11.2. A tree with counters at the nodes

The difference between any two counters is at most equal to 1	FUN-2

An additional constraint of our distributed algorithm states that each process can *read the counters of its immediate neighbors only*:

Each node can only read the counter of its immediate neighbors in the tree	FUN-3

Moreover, each process is *allowed to modify its own counter only*:

The counter of a node can be modified by this node only	FUN-4

One of the most important aspects of our approach is that the local constraint as expressed in FUN-3 has not to be followed right from the beginning of the construction process. During the early phases, we feel free to magically have access everywhere from any node. During the refining phases however, we shall gradually strengthen the guards of the events so that this local constraint will be obeyed eventually. Again, this reveals an important distinction between a model and a program.

11.2 Initial model

11.2.1 The state

We now proceed with the first formalization. The network is defined from a carrier set N of nodes. Our only property about this set is that it is finite. This is expressed as axiom **axm0_1**:

sets: N	**axm0_1:** finite(N)

At this stage, we do not need to define the tree, the only state variable we have is the function c defining the counter value at each node (all initialized to 0). We now define two invariants involving c. First its basic invariant, **inv0_1**, stating that c is a total function from N to the set $\mathbb{N}$ natural numbers, and then another invariant, **inv0_2**, expressing the basic synchronizing requirement, FUN-2: the difference between two node counters is at most 1, so that each counter value is kept smaller than or equal to the value of any other counter plus 1:

variable: c	**inv0_1:** $c \in N \rightarrow \mathbb{N}$
	inv0_2: $\forall x, y \cdot x \in N \land y \in N \Rightarrow c(x) \leq c(y) + 1$

Invariant **inv0_2** seems a bit surprising at first glance. Does it state that the difference between the values of two counters is at most equal to 1? Let a and b be two such values. If $a \leq b$, then we have $b = a + d$ with $d \geq 0$, then we certainly have $a + d \leq a + 1$ (that is, $d \leq 1$) since $b \leq a + 1$ according to **inv0_2**. In other words, in the case where $a \leq b$, then $b - a \in 0 .. 1$. A similar reasoning would show that if $b \leq a$, then $a - b \in 0 .. 1$.

11.2.2 The events

Besides event init, our only other event, increment, makes explicit the conditions under which a node n can progress. It is obviously the case when its counter $c(n)$ is not greater than that of any other counter m, that is when $c(n) \leq c(m)$. It is in this case only that the node can increment its own counter without destroying the synchronizing invariant **inv0_2**. As can be seen (and as announced above), we have supposed that a given node n has free access to all other nodes in the tree. Again, this is because we are here in an abstraction where every access is still possible. Note how we initialize the counters in event init to be all equal to 0:

$$
\boxed{
\begin{array}{l}
\text{init} \\
\quad c := N \times \{0\}
\end{array}
}
$$

$$
\boxed{
\begin{array}{l}
\text{increment} \\
\quad \textbf{any} \ \ n \ \ \textbf{where} \\
\qquad n \in N \\
\qquad \forall m \cdot m \in N \ \Rightarrow \ c(n) \leq c(m) \\
\quad \textbf{then} \\
\qquad c(n) := c(n) + 1 \\
\quad \textbf{end}
\end{array}
}
$$

11.2.3 The proofs

The proofs of the statements expressing that event init establishes the invariants are trivial. We shall only informally develop the proof of the statement expressing the preservation of invariant **inv0_2** by event increment. Here is what we have to prove:

Invariant **inv0_1**	$c \in N \to \mathbb{N}$
Invariant **inv0_2**	$\forall x, y \cdot x \in N \ \wedge \ y \in N \ \Rightarrow \ c(x) \leq c(y) + 1$
Guards of	$n \in N$
event increment	$\forall m \cdot m \in N \ \Rightarrow \ c(n) \leq c(m)$
$\vdash$	$\vdash$
Mod. inv. **inv0_2**	$\forall x, y \cdot x \in N \ \wedge \ y \in N \ \Rightarrow \ (c \mathbin{\lhd\mkern-9mu-} \{n \mapsto c(n) + 1\})(x) \leq$
	$\qquad\qquad\qquad\qquad\qquad (c \mathbin{\lhd\mkern-9mu-} \{n \mapsto c(n) + 1\})(y) + 1$

This statement can be simplified to the following by removing the universal quantification in the consequent and then moving both predicates $x \in N$ and $y \in N$ in the antecedent (rules ALL_R and IMP_R):

$$c \in N \to \mathbb{N}$$
$$\forall x, y \cdot x \in N \wedge y \in N \ \Rightarrow\ c(x) \leq c(y) + 1$$
$$n \in N$$
$$\forall m \cdot m \in N \ \Rightarrow\ c(n) \leq c(m)$$
$$x \in N$$
$$y \in N$$
$$\vdash$$
$$(c \lessdot \{n \mapsto c(n) + 1\})(x) \ \leq\ (c \lessdot \{n \mapsto c(n) + 1\})(y) + 1$$

The proof now proceeds by cases (four of them, in fact) as is usual when we deal with the overriding operator $\lessdot$:

(1) When x and y are both equal to n, then it results in the following goal, which is trivial:

$$c(n) + 1 \ \leq\ c(n) + 1 + 1.$$

(2) When x is equal to n while y is not, then it results in the following goal, which is trivial according to the guarding condition, $\forall m \cdot m \in N \ \Rightarrow\ c(n) \leq c(m)$ of event ascending (instantiate m with y):

$$c(n) + 1 \ \leq\ c(y) + 1.$$

(3) When x is not equal to n while y is, then it results in the following goal, which is trivial according to invariant **inv0_2** (instantiate x with x and y with n):

$$c(x) \ \leq\ c(n) + 1.$$

(4) When x and y are both not equal to n, then it results in the following goal, which is trivial according to invariant **inv0_2** (instantiate x with x and y with y):

$$c(x) \ \leq\ c(y) + 1.$$

Note that such a proof can be done automatically by a prover.

11.3 First refinement

11.3.1 The state

The problem with the guard of the event ascending proposed in the previous section (it is copied below) is that we have to compare the value $c(n)$ of the counter at node

n, with that of *all* other counters $c(m)$.

```
increment
    any  n  where
        n ∈ N
        ∀m · m ∈ N  ⇒  c(n) ≤ c(m)
    then
        c(n) := c(n) + 1
    end
```

In order to solve this problem (partially in this refinement), we have to introduce the tree structure of the network. This is what we are going to do in this section. The tree is defined by three constants: its root r, a set of leafs L, and also its parent function f. We borrow the axiomatic definition of finite trees as well as the tree induction rule presented in Section 9.7.7 of Chapter 9.

$$\textbf{constants:}\quad r$$
$$L$$
$$f$$

axm1_1 : $r \in N$

axm1_2 : $L \subseteq N$

axm1_3 : $f \in N \setminus \{r\} \twoheadrightarrow N \setminus L$

axm1_4 : $\forall T \cdot r \in T \wedge f^{-1}[T] \subseteq T \Rightarrow N \subseteq T$

In order to limit the number of comparisons which a node had to perform in the abstract version of event **increment**, the idea is to suppose that the value $c(r)$ of the counter at the root r of the tree is always smaller than or equal to that of any other counter. We have thus $c(r) \le c(m)$ for *all* nodes m. In that case, it is sufficient to reduce the guard of event **increment** to a mere comparison of $c(n)$ with $c(r)$. When the equality holds, that is when we have $c(n) = c(r)$, then clearly $c(n) \le c(m)$ holds for *all* nodes m and we can thus safely increment the counter of n. We could have stated the above rule – that is, $c(r) \le c(m)$ for all nodes m – as an invariant, but we choose to have the following more primitive invariant **inv1_1**:

inv1_1: $\forall m \cdot m \in N \setminus \{r\} \Rightarrow c(f(m)) \le c(m)$

In order to maintain the property $c(r) \le c(m)$ for *all* nodes m, it is sufficient to have the counter of the parent of each node m (except the root which has no parent) being kept smaller than or equal to that of its offspring m. In other words, $c(f(m)) \leq c(m)$ must hold for each node m except the root r: this is invariant **inv1_1**. As a consequence, the counters are incremented by *waves* moving up as illustrated in Fig. 11.3. Here is the theorem we want eventually to prove:

$$\textbf{thm1\_1:} \quad \forall m \cdot m \in N \Rightarrow c(r) \leq c(m)$$

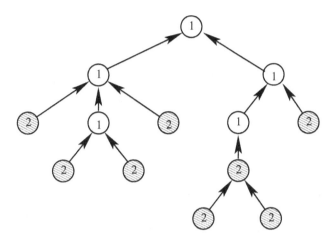

Fig. 11.3. An ascending wave

11.3.2 The events

In order to maintain our new invariant **inv1_1**, we have to strengthen the guard of event ascending (a new name for abstract event increment) by ensuring that the counter of node n is distinct from that of each of its offspring:

```
init
    c := N × {0}
```

```
ascending
    refines
        increment
    any n where
        n ∈ N
        c(n) = c(r)
        ∀m · m ∈ f⁻¹[{n}] ⇒ c(n) ≠ c(m)
    then
        c(n) := c(n) + 1
    end
```

Note that the comparisons of $c(n)$ in node n are now limited to the counters $c(m)$ of the set of children, $f^{-1}[\{n\}]$, of node n, which is allowed according to requirement FUN-3 since node n and m are next to each other. But we also compare $c(n)$ with $c(r)$, which is not acceptable since nodes n and r are not in general next to each other. This problem will be solved in the next refinement.

11.3.3 *The proofs*

In order to ease the proof, we introduce the following two theorems, which are easily deductible from the invariants:

$$\textbf{thm1\_2:} \quad \forall n \cdot n \in N \; \Rightarrow \; c(n) \; \in \; c(r) \mathbin{..} c(r) + 1$$

$$\textbf{thm1\_3:} \quad \forall n \cdot n \in N \setminus \{r\} \; \Rightarrow \; c(n) \; \in \; c(f(n)) \mathbin{..} c(f(n)) + 1$$

The proof of **thm1_1** is done by tree induction under the assumption of **inv1_1**. Let us recall that the tree induction rule IND_TREE, which was introduced in Section 9.7.6 of Chapter 9. We adapt it by instantiating V to N, t to r, p to f, and x to m yielding:

$$\frac{\text{H} \vdash \text{P}(r) \qquad \text{H}, \; m \in N \setminus \{r\}, \; \text{P}(f(m)) \vdash \text{P}(m)}{\text{H}, \; m \in N \vdash \text{P}(m)} \quad \begin{array}{l} \text{IND\_TREE} \\[4pt] (\text{m } \underline{\text{nfin}} \text{ H}) \end{array}$$

Here $\text{P}(m)$ is $c(r) \leq c(m)$. Next is the proof of **thm1_1** after applying rules ALL_R and IMP_R:

$$
\begin{array}{l}
\forall m \cdot m \in N \setminus \{r\} \Rightarrow c(f(m)) \leq c(m) \\
m \in N \\
\vdash \\
c(r) \leq c(m)
\end{array}
\quad \text{IND\_TREE}
\left\{
\begin{array}{l}
\begin{array}{l}
\forall m \cdot m \in N \setminus \{r\} \Rightarrow c(f(m)) \leq c(m) \\
\vdash \\
c(r) \leq c(r)
\end{array} \quad \text{ARI} \\[20pt]
\begin{array}{l}
\forall m \cdot m \in N \setminus \{r\} \Rightarrow c(f(m)) \leq c(m) \\
m \in N \setminus \{r\} \\
c(r) \leq c(f(m)) \\
\vdash \\
c(r) \leq c(m)
\end{array} \quad \text{ALL\_L} \ldots
\end{array}
\right.
$$

We instantiate now m in the first assumption with m:

$$\dots \quad \frac{\begin{array}{l} m \in N \setminus \{r\} \Rightarrow c(f(m)) \leq c(m) \\ m \in N \setminus \{r\} \\ c(r) \leq c(f(m)) \\ \vdash \\ c(r) \leq c(m) \end{array}}{} \quad \text{IMP\_L} \quad \frac{\begin{array}{l} c(f(m)) \leq c(m) \\ m \in N \setminus \{r\} \\ c(r) \leq c(f(m)) \\ \vdash \\ c(r) \leq c(m) \end{array}}{} \quad \text{ARI} \quad \frac{\begin{array}{l} c(f(m)) \leq c(m) \\ x \in N \setminus \{r\} \\ c(r) \leq c(f(m)) \\ c(r) \leq c(m) \\ \vdash \\ c(r) \leq c(m) \end{array}}{} \quad \text{HYP}$$

11.4 Second refinement

It remains now for us to replace the test $c(r) = c(n)$ in the guard of the previous version of event ascending (copied below) by a more local test.

---

ascending
   any n **where**
      $n \in N$
      $c(n) = c(r)$
      $\forall m \cdot m \in f^{-1}[\{n\}] \Rightarrow c(n) \neq c(m)$
   then
      $c(n) := c(n) + 1$
   end

The problem is that of having the nodes informed that the value of the counter at the root is indeed equal to that of their local counter. This is clearly the case when an incrementing wave has reached the root, where then all nodes have the same value.

When this situation is reached, the idea is to have a second wave going down and gradually informing the nodes that the value of the c counter at the root r is the same as the value of all other c counters. For this, we need a second counter d at each node to hold the second descending wave. This is indicated in Fig. 11.4, where the second counter d is the one indicated on the left of each node.

This second wave goes down as illustrated in Fig. 11.5. In this refinement, we shall just define the d counters (this is done in invariant **inv2_1** below) together with the basic property that the difference between two d counters does not exceed 1 (invariant **inv2_2**). Note that this property is of the same nature as that expressed in invariant **inv0_1** in the initial model for c counters. Formally:

---

variable: c, d

---

inv2_1: $d \in N \rightarrow \mathbb{N}$

inv2_2: $\forall x, y \cdot x \in N \wedge y \in N \Rightarrow d(x) \leq d(y) + 1$

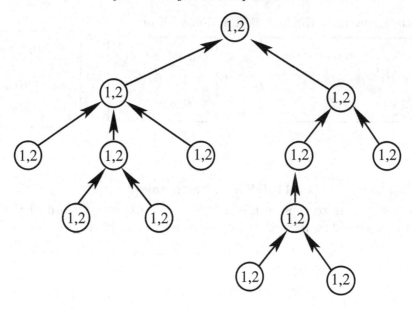

Fig. 11.4. Enlarging the state with a second counter

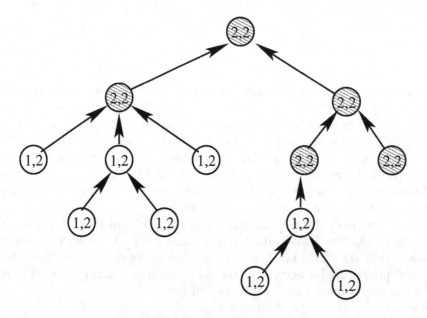

Fig. 11.5. The descending wave

We now have to extend event **init** in a straightforward fashion and also add a new event, **descending**, corresponding to the incrementation of the d counters when appropriate. Again, note the analogy with what we did in the initial model with the c counters:

$$
\boxed{
\begin{aligned}
&\text{init} \\
&\quad c \;:=\; N \times \{0\} \\
&\quad d \;:=\; N \times \{0\}
\end{aligned}
}
$$

$$
\boxed{
\begin{aligned}
&\text{descending} \\
&\quad \textbf{any} \quad n \quad \textbf{where} \\
&\qquad n \in N \\
&\qquad \forall m \cdot m \in N \;\Rightarrow\; d(n) \le d(m) \\
&\quad \textbf{then} \\
&\qquad d(n) := d(n) + 1 \\
&\quad \textbf{end}
\end{aligned}
}
$$

Event ascending has not been touched in this refinement; hence we have not copied it above. We leave it to the reader to prove that this superposition refinement is correct. Do not forget to prove that the new event does not diverge and also that the system does not deadlock.

11.5 Third refinement

In this third refinement, we are going to perform two tasks: first, we construct the descending wave of the d counters incrementation very much in the same way as we did for the ascending wave of the c counters incrementation in Section 3; and, second, we establish the relationship between the c and the d counters. Note that we do not extend the state. We have thus here a special case of superposition: the concrete state is exactly the same as the abstract one.

11.5.1 *Refining event* ascending

The first invariant we introduce, **inv3_1**, is very much of the same nature as invariant **inv1_1**, introduced in the first refinement for the c counters (Section 11.3.1), which we repeat:

$$
\boxed{\textbf{inv1\_1:} \quad \forall m \cdot m \in N \setminus \{r\} \;\Rightarrow\; c(f(m)) \le c(m)}
$$

The d counter at a node m is not greater than that of its parent node $f(m)$. It is what makes the wave descending:

$$
\boxed{\textbf{inv3\_1:} \quad \forall m \cdot m \in N \setminus \{r\} \;\Rightarrow\; d(m) \le d(f(m))}
$$

With this invariant and the induction rule IND_TREE mentioned in Section 11.5.3, we can easily prove the following theorem, which is of the same nature as **thm1_1** of Section 11.5.3. It says that the d counters are are not greater than the value $d(r)$:

$$\boxed{\textbf{thm3\_1:} \quad \forall n \cdot n \in N \Rightarrow d(n) \leq d(r)}$$

It remains for us to establish the connection between $c(r)$ and $d(r)$. In fact, the latter is never greater than the former. It is expressed in the following invariant:

$$\boxed{\textbf{inv3\_2:} \quad d(r) \leq c(r)}$$

Thanks to these invariants, we can refine event **ascending** as follows:

(abstract-)ascending	(concrete-)ascending
any n **where**	**any** n **where**
$\quad n \in N$	$\quad n \in N$
$\quad c(n) = c(r)$	$\quad c(n) = d(n)$
$\quad \forall m \cdot m \in f^{-1}[\{n\}] \Rightarrow c(n) \neq c(m)$	$\quad \forall m \cdot m \in f^{-1}[\{n\}] \Rightarrow c(n) \neq c(m)$
then	**then**
$\quad c(n) := c(n) + 1$	$\quad c(n) := c(n) + 1$
end	**end**

As can be seen, the only difference between the abstract and concrete versions of these events is the replacement of the abstract guard $c(n) = c(r)$ by the concrete one $c(n) = d(n)$. As a consequence, we just have to prove that the latter implies the former (guard strengthening), which is trivial:

$$
\begin{array}{ll}
\text{concrete guard} & c(n) = d(n) \\
\text{according to } \textbf{thm3\_1} & d(n) \leq d(r) \\
\text{invariant } \textbf{inv3\_2} & d(r) \leq c(r) \\
\text{according to } \textbf{thm1\_1} & c(r) \leq c(n) \\
\vdash & \vdash \\
\text{abstract guard} & c(n) = c(r)
\end{array}
$$

We have now reached our goal concerning event **ascending**: it is indeed accessing its neighbors' counters only as required by requirement FUN-3.

11.5.2 Refining event descending

We now turn our attention to event **descending**. In fact, the abstract **descending** event has to be split into two events: one dealing with any node n except the root r and another one dealing with the root node r. Here is the proposal for the first case together with the abstraction:

```
(abstract-)descending
    any  n  where
        n ∈ N
        ∀m · m ∈ N ⇒ d(n) ≤ d(m)
    then
        d(n) := d(n) + 1
    end
```

```
(concrete-)descending_1
    any  n  where
        n ∈ N \ {r}
        d(n) ≠ d(f(n))
    then
        d(n) := d(n) + 1
    end
```

We notice that in the concrete version the node n follows requirement FUN-3: it only accesses the value of counters d at n and at $f(n)$, the parent node of n. The only difference between the two versions concerns again the guards. The abstract guard $\forall m \cdot m \in N \Rightarrow d(n) \leq d(m)$ is replaced by the concrete one $d(n) \neq d(f(n))$. We have then again just to prove that the concrete guard implies the abstract one. It amounts to proving:

$$n \in N \setminus \{r\}$$
$$d(n) \neq d(f(n))$$
$$m \in N$$
$$\vdash$$
$$d(n) \leq d(m)$$

To prove this statement, we can first prove the following simple theorems:

thm3_2: $\forall n \cdot n \in N \setminus \{r\} \Rightarrow d(f(n)) \in d(n) .. d(n) + 1$

thm3_3: $\forall n \cdot n \in N \Rightarrow d(r) \in d(n) .. d(n) + 1$

From $d(n) \neq d(f(n))$ and **thm3_2**, we deduce $d(f(n)) = d(n) + 1$. By instantiating n in **thm3_3** successively with $\overline{f}(n)$ and m, we obtain $d(r) \in d(f(n)) .. d(f(n)) + 1$ and $d(r) \in d(m) .. d(m) + 1$. We are thus left to prove the following, which is trivial (the assumptions yield: $d(n) + 1 \leq d(r) \leq d(m) + 1$):

$$d(r) \in d(n) + 1 \mathrel{..} d(n) + 2$$
$$d(r) \in d(m) \mathrel{..} d(m) + 1$$
$$\vdash$$
$$d(n) \leq d(m)$$

We now have to consider the second case for the **descending** event. Here is the proposal:

(abstract-)descending
  any n **where**
    $n \in N$
    $\forall m \cdot m \in N \Rightarrow d(n) \leq d(m)$
  then
    $d(n) := d(n) + 1$
  end

(concrete-)descending_2
  when
    $d(r) \neq c(r)$
  then
    $d(r) := d(r) + 1$
  end

Again, the concrete version follows requirement **FUN-3** as node r only accesses the c and d counters of this node. We have a case here where the abstract event is introduced by an **any** construct, whereas the concrete one is introduced by a **when** construct. We have to provide a witness, which is clearly r for n in the abstraction. As a consequence, the two actions are now the same and the only statement to prove is again the strengthening of the guard. After some simplification, it amounts to proving:

$$d(r) \neq c(r)$$
$$m \in N$$
$$\Rightarrow$$
$$d(r) \leq d(m)$$

Now suppose that we have the following theorem:

thm3_4: $\forall n \cdot n \in N \Rightarrow c(r) \in d(n) \mathrel{..} d(n) + 1$

We can instantiate this theorem first with r yielding $c(r) \in d(r) \mathrel{..} d(r) + 1$. But we have $d(r) \neq c(r)$. As a consequence, we have $c(r) = d(r) + 1$. We now instantiate **thm3_4** with m yielding $c(r) \in d(m) \mathrel{..} d(m) + 1$. We are thus left to prove the following, which is trivial:

$$d(r) + 1 \in d(m) \mathrel{..} d(m) + 1$$
$$\vdash$$
$$d(r) \leq d(m)$$

11.5.3 Proving theorem thm3_4

It now remains for us to prove **thm3_4**. For this we have to introduce a new invariant, namely:

$$\boxed{\textbf{inv3\_3:} \quad \forall n \cdot n \in N \;\Rightarrow\; c(n) \in d(n)\,..\,d(n)+1}$$

Note that invariant **inv3_2**, stating that $d(r)$ is not greater than $c(r)$, can be transformed into a mere theorem as it is clearly implied by invariant **inv3_3**. Theorem **thm3_4** can now be proved from invariant **inv3_3** and theorems **thm3_1** and **thm1_2**. Here is what we have to prove:

Theorem **thm3_1**	$\forall n \cdot n \in N \;\Rightarrow\; d(n) \le d(r)$
Invariant **inv3_3**	$\forall n \cdot n \in N \;\Rightarrow\; c(n) \in d(n)\,..\,d(n)+1$
Theorem **thm1_2**	$\forall n \cdot n \in N \;\Rightarrow\; c(n) \in c(r)\,..\,c(r)+1$
$\vdash$	$\vdash$
Theorem **thm3_4**	$\forall n \cdot n \in N \;\Rightarrow\; c(r) \in d(n)\,..\,d(n)+1$

By properly instantiating and simplifying the previous statement, we obtain the following, which is trivially true (the two first antecedents yields $d(n) \le d(r) \le c(r)$, whereas the last two yields $c(r) \le c(n) \le d(n)+1$):

Theorem **thm3_1** instantiated with n	$d(n) \le d(r)$
Invariant **inv3_3** instantiated with r	$c(r) \in d(r)\,..\,d(r)+1$
Theorem **thm1_2** instantiated with n	$c(n) \in c(r)\,..\,c(r)+1$
Invariant **inv3_3** instantiated with n	$c(n) \in d(n)\,..\,d(n)+1$
$\vdash$	$\vdash$
Theorem **thm3_4**	$c(r) \in d(n)\,..\,d(n)+1$

11.5.4 Proving preservation of invariant inv3_3

It remains now for us to prove that the new invariant **inv3_3** is indeed preserved by the proposed events. Here is what we have to prove for event **ascending** to preserve invariant **inv3_3**:

Invariant **inv3_3**	$\forall m \cdot m \in N \;\Rightarrow\; c(m) \in d(m)\,..\,d(m)+1$
Guard of **ascending**	$n \in N$
	$c(n) = d(n)$
	$\forall m \cdot m \in f^{-1}[\{n\}] \;\Rightarrow\; c(n) \neq c(m)$
$\vdash$	$\vdash$
Mod. inv. **inv3_3**	$\forall n \cdot m \in N \;\Rightarrow\; (c \lhdminus \{n \mapsto c(n)+1\})(m) \in d(m)\,..\,d(m)+1$

This can be rearranged as:

$$\begin{array}{l} \forall m \cdot m \in N \;\Rightarrow\; c(m) \;\in\; d(m) \ldots d(m) + 1 \\ n \in N \\ c(n) = d(n) \\ m \in N \\ \vdash \\ c \nleftarrow \{n \mapsto c(n) + 1\})(m) \;\in\; d(m) \ldots d(m) + 1 \end{array}$$

As usual in the presence of the overriding operator $\nleftarrow$, we have to do a proof case by case. First case: $m = n$, and second case: $m \neq n$. The first case leads to the following, which is trivial:

$$\begin{array}{l} c(n) = d(n) \\ n \in N \\ \vdash \\ c(n) + 1 \;\in\; d(n) \ldots d(n) + 1 \end{array}$$

The second case is solved by instantiating m in the universal quantification with m, leading to the following, which is trivial:

$$\begin{array}{l} c(m) \;\in\; d(m) \ldots d(m) + 1 \\ m \in N \\ \vdash \\ c(m) \;\in\; d(m) \ldots d(m) + 1 \end{array}$$

We now prove that invariant **inv3_3** is preserved by event **descending_1**. It amounts to proving:

Invariant **inv3_3**	$\forall m \cdot m \in N \;\Rightarrow\; c(m) \;\in\; d(m) \ldots d(m) + 1$
Guard of **descending_1**	$n \in N \setminus \{r\}$
	$d(n) \neq d(f(n))$
$\vdash$	$\vdash$
Mod. inv. **inv3_3**	$\forall m \cdot m \in N \;\Rightarrow\; c(m) \;\in\; (d \nleftarrow \{n \mapsto d(n) + 1\})(m) \ldots$
	$(d \nleftarrow \{n \mapsto d(n) + 1\})(m) + 1$

This can be rearranged as:

$$\begin{array}{l} \forall m \cdot m \in N \;\Rightarrow\; c(m) \;\in\; d(m) \ldots d(m) + 1 \\ n \in N \setminus \{r\} \\ d(n) \neq d(f(n)) \\ m \in N \\ \vdash \\ c(m) \;\in\; (d \nleftarrow \{n \mapsto d(n) + 1\})(m) \ldots (d \nleftarrow \{n \mapsto d(n) + 1\})(m) + 1 \end{array}$$

We prove this by cases: first case $m = n$; second case $m \neq n$. Here is what the first case yields:

$$n \in N \setminus \{r\}$$
$$d(n) \neq d(f(n))$$
$$\Rightarrow$$
$$c(n) \in d(n) + 1 \mathbin{..} d(n) + 2$$

By instantiating **thm3_2** with n, we obtain $d(f(n)) \in d(n) \mathbin{..} d(n)+1$, which together with $d(n) \neq d(f(n))$ yields $d(f(n)) = d(n) + 1$. Instantiating then **thm3_1** with $f(n)$ yields $d(f(n)) \leq d(r)$, that is $d(n) + 1 \leq d(r)$. We are thus left to prove the following where we have added some theorems and invariant instantiations. This is trivially true (the three first antecedents yield $d(n) + 1 \leq d(r) \leq c(r) \leq c(n)$, whereas the last antecedent yields $c(n) \leq d(n+1)$; therefore we have $c(n) = d(n) + 1$):

$$
\begin{array}{ll}
 & d(n) + 1 \leq d(r) \\
\textbf{inv3\_3} \text{ instantiated with } r & c(r) \in d(r) \mathbin{..} d(r) + 1 \\
\textbf{thm1\_2} \text{ instantiated with } n & c(n) \in c(r) \mathbin{..} c(r) + 1 \\
\textbf{inv3\_3} \text{ instantiated with } n & c(n) \in d(n) \mathbin{..} d(n) + 1 \\
 & \vdash \\
 & c(n) \in d(n) + 1 \mathbin{..} d(n) + 2.
\end{array}
$$

The second case ($m \neq n$) yields the following, which is trivially true:

$$\forall m \cdot m \in N \Rightarrow c(m) \in d(m) \mathbin{..} d(m) + 1$$
$$n \in N \setminus \{r\}$$
$$d(n) \neq d(f(n))$$
$$m \in N$$
$$\vdash$$
$$c(m) \in d(m) \mathbin{..} d(m) + 1.$$

It remains finally for us to prove that invariant **inv3_3** is preserved by event descending_2. It amounts to proving:

$$
\begin{array}{ll}
\text{Invariant } \textbf{inv3\_3} & \forall m \cdot m \in N \Rightarrow c(m) \in d(m) \mathbin{..} d(m) + 1 \\
\text{Guard of descending\_2} & d(r) \neq c(r) \\
 & \vdash \\
\vdash & \forall m \cdot m \in N \Rightarrow c(m) \in (d \mathbin{\substack{\lhd\\-}} \{r \mapsto d(r) + 1\})(m) \mathbin{..} \\
\text{Mod. inv. } \textbf{inv3\_3} & \qquad\qquad\qquad\qquad (d \mathbin{\substack{\lhd\\-}} \{r \mapsto d(r) + 1\})(m) + 1.
\end{array}
$$

This can be rearranged as follows:

$$\forall m \cdot m \in N \Rightarrow c(m) \in d(m) .. d(m) + 1$$
$$d(r) \neq c(r)$$
$$m \in N$$
$$\vdash$$
$$c(m) \in (d \nleftarrow \{r \mapsto d(r) + 1\})(m) .. (d \nleftarrow \{r \mapsto d(r) + 1\})(m) + 1.$$

The proof proceeds again by cases. The first case ($m = r$), leads to the following, which is trivially true:

Theorem **thm3_1** instantiated with r
$$d(r) \neq c(r)$$
$$c(r) \in d(r) .. d(r) + 1$$
$$\vdash$$
$$c(r) \in d(r) + 1 .. d(r) + 1 + 1.$$

The second case ($m \neq r$), leads to the following, which is also trivially true:

Invariant **inv3_3** instantiated with m
$$c(m) \in d(m) .. d(m) + 1$$
$$\vdash$$
$$c(m) \in d(m) .. (d(m) + 1).$$

11.6 Fourth refinements

The idea of the next refinement comes from a careful observation of the three events we have obtained in the previous section. Let us copy them here again (note that we have changed the guard of event ascending to an equivalent one):

```
ascending
  any n where
    n ∈ N
    c(n) = d(n)
             ⎛  m ∈ N        ⎞
             ⎜  n = f(m)     ⎟
    ∀m ·     ⎜  ⇒            ⎟
             ⎝  c(f(m)) ≠ c(m) ⎠
  then
    c(n) := c(n) + 1
end
```

```
descending_1
  any  n  where
    n ∈ N \ {r}
    d(n) ≠ d(f(n))
  then
    d(n) := d(n) + 1
end
```

```
descending_2
  when
    d(r) ≠ c(r)
  then
    d(r) := d(r) + 1
end.
```

In event ascending, we observe a comparison of $c(n)$ and $d(n)$, and also a comparison of $c(m)$ and $c(f(m))$. In event descending_1, we observe that the guard contains a comparison of $d(n)$ and $d(f(n))$, and in event descending_2, we observe that the guard contains a comparison of $d(r)$ and $c(r)$. Moreover, the counters c or d are incremented in all events.

We have the impression to encounter a situation which is very similar to the one already encountered in the file transfer protocol example in Chapters 4 and 6. Should this impression be confirmed, then we could replace the values of the counters c and d simply by their parities. It is certainly an interesting transformation since then we have no more risk of such counters becoming too big. But in order to be able to do this refinement, we must be sure that the *difference between the compared values is not greater than one*. In the following table, we state that it is indeed the case:

Comparison	Justifying theorem
$c(n)$ and $d(n)$	**inv3_3:** $\forall n \cdot n \in N \Rightarrow c(n) \in d(n)..d(n)+1$
$c(m)$ and $c(f(m))$	**thm1_3:** $\forall n \cdot n \in N \setminus \{r\} \Rightarrow c(n) \in c(f(n))..c(f(n))+1$
$d(n)$ and $d(f(n))$	**thm3_2:** $\forall n \cdot n \in N \setminus \{r\} \Rightarrow d(f(n)) \in d(n)..d(n)+1$
$d(r)$ and $c(r)$	**thm3_4:** $\forall n \cdot n \in N \Rightarrow c(r) \in d(n)..d(n)+1$

The fourth refinement is now mere routine. We copy here the properties and basic theorem concerning parities:

$$\textbf{constants:} \quad r, f, parity$$

axm4_1: $parity \subset \mathbb{N} \rightarrow \{0,1\}$

axm4_2: $parity(0) = 0$

axm4_3: $\forall x \cdot x \in \mathbb{N} \Rightarrow parity(x+1) = 1 - parity(x)$

thm4_1: $\forall x, y \cdot x \in \mathbb{N} \wedge y \in \mathbb{N} \wedge x \in y..y+1 \wedge parity(x) = parity(y) \Rightarrow x = y$

And we define the parities $p(n)$ and $q(n)$ of $c(n)$ and $d(n)$:

variables: p
$\qquad\qquad q$

> **inv4_1:** $\quad p \in N \to \{0,1\}$
>
> **inv4_2:** $\quad q \in N \to \{0,1\}$
>
> **inv4_3:** $\quad \forall n \cdot (n \in N \Rightarrow p(n) = parity(c(n)))$
>
> **inv4_4:** $\quad \forall n \cdot (n \in N \Rightarrow q(n) = parity(d(n)))$

The final events are as follows:

init
$\quad p := N \times \{0\}$
$\quad q := N \times \{0\}$

ascending
$\quad$ **any** n **where**
$\qquad n \in N$
$\qquad p(n) = q(n)$
$\qquad \forall m \cdot m \in N \ \land \ f(m) = n \ \Rightarrow \ p(n) \neq p(m)$
$\quad$ **then**
$\qquad p(n) := 1 - p(n)$
$\quad$ **end**

descending_1
$\quad$ **any** n **where**
$\qquad n \in N \setminus \{r\}$
$\qquad q(n) \neq q(f(n))$
$\quad$ **then**
$\qquad q(n) := 1 - q(n)$
$\quad$ **end**

descending_2
$\quad$ **when**
$\qquad q(r) \neq p(r)$
$\quad$ **then**
$\qquad q(r) := 1 - q(r)$
$\quad$ **end**

11.7 References

[1] N. Lynch. *Distributed Algorithms*. Morgan Kaufmann Publishers, 1996.

[2] W. H. J. Feijen and A. J. M. van Gasteren. *On a Method of Multi-programming*. Springer, 1999.

12

Routing algorithm for a mobile agent

The purpose of the example developed in this chapter is to present an interesting routing algorithm for sending messages to a mobile phone. In this example, we shall again encounter a tree structure as in the previous chapter, but this time the tree structure will be modified dynamically. We shall also encounter another example (besides the bounded re-transmission protocol in Chapter 6) where the usage of clocks will play a fundamental role. This example is taken from [1].

12.1 Informal description of the problem

A, so-called, *mobile agent* $\mathcal{M}$ is supposed to travel between various sites. Fixed agents situated in the sites in question want to establish some communications with it. To simplify matters, such communications are supposed to be unidirectional: they take the practical form of messages sent from the fixed agents to $\mathcal{M}$.

12.1.1 Abstract informal specification

In an ideal *abstract* world, the moves of the mobile agent $\mathcal{M}$ from one site to another are instantaneous. Likewise, the knowledge by the fixed agents of the exact position of $\mathcal{M}$ is also supposed to be instantaneous. In that case, the fixed agents follow the mobile agent $\mathcal{M}$ by sending messages where it currently is. Notice that such messages are (for the moment) received immediately by $\mathcal{M}$. This is illustrated in Fig. 12.1 where the mobile agent $\mathcal{M}$ (represented by a black square) originally situated at site c, moves then successively to sites d, a, c, and b. The arrows indicate where each fixed agent is sending messages: they just follow $\mathcal{M}$ since they immediately know where it is.

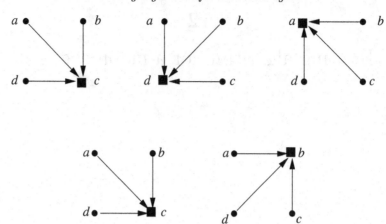

Fig. 12.1. First abstraction: the fixed agents always know where the mobile agent is

12.1.2 *First informal refinement*

In a more realistic *concrete* world, the moves of M from one site to another are still instantaneous, but the only site to know where M is, is the site that M has just left. The other sites are not aware of the move, they continue thus to send messages to the site where they still *believe* that M resides. Then it is quite possible that some messages arrive at a destination which is not currently that of M. As a consequence, each site, besides sending its own messages, is thus also in charge of possibly *forwarding* the messages received while M is not present any more locally. It is quite possible that several such intermediate transmissions take place before a message eventually reaches M. This is illustrated in Fig. 12.2.

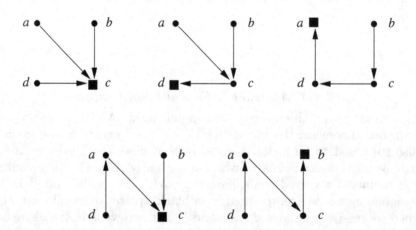

Fig. 12.2. First refinement: fixed agents do not know the exact position of the mobile agent

As can be seen, when $\mathcal{M}$ reaches a new site, that site destroys the previous knowledge it has concerning the location of $\mathcal{M}$. For instance, in the third snapshot, where $\mathcal{M}$ has just moved to site a coming from site d, the link between a and c that existed in the previous situation is removed. Similarly, when $\mathcal{M}$ leaves a site, that site re-actualizes its knowledge by storing the new location of $\mathcal{M}$ (again, supposed to be known instantaneously). For instance, in the fourth snapshot above, where $\mathcal{M}$ has just moved from a to c, a new link between a and c is established.

Intuitively for the moment, we can figure out that the communication channels are dynamically modified, while maintaining a *tree structure* whose root is the actual site of $\mathcal{M}$. This is illustrated in Fig. 12.3 where we have reordered the sites to show more clearly the tree structure. Each site is then indirectly *connected* to the site of $\mathcal{M}$ and there exists *no cycles* that might put some forwarded messages in an endless loop.

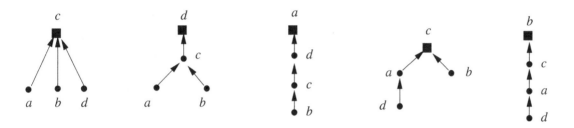

Fig. 12.3. The tree structure

12.1.3 Second informal refinement: a problem

In a still more realistic world, the moves of $\mathcal{M}$ between sites are not instantaneous anymore. In fact, when $\mathcal{M}$ leaves a site, it does not know necessarily where it is going. Only when $\mathcal{M}$ arrives at its destination, is it able to send a *service message* to its previous site in order to inform it of its present location. Of course, the service message in question does not itself travel instantaneously. Communication messages are thus still forwarded from sites to sites, but that forwarding might be *suspended* in some sites, which $\mathcal{M}$ has left in the past, until such sites receive service messages informing them of the "present" location of $\mathcal{M}$ ("present", however, meaning when the service message was sent, which may not be the situation any more when it is received).

We have no control over the relative speed of the service messages: some of them can reach their destination quite quickly, while some others might take more time (but we suppose that they will eventually arrive at their destination). In Fig. 12.4, we have put some dashed lines to indicate that the corresponding service messages have not yet arrived: notice that service messages following the dashed lines circulate in a direction which is the opposite of that followed by the communication messages that will be established upon reception of the service message. In fact, when a service message arrives at its destination, the corresponding dashed line is transformed into a "plain" line going in the opposite direction.

In Fig. 12.4, we have shown a series of snapshots where all service messages are pending. Notice that the situation pictured in the last snapshot contains a potential problem. This is because site c is expected to receive two service messages, one from d and another one from b. As a matter of fact, a site might expect as many service messages as there has been past visits of that site by the mobile agent $\mathcal{M}$.

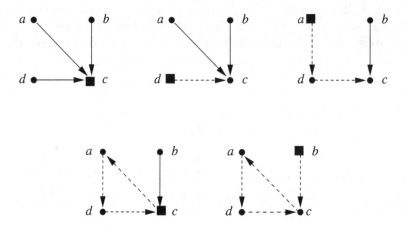

Fig. 12.4. Second refinement: the mobile agent sends a service message with its new position

In Fig. 12.5, we show various snapshots corresponding to the arrival of some service messages. The last snapshot shows a situation were all service messages have reached their destination except the ones, $sm1$ and $sm2$, supposed to reach site c form d and b respectively.

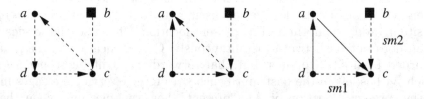

Fig. 12.5. Service messages messages $sm2$ from b to c and $sm1$ from d to c have not yet arrived

If the service message $sm1$ between d and c is very late (arriving after the service message $sm2$ between b and c although sent before $sm2$), then, upon arrival, $sm1$ may have the disastrous effect: first, isolating completely site b, and, second, forming a cycle within which communication messages may circulate for ever. This is illustrated in

Fig. 12.6 where the two snapshots show the arrival of service message *sm2* followed by that of service message *sm1*.

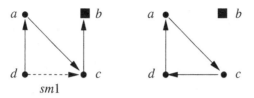

Fig. 12.6. Arrival of service message *sm2* before *sm1*

This failure is due to the fact that site *c* is misled by service message *sm1* from site *d*. In fact, message *sm1* should have been *discarded* by site *b* when sending service message *sm2* to *c*. But how can site *b* know about the existence of such a pending service message *sm1* whose destination is also *c*?

12.1.4 Third informal refinement: the solution

The purpose of the distributed routing algorithm presented here and developed by L. Moreau in [1] is precisely to solve the potential problem we revealed above. The idea is to have the mobile agent $\mathcal{M}$ traveling with a *logical clock* which is incremented each time it arrives at a new site. Upon arrival in a site, the value of the logical clock is stored (after being incremented). It thus records the time of the last visit of the mobile agent $\mathcal{M}$ at this site. When $\mathcal{M}$ sends its service message to its previous site, it stamps that message with the new time (the one that has just been incremented and recorded in the new site). This is illustrated in Fig. 12.7 where the local time stored in each site

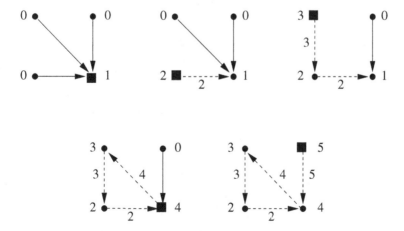

Fig. 12.7. Introducing the clock

can be seen next to each of them. The stamp value on the service messages are shown next to the middle of the corresponding arrow (they are all equal as expected to the value of the clock stored at the origin of the message).

As a consequence, a new service message is stamped with a value that is certainly greater than that recorded in its destination. When the service message arrives, it is filtered: if the stamp is smaller than or equal to the local time of the destination, then it is discarded because it is clearly a late service message. If the stamp of a service message is greater than the local time, then the message is accepted and, simultaneously, the local clock of the site is updated with the value of the stamp traveling with the service message. Thanks to this, the message could not be used a second time (in case of misbehavior of the network). Figure 12.8 shows the series of situations corresponding to the arrival of the service messages. We have decorated these situations with the clocks and the stamps.

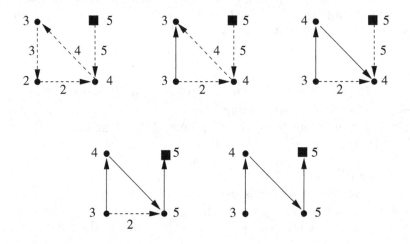

Fig. 12.8. Arrival of the service messages

As can be seen, the last service message is discarded because its stamp value, 2, is smaller than the local clock, 5, at destination. We have reversed from the potential failure presented earlier. This is due to the presence of the clock and stamps, and of the particular adopted strategy.

The system we have described seems to work, at least according to our informal explanations. But it is certainly important to develop it formally so as to be sure that it behaves in a correct fashion. This is the purpose of the coming sections.

12.2 Initial model

Now, we have enough information to start the formal construction of this routing protocol. The first question that we must ask ourselves with an example such as this one (and many others) is that concerning the *level of description* we have to start from. It is out of the question to start from the final solution, because then nothing really can be proved. We must start from an abstract enough level, which must be pretty obvious (and where no technical difficulties exist yet, in particular those dealing with time and distances), so that the proposed solution can be proved to indeed solve the problem that has been informally described.

In the present case, we are going to start from the second abstract informal level described in Section 12.1.2, where the exact position of the mobile is only known by its previous site. This level is quite simple: the communication channels, as we have said informally, form a tree structure (an invariant that has to be proved, of course), the moves of the mobile agent are timeless, and finally the knowledge concerning the new location of the mobile agent is instantaneously communicated to its previous site (no service message thus). Further refinements will introduce more realistic constraints.

12.2.1 The state

We have two carrier sets S and M: the set S denotes the set of sites and M the set of communication messages. To have a carrier set representing the set of communication messages is a really useful abstraction since we are not interested in the contents of these messages: we can then suppose that they are all distinct. Initially the mobile is at some *initial location* denoted by the constant il (**axm0_1**):

sets: S M	**constant:** il	**axm0_1:** $il \in S$

We have three variables in our initial model: l, c, and p. The variable l denotes the actual location of the mobile agent (**inv0_1**). The variable c denotes the dynamically changing communication channels between sites: it is a total function from sites to sites (**inv0_2**). Notice that this function is obviously not meaningful at l. Finally, the variable p denotes the pool of messages that are waiting to be forwarded on each site: clearly a given message is at most in one site at a time, so that p is a partial function from messages to sites (**inv0_3**). Formally:

variables: l, c, p	**inv0_1:** $l \in S$
	inv0_2: $c \in S \setminus \{l\} \to S$
	inv0_3: $p \in M \nrightarrow S$

It remains now for us to formalize the tree structure of the communication channels. The root of the tree is l and the parent function is the function c. We shall use exactly the same formulation as the one introduced in Section 9.7.7, namely **inv0_4**:

$$\textbf{inv0\_4:} \quad \forall T \cdot T \subseteq c^{-1}[T] \Rightarrow T = \varnothing$$

We can see the difference with the previous chapter: in this one, this statement is an invariant, not an axiom.

12.2.2 The events

We have four events besides event init which show that all nodes (except il) are pointing to the initial position of the mobile $\mathcal{M}$. Event rcv_agt corresponds to the mobile moving instantaneously from the site l to another one (different from l). Event snd_msg corresponds to a new communication message m sent from one site s to the mobile. Event fwd_msg corresponds to a communication message m being forwarded from one site s to another one by means of the corresponding channel (note that this transfer is also instantaneous for the moment). And finally event dlv_msg corresponds to a communication message m being delivered to the mobile. Here are these events:

```
init
    l := il
    c := (S \ {il}) × {il}
    p := ∅
```

```
rcv_agt
    any s where
        s ∈ S \ {l}
    then
        l := s
        c := ({s} ⩤ c) ∪ {l ↦ s}
    end
```

```
snd_msg
    any s, m where
        s ∈ S
        m ∈ M \ dom(p)
    then
        p(m) := s
    end
```

```
fwd_msg
    any m where
        m ∈ dom(p)
        p(m) ≠ l
    then
        p(m) := c(p(m))
    end
```

```
dlv_msg
    any m where
        m ∈ dom(p)
        p(m) = l
    then
        p := {m} ⩤ p
    end
```

12.2.3 The proofs

The only interesting proof at this level is that of the preservation of invariant **inv0_4** by event rcv_agt. Here is what we have to prove:

$$
\cdots
$$

Invariant **inv0_4**

$$
\left(
\begin{array}{l}
\forall T \cdot\ T \subseteq S \\
\qquad T \subseteq c^{-1}[T] \\
\quad \Rightarrow \\
\qquad T = \varnothing
\end{array}
\right)
$$

Guard of rcv_agt $\qquad s \in S \setminus \{l\}$

$\vdash \qquad\qquad\qquad \vdash$

Modified invariant **inv0_4**

$$
\left(
\begin{array}{l}
\forall T \cdot\ T \subseteq S \\
\qquad T \subseteq (\{s\} \lessdot c) \cup \{l \mapsto s\})^{-1}[T] \\
\quad \Rightarrow \\
\qquad T = \varnothing
\end{array}
\right)
$$

We can remove the universal quantification in the consequent of this implication by using rules ALL_R and IMP_R. The proof proceeds then as follows:

$$
\cdots
$$
$$
\left(
\begin{array}{l}
\forall T \cdot\ T \subseteq S \\
\qquad T \subseteq c^{-1}[T] \\
\quad \Rightarrow \\
\qquad T = \varnothing
\end{array}
\right)
$$
$$
s \in S \setminus \{l\}
$$
$$
T \subseteq S
$$
$$
T \subseteq (\{s\} \lessdot c) \cup \{l \mapsto s\})^{-1}[T]
$$
$$
\vdash
$$
$$
T = \varnothing
$$

ALL_L

$$
\cdots
$$
$$
\left(
\begin{array}{l}
T \subseteq S \\
T \subseteq c^{-1}[T] \\
\Rightarrow \\
T = \varnothing
\end{array}
\right)
$$
$$
s \in S \setminus \{l\}
$$
$$
T \subseteq S
$$
$$
T \subseteq (\{s\} \lessdot c) \cup \{l \mapsto s\})^{-1}[T]
$$
$$
\vdash
$$
$$
T = \varnothing
$$

SET ...

$$
\cdots
$$
$$
\left(
\begin{array}{l}
T \subseteq S \\
T \subseteq c^{-1}[T] \\
\Rightarrow \\
T = \varnothing
\end{array}
\right)
$$
$$
s \in S \setminus \{l\}
$$
$$
T \subseteq S
$$
$$
T \subseteq (\{s\} \lessdot c) \cup \{l \mapsto s\})^{-1}[T]
$$
$$
T \subseteq c^{-1}[T]
$$
$$
\vdash
$$
$$
T = \varnothing
$$

IMP_L

$$
\cdots
$$
$$
T = \varnothing
$$
$$
s \in S \setminus \{l\}
$$
$$
T \subseteq S
$$
$$
T \subseteq (\{s\} \lessdot c) \cup \{l \mapsto s\})^{-1}[T]
$$
$$
T \subseteq c^{-1}[T]
$$
$$
\vdash
$$
$$
T = \varnothing
$$

HYP.

The key of this proof is the following lemma whose proof is sketched below.

$$
\begin{array}{l}
\ldots \\
s \in S \setminus \{l\} \\
T \subseteq (\{s\} \lhd c) \cup \{l \mapsto s\})^{-1}[T] \\
\vdash \\
\quad T \subseteq c^{-1}[T]
\end{array}
$$

Consider two cases successively $s \notin T$ and $s \in T$. In the first case, $T \subseteq (\{s\} \lhd c) \cup \{l \mapsto s\})^{-1}[T]$ reduces to $T \subseteq (c^{-1} \rhd \{s\})[T]$, hence $T \subseteq c^{-1}[T]$. In the second case, $T \subseteq (\{s\} \lhd c) \cup \{l \mapsto s\})^{-1}[T]$ reduces to $T \subseteq (c^{-1} \rhd \{s\})[T] \cup \{l\}$ which contradicts $s \in T$ since $s \notin (c^{-1} \rhd \{s\})[T]$ and $s \neq l$.

12.3 First refinement

In this first refinement, we are more concrete. The movements of the mobile will not be instantaneous any more, it will be made in two steps: first the mobile agent leaves the site l (new event leave_agt), and then arrives at a new site s different from l (old event rcv_agt).

In that second case, the knowledge by the previous site l of the new position s of the mobile agent will not be instantaneous any more as was the case in the initial model. In fact, as we said in Section 12.1.3, the mobile agent will send a *service message* to its previous site s, in order for that site to update its forward pointer to the new site. But during the traveling delay of the mobile agent and then the transmission delay of the service message, site s cannot transmit any forward message because it does not know where the agent is. Site s only knows that it is expecting a service message. The site corresponding to the previous position of $\mathcal{M}$ will eventually receive the service message (new event rcv_srv).

12.3.1 The state

Clearly, the channel structure in this new refined model is not in phase with that of the previous model where it was modified when the mobile agent arrived at its new destination: this was done by event rcv_agt (in the previous model, we had no traveling time and no transmission of a service message). In this refinement, we have thus to add a new variable, d, denoting this new channel structure (**inv1_1**), which will only be updated as a consequence of the new event rcv_srv.

We have a new variable, a, denoting the service channel containing the service messages mentioned in the informal description. It is a partial function from sites to sites (**inv1_2**); more precisely, from the site *where the mobile was before moving* (it cannot be l) to the site *where it currently is*. This function contains the *future* of the communication channel. We shall make precise in what follows the reason why a is such a *function*, which is far from being obvious *a priori*: we shall see that, in this abstraction, this channel has a rather magic behavior.

The next invariant, **inv1_3**, establishes the connection between the abstract communication channel c and its concrete counterpart d. It says that the abstract channel c corresponds to the concrete one, d, *overridden* by the service channel a. Formally:

variables:	l
	p
	d
	a
	da

inv1_1:	$d \in S \setminus \{l\} \rightarrowtail S$
inv1_2:	$a \in S \setminus \{l\} \rightarrowtail S$
inv1_3:	$c = d \oplus a$

We introduce another variable da which records the sites at which the current forwarding direction for information messages is not meaningful any more. This is because the mobile has left these sites while none of them has received yet the expected service message. For these reasons, the sites of da cannot forward any messages. Formally:

inv1_4:	$\mathrm{dom}(a) = da \setminus \{l\}$

12.3.2 The events

The various concrete events are very close to their abstraction. As event snd_msg does not change, we have not copied it in what follows. Here are the first ones:

init
$$l := il$$
$$p := \varnothing$$
$$d := (S \setminus \{il\}) \times \{il\}$$
$$a := \varnothing$$
$$da := \varnothing$$

dlv_msg
  any m **where**
  $$m \in \mathrm{dom}(p)$$
  $$p(m) \notin da$$
  $$p(m) = l$$
  then
  $$p := \{m\} \lhd p$$
  end

fwd_msg
  any m **where**
  $$m \in \mathrm{dom}(p)$$
  $$p(m) \notin da$$
  $$p(m) \neq l$$
  then
  $$p(m) := d(p(m))$$
  end

Event fwd_msg has a stronger guard than its abstraction. More precisely, a message m whose site is $p(m)$ can only be forwarded if this site is not in da, since then the destination is not known, and also different from l, since then it can be delivered directly by event dlv_msg.

We have a new event called leave_agt. It corresponds to the mobile leaving its site l. Of course, it can only happen when l is not in da since otherwise the mobile would have been already in transit. As can be seen, site l is now expecting a service message (assignment $da := da \cup \{l\}$).

leave_agt
  when
  $$l \notin da$$
  then
  $$da := da \cup \{l\}$$
  end

rcv_agt
  any s **where**
  $$s \in S \setminus \{l\}$$
  $$l \in da$$
  then
  $$l := s$$
  $$a := (\{s\} \lhd a) \lhd\!\!\!- \{l \mapsto s\}$$
  $$d := \{s\} \lhd d$$
  $$da := da \setminus \{s\}$$
  end

rcv_srv
  any s **where**
  $$s \in \mathrm{dom}(a)$$
  $$l \neq s$$
  then
  $$d(s) := a(s)$$
  $$a := \{s\} \lhd a$$
  $$da := da \setminus \{s\}$$
  end

Event rcv_agt has a very interesting behavior. We note that when putting a new message $\{l \mapsto s\}$ in the service channel a (this message goes from the new site s of the mobile agent to its previous site l), we magically *remove the previous pair, if any, whose first component was l*: In other words, we clean the channel by removing pending service messages to l, which might not have been delivered yet at l. In this way, there is at most one service message pointing to a given site, and there is thus no risk of having a pending message arriving late (that is, after a more recent one) and having the kind of bad effect we have described in Section 12.1.3. Of course, this is quite magic for the moment. What we only wanted to express at this level is the intended behavior of the channel. It will remain, of course, for us to implement this magical behavior, which is another matter. This will be the business of the next refinement.

Finally, we have a new event, rcv_srv, corresponding to the reception by a site s of a service message informing s of the new location $a(s)$ of the mobile at the time this service message was sent. Notice that the move from s to $a(s)$ is indeed the most recent move by the mobile from s since all other pending service messages to s have been discarded by event rcv_agt. The communication channel is updated and the service message removed from the service channel.

12.3.3 The proofs

The proofs are left to the reader.

12.4 Second refinement

In the next refinement, we shall implement the magic service channel of the previous abstraction. This is the heart of the development.

12.4.1 The state

We now have a clock k traveling with the agent (**inv2_1**). We also have in each site a variable, t, recording the time of the last visit of the mobile in the corresponding site (**inv2_2**). Formally:

variables:	...
	b
	k
	t

inv2_1: $k \in \mathbb{N}$
inv2_2: $t \in S \to \mathbb{N}$

The new service channel b replacing a has now a structure far richer than its abstraction. It may contain several stamped messages to the same site s. It is formalized as indicated in the following example:

$$s \mapsto \{3 \mapsto s1, 5 \mapsto s2, 9 \mapsto s3, \ldots\}.$$

This means that there has been a message $s \mapsto s1$ emitted at time 3, a message $s \mapsto s2$ emitted at time 5, a message $s \mapsto s3$ emitted at time 9, etc. The channel b is thus typed as follows:

$$\boxed{\textbf{inv2\_3:} \ \ b \in S \to (\mathbb{N} \rightarrowtail S)}$$

Next comes the invariant **inv2_4** connecting the abstract service channel a and the concrete one b; the service message to s in the abstract channel a corresponds, among all service messages to s in the concrete channel b, to the one with the *greatest time* (the most recent one):

$$
\boxed{
\begin{array}{l}
\textbf{inv2\_4:} \ \ \forall s \cdot \ \ s \in \mathrm{dom}(a) \\
\qquad\qquad \Rightarrow \\
\qquad\qquad\quad \mathrm{dom}(b(s)) \neq \varnothing \\
\qquad\qquad\quad a(s) = b(s)(\max(\mathrm{dom}(b(s))))
\end{array}
}
$$

When the time of the last visit $t(s)$ of the recipient s of a service message is strictly smaller than the maximum time of the pending service messages for that recipient, that is $\max(\mathrm{dom}(b(s)))$, then the recipient s in question is indeed expecting a real message as in the abstraction. This is formalized in the following invariant **inv2_5**:

$$
\boxed{
\begin{array}{l}
\textbf{inv2\_5:} \ \ \forall s \cdot \ \ s \in S \\
\qquad\qquad\quad \mathrm{dom}(b(s)) \neq \varnothing \\
\qquad\qquad\quad t(s) < \max(\mathrm{dom}(b(s))) \\
\qquad\qquad \Rightarrow \\
\qquad\qquad\quad s \in \mathrm{dom}(a)
\end{array}
}
$$

But the problem, of course, is that, *a priori*, the recipient does not know that it is indeed receiving the maximum in question. This difficulty will be circumvented below in the last invariant **inv2_9**. Invariant **inv2_5** allows us to prove the guard strengthening of event rcv_srv, with the help of invariant **inv2_9** below.

We now have three more invariants concerned with the time of the last visit t and the clock k: (1) the times in the pending service messages are never bigger than the clock (**inv2_6**), (2) the time of the last visit is equal to the clock at the site of the Mobile (**inv2_7**), and (3) in other sites, the time of the last visit is at most equal to the clock (**inv2_8**):

---

inv2_6: $\forall s \cdot s \in S \,\wedge\, \text{dom}(b(s)) \neq \varnothing \,\Rightarrow\, \max(\text{dom}(b(s))) \leq k$

inv2_7: $t(l) = k$

inv2_8: $\forall s \cdot s \in S \setminus \{l\} \,\Rightarrow\, t(s) \leq k$

Now comes at last the *key invariant* **inv2_9**. When the recipient s of a service message receives a message with a time n that is strictly greater than the time of its own last visit $t(s)$, then it can be *absolutely certain* that it is indeed receiving the message with the greatest time, therefore the same message as in the abstraction according to invariant **inv2_4**.

---

inv2_9: $\forall\, s, n \cdot \quad s \in S$
$\qquad\qquad\qquad\quad n \in \text{dom}(b(s))$
$\qquad\qquad\qquad\quad t(s) < n$
$\qquad\qquad\qquad\Rightarrow$
$\qquad\qquad\qquad\quad n = \max(\text{dom}(b(s)))$

This invariant is far from being completely intuitive. The informal explanation is as follows. If several service messages are expected at a site s, then it means that the mobile agent has visited s several times. And on each such visit it has updated the time of last visit of s with the most recent value of the clock. Upon leaving site s, it has sent to s (when arriving at its new location) a service message with a stamp value which is one more than that of the time of last visit of s. So, during its *previous* visit to s, which has certainly taken place *after* the sending (not necessarily the receiving) of the previous service messages to s, the updated value of the time of the last visit of s is then certainly greater than that of the stamp of any pending service messages to s. As a consequence, when the mobile leaves s again for the last time, it sends (upon arrival at its new location) yet another service message, which is then *the only one* with a stamp greater than the value of the time of the last visit at s. *All this, clearly, needs confirmation from a formal proof.* Thanks to this invariant, we can implement the magic abstract channel a with the concrete channel b.

12.4.2 The events

Here is first the last version of event init:

$$
\boxed{
\begin{aligned}
&\text{init} \\
&\quad l := il \\
&\quad p := \varnothing \\
&\quad d := (S \setminus \{il\}) \times \{il\} \\
&\quad b := S \times \{\varnothing\} \\
&\quad da := \varnothing \\
&\quad k := 1 \\
&\quad t := S \times \{0\} \; \Leftarrow \; \{il \mapsto 1\}
\end{aligned}
}
$$

Next comes event `rcv_agt` together with its previous abstract version:

$$
\boxed{
\begin{aligned}
&\text{(abstract-)}\text{rcv\_agt} \\
&\quad \textbf{any } s \textbf{ where} \\
&\quad\quad s \in S \setminus \{l\} \\
&\quad\quad l \in da \\
&\quad \textbf{then} \\
&\quad\quad l := s \\
&\quad\quad a(l) := s \\
&\quad\quad d := \{s\} \lhd d \\
&\quad\quad da := da \setminus \{s\}
\end{aligned}
}
\qquad
\boxed{
\begin{aligned}
&\text{(concrete-)}\text{rcv\_agt} \\
&\quad \textbf{any } s \textbf{ where} \\
&\quad\quad s \in S \setminus \{l\} \\
&\quad\quad l \in da \\
&\quad \textbf{then} \\
&\quad\quad l := s \\
&\quad\quad t(s) := k + 1 \\
&\quad\quad k := k + 1 \\
&\quad\quad b(l)(k + 1) := s \\
&\quad\quad d := \{s\} \lhd d \\
&\quad\quad da := da \setminus \{s\} \\
&\quad \textbf{end}
\end{aligned}
}
$$

Notice the incrementation of the clock k and the storing of it in $t(s)$. And now we propose event `rcv_srv`, again together with its previous abstract version:

$$
\boxed{
\begin{aligned}
&\text{(abstract-)}\text{rcv\_srv} \\
&\quad \textbf{any } s \textbf{ where} \\
&\quad\quad s \in \mathrm{dom}(a) \\
&\quad\quad l \neq s \\
&\quad \textbf{then} \\
&\quad\quad d(s) := a(s) \\
&\quad\quad a := \{s\} \lhd a \\
&\quad\quad da := da \setminus \{s\} \\
&\quad \textbf{end}
\end{aligned}
}
\qquad
\boxed{
\begin{aligned}
&\text{(concrete-)}\text{rcv\_srv} \\
&\quad \textbf{any } s, n \textbf{ where} \\
&\quad\quad s \in S \\
&\quad\quad n \in \mathrm{dom}(b(s)) \\
&\quad\quad t(s) < n \\
&\quad \textbf{then} \\
&\quad\quad d(s) := b(s)(n) \\
&\quad\quad t(s) := n \\
&\quad\quad da := da \setminus \{s\} \\
&\quad \textbf{end}
\end{aligned}
}
$$

We again copy below **inv2_5** and **inv2_9** in order to show how part of guard strengthening, namely $s \in \text{dom}(a)$, can be proved:

$$\textbf{inv2\_5:} \ \forall s \cdot \begin{pmatrix} s \in S \\ \text{dom}(b(s)) \neq \varnothing \\ t(s) < \max(\text{dom}(b(s))) \\ \Rightarrow \\ s \in \text{dom}(a) \end{pmatrix} \qquad \textbf{inv2\_9:} \ \forall s, n \cdot \begin{pmatrix} s \in S \\ n \in \text{dom}(b(s)) \\ t(s) < n \\ \Rightarrow \\ n = \max(\text{dom}(b(s))) \end{pmatrix}$$

In fact, putting together **inv2_9** and **inv2_5**, we easily obtain the following theorem:

$$\textbf{thm2\_1:} \quad \forall s, n \cdot \quad \begin{aligned} & s \in S \\ & n \in \text{dom}(b(s)) \\ & t(s) < n \\ & \Rightarrow \\ & s \in \text{dom}(a) \end{aligned}$$

The second part of guard strengthening, namely $l \neq s$, can be proved according to **inv2_7**, **inv2_6** and again **inv2_9**. The proof is by contradiction: we suppose $l = s$ and derive a contradiction.

Note that, to simplify matters, we do not clean the channel b in event rcv_srv. As a matter of fact, *it is not necessary*. Since the abstract channel was cleaned (the refinement is correct), this means that the message will not be accepted another time. This is because of the updating of the time of the last visit ($t(s) := n$). This gives us a cleaning effect.

12.4.3 The proofs

Proofs are left to the reader.

12.5 Third refinement: data refinement

In this refinement, we transform the set da into a boolean function. In fact we then localize this information in each site.

12.5.1 The state

We introduce the variable dab (**inv3_1**), replacing abstract variables da. Invariant **inv3_2** defines the boolean function as the characteristic function of the corresponding set.

variables: ... dab	**inv3_1:** $dab \in S \to \mathrm{BOOL}$ **inv3_2:** $\forall x \cdot x \in S \Rightarrow (x \in da \Leftrightarrow dab(x) = \mathrm{TRUE})$

12.5.2 The events

The events are now refined in a straightforward way as follows (note how the function dab is initialized):

```
init
    l := il
    p := ∅
    d := (S \ {il}) × {il}
    b := S × {∅}
    dab := S × {FALSE}
    k := 1
    t := S × {0} ⊰ {il ↦ 1}
```

```
leave_agt
    when
        dab(l) = FALSE
    then
        dab(l) := TRUE
    end
```

```
rcv_agt
    any s where
        s ∈ S \ {l}
        dab(l) = TRUE
    then
        l := s
        t(s) := k + 1
        k := k + 1
        b(l)(k + 1) := s
        d := {s} ⊲ d
        dab(s) := FALSE
    end
```

```
rcv_srv
    any s, n where
        s ∈ S
        n ∈ dom(b(s))
        t(s) < n
    then
        d(s) := b(s)(n)
        t(s) := n
        dab(s) := FALSE
    end
```

```
dlv_msg
   any m where
      m ∈ dom(p)
      dab(p(m)) = FALSE
      p(m) = l
   then
      p := {m} ◁ p
   end
```

```
fwd_msg
   any m where
      m ∈ dom(p)
      dab(p(m)) = FALSE
      p(m) ≠ l
   then
      p(m) := d(p(m))
   end
```

12.5.3 The proofs

Proofs are left to the reader.

12.6 Fourth refinement

There is one more refinement where we implement the effective migration of the forwarded communication messages. We leave it as an exercise to the reader to develop this refinement.

12.7 References

[1]   L. Moreau. Distributed directory service and message routers for mobile agent. *Science of Computer Programming* **39** (2–3): 249–272, 2001.

13

Leader election on a connected graph network

The goal of the IEEE-1394 protocol is to elect in a *finite time* a specific node, called the *leader*, in a network made of a finite number of nodes linked by some communication channels.

We are given a finite network of nodes. The goal of the protocol is to elect a leader	FUN-1

The network has got some specific properties: as a mathematical structure, it is called a *free tree*.

The graph representing the network is a free tree	FUN-2

Such a free tree is shown in Fig. 13.1

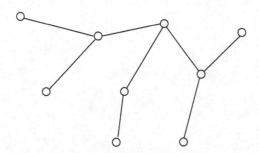

Fig. 13.1. A free tree

13.1 Initial model

13.1.1 The state

This initial steps just contain the definition of the finite set N of nodes. A variable l will be assigned the leader in a one shot action.

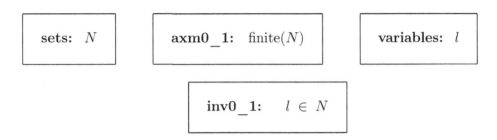

13.1.2 Events

The dynamic aspect of the protocol is essentially made of one *event*, called elect, which claims *what the result of the protocol is, when it is completed*. In other words, at this level, there is no protocol, just the formal definition of its intended result, namely a node l chosen non-deterministically to be the leader.

13.2 First refinement

13.2.1 Defining the free tree

The constant graph g is introduced as a free tree. To do this, we copy the axiomatization of free trees we performed in Section 7.8 of Chapter 9.

$$\text{axm1\_1:} \quad g \in N \leftrightarrow N$$

$$\text{axm1\_2:} \quad g = g^{-1}$$

$$\text{axm1\_3:} \quad g \cap \mathrm{id}(N) = \varnothing$$

$$\text{axm1\_4:} \quad \forall s \cdot \begin{array}{l} S \subseteq N \\ S \neq \varnothing \\ g[S] \subseteq S \\ \Rightarrow \\ N \subseteq S \end{array}$$

$$\text{axm1\_5:} \quad \forall h, S \cdot \begin{array}{l} h \subseteq g \\ h \cap h^{-1} = \varnothing \\ S \subseteq h[S] \\ \Rightarrow \\ S = \varnothing \end{array}$$

constant: g

13.2.2 Extending the state

We extend the state with a subset n of the carrier set N. The variable n is initialized to N. The invariant states that the graph $n \lhd g \rhd n$ remains a free tree until it becomes empty (when n is reduced to a single element).

constant: l
          n

$$\text{inv1\_1:} \quad n \subseteq N$$

$$\text{inv1\_2:} \quad \forall s \cdot \begin{array}{l} S \subseteq n \\ S \neq \varnothing \\ (n \lhd g \rhd n)[S] \subseteq S \\ \Rightarrow \\ n \subseteq S \end{array}$$

13.2.3 The events of the first refinement

We introduce a new event, **progress**, which removes from the set n an element x which happens to be an outer node of the free tree (Section 9.7.8 of Chapter 9). This is illustrated in Fig. 13.2.

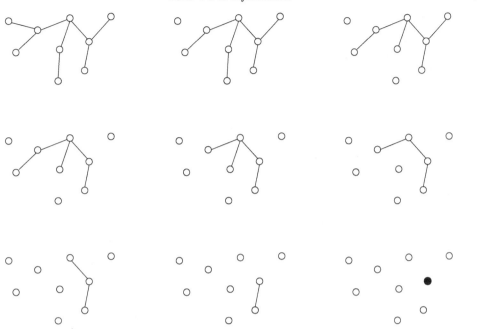

Fig. 13.2. Illustration of the distributed algorithm

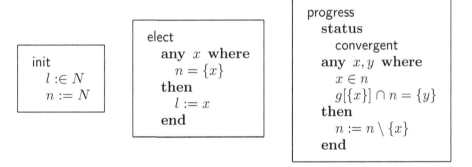

13.2.4 Proofs of the first refinement

The proofs are not difficult except that of the preservation of invariant **inv1_2** by event **progress**, which is a bit tedious. The variant for the convergence of event **progress** is obvious: this is the set n, which is clearly finite and decreasing.

The deadlock freeness proof is a direct consequence of theorem **thm_1** of Section 9.7.8 of Chapter 9 on free trees. It says that the set of outer nodes of a free tree is not empty, provided the free tree is itself not empty.

13.3 Second refinement

In the previous refinement, event **progress** was still very abstract. When a node x detects that it is an outer node of the free tree $n \lhd g \rhd n$, then x is removed from the set n. In the real protocol, things works differently: once a node x detects that it is an outer node of the free tree $n \lhd g \rhd n$, it sends a *message* to the only node y to which it is connected by means of $n \lhd g \rhd n$. When receiving this message, node y finalizes the job by removing x from n.

13.3.1 The state of the second refinement

In order to establish this distributed connection between nodes, we need to define a new variable, m, to handle the message: m represents the channels between nodes. Variable m is a partial function from n to itself. When a pair $x \mapsto y$ belongs to m, it means that node x has sent a message to node y; the fact that m is a function is because x is only connected to a single node y by means of $n \lhd g \rhd n$. Clearly, m is also included in the graph g (invariant **inv2_1**). All this can be formalized as follows:

variables: l, n, m

inv2_1:	$m \subseteq g$
inv2_2:	$m \in n \rightarrowtail n$
inv2_3:	$\forall x, y \cdot x \mapsto y \in m \Rightarrow x \in n$
inv2_4:	$\forall x, y \cdot x \mapsto y \in m \Rightarrow g[\{x\}] \cap n = \{y\}$

13.3.2 Events

A new event is defined in order to manage messages: **send_msg**. As we shall see, event **progress** is modified, whereas event **elect** is left unchanged. Here is the new event send_msg and the refined version of event progress:

```
send_msg
    any x, y where
        x ∈ n
        g[{x}] ∩ n = {y}
        x ∉ dom(m)
    then
        m := m ∪ {x ↦ y}
    end
```

```
progress
    any x, y where
        x ↦ y ∈ m
        y ∉ dom(m)
    then
        n := n \ {x}
        m := m \ {x ↦ y}
    end
```

Event send_msg is enabled when a node x of n discovers that it is an outer node of the tree $n \lhd g \rhd n$. These conditions were the guards of the abstraction of event progress. Moreover, node x must not have already sent a message, that is condition $x \notin \text{dom}(m)$ must hold. When these conditions are fulfilled, then the pair $x \mapsto y$ is added to m.

Event progress is enabled when a node y receives a message from node x, that is when condition $x \mapsto y \in m$ holds. Moreover, node y itself has not sent a message, that is condition $y \notin \text{dom}(m)$ must hold. When these conditions are fulfilled then node y removes x from n and $x \mapsto y$ from m.

13.3.3 Proofs

Proofs of events send_msg New event send_msg clearly refines skip since it only works with the new variable m. Moreover, its action increments the cardinal of m (this cardinal is bounded by that of g); therefore, it does not diverge. It is also easily provable that it maintains invariants **inv2_1** to **inv2_4**

Proof of event progress Here are the concrete and abstract versions of event progress:

```
(abstract-)progress
    any x, y where
        x ∈ n
        g[{x}] ∩ n = {y}
    then
        n := n \ {x ↦ y}
    end
```

```
(concrete-)progress
    any x, y where
        x ↦ y ∈ m
        y ∉ dom(m)
    then
        n := n \ {x}
        m := m \ {x ↦ y}
    end
```

The action on variable n being the same, we have just to prove that the concrete guard implies the abstract one, which is obvious according to invariants **inv2_3** and **inv2_4**

13.4 Third refinement: the problem of contention

13.4.1 Introduction

Here is the event progress, which we copy again from Section 13.3.2. This event explains when node x can be removed from set n.

```
progress
    any x, y where
        x ↦ y ∈ m
        y ∉ dom(m)
    then
        n := n \ {x}
        m := m \ {x ↦ y}
    end
```

As can be seen, this event contains the guarding condition $y \notin \mathrm{dom}(m)$. It means that node x can be removed from n provided node y *has not itself sent a message*. If y has sent a message to x while the other guarding conditions hold, that is $x \mapsto y \in m$, then clearly (1) x has sent a message to y, and (2) y has sent a message to x. In other words, the situation is *completely symmetric* between the two: each one of them wants the other to remove x or y from n.

In this case, no action can take place. The solution consists in the two nodes x and y retrying to send a message to the other (as if it were not already the case), hoping to introduce some sort of asymmetry. Figure 13.3 shows when the contention problem does occur, that is when there remain only two nodes to be potential leader candidates.

In the real protocol, the problem is solved by means of timers. As soon as a node y discovers a contention with node x, it waits for a very short delay in order to be certain that the other node x has also discovered the problem. The very short delay in question is at least equal to the message transfer time between nodes (such a time is supposed to be *bounded*). After this, each node randomly chooses (with probability $1/2$) to wait for a second delay, which is either a "short" or a "large" delay (the difference between the two is at least twice the message transfer time). After the chosen delay has passed, each node sends a new message to the other.

Clearly, if both nodes choose the same second delay, the contention situation will reappear. However, if they do not choose the same delay, then the one that has

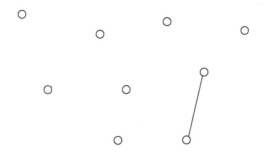

Fig. 13.3. The contention

chosen the largest delay becomes the winner: when it wakes up, it discovers the message from the other, while it has not itself already sent its own message; it can therefore remove the other from n. According to the *law of large numbers*, the probability that both nodes will *indefinitely choose the same delay* is zero. Thus, at some point, they will (in probability) choose different delays and one of them will thus become the leader.

13.4.2 The state for contention

We shall only present here a partial formalization of the contention problem. The idea is to introduce a *virtual contention channel*, called c. When this "channel" c contains a pair $x \mapsto y$, it means that y has discovered the contention with node x. When both pairs $x \mapsto y$ and $y \mapsto x$ are present in c, it means that both nodes x and y have discovered the contention. Notice that c and m are incompatible and that their union is a function. We also introduce a set bm, which is equal to the domain of $m \cup c$. These invariants are shown below:

variables: l, n, m, c, bm

inv3_1:	$c \subseteq g$
inv3_2:	$m \cup c \in n \nrightarrow n$
inv3_3:	$m \cap c = \varnothing$
inv3_4:	$bm = \mathrm{dom}(m \cup c)$

13.4.3 The events for contention

We have thus to modify our previous events as follows:

```
send_msg
    any x, y where
        x ∈ n
        g[{x}] ∩ n = {y}
        x ∉ bm
    then
        m := m ∪ {x ↦ y}
        bm := bm ∪ {x}
    end
```

```
progress
    any x, y where
        x ↦ y ∈ m
        y ∉ bm
    then
        n := n \ {x}
        m := m \ {x ↦ y}
        bm := bm \ {x}
    end
```

In event **send_msg**, the guard $x \notin bm$ replaces the weaker guard $x \notin \mathrm{dom}(m)$. In event **progress**, the guard $y \notin bm$ replaces the weaker guards $y \notin \mathrm{dom}(m)$.

We have two new events. The first one is called **discover_contention**. The only difference with the guard of this event and that of event **progress** concerns the condition $y \in bm$, which is true in **discover_contention** and false in **progress**. The action of this event adds the pair $x \mapsto y$ to c. The second new event is called **solve_contention**. It is enabled when both pairs $x \mapsto y$ and $y \mapsto x$ are present in c. This event resets c and removes x and y from bm. This formalizes what happens after the "very short delay". Notice that this event is not part of the protocol: it corresponds to a "daemon" acting when the very short delay has just passed. Here are the events:

```
discover_contention
    any x, y where
        x ↦ y ∈ m
        y ∈ bm
    then
        c := c ∪ {x ↦ y}
        m := m \ {x ↦ y}
    end
```

```
solve_contention
    any x, y where
        c = {x ↦ y, y ↦ x}
    then
        c := ∅
        bm := bm \ {x, y}
    end
```

All invariants are proved to be maintained easily.

13.5 Fourth refinement: simplification

In this refinement, we data-refine the previous model. In fact, the guard

$$g[\{x\}] \cap n = \{y\}$$

is simplified by introducing a variable d replacing n. Here are the new invariants:

---

variables: l, d, m, c, bm

---

inv4_1: $d \in n \to \mathbb{P}(n)$

inv4_2: $\forall x \cdot x \in n \Rightarrow d(x) = g[\{x\}] \cap n$

Here are the impacted events:

---

init
$\quad l :\in N$
$\quad d :| \left(\begin{array}{l} d' \in N \to \mathbb{P}(N) \\ \forall x \cdot (x \in N \Rightarrow d'(x) = g[\{x\}]) \end{array} \right)$
$\quad m := \varnothing$
$\quad c := \varnothing$
$\quad bm := \varnothing$

---

elect
$\quad$**any** x **where**
$\quad\quad x \in \text{dom}(d)$
$\quad\quad d(x) = \varnothing$
$\quad$**then**
$\quad\quad l := x$
$\quad$**end**

---

send_msg
$\quad$**any** x, y **where**
$\quad\quad x \in \text{dom}(d)$
$\quad\quad d(x) = \{y\}$
$\quad\quad x \notin bm$
$\quad$**then**
$\quad\quad m := m \cup \{x \mapsto y\}$
$\quad\quad bm := bm \cup \{x\}$
$\quad$**end**

---

progress
$\quad$**any** x, y **where**
$\quad\quad x \mapsto y \in m$
$\quad\quad y \notin bm$
$\quad$**then**
$\quad\quad d := (\{x\} \mathbin{\lhd\mkern-9mu-} d) \mathbin{\lhd\mkern-9mu-} \{y \mapsto d(y) \setminus \{x\}\}$
$\quad\quad m := m \setminus \{x \mapsto y\}$
$\quad\quad bm := bm \setminus \{x\}$
$\quad$**end**

The proofs that these events correctly refine their respective abstractions are easy.

13.6 Fifth refinement: introducing cardinality

In the guard of events **elect** or **send_msg**, it is checked that the set $d(x)$ is either empty or a singleton. In most cases, such tests can be simplified by just checking that the cardinality of $d(x)$ is either equal to 1 or 0. The purpose of this simple refinement is to introduce this optimization. Here is the new state:

variables: l, d, m, c, bm, r

inv5_1: $\quad r \in N \to \mathbb{N}$

inv5_2: $\quad \forall x \cdot (x \in N \Rightarrow r(x) = \mathrm{card}(d(x)))$

Here are the impacted events:

init
$\quad l :\in N$
$\quad d :\mid \left(\begin{array}{l} d' \in N \to \mathbb{P}(N) \\ \forall x \cdot (x \in N \Rightarrow d'(x) = g[\{x\}]) \end{array} \right)$
$\quad m := \varnothing$
$\quad c := \varnothing$
$\quad bm := \varnothing$
$\quad r :\mid \left(\begin{array}{l} r' \in N \to \mathbb{N} \\ \forall x \cdot (x \in N \Rightarrow r'(x) = \mathrm{card}(g[\{x\}])) \end{array} \right)$

elect
$\quad$**any** x **where**
$\qquad x \in N$
$\qquad r(x) = 0$
$\quad$**then**
$\qquad l := x$
$\quad$**end**

send_msg
$\quad$**any** x, y **where**
$\qquad x \in N$
$\qquad r(x) = 1$
$\qquad y \in d(x)$
$\qquad x \notin bm$
$\quad$**then**
$\qquad m := m \cup \{x \mapsto y\}$
$\qquad bm := bm \cup \{x\}$
$\quad$**end**

progress
$\quad$**any** x, y **where**
$\qquad x \mapsto y \in m$
$\qquad y \notin bm$
$\quad$**then**
$\qquad d := (\{x\} \lhd d) \Lleftarrow \{y \mapsto d(y) \setminus \{x\}\}$
$\qquad r := (\{x\} \lhd r) \Lleftarrow \{y \mapsto r(y) - 1\}$
$\qquad m := m \setminus \{x \mapsto y\}$
$\quad$**end**

14

Mathematical models for proof obligations

14.1 Introduction

This chapter contains the mathematical justification of the proof obligation rules used in this book. More precisely, we are going to give solid mathematical definitions to the following proof obligation rules:

Rules	Chapter 5	This Chapter	Rules	Chapter 5	This Chapter
INV	§2.2	§2	FIN	§2.8	§6.3
FIS	§2.3	§2	VAR	§2.9	§6.3
GRD	§2.4	§5.3	WFIS	§2.10	§5.3
MRG	§2.5	§6.2	THM	§2.11	
SIM	§2.6	§5.3	WD	§2.12	
NAT	§2.7	§6.3	DLF		§2

In this presentation, to simplify matters, we suppose that we have models defined without constants.

14.2 Proof obligation rules for invariant preservation

In this section, our intention is to *formally justify* the invariant proof obligation rules, namely INV, FIS, and DLF, which we use throughout this book. For this, we develop a set-theoretic representation of the discrete models and then we establish a connection between this representation and the event models.

We suppose that the state variables v are constrained by the invariant $I(v)$. The initialization event init is defined by means of the after-predicate $K(v')$. Each event, say $event_i$, different from init, is defined by means of its guard $G_i(v)$ and before–after predicate $R_i(v, v')$. This can be stated as follows:

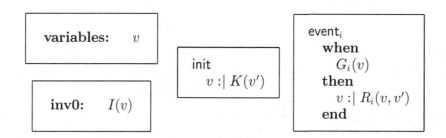

Our mathematical model is made of three items: (1) a set S on which the variables v are moving; (2) a non-empty initializing set L; and (3) a certain binary relation ae_i for each event $event_i$. The fact that the invariant $I(v)$ is established by the initializing event init and preserved by the event $event_i$ is simply formalized by saying that L is included in S and ae_i is a binary relation built on S:

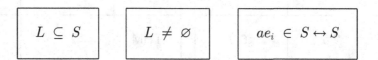

In order to link this set-theoretic representation with the proof obligation rules we have used, it suffices to formally define S, L, and ae_i. It involves the invariant $I(v)$ for the set S, the after predicate $K(v')$ for the set L, and the guard $G_i(v)$ and before–after predicate $R_i(v, v')$ for the relation ae_i. This yields:

$$
\begin{aligned}
S &= \{\, v \mid I(v)\,\} \\[2mm]
L &= \{\, v \mid K(v)\,\} \\[2mm]
ae_i &= \{\, v \mapsto v' \mid I(v) \wedge G_i(v) \wedge R_i(v, v')\,\} \\[2mm]
\mathrm{dom}\,(ae_i) &= \{\, v \mid I(v) \wedge G_i(v)\,\}
\end{aligned}
$$

The fact that the set L is not empty leads to the following, which is exactly the proof obligation FIS for the init event:

$\vdash\ \exists v \cdot K(v)$	FIS

The translation of the condition $L \subseteq S$ yields the proof obligation rule INV for the init event, namely:

$K(v)\ \vdash\ I(v)$	INV

The last definition above states that $G_i(v)$ and $I(v)$ together denote the genuine domain of the relation ae_i. But the domain of ae_i is defined to be the set:

$$
v \mid I(v) \wedge G_i(v) \wedge \exists v' \cdot R_i(v, v')\,\}
$$

This leads to the following, which is exactly the proof obligation FIS for events:

$\begin{aligned}&I(v)\\&G_i(v)\\ \vdash\ &\\ &\exists v' \cdot R_i(v, v')\end{aligned}$	FIS

Finally, the translation of the predicate $ae_i \in S \leftrightarrow S$ yields exactly the proof obligation rule INV, namely:

$$
\begin{array}{|l|l|}
\hline
\begin{array}{l} I(v) \\ G_i(v) \\ \quad R_i(v, v') \\ \vdash \\ \quad I(v') \end{array} & \text{INV} \\
\hline
\end{array}
$$

In case the invariant $I(v)$ is made of several sub-invariants $I_1(v), \ldots, I_n(v)$, then the previous rule splits into n separate rules (one for each sub-invariant).

Sometimes we want to prove that the transition system does not deadlock, namely that it is always possible to have an event enabled. For this, we have to consider the global transition relation ae of our model; it is the union of all the individual transition relations corresponding to each event, formally:

$$ ae \;=\; ae_1 \;\cup\; \ldots \;\cup\; ae_n. $$

We have then just to prove that the domain of the relation ae is exactly the set S, that is:

$$ \mathrm{dom}(ae) \;=\; \{\, v \mid I(v) \wedge (G_1(v) \vee \ldots \vee G_n(v)) \,\} \;=\; \{\, v \mid I(v) \,\}. $$

This yields the following, which is exactly proof obligation rule DLF:

$$
\begin{array}{|l|l|}
\hline
\begin{array}{l} I(v) \\ \vdash \\ \quad G_1(v) \vee \ldots \vee G_n(v) \end{array} & \text{DLF} \\
\hline
\end{array}
$$

14.3 Observing the evolution of discrete transition systems: traces

In this section, we introduce the well-known concept of *trace*. A trace is a record of the history of what can be observed of a "running" discrete system after the occurrence of each transition. First, this concept will be presented by means of an example. After that, the example will be generalized. Finally, the concept will be given a solid mathematical definition. The concept of trace is introduced here because it has been used on many occasions to help define the notion of *refinement*. In Section 14.4, we shall present a simple refinement using traces. At the end of that section, we shall show that the use of trace is not really necessary however.

14.3.1 First example

As an introductory example, let us take the "action/weak-reaction" pattern, which is described in Chapter 3. The state is made of two variables a (for action) and r (for reaction) both ranging over the set $\{0, 1\}$. Here are the various events making this little system:

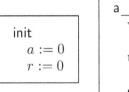
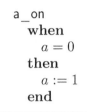
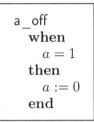

The reaction, represented by events r_on and r_off, is said to be *weak*. This can be explained as follows. When both action and reaction are "off" (0), the action, represented by events a_on and a_off, may alternate (after moving to "on" (1)) zero or more times between "off" (0) and "on" (1) before the reaction indeed reacts and moves to "on" (1). A similar symmetric effect can be observed in the other direction: when both action and reaction are "on" (1), the action (after moving to "off" (0)) may alternate zero or more times between "on" (1) and "off" (0) before the reaction indeed reacts and itself moves to "off" (0). This can be illustrated on the following figure:

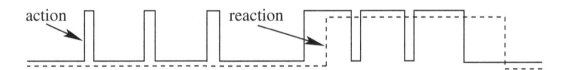

14.3.2 Traces

A more formal way to consider this is to record the finite succession of states, which *an external person can observe* from the beginning of operations until "now". In our example, let us illustrate the state by means of the following "circle" with the two values a and r inside it as follows:

With this convention, we show below a succession of states which can be observed after eight moves (among many others which can be observed):

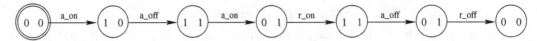

Such a succession of states is called a *trace*.

14.3.3 Characterizing traces

Let T be the set of all such traces. A trace t in T can be characterized in the following way:

(i) It is a finite sequence of size at least 1.
(ii) The first element of it is a member of the initial set of states as defined by the init event.
(iii) Two successive elements in it are related by the before–after predicate defined by the events.

Moreover, when a trace t belongs to T, then all prefixes of t except the empty sequence are also members of T. This is very intuitive: clearly, the recording of what we have observed till now must contain what we have observed before. Finally, the entire set of traces T is characterized in three different ways:

(i) In some discrete systems, the number of traces is limited: in fact, such systems are due to eventually deadlock (when all event guards become false) after some time.
(ii) In other systems, however, each trace can always be extended. The number of traces is not limited and the system is running for ever.
(iii) There are some intermediate cases where some traces can be extended while others cannot. It simply means that, in some circumstances, such systems deadlock while in others they run for ever.

In the proposed example above, our "action/weak-reaction" system is in case (2); any trace can always be extended. The system always "runs" for ever.

14.3.4 Graph of evolution

Another way to look at the evolution of a discrete transition system is to show its *graph of evolution*. In our example, this graph is finite since the set of states is finite too; we have four different states only. Here is an illustration of this graph:

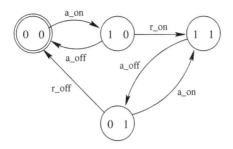

As can be seen, a trace corresponds to a finite path, which can be followed in this graph from an initial state till a certain point. Notice that in the previous figure we have emphasized the initial state, which is unique in this case (but this is not always the case).

14.3.5 Mathematical representation

All this can be further formalized by defining directly the various binary relations corresponding to the events. The initialization is expressed under the form of an initial set L of states. In the case of our example, we obtain the following:

$$
\begin{array}{lll}
L \;=\; \{0 \mapsto 0\} &
\begin{array}{lcl}
\mathsf{a\_on\_rel} & = & \{(0 \mapsto 0) \mapsto (1 \mapsto 0), (0 \mapsto 1) \mapsto (1 \mapsto 1)\} \\
\mathsf{a\_off\_rel} & = & \{(1 \mapsto 0) \mapsto (0 \mapsto 0), (1 \mapsto 1) \mapsto (0 \mapsto 1)\} \\
\mathsf{r\_on\_rel} & = & \{(1 \mapsto 0) \mapsto (1 \mapsto 1)\} \\
\mathsf{r\_off\_rel} & = & \{(0 \mapsto 1) \mapsto (0 \mapsto 0)\}.
\end{array}
\end{array}
$$

By taking the union of all these relations, we obtain the relation ae corresponding to all transitions:

$$
ae \;=\; \{ \;
\begin{aligned}
& (0 \mapsto 0) \mapsto (1 \mapsto 0), \\
& (0 \mapsto 1) \mapsto (1 \mapsto 1), \\
& (1 \mapsto 0) \mapsto (0 \mapsto 0), \\
& (1 \mapsto 1) \mapsto (0 \mapsto 1), \\
& (1 \mapsto 0) \mapsto (1 \mapsto 1), \\
& (0 \mapsto 1) \mapsto (0 \mapsto 0) \; \}.
\end{aligned}
$$

Given a discrete transition system built on a set S and defined by means of an initializing set L and a transition relation ae, the corresponding set of traces $T(L \mapsto ae)$ can be defined as follows:

$$
T(L \mapsto ae) \;\subseteq\; \mathbb{N}_1 \times (\mathbb{N}_1 \nrightarrow S).
$$

The pair $n \mapsto t$ made of a positive natural number n and a trace t belongs to the set $T(L \mapsto ae)$ if the following holds:

$$
n \mapsto t \ \in \ T(L \mapsto ae) \quad \Leftrightarrow \quad
\left(
\begin{array}{l}
n \in \mathbb{N}_1 \\
t \in 1 .. n \to S \\
t(1) \in L \\
\forall i \cdot i \in 1 .. n - 1 \ \Rightarrow \ t(i) \mapsto t(i+1) \ \in \ ae
\end{array}
\right)
$$

This formal definition corresponds to the informal characterization we gave in Section 14.3.3, namely:

(i) It is a finite sequence of size at least 1.
(ii) The first element of it is a member of the initial set of states as defined by the init event.
(iii) Two successive elements in it are related by the before–after predicate defined by the events.

From this definition, it is easy to prove that any non-empty prefix of t of size m is also a member of the set $T(L \mapsto ae)$.

14.4 Presentation of simple refinement by means of traces

In this section, we now present the concept of *simple refinement* between two discrete transition systems. As above with the notion of trace, simple refinement will be explained first through an example, which will be generalized afterwards until we obtain a solid mathematical definition. At the end of the section, we show that simple refinement as introduced so far is *relative to what can be observed from the state*, which is not necessarily the entire set of states.

14.4.1 Second example

As a second example, let us take the "action/strong-reaction" pattern, which is also presented in Chapter 3. The state is the same as in the previous example; it is defined by means of two variables a and r, both ranging over the set $\{0, 1\}$. The events are the same except that events a_on and a_off have stronger guards as shown below:

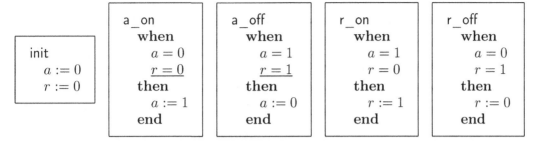

This time, the reaction is said to be "strong". When both action and reaction are "off" (0), the action can move to "on" (1). But it cannot move to "off" (0) again unless the reaction has itself moved to "on" (1). We have a similar symmetric situation in the other direction; the action cannot move to "on" (1) unless the reaction has already moved to "off" (0). As can be seen, the reaction follows the action and the action follows the reaction. This can be illustrated in the following figure:

Here is a trace which shows the described behavior after four transitions:

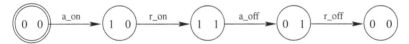

We can also abstract the traces by means of a complete picture of the transition graph:

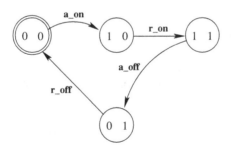

Finally, we might directly define this discrete system by means of the following initializing state M and binary relation re:

$$M = \{0 \mapsto 0\}$$

$$re = \{ \quad (0 \mapsto 0) \mapsto (1 \mapsto 0),$$
$$(1 \mapsto 0) \mapsto (1 \mapsto 1),$$
$$(1 \mapsto 1) \mapsto (0 \mapsto 1),$$
$$(0 \mapsto 1) \mapsto (0 \mapsto 0) \}$$

14.4.2 Comparing the two examples

When putting next to each other the two graphs representing the examples, we can see immediately that the second one is included in the first one. As a consequence, any trace of the second example is also a trace of the first one. In other words, observing a trace of the second example is not sufficient to discover which system has produced it; when we observe a trace of the second example– we cannot say for sure that it comes from that example – the first example could have produced it as well.

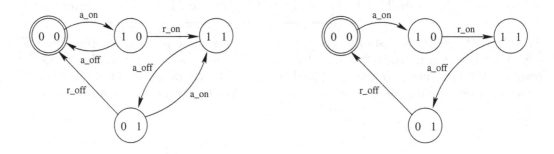

It is said (informally for the moment) that the second example is a *refinement* of the first one. And, conversely, the first example is said to be an *abstraction* of the second one. The idea presented at the beginning of this section is the essence of refinement: *acquiring a refined model instead of an abstraction must not be perceptible by the "buyer"*.

14.4.3 Simple refinement: informal approach

Our goal in this section is to try to characterize more accurately refinement in terms of trace comparisons. As said above, any trace of a refined model must also be a trace of the abstraction. But, on the other hand, saying that the set of traces of the refined model is included in the set of traces of the abstraction is clearly too strong since that would imply that a model with an empty set of traces could be a refinement of any abstraction, which is clearly counter-intuitive!

In order to proceed and obtain a more accurate definition, we have to rely on the original idea consisting in comparing behaviors: an observation of the behavior of the potential refinement must not allow us to deduce whether we observe the refinement or the abstraction (notice that the contrary is not true). So, if we cannot observe anything from a certain model, although we can observe something from a potential abstraction, then we can deduce that we are not observing the abstraction. This precludes the empty set of traces for the refinement.

But we can push this idea a bit further. If we can observe a certain trace, and then cannot observe anything any more after it (no additional evolution), then, if this is not the case in the abstraction where the same trace can be extended, then we can deduce that we are not observing the abstraction. This precludes any deadlock of the refinement which is not itself a deadlock of the abstraction. This property is called *relative deadlock freedom*.

Finally, we have also to consider the initial set. It is possible to have an initial set which is smaller in the refinement (M) than in the abstraction (L). But of course the initial refinement set must not be empty.

14.4.4 Simple refinement: formal definition

We are now ready to give the precise definition of simple refinement. Given a carrier set S, we have an abstraction consisting of an initial set L included in S and a transition relation ae from S to S. We have a potential refinement consisting of an initial set M included in S and a transition relation re from S to S. This can be formalized as follows:

$$L \subseteq S \qquad\qquad M \subseteq S$$

$$ae \in S \leftrightarrow S \qquad\qquad re \in S \leftrightarrow S$$

As said above, we first require that M is included in L and that M is not empty:

$$M \subseteq L \qquad\qquad M \neq \varnothing$$

We have now to consider the space on which the potential refinement states are moving: this is the union of M with the image of the initial set M under the transitive closure of the relation ae, namely $M \cup \mathrm{cl}(ae)[M]$. Clearly, this set contains exactly the elements of all traces of the refined model. Since we want that a refined trace is also an abstract one, we thus have the following additional property:

$$(M \cup \mathrm{cl}(ae)[M]) \triangleleft re \subseteq ae$$

Finally, we do not want a refined trace to be unable to be extended if the corresponding abstract one is able to be extended. This requires that the domain of the abstract transition relation ae intersected with the set $M \cup \mathrm{cl}(ae)[M]$ is included in the domain of the refined transition relation re also intersected with the same set $M \cup \mathrm{cl}(ae)[M]$; formally:

$$(M \cup \mathrm{cl}(ae)[M]) \cap \mathrm{dom}(ae) \subseteq (M \cup \mathrm{cl}(ae)[M]) \cap \mathrm{dom}(re)$$

The last two conditions are not so easy to deal with because of the presence of the set $M \cup \mathrm{cl}(ae)[M]$. As a consequence, we forget about this set and get the following slightly stronger (but far simpler) conditions:

$$
\begin{array}{l}
M \subseteq L \\[2mm]
M \neq \varnothing \\[2mm]
re \subseteq ae \\[2mm]
\mathrm{dom}(ae) \subseteq \mathrm{dom}(re)
\end{array}
\qquad (I)
$$

Going back to our examples, we can now clearly prove that the second one is a refinement of the first one:

$$L = \{0 \mapsto 0\}$$

$$M = \{0 \mapsto 0\}$$

$$
ae = \{ \begin{array}[t]{l}
(0 \mapsto 0) \mapsto (1 \mapsto 0), \\
(0 \mapsto 1) \mapsto (1 \mapsto 1), \\
(1 \mapsto 0) \mapsto (0 \mapsto 0), \\
(1 \mapsto 1) \mapsto (0 \mapsto 1), \\
(1 \mapsto 0) \mapsto (1 \mapsto 1), \\
(0 \mapsto 1) \mapsto (0 \mapsto 0) \}
\end{array}
$$

$$
re = \{ \begin{array}[t]{l}
(0 \mapsto 0) \mapsto (1 \mapsto 0), \\
(1 \mapsto 1) \mapsto (0 \mapsto 1), \\
(1 \mapsto 0) \mapsto (1 \mapsto 1), \\
(0 \mapsto 1) \mapsto (0 \mapsto 0) \}
\end{array}
$$

In conclusion, we have seen that traces allowed us to informally reason about a refinement by making explicit what can be observed in a refinement and in an abstraction. But, on the other hand, we end up with conditions (I), which do not depend on the traces, but rather on the initial sets and on the transition relations of both the abstraction and the refinement.

14.4.5 Considering the individual events

In the previous section, we considered the abstract and concrete relation ae and re obtained after taking the union of the various relations $ae_1, \ldots, ae_n$ making the abstract events and $re_1, \ldots, re_n$ making the corresponding concrete events; formally:

$$ae = ae_1 \cup \cdots \cup ae_n \qquad re = re_1 \cup \cdots \cup re_n.$$

The above condition $re \subseteq ae$ is made stronger by imposing that the containment is constrained at the finer level of each individual events, namely:

$$re_1 \subseteq ae_1 \ \wedge \ \ldots \ \wedge \ re_n \subseteq ae_n.$$

Such conditions clearly imply $re \subseteq ae$. We could have imposed some similar stronger conditions dealing with the domains as well, namely:

$$\mathrm{dom}(ae_1) \subseteq \mathrm{dom}(re_1) \ \wedge \ \ldots \ \wedge \ \mathrm{dom}(ae_n) \subseteq \mathrm{dom}(re_n).$$

But this happens to be sometimes too strong. Refinement conditions (I) can be re-written as follows:

$$
\boxed{
\begin{array}{l}
M \subseteq L \\[1ex]
M \neq \varnothing \\[1ex]
re_1 \subseteq ae_1 \\[1ex]
\ldots \\[1ex]
re_n \subseteq ae_n \\[1ex]
\mathrm{dom}(ae) \subseteq \mathrm{dom}(re)
\end{array}
}
\qquad (II)
$$

In doing so, we impose (for the moment) that to each concrete event formalized by the relation re_i there corresponds an abstract event formalized by the relation ae_i. Notice that this constraint will be made more liberal in Section 14.6, where we shall study three possible extensions: (1) the *splitting* of an abstract event into several concrete ones, (2) the *merging* of several abstract events into a single concrete one, and (3) the introduction in a refinement of *new events*, which have no counterparts in the abstraction.

14.4.6 External and internal variables

In the previous section, we defined a refinement by considering what we can observe from our discrete transition systems. But, what we can observe is just a *convention* we give ourselves. In fact, the state can be more complicated than what we can observe of it. In the "action/reaction" examples, as they are developed in Chapter 3, we have a more complicated state containing, besides variables a and r, two additional variables ca and cr recording the number of times the action and the reaction are "on" (1) respectively. Such variables ca and cr are said to be *internal variables*, whereas variables a and r are said to be *external variables*. If we represent the state with a circle containing four values as shown below:

then the transition relation corresponding to the first example can be illustrated partially (because it is now infinite) as follows:

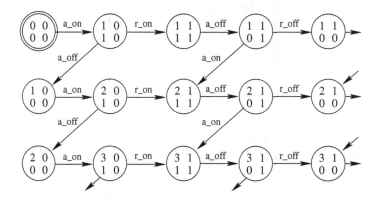

In summary, to define the refinement we are only interested in comparing the two sets of traces, recording only those parts of the states that correspond to the variables we decide are *external*.

14.4.7 External set

In order to formalize what has been explained in the previous section, we consider the set of states S and a total function f projecting S on an *external set* E:

$$f \in S \to E$$

This projection function is applied systematically in order to define the transition relations used to define the refinement between two discrete transition systems. We do not compare directly the re_i with the ae_i, but rather their projections on the external set E by means of the function f, that is: $f^{-1} \; ; \; re_i \; ; \; f$ and $f^{-1} \; ; \; ae_i \; ; \; f$. This can be illustrated in the following diagram where an abstract event is represented by the relation named ae_i and the corresponding refined event is represented by the relation named re_i:

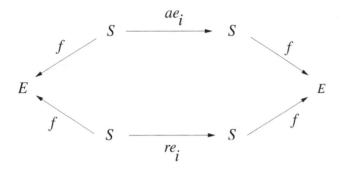

In other words, what has been defined as the simple refinement conditions (II) in Section 14.4.3 remains valid, provided we replace the set S by the external set E. This is formalized in the following conditions:

$$
\begin{array}{l}
M \subseteq L \\[1ex]
M \neq \varnothing \\[1ex]
f^{-1} ; re_1 ; f \ \subseteq \ f^{-1} ; ae_1 ; f \\[1ex]
\dots \\[1ex]
f^{-1} ; re_n ; f \ \subseteq \ f^{-1} ; ae_n ; f \\[1ex]
\mathrm{dom}(ae) \subseteq \mathrm{dom}(re)
\end{array}
$$

$$(III)$$

An additional sophistication consists in changing the set of state S to another T when we refine. The purpose of the next section is to explain how we can define *general refinement*, also called data refinement in such a case.

14.5 General refinement set-theoretic representation

As in the Section 14.2 for invariants, our intention is to formally *justify* in this section the refinement proof obligation rules, namely FIS, GRD, INV, and SIM, that we use in this book. For this, we shall extend the set-theoretic representation of Section 14.2.

14.5.1 Introduction

We suppose, as above, that the abstract state variables v are together moving within a certain set S. But we now have to introduce the *external* set. In fact, the set S is able to be projected on an external set E. As said in the previous sections, the external sets E defines what can be *observed* in a model. Similarly, the refined state variables w are together moving within a certain set T, which is also able to be projected on an external set F (notice that now external sets E and F are not identical). Let f and g denote the functions projecting the set S on the set E and the set T on the set F respectively:

$$
\begin{array}{l}
f \in S \to E \\[2mm]
g \in T \to F
\end{array}
$$

The external sets E and F are related by a certain *total function* h. The reason for h to be a *function* is that we want to be able to *reconstruct* the abstract observation from the concrete one. In other words, we do not want to loose in the concrete state what can be observed in the abstract one. The function h is thus typed as follows:

$$
h \in F \to E
$$

Let ae_i denote a binary relation corresponding to an abstract event event$_i$ and let re_i be the corresponding refined event binary relation. The initializing set L is not empty and included in S, whereas the refined initializing set M is not empty and included in T. We then have the following typing constraints:

$$
\begin{array}{l}
L \subseteq S \\[2mm]
M \subseteq T
\end{array}
\qquad
\begin{array}{l}
L \neq \varnothing \\[2mm]
M \neq \varnothing
\end{array}
\qquad
\begin{array}{l}
ae_i \in S \leftrightarrow S \\[2mm]
re_i \in T \leftrightarrow T
\end{array}
$$

All this can be illustrated in the following diagram:

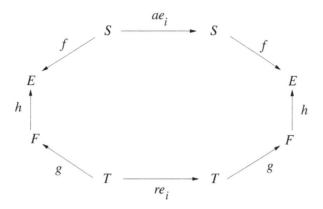

In this diagram, the initializing case can be obtained by assuming that the relation ae_i is $S \times L$ and the relation re_i is $T \times M$.

14.5.2 Formal definition of refinement

We now present a formal definition of refinement that is entirely based on the external sets. This will result in a kind of ultimate definition of refinement. In the next section we shall however derive some *sufficient refinement conditions* implying a formalization of the gluing invariant.

The previous diagram shows how we can link the external set F to itself by navigating either through h, f^{-1}, ae_i, f, and h^{-1} in the abstraction or through g^{-1}, re_i, and g in the refinement. These two compositions result in two binary relations built on F. The definition of refinement follows: the event represented by the relation ae_i is refined by that represented by the relation re_i if the relation $g^{-1}\,; re_i\,; g$ is *included* in the relation $h\,; f^{-1}\,; ae_i\,; f\,; h^{-1}$. As can be seen, refinement is clearly defined *relative to the external sets*. The initializing case simplifies to $g[M] \subseteq h^{-1}[f[L]]$:

$$
\begin{array}{l}
g[M] \;\subseteq\; h^{-1}[f[L]] \\[4pt]
M \neq \varnothing \\[4pt]
g^{-1}\,, re_1\,; g \;\subseteq\; h\,; f^{-1}\,; ae_1\,; f\,; h^{-1} \\[4pt]
\dots \\[4pt]
g^{-1}\,; re_n\,; g \;\subseteq\; h\,; f^{-1}\,; ae_n\,; f\,; h^{-1} \\[4pt]
h^{-1}[f[\mathrm{dom}(ae)]] \;\subseteq\; g[\mathrm{dom}(re)]
\end{array}
$$

(IV)

If a pair of external values is linked through the refined event re_i, it must also be linked through the abstract event ae_i. In other words, the refined event must not contradict the abstract one *from the point of view of the external sets.*

14.5.3 Sufficient refinement conditions: forward simulation

We are now going to define a sufficient refinement condition for refinement: it is called *forward simulation*. In the next section, we shall see another sufficient condition called *backward simulation*. Let r be a *total* binary relation from the concrete set T to the abstract set S. This relation formalizes the gluing invariant between the refined state and the abstract one. Formally:

$$r \in T \leftrightarrow S$$

Note that the symbol "$\leftrightarrow$" is used to define the set of *total binary relations* from one set to another. The introduction of the relation r leads to the following diagram:

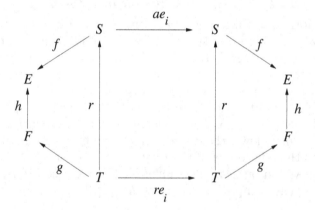

The relation r must be *compatible* with the function h linking the external sets F and E. In other words, if y is linked to x through r, then $g(y)$ must be linked to $f(x)$ through h, that is to say: $f(x) = h(g(y))$. This can be formalized by means of the following condition:

$$\forall x, y \cdot (y \mapsto x \in r \;\Rightarrow\; f(x) = h(g(y)))$$

The previous condition can be simplified to the following equivalent one:

$$r^{-1}\,;g \;\subseteq\; f\,;h^{-1} \qquad \text{C1}$$

Here is the proof (it uses simple predicate calculus rules):

$$\forall x, y \cdot (y \mapsto x \in r \; \Rightarrow \; f(x) = h(g(y)))$$
$\Leftrightarrow$
$$\forall x, y \cdot (y \mapsto x \in r \; \Rightarrow \; g(y) \mapsto f(x) \in h)$$
$\Leftrightarrow$
$$\forall x, y, z \cdot (z = g(y) \; \wedge \; y \mapsto x \in r \; \Rightarrow \; z \mapsto f(x) \in h)$$
$\Leftrightarrow$
$$\forall x, z \cdot (\exists y \cdot (z = g(y) \; \wedge \; y \mapsto x \in r) \; \Rightarrow \; z \mapsto f(x) \in h)$$
$\Leftrightarrow$
$$\forall x, z \cdot (\exists y \cdot (z = g(y) \; \wedge \; y \mapsto x \in r) \; \Rightarrow \; \exists u \cdot (u = f(x) \; \wedge \; z \mapsto u \in h))$$
$\Leftrightarrow$
$$\forall x, z \cdot (\exists y \cdot (x \mapsto y \in r^{-1} \; \wedge \; y \mapsto z \in g) \; \Rightarrow \; \exists u \cdot (x \mapsto u \in f \; \wedge \; u \mapsto z \in h^{-1}))$$
$\Leftrightarrow$
$$\forall x, z \cdot (x \mapsto z \in (r^{-1} ; g) \; \Rightarrow \; x \mapsto z \in (f ; h^{-1}))$$
$\Leftrightarrow$
$$r^{-1} ; g \; \subseteq \; f ; h^{-1}$$

We now suppose that the following two additional conditions hold:

$r^{-1} ; re_i \; \subseteq \; ae_i ; r^{-1}$	C2
$g^{-1} \; \subseteq \; h ; f^{-1} ; r^{-1}$	C3

It is then easy to prove that conditions C1, C2, and C3 are together *sufficient to ensure refinement*, namely condition (IV) above. It relies on the monotonicity of composition with regards to set inclusion and also on the associativity of composition. Here is the proof:

$$g^{-1} ; re_i ; g$$
$\subseteq$ C3
$$h ; f^{-1} ; r^{-1} ; re_i ; g$$
$\subseteq$ C2
$$h ; f^{-1} ; ae_i ; r^{-1} ; g$$
$\subseteq$ C1
$$h ; f^{-1} ; ae_i ; f ; h^{-1}$$

But it happens that condition **C3** can be deduced from condition **C1** and from the totality of r. Here is the proof:

$$r^{-1};g \;\subseteq\; f;h^{-1}$$

$\Rightarrow$ **C1**

Set theory

$$r;r^{-1};g \;\subseteq\; r;f;h^{-1}$$

$\Rightarrow$ $\mathrm{id} \subseteq r;r^{-1}$ since $r \in T \leftrightarrow S$

$$g \;\subseteq\; r;f;h^{-1}$$

$\Leftrightarrow$ Set theory

$$g^{-1} \;\subseteq\; h;f^{-1};r^{-1}$$ **C3**

The relationship between the initializing sets L and M can be deduced from rule **C2** by replacing ae_i by $S \times L$ and re_i by $T \times M$. We leave it to the reader to show that it yields:

$$M \;\subseteq\; r^{-1}[L]$$

As a consequence, there only remains condition **C2**. In order to translate this condition and thus establish our proof obligation rules, it suffices to link S, T, ae_i, re_i, and r with this new formulation. We suppose to have the following abstract model as defined in Section 14.2:

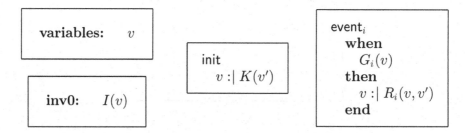

The following model is supposed to refine the previous one. Notice the **with** clause in event$_i$. It defines a *non-deterministic witness* for v'.

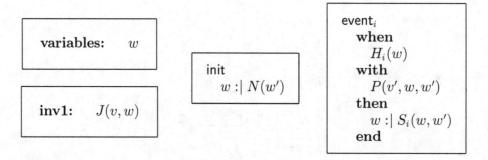

This yields:

$$
\begin{aligned}
S &= \{\, v \mid I(v) \,\} \\[2mm]
T &= \{\, w \mid \exists v \cdot (\, I(v) \;\wedge\; J(v,w) \,) \,\} \\[2mm]
L &= \{\, v \mid K(v) \,\} \\[2mm]
M &= \{\, w \mid N(w) \,\} \\[2mm]
ae_i &= \{\, v \mapsto v' \mid I(v) \;\wedge\; G_i(v) \;\wedge\; R_i(v,v') \,\} \\[2mm]
re_i &= \{\, w \mapsto w' \mid (\, \exists v \cdot I(v) \;\wedge\; J(v,w) \,) \;\wedge\; H_i(w) \;\wedge\; S_i(w,w') \,\} \\[2mm]
r &= \{\, w \mapsto v \mid I(v) \;\wedge\; J(v,w) \,\} \\[2mm]
\mathrm{dom}\,(ae_i) &= \{\, v \mid I(v) \;\wedge\; G_i(v) \,\} \\[2mm]
\mathrm{dom}\,(re_i) &= \{\, w \mid \exists v \cdot (\, I(v) \;\wedge\; J(v,w) \,) \;\wedge\; H_i(w) \,\}
\end{aligned}
$$

The translation of $M \subseteq r^{-1}[L]$ gives us the following, which is exactly rule INV in the case of initializing a refinement:

$$
\begin{array}{|l|l|}
\hline
\begin{array}{l}
N(w) \\
\vdash \\
\exists v \cdot (\; K(v) \;\wedge\; J(v,w) \;)
\end{array}
& \text{INV} \\
\hline
\end{array}
$$

Note that the domain of the binary relation r is T. The binary relation r is thus indeed a total relation as required. The domain of the binary relation re_i is the set:

$$
\{\, w \mid \exists v \cdot (\, I(v) \;\wedge\; J(v,w) \,) \;\wedge\; H_i(w) \;\wedge\; \exists w' \cdot S_i(w,w') \,\}
$$

Thus our last constraint on the domain of re_i leads to the following, which is exactly FIS in the case of a refinement:

$$
\begin{array}{|l|l|}
\hline
\begin{array}{l}
I(v) \\
J(v,w) \\
H_i(w) \\
\vdash \\
\exists w' \cdot S_i(w,w')
\end{array}
& \text{FIS} \\
\hline
\end{array}
$$

The translation of condition **C2**, namely $r^{-1} ; re_i \subseteq ae_i ; r^{-1}$, yields:

$$I(v) \ \wedge \ J(v,w) \ \wedge \ H_i(w) \ \wedge \ S_i(w,w') \ \vdash \ G_i(v) \ \wedge \ \exists v' \cdot (\, R_i(v,v') \ \wedge \ J(v',w') \,)$$

It can be split as follows yielding exactly proof obligation GRD:

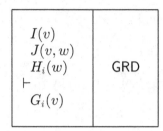

$$
\begin{array}{|c|c|}
\hline
\begin{array}{l} I(v) \\ J(v,w) \\ H_i(w) \\ \vdash \\ G_i(v) \end{array} & \text{GRD} \\
\hline
\end{array}
$$

The second half is the following. As can be seen, the goal contains an existential quantification:

$$
\begin{array}{l}
I(v) \\
J(v,w) \\
H_i(w) \\
S_i(w,w') \\
\vdash \\
\exists v' \cdot (\, R_i(v,v') \ \wedge \ J(v',w') \,)
\end{array}
$$

Thanks to the witness predicate $P(v',w,w')$ provided in the refined event, this sequent can be decomposed into the following three proof obligation rules:

$$
\begin{array}{|c|c|}
\hline
\begin{array}{l} I(v) \\ J(v,w) \\ H_i(w) \\ S_i(w,w') \\ \vdash \\ \exists v' \cdot P(v',w,w') \end{array} & \text{WFIS} \\
\hline
\end{array}
\qquad
\begin{array}{|c|c|}
\hline
\begin{array}{l} I(v) \\ J(v,w) \\ H_i(w) \\ S_i(w,w') \\ P(v',w,w') \\ \vdash \\ R_i(v,v') \end{array} & \text{SIM} \\
\hline
\end{array}
\qquad
\begin{array}{|c|c|}
\hline
\begin{array}{l} I(v) \\ J(v,w) \\ H_i(w) \\ S_i(w,w') \\ P(v',w,w') \\ \vdash \\ J(v',w') \end{array} & \text{INV} \\
\hline
\end{array}
$$

This decomposition is a direct consequence of applying the derived inference rule **CUT_EXT** proved at the end of Section 9.4.2 of Chapter 9. It remains now for us to formalize relative deadlock freedom. This corresponds to the condition:

$$r^{-1}[\mathrm{dom}(ae)] \subseteq \mathrm{dom}(re)$$

This is translated trivially as follows:

$$
\begin{array}{|l|c|}
\hline
\begin{array}{l}
I(v) \\
J(v, w) \\
G_1(v) \ \lor \ \ldots \ \lor \ G_n(v) \\
\vdash \\
\quad H_1(w) \ \lor \ \ldots \ \lor \ H_n(w)
\end{array} & \text{DLF} \\
\hline
\end{array}
$$

Note that a stronger deadlock freedom rule could have been defined requiring that each individual abstract guard implies the concrete one; formally:

$$
\begin{array}{|l|c|}
\hline
\begin{array}{l}
I(v) \\
J(v, w) \\
G_i(v) \\
\vdash \\
\quad H_i(w)
\end{array} & \text{DLF} \\
\hline
\end{array}
$$

14.5.4 Another sufficient refinement conditions: backward simulation

There exists another sufficient condition for refinement: it is called *backward simulation*. Relation r has got the same property as in previous section: it is a total relation from T to S. Conditions **C1** and **C3** of previous section are the same, only condition **C2** is changed to condition **C2'**. Next is a copy of the conditions of previous section together with the new ones:

$$
\begin{array}{|l|c|}
\hline
r^{-1} \, ; g \ \subseteq \ f \, ; h^{-1} & \text{C1} \\
\hline
r^{-1} \, ; re_i \ \subseteq \ ae_i \, ; r^{-1} & \text{C2} \\
\hline
g^{-1} \ \subseteq \ h \, ; f^{-1} \, ; r^{-1} & \text{C3} \\
\hline
\end{array}
\qquad
\begin{array}{|l|c|}
\hline
r^{-1} \, ; g \ \subseteq \ f \, ; h^{-1} & \text{C1} \\
\hline
r^{-1} \, ; re_i^{-1} \ \subseteq \ ae_i^{-1} \, ; r^{-1} & \text{C2'} \\
\hline
g^{-1} \ \subseteq \ h \, ; f^{-1} \, ; r^{-1} & \text{C3} \\
\hline
\end{array}
$$

Conditions C1, C2', and C3 can be put under the following equivalent forms D1, D2', and D3:

$g^{-1}\,;r\ \subseteq\ h\,;f^{-1}$	D1
$re_i\,;r\ \subseteq\ r\,;ae_i$	D2'
$g\ \subseteq\ r\,;f\,;h^{-1}$	D3

Next is the proof stating that conditions D1, D2', and D3 are sufficient to prove refinement:

$$g^{-1}\,;re_i\,;\underline{g}$$
$$\subseteq \qquad\qquad\qquad\qquad\text{D3}$$
$$g^{-1}\,;\underline{re_i\,;r}\,;f\,;h^{-1}$$
$$\subseteq \qquad\qquad\qquad\qquad\text{D2'}$$
$$\underline{g^{-1}\,;r}\,;ae_i\,;f\,;h^{-1}$$
$$\subseteq \qquad\qquad\qquad\qquad\text{D1}$$
$$h\,;f^{-1}\,;ae_i\,;f\,;h^{-1}$$

The reason for calling condition C2' "backward simulation" must be clear now by comparing it with C2. In C2 (forward), we are using re_i and ae_i, whereas in C2' (backward), we are using re_i^{-1} and ae_i^{-1}. In the sequel, we shall not use backward simulation.

14.5.5 *Refining a trace*

Forward (and backward) simulation allows one to prove that individual event refinements are generalizable to trace refinements. In this section, it is shown that it is the case for a trace comprising two events: it can clearly be extended trivially to traces containing more events. A trace with two events and its refinement is illustrated in the following diagram:

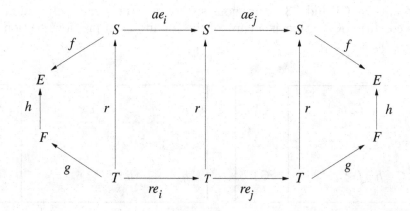

In order to verify (by forward simulation) that the trace ae_i ; ae_j is refined to the trace re_i ; re_j, it is sufficient to prove the following (this is condition C2 of Section 14.5.3):

$$r^{-1} ; re_i ; re_j \quad \subseteq \quad ae_i ; ae_j ; r^{-1}$$

But ae_i is refined to re_i, thus we have:

$$r^{-1} ; re_i \quad \subseteq \quad ae_i ; r^{-1}$$

Hence:

$$r^{-1} ; re_i ; re_j \quad \subseteq \quad ae_i ; r^{-1} ; re_j$$

And ae_j is refined to re_j, thus we have:

$$r^{-1} ; re_j \quad \subseteq \quad ae_j ; r^{-1}$$

Hence:

$$r^{-1} ; re_i ; re_j \quad \subseteq \quad ae_i ; r^{-1} ; re_j \quad \subseteq \quad ae_i ; ae_j ; r^{-1}$$

The proof with backward simulation is obtained in the same way.

14.6 Breaking the one-to-one relationship between abstract and concrete events

14.6.1 Splitting an abstract event

When refining an abstract event ae_i, it can be split into two (or more) events, say re_{i1} and re_{i2}. We simply prove that these events both refine ae_i.

14.6.2 Merging several abstract events

It is also possible to merge two abstract events ae_i and ae_j to form a single refined event re_{ij}. We simply have to prove that re_{ij} refines $ae_i \cup ae_j$. We insist that events event$_i$ and event$_j$ work in the model with the same variables v with invariant $I(v)$ and that they both have the same actions as shown below:

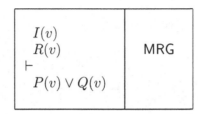

event$_i$
when
   $P(v)$
then
   S
end

event$_j$
when
   $Q(v)$
then
   S
end

The merging yields the following event:

event$_{ij}$
refines
   event$_i$
   event$_j$
when
   $R(v)$
then
   S
end

As a consequence the merging proof obligation rule is straightforward:

$$
\begin{array}{l}
I(v)\\
R(v)\\
\vdash\\
\quad P(v) \vee Q(v)
\end{array}
\qquad \text{MRG}
$$

14.6.3 Introducing new events

Besides changing the state in a refinement and also establishing a certain relationship between the concrete and abstract states by means of the, so-called, "gluing invariant", it is also possible to add new events in a refinement. Such new events have no counterpart in the abstraction, they correspond to transitions which can be observed in the concrete space but could not be observed in the abstraction. By having new events, we are observing our discrete system in the refinement with a finer grain than in the abstraction.

It is not so clear to see what it means for a model (with new events) to refine another more abstract one. We have to go back to the set of traces and consider what we can observe in the abstraction and what we can observe in the refinement. In order to simplify, we shall suppose in this approach that we have no event splitting or merging. Thus if "old" events in the abstraction are represented by the relation $ae_1, \ldots, ae_i, \ldots,$ ae_n, then these events exist in the refinement where they are represented by the relations $re_1, \ldots, re_i, \ldots, re_n$. The "new" events are represented in the refinement only by the binary relations $ne_1, \ldots, ne_k, \ldots, ne_m$. Next is an illustration of a short abstract trace with event ae_i followed ae_j. In the concrete space, we have event re_i followed by re_j, but between the two we have the new event ne_k, which could not be observed in the abstraction.

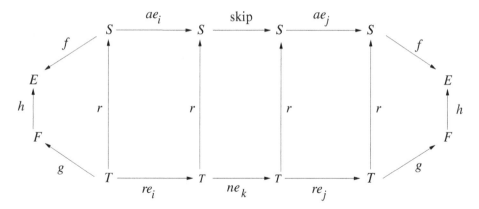

In fact, this new event simply refines a pseudo-event that does nothing (skip). We have thus the following forward simulation proof to perform:

$$r^{-1} \, ; ne_k \quad \subseteq \quad r^{-1}$$

From this, it is trivial to prove that the abstract trace $ae_i \, ; ae_j$ is refined to the concrete trace $re_i \, ; ne_k \, ; re_j$. It is simply an application of the technique we have already applied in Section 14.5.5. Suppose we have a new event of the following shape:

$$
\boxed{
\begin{array}{l}
\textsf{new\_event}_k \\
\quad \textbf{when} \\
\qquad N_k(w) \\
\quad \textbf{then} \\
\qquad w :| \; T_k(w, w') \\
\quad \textbf{end}
\end{array}
}
$$

What we have to prove for invariant preservation is an adaptation of rule INV:

$$
\boxed{
\begin{array}{l|l}
\begin{array}{l}
I(v) \\
J(v, w) \\
N_k(w) \\
T_k(w, w') \\
\vdash \\
J(v, w')
\end{array}
& \text{INV}
\end{array}
}
$$

The introduction of new events requires a slight modification in the relative deadlock freedom rule as we have to take into account the guards of the new events. We suppose that the guarding predicates of the new events are denoted by: $N_1(w)$, ..., $N_m(w)$.

The rule is modified so:

$$
\begin{array}{|l|c|}
\hline
\begin{array}{l}
I(v) \\
J(v, w) \\
G_1(v) \ \vee \ \ldots \ \vee \ G_n(v) \\
\vdash \\
\quad H_1(w) \ \vee \ \ldots \ \vee \ H_n(w) \ \vee \ N_1(w) \ \vee \ \ldots \ \vee \ N_m(w)
\end{array}
& \text{DLF} \\
\hline
\end{array}
$$

The stronger rule is modified as follows:

$$
\begin{array}{|l|c|}
\hline
\begin{array}{l}
I(v) \\
J(v, w) \\
G_i(v) \\
\vdash \\
\quad H_i(w) \ \vee \ N_1(w) \ \vee \ \ldots \ \vee \ N_m(w)
\end{array}
& \text{DLF} \\
\hline
\end{array}
$$

Notice that between two occurrences of concrete events represented by binary relations re_i and re_j there might be several occurrences of new events as indicated in the following figure:

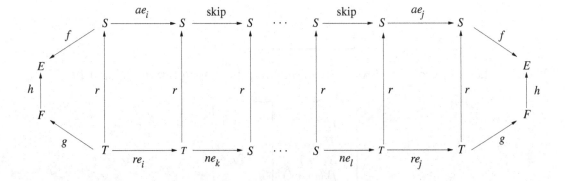

Clearly, we do not want this sequence of new events being possibly *infinite*, because the corresponding trace could not be a refinement of an abstract trace where the abstract event represented by the relation ae_i is indeed followed by the event represented by the binary relation ae_j. In other words, event re_j must be *reachable* after event re_i. This is the reason for introducing the two rules NAT and VAR. We must exhibit a natural number variant $V(w)$, which is a natural number. Each new event of the following form must decrease this variant:

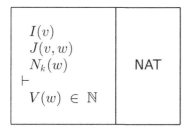

Here are the corresponding proof obligation rules:

$$
\begin{array}{|l|c|}
\hline
\begin{array}{l} I(v) \\ J(v,w) \\ N_k(w) \\ \vdash \\ \quad V(w) \ \in \ \mathbb{N} \end{array} & \text{NAT} \\
\hline
\end{array}
\qquad
\begin{array}{|l|c|}
\hline
\begin{array}{l} I(v) \\ J(v,w) \\ N_k(w) \\ T_k(w,w') \\ \vdash \\ \quad V(w') < V(w) \end{array} & \text{VAR} \\
\hline
\end{array}
$$

The variant decreasing can be generalized to the strict decreasing (strict inclusion) of a finite set $S(w)$. This yields the following two rules:

$$
\begin{array}{|l|c|}
\hline
\begin{array}{l} I(v) \\ J(v,w) \\ N_k(w) \\ \vdash \\ \quad \text{finite}(S(w)) \end{array} & \text{FIN} \\
\hline
\end{array}
\qquad
\begin{array}{|l|c|}
\hline
\begin{array}{l} I(v) \\ J(v,w) \\ N_k(w) \\ T_k(w,w') \\ \vdash \\ \quad S(w') \subset S(w) \end{array} & \text{VAR} \\
\hline
\end{array}
$$

15

Development of sequential programs

In this chapter, we shall see how to develop *sequential programs*. We present the approach we shall use, and then we propose a large number of examples.

Sequential programs (e.g. loops), when formally constructed, are usually developed gradually by means of a series of progressively more refined "sketches" starting with the formal specification and ending in the final program. Each such sketch is already (although often in a highly non-deterministic form) a monolithic description which resumes the final intended program in terms of a single formula. This is precisely that initial "formula", that is gradually transformed into the final program.

We are not going to use this approach here. After all, in order to prove a large formula, a logician usually breaks it down into various pieces, on which he performs some simple manipulations before putting them together again in a final proof.

15.1 A systematic approach to sequential program development

15.1.1 Components of a sequential program

A sequential program is essentially made up of a number of *individual assignments* that are glued together by means of various constructs. Typical constructs are sequential composition (;), loop (**while**), and condition (**if**). Their role is to explicitly *schedule* these assignments in a proper order so that the execution of the program can achieve its intended goal. Here is an example of a sequential program where the various assignments have been emphasized:

$$
\begin{aligned}
&\textbf{while} \quad j \neq m \quad \textbf{do} \\
&\quad \textbf{if} \quad g(j+1) > x \quad \textbf{then} \\
&\qquad \boxed{j := j+1} \\
&\quad \textbf{elsif} \quad k = j \quad \textbf{then} \\
&\qquad \boxed{k, j := k+1, j+1} \\
&\quad \textbf{else} \\
&\qquad \boxed{k, j, g := k+1, j+1, \mathsf{swap}\,(g, k+1, j+1)} \\
&\quad \textbf{end} \\
&\textbf{end}\,; \\
&\boxed{p := k}
\end{aligned}
$$

Note that, to simplify matters, we use a pidgin imperative language allowing us to have multiple assignments as in:

$$k, j := k + 1, j + 1 k, j, g := k + 1, j + 1, \mathsf{swap}\,(g, k+1, j+1)$$

Although it is not important for what we want to explain here, note that the expression $\mathsf{swap}\,(g, k+1, j+1)$ stands for the swapping of the values $g(k+1)$ and $g(j+1)$ in the array g. Also note that we have used a syntax with opening (**while**, **if**), intermediate (**do**, **then**, **elsif**, **else**), and closing (**end**) keywords. We could have used another syntax which would have been more appealing to Java or C programmers. In fact, the syntax used here in not important as long as we understand what we are writing.

In summary, we shall develop programs written in a simple pidgin programming language with the following syntax for program statements:

$$
\begin{aligned}
&< variable > := < expressions > \\
\\
&< statement > \,;\, < statement > \\
\\
&\textbf{if} \ < condition > \ \textbf{then} \ < statement > \ \textbf{else} \ < statement > \ \textbf{end} \\
\\
&\textbf{if} \ < condition > \ \textbf{then} \ < statement > \ \textbf{elsif} \ \ldots \ \textbf{else} \ < statement > \ \textbf{end} \\
\\
&\textbf{while} \ \ < condition > \ \ \textbf{do} \ \ < statement > \ \ \textbf{end}
\end{aligned}
$$

Moreover, expressions will denote natural numbers, arrays, and also pointers.

15.1.2 Decomposing a sequential program into individual events

The approach we present here is to completely separate, during the design, these individual assignments from their scheduling. This approach is thus essentially one where we favor an initial implicit *distribution of the computation* over a centralized explicit one. At a certain stage, the "program" will just be made of a number of naked events, performing some actions under the control of certain guarding conditions. And at this point the synchronization of these events is not our concern. Thinking operationally, it is done *implicitly* by a hidden scheduler, which *may fire* an event once its guard holds. We can express as follows the various naked events corresponding to the previous example:

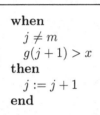

$$
\begin{array}{|l|}
\hline
\textbf{when} \\
\quad j \neq m \\
\quad g(j+1) > x \\
\textbf{then} \\
\quad j := j+1 \\
\textbf{end} \\
\hline
\end{array}
\qquad
\begin{array}{|l|}
\hline
\textbf{when} \\
\quad j \neq m \\
\quad g(j+1) \leq x \\
\quad k = j \\
\textbf{then} \\
\quad k := k+1 \\
\quad j := j+1 \\
\textbf{end} \\
\hline
\end{array}
\qquad
\begin{array}{|l|}
\hline
\textbf{when} \\
\quad j \neq m \\
\quad g(j+1) \leq x \\
\quad k \neq j \\
\textbf{then} \\
\quad k := k+1 \\
\quad j := j+1 \\
\quad g := \mathsf{swap}\,(g, k+1, j+1) \\
\textbf{end} \\
\hline
\end{array}
\qquad
\begin{array}{|l|}
\hline
\textbf{when} \\
\quad j = m \\
\textbf{then} \\
\quad p := k \\
\textbf{end} \\
\hline
\end{array}
$$

This decomposition has been done in a very systematic fashion. As can be seen, the guard of each event has been obtained by collecting the conditions that are introduced by the **while** and **if** statements. For instance, the second event dealing with assignments $k := k+1$ and $j := j+1$ has got the following guards:

$j \neq m$, because this assignment is inside the loop starting with **while** $j \neq m$ **do** ... **end**.

$g(j+1) \leq x$, because we are *not* in the first branch of the **if** $x < g(j+1)$ **then** ... **end** statement.

$k = j$, because we are in the first branch of the **elsif** $k = j$ **then** ... **end** statement.

Conversely, it seems easy to build the initial program of the previous section from these four naked events. But, of course, this process will have to be made systematic later in Section 15.3.

15.1.3 Sketch of the approach

After what has just been said, the approach we are going to take can be divided up into three distinct phases:

1. At the beginning of the development process, the event system, besides an initializing event, is made of a single guarded event with no action. This event represents the specification of our future program. At this step, we might also define an **anticipated** event (see Section 15.2).
2. During the development process, other events might be added or some abstract **anticipated** events might become **convergent** (see Section 15.2).
3. When all the individual pieces are "on the table" (this is the situation shown in the previous section), and only then, we start to be interested in their *explicit* scheduling. This will have the effect of minimizing guard evaluations in the scheduling. For this, we apply certain systematic rules (section 15.3) whose role is to gradually *merge the events* and thus organize them into a single entity forming our final program. The application of these rules has the effect of gradually eliminating the various predicates making the guards. At the end of the development, it results in a single guardless final "event".

What is interesting about this approach is that it gives us full freedom to refine small pieces of the future program, and also to create new ones, *without being disturbed by others*; the program is developed by means of small *independent* parts that so remain until they are eventually put together systematically at the end of the process. This can be illustrated as follows:

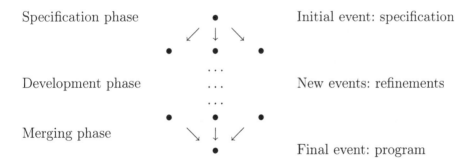

15.1.4 Sequential program specification: pre- and post-condition

A sequential program P with some input parameters and some results is often specified by using a so-called Hoare-triple, of the following shape:

$$\{Pre\} \quad \mathsf{P} \quad \{Post\}$$

Here *Pre* denotes the *pre-condition* of the program P, while *Post* denotes its *post-condition*. The pre-condition defines the condition we can assume concerning the parameters of the program, and the post-condition denotes what we can expect concerning the outcome of the program.

It is very simple to have an Hoare-triple being encoded within an event system. The parameters are constants and the pre-conditions are the axioms of these constants. The results are variables and the program is represented by an event containing the post-condition in its guard together with a **skip** action. We illustrate this in the next section with a very simple example.

15.2 A very simple example

15.2.1 Specification

Suppose we want to specify a program, named **search**, with the following parameters: an array f of size n, and a certain value v guaranteed to be within the range of the array f. The result of our program **search** is denoted by r, which is an index of the array f such that $f(r) = v$. This informal specification can be made a little more formal by the following Hoare-triple:

$$\left\{ \begin{array}{l} n \in \mathbb{N} \\ f \in 1 .. n \to S \\ v \in \mathrm{ran}(f) \end{array} \right\} \qquad \text{search} \qquad \left\{ \begin{array}{l} r \in 1 .. n \\ f(r) = v \end{array} \right\}$$

The previous example can then be encoded in a straightforward fashion as follows. Here is the encoding of the pre-condition:

sets: S **constants:** n, f, v	**axm0_1:** $n \in \mathbb{N}$ **axm0_2:** $f \in 1 .. n \to S$ **axm0_3:** $v \in \mathrm{ran}(f)$ **thm0_1:** $n \geq 1$

As can be seen, the three predicates making the pre-conditions have become three axioms **axm0_1** to **axm0_3**. Notice the theorem **thm0_1** we have stated. Now comes the post-condition encoding. First the definition of the result variable r:

variables: r	**inv0_1:** $r \in \mathbb{N}$

As can be seen, the invariant is very weak, we just say in invariant **inv0_1** that the result r is a natural number. Next are the two events named init and final:

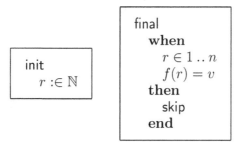

The two predicates making the post-condition have become guards of the final event, which has no action. Finally, we introduce the following anticipated event progress:

```
progress
    status
        anticipated
    then
        r :∈ ℕ
    end
```

This event modifies variable r in a totally non-deterministic way. This is a technique we introduced in Section 7 of Chapter 4 and reused again in Section 4.2 of Chapter 6. We are going to use this technique systematically throughout this chapter.

15.2.2 Refinement

The development of sequential programs will exactly follow the same lines as those we have already followed in previous chapters: namely doing some refinements by looking more carefully at the state and introducing new events or (in the present case) refining an anticipated event.

In this searching example, our refinement will be extremely simple. We do not introduce any new variables: we rather add invariants on r and refine event progress. Variable r ranges over the interval $1 .. n$ (invariant **inv1_1**). The main invariant states that v is not within the set denoting the image of the interval $1 .. r - 1$ under f, that is $f[1 .. r - 1]$ (invariant **inv1_2**). In other words, the interval $1 .. r - 1$ denotes the set of indices we have already explored *unsuccessfully*:

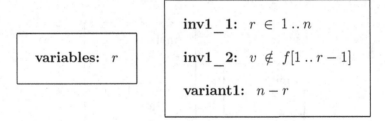

This can be illustrated as follows:

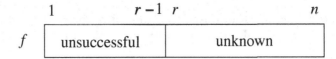

Now we make our previous **anticipated** event **progress**, **convergent**. It increments r when $f(r)$ is not equal to v; notice also the initialization of the result variable r:

init
$r := 1$

final
  when
    $f(r) = v$
  then
    skip
  end

progress
  status
    convergent
  when
    $f(r) \neq v$
  then
    $r := r + 1$
  end

Notice that event **progress** is now **convergent**. For this, we provide variant **variant1**, which is a natural number decreased by event **progress**. All proofs are left to the reader.

15.2.3 Generalization

Note that the previous example can be generalized to the case where the searched value v is not necessarily within the range of the array f. The program may have then two different outcomes: (1) the searched value has not been found; and (2) the searched value has been found and the result is then a corresponding index. This will be represented in the abstraction by two distinct events and an additional boolean variable *success*, which is equal to true when v is in the range of f, false otherwise.

It is also possible to re-arrange the previous solution so that both solutions are very close to each other.

15.3 Merging rules

At this point, our development is almost finished. It just remains for us to merge the events in order to obtain our final program. For this we shall define some *merging rules*. We essentially have two merging rules: one for defining a conditional statement (M_IF) and the other one for defining a loop statement (M-WHILE). Here are these rules:

when P Q **then** S **end**	**when** P $\neg Q$ **then** T **end** $\quad \rightsquigarrow$	**when** P **then** **if** Q **then** S **else** T **end** **end**	M_IF

when P Q **then** S **end**	**when** P $\neg Q$ **then** T **end** $\quad \rightsquigarrow$	**when** P **then** **while** Q **do** S **end** ; T **end**	M_WHILE

These rules can be read as follows: if we have an event system where two events have forms corresponding to the ones shown on the left of the $\rightsquigarrow$ symbol in the rule, they can be merged into a single *pseudo-event* corresponding to the right-hand side of the rule. Notice that both rules have the same antecedent events, so that the application of one or the other might be problematic. There is no confusion, however, as the rules have some *incompatible side conditions*, which are the following:

> The second rule (that introducing **while**) requires that the first antecedent event (that giving rise to the "body" S of the loop) appears as *new or non-anticipated, thus convergent* at *one refinement level below that of the second one*. In this way, we are certain that there exists a variant ensuring that the loop terminates. Moreover, *the first event must keep the common condition P invariant*. The merged event is considered to "appear" at the same level as the second antecedent event.

The first rule (that introducing **if**) is applicable when both events have been introduced at the same level. The merged event is considered to bear the same "level" as the component events.

The first rule may take a special form when one of the antecedent events has an **if** form. It is as follows:

when   **when**
    P P
    Q $\neg Q$
 then   **then**
    S **if** R **then** T **else** U **end**
 end   **end**
	$\rightsquigarrow$ **when**
	      P
	    then
	       if Q **then** S **elsif** R **then** T **else** U **end**
	    end

M_ELSIF	

Note that in the three rules, the common guard P is optional. When P is missing then the pseudo-event on the right-hand side of the rule reduces to a non-guarded event. Also note that in the merging rule **M_WHILE**, the action T can be reduced to **skip**. In these cases, the rule simplifies accordingly.

The rules are applied systematically until a single pseudo-event with no guard is left. It then remains for us to apply a last merging rule, called **M_INIT**, consisting in prepending the unique pseudo-event with the initialization event. In our case, it leads to the final program construction:

search_program
    $r := 1;$
    while $f(r) \neq v$ **do**
      $r := r + 1$
    end

15.4 Example: binary search in a sorted array

15.4.1 Initial model

This problem is exactly the same as the previous one: searching for a value in an array. So, the formal specification is (almost) identical to the one of the previous example. The only difference is that, this time, we have more information on the array: it is an array of natural numbers, which is sorted in a non-decreasing way as indicated in

axm0_4. Here is the pre-condition:

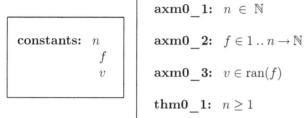

Here is now the post-condition:

$$\boxed{\textbf{variables: } r}$$ $$\boxed{\textbf{inv0\_1: } r \in \mathbb{N}}$$

init
$$r :\in \mathbb{N}$$

final
  when
    $r \in 1..n$
    $f(r) = v$
  then
    skip
  end

We have also an anticipated event:

progress
  status
    anticipated
  then
    $r :\in \mathbb{N}$
  end

15.4.2 First refinement

The state We introduce two new variables p and q. Variables p and q are supposed to be two indices in the array f (**inv1_1** and **inv1_2**). The variable r is within the interval $p..q$ (**inv1_3**). Moreover, the value v is supposed to be a member of the set denoting the image of the interval $p..q$ under f: that is, $f[p..q]$ (**inv1_4**). Here is the state of this refinement:

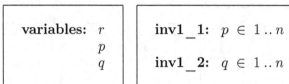

The current situation is illustrated in the following figure:

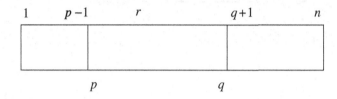

Now, we introduce two events called inc and dec which split abstract anticipated event **progress**. These events are **convergent** (see **variant1** above). They increment or decrement p or q when $f(r)$ is smaller or greater than v. They also move r non-deterministically within the new interval $p .. q$:

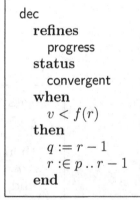
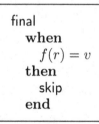

The following figure illustrates the situation encountered by event inc (the arrow indicates the new value of index p), which is guarded by the predicate $f(r) < v$:

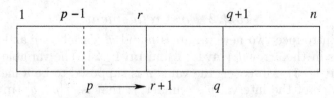

We next illustrate the situation encountered by event **dec** (the arrow indicates the new value of index q), which is guarded by the predicate $v < f(r)$:

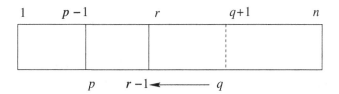

The proofs are simple. We encourage the reader to do them with the Rodin Platform.

15.4.3 Second refinement

The second refinement is very simple. The state is the same as in the abstraction. We only reduce the non-determinism of events **inc** and **dec** by choosing r in the "middle" of the intervals $r + 1 .. q$ or $p .. r - 1$. This leads to the following refinements of these events:

init	inc	dec	final
$p := 1$ $q := 1$ $r := (1 + n)/2$	**when** $\quad f(r) < v$ **then** $\quad p := r + 1$ $\quad r := (r + 1 + q)/2$ **end**	**when** $\quad v < f(r)$ **then** $\quad q := r - 1$ $\quad r := (p + r - 1)/2$ **end**	**when** $\quad f(r) = v$ **then** $\quad$ skip **end**

The main proofs concern the implication of the common actions on r in events **inc** and **dec**. For event **dec**, this amounts to proving $(r + 1 + q)/2 \in r + 1 .. q$, which is obvious since we have already proved in the abstraction that the interval $r + 1 .. q$ was not empty (feasibility of abstract event **dec**). The proof of event **inc** is similar.

15.4.4 Merging

We are now ready to merge events **inc** and **dec**. For this we can use merging rule M_IF thus obtaining (on the left) the following pseudo-event inc_dec. After that, we can merge this pseudo-event with event **final**. For this, we can use merging rule M_WHILE, thus obtaining the pseudo-event situated on the right:

```
inc_dec
  when
    f(r) ≠ v
  then
    if  f(r) < v  then
      p, r := r + 1, (r + 1 + q)/2
    else
      q, r := r − 1, (p + r − 1)/2
    end
  end
```

```
inc_dec_final
  while  f(r) ≠ v  do
    if  f(r) < v  then
      p, r := r + 1, (r + 1 + q)/2
    else
      q, r := r − 1, (p + r − 1)/2
    end
  end
```

The final program is obtained by pre-pending the initialization (rule M-INIT):

```
bin_search_program
  p, q, r := 1, n, (1 + n)/2;
  while  f(r) ≠ v  do
    if  f(r) < v  then
      p, r := r + 1, (r + 1 + q)/2
    else
      q, r := r − 1, (p + r − 1)/2
    end
  end
```

15.5 Example: minimum of an array of natural numbers

15.5.1 Initial model

Our next elementary example consists in looking for the minimum of the range of a non-empty array of natural numbers. Let n and f be two constants, and m a variable. Here is our initial model:

constants: n		variables: m
f		

axm0_1: $0 < n$

axm0_2: $f \in 1..n \to \mathbb{N}$

thm0_1: $\operatorname{ran}(f) \neq \varnothing$

$$\boxed{\textbf{inv0\_1:} \quad m \in \mathbb{N}}$$

$$\boxed{\begin{array}{l} \text{init} \\ \quad m :\in \mathbb{N} \end{array}}$$

$$\boxed{\begin{array}{l} \text{minimum} \\ \quad m := \min(\mathrm{ran}(f)) \end{array}}$$

15.5.2 First refinement

Our first refinement consists in introducing, as in the previous example, two indices p and q where p is not greater than q as indicated in invariant **inv1_3**. Moreover, it is shown in invariant **inv1_4** that the minimum of the array is in the set $f[p .. q]$:

$$\boxed{\begin{array}{l} \textbf{constants:} \quad n, f \\[4pt] \textbf{variables:} \quad m, p, q \end{array}}$$

$$\boxed{\begin{array}{l} \textbf{inv1\_1:} \quad p \in 1 .. n \\[4pt] \textbf{inv1\_2:} \quad q \in 1 .. n \\[4pt] \textbf{inv1\_3:} \quad p \le q \\[4pt] \textbf{inv1\_4:} \quad \min(\mathrm{ran}(f)) \in f[p .. q] \end{array}}$$

We also introduce two new events inc and dec. When p is smaller than q and $f(p)$ is greater than $f(q)$, we can reduce the interval $p .. q$ to $p + 1 .. q$ since $f(p)$ is certainly not the minimum we are looking for. We have a similar effect with invariant dec. The minimum is then found when p is equal to q according to invariant **inv1_4**:

$$\boxed{\begin{array}{l} \text{init} \\ \quad p, q := 1, n \\ \quad m :\in \mathbb{N} \end{array}}$$

$$\boxed{\begin{array}{l} \text{inc} \\ \quad \textbf{when} \\ \qquad p < q \\ \qquad f(p) > f(q) \\ \quad \textbf{then} \\ \qquad p := p + 1 \\ \quad \textbf{end} \end{array}}$$

$$\boxed{\begin{array}{l} \text{dec} \\ \quad \textbf{when} \\ \qquad p < q \\ \qquad f(p) \le f(q) \\ \quad \textbf{then} \\ \qquad q := q - 1 \\ \quad \textbf{end} \end{array}}$$

$$\boxed{\begin{array}{l} \text{minimum} \\ \quad \textbf{when} \\ \qquad p = q \\ \quad \textbf{then} \\ \qquad m := f(p) \\ \quad \textbf{end} \end{array}}$$

We leave it as an exercise for the reader to prove this refinement (do not forget to prove the convergence of events inc and dec) and generate the corresponding final program by applying some merging rules.

15.6 Example: array partitioning

In this example, all proofs are left to the reader.

15.6.1 Initial model

The problem we study now is a variant of the well-known partitioning problem used in Quicksort. Let f be an array of n natural numbers (supposed to be distinct for simplification). Let x be a natural number. We would like to transform f in another array g with exactly the same elements as in the initial array f, in such a way that there exists an index k of the interval $0 .. n$ such that all elements in $g[1 .. k]$ are smaller than or equal to x, while all elements in $g[k + 1 .. n]$ are strictly greater than x. The final result is shown below:

1	$\leq x$	k	$k+1$	$> x$	n

For example, let the array f be the following:

3	7	2	5	8	9	4	1

If we like to partition it with 5, then the transformed array g can be the following with k being set to 5:

3	2	5	4	1	9	7	8

Note that in case all elements of f are greater than x, then k should be equal to 0. And in case all elements are smaller than or equal to x, then k should be equal to n. We now have enough elements to introduce our initial model as follows:

constants: n
$\qquad\qquad f$
$\qquad\qquad x$

axm0_1: $n \in \mathbb{N}$

axm0_2: $f \in 1 .. n \rightarrowtail \mathbb{N}$

axm0_3: $x \in \mathbb{N}$

```
┌─────────────────────┐   ┌─────────────────────────────┐   ┌─────────────────────┐
│                     │   │  inv0_1:  k ∈ ℕ             │   │ init                │
│  variables:  k      │   │                             │   │   k :∈ ℕ            │
│              g      │   │  inv0_2:  g ∈ ℕ ↔ ℕ         │   │   g :∈ ℕ ↔ ℕ       │
└─────────────────────┘   └─────────────────────────────┘   └─────────────────────┘
```

```
┌───────────────────────────────────────────────┐
│ final                                          │
│   when                                         │
│     k ∈ 0 .. n                                 │       ┌─────────────────────────┐
│     g ∈ 1 .. n ↣ ℕ                             │       │ progress                │
│     ran (g) = ran (f)                          │       │   status                │
│     ∀m · m ∈ 1 .. k ⇒ g(m) ≤ x                 │       │     anticipated         │
│     ∀m · m ∈ k + 1 .. n ⇒ g(m) > x             │       │   then                  │
│   then                                         │       │     k :∈ ℕ             │
│     skip                                       │       │     g :∈ ℕ ↔ ℕ        │
│   end                                          │       │   end                   │
└───────────────────────────────────────────────┘       └─────────────────────────┘
```

15.6.2 First refinement

Our next step is to introduce one new variable j. Variables j and k are indices in $0 .. n$. Variable k is supposed to be smaller than or equal to j. We have also two invariants saying that k and j partition the array g as indicated as follows:

1	$\leq x$	k	$k + 1$	$> x$	j	$j + 1$	?	n

As can be seen, the array g is partitioned in the interval $1 .. j$ with k being the intermediate partitioning point. The idea is then to possibly increment j alone or both k and j while maintaining the corresponding invariant. The process is completed when j is equal to n. More formally, this yields the following new state:

```
┌─────────────┐   ┌─────────────────────────┐   ┌─────────────────────────────────────┐
│             │   │ inv1_1:  j ∈ 0 .. n     │   │ inv1_4:  ran(g) = ran(f)            │
│ variables: k│   │                         │   │                                     │
│            g│   │ inv1_2:  k ∈ 0 .. j     │   │ inv1_5:  ∀m · m ∈ 1 .. k ⇒ g(m) ≤ x │
│            j│   │                         │   │                                     │
│             │   │ inv1_3:  g ∈ 1 .. n ↣ ℕ │   │ inv1_6:  ∀m · m ∈ k + 1 .. j ⇒ x < g(m) │
└─────────────┘   └─────────────────────────┘   └─────────────────────────────────────┘
```

Here are the refinements of the events init and final, and the introduction of three convergent events progress_1, progress_2, and progress_3 all refining abstract anticipated event **progress** (guess the variant):

```
init
    j := 0
    k := 0
    g := f
```

```
final
    when
        j = n
    then
        skip
    end
```

```
progress_1
    refines
        progress
    .status
        convergent
    when
        j ≠ n
        g(j + 1) > x
    then
        j := j + 1
    end
```

```
progress_2
    refines
        progress
    status
        convergent
    when
        j ≠ n
        g(j + 1) ≤ x
        k = j
    then
        k := k + 1
        j := j + 1
    end
```

```
progress_3
    refines
        progress
    status
        convergent
    when
        j ≠ n
        g(j + 1) ≤ x
        k ≠ j
    then
        k := k + 1
        j := j + 1
        g := g ⩤ {k + 1 ↦ g(j + 1)} ⩤ {j + 1 ↦ g(k + 1)}
    end
```

15.6.3 Merging

By merging these events, we obtain the following final program:

```
partition_program
    j, k, g := 0, 0, f;
    while j ≠ n do
        if g(j + 1) > x then
            j := j + 1
        elsif k = j then
            k, j := k + 1, j + 1
        else
            k, j, g := k + 1, j + 1, g ⩤ {k + 1 ↦ g(j + 1)} ⩤ {j + 1 ↦ g(l + 1)}
        end
    end
```

15.7 Example: simple sorting

In this example, all proofs are left to the reader.

15.7.1 Initial model

We are not going to develop a very clever sorting algorithm here. Rather, our intention is only to use sorting as an opportunity to develop a little program containing an *embedded loop*. We have two constants: n, which is a positive natural number, and f, which is a total injective function from $1\,..\,n$ to the natural numbers. We have a result variable g which must be sorted and have the same elements as f. Here is our initial state:

$$\boxed{\begin{array}{l}\textbf{constants:}\quad n \\ \hspace{4.5em} f\end{array}}$$

$$\boxed{\begin{array}{l}\textbf{axm0\_1:}\ \ 0 < n \\[1ex] \textbf{axm0\_2:}\ \ f \in 1\,..\,n \rightarrowtail \mathbb{N}\end{array}}$$

$$\boxed{\textbf{variables:}\quad g}$$

$$\boxed{\textbf{inv0\_1:}\ \ g \in \mathbb{N} \leftrightarrow \mathbb{N}}$$

$$\boxed{\begin{array}{l}\text{init} \\ \quad g :\in \mathbb{N} \leftrightarrow \mathbb{N}\end{array}}$$

$$\boxed{\begin{array}{l}\text{final} \\ \quad \textbf{when} \\ \qquad g \in 1\,..\,n \rightarrowtail \mathbb{N} \\ \qquad \mathrm{ran}\,(g) = \mathrm{ran}\,(f) \\ \qquad \forall i,j \cdot\ \ i \in 1\,..\,n-1 \\ \qquad\qquad\qquad j \in i+1\,..\,n \\ \qquad\qquad\quad \Rightarrow \\ \qquad\qquad\qquad g(i) < g(j) \\ \quad \textbf{then} \\ \qquad \text{skip} \\ \quad \textbf{end}\end{array}}$$

$$\boxed{\begin{array}{l}\text{progress} \\ \quad \textbf{status} \\ \qquad \text{anticipated} \\ \quad \textbf{then} \\ \qquad g :\in \mathbb{N} \leftrightarrow \mathbb{N} \\ \quad \textbf{end}\end{array}}$$

The guards in event final stipulate that g has exactly the same elements as the original f, and that it is sorted in ascending order.

15.7.2 First refinement

In our first refinement, we introduce a new index k supposed to be in the interval $1\,..\,n$. Moreover, the elements of the sub-part of g ranging from 1 to $k-1$ are all sorted and also smaller than the elements lying in the other sub-part, namely those ranging from k to n. This can be illustrated as follows:

1	sorted and smaller	$k-1$	k		n

We also introduce a new variable l and a new **anticipated** event **prog**. In the guard of the **convergent** event **progress** (guess the variant), we require that $g(l)$ is the minimum of the set $g[k \mathrel{.\,.} n]$. Our new state and events are as follows. Notice that events init, **progress**, and **prog** all modify l non-deterministically:

variables: g
k
l

inv1_1: $g \in 1 \mathrel{.\,.} n \rightarrowtail \mathbb{N}$

inv1_2: $\mathrm{ran}(g) = \mathrm{ran}(f)$

inv1_3: $k \in 1 \mathrel{.\,.} n$

inv1_4: $\forall i, j \cdot\ i \in 1 \mathrel{.\,.} k-1$
$\qquad j \in i+1 \mathrel{.\,.} n$
$\qquad \Rightarrow$
$\qquad g(i) < g(j)$

inv1_5: $l \in \mathbb{N}$

init
$\quad g := f$
$\quad k := 1$
$\quad l :\in \mathbb{N}$

final
$\quad$**when**
$\qquad k = n$
$\quad$**then**
$\qquad$skip
$\quad$**end**

progress
$\quad$**status**
$\qquad$convergent
$\quad$**when**
$\qquad k \neq n$
$\qquad l \in k \mathrel{.\,.} n$
$\qquad g(l) = \min(g[k \mathrel{.\,.} n])$
$\quad$**then**
$\qquad g := g \mathbin{\lhd\!\!\!-} \{k \mapsto g(l)\} \mathbin{\lhd\!\!\!-} \{l \mapsto g(k)\}$
$\qquad k := k + 1$
$\qquad l :\in \mathbb{N}$
$\quad$**end**

prog
$\quad$**status**
$\qquad$anticipated
$\quad$**then**
$\qquad l :\in \mathbb{N}$
$\quad$**end**

15.7.3 Second refinement

Our next step consists in determining the minimum chosen arbitrarily in the previous section. For this, we introduce an additional index j. The index j ranges from k to n, whereas l ranges from k to j. The value of g at index l is supposed to be the minimum of g on the sub-part of it ranging from k to j. Here is our new state:

| **variables:** g |
| k |
| l |
| j |

inv2_1: $j \in k \mathinner{..} n$

inv2_2: $l \in k \mathinner{..} j$

inv2_3: $g(l) = \min(g[k \mathinner{..} j])$

Invariant **inv2_3** is illustrated as so:

1	**sorted and smaller**	$k-1$	k	$g(l)$ **is the minimum**	j		n

Next are the refinements of the abstract events:

```
init
    g := f
    k := 1
    l := 1
    j := 1
```

```
final
    when
        k = n
    then
        skip
    end
```

```
progress
    when
        k ≠ n
        j = n
    then
        g := g ⩤ {k ↦ g(l)} ⩤ {l ↦ g(k)}
        k := k + 1
        j := k + 1
        l := k + 1
    end
```

In the concrete event **progress**, the strengthening of the guard (with condition $j = n$) implies that the value of the variable l corresponds exactly to the minimum chosen arbitrarily in the abstraction. Here are the new convergent events **prog1** and **prog2** (guess the variant) both refining abstract **anticipated** event **prog**:

```
prog1
  refines
     prog
  status
     convergent
  when
     k ≠ n
     j ≠ n
     g(l) ≤ g(j + 1)
  then
     j := j + 1
  end
```

```
prog2
  refines
     prog
  status
     convergent
  when
     k ≠ n
     j ≠ n
     g(j + 1) < g(l)
  then
     j := j + 1
     l := j + 1
  end
```

15.7.4 Merging

After applying the merging rule we obtain the following final program:

```
sort_program
  g, k, j, l := f, 1, 1, 1
  while k ≠ n do
     while j ≠ n do
        if g(l) ≤ g(j + 1) then
           j := j + 1
        else
           j, l := j + 1, j + 1
        end
     end ;
     k, j, l, g := k + 1, k + 1, k + 1, g ⩤ {k ↦ g(l)} ⩤ {l ↦ g(k)}
  end
```

Note that the initialization of the inner loop variables, namely j and l, is made in two different places: either in the proper initialization at the beginning of the program, or in the trailing statement after the inner loop itself.

15.8 Example: array reversing

In this example, all proofs are left to the reader.

15.8.1 *Initial model*

Our next example is the classical array reversing. We are given a carrier set S, and two constants n and f, and a variable g. Here is the state:

sets: S constants: n, f	**axm0_1:** $n \in \mathbb{N}$ **axm0_2:** $0 < n$ **axm0_3:** $f \in 1 .. n \to S$	**variables:** g **inv0_1:** $g \in \mathbb{N} \leftrightarrow S$

Here are the events:

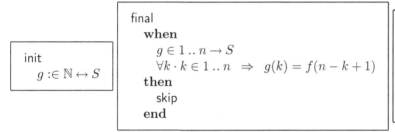

```
init
    g :∈ ℕ ↔ S
```

```
final
    when
        g ∈ 1 .. n → S
        ∀k · k ∈ 1 .. n  ⇒  g(k) = f(n − k + 1)
    then
        skip
    end
```

```
progress
    status
        anticipated
    then
        g :∈ ℕ ↔ S
    end
```

15.8.2 *First refinement*

Our first refinement consists in introducing two indices i, starting at 1, and j, starting at n. The indices i and j move towards each other. The array g is gradually reversed by swapping elements $g(i)$ and $g(j)$ while, of course, i is strictly smaller than j. This is done in the event **progress**. In this way, the sub-arrays of g ranging from 1 to $i - 1$ and from $j + 1$ to n respectively have all their elements reversed with regard to the original array f. And the middle part is still unchanged with regards to f. This is illustrated as follows:

1	**reversed**	i	**unchanged**	j	**reversed**	n

Notice that the quantity $i + j$ is always equal to $n + 1$. At the end of the process, either i is equal to j when n is odd, or i is equal to $j + 1$ when n is even. But, in both cases, we have $i \geq j$. Here is the new state:

---

variables: g
$\quad\quad\quad\quad i$
$\quad\quad\quad\quad j$

---

inv1_1: $g \in 1..n \rightarrow S$

inv1_2: $i \in 1..n$

inv1_3: $j \in 1..n$

inv1_4: $i + j = n + 1$

inv1_5: $i \leq j + 1$

inv1_6: $\forall k \cdot k \in 1..i-1 \Rightarrow g(k) = f(n-k+1)$

inv1_7: $\forall k \cdot k \in i..j \Rightarrow g(k) = f(k)$

inv1_8: $\forall k \cdot k \in j+1..n \Rightarrow g(k) = f(n-k+1)$

Here are the refined events (guess the variant for event **progress**):

---

init
$\quad i := 1$
$\quad j := n$
$\quad g := f$

---

final
$\quad$**when**
$\quad\quad j \leq i$
$\quad$**then**
$\quad\quad$skip
$\quad$**end**

---

progress
$\quad$**status**
$\quad\quad$convergent
$\quad$**when**
$\quad\quad i < j$
$\quad$**then**
$\quad\quad g := g \ensuremath{\Lleftarrow} \{i \mapsto g(j)\} \ensuremath{\Lleftarrow} \{j \mapsto g(i)\}$
$\quad\quad i := i + 1$
$\quad\quad j := j - 1$
$\quad$**end**

Now, we can apply the merging rules and obtain the following final program:

---

reverse_program
$\quad i, j, g := 1, n, f;$
$\quad$**while** $i < j$ **do**
$\quad\quad i, j, g := i+1, j-1, g \ensuremath{\Lleftarrow} \{i \mapsto g(j)\} \ensuremath{\Lleftarrow} \{j \mapsto g(i)\}$
$\quad$**end**

15.9 Example: reversing a linked list

So far, all our examples were dealing with arrays and corresponding indices. As a consequence, some of the proofs relied on elementary arithmetic properties. In this example, we experiment with a data structure that deals with pointers. The problem we shall tackle is very classical and simple: we just want to reverse a linear chain. Notice that to simplify matters, the chain is made of pointers only. In other words, a node of the chain has no information field.

15.9.1 Initial model

Each node in the chain points to its immediate successor (if any). The chain starts with a node called f (for "first") and ends with a node called l (for "last"). All this can be represented as follows:

$$\boxed{\;f\;} \rightarrow \boxed{\;x\;} \rightarrow \ldots \rightarrow \boxed{\;z\;} \rightarrow \boxed{\;l\;}$$

Before engaging in our problem, we first have to formalize what we have just introduced. After renaming its constants, we simply copy the axioms which have been presented in Section 9.7.4 of Chapter 9:

sets: S	
constants: d, f, l, c	

axm0_1:	$d \subseteq S$
axm0_2:	$f \in d$
axm0_3:	$l \in d$
axm0_4:	$f \neq l$
axm0_5:	$c \in d \setminus \{l\} \rightarrowtail\!\!\!\!\rightarrow d \setminus \{f\}$
axm0_6:	$\forall T \cdot T \subseteq c[T] \Rightarrow T = \varnothing$

We would like to reverse this chain. So, if the initial chain is

$$\boxed{\;f\;} \rightarrow \boxed{\;x\;} \rightarrow \ldots \rightarrow \boxed{\;z\;} \rightarrow \boxed{\;l\;},$$

then the transformed chain r should look like this:

$$\boxed{\;f\;} \leftarrow \boxed{\;x\;} \leftarrow \ldots \leftarrow \boxed{\;z\;} \leftarrow \boxed{\;l\;}$$

Here is the definition of the result r together with the event **reverse** doing the job in one shot: r is exactly the converse of c.

variables: r	**inv0_1:** $r \in S \leftrightarrow S$	init $r :\in S \leftrightarrow S$	reverse $r := c^{-1}$

15.9.2 First refinement

In this first refinement, we introduce two additional chains a and b and a pointer p. Chain a corresponds to the part of chain c that has already been reversed, whereas chain b corresponds to the part of chain c that has not yet been reversed. Node p is the starting node of both chains. Here is the situation:

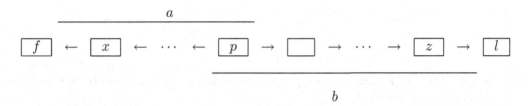

Progress is obtained by moving p one step to the right and reversing the first pointer of chain b. This is indicated as follows:

At the start, p is equal to f, a is empty, and b is equal to c:

At the end, p is equal to l, a is the reversed chain, and b is empty:

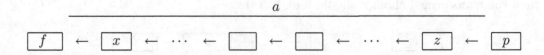

Formalizing what we have just informally presented is simple: we define both chains a and b and their relationship with c. Notice that we use $\mathrm{cl}(c)$ and $\mathrm{cl}(c^{-1})$, which are the irreflexive transitive closures of c and c^{-1} (cl is defined in Section 9.7.1 of Chapter 9).

variables: r
a
b
p

inv1_1: $p \in d$

inv1_2: $a \in (\mathrm{cl}(c^{-1})[\{p\}] \cup \{p\}) \setminus \{f\} \rightarrowtail \mathrm{cl}(c^{-1})[\{p\}]$

inv1_3: $b \in (\mathrm{cl}(c)[\{p\}] \cup \{p\}) \setminus \{l\} \rightarrowtail \mathrm{cl}(c)[\{p\}]$

inv1_4: $c = a^{-1} \cup b$

Here are the refinements of the previous events and also the introduction of the new event progress:

init
$r :\in S \leftrightarrow S$
$a, b, p := \varnothing, c, f$

reverse
when
$b = \varnothing$
then
$r := a$
end

progress
when
$p \in \mathrm{dom}(b)$
then
$p := b(p)$
$a(b(p)) := p$
$b := \{p\} \lhd b$
end

As can be seen in event progress, p is moved to the right (that is $p := b(p)$), the pair $b(p) \mapsto p$ is added to the chain a (that is $a(b(p)) := p$), and, finally, node p is removed from chain b (that is $b := \{p\} \lhd b$).

15.9.3 Second refinement

In this refinement, we introduce a special constant node named *nil* (**axm2_1**), which is supposed to be outside the set d. We also replace the chain b by the chain bn which is equal to $b \cup \{l \mapsto nil\}$ (**inv2_1**). Finally, we introduce a second pointer, q, which is equal to $bn(p)$. This is represented as follows:

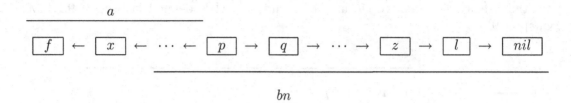

Here is the new state:

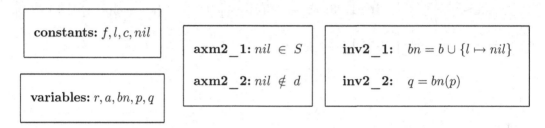

Here are the refinements of the events. Notice that the guards have been made independent of the chain b:

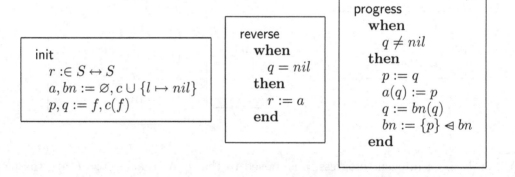

15.9.4 Third refinement

We now remove chains a and bn and replace them by a unique chain, e, containing both chains a and bn. Here is the new situation:

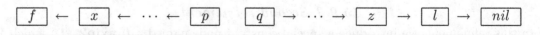

Next is the refined state with the definition of the new variable e in terms of the abstract variables a and bn:

variables: r, p, q, e

inv3_1: $e = (\{f\} \lhd bn) \lhd a$

The events correspond to straightforward transformations of the previous one:

init
$\quad r :\in S \leftrightarrow S$
$\quad e := \{f\} \lhd (c \cup \{l \mapsto nil\}$
$\quad p := f$
$\quad q := c(f)$

reverse
$\quad$ **when**
$\qquad q = nil$
$\quad$ **then**
$\qquad r := e \rhd \{nil\}$
$\quad$ **end**

progress
$\quad$ **when**
$\qquad q \neq nil$
$\quad$ **then**
$\qquad p := q$
$\qquad e(q) := p$
$\qquad q := e(q)$
$\quad$ **end**

15.9.5 Merging

The last refinement leads to the following final program:

reverse_program
$\quad p, q, e := f, c(f), \{f\} \lhd (c \cup \{l \mapsto nil\});$
$\quad$ **while** $q \neq nil$ **do**
$\qquad p := q$
$\qquad e(q) := p$
$\qquad q := e(q)$
$\quad$ **end**;
$\quad r := e \rhd \{nil\}$

15.10 Example: simple numerical program computing the square root

We have not yet tried our approach on a numerical example. This is the purpose of this section. Given a natural number n, we want to compute its natural number square root by defect; that is, a number r such that:

$$r^2 \leq n < (r+1)^2.$$

15.10.1 Initial model

Our first model is simply the following:

constants: n	axm0_1: $n \in \mathbb{N}$	variables: r	inv0_1: $r \in \mathbb{N}$

```
init
    r :∈ ℕ
```

```
final
    when
        r² ≤ n
        n < (r + 1)²
    then
        skip
    end
```

```
progress
    status
        anticipated
    then
        r :∈ ℕ
    end
```

15.10.2 First refinement

variables: r	inv1_1: $r^2 \leq n$

```
init
    r := 0
```

```
final
    when
        n < (r + 1)²
    then
        skip
    end
```

```
progress
    status
        convergent
    when
        (r + 1)² ≤ n
    then
        r := r + 1
    end
```

The proof of this refinement is straightforward but do not forget to prove the convergence of event progress. We obtain the following program:

```
square_root_program
    r := 0;
    while  (r + 1)² ≤ n  do
        r := r + 1
    end
```

15.10.3 Second refinement

The previous solution, although correct, is a bit heavy because we have to compute $(r + 1)^2$ at each step of the computation. We would like to investigate whether it would be possible to refine the previous solution by computing this quantity in a less expensive way. The idea relies on the following equalities:

$$((r + 1) + 1)^2 = (r + 1)^2 + (2r + 3)$$

$$2(r + 1) + 3 = (2r + 3) + 2$$

We are thus extending our state with two more variables a and b recording in advance respectively $(r + 1)^2$ and $2r + 3$. Here is the new state and the new program:

```
variables:  r
            a
            b
```

```
inv2_1:   a = (r + 1)²

inv2_2:   b = 2r + 3
```

```
init
    r := 0
    a := 1
    b := 3
```

```
final
    when
        n < a
    then
        skip
    end
```

```
progress
    when
        a ≤ n
    then
        r := r + 1
        a := a + b
        b := b + 2
    end
```

We obtain the following program:

```
square_root_program
  r, a, b := 0, 1, 3;
  while  a ≤ n  do
    r, a, b := r + 1, a + b, b + 2
  end
```

15.11 Example: the inverse of an injective numerical function

In this example we are trying to borrow some ideas coming from the binary search example of Section 15.4. We want to compute the inverse by defect of an injective numerical function defined on all natural numbers.

15.11.1 Initial model

This is a generalization of the previous example where the function in question was the squaring function. In this model, we are a bit more specific than was announced: our function f is not stated to be injective to begin with. It is only defined to be a total function in **axm0_1**. But it is said in **axm0_2** that this numerical function f is strictly increasing. As a consequence, it can be proved to be injective, i.e. that its inverse is also a function; this is stated in **thm0_1**:

axm0_1: $f \in \mathbb{N} \to \mathbb{N}$

axm0_2: $\forall i, j \cdot\ i \in \mathbb{N}$
$\qquad\qquad\quad j \in \mathbb{N}$
$\qquad\qquad\quad i < j$
$\qquad\qquad\quad \Rightarrow$
$\qquad\qquad\qquad f(i) < f(j)$

axm0_3: $n \in \mathbb{N}$

thm0_1: $f \in \mathbb{N} \rightarrowtail \mathbb{N}$

constants: n
$\qquad\qquad\quad f$

variables: r

inv0_1: $r \in \mathbb{N}$

Event **final** calculates the inverse by defect of f at n in one shot which is just a generalization of what was defined in the previous example.

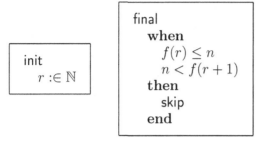

15.11.2 First refinement

The idea of this refinement is to suppose first that we can exhibit two numerical constants a and b such that:

$$f(a) \leq n < f(b+1)$$

We are certain then that our result r is within the interval $a \mathbin{..} b$ since f is defined everywhere and increasing. The idea of the refinement is then to narrow this initial interval. For this, we introduce a new variable q initially set to b, whereas variable r is initially set to a. These two variables will have the following invariant property:

$$f(r) \leq n < f(q+1)$$

When r and q are equal, we are done. When r and q are distinct we are left to perform a search in the interval $r \mathbin{..} q$. For this we shall use a technique very close to the one we used in Section 15.4 for binary search. Here is the state of this refinement:

constants: f, n, a, b	**axm1_1:** $a \in \mathbb{N}$	**inv1_1:** $q \in \mathbb{N}$
	axm1_2: $b \in \mathbb{N}$	**inv1_2:** $r \leq q$
variables: r, p, q	**axm1_3:** $f(a) \leq n$	**inv1_3:** $f(r) \leq n$
	axm1_4: $n < f(b+1)$	**inv1_4:** $n < f(q+1)$

We introduce two new events **inc** and **dec**. As can be seen, a number x is chosen nondeterministically in the interval $p+1 \mathbin{..} q$. Then n is compared with $f(x)$ and an action is done accordingly on q or on p:

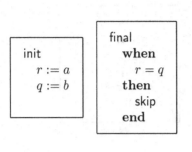

```
init
    r := a
    q := b
```

```
final
    when
        r = q
    then
        skip
    end
```

```
dec
    refines
        progress
    status
        convergent
    any  x  where
        r ≠ q
        x ∈ r + 1 .. q
        n < f(x)
    then
        q := x - 1
    end
```

```
inc
    refines
        progress
    status
        convergent
    any  x  where
        r ≠ q
        x ∈ r + 1 .. q
        f(x) ≤ n
    then
        r := x
    end
```

The proof of this refinement is not difficult. We have to exhibit a variant and prove that it is decreased by the new events. This variant is not difficult to guess.

15.11.3 Second refinement

In this second refinement, we are going to remove the non-determinacy in the events inc and dec. This will be done by choosing for the local variable x the "middle" of the interval $r + 1 .. q$. In this refinement, we do not change the state, only the events dec and inc as follows:

```
dec
    when
        r ≠ q
        n < f((r + 1 + q)/2)
    with
        x = (r + 1 + q)/2
    then
        q := (r + 1 + q)/2 - 1
    end
```

```
inc
    when
        r ≠ q
        f((r + 1 + q)/2) ≤ n
    with
        x = (r + 1 + q)/2
    then
        r := (r + 1 + q)/2
    end
```

In order to prove this refinement the following theorem can be useful:

$$
\textbf{thm2\_1:} \quad \forall x, y \cdot \; x \in \mathbb{N}
$$
$$
y \in \mathbb{N}
$$
$$
x \leq y
$$
$$
\Rightarrow
$$
$$
(x + y)/2 \in x .. y
$$

As a result, we obtain, by using some of the merging rules, the following program:

```
inverse_program
  r, q := a, b;
    while  r ≠ q  do
      if  n < f((r + 1 + q)/2)  then
        q := (r + 1 + q)/2 − 1
      else
        r := (r + 1 + q)/2
      end
    end
```

15.11.4 Instantiation

The development we have done in this example is interesting because it is *generic*. By this, it is meant that is can be *instantiated*. For this, it is sufficient to provide some values to the constants and to provide proofs that the proposed values are obeying the properties that were given for these constants.

In our case, the constants to be instantiated are f, a, and b. The constant n will remain as it is since it corresponds to the quantity for which we want to compute the inverse function value. And the *properties we have to prove* for the proposed instantiations are **axm0_1** (f is a total function defined on $\mathbb{N}$), **axm0_2** (f is an increasing function), **axm1_3** ($f(a) \leq n$), and **axm1_4** ($n < f(b + 1)$).

15.11.5 First instantiation

If we take for f the squaring function, then the computation will provide the square root of n by defect. More precisely, we shall compute a quantity r such that:

$$r^2 \leq n < (r + 1)^2$$

We have thus to prove that the squaring function is total and increasing, which is trivial. Now, given a value n we have to find two numbers a and b such that:

$$a^2 \leq n < (b + 1)^2$$

It is easy to see that a can be instantiated to 0 and b to n. As a result, we have *for free* the following program calculating the square root of n:

```
square_root_program
  r, q := 0, n;
  while  r ≠ q  do
    if  n < ((r + 1 + q)/2)²   then
      q := (r + 1 + q)/2 − 1
    else
      r := (r + 1 + q)/2
    end
  end
```

15.11.6 Second instantiation

If we take for f the function "multiply by m", *where m is a positive natural number*, then the computation will provide the integer division of n by m. More precisely, we shall compute a quantity r such that:

$$m \times r \ \leq \ n \ < \ m \times (r + 1)$$

We have thus to prove that this function is total and increasing, which is trivial. Now, given a value n we have to find two numbers a and b such that:

$$m \times a \ \leq \ n \ < \ m \times (b + 1).$$

It is easy to see that a can be instantiated to 0 and b to n (remember, m is a *positive* natural number). As a result, we have *for free* the following program calculating the integer division of n by m:

```
integer_division_program
  r, q := 0, n;
  while  r ≠ q  do
    if  n < m × (p + 1 + q)/2   then
      q := (r + 1 + q)/2 − 1
    else
      r := (r + 1 + q)/2
    end
  end.
```

16

A location access controller

The purpose of this chapter is to study yet another example dealing with a complete system like the one we studied in Chapter 2, where we controlled cars on a bridge, and in Chapter 3, where we studied a mechanical press controller. The system we study now is a little more complicated than the previous ones. In particular, the mathematical data structure we are going to use is more advanced. Our intention is also to show that during the reasoning on the model we shall discover a number of important missing points in the requirement document.

16.1 Requirement document

We shall construct a system which will be able to control the access of certain people to different locations of a "workplace"; for example, a university campus, an industrial site, a military compound, a shopping mall, etc. Thus:

The system concerns people and locations	FUN-1

The control takes place on the basis of the authorization that each person concerned is supposed to possess. This authorization should allow him, controlled by the system, to penetrate into certain locations, and not into others. For example, a certain person p_1 is authorized to enter location l_1 and not location l_2; however, another person p_2 is allowed to enter both locations. These authorizations are given on a "permanent" basis; in other words, they will not change during a normal functioning of the system:

People are permanently assigned the authorization to access certain locations	FUN-2

A person who is in a location must be authorized to be there	FUN-3

When someone is inside a location, his eventual exit must also be controlled by the system, so as to be able to know at any moment who is inside a given location. Each person involved receives a magnetic card with a unique identifying sign, which is engraved on the card itself:

Each person receives a personal magnetic card	EQP-1

Card readers are installed at each entrance and at each exit of the locations concerned. Near to each reader, two control lights can be found: a red one and a green one. Each one of these lights can be on or off:

Each entrance and exit of a location is equipped with a card reader	EQP-2

Each card reader has two lights: one green light and one red light	EQP-3

Each light can be "on" or "off".	EQP-4

The transfer of people from one location to another takes place thanks to "turnstiles" which are normally blocked; nobody can get through them without being controlled by the system, any person getting through is detected by a sensor:

Locations communicate via one-way turnstiles	EQP-5

Each turnstile is dedicated to a single task, either entry or exit; there are no "two-way" turnstiles. Turnstiles and card readers are illustrated in Fig. 16.1.

A sensor detects the passage of a person through a turnstile	EQP-6

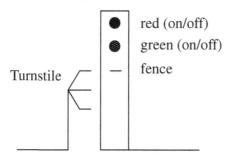

Fig. 16.1. Turnstile and card reader

Turnstiles are normally blocked	FUN-4

The entry or the exit of a location follows a systematic procedure composed of a suite of events. A person wishing to enter or exit a location puts his card into the card reader on the appropriate turnstile. We are then faced with the following two alternatives:

1. If the person is authorized to pass through the turnstile, the green control light is lit and the turnstile is opened within 30 seconds. We are now faced with the following situation:

   - As soon as the individual gets through the turnstile within the 30 seconds limit, the green control light goes out immediately and the turnstile is blocked.
   - If, however, 30 seconds go by without anybody going through the turnstile, the control light goes out and the turnstile is also blocked.

2. If the person is not authorized to pass through the turnstile, the red control light goes on for two seconds and, of course, the turnstile remains blocked.

A person willing to pass through a turnstile puts his/her card in the fence of the card reader	FUN-5

If the person is accepted, the green light is lit and the turnstile is unblocked for at most 30 seconds.	FUN-6

If the person is not accepted, the red light is lit for 2 seconds and the turnstile remains blocked	FUN-7

As soon as an accepted person has gone through an unblocked turnstile, the green light is turned off and the turnstile is blocked again	FUN-8

If nobody goes through an unblocked turnstile during the 30 seconds period, the green light is turned off and the turnstile is blocked again	FUN-9

16.2 Discussion

The above informal presentation of the system does not pretend to be complete, or to have raised all the technical options. Indeed, it is merely the minimal starting point for the realization of the future control software, but clearly there remain many unknowns concerning, among others, the hardware and its links with the software. We give precisions hereafter as to the role of the study which we shall undertake during the construction of the formal model.

16.2.1 Sharing out of the control

An important question which should be asked at the outset about such a system concerns the distribution, which is more or less important, of control between the software and the diverse peripherals (turnstiles, readers).

For example, there can be a computer at each turnstile; in this case, the control is entirely decentralized. Inversely, a single computer can entirely centralize the control. Of course, there are intermediate situations in which each turnstile has a certain form of autonomy; an example consists in equipping each turnstile with a clock which conditions part of its behavior.

16.2.2 Construction of a closed model

In any case, technical argumentation which can lead to such and such a decision can only be realized *by analyzing the system as a whole*. It is to be noted that this technical argumentation must also be nourished by information concerning the equipment available on the market (it can also be decided to utilize new equipment).

For this we shall therefore build a *closed model* of our future system and *prove* that its *characteristic properties* (which will have to be precisely explained) are in fact assured.

16.2.3 Behavior of the equipment

An important result of this study concerns the behavioral specification of the different equipment. So as to conduct this study correctly, we will be obliged to introduce into the model a certain amount of supposition concerning the equipment. For example, does the turnstile block of its own accord after the pass of a single person, or does it block only after the reception of an order from the software? Of course, the chosen option will condition the organization of the software. This option makes up a hypothesis under which the software can function correctly.

Thus, it will be necessary to make a certain number of choices concerning the behavior of the equipment. These choices will result, among other things, in the definition of a receipt procedure aimed at verifying that all the equipment that has been installed has in fact the expected qualities. If this were not the case, it is clear that the union of the software and the hardware would have no chance of working correctly as had been demonstrated in the model. This demonstration will therefore have been useless.

16.2.4 Tackling safety questions

An important question which is not tackled at all in the requirement document concerns the safety of people implicated in this system. We would like the model to inform us on this point, or at least that it asks a certain number of pertinent questions. For example, can people be blocked for ever in a location? How can we guarantee the contrary?

16.2.5 Synchronization problems

On a more technical level, the informal presentation says nothing about the details of the timing of the transfer operation. For example, what time-lag is there between the lighting up of the green control light, the acceptance of the turnstile and the start of the 30 second countdown? Could the green light go on while the turnstile is still blocked, or could it go out while the turnstile is still accepted?

The question is not so much to find out if the previous behavior is good or bad, it is rather to recognize the existence of a certain behavior and to know in advance if it can occur (even in a fugitive form) in the final system which will be installed.

16.2.6 Functioning at the limits

Another question not treated in the requirement document is what happens when the system functions "at the limits". For example, what is the reaction of the system when a card is introduced into the reader, whilst the green or red lights are still lit (that is to say, before the preceding *action* is finished)? More generally, we would like to be able to understand and predict how the system reacts when faced with "hostile" behavior of certain users. In this sort of system, we must not count upon hypotheses that rely too much upon the "good" behavior of users. Some users certainly do behave in a "strange" way.

16.3 Initial model of the system

We are now going to proceed to the initial formal description of our system by constructing a first, very abstract, model in which the separation between the software and the hardware is not the current issue.

In this first model, we introduce the set P of people and the set L of locations as carrier sets. We remind the reader that a carrier set has the implicit unique property of being non-empty. We introduce a constant *aut* denoting the authorization permanently given to people; it is a binary relation built on the sets P and L as stated in **axm0_1**. We also introduce a special location, *out*, denoting the outside. We ensure in **axm0_3** that everyone is authorized to be in location *out*!

Finally, we introduce a variable, *sit*, denoting the location where each person is. Note that this is a total function as stated in **inv0_1**: a person cannot be in two locations at a time and a person is always somewhere (thanks to *out*). Finally, the main property of our system is stated in invariant **inv0_2**: every person, which in a certain location, is authorized to be there. This invariant formalizes requirement FUN_3. Here is our initial formal state:

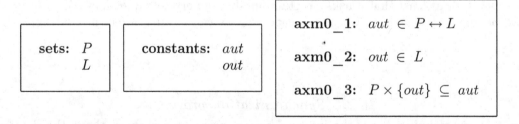

$$\textbf{sets:} \quad P \atop L$$

$$\textbf{constants:} \quad aut \atop out$$

$$\textbf{axm0\_1:} \quad aut \in P \leftrightarrow L$$
$$\textbf{axm0\_2:} \quad out \in L$$
$$\textbf{axm0\_3:} \quad P \times \{out\} \subseteq aut$$

$$\textbf{variables:} \quad sit$$

$$\textbf{inv0\_1:} \quad sit \in P \to L$$
$$\textbf{inv0\_2:} \quad sit \subseteq aut$$

Initially, everyone is outside as indicated in event init. We have a unique normal event, **pass**, corresponding to a person going from one location to another different one:

init
$$sit := P \times \{out\}$$

pass
  any p, l **where**
    $p \mapsto l \in aut$
    $sit(p) \neq l$
  then
    $sit(p) := l$
  end

To illustrate this, let us suppose that we have four locations l1, l2, l3, and l4 and three people p1, p2, and p3 together with the following authorizations:

p1	l2, l4
p2	l1, l3, l4
p3	l2, l3, l4

The following situations can therefore represent a satisfying evolution of the system since, as can be noted, invariant **inv0_1** and **inv0_2** are respected:

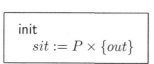

p1	l4
p2	l4
p3	l4

p1	l2
p2	l4
p3	l4

p1	l2
p2	l1
p3	l4

p1	l4
p2	l1
p3	l4

p1	l4
p2	l1
p3	l3

Situation 1   **Situation 2**   **Situation 3**   **Situation 4**   **Situation 5**

It is easy to *prove* that the invariants are well preserved by the above transitions when they happen. It is to be remarked that the event **pass** is very abstract; we do not know by which process the person p enters the location l. Neither do we know if the location, in which the person p is, communicates with location l, in which he wishes to go. In fact, we cannot express this property because we have not yet formalized the "geometry" of the locations.

The only important element of the present model is the expression of fundamental rules of the system in invariant **inv0_1** and **inv0_2**, and the proof that the unique observable and interesting event at this level (**pass**) maintains these conditions. We are already sure that the future models will respect these conditions, if, of course, we can *prove* that they constitute *correct refinements* of the present model.

16.4 First refinement

16.4.1 State and event

We are now going to proceed to our first refinement, which will consist in introducing into the model the notion of possible direct communication between two locations. For this, we introduce a new constant, *com*, denoting the direct communication between two locations. This is a binary relation built on the set L. A location does not "communicate" with itself as stated in **axm1_2**:

constants: ...
           com

axm1_1: $com \in L \leftrightarrow L$

axm1_2: $com \cap \mathrm{id} = \varnothing$

The initialization event does not change, and the event **pass** is refined in a straightforward way; we stipulate that a person can move to another location l if it has the authorization to be in l (as already stated in the abstraction) and also if location l communicates with the location where p is now, that is $sit(p)$:

init
    $sit := P \times \{out\}$

pass
  any p, l **where**
    $p \mapsto l \in aut$
    $sit(p) \mapsto l \in com$
  then
    $sit(p) := l$
  end

This event is quite simply a refinement of the previous version because the action is identical in both cases ($sit(p) := l$) and the guard of the second is stronger than that of the first as we have:

$$sit(p) \mapsto l \in com \;\Rightarrow\; sit(p) \neq l$$

since a location cannot communicate with itself according to **axm1_2**.

16.4.2 Deadlock freeness

It must now be proved that, in the absence of new events in this refinement, the concrete event **pass** does not happen less often than its abstract homologue (we recall that this is a necessary condition of the refinement). In fact, we are obviously faced with a difficulty here; it is not possible to prove that the refined event **pass** does not happen less often than its more abstract homologue. To demonstrate this, we would have to prove that the guard of the abstract event implies that of the concrete event; that is,

$$\exists p, l \cdot p \mapsto l \in aut \;\wedge\; sit(p) \neq l \;\vdash\; \exists p, l \cdot p \mapsto l \in aut \;\wedge\; sit(p) \mapsto l \in com$$

It is clear that this condition cannot be verified in general. A counter-example is easy to exhibit. Suppose we only have one person, p, in our system, and suppose that p is in a location $sit(p)$ where it is possible to enter (p did it). Now if this location has no exit, then p cannot leave it for another location l, although it could do it in the abstraction because the constraints about communication between locations did not exist.

The failure to prove the above condition indicates that *there are possibilities that some people could stay permanently blocked in locations.* And to be more precise, this could be the case even if this possibility did not exist in the abstraction, that is to say even if the authorizations are well defined to begin with so that it cannot happen. In fact, the geometry of communication between locations clearly adds an additional constraint limiting the way people can move.

Indeed, if a person is in a location l and has no authorization allowing him to be in any of the locations which communicate with l, then that person is blocked in l. The impossibility to make the above proof has brought up a safety problem, which can be set out in the form of a safety requirement which the system must satisfy:

No persons must remain blocked in a location	SAF-1

Notice that, what is stated here is stronger than what would have been needed, strictly speaking, to allow us to perform the proof that failed. That weaker statement would have been the following: "The geometry of locations does not introduce additional possibilities of blockage beyond those already present without this constraint." As a matter of fact, the mathematics of our approach has revealed a problem that gives us the idea of a wider safety question that was totally ignored in the requirement document.

16.4.3 A first solution

So we must find a sufficient constraint so that this requirement SAF-1 is practically satisfied. The previous proof obligation, namely:

$$\exists p, l \cdot p \mapsto l \in aut \ \wedge \ sit(p) \neq l \ \vdash \ \exists p, l \cdot p \mapsto l \in aut \ \wedge \ sit(p) \mapsto l \in com,$$

will serve as a model for this constraint. It is sufficient to prove the consequence of this implication:

$$\exists q, m \cdot q \mapsto m \in aut \ \wedge \ sit(q) \mapsto m \in com$$

which can be re-written as:

$$(aut \ \cap \ (sit; com)) \neq \varnothing$$

or, in an equivalent way:

$$((aut; com^{-1}) \ \cap \ sit) \neq \varnothing.$$

So as to prove this condition, it is sufficient to prove the following (since the condition $P \neq \varnothing$ implies that the total function sit is not empty):

$$sit \subseteq (aut; com^{-1}).$$

What does this condition say? If we develop it, we obtain:

$$\forall p \cdot \exists l \cdot (p \mapsto l \in aut \ \wedge \ sit(p) \mapsto l \in com).$$

In other words, the location $sit(p)$, in which each person p is situated at any moment, is in communication with at least one other location, l, in which p is authorized to go: the person p can therefore go out of the the location $sit(p)$, in which he is, via l.

This condition could be imposed as a new invariant of the system; however, it would be necessary to reinforce the guard for the **pass** event so as to admit in any one location only the people authorized to enter it (this is already the case), and who would also be authorized to exit. If faced with an interdiction, the authorization to enter such a location, which the person concerned would hold, would not be of much use since access would be refused anyway. So, it would be preferable to have a (sufficient) condition *which would be independent of the situation of people*. Indeed, this is possible, because we already have the invariant property $sit \subseteq aut$. So as to prove the condition

$sit \subseteq (aut; com^{-1})$ above, it is sufficient to prove the following, by transitivity of the inclusion:

$$aut \subseteq aut; com^{-1}$$

This condition makes up a further invariant, which can be translated as follows:

$$\forall p, l \cdot p \mapsto l \in aut \implies (\exists m \cdot p \mapsto m \in aut \land l \mapsto m \in com).$$

The interpretation of this invariant is quite instructive; it can be remarked that whenever the pair $p \mapsto l$ belongs to aut (the person p could therefore be in the location l since he is authorized to be there), there is a location m such as $p \mapsto m$ belongs to aut (the same person p is therefore authorized to enter the location m) and, moreover, such that the pair $l \mapsto m$ belongs to com (so the two locations l and m do communicate). When all is said and done, the person p, who could be in the location l, would not remain blocked indefinitely since he is also authorized to enter the location m which communicates with l. So this person can leave l via m. As can be seen, requirement SAF-1 has now been satisfied thanks to a stronger requirement whose expression has been determined (calculated) before being expressed as follows:

Any person authorized to be in a location must also be authorized to go in another location which communicates with the first one.	SAF-2

16.4.4 Second solution

Note that the previous solution is not satisfactory. It should be widened to guarantee that any person in a location, cannot only go out of it but, more generally, can also get outside. For this we extend our constant by introducing a function, *exit*, connecting locations to locations and defined at every location except *out* (this is property **axm1_3** below). More precisely, exit defines a tree structure. As a consequence, we can copy the tree axioms as defined in Section 7.6 of Chapter 9. Moreover, *exit* must be compatible with *com* (**axm1_5**). Finally, we must state that people must be authorized to follow the exit sign (**axm1_6**). All this leads to the following axioms:

<table>
<tr><td>constants: ...
   exit</td><td>**axm1_3**: $exit \in L \setminus \{out\} \rightarrow L$

axm1_4: $\forall s \cdot s \subseteq exit^{-1}[s] \Rightarrow s = \varnothing$

axm1_5: $exit \subseteq com$

axm1_6: $aut \rhd \{out\} \subseteq aut \,;\, exit^{-1}$</td></tr>
</table>

The last property could be promoted to a requirement replacing the one we defined above:

Any person authorized to be in a location which is not "outside", must also be authorized to be in another location communicating with the former and leading towards outside.	SAF-3

16.4.5 Revisiting deadlock freeness

Earlier, we proved that people who are in any location (except "outside") can always go outside. But we have not proved that we have no deadlock for people who are outside! We must prove that people can enter into the building. This is formalized by means of the following additional property:

axm1_7: $\forall p \cdot p \in P \Rightarrow (\exists l \cdot p \mapsto l \subseteq aut \ \wedge \ out \mapsto l \in com)$

16.5 Second refinement

16.5.1 State and events

During this second refinement, we are going to introduce one-way doors to communicate from one location to another. The formalization goes through the introduction of a new carrier set D which makes models of the doors. Each door is associated with a location of origin, represented by the total function *org* (property **axm2_1**) and a destination location represented by the total function *dst* (property **axm2_2**). For all these doors, the locations of origin and destination represent exactly the pairs of locations implied in the relation *com* introduced during the previous refinement (property **axm2_3**). This is formalized as follows:

$$
\begin{array}{l}
\textbf{sets:} \quad \ldots \\
\qquad D
\end{array}
\qquad
\begin{array}{l}
\textbf{constants:} \quad \ldots \\
\qquad org \\
\qquad dst
\end{array}
\qquad
\begin{array}{ll}
\textbf{axm2\_1:} & org \in D \rightarrow L \\[2mm]
\textbf{axm2\_2:} & dst \in D \rightarrow L \\[2mm]
\textbf{axm2\_3:} & com = (org^{-1} \,;\, dst)
\end{array}
$$

We introduce three new variables in this refinement, namely *dap*, *grn*, and *red*. The variable *dap* is a partial function from the set P of persons to the set D of doors:

$$
\begin{array}{l}
\textbf{variables:} \quad \ldots \\
\qquad\qquad dap
\end{array}
\qquad
\begin{array}{ll}
\textbf{inv2\_1:} & dap \in P \rightarrowtail D \\[2mm]
\textbf{inv2\_2:} & (dap \,;\, org) \subseteq sit \\[2mm]
\textbf{inv2\_3:} & (dap \,;\, dst) \subseteq aut
\end{array}
$$

It corresponds to the temporary connection that exists between a person p willing to go through a door d, but who has not passed yet through the door d. This connection exists between the moment where that person is "accepted" by the door (new event accept) and the subsequent moment where either that person passes through the door (event pass) or the 30 seconds delay is over (new event off_grn). The variable *dap* is a function (invariant **inv2_1**) because we do not want a person to be involved with more than one door at a time (since otherwise some additional people could be admitted into locations without cards). And it is also an injective function (invariant **inv2_1**) because we do not want to have a door involved with more than one person at a time (since otherwise people could be confused with the meaning of the green and red lights). Moreover, the origin of the door involved in this relationship correspond to the actual situation of the person (invariant **inv2_2**) and the destination of the door is a location where the person is authorized to be (invariant **inv2_3**):

The other two variables *grn* and *red* denote the subsets of the doors where the green or red light is lit (invariants **inv2_4** and **inv2_5**). Note that the set of green doors exactly corresponds to the range of the variables *dap* (invariant **inv2_6**). Also notice that both lights cannot be lit simultaneously (invariant **inv2_7**):

variables:	...
	grn
	red

inv2_4 :	$grn \subseteq D$
inv2_5 :	$red \subseteq D$
inv2_6 :	$grn = \text{ran}(dap)$
inv2_7 :	$grn \cap red = \varnothing$

We have two new events, accept and refuse, defined below:

```
accept
   any p, d where
      p ∈ P
      d ∈ D
      d ∉ grn ∪ red
      sit(p) = org(d)
      p ↦ dst(d) ∈ aut
      p ∉ dom (dap)
   then
      dap(p) := d
      grn := grn ∪ {d}
   end
```

```
refuse
   any p, d where
      p ∈ P
      d ∈ D
      d ∉ grn ∪ red
      ¬ ( sit(p) = org(d)
         p ↦ dst(d) ∈ aut
         p ∉ dom (dap) )
   then
      red := red ∪ {d}
   end
```

Both events involve a person p and a door d where red and green lights are both off. Event pass has three additional guards which make the door d possibly accept the person p: (1) person p must be situated at the origin of d, (2) person p is authorized to be at the destination of d, and finally (3) person p is not already involved with a door. Event refuse has an additional guard which is the negation of the conjunction of the three previous guards.

Next are the definitions of two new events, off_grn and off_red, and also the refinement of the abstract event pass:

off_grn
  any d **where**
    $d \in grn$
  then
    $dap := dap \rhd \{d\}$
    $grn := grn \setminus \{d\}$
  end

off_red
  any d **where**
    $d \in red$
  then
    $red := red \setminus \{d\}$
  end

pass
  any d **where**
    $d \in grn$
  with
    $p = dap^{-1}(d)$
    $l = dst(d)$
  then
    $sit(dap^{-1}(d)) := dst(d)$
    $dap := dap \rhd \{d\}$
    $grn := grn \setminus \{d\}$
  end

Event off_grn corresponds to the green light being put off when the 30 seconds delay has passed. Event off_red corresponds to the red light being put off when the 2 seconds delay has passed. Event pass corresponds to the person p associated with a green door d passing through that door. The person p in question is $dap^{-1}(d)$. The green light of d is put off and the association between p and d is removed.

16.5.2 Synchronization

As illustrated in the following diagram, the synchronization between the different events is quite weak for the moment.

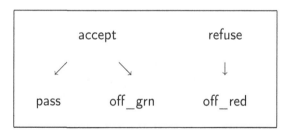

16.5.3 Proofs

It is easy to prove that the new version of the event pass refines its abstraction. It is also easy to prove that the new events all refine the event which does nothing, skip. Two things remain to be proved:

(1) that the event pass does not happen less often than its abstraction, taking into account, of course, the new events;

(2) that the new events cannot take control indefinitely, thus preventing the event **pass** from taking place.

In fact, the proof of (1) is relatively easy; however that of (2) is quite simply *impossible*. We have here a new difficulty which we will have to investigate and probably correct by additional requirements.

16.5.4 Risk of permanent obstruction of card readers

Taking into account the initial informal presentation, we now know that the event **pass** envisaged above is not the only "basic" event that can be observed. We know that the entrance of a person can be refused and also that a person who wishes to enter a location can change his mind just before passing – in this last case the door is automatically blocked again after 30 seconds. This corresponds to the events **refuse** and **off_grn** envisaged above.

However, during their introduction, it must be proved that these two events cannot prevent indefinitely the event **pass** from happening (that is to say, their guards are not indefinitely true at the same time as those of the event **pass**), which, in theory rather than in practice, is not impossible.

Indeed, we can imagine observing strange behavior of the system where nobody could ever enter the locations, either because people without the necessary authorizations keep trying to get in, or because other people, who are authorized put their cards in the reader but change their minds at the last minute. So as to prove that this behavior is not indefinitely possible, we must propose something to prevent them.

16.5.5 Propositions for preventing permanent obstruction

A first way of proceeding would be to formalize a mechanism whereby the "system" (at large) would force, in one way or another, people who are not allowed to access a location not to keep on trying *indefinitely* to get in (meeting indefinitely with refuse). In the same way, should the system force, in one way or another, those who have the right not to give up at the last minute (thus provoking *indefinitely* a new blockage)? This type of drastic behavior, in all evidence, is not part of the specification of the system we are analyzing.

A second way of proceeding, more gentle but also more efficient, would consist in eliminating from the system people who tend to behave in this way too frequently. They would simply no longer be allowed to enter any location at all. Their authorization to enter any location at all would be taken away. These people would therefore be confined to the location in which they find themselves, for example "outside". This is very easy to formalize and then to realize; moreover, this is the situation to be found in most smart card systems. For example, after three successive unfruitful tries with a cash dispenser, the card is "snatched", which is a very efficient way of preventing the person in question from blocking indefinitely access to the dispenser. Note however that such a drastic solution has its drawbacks in our case: the person whose card has been removed simply cannot leave the location where this has happened, causing yet another safety problem.

16.5.6 Final decision

We decide not to envisage this last possibility which would make the card readers too complicated (too expensive) and would introduce an additional safety problem. In other words, we accept, for financial (and safety) reasons, a risk of indefinite obstruction, which, despite everything, will probably never happen in reality. In other words, the system we are going to construct will not prevent people from blocking doors indefinitely either by trying indefinitely to enter locations into which they are not authorized to enter, or by abandoning "on the way" their intention to enter the locations in which they are in fact authorized to enter.

Clearly, the system we are going to construct is thus not totally correct according to our theoretical criteria. We accept this, but, and this is very important, we have taken great care to make it known, and to point it out explicitly by a clearly expressed decision.

16.6 Third refinement

16.6.1 Introducing the card readers

We now introduce the card readers into the model. This is the first time we will have been taking into account such a material element. This device can be characterized by: (i) the capture of information which is read on the card introduced by the user and (ii) the expedition of this information towards the controlling computer by means of a networked message. Moreover, when a card is read, it can be supposed that the reader is physically blocked (the slot is obstructed) until it receives an acknowledgement message coming from the control system.

All this corresponds to the following behavioral decision for card readers: each card reader is supposed to stay physically blocked (slot obstructed) between the moment when the contents of a card is sent to the system and the reception by this reader of the corresponding acknowledgement. This comes when the pass protocol has been entirely completed (successfully or not).

By this decision, we are making sure that no-one will be able to introduce a card into a reader at random. It is to be noted that we must pay a certain price for this, that of the installation of readers with obstructable slots (they do not all belong to this category).

16.6.2 Assumptions concerning the communication network

We will only make minimal assumptions concerning the forwarding of messages through the network. For example, we suppose that the network does not guarantee that the messages be received in the order in which they have been sent. However, it can be supposed that the messages sent along the network are not lost, or modified, or duplicated. Of course, we could take into account these particular constraints, but then the model would be more complicated. In any case, such constraints would only be introduced during ulterior refinements.

16.6.3 Variables and invariant

We will identify in the model each physical reader with the door it is associated with. Therefore, it is not necessary to have a particular set for the readers. The set of blocked readers is represented by a subset of doors which we will name BLR (for blocked readers). This is invariant **inv3_1** below.

The messages which are sent from the readers towards the control system are "door-person" pairs represented collectively by the variable $mCard$ (each one of these pairs $d \mapsto p$ represents what the reader associated with the door d has read on the card of the person p). They make up a partial function from the set D of doors to the set P of persons (invariant **inv3_2**); intuitively, this comes from the fact that no reader can implicate more than one person in the messages it sends because its slot is obstructed as seen above. However, this is not an injective function because nothing prevents a person from sliding his card into another reader when he has not gone through the door associated to the first one and the 30 seconds corresponding to this are not over (this is a case of strange behavior that cannot be eliminated).

Lastly, the set of acknowledgement messages is represented by the set $mAckn$, which is therefore a subset of doors (invariant **inv3_3**). These elements are formally defined as follows:

variables: ...
BLR
$mCard$
$mAckn$

inv3_1 :	$BLR \subseteq D$
inv3_2 :	$mCard \in D \nrightarrow P$
inv3_3 :	$mAckn \subseteq D$

While a reader is obstructed, the door in question is in one of the four following *exclusive* situations: (1) it is consigned in an input message as yet untreated by the system, (2) its green light is on, (3) its red light is on, (4) it is consigned in an acknowledgement message as yet untreated by the reader. These different states characterize the progression of the information through the system. They correspond to the following supplementary invariants:

---

inv3_4 : $\mathsf{dom}\,(mCard) \ \cup\ grn\ \cup\ red\ \cup\ mAckn\ =\ BLR$

inv3_5 : $\mathsf{dom}\,(mCard) \ \cap\ (grn\ \cup\ red\ \cup\ mAckn)\ =\ \varnothing$

inv3_6 : $mAckn\ \cap\ (grn\ \cup\ red)\ =\ \varnothing$

Since we already know that the sets grn and red are disjoint (this is invariant **inv2_7**), we can say that the four sets $\mathsf{dom}\,(mCard)$, grn, red, and $mAckn$ form a *partition* of the set BLR.

16.6.4 Events

The new event we are introducing at this stage is the one that corresponds to the reading of a card. It is a "physical" event:

CARD
   any p, d **where**
      $p \in P$
      $d \in D \setminus BLR$
   then
      $BLR := BLR \cup \{d\}$
      $mCard := mCard \cup \{d \mapsto p\}$
   end

Note the the guard $d \in D \setminus BLR$ indicates that no card can be introduced in the reader while it is blocked. This is a "physical" guard.

We can now find the refinements of two events **accept** and **refuse**. They are almost identical to their previous versions except that now the implied elements p and d are those read on a message coming from a card reader:

```
accept
   any p, d where
      d ↦ p ∈ mCard
      sit(p) = org(d)
      p ↦ dst(d) ∈ aut
      p ∉ dom (dap)
   then
      dap(p) := d
      grn := grn ∪ {d}
      mCard := mCard \ {d ↦ p}
   end
```

```
refuse
   any p, d where
      d ↦ p ∈ mCard
      ¬ ( sit(p) = org(d)
          p ↦ dst(d) ∈ aut
          p ∉ dom (dap) )
   then
      red := red ∪ {d}
      mCard := mCard \ {d ↦ p}
   end
```

Note that the message $d \mapsto p$, once read, is removed from the "channel" $mCard$. The event **pass** is almost identical to its previous versions. The reading of the card is only confirmed by the dispatch of the corresponding acknowledgement message towards the corresponding reader by means of the "channel" $mAckn$:

```
pass
   any d where
      d ∈ grn
   then
      sit(dap⁻¹(d)) := dst(d)
      dap := dap ⊳ {d}
      grn := grn \ {d}
      mAckn := mAckn ∪ {d}
   end
```

Likewise the two events **off_grn** and **off_red** also contain the dispatching of an acknowledgement message to the card reader.

```
off_grn
   any d where
      d ∈ grn
   then
      dap := dap ⊳ {d}
      grn := grn \ {d}
      mAckn := mAckn ∪ {d}
   end
```

```
off_red
   any d where
      d ∈ red
   then
      red := red \ {d}
      mAckn := mAckn ∪ {d}
   end
```

Lastly, a new physical event **ACKN** closes the protocol by unblocking the corresponding reader:

```
ACKN
    any d where
       d ∈ mAckn
    then
       BLR := BLR \ {d}
       mAckn := mAckn \ {d}
    end
```

16.6.5 Synchronization

The various events of this refinement are now synchronized as follows:

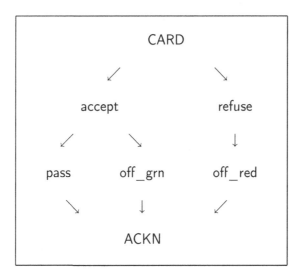

16.6.6 Proofs

The proof of this refinement does not induce any particular problem.

16.7 Fourth refinement

16.7.1 Decisions concerning the physical doors

We are now introducing the physical controls of the door (blocking and acceptance) as well as those for the detection of pass. We are also taking the following decision concerning "local" behavior of doors: when a door has been cleared, it blocks itself automatically without any intervention from the control system.

We are also making another important decision, which is the following: it is supposed that each door incorporates a local clock which assures temporized blocking after 30 seconds together with the extinction of the green light, or the extinction of the red light after 2 seconds.

16.7.2 Variables and invariant: the green chain

The formalization takes place thanks to a certain number of new variables. First the set *mAccept* of messages sent by the control system to accept the doors. As we have seen above with the card readers, the set of accepted doors is introduced: it is called *GRN* since it corresponds to the *doors whose green light is physically on*. Then we have the set *mPass* of messages sent by each door after detection of clearing. Lastly, we have the set *mOff_grn* of messages sent by the doors to signal automatic re-blocking after 30 seconds. The following invariant is obtained:

$$
\begin{array}{ll}
\textbf{variables:} & \ldots \\
& GRN \\
& mAccept \\
& mOff\_grn \\
& mPass
\end{array}
$$

These sets are exclusive and their union is equal to the set *grn* of doors whose *green light is logically on*. As in the previous section, these properties show the progression of the information. Also notice that *GRN* is included in *mAccept*:

$$
\begin{array}{ll}
\textbf{inv4\_1}: & mAccept \cup mPass \cup mOff\_grn = grn \\[2mm]
\textbf{inv4\_2}: & mAccept \cap (mPass \cup mOff\_grn) = \varnothing \\[2mm]
\textbf{inv4\_3}: & mPass \cap mOff\_grn = \varnothing \\[2mm]
\textbf{inv4\_4}: & GRN \subseteq mAccept
\end{array}
$$

As can be seen, it is possible for a door to be logically green while it is not yet or not any more physically green. Moreover, invariant **inv4_1** makes the variable *grn* useless in this refinement.

16.7.3 Variables and invariant: the red chain

In a completely symmetrical way to the "green chain", we are now going to study the "red chain". The following variables are to be found. First the set $mRefuse$ of messages used to send to a door the order to put on its red light. Then the set RED of doors whose red light is physically on. Finally, we have the set of messages $mOff\_red$ used for sending the corresponding information to the part of the software concerned with the extinction of the red light. These last messages are sent automatically by the door 2 seconds after the red light goes on. The following invariant is obtained:

$$
\begin{aligned}
&\textbf{variables:} \quad \ldots \\
&\qquad\qquad RED \\
&\qquad\qquad mRefuse \\
&\qquad\qquad mOff\_red
\end{aligned}
$$

These sets are exclusive and their union is equal to the set red of doors whose red lights are logically on. As before, these properties show the progression of information. Moreover RED is included in $mRefuse$:

$$
\begin{aligned}
&\textbf{inv4\_5:} \qquad mRefuse \ \cup\ mOff\_red \ =\ red \\
\\
&\textbf{inv4\_6:} \qquad mRefuse \ \cap\ mOff\_red \ =\ \varnothing \\
\\
&\textbf{inv4\_7:} \qquad RED \ \subseteq\ mRefuse
\end{aligned}
$$

As can be seen, it is possible for a door to be logically red while it is not yet or not any more physically red. Moreover, invariant **inv4_5** makes the variable red useless in this refinement.

16.7.4 The events

Let us now consider the events. Those which correspond to card readers which have not been changed in this refinement will not be copied here. Inversely, the event accept has been slightly modified. The sending of a physical acceptance message to the doors has been added:

```
accept
    any p, d where
        d ↦ p ∈ mCard
        sit(p) = org(d)
        p ↦ dst(d) ∈ aut
        p ∉ dom (dap)
    then
        dap(p) := d
        mCard := mCard \ {d ↦ p}
        mAccept := mAccept ∪ {d}
    end
```

We now find the physical event of acceptance to a door and the physical lighting of a green light:

```
ACCEPT
    any d where
        d ∈ mAccept
    then
        GRN := GRN ∪ {d}
    end
```

It is interesting to remark on the gap between the logical acceptance of the door (accept event in the software) and the physical acceptance (event ACCEPT of the hardware). This gap evokes a major problem of distributed systems which is that of distinguishing between the intention (software) and the real action (hardware). We now find the physical event corresponding to the clearing of the door. Note that the door does not "know" who is clearing it.

```
PASS
    any d where
        d ∈ GRN
    then
        GRN := GRN \ {d}
        mPass := mPass ∪ {d}
        mAccept := mAccept \ {d}
    end
```

This physical pass is followed by a logical pass which is almost identical to its version during the previous refinement. The only difference corresponds to the fact that the launching of this event is now due to the reception of a message. It is to be noted here that the event **pass** "knows" who is passing; we are dealing with the person implied in acceptance of the door. Once again we may note a gap between physical detection (PASS event of the hardware) and its logical effect (**pass** event of the software):

```
pass
    any d where
       d ∈ mPass
    then
       sit(dap⁻¹(d)) := dst(d)
       dap := dap ⩤ {d}
       mAckn := mAckn ∪ {d}
       mPass := mPass \ {d}
    end
```

The event which consists in physically blocking the door (from a clock supposedly inside the door which starts up 30 seconds after its acceptance if no one has cleared it in the meantime) is the following. The message of re-blocking is sent to the software.

```
OFF_GRN
    any d where
       d ∈ GRN
    then
       GRN := GRN \ {d}
       mOff_grn := mOff_grn ∪ {d}
       mAccept := mAccept \ {d}
    end
```

Finally, we can find a new version of the event **off_grn**, which gets underway on reception of the previous message.

```
off_grn
    any d where
       d ∈ mOff_grn
    then
       dap := dap ⩤ {d}
       mAckn := mAckn ∪ {d}
       mOff_grn := mOff_grn \ {d}
    end
```

The event **refuse** is slightly modified so as to allow a message concerning the lighting of the red light to be sent:

```
refuse
    any p, d where
        d ↦ p ∈ mCard
        ¬ ( sit(p) = org(d)
            p ↦ dst(d) ∈ aut
            p ∉ dom (dap) )
    then
        mCard := mCard \ {q ↦ p}
        mRefuse := mRefuse ∪ {q}
    end
```

The first hardware event after this corresponds to the reception of the previous message and the effective lighting up of the red light. The automatic extinction of the red light after 2 seconds corresponds to the following second event which sends a message to the software so as to warn it:

```
REFUSE
    any d where
        d ∈ mRefuse
    then
        RED := RED ∪ {d}
    end
```

```
OFF_RED
    any d where
        d ∈ RED
    then
        RED := RED \ {d}
        mOff_red := mOff_red ∪ {d}
        mRefuse := mRefuse \ {d}
    end
```

The event **off_red** is slightly modified as regards its previous version; it is now set off by the reception of the previous message:

```
off_red
    any d where
        d ∈ mOff_red
    then
        mAckn := mAckn ∪ {d}
        mOff_red := mOff_red \ {d}
    end
```

16.7.5 Synchronization

We now obtain the following complete synchronization between the software and the hardware:

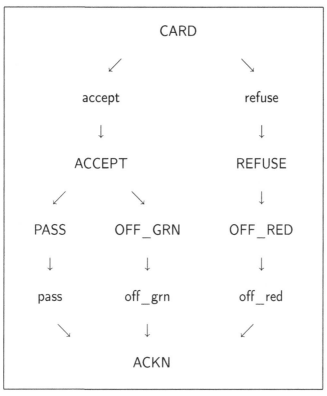

17

Train system

17.1 Informal introduction

The purpose of this chapter is to show the specification and construction of a complete computerized system. The example we are interested in is called a *train system*. By this, we mean a system that is practically managed by a *train agent*, whose role is to control the various trains crossing part of a certain *track network* situated under his supervision. The computerized system we want to construct is supposed to help the train agent in doing this task.

Before entering in the informal description of this system (followed by its formal construction), it might be useful to explain the reason why we think it is important to present such a case study in great detail. There are at least four reasons which are the following:

(i) This example presents an interesting case of quite complex data structures (the track network), whose mathematical properties have to be defined with great care: we want to show that this is possible.

(ii) This example also shows a very interesting case where the reliability of the final product is absolutely fundamental: several trains have to be able to cross the network safely under the complete automatic guidance of the software product we want to construct. For this reason, it will be important to study the bad incidents that could happen and which we want either to avoid completely or manage safely. In this chapter, however, we are more concerned by *fault prevention* than *fault tolerance*. We shall come back to this in the conclusion.

(iii) The software must take account of the external environment that is to be carefully controlled. As a consequence, the formal modeling we propose here will contain not only a model of the future software we want to construct, but also a detailed model of its environment. Our ultimate goal is to have the software working in perfect synchronization with the external equipment, namely the track circuits, the points (switches), the signals, and also the train drivers. We want to *prove*

508

that trains obeying the signals, set by the software controller, and then (blindly) circulating on the tracks whose points have been positioned, again by the software controller, will do so in a completely safe manner.

(iv) Together with this study, the reader will be able to understand the kind of methodology we recommend. It should be described, we hope, in sufficiently general terms so that he will be able to use this approach in similar examples.

We now proceed with the informal description of this train system together with its informal (but very precise) definitions and requirements. We first define a typical track network, which we shall use as a running example throughout the chapter. We then study the two main components of tracks, namely points (switches) and crossings. The important concepts of blocks, routes, and signals are then presented together with their main properties. The central notions of route and block reservations are proposed. Safety conditions are then studied.This is followed by the complementary train moving conditions, allowing several trains to be present in the network at the same time. We propose a number of assumptions about the way trains behave. Finally, we present possible failures that could happen and the way such problems are solved.

The formal development (model construction) is preceded by the *refinement strategy* we shall adopt in order to proceed in a gentle and structured manner. This is followed by the formal model construction.

17.1.1 Methodological conventions for the informal presentation

In the following sections, we give an informal description of this train system, and, together with this description, we state what its main *definitions and requirements* are. Such definitions and requirements will be inserted as separate labeled boxes in the middle of an explanatory text. These boxes must all together clearly define what is to be taken into account by people doing the formal development. The various definitions and requirements will be labeled according to the following taxonomy:

ENV	Environment		MVT	Movement
FUN	Functional		TRN	Train
SAF	Safety		FLR	Failure

- "Environment" definitions and requirements are concerned with the structure of the track network and its components.

- "Functional" definitions and requirements are dealing with the main functions of the system.
- "Safety" definitions and requirements define the properties ensuring that no classical accidents could happen.
- "Movement" definitions and requirements ensure that a large number of trains may cross the network at the same time.
- "Train" definitions and requirements define the implicit assumptions about the behavior of trains.
- "Failure" definitions and requirements finally define the various failures against which the system is able to react without incidents.

Here is our first very general requirement:

The goal of the train system is to safely control trains moving on a track network	FUN-1

17.1.2 Network associated with a controlling agent

Here is a typical track network that a train agent is able to control. In what follows, we are going to use that network as a running example:

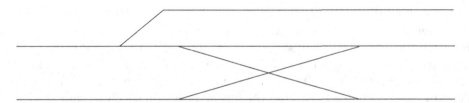

17.1.3 Special components of a network: points and crossings

Such a network contains a number of *special components*: these are the *points* and the *crossings* as illustrated in the following figure (five points and one crossing).

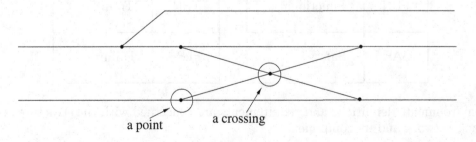

A point is a device allowing a track to split in two distinct directions. A crossing, as its name indicates, is a device that makes two different tracks cross each other. In what follows, we briefly describe points and crossings.

A track network may contain some special components: points and crossings	ENV-1

Point A point special component can be in three different positions: left, right, or unknown. This is indicated in the following figure.

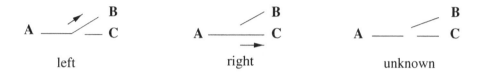

Note that the orientation from **A** to **C** is sometimes called the *direct track*, whereas the one from **A** to **B** is called the *diverted track*. In what follows, however, we shall continue to call them right and left respectively as there is no ambiguity in doing so.

In the first two cases above, the arrow in the figure shows the convention we shall use to indicate the orientation of the point. Note that these arrows do not indicate the direction followed by a train. For example, in the first case, it is said that a train coming from **A** will turn left, a train coming from **B** will turn right, and a train coming from **C** *will probably have some troubles!* Also note that a train encountering a point oriented in an unknown direction (third case) might have some trouble too, even more if a point suddenly changes position while a train is on it (we shall come to this in Section 17.1.8).

The last case is the one that holds when the point is moving from left to right or vice-versa. This is because this movement is supposed to take some time; it is performed by means of a motor which is part of the point. When the point has reached its final position (left or right) it is locked, whereas when it is moving it is unlocked. Note, however, that in the coming development, we shall not take this into account. In other words, we shall suppose, as a simplification, that a *point moves instantaneously and that it is thus always locked*; that is, the unknown case is not treated. We then just require in this development that a point may have only two positions: left or right:

A point may have two positions: left or right	ENV-2

Crossing A crossing special component is completely static; it has no state as points have. The way a crossing behaves is illustrated in the following figure: trains can go from **A** to **B** and vice-versa, and from **C** to **D** and vice-versa.

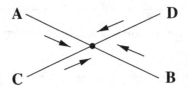

17.1.4 The concept of block

The controlled network is statically divided into a fixed number of *named blocks* as indicated in the following figure where we have 14 blocks named by single letters from *A* to *N*:

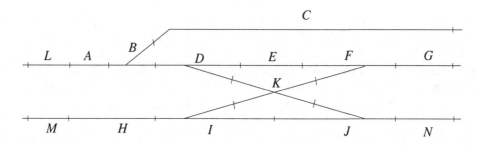

A track network is made of a number of fixed blocks	ENV-3

Each block may contain at most one special component (points or crossings):

A special component (points or crossings) is always attached to a given block. And a block contains at most one special component	ENV-4

For example, in our case, block *C* does not contain any special component, whereas block *D* contains one point, and block *K* contains a crossing. Each block is equipped with a, so-called, *track circuit*, which is able to detect the presence of a train on it. A block can thus be in two distinct states: unoccupied (no train on it) or occupied (a train is on it).

A block may be occupied or unoccupied by a train	ENV-5

In the following figure, you can see that a train is occupying the two adjacent blocks D and K (this is indicated in the figure by the fact that the blocks in question are emphasized).

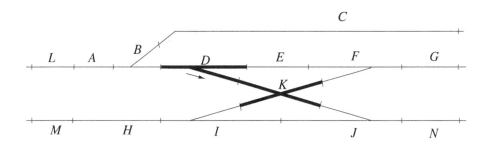

Notice that when a train is detected in a block, we do not know a priori the precise position of the train in it, nor do we know whether the train is stopped or moving. Moreover, in the last case, we do not know in which direction the train is moving. But all such information is not important for us; as will be seen in this development, it is only sufficient for our purpose to know that a block is occupied or not.

17.1.5 The concept of route

The blocks defined in the previous section are always structured in a number of statically *pre-defined routes*. Each route represents a possible path that a train may follow within the network controlled by the train agent. In other words, the routes define the various ways a train can traverse the network. A route is composed of a number of adjacent blocks forming an ordered sequence:

A network has a fixed number of routes. Each route is characterized by a sequence of adjacent blocks	ENV-6

A train following a route is supposed to occupy in turn each block of that route. Note that a train may occupy several adjacent blocks at the same time (even a short train). Also note that a given block can be part of several routes. All this is shown below in the following table where ten pre-defined routes are proposed:

R1	*L A B C*	R6	*C B A L*
R2	*L A B D E F G*	R7	*G F E D B A L*
R3	*L A B D K J N*	R8	*N J K D B A L*
R4	*M H I K F G*	R9	*G F K I H M*
R5	*M H I J N*	R10	*N J I H M*

Besides being characterized by the sequence of blocks composing it, a route is also statically characterized by the positions of the points which are parts of the corresponding blocks. For example, route *R3* (*L A B D K J N*) is characterized as follows:

- the point in block *B* is positioned to right,
- the point in block *D* is positioned to right,
- the point in block *J* is positioned to right.

This is illustrated in the following figure where route *R3* (*L A B D K J N*) is emphasized. The little arrows situated next to the points of blocks *B*, *D*, and *J* indicate their position:

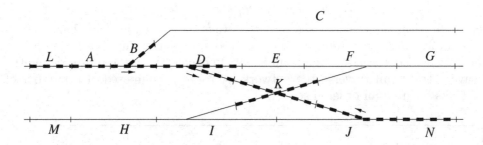

A route is also characterized by the positions of the points which are situated in blocks composing it	ENV-7

Routes have two additional properties. The first concerns the first block of a route:

The first block of a route cannot be part of another route unless it is also the first or last block of that route	ENV-8

And the second one concerns the last block of a route:

The last block of a route cannot be part of another route unless it is also the first or last block of that route	ENV-9

At the end of the next section, we shall explain why the constraints we have presented just now are important. Finally, a route has some obvious continuity property:

A route connects its first block to its last one in a continuous manner	ENV-10

and it has no cycle:

A route contains no cycles	ENV-11

17.1.6 The concept of signal

Each route is protected by a *signal*, which can be red or green. This signal is situated just before the first block of each route. It must be clearly visible from the train drivers:

Each route is protected by a signal situated just before its first block	ENV-12

When a signal is red, then, by convention, the corresponding route cannot be used by an incoming train. Of course, the train driver must obey this very fundamental requirement:

A signal can be red or green. Trains are supposed to stop at red signals	ENV-13

In the next figure, you can see the signal protecting each route:

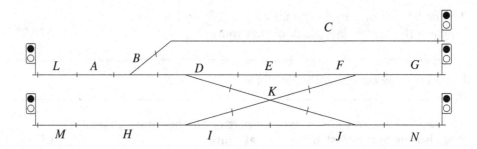

Notice that a given signal can protect several routes. For example, the signal situated on the left of block L protects route $R1$ (L A B C), $R2$ (L A B D E F G), and $R3$ (L A B D K J N); this is because each of these routes starts with the same block, namely block L:

Routes having the same first block share the same signal	ENV-14

In the previous figure and in the coming ones, we use the convention that a signal situated to the left of its pole protects the routes situated on its right and vice-versa. For example, the signal situated on the right-hand side of block C protects route $R6$, namely (C B A L).

A last important property of a signal protecting the first block of a route is that, when green, it turns back automatically to red as soon as a train enters into the protected block.

A green signal turns back to red automatically as soon as the first block is made occupied	ENV-15

The reason for the constraints defined at the end of Section 17.1.5 must now be clear: we want a signal, which is always situated just before the first block of a route, to clearly identify the protection of that route. If a route, say $r1$, starts in the middle of another one, say $r2$, then the signal protecting $r1$ will cause some trouble for the train situated in route $r2$. As very often the reverse of a route is also used as a route, the previous constraint applies for the last block of a route; it cannot be common to another route except if it is also the last block of that route.

17.1.7 Route and block reservations

The train agent is provided with a panel offering a number of commands corresponding to the different routes he can assign to trains traversing his "territory".

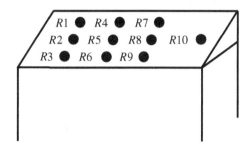

When a train is approaching the network, the train agent is told that this train will cross the network by using a certain route. The train agent then presses the corresponding command in order to *reserve* that route. Note that other trains might already be crossing the network, while the train agent is pressing that command. As a consequence, the situation faced by the train agent is potentially dangerous; we shall come back to this very important fact in Section 17.1.8. This is the reason why the forthcoming reservation process is entirely controlled by the software we want to construct.

A route can be reserved for a train. The software is in charge of controlling the reservation process	FUN-2

The reservation process of a route r is made of three phases:

  (i) the individual reservation of the various blocks composing route r is performed,
 (ii) the positioning of the relevant points of route r is accomplished,
(iii) the turning to green of the signal protecting route r is done.

When the first phase is not possible (see next section), the reservation fails and the two other phases are then canceled. In this case, the reservation has to be re-tried later by the train agent. Let us now describe these phases in more detail.

Phase 1: Block reservation The block reservation performed during the first phase induces another state for a block (besides being occupied or unoccupied by a train, as seen in Section 1.3), that is a block can be reserved or free:

A block can be reserved or free	FUN-3

Note that an occupied block must clearly be already reserved:

An occupied block is always reserved	FUN-4

At the end of this first successful phase, the route is said to be *reserved*, but it is not ready yet to accept a train:

Reserving a route consists in reserving the individual blocks it is made of. Once this is done, the route is said to be *reserved*	FUN-5

Phase 2: Point positioning When the reservation of all blocks of a route r is successful, the reservation process proceeds with the second phase, namely the positioning of the corresponding points in the direction corresponding to the route r. When all points of r are properly positioned, the route is said to be *formed*:

Once it is reserved, a route has to be *formed* by properly positioning its points	FUN-6

Note that a formed route remains reserved:

A formed route is always a reserved route	FUN-7

Phase 3: Turning signal to green Once a route r is formed, the third and last phase of the reservation can be done: the signal controlling route r is turned green; a train can be accepted in it. A train driver, looking at the green signal, then leads the train within the reserved and formed route. We already know from requirement ENV-15 that the signal will then turn red immediately:

Once it is formed, a route is made available for the incoming train by turning its signal to green	FUN-8

17.1.8 Safety conditions

As several trains can cross the network at the same time, and as the train agent (or rather the software he uses) is sometimes re-positioning a point when forming a route, there are clearly some serious risks of bad incidents. This is the reason why we must clearly identify such risks and see how we can safely avoid them. This is, in fact, the main purpose of the software we would like to build in order to help the train agent in a systematic fashion. There are three main risks which are the following:

(1) Two (or more) trains traversing the network at the same time hit each other in various ways.
(2) A point may change position under a train.
(3) The point of a route may change position in front of a train using that route. In other words, the train has not yet occupied the block at this point, but it will do so in the near future since that block is situated on that route.

Case (1) is obviously very bad since the crashed trains may derail. Case (2) would have the consequence to cut the train into two parts and, most probably, the train will derail too. Case (3) may have two distinct consequences: either to move the train outside its current route so that it can now hit another train (Case (1)), or to have the train derail in case the point now disconnects the current route. We are thus going to set up a number of safety conditions in order to prevent such risks from happening. The first risk (train hitting) is avoided by ensuring two safety conditions:

(i) a given block *can only be reserved for at most one route at a time,*

A block can be reserved for *at most one* route	SAF-1

(ii) the signal of a route is green *only* when the various blocks of that route are all reserved for it and are unoccupied, and when all points of that route are set in the proper direction.

The signal of a route can *only be green* when all blocks of that route are reserved for it and are unoccupied, and when all points of this route are properly positioned	SAF-2

As a consequence (and also thanks to requirement FUN-4 stating that an occupied block is always a reserved block), several trains never occupy the same block at the same time, *provided, of course, that train drivers do not overpass a red signal*. We shall come back to this important point in Section 17.1.11.

The second and third risks (points changing direction under certain circumstances) are avoided by ensuring that a point can only be maneuvered when the corresponding block is that of a route which is *reserved (all its blocks being reserved) but not yet formed*:

A point can *only be re-positioned* if it belongs to a block which is in a reserved but not yet formed route	SAF-3

The last safety requirement ensures that no blocks of a reserved, but not yet formed, route are occupied by a train.

No blocks of a reserved, but not yet formed, route are occupied	SAF-4

A consequence of this last safety requirement is that the re-positioning of a point, done according to requirement SAF_3, is always safe.

17.1.9 Moving conditions

In spite of the safety conditions (which could be preserved by not allowing any train to cross the network!), we want to allow a large number of trains to be present in the network at the same time without danger. For this, we allow each block of a reserved route to be freed as soon as the train does not occupy it any more:

Once a block of a formed route is made unoccupied, it is also freed	MVT-1

As a result, the only reserved blocks of a formed route are those blocks which are occupied by the train or those blocks of the route which are not yet occupied by the train:

A route remains formed as long as there are some reserved blocks in it	MVT-2

When no block of a formed route is reserved any more for that route, it means that the train has left the route, which can thus be made free:

A formed route can be made free (not formed and not reserved any more) when no blocks are reserved for it any more	MVT-3

17.1.10 Train assumptions

Note that it is very important that a block once freed for a route (after being occupied and subsequently unoccupied) *cannot be made occupied again for this route* unless the route is first made free and then formed again. The reason for this is that the freed block in question can be assigned to another route. To achieve this, we must assume that trains obey two properties. First, a train cannot split in two or more parts while in the network:

A train cannot split while in the network	TRN-1

And second, a train cannot move backwards while in the network:

A train cannot move backwards while in the network	TRN-2

This is so because in both cases a freed block can be made occupied again. Note that clearly trains do split and move backwards (for example, in the main station of most towns); it simply means that the blocks where they do so are not within the network controlled by a train system.

Another important implicit assumption about trains is that they cannot enter "in the middle" of a route (it cannot land on a route!):

A train cannot enter in the middle of a route. It has to do so through its first block.	TRN-3

Likewise, a train cannot disappear in the middle of a route (it cannot take off!):

A train cannot leave a route without first occupying then freeing all its blocks	TRN-4

17.1.11 Failures

In this section, we study a number of abnormal cases which could happen. The fact that their probabilities are very low is not a reason to preclude these cases.

The first and most important case of failure is obviously the one where, for some reason, the driver of a train does not obey the red signal guarding a route. In Section 17.1.6 we said in requirement ENV_14 that "trains are supposed to stop at red signals". Now, is it always the case?

The solution to this problem is local to the train. This case is detected within the faulty train by a device called the automatic train protection. As soon as this device detects that the train passes a red signal, it automatically activates the emergency brakes of the train. The distance between the signal and the first block of the route it protects is calculated so that we can be sure that the train will stop before entering that first block. Note that this protection is not certain as the automatic train protection could be broken while the train does not stop at a red signal!

Trains are equipped with the automatic train protection system, which guarantees that they cannot enter a route guarded by a red signal	FLR-1

In Section 17.1.10, we claimed in requirement TRN_1 that "a train cannot split while in the network". Is it possible that it happens nevertheless by accident? The solution to this problem is again local to the train. Each train is now equipped with special bindings so that it forms a continuous body that cannot be mechanically broken. Here again, the solution is not certain but professionals claim that the risk is extremely low:

Trains are equipped with special bindings, which guarantee that they cannot be mechanically broken.	FLR-2

Another case raised in Section 17.1.10 is requirement TRN_2 claiming that "a train cannot move backwards while in the network". Here again, the automatic train protection system is used. It detects immediately any backward move and in that case activates automatically the emergency brakes. But we have to be sure that the train nevertheless does not occupy a block again that it has recently freed. This is guaranteed by the fact that the transmission of the occupancy of a block by the track circuit is slightly delayed. As a consequence, when the train has physically left a block, this fact is not immediately transmitted to the controller; it is only done when the back of the train has moved a certain distance. If the train moves backwards slightly, then it does not occupy the block again since it did not leave it (as "seen" from the software controller):

The automatic protection system and a slight delay observed by the track circuit guarantee that a train moving backward cannot occupy again a block which has been physically freed.	FLR-3

In Section 17.1.10, we said in requirement **TRN-3** that "a train cannot enter in the middle of a route". This is certainly the case for trains. The problem is that the software controller does not "see" trains. It only detects that a block is occupied or freed by means of track circuits connections. As a consequence, it is possible that, for some reason, a block is detected to be occupied by its track circuit because a piece of metal is put on the rail. The software controller can detect such a faulty occupancy. In that case the train agent can take some emergency action. But this is not always the case however. This risk is therefore accepted but not treated here:

The risk of a faulty detection of a block occupancy is not treated	FLR-4

In Section 17.1.10, we said in requirement **TRN-4** that "a train cannot leave a route without first occupying then freeing all its block". This is not always the case; however, in the very rare circumstance where a short train (say a single engine) derails and then falls down it suddenly quits the block where it is situated! This case can certainly be detected by the software controller and some emergency action can be taken by the train agent. We do not treat this case here however:

The case where a short train derails and leaves its block is not treated here	FLR-5

Note that the last two cases of failure raise a difficult problem which is the one of restarting the system after an emergency. It seems that the only solution consists in carefully inspecting the network to decide whether a normal situation has been reached again.

17.1.12 Examples

We now illustrate the previous concepts with examples of trains safely crossing the network.

To begin with, we can see a train $T1$ approaching block L. This is indicated by a little thick line on the left of block L. The train cannot continue since the signal is red.

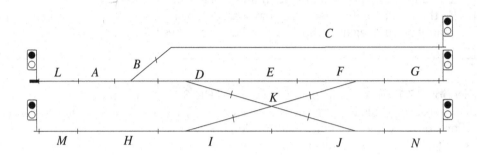

The train agent is told to form route $R3$, that is L A B D K J N. This consists in checking that the various blocks of this route are not reserved for another route and that the points are oriented in the proper directions. Once this is done, the corresponding signal is turned green; route $R3$ is indeed formed. In the following figure,† we can see the situation just after the "formation" of route $R3$:

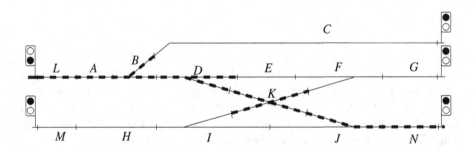

Train $T1$ now enters route $R3$. It occupies block L.‡ The signal protecting route $R3$ has been turned to red again so that no train can enter this route any more.

---

† In subsequent figures, we use the following convention: a reserved, but not yet occupied, block is represented by a thick dashed line (we have already seen in Section 17.1.3 that a reserved and occupied block is represented by a thick plain line)

‡ In this running example, we suppose that trains never occupy more than one block at a time. This is a simplification that does not correspond to the reality; a train can clearly occupy two adjacent blocks when a car is covering the transition between them. We use this simplification here just to make the examples shorter.

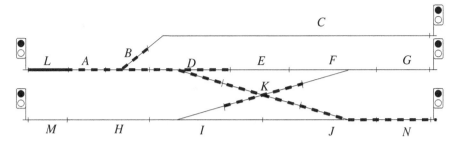

Train $T1$ moves further to block A (this is skipped) and then to block B. Block L and A are freed as soon as the train does not occupy them any more.

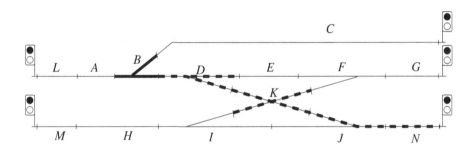

Train $T1$ moves further to block D. Block B is freed. A second train, $T2$, arrives and approaches block C. The train agent is told to form route $R6$, that is C B A L, for that new train. This is possible because there is no conflict with the already reserved blocks. The corresponding points are set properly and the signal protecting route $R6$ has turned green.

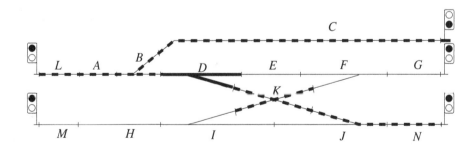

Train $T1$ moves to block K. Train $T2$ enters route $R6$. It occupies block C. The signal protecting route $R6$ is turned red:

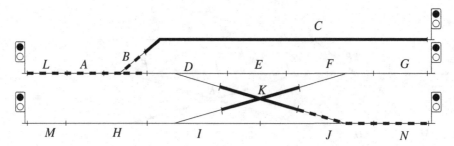

Train $T1$ now occupies block J and frees block K, and train $T2$ still occupies block C. A third train, $T3$, approaches block M. The train agent is told to form route $R4$; that is, M H I K F G, for that new train. This is possible because there is no conflict with already reserved blocks. The corresponding points are set properly and the signal protecting route $R4$ is turned green.

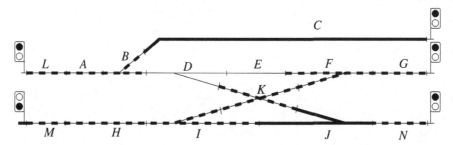

Train $T3$ enters route $R4$ by occupying block M. The signal protecting route $R4$ turns back to red. The other trains are moving in their respective routes.

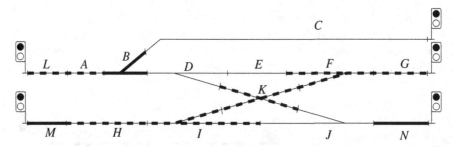

Train $T1$ now leaves route $R3$. Trains $T2$ and $T3$ continue to move.

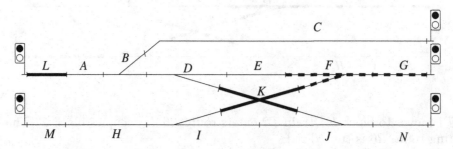

Eventually trains $T2$ and $T3$ leave their routes.

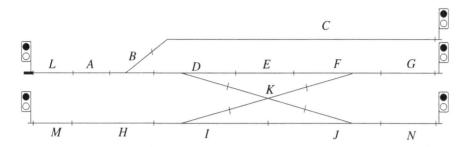

17.2 Refinement strategy

The summary of the various informal requirements we have seen in previous sections is as indicated below. We have all together 39 requirements. Of course, a real train system might have far more requirements than this; it must be clear that what we are presenting here is only a very simplified version of such a train system:

ENV	Environment	15	MVT	Movement	3
FUN	Functional	8	TRN	Train	4
SAF	Safety	4	FLR	Failure	5

The role of the formal phase, which we start now, is to build models able to take account of these requirements. As it is out of the question to incorporate all of them at ounce, we are going to proceed by successive approximations, which are called *refinements*. In this section, we define the refinement strategy we are going to follow. It is very important indeed to define the order in which we are going to extract the various requirements which have been exhibited in the previous phase.

(i) In the initial model, the blocks, and route concepts are formalized. Blocks are defined from a logical point of view however.

(ii) In the first refinement we introduce the physical blocks and thus start to formalize part of the environment. We establish the connection between the logical blocks and the physical ones. This is done in an abstract way, however, as we do not yet introduce the points.

(iii) In the second refinement, we introduce the notion of readiness for a route. This corresponds to an abstract view of the green signals.

(iv) In the third refinement, we introduce the physical signals. We data-refine (implement) the readiness of a route by means of green signals.

(v) In the fourth refinement, we introduce the points.

(vi) Some other refinements are needed in order to finalize details. Such refinements are not treated in this chapter however.

17.3 Initial model

17.3.1 The state

The state is made up of a number of carrier sets, constants, and variables, which we study in the following sections.

Carrier sets The initial model is concerned with blocks and routes. We thus take account of requirement **ENV-3** of Section 17.1.4, and of requirement **ENV-6** of Section 17.1.5. We do not take account of points or signals for the moment; this will be done in further refinements. We have thus only two carrier sets, B and R, standing for blocks and routes. In what follows, we shall use the convention that carrier sets are named using single upper case letters:

$$
\begin{array}{ll}
\textbf{sets:} & B \\
& R
\end{array}
$$

Constants The organization of the track network, which is made of a number of routes, is formalized by means of two constant: $rtbl$ ("routes of blocks") relating routes to blocks and nxt ("next") relating blocks to blocks for each route:

$$
\begin{array}{ll}
\textbf{constants:} & rtbl \\
& nxt
\end{array}
$$

The constant $rtbl$ is a total (all routes are concerned) and surjective (all blocks are concerned) binary relation from B to R (**axm0_1**). This is so because a route may have many blocks and a block can belong to several routes:

$$
\textbf{axm0\_1:} \quad rtbl \in B \leftrightarrow\!\!\!\rightarrow R
$$

The constant nxt denotes the succession of each blocks associated with a route (**ENV-6**). This succession forms an injective function from blocks to blocks (that is, a function whose inverse is also a function):

$$\mathbf{axm0\_2:} \quad nxt \in R \to (B \rightarrowtail B)$$

For example, a route such as route $R3$ comprising the following blocks L A B D K J N in that order:

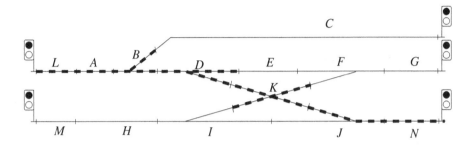

is represented as follows by the injective function $nxt(R3)$. As can be seen, the function $nxt(R3)$ establishes a continuous connection between the first block L and last block N of route $R3$:

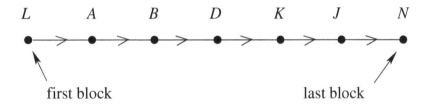

As the first and last block of a route will play a certain role in further properties, we have to introduce them explicitly in our state by means of some new constants. We thus extend our set of constants by introducing the first and last block of each route r: fst and lst

$$\begin{array}{ll} \mathbf{constants:} & \cdots \\ & fst \\ & lst \end{array}$$

These first and last elements of a route enjoy the following obvious properties: they are defined for each route (**axm0_3** and **axm0_4**) and they are genuine blocks of the route (**axm0_5** and **axm0_6**). Moreover the first and last block of a route are distinct (**axm0_7**):

axm0_3: $fst \in R \rightarrow B$

axm0_4: $lst \in R \rightarrow B$

axm0_5: $fst^{-1} \subseteq rtbl$

axm0_6: $lst^{-1} \subseteq rtbl$

axm0_7: $\forall r \cdot r \in R \Rightarrow fst(r) \neq lst(r)$

As illustrated in the previous figure, we want the connection represented by the function $nxt(r)$ for each route r, to be continuous as required by requirement **ENV-10** of Section 17.1.5. In other words, we want to exclude cases like this, which do not make sense for a route:

Moreover, we want to express that the blocks of a route r, which are present in the domain and range of the injection $nxt(r)$, are exactly the blocks of route r, namely $rtbl^{-1}[\{r\}]$. In order to express all this, we just say that the injection $nxt(r)$ is indeed a bijection from $rtbl^{-1}[\{r\}] \setminus \{lst(r)\}$ to $rtbl^{-1}[\{r\}] \setminus \{fst(r)\}$:

axm0_8: $\forall r \cdot r \in R \Rightarrow nxt(r) \in s \setminus \{lst(r)\} \rightarrowtail\!\!\!\rightarrow s \setminus \{fst(r)\}$

where s is $rtbl^{-1}[\{r\}]$

But this is not sufficient, as the following pathological case can happen:

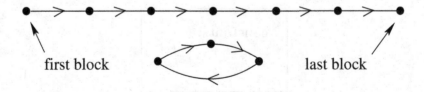

We have then to express that there is no such cycles in the connection. This corresponds to requirement **ENV-11** of Section 17.1.5. This can be done by stating that the only subset S of B which is included in its image under $nxt(r)$, that is $nxt(r)[S]$, is the empty set (a genuine cycle is indeed equal to its image under $nxt(r)$):

$$\textbf{axm0\_9:} \quad \forall r \cdot r \in R \; \Rightarrow \; (\forall S \cdot S \subseteq nxt(r)[S] \; \Rightarrow \; S = \varnothing)$$

A final property of the routes is that they cannot depart or arrive in the *middle* of another one. However several routes can depart from the same block or arrive at the same block. All this corresponds to requirements **ENV-8** and **ENV-9** of Section 17.1.5. It is expressed by the following two properties:

$$
\begin{aligned}
\textbf{axm0\_10:} \quad & \forall r, s \cdot r \in R \\
& \qquad\quad s \in R \\
& \qquad\quad r \neq s \\
& \qquad\quad \Rightarrow \\
& \qquad\quad fst(r) \notin rtbl^{-1}[\{s\}] \setminus \{fst(s), lst(s)\} \\[2mm]
\textbf{axm0\_11:} \quad & \forall r, s \cdot r \in R \\
& \qquad\quad s \in R \\
& \qquad\quad r \neq s \\
& \qquad\quad \Rightarrow \\
& \qquad\quad lst(r) \notin rtbl^{-1}[\{s\}] \setminus \{fst(s), lst(s)\}
\end{aligned}
$$

Note that the previous properties do not preclude two routes from having the same first or last blocks.

Variables In this initial model, we have four variables named $resrt$, $resbl$, $rsrtbl$, and OCC (see below, the box entitled **variables**). In what follows, we shall use the convention that *physical variables* are named using upper case letters only. By "physical variable", we mean a variable representing part of the external equipment (here OCC denotes the set of physical blocks which are occupied by trains). The other variables (named using lower case letters only) are called the *logical variables*: they represent variables that will be part of the future software controller. The invariants corresponding to all these variables can be seen on the right table below (these invariants are explained below):

<table>
<tr><td>variables:</td><td>*resrt*
resbl
rsrtbl
OCC</td></tr>
</table>

inv0_1: $resrt \subseteq R$

inv0_2: $resbl \subseteq B$

inv0_3: $rsrtbl \in resbl \rightarrow resrt$

inv0_4: $rsrtbl \subseteq rtbl$

inv0_5: $OCC \subseteq resbl$

The variable *resrt* (reserved routes) denotes the reserved routes (**inv0_1**): this is coherent with requirement **FUN-2** of Section 17.1.7, which says that a route can be reserved for a train.

The second variable, *resbl* (reserved blocks), denotes the set of reserved blocks (**inv0_2**). This is coherent with requirement **FUN-3** of Section 17.1.7, which states that a block can be reserved for a route.

Our third variable, *rsrtbl* (reserved routes of reserved blocks), relates reserved blocks to reserved routes: it is a *total function* from reserved blocks to reserved routes (**inv0_3**). This is coherent with requirement **SAF-1** stating that a block cannot be reserved for more than one route. Of course, this connection is compatible with the static relationship *rtbl* between blocks and routes (**inv0_4**): a reserved block for a route is a block of that route.

Finally, variable *OCC* denotes the set of occupied blocks. This is coherent with requirement **ENV-5** stating that a block might be occupied by a train. Such occupied blocks are obviously reserved for some route (**inv0_5**). This is coherent with requirement **FUN-4** of Section 17.1.7 stating that an occupied block is always reserved.

We have to define now more invariants corresponding to the way a train can occupy a reserved route. The general situation is illustrated on the following figure:

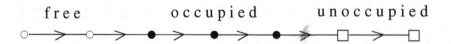

free   occupied   unoccupied

The blocks of a reserved route are divided in three areas:

(i) In the first area (on the left, where the blocks are represented by white circles), the blocks are freed by that route because the train does not occupy them any more. They can readily be reused (and maybe they are already) for another reserved route.

(ii) In the second area (in the centre, where the blocks are represented by black circles), the blocks are all reserved and occupied by a train.

(iii) In the third area (on the right, where the blocks are represented by white squares), the block are all reserved, but not occupied yet by a train.

There are other situations corresponding to some special cases of the general situation depicted in the previous figure. In the first special case, areas 1 and 2 are empty; the route is reserved, but the train has not yet entered the route:

The second special case is the one where area 1 is empty, but not areas 2 and 3. In fact, the train is entering the route as illustrated in the following figure:

A third special case is one where a (long) train occupies all blocks in a route:

The fourth special case it the one where the train is leaving the route:

The last special case is the one where all blocks in the reserved route have been freed by that route. The route itself is then ready to be freed

More formally, let us call M the set of *free blocks* in a reserved route (those behind the train), N the set of *occupied blocks* in a reserved route, and finally P the set of reserved but *unoccupied blocks* of a reserved route (those situated in front of a train). Sets M, N, and P are formally defined as follows for a given reserved route r:

$$M = rtbl^{-1}[\{r\}] \setminus rsrtbl^{-1}[\{r\}]$$

$$N = rsrtbl^{-1}[\{r\}] \cap OCC$$

$$P = rsrtbl^{-1}[\{r\}] \setminus OCC$$

Note that M, N, and P partition $rtbl^{-1}[\{r\}]$. According to the previous presentation, the only transitions that are allowed are the following:

$$M \to M \qquad M \to N \qquad N \to N \qquad N \to P \qquad P \to P$$

This can be represented by the following conditions:

$$nxt(r)[M] \subseteq M \cup N \qquad nxt(r)[N] \subseteq N \cup P \qquad nxt(r)[P] \subseteq P$$

Such conditions are equivalent to the following ones (since $nxt(r)[rtbl^{-1}[\{r\}]]$ is included in $rtbl^{-1}[\{r\}]$ according to **axm0_8**):

$$nxt(r)[M] \cap P = \varnothing \qquad nxt(r)[N \cup P] \subseteq N \cup P \qquad nxt(r)[P] \subseteq P$$

All this is eventually formalized in the following invariants:

---

inv0_6: $\forall r \cdot r \in R \;\Rightarrow\; nxt(r)[rtbl^{-1}[\{r\}] \setminus s] \cap (s \setminus OCC) = \varnothing$

inv0_7: $\forall r \cdot r \in R \;\Rightarrow\; nxt(r)[s] \subseteq s$

inv0_8: $\forall r \cdot r \in R \;\Rightarrow\; nxt(r)[s \setminus OCC] \subseteq s \setminus OCC$

where s is $rsrtbl^{-1}[\{r\}]$

These invariants are coherent with the train requirements TRN-1 to TRN-4 defined in Section 17.1.10.

17.3.2 The events

The four variables *resrt*, *resbl*, *rsrtbl*, and *OCC* are initialized to the empty set. Initially, no trains are in the network and no routes or blocks are reserved. Besides the initialization event (which we do not present here), we have five normal events. Events define transitions which can be observed. In what follows, we shall use the convention that physical events corresponding to transitions occurring in the environment are named using upper case letters only. Here are the events of the initial model:

- route_reservation,
- route_freeing,
- FRONT_MOVE_1,
- FRONT_MOVE_2,
- BACK_MOVE.

Event route_reservation corresponds to the reservation of a route r. It is done on an unreserved route (i.e. $r \in R \setminus resrt$) whose blocks are not already reserved for a route (i.e. $rtbl^{-1}[\{r\}] \cap resbl = \varnothing$). Route r is then reserved together with its blocks. This is coherent with requirement FUN-5, which says that a route can be reserved as soon as all its blocks are themselves reserved:

---

route_reservation
  any r **where**
    $r \in R \setminus resrt$
    $rtbl^{-1}[\{r\}] \cap resbl = \varnothing$
  then
    $resrt := resrt \cup \{r\}$
    $rsrtbl := rsrtbl \cup rtbl \rhd \{r\}$
    $resbl := resbl \cup rtbl^{-1}[\{r\}]$
  end

---

route_freeing
  any r **where**
    $r \in resrt \setminus \mathrm{ran}(rsrtbl)$
  then
    $resrt := resrt \setminus \{r\}$
  end

Event route_freeing makes a reserved route free when it does not contain reserved blocks any more. This is coherent with requirement MVT-3, which says that a route can be made free when no blocks are reserved for it any more.

Event FRONT_MOVE_1 corresponds to a train entering a reserved route r. The first block of r must be reserved and unoccupied. Moreover, the reserved route corresponding to the first block of r must be r itself. The first block is made occupied:

FRONT_MOVE_1
  any r **where**
    $r \in resrt$
    $fst(r) \in resbl \setminus OCC$
    $rsrtbl(fst(r)) = r$
  then
    $OCC := OCC \cup \{fst(r)\}$
  end

FRONT_MOVE_2
  any b, c **where**
    $b \in OCC$
    $c \in B \setminus OCC$
    $b \mapsto c \in nxt(rsrtbl(b))$
  then
    $OCC := OCC \cup \{c\}$
  end

Event FRONT_MOVE_2 corresponds to the occupancy of a block, which happens to be different from the first block of a reserved route. Given a block b, which is occupied and preceded (in the same route) by a block, say c, which is not occupied, then c is made occupied.

Finally, event BACK_MOVE corresponds to the move of the rear part of the train. This happens for a block b which is occupied and is the last block of a train. This is detected when block b has a follower in the route r reserved for b and that follower, if reserved, is not reserved for r (this corresponds to the big implicative guard). Moreover, when b has a predecessor, that predecessor must be occupied so that the train does not disappear before reaching the end of route r (this corresponds to the last guard). The action corresponding to that event makes b unoccupied and unreserved. This is coherent with requirement MVT-1, which says that "once a block of a formed route is made unoccupied, it is also freed":

$$
\boxed{
\begin{array}{l}
\text{BACK\_MOVE} \\
\quad \textbf{any} \ \ b, n \ \ \textbf{where} \\
\qquad b \ \in OCC \\
\qquad n = nxt(rsrtbl(b)) \\
\qquad \left(\begin{array}{l}
b \in \mathrm{ran}(n) \ \wedge \\
n^{-1}(b) \in \mathrm{dom}(rsrtbl) \\
\Rightarrow \\
rsrtbl(n^{-1}(b)) \neq rsrtbl(b)
\end{array} \right) \\
\qquad b \in \mathrm{dom}(n) \ \Rightarrow \ n(b) \ \in OCC \\
\quad \textbf{then} \\
\qquad OCC := OCC \setminus \{b\} \\
\qquad rsrtbl := \{b\} \lhd rsrtbl \\
\qquad resbl := resbl \setminus \{b\} \\
\quad \textbf{end}
\end{array}
}
$$

Important remark It might seem strange at first glance (and even incorrect) to have physical events such as FRONT_MOVE_1, FRONT_MOVE_2, and BACK_MOVE using non-physical variables in their guards. Clearly, a physical event can be enabled under certain conditions depending on physical variables only: a physical event cannot magically "see" the non-physical variables. The reason for having non-physical variables in the guards here is that we are still in an abstract version where such abnormalities are possible. Of course, in the final refined version of physical events we have to check that it is not the case any more.

17.4 First refinement

In this first refinement, we introduce the *physical tracks*. So that the movements of the train will correspond entirely on the physical situation of the track. Note however that we do not yet introduce the points and the signals.

17.4.1 *The state*

We do not introduce new carrier sets or new constants in this refinement.

Variables In this refinement, we have three new variables named TRK (track), frm (formed routes), and LBT (last blocks of trains). Notice that the variables introduced in the initial models, namely $resrt$, $resbl$, $rsrtbl$, and OCC, are kept in this refinement:

$$\begin{array}{ll} \textbf{variables:} & \cdots \\ & TRK \\ & frm \\ & LBT \end{array}$$

The variable TRK is a partial injection (**inv1_1**) from blocks to blocks defining the *physical succession of blocks*. It also contains the direction taken by trains following the tracks. Note that this last information is not "physical" (you cannot "see" it on the track); it corresponds however to the physical movements of trains on the physical tracks. Next is the invariant defining variable TRK as an injective function:

$$\textbf{inv1\_1:} \quad TRK \in B \rightarrowtail B$$

Here is an illustration of the variable TRK in a certain situation:

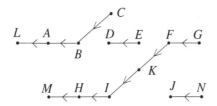

As can be seen, route $R9$ (G F K I H H M) is now established on the physical track. In Section 17.4.2, we shall see how the event, which is positioning the points will modify this situation. Note that the crossing in block K is "broken" and that the physical track "remembers" the direction followed by trains circulating on it; of course, this is not what happen in the real tracks, but this is a convenient abstraction.

Finally, all pairs belonging to TRK also belong to $nxt(r)$ for some route r (**inv_2**):

$$\textbf{inv1\_2:} \quad \forall x, y \cdot x \mapsto y \in TRK \;\Rightarrow\; (\exists r \cdot r \in R \;\wedge\; x \mapsto y \in nxt(r))$$

The variable frm represents the set of formed routes; it is a subset of the reserved routes (**inv1_3**). This is coherent with requirement FUN-7, which says that "a formed route is always a reserved route". We have a number of invariants involving the formed routes. The reserved routes of occupied blocks are formed routes (**inv1_4**). A route r, which is reserved but not yet formed, is such that its reserved blocks are exactly the constant reserved blocks associated with r (**inv1_5**). The two previous invariants are coherent with requirements SAF-4, which says that "no blocks of a reserved but not yet formed route are occupied":

$$\textbf{inv1\_3:} \quad frm \subseteq resrt$$

$$\textbf{inv1\_4:} \quad rsrtbl[OCC] \subseteq frm$$

$$\textbf{inv1\_5:} \quad \forall r \cdot r \in resrt \setminus frm \Rightarrow rtbl \rhd \{r\} = rsrtbl \rhd \{r\}$$

Now comes the most important invariant (**inv1_6**); it relates the logical succession of blocks on a route (represented by the function $nxt(r)$ for each route r) to the physical tracks on the terrain (represented by the variable TRK). It says that for each formed route r, the logical succession of blocks (where the train is supposed to be and where it has to go when proceeding through route r) *agrees with the physical tracks on the terrain*. In other words, when a route r is formed, then the portion of the physical blocks where the train is or where it will be in the future when proceeding along this route corresponds to what is expected in the logical blocks as recorded by the controller:

$$\textbf{inv1\_6:} \quad \forall r \cdot r \in frm \Rightarrow rsrtbl^{-1}[\{r\}] \lhd nxt(r) = rsrtbl^{-1}[\{r\}] \lhd TRK$$

Finally, variable LBT denotes the set of blocks occupied by the back of each train; this is also a "physical" variable like variable TRK. The first invariant (**inv1_7**) concerning this variable, quite naturally says that the last block of a train is indeed occupied by a train:

$$\textbf{inv1\_7:} \quad LBT \subseteq OCC$$

And now we state (**inv1_8**) that the last block b of a train, if it has a follower a on its route, then a, if reserved, is not reserved for the route of b:

$$
\begin{aligned}
\textbf{inv1\_8:} \quad \forall a, b \cdot\ & b\ \in\ LBT \\
& b\ \in\ \mathrm{ran}(nxt(rsrtbl(b))) \\
& a = nxt(rsrtbl(b))^{-1}(b) \\
& a \in \mathrm{dom}(rsrtbl) \\
& \Rightarrow \\
& rsrtbl(a) \neq rsrtbl(b)
\end{aligned}
$$

Thanks to the introduction of the physical variables TRK and LBT, we shall be able to define the movements of the train based only on what the train finds on the terrain, namely the physical blocks. Notice that a train "knows" that the last part of it occupies a block belonging to LBT.

17.4.2 The events

Event route_reservation is not modified in this refinement. Other events are modified as shown below. We also introduce two more events:

- point_positioning,
- route_formation

Event point_positioning is still very abstract in this refinement. It conveys however the essence of the communication between the future software and the outside equipment; the physical TRK is modified according to the logical route $nxt(r)$. This event is coherent with requirement **SAF-3**, which says that "a point can *only be re-positioned* if it belongs to a block that is in a reserved but not yet formed route". In further refinements, this modification of the physical track will correspond to the controller action modifying the point positions:

point_positioning
  any r **where**
    $r \in resrt \setminus frm$
  then
    $TRK := (\mathrm{dom}(nxt(r)) \lhd TRK \rhd \mathrm{ran}(nxt(r))) \cup nxt(r)$
  end

As can be seen, this logical event has an effect on the physical variable TRK. This is due to the fact that this event is effectively changing (at ounce for the moment) the physical position of the points of route r.

Next is an illustration of the physical situations just before and just after an occurrence of event **point_positioning**. As can be seen, after this occurrence we have three properties: (1) route $R3$ (L A B K J N) is established on the physical track, (2) the points have been modified accordingly, and (3) the crossing situated in block K has been "reorganized":

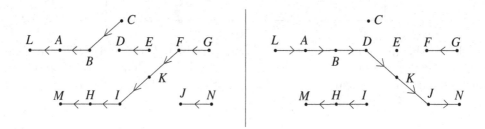

Event **route_formation** explains when a route r can be "formed", namely when the physical and logical track agree, that is after event **point_positioning** has acted on route r:

$$
\begin{array}{|l|}
\hline
\text{route\_formation} \\
\quad \textbf{any}\;\; r\;\; \textbf{where} \\
\qquad r \in resrt \setminus frm \\
\qquad rsrtbl^{-1}[\{r\}] \lhd nxt(r) \;=\; rsrtbl^{-1}[\{r\}] \lhd TRK \\
\quad \textbf{then} \\
\qquad frm := frm \,\cup\, \{r\} \\
\quad \textbf{end} \\
\hline
\end{array}
$$

It can be seen that this event refers to the physical variable TRK in its guard. This is due to the fact that this event is enabled when the controller detects (here at ounce for the moment) that all points of route r are correctly positioned.

Event **route_freeing** is slightly extended by making the freed route not formed any more. This is coherent with requirement MVT_2, which says that "a route remains formed as long as there are some reserved blocks in it" and MVT-3, which says that "a formed route can be made free (not formed and not reserved any more) when no blocks are reserved for it any more":

```
route_freeing
  any  r  where
    r ∈ resrt \ ran(rsrtbl)
  then
    resrt := resrt \ {r}
    frm := frm \ {r}
  end
```

Event FRONT_MOVE_1 is only slightly modified for the moment as we have not introduced the signals yet; this will be done in further refinements. The present modification consists in extending the set LBT by adding to it the singleton $\{fst(r)\}$. As a matter of fact, when a train is entering a route, the last block of the train for that route is certainly the first block of the route until that block is freed when the back of the train will move in event BACK_MOVE.

```
FRONT_MOVE_1
  any  r  where
    r ∈ frm
    fst(r) ∈ resbl \ OCC
    rsrtbl(fst(r)) = r
  then
    OCC := OCC ∪ {fst(r)}
    LBT := LBT ∪ {fst(r)}
  end
```

```
FRONT_MOVE_2
  any  b  where
    b ∈ OCC
    b ∈ dom(TRK)
    TRK(b) ∉ OCC
  then
    OCC := OCC ∪ {TRK(b)}
  end
```

Event FRONT_MOVE_2 is now following the physical situation on the real track. We shall have to prove that it refines its abstraction however. As can be seen, all guards are now defined in terms of physical variables.

Event BACK_MOVE is split into two events. Event BACK_MOVE_1 corresponds to the last block of the train leaving the route. Event BACK_MOVE_2 corresponds to the last block of the train progressing in the route.

```
BACK_MOVE_1
    any  b  where
        b ∈ LBT
        b ∉ dom(TRK)
    then
        OCC := OCC \ {b}
        rsrtbl := {b} ⩤ rsrtbl
        resbl := resbl \ {b}
        LBT := LBT \ {b}
    end
```

```
BACK_MOVE_2
    any  b  where
        b ∈ LBT
        b ∈ dom(TRK)
        TRK(b) ∈ OCC
    then
        OCC := OCC \ {b}
        rsrtbl := {b} ⩤ rsrtbl
        resbl := resbl \ {b}
        LBT := (LBT \ {b}) ∪ {TRK(b)}
    end
```

Remark 1 As can be seen, the guards of physical events FRONT_MOVE_2, BACK_MOVE_1, and BACK_MOVE_2 are all now involving physical variables only (remember our "important remark" at the end of Section 17.3.2). It is still not the case for event FRONT_MOVE_1 however. Wait until refinement 3 in Section 17.6 where we shall see that event FRONT_MOVE_1 will be enabled as a consequence of a green signal, which clearly is a physical condition.

Remark 2 We notice that physical events BACK_MOVE_1 and BACK_MOVE_2 both make reference to some non-physical variables in their action part (*rsrtbl* and *resbl*). We wonder whether this is allowed. It would seem obvious that a physical event cannot modify controller variables. The reason to have some non-physical variables still present in the action parts of these events is because these events *have still to be decomposed* into two events: the "pure" physical event and a corresponding event in the controller. The reason can clearly be seen here: when the train does a physical back move, the controller has to react by freeing the corresponding logical block. The connection between the physical move and the (separate) logical reaction in the controller will be done later (in some refinement step to be done, but not presented in this chapter) by having the physical track circuit *sending a message to the controller* when it is physically made unoccupied. Upon receiving this message, the controller can then react.

Remark 3 Notice that both events FRONT_MOVE_1 and FRONT_MOVE_2 do not make any reference in their action part to some non-physical variables. It means that such events have no influence on the controller. This is quite understandable, when the front of the train proceeds, we have nothing to do in the controller, whereas when the back of the train proceeds we have something to do (block freeing).

17.5 Second refinement

In this refinement, we introduce the notion of *readiness* for a route. A route is ready when it is able to accept a new train. In the next refinement, we shall introduce the signals. As we shall see, the ready routes will have a green signal.

17.5.1 The state

We do not introduce new carrier sets or new constants.

Variables In this refinement, we introduce the new variable rdy, which denotes the set of ready routes.

$$
\begin{array}{ll}
\textbf{variables:} & \cdots, \\
& rdy
\end{array}
$$

Here are the basic properties of a ready route. A ready route is one which is formed (**inv2_1**), has all its blocks reserved for it (**inv2_2**), and has all its blocks unoccupied (**inv2_3**):

$$
\begin{array}{ll}
\textbf{inv2\_1:} & rdy \subseteq frm \\[2mm]
\textbf{inv2\_2:} & \forall r \cdot r \in rdy \Rightarrow rtbl \rhd \{r\} \subseteq rsrtbl \rhd \{r\} \\[2mm]
\textbf{inv2\_3:} & \forall r \cdot r \in rdy \Rightarrow \mathrm{dom}(rtbl \rhd \{r\}) \cap OCC = \varnothing
\end{array}
$$

17.5.2 The events

Events point_positioning, route_reservation, route_freeing, FRONT_MOVE_2, BACK_MOVE_1, and BACK_MOVE_2 are not modified in this refinement, they are thus not copied below. Event route_formation is extended by making the corresponding route ready besides being formed (this action was performed in the previous refinement):

```
route_formation
  any r where
    r ∈ resrt \ frm
    rsrtbl⁻¹[{r}] ◁ nxt(r) = rsrtbl⁻¹[{r}] ◁ TRK
  then
    frm := frm ∪ {r}
    rdy := rdy ∪ {r}
  end
```

The guards of event FRONT_MOVE_1 are simplified (and made stronger) by stating that the route r is a ready route (this event will be further simplified in the next refinement where we introduce the signals). We put the abstract version of this event next to the refined one to show the differences between the two guards:

(abstract-)FRONT_MOVE_1
   any r **where**
     $r \in frm$
     $fst(r) \in resbl \setminus OCC$
     $rsrtbl(fst(r)) = r$
   then
     $OCC := OCC \cup \{fst(r)\}$
     $LBT := LBT \cup \{fst(r)\}$
   end

(concrete-)FRONT_MOVE_1
   any r **where**
     $r \in rdy$
     $rsrtbl(fst(r)) = r$
   then
     $OCC := OCC \cup \{fst(r)\}$
     $LBT := LBT \cup \{fst(r)\}$
     $rdy := rdy \setminus \{r\}$
   end

17.6 Third refinement

In this refinement, we define the signals. The role of a signal is to express, when green, that a route is ready.

17.6.1 The state

Carrier sets We introduce the new carrier set S defining the signals:

sets: B, R, S

Constants In this refinement, we define one constant named SIG (pronounced "signal of first block"). This constant yields the unique signal associated with the first block of a route (**axm3_1**). This corresponds to requirements **ENV-12** and **ENV-14** of section 17.1.6. It is a bijection since every signal is uniquely associated with the corresponding first block of a route. Notice that routes sharing the same first block share the same signal:

constants: $\cdots$ SIG

axm3_1: $SIG \in \mathrm{ran}(fst) \rightarrowtail\!\!\!\rightarrow S$

Variables In this refinement, we introduce the variable GRN denoting the set of green signals (**inv3_1**). This variable data-refines variable rdy which disappears. The connection between the two is established by saying that signals of the first blocks of ready routes are exactly the green signals (**inv3_2**). We have thus established a correspondence between the abstract notion of ready routes and the physical notion of green signals:

variables: $\cdots$
GRN

inv3_1: $\quad GRN \subseteq S$
inv3_2: $\quad SIG[fst[rdy]] = GRN$

17.6.2 The events

The only two events that are modified in this refinement are events route_formation and FRONT_MOVE_1. Event route_formation is refined by turning to green the signal associated with the first block of the newly formed route. This is coherent with requirement FUN-8, which says that "once it is formed, a route is made available for the incoming train by turning its signal to green". This event is also coherent with requirement SAF-2, which says that "the signal of a route can *only be green* when all blocks of that route are reserved for it and are unoccupied". This is due to invariant **inv3_2** equating the blocks with green signals with ready routes, and invariants **inv2_2** and **inv2_3** saying that ready routes have all their blocks reserved and unoccupied:

```
route_formation
    any  r  where
      r ∈ resrt \ frm
      rsrtbl⁻¹[{r}] ◁ nxt(r)  =  rsrtbl⁻¹[{r}] ◁ TRK
    then
      frm :— frm ∪ {r}
      GRN := GRN ∪ {SIG(fst(r))}
    end
```

This logical event acts on the physical variable GRN. It corresponds to the controller sending a command to turn the physical signal of the first block of route r to green.

Event FRONT_MOVE_1 now reacts to a green signal rather than to a ready route as in the previous refinement. We take at last account of requirement ENV-13:

```
FRONT_MOVE_1
  any  b  where
      b ∈ dom(SIG)
      SIG(b) ∈ GRN
  then
      OCC := OCC ∪ {b}
      LBT := LBT ∪ {b}
      GRN := GRN \ {SIG(b)}
  end
```

As can be seen, the physical movement of trains follows the indication of green signals. Note that a green signal is *automatically turned red* when the train enters the corresponding block: this is coherent with requirement ENV-15.

17.7 Fourth refinement

17.7.1 The state

In this refinement, we introduce the points from an abstract point of view for the moment. They are denoted by the set of blocks which contain points. We know from requirement ENV-4 that a block may contain at most one special component: point or crossing.

Constants We introduce three constants in this refinement: $blpt$, lft, and rht. Constant $blpt$ (pronounced "blocks with points") denotes the set of blocks containing points (**axm4_1**). Each block b containing a point is connected to another block situated on the left of b and another block situated on its right. This is represented by two total functions lft and rht from $blpt$ to B (**axm4_2** and **axm4_3**). Notice that the two function lft and rht are disjoint (**axm4_4**) because a block cannot be situated simultaneously to the left and to the right of a point:

```
constants:  · · ·
              blpt,
              lft,
              rht
```

axm4_1: $blpt \subseteq B$

axm4_2: $lft \in blpt \rightarrow B$

axm4_3: $rht \in blpt \rightarrow B$

axm4_4: $lft \cap rht = \varnothing$

Let us recall our usual example network:

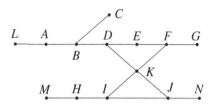

Next are the set *blpt* and both functions *lft* and *rht* corresponding to this example:

$$blpt = \{\, B, D, F, I, J \,\}$$

$$lft = \{\, B \mapsto C,\ D \mapsto E,\ F \mapsto K,\ I \mapsto K,\ J \mapsto I \,\}$$

$$rht = \{\, B \mapsto D,\ D \mapsto K,\ F \mapsto E,\ I \mapsto J,\ J \mapsto K \,\}$$

Each point situated in a route is either in the "direct" or "inverse" direction of this route. This is illustrated in the following figure where you can see fragments of two routes: on the left, we have a point oriented "direct-right", and on the right we have a point oriented "inverse-right".

More precisely, a point is represented in a route by either the left or the right connection, and also on the direct direction of the route or the inverse one. For example, in route $R2$ (L A B D E F G), there are three points: in B, in D, and in F. The one in B is direct and represented by the pair $B \mapsto D$ which is a member of *rht*, the one in D is direct and represented by the pair $D \mapsto E$ which is a member of *lft*, and finally the one in F is inverse and represented by the pair $F \mapsto E$ which is a member of *rht*. The connection of each point-block to the next one in a route must be functional (since the point is either in the right or in the left position). This can be formalized as follows:

---

axm4_5: $\forall r \cdot r \in R \Rightarrow (lft\ \cup\ rht) \cap (nxt(r)\ \cup\ nxt(r)^{-1}) \in blpt \nrightarrow B$

Notice that the position of each point relative to a given route r is the following: $(lft\ \cup\ rht) \cap (nxt(r)\ \cup\ nxt(r)^{-1})$.

We also have to add a technical property saying that there is no point in the first or last block of a route (**axm4_6** and **axm4_7**):

$$\textbf{axm4\_6:} \quad blpt \ \cap \ \mathrm{ran}(fst) \ = \ \varnothing$$

$$\textbf{axm4\_7:} \quad blpt \ \cap \ \mathrm{ran}(lst) \ = \ \varnothing$$

Variable We have no new variable in this refinement, only a new invariant expressing that the point positioning is, as expected, functional in the real track. This is expressed by the invariant **inv4_1**:

$$\textbf{inv4\_1:} \quad (lft \ \cup \ rht) \ \cap \ (TRK \ \cup \ TRK^{-1}) \ \in \ blpt \nrightarrow B$$

Notice that the function is partial only: this is due to the crossing. It is not difficult to prove that this invariant is maintained by event point_positioning, which is recalled now:

```
point_positioning
   any  r  where
     r ∈ resrt \ frm
   then
     TRK := (dom(nxt(r)) ◁ TRK ▷ ran(nxt(r))) ∪ nxt(r)
   end
```

A few additional refinements are clearly needed in order to complete this modeling development. It should contain the decomposition of events route_reservation, route_formation, and point_positioning in more atomic events so as to construct corresponding loops.

17.8 Conclusion

As was said in the introduction, this chapter contains more material on fault prevention than on fault tolerance. This is essentially due to the problem at hand where faults have to be avoided by all means. But faults can happen as was explained in Section 17.1.11, so it is interesting to see how this could have been taken into account in the modeling process.

It would not have been difficult to incorporate the Automatic Train Protection System (alluded above in Section 17.1.11) within the formal models because we have a global approach taking account of the environment. This would take care of requirements FLR-1 (drivers passing a red signal) and FLR-3 (trains moving backwards) which are protected by the Automatic Train Protection System.

As much as I understand from experts, the other failures are not treated, simply because people consider that their probability is extremely low. However, such failures could sometimes be detected in the case of FLR-4 (wrong block occupancy) and that of FLR-5 (train leaving a block). In these cases, the controller has to stop the system by not allowing any signal to be turned green and by not doing any point positioning. This default phase is to last until the environment is inspected and the system is reset. It would be also very easy to model this.

What we have presented here is very close to similar studies found in [1] and [3]. The approach of [1] itself follows from original approaches done in the past by applying the "Action System" methodology [2]. The important lesson learned from Action System is the idea of reasoning at a global level by introducing not only the intended software into the picture but also its *physical environment*.

In the present study, we insisted on the preliminary informal phase consisting in presenting the structured "definitions and requirements" of the system we want to build. We think that it is extremely important from a methodological point of view, as it is quite frequently a very weak point in similar industrial applications. It seems that we have also made a more complete mathematical treatment of the track network model.

17.9 References

[1] M. Butler. A system-based approach to the formal development of embedded controllers for a railway. *Design Automation for Embedded Systems* **6**, 2002.

[2] M. Butler, E. Sekerinski, and K. Sere. An action system approach to the steam boiler problem. In *Formal Methods for Industrial Applications*. Lecture Notes in Computer Science 1165. Springer-verlag, 1996.

[3] A. E. Haxthausen and J. Peleska. *Formal Development and Verification of a Distributed Railway Control System*. FM'99, Lecture Notes in Computer Science Volume 1709. Springer-verlag, 1999.

18

Problems

This final chapter is entirely devoted to problems which you might try solving. They are all to be done with the Rodin Platform, which you can download from the web site "event-b.org". We recommend beginners who are downloading the Rodin Platform for the first time to "perform" the tutorial which is included on this site before engaging in any of the problems presented in this chapter.

These problems are divided up into three categories called *Exercises* (Section 1), *Projects* (Section 2), and *Mathematical developments* (Section 3).

Exercises are small and easy developments, mainly corresponding to the construction of simple sequential programs. But we also find models of simple complete systems and even the development of a small electronic circuit. Exercises can be proposed in a beginner course.

Projects are more serious problems, which require more investment than exercises. They can be proposed in an advanced course.

Mathematical developments come from pure mathematics. They involve more complicated proofs than in the two previous cases; most of them are not performed automatically by the provers of the Rodin Platform. As such, they represent excellent exercises to improve our ability to perform interactive proofs.

For *Exercises* and *Projects*, we are required to write a requirements document as well as a refinement strategy before engaging in the formal development with the Rodin Platform. Most of the time, we will have to use some contexts to define the carrier sets and the constants of the problem at hand. The various machines we will define then represent our development by means of successive refinements. Many proofs can be done automatically by the Rodin Platform.

In the case of *Mathematical developments*, we will only define contexts since the issue is not to define transition systems but just to answer mathematical questions.

18.1 Exercises

18.1.1 Bank

Develop the simple model of a bank where people (customers of the bank) can open or close an account and make a deposit or withdraw some money on their account. It is not allowed to have a negative balance.

We might define two carrier sets *PERSON* and *ACCOUNT* in a context. We might define a variable *client* representing the set of clients of the bank, and a variable *account* representing the set of open accounts in the bank. Each such *account* must be connected to a single *client*. Persons can become clients of the banks and then successively open one or several accounts.

18.1.2 Birthday book

A birthday book contains the names and dates of birth of certain persons. In this exercise, we can consider that *NAME* and *DATE* are abstract sets.

It will be possible to add a new record (name, date) in the birthday book and also to remove a record from the book.

As a refinement, the book is made of a number of consecutive numbered pages. Each page contains a person's record. When removing a person, the last page of the book is moved in place of the missing page.

18.1.3 Numerical matrix with a row of 0s

We are given a numerical matrix with m rows and n columns. We would like to find out whether there is a row in this matrix in which all n elements are equal to 0.

First define a context with the matrix definition.

Then define an initial machine with two events corresponding to the specification of the possible outcomes: success (such a row does exist) or failure (such a row does not exist).

Refine this machine by introducing a row index r and a column index c. Initially, r and c are both equal to 1. Define two invariants stating that the first $r - 1$ rows are not successful (these rows are not made of 0 only), whereas the $c - 1$ first columns of row r are successful (containing 0). This refinement has two new events making r and c progressing in certain circumstances.

18.1.4 Search in an ordered numerical matrix

We are given a numerical matrix with m rows and n columns. We suppose that this matrix is ordered both row-wise and column-wise in ascending order. We are also given a numeric constant x. We would like to know whether this number x is in the matrix.

First define a context with the matrix definition and property, together with the constant x.

Then define a machine with two events corresponding to the specification of the possible results: success (x is in the matrix) or failure (x is not in the matrix).

Refine this machine by introducing a row index r and a column index c. Initially, r is equal to m, whereas c is equal to 1. Define an invariant stating that x is not in the sub-matrix $(1..r, 1..c-1)$ and also in the rows from $r+1$ to m. In other words, the search is concentrated in the sub-matrix $(1..r, c..n)$. This is indicated in Fig. 18.1. Introduce two new events incrementing c or r according to the comparison with x (greater or smaller) of the value of the matrix at row r and column c.

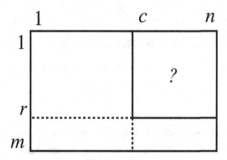

Fig. 18.1. Searching in a matrix

18.1.5 The celebrity problem

Among a set P of persons, there is a celebrity c. We are given a binary relation *knows* between two different persons. More precisely if the pair $p \mapsto q$ belongs to *knows*, it means that person p knows person q. The characteristic property of the celebrity c is that everyone knows c, whereas c does not know anybody. We would like to search for the celebrity by asking who knows or does not know who.

Define a context with the finite set of persons P, the relation *knows* and the celebrity c. For reasons which will be clearer later we suppose that P is a set of natural numbers.

Define an initial machine with a single event **find** setting a result variable r to the celebrity c.

Refine the previous machine. Introduce a variable Q, which is supposed to be a subset of P containing the celebrity c. Initially Q is equal to P. The purpose of this machine is to introduce two new events, gradually removing elements from the set Q. The first event removes a person p from Q if p knows another person q of Q. The second event removes a person q from Q if q is not known from another person p of Q. First give an informal justification for these removals and then do the corresponding formal proofs.

Refine the previous machine by introducing two variables R and b. Variable R is a subset of the set P and variable b is a person which is not in R. Variable Q disappears but it is related to Q and b as follows: $Q = R \cup \{b\}$. Refine the events of previous machine. Do the proofs.

In the next refinement, we suppose that the set P is exactly the interval $0 \mathinner{..} n$ for some positive number n. We introduce a new variable a which is a number in the interval $1 \mathinner{..} n + 1$. Initially, a is equal to 1 and b is equal to 0. The set R disappears. It is related to a and n as follows: $R = a \mathinner{..} n$. Refine the events of previous machine. Do the proofs.

18.1.6 *Find a common element in two intersecting finite sets of numbers [1]*

We are given two finite sets a and b of natural numbers. The intersection of these two sets is supposed to be non-empty. We would like to find any number r such that $r \in a \cap b$.

Define a context with the two sets.

Define an initial machine with variable r and a single event find assigning r to any value x in $a \cap b$.

Refine the previous machine. For this, introduce two new variables c and d. Variable c is a subset of a and variable d is a subset of b. Moreover, the intersection of c and d is equal to the intersection of a and b. Initially, c is set to a and d is set to b. We introduce two new events, which remove gradually elements in c and d. These elements are chosen non-deterministically.

Refine the previous machine. The previous non-deterministic removing events are made deterministic. We remove the minimum of c if it is smaller than the minimum of d and we remove the minimum of d if it is smaller than the minimum of c. When both minima are equal, then we have found a common element.

Now we extend the context. We suppose that the sets a and b are the range of two bijections f and g from $1 \mathinner{..} m$ and $1 \mathinner{..} n$ respectively:

$$f \in 1 \mathinner{..} m \twoheadrightarrow a$$

$$g \in 1 \mathinner{..} n \twoheadrightarrow b$$

We suppose that these bijections are ordered, that is:

$$\forall i, j \cdot i \in 1 \mathinner{..} m \ \wedge \ j \in 1 \mathinner{..} m \ \wedge \ i \leq j \ \Rightarrow \ f(i) \leq f(j)$$

$$\forall i, j \cdot i \in 1 \mathinner{..} n \ \wedge \ j \in 1 \mathinner{..} n \ \wedge \ i \leq j \ \Rightarrow \ g(i) \leq g(j)$$

Prove the following theorems:

$$\forall k \cdot k \in 1 \mathinner{\ldotp\ldotp} m \;\Rightarrow\; f(k) = \min(f[k \mathinner{\ldotp\ldotp} m])$$

$$\forall l \cdot l \in 1 \mathinner{\ldotp\ldotp} n \;\Rightarrow\; g(l) = \min(g[l \mathinner{\ldotp\ldotp} n]).$$

Now, we refine the previous machine. For this, we introduce two new variables i and j. These variables are in the intervals $1 \mathinner{\ldotp\ldotp} m$ and $1 \mathinner{\ldotp\ldotp} n$ respectively. Initially, they are both equal to 1. The variables c and d disappear. They are related to i and j as follows:

$$c = f[i \mathinner{\ldotp\ldotp} m]$$

$$d = g[i \mathinner{\ldotp\ldotp} n].$$

Refine the events.

18.1.7 A simple access control system

We want to define the requirements document of a simple access control system. Here is the informal (poor) description of this system.

We have a building made of different rooms. Each room is connected to some other rooms by means of doors. There is a special room called the hallway: it is connected to all rooms.

This building is supposed to be used by a group of people. Each person in this group receives the authorization to be in certain rooms only. Note that everybody can be in the hallway.

People can enter and leave rooms by means of a magnetic card with an adequate identification. In order to do so they have to put their card into a machine situated at each door. If they are authorized to enter the room, then the door will be open for a while.

Define a more precise requirements document. Each requirement will be labeled as being an equipment requirement (EQP), or a functional requirement (FUN), or else a safety requirement (SAF).

Develop a model of this system by means of several refinements.

18.1.8 A simple library [2]

A library is made of books which can be acquired or discarded by the library. People can be made members of this library. Members can also leave the library.

Books can be borrowed by members. But members cannot borrow more than a certain fixed number of books. Members return books which they have borrowed.

When a book which a member wants to borrow is not available (borrowed by another person), the member is put on a waiting queue associated with this book. Members can quit a waiting queue. The member in a waiting queue who has been waiting the longest is served when the book is returned.

Define a proper requirements document for this system.

Develop a model by means of several refinements.

18.1.9 A simple circuit [3]

We want to construct a simple circuit which is sketched in Fig. 18.2. This circuit has four inputs a_in, b_in, r_in, and t_in and one output o, which are all boolean (TRUE or FALSE). For the sake of simplification, we suppose that only one input can be set to TRUE at a time.

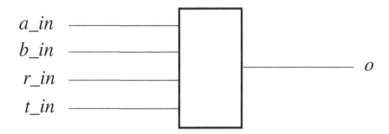

Fig. 18.2. A simple circuit

The circuit might be said to be open or closed. When it is closed, if input t_in is set to TRUE, then the circuit is made open. When it is open, if input t_in is set to TRUE, then the circuit is made closed.

When the circuit is open, the output o is set to TRUE as soon as the circuit has received a TRUE signal on both inputs a_in and b_in in any order while the circuit was open.

When the circuit is open, a TRUE signal on input r_in resets the circuit. More precisely, the memory of input a_in and/or b_in are lost. In case the output o is TRUE, then it is reset to FALSE.

When the circuit is made open, it is reset. In other words, it looses the memory of what has happened when it was previously open.

Define an initial machine with four boolean variables: a, b, t, and o. The variable t records whether the circuit is open (TRUE) or closed (FALSE). Note that the four inputs have not yet been introduced in this machine. The variable a (or b) records the fact that input a_in (or b_in) was set to TRUE when the circuit was open. The variable o is the output. Define the invariants relating these variables. Define events A1, A2, B1, B2, R, T, and S. Events A1 correspond to input a_in being TRUE, while b is still FALSE: it makes a become TRUE. Events A2 corresponds to input a_in being TRUE, while b is True: it makes a become TRUE and o become TRUE. Events B1 and B2 have similar behavior as events A1 and A2 with input b_in. Event R resets the circuit. Event T closes the circuit and event S opens it.

Refine the previous machine. Introduce a technical boolean variable cir, which is TRUE when the circuit reacts to the environment and FALSE when the environment sets the inputs. Introduce the four input variables a_in, b_in, r_in, and t_in. Define the invariants stating that at most one input is TRUE at a time and that one input is always TRUE. Introduce the environment events push_a, push_b, push_r, and push_t. Introduce another circuit event N that does nothing. Refine the events of the previous machine.

Refine the previous machine by using the technique developed in Chapter 8 so that all circuit events have the same action.

Refine the previous machine by merging the circuit events into a single event.

18.1.10 An alarm clock

In this exercise, we want to build the model of a telephone alarm clock. We have two processes: the *user* and the *alarm clock*. These processes are communicating through a telephone line.

In order to ask for an alarm, the user calls for an alarm call, giving (by dialling) the time he wants to be woken up. The telephone answers that it has established the requirement.

From here there are two possibilities:

- the user calls up again before being woken up to cancel the demand;
- the bell of the telephone alarm clock rings.

Note that these two events might be competing. Define and prove the corresponding formal model.

18.1.11 Analysis of a continuous signal

The purpose of this exercise is to construct the model of a system analysing a continuous signal in order to transform it into a a "step" signal.

In Fig. 18.3, you can see a continuous input signal being sampled every other CT second (CT stands for the cycling time): this is indicated by the black dots. An output signal will be generated as a result of the sampling. Initially, the output signal is *off*.

If the sampling detects that the threshold RTH (rising threshold) has been passed between two successive samplings and that the input signal is above RTH for a time BT (debounce time) immediately after this detection, then the output signal moves from *off* to *on*. We have a symmetric situation with the threshold FTH (falling threshold) and the output signal moving from *on* to *off*. We suppose that the integer ratio $n = BT/CT$ is well defined and positive.

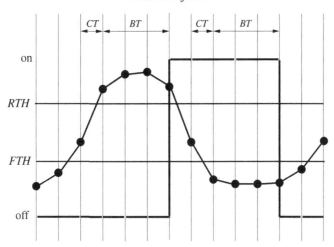

Fig. 18.3. Sampling

Construct a model of this system producing an adequate output for each detected input. Each event will correspond to a reaction of the system to an input. There will be many different events as there are many different situations in which an input may occur.

Define the model by successive refinements. Do not forget to write an initial requirements document as well as a refinement strategy before embarking on the formal development.

18.2 Projects

18.2.1 An electronic hotel key system [4] [5]

The purpose of this project is to develop the model of an hotel electronic key system.

The purpose of such a system is to guarantee that between your check-in and check-out in an hotel, you can enter the room you booked and no one else can do so. Note that this is not the case with a metallic key system since a previous user of the room may have duplicated the metallic key.

A proposed implementation is defined as follows:

(1) Each hotel room door is equipped with an independent electronic lock which holds an electronic key. The lock has a fence in which one may insert a magnetic card.
(2) Each check-in starts a new booking of a certain room. To each booking is associated a magnetic card containing two electronic keys: a guaranteed new key, and the electronic key presently stored in the lock of the room (a centralized dynamic system is supposed to hold the keys stored in the room locks). To enter the room, you insert your card in the fence of the lock. The lock reads your card and opens

the door provided its own electronic key is one of the keys on your card. The electronic key is replaced by the new key which is on your card.

In Fig. 18.4 a new card is introduced in the fence. It contains the new key $k2$ and the key $k1$ of the lock. The card is accepted and the electronic key of the lock becomes $k2$. The owner of the card can now re-enter his room with the same card (since it contains key $k2$).

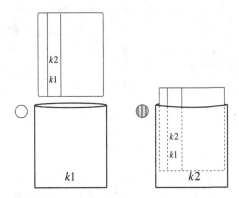

Fig. 18.4. A door lock and a new card being inserted

The proposed implementation with the cards requires that people effectively use the room. If someone does not use the room he booked, then the next client cannot enter the room.

Develop a model for this system. Do not introduce the card and the key at the beginning. You rather make an abstraction were the main property is expressed: a person who has booked a room is guaranteed that no one else can enter this room.

In subsequent refinements, express the fact that clients are served according to their arrival (hotel policy). Then finally, introduce the card system which implements this policy.

You might define various events: check-in, check-out, enter_room, leave_room. Consider also a master entering in the room (under the responsibility of the hotel).

18.2.2 Earley parser [6]

The purpose of this project is to develop a formal model for an Earley parser.

For this we have to define first what a syntax is. We are given a set S of symbols. A subset N of S contains the so-called non-terminal symbols. The complement T of N (that is, $S \setminus N$) contains the so-called terminal symbols.

We are given a set P of productions. A production has got a *left*-hand part which is a non-terminal symbol. It has got also a *right*-hand part which is a non-empty sequence of symbols. Finally, there is a special production called the *axiom*. This can be defined as follows:

$$left \in P \to N$$

$$right \in P \to (\mathbb{N} \twoheadrightarrow S)$$

$$size \in P \to \mathbb{N}_1$$

$$\forall p \cdot right(p) \in 1 \mathbin{..} size(p) \to S$$

$$axiom \in P$$

A syntax is just a set of productions defined on a set S of symbols.

We define now what it means for a sequence of symbols to *match* a sequence of terminal symbols. For this, we use the following binary relation:

$$match \in (\mathbb{N} \twoheadrightarrow S) \leftrightarrow (\mathbb{N} \twoheadrightarrow T)$$

The relation *match* is defined by means of three axioms, which are the following:

$$\varnothing \mapsto \varnothing \in match$$

$$\forall i, j, k, l, n1, n2, s1, s2 \cdot \quad \begin{aligned} &i \in 1 \mathbin{..} n1 \\ &j \in 0 \mathbin{..} n1 - 1 \\ &k \in 1 \mathbin{..} n2 \\ &l \in 0 \mathbin{..} n2 - 1 \\ &s1 \in 1 \mathbin{..} n1 \to S \\ &s2 \in 1 \mathbin{..} n2 \to T \\ &s1(j+1) = s2(l+1) \\ &i \mathbin{..} j \vartriangleleft s1 \mapsto k \mathbin{..} l \vartriangleleft s2 \in match \\ &\Rightarrow \\ &i \mathbin{..} j+1 \vartriangleleft s1 \mapsto k \mathbin{..} l+1 \vartriangleleft s2 \in match \end{aligned}$$

$$\forall i, j, k, l, n1, n2, s1, s2, m, p \cdot \begin{array}{l} i \in 1 \mathbin{..} n1 \\ j \in 0 \mathbin{..} n1 - 1 \\ k \in 1 \mathbin{..} n2 \\ l \in 0 \mathbin{..} n2 - 1 \\ s1 \in 1 \mathbin{..} n1 \to S \\ s2 \in 1 \mathbin{..} n2 \to T \\ m \in l \mathbin{..} n2 \\ left(p) = s1(j + 1) \\ right(p) \mapsto l + 1 \mathbin{..} m \lhd s2 \in match \\ i \mathbin{..} j \lhd s1 \mapsto k \mathbin{..} l \lhd s2 \in match \\ \Rightarrow \\ i \mathbin{..} j + 1 \lhd s1 \mapsto k \mathbin{..} m \lhd s2 \in match \end{array}$$

Finally, we define the *input* as a sequence of terminal symbol of size s: formally,

$$s \in \mathbb{N}$$

$$input \in 1 \mathbin{..} s \to T$$

All previous modeling components can be entered in a context.

The *input* is said to be recognized by the syntax if the following holds:

$$right(axiom) \mapsto input \in match$$

Define an initial machine that does the recognition in one shot. This can be done by means of the following event:

```
parser
    when
        right(axiom) ↦ input ∈ match
    then
        r := TRUE
    end
```

The purpose of this project is to perform a complete model of this parser.

The first refinement contains the essence of the Earley parser. For this we introduce a variable *item*, which is a binary relation defined as follows:

$$item \in (P \times \mathbb{N}) \leftrightarrow (\mathbb{N} \times \mathbb{N})$$

together with the following invariant:

$$\forall p, k, i, j \cdot \ (p \mapsto k) \mapsto (i \mapsto j) \ \in \ item$$
$$\Rightarrow$$
$$k \in 0 \mathrel{..} size(p)$$
$$i \in 0 \mathrel{..} s$$
$$j \in 0 \mathrel{..} s$$
$$i \leq j$$
$$1 \mathrel{..} k \lhd right(p) \mapsto i+1 \mathrel{..} j \lhd input \ \in \ match$$

Besides the refinement of the **parser** event, this first refinement is made of three events called: the **scanner**, the **predictor**, and the **completer**.

The **scanner** adds a new "item" $(p \mapsto k+1) \mapsto (i \mapsto j+1)$ provided $(p \mapsto k) \mapsto (i \mapsto j)$ (where $k < size(p)$ and $j < s$) is already stored and $right(p)(k+1) = input(j+1)$ holds.

The **predictor** adds a new "item" $(q \mapsto 0) \mapsto (j \mapsto j)$ provided $(p \mapsto k) \mapsto (i \mapsto j)$ (where $k < size(p)$) is already stored and there is a production q such that $left(q) = right(p)(k+1)$.

The **completer** adds a new "item" $(q \mapsto kp+1) \mapsto (ip \mapsto j)$ provided $(p \mapsto size(p)) \mapsto (i \mapsto j)$ is already stored and $(q \mapsto kp) \mapsto (ip \mapsto i)$ (where $kp < size(q)$) is also already stored, and finally $right(q)(kp+1) = left(p)$ holds.

Prove (informally first) with the help of the axioms for *match* that these events maintain the main invariant. Refine event **parser**. As can be seen, this first refinement is highly non-deterministic.

The goal of the project is to perform a number of refinements in order to obtain an efficient parser implemented as a final sequential program.

18.2.3 The Schorr–Wait Algorithm [7]

The purpose of this project is to make a model for the Schorr–Wait algorithm.

We are given a finite set N of node, a binary relation g (for "graph") built on this set, and a special node t (for "top"). Let r be the image of $\{t\}$ under the irreflexive transitive closure of g: $r = \mathsf{cl}(g)[\{t\}]$. We want to mark (in black) all elements of r.

Define an initial machine with a "one shot" event **mark** performing this task.

Refine this machine by introducing a non-deterministic event **progress**. Initially only node t is marked. Event **progress** marks a node which is related to an already marked node by means of relation g. Introduce the necessary invariant and refine event **mark**.

Refine this machine by making it work in a "depth-first" fashion. For this introduce a "current" node and also a stack which is a linear list. Give invariant properties of the stack.

Simplify this machine by supposing the graph g is a binary graph. In other words, each node is connected to at most two nodes by means of two partial functions *left* and *right*.

Continue to refine by temporary storing the stack in the graph (this is the essence of the Schorr–Waite algorithm).

18.2.4 Linear list encapsulation [8]

The purpose of this project is to develop the model of a linear list "encapsulation".

We are given a finite set N of node.

We define an initial machine with a finite linear list of such nodes. This list is defined as follows by means of the *next* variable:

$$next \in N \rightarrowtail N$$

Add some other variables in order to define this linear list more precisely. Give some invariant properties. Initially, the list is empty.

Provide a number of events for inserting or removing nodes at the beginning, at the end, or in the middle of this list. In the last case, it is possible to use $next^{-1}$.

This machine is then refined so that inserting or removing a node in the middle of the list does not use $next^{-1}$

18.2.5 Concurrent access to a queue [9]

This project consists in developing a model for a concurrent access to a queue. The technique to be used is similar to the one developed in Chapter 7. The problem is described in full detail in [9]. The reader is encouraged to have a look at this paper.

The queue is made of a number of nodes linked by pointers called *Next*. The final element of the queue is a dummy node called *Null*. The queue is accessed through two additional pointers called *Head* and *Tail*. Normally *Tail* points to the node preceding *Null* in the queue. When *Head* and *Tail* are the same, the queue is said to be degraded. All this can be seen in Fig. 18.5.

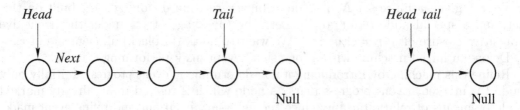

Fig. 18.5. The queue (normal and degraded)

We may perform three operations on this queue: Enqueue, Dequeue, and Adapt. These operations are described below in a pidgin programming language:

Dequeue
if $Next \neq Tail$ **then**
  $Head := Next(Head)$
end

Enqueue
  if $Next(Tail) = Null$ **then**
    $node := $ new_node;
    $Next(node) := Null;$
    $Next(Tail) := node$
  end

Adapt
  if $Next(Tail) \neq Null$ **then**
    $Tail := Next(Tail)$
  end

We suppose that a number of processes have a concurrent access to this queue. They all perform "simultaneously" the previous operations ignoring each other. In the mentioned paper you will see how these processes can interrupt each other according to some precise definition of their atomicity.

Follow the description of the paper to define the initial machine and its various refinements. Perform all proofs with the Rodin Platform.

18.2.6 Almost linear sorting

Normally the expected time to sort n item is proportional to $n \log n$. But, in certain circumstances, it can be made "almost" proportional to n. The purpose of this project is to develop the model of such an almost linear sorting algorithm.

Suppose we have to sort n distinct numbers ranging exactly from 1 to n. The sorting is clearly linear: simply put each number i at the ith position. This is illustrated in Fig. 18.6.

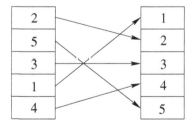

Fig. 18.6. Linear sorting

Now suppose we have to sort n distinct numbers ranging from 1 to m where m is slightly greater than n. For instance, n is equal to 5 but m is now equal to 7 as shown in Fig. 18.7. We can suppose that this assumption about a slight difference only between m and n could help in designing an almost linear sorting. This is so because there is no reason for that small difference between n and m to suddenly induce a large difference in the sorting time with respect to the linear time we had when n and m were identical.

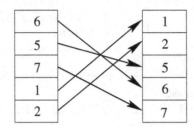

Fig. 18.7. Almost linear sorting

First define a context introducing n, m, and the array f to sort:

$$n > 0$$

$$m > 0$$

$$f \in 1 \mathinner{.\,.} n \rightarrowtail 1 \mathinner{.\,.} m$$

Define an initial machine doing the sorting in one shot. For this, define a variable array g which is a function from $1 \mathinner{.\,.} n$ to $1 \mathinner{.\,.} m$. Also define an event **sort** and an anticipating event **progress** as follows:

```
sort
    any  h  where
        h ∈ 1 .. n → 1 .. m
        ran(h) = ran(f)
        ∀i · i ∈ 1 .. n − 1  ⇒  h(i) < h(i + 1)
    then
        g := h
    end
```

```
progress
    status
        anticipated
    begin
        g :∈ 1 .. n → 1 .. m
    end
```

Refine the initial machine. For this, introduce a variable k situated in $0 \mathinner{.\,.} m$ and a variable l situated in $0 \mathinner{.\,.} n$. Initially, these variables are set to 0. As an invariant, state that the array g is sorted from 1 to l. Also state that the image $g[1 \mathinner{..} l]$ is equal to $\mathrm{ran}(f) \cap 1 \mathinner{..} k$, and that the cardinal of $\mathrm{dom}(f \rhd 1 \mathinner{..} k))$ is exactly equal to l. Refine the events. Split the anticipated event **progress**: the two resulting events become **convergent**. Prove this refinement.

Add another refinement with an event **scan** constructing a boolean array r from $1 \mathinner{..} m$ to BOOL where we eventually have $r(x)$ being TRUE if and only if x is in the range of f. Refine the events. Prove this refinement. Perform an animation. The sorting is proportional to $m + n$, so roughly $2n$ when n and m are almost equal.

18.2.7 Termination detection [12]

The purpose of this small project is to develop a simple model of the Dijkstra-Scholten termination detection algorithm.

We are given a set P of processes. A subset of these processes are *sleeping*. The purpose of the algorithm is to determine whether all processes are sleeping.

Define a context with the set P of processes. Define an initial machine with the variable *sleeping* and a boolean d which when TRUE implies that all processes are sleeping:

$$d = \mathrm{TRUE} \;\Rightarrow\; sleeping = P$$

This machine has three events: **awake**, **make_asleep**, and **detection**. The last one is as follows:

```
detection
   when
      sleeping = P
   then
      d; = TRUE
   end
```

In this version, the entire set of processes has to be considered. We would like to have a more economical version where only one process is considered.

We extend our initial context by introducing a special constant process r, which is supposed to be always sleeping. The non-sleeping processes are supposed to be all in a dynamic tree rooted at r. The tree might contain some sleeping processes as well. But these processes are eliminated when they are leafs of the tree. For this, we introduce an additional event **shrink** removing a sleeping leaf of this tree. The tree is defined by means of a function f as follows (Section 9.7.7 of Chapter 9):

$$f \;\in\; P \setminus \{r\} \rightarrowtail \mathrm{dom}(f) \cup \{r\}$$

together with the usual tree property:

$$\forall S \cdot S \subseteq f^{-1}[S] \implies S = \varnothing$$

The guard of the refined version of the **detection** event becomes:

$$r \notin \mathrm{ran}(f)$$

In other words, the root of the tree has no children. Finalize and prove this refined machine.

18.2.8 Distributed mutual exclusion [10]

We, supposedly, have a number of processes running in parallel. From time to time some of them want to access a certain "resource" (whose exact nature is not important) in an *exclusive* way. We want to develop a model that handles this constraint.

The processes in question are all members of a certain fixed set P of processes. Each such process x is supposed to cycle indefinitely on the following three successive phases:

- x is in the, so-called, *non-critical* section – it is thus not using or willing to use the resource;
- x is in the *pre-critical* section – this corresponds to the process willing to access the resource. It is thus competing with other processes, which are also in the pre-critical section waiting to be admitted into the critical section where the mentioned resource is supposed to be granted exclusively to a single process;
- x is in the *critical* section – it is using the resource.

We shall represent the transitions between these phases by means of the following three events as illustrated in Fig. 18.8:

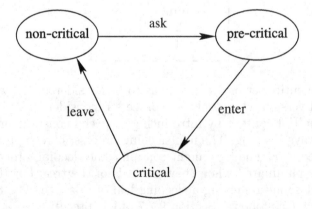

Fig. 18.8. Transitions between the three phases

- event **ask** corresponds to the transition *non-critical* $\longrightarrow$ *pre-critical*;
- event **enter** corresponds to the transition *pre-critical* $\longrightarrow$ *critical*;
- event **leave** corresponds to the transition *critical* $\longrightarrow$ *non-critical*.

There are three fundamental constraints in this problem, which are the following:

- a process, supposed to be blocked in the non-critical section, *must not block* the processes that are in the pre-critical section – this excludes solutions where each process is given a pre-defined ordered access to the resource;
- a process *must not wait for ever* in the pre-critical section – this encourages solutions where a certain dynamic re-ordering between the processes is realized;
- the critical section contains *at most one process* – this is the basic mutual exclusion property.

We define an initial machine. The problem is formalized by means of a set variable p containing the processes in the pre-critical section *as well as the process in the critical section*. The set of processes in the critical section is denoted by the variable c. This is expressed in invariants **inv0_1** and **inv0_2**. The critical section should have at most one member (invariant **inv0_3**):

$$\textbf{inv0\_1}: \quad p \subseteq P$$

$$\textbf{inv0\_2}: \quad c \subseteq p$$

$$\textbf{inv0\_3}: \quad c \neq \varnothing \Rightarrow \exists x \cdot c = \{x\}$$

We also define a variable holding a *precedence* relation r, which possibly holds between members of the set P of processes and members of the set of processes in the pre-critical section p except the one (if any) in the critical section. When a pair x, y belongs to r this means that x must not enter the critical section before y (or that y should precede x in entering the critical section). The reason for having y to precede x is because last time x was in the critical section, y was already waiting in the pre-critical section. And, since then, y is still waiting. Consequently, if x re-enters the pre-critical section, it will be unfair to allow it to enter the critical section before y, since otherwise y could be indefinitely blocked in the pre-critical section. Clearly, the relation r should be a *strict partial order*. That is, if z precedes y and y precedes x, then z should precede x (otherwise we might have some risk of deadlock), and x cannot be preceded by itself. All this is formalized as:

$$\mathbf{inv0\_4}: \; r \in P \leftrightarrow p \setminus c$$

$$\mathbf{inv0\_5}: \; r \, ; r \subseteq r$$

$$\mathbf{inv0\_6}: \; r \cap r^{-1} = \varnothing$$

The three events of our initial machine are:

ask
  any x **where**
    $x \in P \setminus p$
  then
    $p := p \cup \{x\}$
  end

enter
  any x **where**
    $x \in p$
    $c = \varnothing$
    $x \notin \mathsf{dom}\,(r)$
  then
    $c := \{x\}$
    $r := r \rhd \{x\}$
  end

leave
  any x **where**
    $x \in c$
  then
    $c := \varnothing$
    $p := p \setminus \{x\}$
    $r := r \, \cup \, \{x\} \times (p \setminus \{x\})$
  end

Here are some comments concerning the guard of the previous events. A process x can execute **ask** if it is not already in the pre-critical section. A process x can execute **enter** if it is in the pre-critical section, if the critical section is empty, and if x is not preceded by any other process (thus x is not in the domain of the precedence relation r). Finally, a process x can execute **leave** if it is in the critical section.

Notice that we have a certain non-determinism in the possible executions of the event **leave** as there might exist several candidates in the pre-critical section, which are not preceded by other processes (remember, r is only a *partial* order).

When a process x enters the critical section (event **enter**) each pair of processes of the form $y \mapsto x$ should be removed from the relation r since x should not precede any other process as it is now in the critical section. The other modification of the relation r takes place when a process leaves the critical section (event **leave**); all processes present in the pre-critical section should now precede x for entering the critical section.

Prove this initial machine.

The development of a specific mutual exclusion algorithm may implement the relation r by means of a more concrete relation, which only needs to be *weaker* than r (i.e. with more pairs). Thus, the concrete relation has a domain including that of r. As a consequence, we shall be able to replace the guard $x \notin \mathsf{dom}\,(r)$ in event **enter** by the stronger guard "x is not in the domain of the concrete guard". This is because a process x which is *not* in the domain of the concrete relation, is not in the domain of r.

Before developing the first refinement, we extend our initial context where the set P of processes is defined. In this extension, the processes form a ring. For this use the definition of rings described in Section 9.7.5 of Chapter 9. The ring is defined by means of a bijection n between processes. You might also prove a few more interesting lemmas on rings. In particular, you need to copy the definition of an interval $itv(a \mapsto b)$ between two nodes a and b in a ring.

In the first refinement, the variable r is removed. It is "replaced" by a variable w which is a process. More precisely, w denotes either the process which sits in the critical section or, in case the critical section is empty, the process which was last in the critical section. The gluing invariant between r and w is as follows:

$$\forall x, y \cdot x \mapsto y \in r \;\Rightarrow\; y \in p \,\wedge\; x \neq y \,\wedge\; y \in itv(n(w) \mapsto x)$$

This is illustrated in Fig. 18.9. An additional invariant states that w is not in the range of r. Refined the three events.

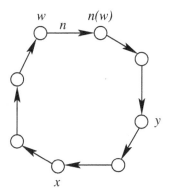

Fig. 18.9. The ring

Develop further refinements defining the loop which is concentrated in event **enter**.

18.2.9 Lift

The informal description of an elevator system is given below. It's quite clumsy and poorly written. Sometimes, some basic requirements might be omitted (when they have been considered trivial). This is on purpose. It reflects the average user's requirements document encountered in practice.

The elevator system consists of the following parts:

- an elevator,
- a door for the elevator,

- a cable and an engine for moving the elevator,
- sensors for detecting that the elevator has reached some floor,
- an engine for opening and closing the door,
- sensors for detecting if the door is open or closed,
- $N + 1$ floors,
- buttons on floors for calling the elevator,
- buttons in the elevator for choosing floors,
- a controller that controls the system,
- copper wires between them.

In order for the user to know that his request is acknowledged by the system, all buttons have a small light attached to them. That light should be switched on when the user presses the corresponding button. Conversely, it should be switched off once the request has been served.

Floors have two buttons (one for each direction of the elevator), unless only one button is needed. There are exactly $N + 1$ buttons in the elevator (one for each floor).

Finally, to prevent accidents, the elevator should always move with the door engine working towards closing the doors; this prevents users from opening the doors while the elevator is moving.

The inputs of the controller are:

- the status of the cable engine (winding, unwinding, or stopped),
- the status of the door engine (opening, closing, or stopped),
- the status of the floor sensors (the number of the floor that the elevator has reached or -1 if the elevator is between two floors; floors are counted from 0 to N),
- the status of the door sensors (fully open, half open, or closed),
- the status of the buttons (pressed or not: boolean).

The outputs of the controller are:

- the command of the cable engine (wind, unwind, or stop),
- the command of the door engine (open, close, or stop),
- the command of the lights of the buttons (on or off: boolean).

Out of that description, you should write a clean requirements document. You should use the following taxonomy of requirements:

- **EQP** for equipment,
- **FUN** for functional,
- **SAF** for safety requirements.

Pursue this project by proposing a refinement strategy and then develop the corresponding model by means of several refinements.

18.2.10 A business protocol [11]

This project aims at constructing the model of a business protocol. The idea is also to use the *design pattern* technique which was presented in Chapter 3.

This protocol determines the negotiation taking place between a buyer and a seller. The outcome of the protocol might be as follows:

- the two parties agree on a final agreement by which the seller sells a certain quantity of a certain product to the buyer at a certain price. Note that the product, the quantity, and the price are all abstracted here as an INFO exchanged between the participants;
- the two parties might end up by not succeeding in finding an agreement;
- whatever the final result (agreement or no agreement), the buyer might always cancel the protocol.

The protocol is divided up into four phases: the *initial phase*, the *free game* phase, the *last proposal* phase, and the *termination* phase.

- In the initial phase, the buyer starts the protocol by sending a proposal to the seller.
- After this initial proposal has been received by the seller, the protocol enters the free game phase. In this second phase buyer and seller can send counter-proposal or acceptance to the other partner proposal in a fully asynchronous way. In this phase, an acceptance or a counter-proposal by either party is never definitive.
- The last proposal phase is at the initiative of the buyer which makes it clear to the seller that the proposal sent to it is the last one; the seller can either accept it or reject it. It cannot send a counter-proposal.
- The termination phase is the one by which the buyer sends a termination message, which the seller has to acknowledge.

During the three first phases, the buyer can always cancel the protocol by sending a message to the seller, which needs to acknowledge it. This has the immediate effect to move the protocol to the termination phase.

When the seller or the buyer sends a counter-proposal it must mention in the corresponding message to which proposal of the other party it corresponds.

The channels between the seller and the buyer are not reliable: messages can be lost, copied and do not arrive necessarily at their destination in the same order in which they have been sent.

Use design patterns to handle the sending of messages, the response to a message, or both. Use these patterns in a systematic fashion to model the various phases of the protocol.

Do not perform the modeling in a flat manner; use various refinements to structure your formal model. Do not forget to write a precise requirements document as well as a refinement strategy.

18.3 Mathematical developments

18.3.1 *Well-founded sets and relations*

Characteristic properties Given a set S, a binary relation r built on S is set to be *well founded* if all paths built on r and starting from any point x of S are finite. A relation which is not well founded thus contains infinite paths built on r. A subset p of S contains infinite paths if for any point x in p, there exists a point y, also in p, related to x by means of r; formally:

$$\forall x \cdot x \in p \Rightarrow (\exists y \cdot y \in p \land x \mapsto y \in r):$$

that is:

$$p \subseteq r^{-1}[p].$$

Since the empty set enjoys this property, we can define a well-founded relation r as one where the only set p enjoying that property is the empty set:

$$\boxed{\forall p \cdot p \subseteq r^{-1}[p] \Rightarrow p = \varnothing} \qquad (1)$$

Another characteristic property of a well-founded relation r states that every non-empty subset of S has an r-minimal element; formally:

$$\boxed{\forall p \cdot p \neq \varnothing \Rightarrow \exists x \cdot x \in p \land (\forall y \cdot y \in p \Rightarrow x \mapsto y \notin r)} \qquad (2)$$

Prove that (1) and (2) are equivalent.

Induction principle Given a well-founded relation r built on a set S, we can define a general induction principle stated as follows:

$$\boxed{\forall q \cdot (\forall x \cdot r[\{x\}] \subseteq q \Rightarrow x \in q) \Rightarrow S = q} \qquad (3)$$

Prove that (1) or (2) implies (3).

Proving well-foundedness We now establish a few results for proving well-foundedness.

If a relation b built on a set S is well-founded, then any relation a included in b is also well-founded; formally:

$$
\begin{array}{l}
\forall p \cdot p \subseteq b^{-1}[p] \;\Rightarrow\; p = \varnothing \\
a \subseteq b \\
\Rightarrow \\
\forall p \cdot p \subseteq a^{-1}[p] \;\Rightarrow\; p = \varnothing
\end{array}
\tag{4}
$$

Prove property (4). As a more general result, suppose we have a well-founded relation b built on a set T, and a total binary relation from a set S to T. A binary relation a built on S is well-founded provided $v^{-1}\,;a \subseteq b\,;v^{-1}$ holds; formally:

$$
\begin{array}{l}
\forall p \cdot p \subseteq b^{-1}[p] \;\Rightarrow\; p = \varnothing \\
v \in S \leftrightarrow T \\
v^{-1}\,;a \subseteq b\,;v^{-1} \\
\Rightarrow \\
\forall p \cdot p \subseteq a^{-1}[p] \;\Rightarrow\; p = \varnothing
\end{array}
\tag{5}
$$

Prove property (5). A special case of (5) is when v is a total function from S to T; formally:

$$
\begin{array}{l}
a \in S \leftrightarrow S \\
b \in T \leftrightarrow T \\
v \in S \rightarrow T \\
\forall x, y \cdot x \mapsto y \in a \;\Rightarrow\; v(x) \mapsto v(y) \in b \\
\Rightarrow \\
v^{-1}\,;a \subseteq b\,;v^{-1}
\end{array}
\tag{6}
$$

Prove property (6). The relation "$<$" on natural numbers is well-founded; formally:

$$
\begin{array}{l}
\forall x, y \cdot x \in \mathbb{N} \,\wedge\, y \in \mathbb{N} \;\Rightarrow\; x \mapsto y \in b \;\Leftrightarrow\; y < x \\
\Rightarrow \\
\forall q \cdot q \subseteq b^{-1}[q] \;\Rightarrow\; q = \varnothing
\end{array}
\tag{7}
$$

Prove property (7). Putting (6) and (7) together, we obtain the following:

$$
\begin{aligned}
&a \in S \leftrightarrow S \\
&v \in S \to \mathbb{N} \\
&\forall x, y \cdot x \mapsto y \in a \;\Rightarrow\; v(y) < v(x) \\
&\Rightarrow \\
&\forall a \cdot a \subseteq p^{-1}[a] \;\Rightarrow\; a = \varnothing
\end{aligned}
\tag{8}
$$

Prove property (8).

18.3.2 Fixpoints

Definition We are given a set S and a total function f from $\mathbb{P}(S)$ to itself:

$$f \in \mathbb{P}(S) \to \mathbb{P}(S).$$

We would like to construct a subset $fix(f)$ of S such that the following holds:

$$fix(f) = f(fix(f))$$

Here is a proposed definition of $fix(f)$:

$$
fix(f) \;=\; \mathrm{inter}(\{s \mid s \subseteq f(s)\})
\tag{9}
$$

Prove that this definition is well defined.

Properties Now come two useful lemmas. First, $fix(f)$ is a *lower bound* of the set $\{s \mid s \subseteq f(s)\}$; formally:

$$
\forall s \cdot f(s) \subseteq s \;\Rightarrow\; fix(f) \subseteq s
\tag{10}
$$

Second, $fix(f)$ is the *greatest lower bound* of this set; formally:

$$
\forall v \cdot (\forall s \cdot f(s) \subseteq s \;\Rightarrow\; v \subseteq s) \;\Rightarrow\; v \subseteq fix(f)
\tag{11}
$$

Prove (10) and (11). The theorem of Knaster and Tarski states that $fix(f)$ is indeed a fixpoint provided the function f is *monotone*:

$$
\begin{array}{l}
\forall a, b \cdot a \subseteq b \;\Rightarrow\; f(a) \subseteq f(b) \\
\Rightarrow \\
fix(f) = f(fix(f))
\end{array}
\tag{12}
$$

Prove (12). Moreover, $fix(f)$ is the least fixpoint:

$$
\forall t \cdot t = f(t) \;\Rightarrow\; fix(f) \subseteq t
\tag{13}
$$

Prove (13). Develop similar results for the greatest fixpoint $FIX(f)$ defined as:

$$
FIX(f) \;=\; \mathrm{union}(\{s \mid f(s) \subseteq s\})
\tag{14}
$$

Let *dual* be the following function:

$$
dual \in (\mathbb{P}(S) \to \mathbb{P}(S)) \to (\mathbb{P}(S) \to \mathbb{P}(S))
$$

$$
\forall f, x \cdot dual(f)(x) = S \setminus f(S \setminus x).
$$

Prove:

$$
FIX(f) = S \setminus fix(dual(f)).
$$

18.3.3 Recursion

We are given two sets S and T, a well-founded binary relation r built on S, and a function g which is:

$$
g \in (S \nrightarrow T) \to T.
$$

We would like to construct a total function f from S to T with the following property:

$$
f \in S \to T
$$

$$
\forall x \cdot x \in T \;\Rightarrow\; f(x) = g(r[\{x\}] \lhd f).
$$

In other words, the value of the function f at x depends on its values on points of the set $r[\{x\}]$. First, we define a function *img*:

$$img \in S \to \mathbb{P}(S)$$

$$\forall x \cdot x \in S \implies img(x) = r[\{x\}].$$

Second, we define a function *res*:

$$res \in (S \leftrightarrow T) \to (\mathbb{P}(S) \leftrightarrow (S \to T))$$

$$\forall p \cdot p \in S \leftrightarrow T \implies res(p) = \{a \mapsto h \mid h \in a \to T \ \wedge \ h \subseteq a \lhd p\}.$$

Third, we define a function *genf*:

$$genf \in (S \leftrightarrow T) \to (S \leftrightarrow T)$$

$$\forall p \cdot p \in S \leftrightarrow T \implies genf(p) = img \,;\, res(p) \,;\, g.$$

Prove that *genf* is monotone. We now define f to be a binary relation defined as follows:

$$f \ = \ fix(genf).$$

Prove:

$$\forall z \cdot z \in S \implies \{z\} \lhd f \in \{z\} \to T.$$

Hint: Use the well-founded induction rule defined by the well-founded relation r. From this, prove:

$$f \in S \to T.$$

Finally, prove:

$$\forall x \cdot x \in S \implies f(x) = g(r[\{x\}] \lhd f).$$

18.3.4 *Transitive closure*

Given a set S and a binary relation r built on S, we define the function f:

$$f \in (S \leftrightarrow S) \to (S \leftrightarrow S)$$

$$\forall s \cdot s \in S \leftrightarrow S \implies f(s) = r \cup (s \,;\, r)$$

Prove that f is monotone. Now define $\mathsf{cl}(r)$:

$$\mathsf{cl}(r) = fix(f)$$

Prove the following properties:

$$r \subseteq \mathsf{cl}(r)$$

$$\mathsf{cl}(r) \,;\, r \subseteq \mathsf{cl}(r)$$

$$\forall s \cdot r \subseteq s \;\wedge\; s \,;\, r \subseteq s \;\Rightarrow\; \mathsf{cl}\,(r) \subseteq s$$

$$\mathsf{cl}(r) \,;\, \mathsf{cl}(r) \subseteq \mathsf{cl}(r)$$

$$\mathsf{cl}(r) = r \cup \mathsf{cl}(r) \,;\, r$$

$$\mathsf{cl}(r) = r \cup r \,;\, \mathsf{cl}(r)$$

$$\mathsf{cl}(r^{-1}) = \mathsf{cl}(r)^{-1}$$

18.3.5 Filters and ultrafilters

Given a set S, a filter f is a set of subsets of S such that:

- if a set A belongs to f, then all supersets B of A also belong to f;
- if two sets C and D belong to f, then so does their intersection;
- S belong to f;
- $\varnothing$ does not belong to f.

Then the set *filter* of all filters built on S can be defined as follows:

$$
\begin{aligned}
filter \;=\; \{f \,|\, &(\forall A, B \cdot A \in f \;\wedge\; A \subseteq B \;\Rightarrow\; B \in f) \;\wedge\; \\
&(\forall C, D \cdot C \in f \;\wedge\; D \in f \;\Rightarrow\; C \cap D \in f) \;\wedge\; \\
&S \in f \;\wedge\; \\
&\varnothing \notin f\}
\end{aligned}
$$

An ultrafilter is a filter which has no bigger filters. Then the set *ultra* of ultrafilters can be defined as:

$$ultra \;=\; \{f \,|\, f \in filter \;\wedge\; \forall g \cdot g \in filter \;\wedge\; f \subseteq g \;\Rightarrow\; g = f\}.$$

One of the main properties of ultrafilters is:

$$\forall f, M, N \cdot f \in ultra \;\wedge\; M \cup N \in f \;\Rightarrow\; M \in f \;\vee\; N \in f.$$

Prove this property. Hint: Perform a proof by contradiction and then instantiate g in the predicate:

$$\forall y \cdot y \in filter \;\wedge\; f \subseteq g \;\Rightarrow\; g = f$$

with the set $\{X \,|\, M \cup X \in f\}$.

18.3.6 Topology

Topologies can be defined in different equivalent ways. We would like to investigate this and prove equivalences of these definitions.

Definitions Given a set S, a topological space built on S is defined by means of a set O of subsets of S as follows. The members of O are said to be *open*:

- the intersection of two sets in O is also in O,
- the generalized union of a subset of O is also in O,
- the empty set $\varnothing$ is in O,
- the set S is in O.

A set is said to be *closed* if it is the complement of an open set. Let C be the set of closed sets. Prove:

- the union of two sets in C is also in C,
- the generalized intersection of a non-empty subset of C is also in C,
- the empty set $\varnothing$ is in C,
- the set S is in C.

Prove that a topology can be axiomatized equivalently by means of the set C of closed sets.

The *neighborhood* of a point x of S is any set that contains an open set containing x. Investigate from a mathematics book the properties of neighborhoods and prove them. Prove that a topology can be axiomatized by means of neighborhoods.

Interior, closure, and border We are given a topology built on a set S. Here are a few definitions.

- The *interior* of a set X is the set of points x of X such that X is a neighborhood of x.
- The *closure* of a set X is the set of points x whose neighborhoods have a common point with X.
- The *border* of a set X is the intersection of the closure of X with that of $S \setminus X$.

Prove the following properties:

- The interior of a set X is the union of the open sets included into X.
- An open set is one that is equal to its interior.
- The interior of the intersection of two sets in the intersection of their interiors.
- The interior of an interior is that interior.
- The closure of a closure is that closure.
- The complement of the closure of a set X is the interior of the complement of X.

- A closed set is one that is equal to its closure.
- The closure of a set X it the union of X with the border of X
- The intersection of the interior of a set X with the border of X is empty.

Continuous functions We are given two topological spaces built on S and T respectively. Note: to simplify matters, we can take S and T to be the same set.

A total function from S to T is said to be *continuous*, if for all point x of S and all neighborhoods n of $f(x)$ there exists a neighbourhood m of x such that m is included in the inverse image of n under f.

Prove the following properties of a total function f between S and T (note the circularity of these properties which means that they are all equivalent):

- If f is continuous, then for all subset a of S the image of the closure of a under f is included in the closure of the image of a under f.
- If f is continuous and if for all subset a of S the image of the closure of a under f is included in the closure of the image of a under f, then the inverse image of a closed set under f is closed.
- If the inverse image of a closed set under f is closed, then the inverse image of an open set under f is open.
- If the inverse image of an open set under f is open, then the function f is continuous.

Given three topological spaces, prove that the composition of two continuous functions is continuous.

18.3.7 Cantor–Bernstein theorem

We are given two sets S and T and two total injective functions f and g:

$$f \in S \rightarrowtail T$$

$$g \in T \rightarrowtail S.$$

We are also given two subsets x and y from S and T respectively, such that:

$$f[x] = T \setminus y$$

$$g[y] = S \setminus x.$$

Prove:

$$(x \vartriangleleft f) \cup (y \vartriangleleft g)^{-1} \in S \rightarrowtail\!\!\!\rightarrow T.$$

Prove:

$$\forall a, b \cdot a \subseteq b \implies S \setminus g[T \setminus f[a]] \subseteq S \setminus g[T \setminus f[b]].$$

From the previous properties, deduce the Cantor–Bernstein theorem:

$$\exists f \cdot f \in S \rightarrowtail T$$
$$\exists g \cdot g \in T \rightarrowtail S$$
$$\Rightarrow$$
$$\exists h \cdot h \in S \rightarrowtail\mkern-14mu\rightarrow T.$$

18.3.8 Zermelo's theorem [13]

Transporting a well-order We are given two sets S and T and a well-order relation q built on T; formally:

$$q \in S \leftrightarrow T$$

$$\text{id} \subseteq q$$

$$q \cap q^{-1} \subseteq \text{id}$$

$$q \,;\, q \subseteq q$$

$$\forall B \cdot B \neq \varnothing \;\Rightarrow\; \exists y \cdot y \in B \,\wedge\, B \subseteq q[y].$$

Let f be a total injection between S and T:

$$f \in S \rightarrowtail T.$$

Prove that the relation $f \,;\, q \,;\, f^{-1}$ well-orders the set S.

Strategy for proving Zermelo's theorem We would like to prove that any set S can be well-ordered: this is Zermelo's theorem. The idea is to perform this proof as follows.

- We define a set T.
- We build a well-order q on T.
- We build a total injection f from S to T.

If we succeed in doing that, then, according to the above, the set S can be well-ordered.

Building the set T and the well-order q The set T is a set of subsets of S:

$$T \subseteq \mathbb{P}(S).$$

Let q be the set inclusion relation built on T:

$$\forall a, b \cdot a \in T \,\wedge\, b \in T \;\Rightarrow\; (a \mapsto b \in q \Leftrightarrow a \subseteq b).$$

Moreover, we suppose the following:

$$\forall A \cdot A \subseteq T \ \wedge \ A \neq \varnothing \ \Rightarrow \ \text{inter}(A) \in A. \qquad \textbf{Assumption 1}$$

Prove that relation q well-orders T under Assumption 1.

Defining a total injection between S and T We define f as a total function from S to T:

$$f \in S \rightarrow T.$$

with the following property:

$$\forall z \cdot z \in S \ \Rightarrow \ f(z) = \text{union}(\{x \mid x \in T \ \wedge \ z \notin x\}).$$

In order to prove that f is an injection, we need more assumptions concerning sets S and T. First, we need the following, for any subset A of T:

$$\forall A \cdot A \subseteq T \ \Rightarrow \ \text{union}(A) \in T \qquad \textbf{Assumption 2}$$

Second, we suppose that the set S can be equipped with a *choice function* c defined as follows:

$$c \in \mathbb{P}1(S) \rightarrow S$$

$$\textbf{Assumption 3}$$

$$\forall A \cdot A \subseteq S \ \wedge A \neq \varnothing \ \Rightarrow \ c(A) \in S.$$

Now, we define a total function n (for *next*) on $\mathbb{P}(S)$ as follows:

$$n \in \mathbb{P}(S) \rightarrow \mathbb{P}(S).$$

together with the following properties:

$$\left\{ \begin{array}{l} n(S) = S \\[2mm] \forall A \cdot A \subseteq S \ \wedge A \neq S \ \Rightarrow \ n(A) = A \cup \{c(S \setminus A)\} \end{array} \right.$$

Third, we assume that n is closed under T:

$$\forall x \cdot x \in T \ \Rightarrow \ n(x) \subset T. \qquad \textbf{Assumption 4}$$

Prove that under these four assumptions, f is indeed an injection.

According to what we have done so far, S is a well-ordered set under these four assumptions. Our next step consists in giving more structure to the set T so that we can prove Assumptions 1, 2, and 4. Assumption 3 will remain unproved. In other words, the set S has to be equipped with a choice function like c in order to be proved to be well-ordered.

Giving more structure to the set T We define a function $Union$ on $\mathbb{P}(S)$ as follows:

$$Union \in \mathbb{P}(\mathbb{P}(S)) \rightarrow \mathbb{P}(\mathbb{P}(S))$$

$$\forall A \cdot A \subseteq \mathbb{P}(S) \;\Rightarrow\; Union(A) = \mathrm{union}(A).$$

We define another function g on $\mathbb{P}(S)$ as follows:

$$g \in \mathbb{P}(\mathbb{P}(S)) \rightarrow \mathbb{P}(\mathbb{P}(S))$$

$$\forall A \cdot A \subseteq \mathbb{P}(S) \;\Rightarrow\; g(A) = n[A] \cup Union[\mathbb{P}(A)].$$

We suppose:

$$g(T) \subseteq T.$$

Prove Assumption 2 and Assumption 4. Moreover, we suppose the following:

$$\forall x, y \cdot x \subseteq y \;\vee\; y \subseteq x. \qquad\qquad \textbf{Assumption 5}$$

Prove Assumption 1. It remains for us to prove the new Assumption 5. For this we suppose that T is the *least fixpoint* of the function g:

$$T = fix(g)$$

Prove that g is monotone (so that Tarski's theorem can be used). Prove finally Assumption 5. Hint: Use property (10) of Section 18.3.2. This completes the proof of the Zermelo's theorem, that every set equipped with a choice function can be well-ordered.

18.4 References

[1]   D. Gries. *The Science of Programming*. Springer Verlag, 1981
[2]   B. Fraikin, M. Frappier, and R. Laleau. State-Based versus Event-Base Specifications for Information Systems: a Comparison of B and EB^3. *Software and Systems Modeling*, 2005.
[3]   G. Berry. Private Communication, 2008.
[4]   D. Jackson. *Software Abstractions: Logic, Language, and Analysis*. MIT Press, 2006.
[5]   T. Nipkow. *Verifying a Hotel Key Card System*. ICTAC, 2006.
[6]   J. Earley. An Efficient Context-free Parsing Algorithm. *CACM*, 1970
[7]   H. Schorr and W Waite. An Efficient Machine Independent Procedure for Garbage Collection in Various List Structures. *CACM*, 1967.
[8]   K. Robinson Private Communication, 2008.
[9]   J. R. Abrial and D. Cansell. Formal Construction of a Non-blocking Concurrent Queue Algorithm (a Case Study in Atomicity) *J. UCS*, 2005.
[10] N. Lynch. *Distributed Algorithms*. Morgan Kaufmann Publishers, 1996.

[11] S. Wieczorek, A. Roth, A. Stefanescu, and A. Charfi. Precise Steps for Choreography Modeling for SOA Validation and Verification. *Proceedings of the Fourth IEEE International Symposium on Service-Oriented System Engineering*, 2008.

[12] E. W. Dijkstra and C. S. Scholten. Termination Detection for Diffusing Computations. *Information Processing Letters*, 1980.

[13] J. R. Abrial, D. Cansell, and G. Lafitte. *Doing Higher-order Mathematics in B*, 2005

Index

$\times$, 153
$\lhd$, 160
$\lhd\!\!\!-$, 160
$\rightarrowtail\!\!\!\rightarrow$, 154
$\mathbb{P}$, 153
$\rhd$, 160
$\rhd\!\!\!-$, 160
$\rightarrow$, 154
$\leftrightarrow$, 434

abstract state, 51
abstract variable, 51
abstraction, 426
acknowledgement message, 150
action, 19, 30, 105, 118, 121
  multiple, 61
action, deterministic, 184
action, non-deterministic, 184
acyclic graph, 352
antecedent, 306
antecedent of a rule, 36
anticipated event, 172, 213
arbiter, 280
arithmetic language, 310
atomicity, 228
axiom, 36

backward simulation, 434, 439
before–after predicate, 30
binary relation, 153
blueprint, 12
border of a set, 578
bounded re-transmission protocol, BRP, 204

Cantor–Bernstein theorem, 579
carrier set, 151
Cartesian product, 152, 321
choice function, 581
closed model, 20, 25
closed set, 578
closure of a set, 578
complex system, 16
compound name, 33

concrete invariant, 51
concrete state, 51
concrete variable, 51
concrete version, 52
concurrent program, 227
conditional invariant, 71
conjunction, 310
consequent, 306
consequent of a rule, 36
context, 176
context extension, 177
context of a model, 28
continuous function, 579
convergence, 64
convergent event, 162
correct by construction, 24
cutting, 242
cycle, 339

data refinement, 431
deadlock, 19
deadlock freedom, 45, 66
decomposition, 20, 21
discrete model, 18
discrete system, 17
discrete transition system, 176
disjunction, 310
distributed program, 150
domain, 153
domain restriction, 160
domain subtraction, 160
dummy event, 61
dynamic programming, 235

embedded loop, 463
enabling condition, 207
equality language, 310
equality predicate, 319
equivalence, 314
event, 19, 29
existentially quantified predicate, 316
expression, 316
expression, paired, 316

extensionaility axiom, 321
external non-determinism, 19
external set, 430, 432
external variable, 430

falsity, 310
fault prevention, 508
fault tolerance, 204
file transfer protocol, 204
filter, 577
finite depth tree, 349
finite list, 341
fixpoint, 574
fixpoint, least, 582
formal methods, 10, 16
formal models, 16
formed route, 518
forward simulation, 434
Four-slot Fully Asynchronous Mechanism, 228
free tree, 7, 350, 406
free tree, leaves of, 410
function operator, 328

general refinement, 431
generic development, 151
generic instantiation, 20, 479
gluing invariant, 181
goal, 33, 309
graph of evolution, 422
graph, strongly connected, 336
greatest lower bound, 574
guard, 19, 40, 193
guard strengthening, 54

Hoare triple, 449
hypothesis, 309

implication, 310
inference
    rules of, 36
inference rule, 306
    derived, 37
infinite backward chain, 339
infinite list, 338
infinite tree, 345
init, 43
initializing, 43
instantiation, 118
instantiation, generic, 479
interior of a set, 578
interleaving, 233
internal variable, 429
intersection, generalized, 324
invariant, 20, 28
    conditional, 71
irreflexive transitive closure, 335

Knaster–Tarski theorem, 575

laboratory execution, 17
lambda abstraction, 330
leader node, 406

least fixpoint, 582
life cycle, 13
list induction, 341
logical clock, 391
logical variable, 20

machine, 176
machine refinement, 177
machine structure, 180
member, 321
meta-variable, 38, 310
mobile agent, 387
modality, 20
model, 176
    closed, 20, 89
modeling, 49
modeling, 11
modeling elements, 176
monotonicity, 36
multiple action, 61
multiple section, 59

negation, 310
neighborhood, 578
network modeling, 350
node, inner, 352
node, outer, 351
non-deterministic assignment, 169

open set, 578
ordered pair, 152

partial function, 154
partial transfer, 210
pattern, 106
pattern of variables, 330
pattern refinement, 123
Peano axiom, 339
    first, 44
    second, 36, 38
    third, 44
Peano axioms, 332, 339
physical variable, 20
post-condition, 450
power set, 152, 321
pre-condition, 450
predicate, 308, 317
predicate language, 310
predicate, equality, 319
progress event, 186, 409
proof by cases, 46
proof obligation generator, 33, 188
proof obligation rule, 31
propositional language, 310
protocol modeling, 149
protocol specification, 210
pulser, 267

quantified intersection, 324
quantified union, 324
Quicksort, 460

range, 153
range restriction, 160
range subtraction, 160
re-try counter, 205
reachability, 20
reaction, 105, 118, 122
reaction, weak, 421
readiness, 543
receive event, 158
refined version, 52
refinement, 20, 21, 24, 29, 50, 420,
    426
  data, 21
  general, 431
refinement, simple, 424
refinment, 62
relational image, 326
relative deadlock freedom,
    427
requirement document, 13, 14, 210
reserved route, 518
ring, 343, 359
Rodin, 178
route, 513
  formed, 518
  ready, 543
  reserved, 518
rule schema, 310
rules of inference, 36

search event, 186
section
  multiple, 59
sequent, 32, 33, 306
sequent, proof of, 307
sequential program, 227
set, 321
set defined in comprehension, 321
set operations, 322
set-theoretic language, 310, 321
specification, 210
state, 19
  dynamic part, 28
  static part, 28
state of a model, 28
static checker, 188
strongly connected graph, 336
superposition, 71, 73, 123
synchronization, 368

theory, 307
topological space, 578
total binary relation, 434
total function, 151, 154,
    432
total transfer, 210
trace, 420, 422, 426
traceability, 16
track
  direct, 511
  diverted, 511
track circuit, 512
track network, 508
traffic light, 292
train agent, 508
train system, 508
transition, 19
transition system, 17
tree induction, 349
tree, free, 350, 406
turnstile, 33

ultrafilter, 577
UML, 10
universally quantified predicate,
    316
unreliable channels, 204

variable, 316
  external, 430
  internal, 429
  logical, 20
  physical, 20
variables, pattern of, 330
variant, 64
variant expression, 166
verification condition rule, 31
virtual contention channel, 413

weak reaction, 421
weak synchronization, 106
well-definedness, 202, 324
well-founded relation, 572
witness, 183, 201
witness, deterministic, 183
witness, non-deterministic,
    183

Zermelo's theorem, 580

Printed in the United States
by Baker & Taylor Publisher Services